THE WITHDRAWN
BACK STAGE®
ACTOR'S
HANDBOOK

This is a gift from:

*The Danville Library
Foundation*

DANVILLE
LIBRARY
FOUNDATION

D0012368

REFERENCE

THE
BACK STAGE®
ACTOR'S
HANDBOOK

The How-to and Who-to Contact Reference
for Actors, Singers, and Dancers

REVISED AND EXPANDED FOURTH EDITION

COMPILED AND EDITED BY SHERRY EAKER

CONTRA COSTA COUNTY LIBRARY

3 1901 03461 8076

An imprint of Watson-Guptill Publications/New York

In memory of my father, Ira Eaker,
who raised the curtain on my career,
and to my mom, Lee,
who's been coaching me along the way.

Senior Editor: Mark Glubke
Cover Design: Craig Kuperman and Jay Anning
Interior Design: Areta Buk
Production Manager: Hector Campbell

Copyright © 2004 by Back Stage magazine

First published in 2004 by Back Stage Books,
an imprint of Watson-Guptill Publications,
a division of VNU Business Media, Inc.
770 Broadway, New York, NY 10003
www.wgpub.com.com

Library of Congress Control Number: 2004103245

ISBN: 0-8230-7680-6

All rights reserved. No part of this publication may be reproduced
or used in any form or by any means—graphic, electronic, or mechanical,
including photocopying, recording, taping or information storage and
retrieval systems—without written permission of the publisher.

Manufactured in the United States of America

First printing 2004

1 2 3 4 5 6 7 8 9 / 11 10 09 08 07 06 05 04

ACKNOWLEDGEMENTS

Every film and stage production requires a team of players to make it happen. The same has been true for putting this book together. I'd like to acknowledge the editorial team that helped me to create the *Actor's Handbook*.

First and foremost, I owe much gratitude to my associate editor on the project, Mark Dundas Wood. His skilled craftsmanship as an editor, his complete knowledge of the industry, and his enthusiasm for the project helped me turn it into a reality.

Thank you to Mark Glubke, the book editor on this project.

I'd like to thank Bruce B. Morris, editor in chief of *Ross Reports,* who is responsible for many of the updated listings. Thanks, too, to *Back Stage* staffers B. L. Rice, for additional listings, and David Fairhurst, for his keen editing and updating of both articles and lists. I'd also like to thank the entire editorial staff of *Back Stage* who lent me their support during the year that I spent on the handbook.

A sincere acknowledgement to every one of the *Back Stage* writers whose articles were selected for the book, and who assisted in adapting them.

I owe much to all the industry professionals who contributed their expert advice throughout the various chapters.

Thanks, too, to Jon Cryer for his contribution of a foreword to this book.

Much gratitude to all the freelance feature writers, columnists, regional correspondents, and theatre reviewers who have made valuable contributions to *Back Stage* throughout the years.

Finally, thanks to *all* performers who constantly have to deal with the ups and downs of this crazy business, but continue to stick with it because they recognize the importance of their contributions to the art.

Contents

PART 1: TRAINING

ACTING CLASSES

COLLEGE THEATRE PROGRAMS

IMPROVISATION

ACCENTS AND DIALECT TRAINING

PART 2: THE BASIC TOOLS

HEADSHOTS

RÉSUMÉS

PROMOTION

FINANCIAL MATTERS

List of Advertisers

Foreword

The One Thing That Will Guarantee You Success in Show Business

BY JON CRYER

You've got this book, so I guess that means you are looking to have a career as an actor. Well, let me tell you a story.

It's my big break. I'm 18. I'm taking over for Matthew Broderick in his Tony Award–winning role of Eugene in *Brighton Beach Memoirs* on Broadway, and I'm on top of the world, right?

Nuh-uh.

On my way to rehearsal one Tuesday I experience one of those short, sharp shocks that either set you up or lay you low. My pager goes off. My manager is leaving messages for me everywhere he can. I finally reach him from a pay phone on the platform of the 1 Train (downtown side).

"I'm late for rehearsal. What's up?"

"Don't bother. We need to talk."

Long story short: holy crap. I'm getting the axe. The producers have no confidence in me. I'm cocky, occasionally late, and after four weeks of rehearsals I still don't have the lines down cold. In my defense, Eugene is one of the biggest roles south of Hamlet. But you know what? No excuses. It's my job to have them, and I blew it. I'm done.

It will take quite a while for me to figure out what a big favor the producers have done me, but in the span of a few seconds I've learned what six years of school plays, choir practice, drama camp, cleaning toilets at my local Equity rep theatre, and the Royal Academy of Dramatic Art never taught me. The three most important rules of the business:

1 Don't be cocky!

2 Don't be late!

3 Learn your %$#*ing lines!

These things seem pretty obvious in retrospect. But at the time, I was so consumed with breaking into the business that I forgot what I was in the business for: to do good work (and also, I think, to meet girls), neither of which I would be doing much of now that I was unemployed. So I hitched up my pants, dusted myself off, and went on to the next opportunity.

Most of the other lessons I've learned in the twenty years I've been doing this also came by accident, and I'll tell you them all because (a) you've paid good money for this here book, and (b) they've taught me something of immense value.

THE ONE THING THAT WILL GUARANTEE YOU SUCCESS IN SHOW BUSINESS!

Now, I know what you're thinking: "It's been like a page already, get to it!" And I will. But I'm going to dillydally for a minute 'cause, damnit, you need to hear this!

So it's 1996. I'm producing this ultralow-budget independent film that I wrote with a friend. We're auditioning hundreds of people. I'm watching this succession of incredible actors—people I never thought would even consider doing our movie—coming in, putting their butts on the line, and giving it all they've got. Really taking chances. And you know what? Most of them are sucking. Not even in the ballpark. The two percent who nail it, we cast. I'm in shock. I've been watching days and days of great performers whom I've admired for years miss the mark in so many creative ways that I'm thinking I have to reassess why I thought these people were good in the first place. But then it hits me: "These people are still great. They're just not right for these parts. Maybe all those times I agonized over my auditions, worrying about every single choice I made, I should have just stepped up to the plate, taken my swing, and stayed loose for whatever happens next."

I'm not saying, "Don't prepare." I'm just saying:

You'll get the part if you are right for it. So just relax already.

Don't freak out about what's going to happen in the audition room. Just show up, show them your take on the character, and get the hell out of there. If you are the right person for the part, it will be apparent to everyone.

And also, if you ever get a chance, try to find a way to sit on the other side of the table sometime—either volunteer as a reader for a casting director, or direct your own film, or produce free Shakespeare in the park, or whatever. I'm telling you it will completely change the way you feel about auditions when you see that the people for whom you're auditioning want the same thing you do: to do good work (and also, I think, to meet girls . . . or guys, or whatever). The auditioners are not there to make fun of you when you leave the room. They won't remember when you blow it. It'll just be on to the next. And next time, maybe you'll be the one who nails it.

Oh, and one more thing my little independent movie taught me:

Don't just sit there.

Acting often feels like a very passive profession, sitting around waiting for the phone to ring. Don't let it be. When the business didn't seem to want anything to do with me for a while, I scraped together what money I could, found another investor, and embarked on a really stupid journey: making my own movie. It was alternately harrowing, horrible, horrific, and . . . well, something else bad that begins with an H. But when it was done, I had something. It was flawed as all get-out, but it was mine. And I realized, in many ways, I didn't care what people thought of it. I'd been through this incredible ordeal, and I loved every minute of it. The very effort of overcoming these insane obstacles and even more insane people in order to to create something was monumentally fulfilling and ridiculous all at the same time. And there's where it came to me. The big one.

THE ONE THING THAT WILL GUARANTEE YOU SUCCESS IN SHOW BUSINESS

And here it is:

If you can find it in your heart to love the struggle, you will succeed. If you can discover a way to embrace the stupidity, the beauty, the greed, the egos, the luck, the misfortunes, the could-haves, the won't-evers, the fear, the fun, all the lunatic bull$#%&, and revel in it all, you will succeed. Because the one thing it won't be is easy.

By the way, a year after they fired me from *Brighton Beach Memoirs,* I starred in a movie. When the play's producers heard, they asked me back. I did the show . . . for about six times what they paid me the first time.

JON CRYER
Los Angeles, California
2004

Preface

The More Things Change, the More Things Stay the Same

The above statement is particularly true for the performing arts industry, as I have observed in my role as editor of *Back Stage* for the past 27 years and as a keen observer of the scene. What has changed? Technology has certainly affected the way people communicate with one another: agents with actors, producers with casting directors, performers with their potential audiences. There are now more performing opportunities than ever before, and windows have opened to all types of performers in fields where opportunities once were limited or never existed. But along with this comes the demand that today's performer must not only be multi-skilled and talented, but must also be expected to work in virtually every medium and in many different locales.

But the difficulties of a career in the performing arts industry remain. The financial instability, the rejection, the uncertainty of when the next job will come along—all these things are part of the performer's world, and that's something that will probably never change.

The Back Stage® Actor's Handbook: The How-to and Who-to Contact Reference for Actors, Singers, and Dancers has been assembled to help you recognize and better understand these changes, to help you learn to cope with the insecurity of the business, to define for you the talent and business skills required to promote and market yourself, and, hopefully, to help you achieve success in the performing arts industry.

This is also the focus of *Back Stage* and our sister publication, *Back Stage West*, weekly trade papers geared to performing artists all over the country. Each week, aside from carrying audition information for stage, film, and other productions going on in New York, Los Angeles, and sites nationwide, both weeklies feature "how-to" articles designed to help actors, singers, dancers, directors, playwrights, and other talent move ahead in their careers. In fact, most of the chapters you'll read here were originally prepared by *Back Stage* writers and contributors, and then adapted for the handbook.

This is the fourth edition of the handbook that I have compiled and edited. (The first three books were titled *The Back Stage Handbook for Performing Artists* and were published in 1988, 1992, and 1995.) Many of the performance fields that were explored in past editions are introduced again here, though the articles are completely rewritten, reflecting the viewpoints of a new team of industry professionals, and reflecting the changes that have taken place in the various fields. Included are chapters on TV and radio commercial casting; new, improved avenues of communication; voiceovers; and jingle singing.

Many new subject areas are covered. Included among them: choosing material to audition with, breaking into film and television, coping with stage fright, audition tip sheets for singers and dancers, and an overview of theatre and film activity in five of the country's major acting markets.

For the student looking for help in choosing a career in acting, there are chapters on selecting a college theatre program and on choosing an acting teacher.

For the university graduate and the newcomer to the real world of performing, there are chapters on acclimating to life in two of the major markets (New York and Los Angeles), on headshots and résumés, on the performing unions, and on working in student films.

The mid-level performer will benefit from reading about supplementary markets such as live industrials, industrial films, cruise lines, and daytime dramas.

The truly enterprising performer will find most helpful the chapters on tax advice, negotiating your own contract, and promoting yourself using the web, CDs, and video.

As was the case with previous editions, the text is supplemented by lists of agents, casting directors, personal managers, theatre companies, unions and guilds, combined audition sites, and more. Some of them are specific to a particular chapter; others are listed in the appendix at the end of the forty chapters.

In this world of show business that you have decided to become part of, there will always be new ways of going about doing things, new faces to remember, new contacts to make, new trends to follow. And there will definitely be the ever-increasing influence of technology. Hopefully, what you read here will help prepare you for these changes, and will lay a solid foundation for you in the things that don't change. One thing that hopefully won't: your desire to entertain, educate, and engage audiences everywhere.

SHERRY EAKER
New York, New York
2004

Training

1 Acting Teachers:

Helping You Make the Right Selection

BY SHERRY EAKER

How do you go about choosing an acting class? Working actors have a variety of responses to the query.

States Ann Harada: "An actor should have the chance to talk to the acting teacher ahead of time, as well as audit a class to get a sense of the prevailing philosophies and approaches."

Trisha Jeffrey feels that "it's crucial to study in a place where you feel comfortable and which also challenges you. Find out what you want and need, and look at each school to see if it can bring you towards those goals."

Glenn Seven Allen advises that you "look for recommendations from people whose work you respect and who you know take the acting process seriously."

Chris Burner was convinced that the studio he chose was the right one because his interview "was more about me and what I needed. She listened to me, then told me what the school could offer."

Reports Susan McMahon Colbert, "I immediately liked the school's feeling of community and the fact that they are practical about preparing you for auditions."

Brett Douglas says, "The most important thing to remember is you need to be vulnerable, but safe." And Jason Scott Campbell is an advocate of "choosing acting classes intuitively and trusting your instincts."

Choosing an acting teacher to work with is unlike choosing any other service professional: There's so much more at stake emotionally.

The following is a list of questions that you should be asking yourself, your actor friends, and then those that you've decided to interview. Armed with knowing exactly what you're after, and with responses to your questions, you should be able to make a fair assessment about a particular school or teacher.

The first thing you must do is assess your own individual needs. Do you want to study in a multi-year program, or take independent classes? Do you want to work with a coach to help you prepare for an audition, or a role? Are you a musical performer, or do you have a flair for the classics? There are classes in technique, scene study, improvisation, musical theatre auditioning, speech, movement, and so on. You have to decide which class or classes will fulfill your wants, focus on your weak areas, and, most importantly, hone your strengths.

Once you've figured out what you need, start asking your actor friends for teacher references. There are actors that you may not know, but whose work you admire. Try to find out whom they've studied with. There is also a huge variety of books that have been published on acting technique. Read as many as you can. One of these acting philosophies might strike a chord with you, and will give you a specific direction in your quest for the perfect teacher.

Now that you've narrowed down the field somewhat, there are other basic factors to consider and questions to ask your potential instructors when you interview with them or attend their orientations.

Find out if auditing of classes is permitted, but don't be put off if it's not; teachers may feel the need to protect the privacy of their students. Instead, make sure that you have the opportunity to interview with the coach or teacher. And don't feel intimidated. Be direct and honest. Here are some of the questions that you'll need to ask:

1 How long has the school been in existence and/or how long has the teacher been teaching?

2 What are the teacher's credentials? Where did he or she train? What are his or her professional work credits?

3 How large is the class? Also ask about the ability of the other students. It's best when you work with others who are of equal ability, along with those who are on a somewhat higher level than you are.

4 What about costs? And the payment policy? What about a refund policy?

5 Do students need to audition and/or interview before they are accepted? There should be a screening process.

6 Is one allowed to make up for missed classes? One teacher used to tape classes so that if any of her students were out (on jobs, hopefully), they were able to view the tape of their missed class at their own convenience. Also, ask what happens when the teacher misses class.

7 Does the teacher assign material, or is it up to the actor to bring his own material? The teacher is the one to best assess what's most appropriate for the student.

8 Ask the teacher to explain his or her particular method or approach to acting. Does it feel "right" to you? Can you see yourself comfortably adapting to this style? Is the style easily adaptable to TV and film work as well?

9 Does the school or class produce a showcase at the end of the term to which agents and casting directors may be invited? Not all schools do this; it's certainly not obligatory, but it obviously does have its advantages.

Since no overall association monitors acting teachers or schools (aside from such organizations as the National Association of Schools of Theatre, which oversees the theatre training programs at universities), anyone can hang a shingle outside his door and profess to be a teacher. That's why it's practically mandatory that you arm yourself with the above questions.

• • • •

Acting is mostly about instinct and feeling, and that's exactly what it's all about when choosing the person you decide to work with. If working with that person feels right, then that's the person for you. If your gut is telling you something else, trust your gut and move on to someone else. Know, too, that you can gain from every experience, whether positive or negative. All can help to enhance your next encounter and further define your own unique approach to acting.

2 Training, Technique, and the Acting Workplace:

What You Can Take from the Ivory Tower to the Real World

BY MARK DUNDAS WOOD

The very idea of going through a formal training program to become an actor is one that has fluctuated from culture to culture throughout the centuries.

In the Japanese *noh* tradition, actors would engage in disciplined lifelong training befitting a samurai warrior. The traditions were handed down within families, from generation to generation.

In Elizabethan England, young thesps certainly didn't go away to a conservatory to study some primordial version of Viewpoints with the Renaissance equivalent of Anne Bogart. True, members of those academia-rooted "boy troupes" may have received instruction in declamation and the like from their choirmasters/directors. But for the common player, training likely was achieved via an apprenticeship model—with untried players working their way up the ranks toward the starring roles. And consider those boy actors who originated the roles of Juliet and Ophelia. They must have been thrown into those demanding parts with only the most basic training (and in the middle of puberty, no less!). You have to believe that the casting directors at the Globe theatre were looking more for the innate talent in such youngsters than for impressive studio credits listed on their parchment résumés.

In the United States we've always had a sort of split personality when it comes to this issue. On the one hand, we've been fascinated by the "star is born" myth that takes an untutored actor and elevates him or her to celebrity status overnight. Think of Lana Turner waiting to be discovered in Schwab's drugstore. Or of those Ruby Keeler film vehicles in which the heroine manages to invent talent, polish, and poise for herself simply by willing them into being.

This fascination persists even today. Occasionally you'll hear that certain film directors prefer to use "nonactors" for a project, because they don't want that smooth and studied quality they get with seasoned performers. (In fact, Gus Van Sant's 2003 film *Elephant,* which won the *Palme d'Or* at the Cannes Film Festival, was cast with Oregon high school students who had no formal acting training whatsoever.)

On the other hand, at least since the advent of Lee Strasberg, it's seemed important for American performers to get an education in basic acting technique. If you have no scene, movement, or voice study listed on the back of your headshot, can you realistically expect casting directors or agents to give you the time of day? Even if you're simply interested in hawking detergent or diet sodas in commercials, you're expected to have studied something, somewhere, at some point.

Still, just how valuable is formal acting training, really? Are the stakes so different in the acting workplace that actors discard or forget all they've been taught in the insular world of the classroom or studio?

For this chapter, we spoke with working actors who told about their training (both private and academia based) and about the extent to which they relied on it once they were out in the "real world."

CONCENTRATION IS KEY

Less than an hour before the first preview of Paul Simon's 1998 Broadway musical *The Capeman,* a small bomb was dropped on Stephen Lee Anderson. An actor he was understudying had lost his voice. And Anderson (cast in the supporting role of Virgil) was being asked to play two roles that night.

It seemed impossible. At one point only a 30-second interval existed for changing costumes and shifting into the second role. Still, the actor formed a battle plan. He and the crew worked out the details of his quick change, and also concealed lines of dialogue inside his personal props, including a newspaper and a Bible.

Anderson pulled it off—and continued to do so for several nights thereafter. But the fast planning and steel-plated nerves it took didn't come naturally. Concentration had always been a problem for Anderson.

Fortunately, while studying at the Webber Douglas Academy of Dramatic Art in London many years earlier, he had been helped to find ways to enhance his powers of focus.

"I had a teacher there who said, 'I want you to do more chess, and I want you to read mystery books. . . .' They could see that my energy was so high that I had a hard time settling down and concentrating. Same with my stiffness. I was very stiff, so they took me out of ballet and put me into jazz—more free movement—and into a swimming program."

At the end of his time at Webber Douglas, Anderson's vocal instructor, Patsy Rodenburg, told him that he needed to get into a rep company. Anderson eventually joined the Denver Center Theatre Company, and he considers that stint to be his real training. He learned a great deal by watching seasoned actors prepare for a role. For instance, he noticed that many of these veterans could easily feed him his own lines whenever he "went up."

"They knew that text—they knew that scene. Not just their own lines, but what was coming at them. That's something, as a young actor, I had to learn."

ACCEPTING THE GIVENS

When she was performing the role of "the Girl" Off-Broadway in 2001's *The Play About the Baby,* by Edward Albee, Texas-born Kathleen Early wrote a thank-you note to Susan Shaughnessy, one of her professors at the University of Oklahoma. Shanghnessy's course, "Departures from Realism," had included text analysis and scene study of playwrights ranging from Brecht to Ionesco. The students worked to look at every play, however abstract or absurd, on its own terms—to accept the "givens" in any particular dramatic world.

This training turned out to be peculiarly useful for Early when she set to work rehearsing Albee's cryptic tragicomedy. She credits Shaughnessy with helping her become freer to experiment during rehearsals, and to opt for unusual, unexpected choices in a scene.

Early remembers playing Viola Spolin theatre games in Shaughnessy's class, as well as practicing relaxation and focus exercises. Some of the techniques she picked up then helped her make the transition from the cocoon-ish atmosphere of educational theatre to the workaday world of professional acting:

"In educational theatre, we would always get together as a group before a show, and we'd always warm up together and we'd always 'make the connection.' There was something wonderful about that—that environment. But in a professional environment, a lot of people go smoke a cigarette for their warm-up. . . . So you start figuring out what you have to do in order to carry that over. Can I connect with the actors in another way before the show, without having to do an 'exercise'?"

During performances of *Baby,* Early looked back to her training for help in negotiating the moments when inspiration flagged.

"Every once in a while real tears aren't there," she said in an interview shortly before the play closed. "You feel the tears—your body feels the tears—but for some reason they don't come out. It's almost enough to make you cry, the fact that they're not there! There was actually a period of time when that was really hard. You get frustrated and think, gosh, what if it never happens again? What if I've lost it?"

But returning to some of the listening exercises that she'd picked up during her formal training helped Early get back in touch with the emotional reality of the given moment. They even helped her ignore unexpected distractions during the run of *Baby*—such as the time an audience member decided to wave at her during a particularly intense moment.

LEARNING BY DOING

Bowdoin College in Brunswick, Maine, had no real theatre program when Philip Goodwin was a student there, but he did appear in several plays on campus. Just the experience of getting up in front of an audience was useful to the fledgling actor. Still, he felt woefully under-trained when he came to New York City after graduation.

Once in the city, he took a class from an acting teacher named Bob McAndrew. "I remember thinking, I didn't have any theatre training at Bowdoin—I need to have some real technical skills. And I was quite surprised when I went to him and found out that wasn't the most pressing need at that particular point. There were other things that I really needed to address first, certainly. Things like finding out more about myself and what it was deep within me that was going to make me an actor."

After a brief stay in Manhattan—and an experimental phase where he and friends mounted plays in Greenwich, Connecticut—Goodwin found his way to The Drama Studio in London. The program there proved to be "revelatory," he says. Though compressed into one year, the course of study provided a wide-ranging curriculum: basic acting classes, vocal study, mime, ballet, stage combat, makeup, and acting for television.

At the Studio, Goodwin also studied with a teacher named Patrick Tucker, who specialized in the kind of analysis of Elizabethan verse popularized by director-writer John Barton. Shakespearean acting, however, wasn't the real focus of The Drama Studio program—and this would later come as a surprise to Goodwin's American colleagues.

"When you come back to the United States, people figure, if you've gone to train in London in any capacity, you obviously have deep and extensive training in Shakespeare and in classical method—which isn't necessarily true."

Nevertheless, Goodwin and other American students who graduated from The Drama School mounted a production of *The Winter's Tale* in the States, which led to his being hired to perform with The Acting Company—the prestigious rep troupe that had grown out of Juilliard School in the early 1970s.

Once again, he was "learning by doing." His stint with the troupe allowed him to play in both urban centers and small towns. He experienced a true repertory arrangement with rotating shows. And he got the chance to portray characters that were far from his usual type.

"It was my first professional job," he says. "My first Equity job. But it was also a hugely important extension of my training."

KNOWING WHEN TO LEAVE

Like Goodwin, Rodney Scott Hudson learned his craft in part "by doing." He completed four years of study at Southeast Missouri State, followed by an M.A. program at the University of South Dakota. But in the summer he would act in stock at the Black Hills Playhouse. One year, he appeared in 17 separate productions.

The curriculum at South Dakota emphasized a wide array of approaches. "They told me, 'It's your responsibility to have a knowledge of all the different disciplines: Stanislavski, Meisner, Boleslavsky—even Grotowski.'"

At Missouri State, he had originally been a music major, and voice classes proved especially helpful to him in dealing with rhythmic elements in Shakespeare and other classics.

Hudson credits his eclectic background with giving him the flexibility for work with a wide variety of directors: Andrei Serban, JoAnne Akalaitis, Julie Taymor, and Robert Wilson, among many others. He's found he is able to adapt handily to the particular sensibilities of each director.

After finishing his M.A. program, Hudson began Ph.D. studies at the University of Michigan in Ann Arbor. It was there he learned perhaps the most vital lesson of all: that at a certain point when it comes to training, enough is enough. His tutor on this point was—of all people—playwright Arthur Miller.

"Arthur Miller came there, because he's an alumnus. And he was doing this symposium. And in the middle of the last meeting, I asked him, 'You've been here for a couple of weeks—what have you learned about the students?'

"He said, 'You don't know why you're here. You think theatre is a hobby. You should be out doing it.' And he pointed straight to me and said, 'You, young man. What are you doing here? Don't you think it's time that you leave the cocoon of school to find out what you can do in the real world?'

"And I said, 'I guess so, Mr. Miller.' And I quit school the next day."

THE LEE STRASBERG INSTITUTE
"IT'S ABOUT THE WORK"

The legend continues in Film, Television and Theater

- World renowned Actor Training
- Original source for Method Acting
- Quarterly classes available day and evening
- Classes in Audition, Camera, Comedy, Movement and Voice

* All New Lee Strasberg Digital Film School launch in January, 2004

* The Group At Strasberg presents plays, screenings and seminars

* Unique *Young Actors Program* for children & teens

For further details and inquiries on registration call
323-650-7777

www.strasberg.com

7936 Santa Monica Blvd.
Los Angeles, CA 90045

115 E. 15th St.
New York, NY 1000

THE JOY OF ACTING

THE ART OF THE BUSINESS

THE GLORIA GIFFORD CONSERVATORY FOR PERFORMING ARTS

Some of our current students include:

Dion Basco

"Biker Boyz"
"City Guys"–
series regular
five seasons,
"Dahmer"
"Will & Grace"

Monique Lea

"American Dreams"
(recurring)
"The Shield"
"The District"
"8 Simple Rules"
"Wayne Brady Show"

Aaron D. Spears

Two G's and a Key
Half and Half (recurring)
CSI: Miami
Blue Hill Avenue
Girlfriends

Chad Doreck

Greg Brady in 2002
"Bradys in the
White House",
"NYPD Blue",
"State of Grace"

Dante Basco

"Biker Boyz"
"Hook"
"Fakin' Da Funk"
"The Debut"
"Naked Brown Men"
"American Dragon"

Pablo Santos

WB Series
"Greetings from
Tucson" series
regular
"American Family",
"The Shield",
"Law and Order: SVU",
"Alias"

WE PRODUCE 6-8 SHOWCASES PER YEAR

ADVANCED SCENE STUDY, COLD READING,
INTERMEDIATE CLASS (EVENING),
BEGINNERS CLASS ("TYRO")

VOICE: SAUL KOTZUBEI
MOVEMENT: CANDY BROWN

SPEECH: JOEL GOLDES
VIDEO: FAY HAUSER

GLORIA GIFFORD, Artistic Director

T. 310.535.4999   T. 323.465.4427

ACTING IN THE 21ST CENTURY

Out of Control, In Full Command.

DARRYL
HICKMAN'S
ACTING WORKSHOP

For Interview Call:
(818) 344-5796

www.actingandyou.com

Excellence

What else could you expect from
THE STELLA ADLER
TECHNIQUE?

"Acting is hard work. I had done a couple of films, but my career didn't really begin until I studied with Stella. Stella's Technique is very specific. It helped me back up what I said I could do - which is why I have worked ever since."

Melanie Griffith

On Broadway
starring in
"Chicago"

4 sessions per year.
Full program or individual classes.
Technique thru on-going
Advanced Scene Study classes.

The Stella Adler
Academy of Acting
and Stella Adler Theatre

www.stellaadler-la.com
Call Now for Information: (323) 465-4446
6773 Hollywood Blvd., Los Angeles, CA 90028
Irene Gilbert, Director e-mail:
stellaadler@earthlink.net

ADULTS TEENS KIDS

CLIO Award Winning Casting Director

Beverly Long

Casting Since 1974

On-Camera Commercial, Improv & TV/Film Workshops

• 8 Week Sessions • Students Work On-Camera In Every Class
• Advanced and Private Classes Available

Toyota, Sears, KFC, Sprite, Hallmark Cards, Subaru, Milton Bradley, Coca Cola, Huffy Bicycles, Minolta Cameras, Kraft, Budweiser, Kellogg's, Sea World, NewsWatch 11, Ohio Edison, Heinz, Unocal, Snickers, Nutrigrain, Avon, Legos Toys, Whiskas Cat Food, Mars Bars, Head & Shoulders, Hostess Pudding Pies, United Airlines, McDonalds, Gallo Wines, Ponds, Lifesavers, Arizona Lottery, Taco Bell, Kraft Salad Dressing, GTE, Brim, Vick's Formula 44, American Airlines, Burger King, Marrel, Carl's Jr, Home Savings, Puma, Clorox, Panasonic, Firestone, Yamaha, Allstate Insurance, Alert Shampoo, Pillsbury, Healthy Choice, Mott's Apple Sauce …plus many others

"I cover every situation I can possibly dream up that could occur on a commercial audition. By the end of the six weeks you'll be prepared for whatever they might throw at you. It really works."

11425 Moorpark St.
Studio City, California 91602
818-754-6222/FAX 818-754-6226

Look us up @ BeverlyLongCasting.com

ACTORS! SINGERS! DIRECTORS! MUSICIANS!

Come Create with
LINDSAY CROUSE
Academy Award-Nominated Actress
The Verdict, House Of Games, Places In The Heart

Visiting Professor at UCLA's Musical Theater Department and at USC's Graduate and Undergraduate Film Schools.

MONDAY NIGHT CLASSES
at Highways Theater in Santa Monica

Take a fresh new approach to monologues, scenes and auditions! Create original pieces and perform them! Set hearts on fire!

WARNING:
THIS CLASS IS UNLIKE ANY OTHER.

Lindsay also does private acting coaching on or off-set and script analysis for writers.

for information call 310-573-6288
and visit www.lindsaycrouse.org

The Dee Wallace Stone Acting Studio

Positive, Joyful Acting

818.876.0386 ext. 3#

Limited space available.

www.DWSactingstudio.com

Children and Teen Classes
also available.

CHARLES CARROLL

Private Coaching • Small Group Classes • Free Audit

ON CAMERA

"Like there's nobody watching"

"Charles' insight into the acting process is invaluable. He has a gift for finding the nuances it takes to turn a simple character into a fully realized human being."

Jeri Ryan
Boston Public, Voyager

"A wealth of information makes Charles the most valuable source for acting you will ever find. No one else can offer such a complete and complex tuition of all the acting techniques."

Julian McMahon
Nip/Tuck, Profiler

"Charles understands the distinct rhythms of comedy and the depths of drama equally. He has a director's eye, an actor's heart and a writer's understanding of story."

Brenda Strong
The Help, Everwood

323.692.5560

★★★★ Celebrating 20 years of world-class theatre

Circus Theatricals

in residence at the Odyssey Theatre

Alfred Molina
&
Jack Stehlin
in *Richard III*

Alfred Molina, Greg Mullavey,
Jill Gascoine & Stephanie Zimbalist
in *The Cherry Orchard*

Jack Stehlin
&
Daphne Zuniga
in *Tartuffe*

GET READY FOR A CAREER!

• Critically-Acclaimed Theatre Company
• Award-Winning Main Stage Productions
• Exciting New Plays Development
• Intensive Acting Studios
• Career-oriented Workshops *w / working professionals*
• Scene Study Workshop with Performance Showcase

"An actor grows as long as he works" *Stanislavsky*

Circus Theatricals

Jack Stehlin, Artistic Director
Jeannine W. Stehlin, Producing Director
310.226.6144
circustheatricals.com

Circus Theatricals

THE JOANNE LINVILLE STUDIO

"My mentor & teacher."
MARK RUFFALO, Actor

"An inspirational teacher,
one of the best I've had the
pleasure of witnessing."
MARK RYDELL,
Director "ON GOLDEN POND"

Co-founder:
Stella Adler Conservatory, L.A.

Board Member:
Actor's Studio, NYC

Moderator:
Actor's Studio, L.A.

Taught:
USC Actor's Master Program

Beginning & Advanced Classes
Technique ~ Scene Study ~ Master Class
Former students include: Salma Hayek, Michael Richards (Kramer, *Seinfeld*).

8807 Pico Blvd., 2nd Flr., N.W. Corner @ Robertson
(Rental space available.)

310.248.4825   joannelinvillestudio.com

Acting Class with Eddie Kehler

Twenty years acting experience, from New York to Hollywood

- Scene study
- Audition skills
- Character building
- Rehearsal process

310 792 1232
Call for a free audit

"Eddie's teaching really makes a difference!"

Michelle Stafford, Emmy Winner, "The Young and the Restless"

Get where you want to be.

Hollywood Court Theater • 6817 Franklin Avenue (at Highland)

"Art Wolff has a special gift for getting the best out of an actors' talent. He has the understanding of craft to build on that talent and the generosity of spirit to encourage the confidence an actor needs to apply his craft to his talent. " —SEAN PENN

ART WOLFF ACTING STUDIO
at Theatre/Theatre
6425 Hollywood Blvd.

Seven years on the faculty of NYU'S TISCH SCHOOL OF THE ARTS, Director of 5 Broadway Plays and 15 TV Pilots including *SEINFELD*. Art Wolff has coached and directed the top actors in Hollywood including:

Dakota Fanning, Jennifer Love Hewitt, Sean Penn, Matthew Perry, David Hyde Pierce, Matthew Modine, Chazz Palminterri, K.D. Aubert, Courtney Cox, Jerry Seinfeld, Tracey Ullman, Fred Savage, Kathy Najimy, Peter McNichol,Julie Hagerty, Steve Martin, Brian Benben, John Corbet, Jason Alexander, Penn & Teller, John Goodman, Greg German, Bonnie Hunt, Gary Shandling, Pamela Reed,Dan Castellaneta, Ron Silver, Christine Baranski, Joseph Gordon Levitt, Kevin Pollak, Lily Tomlin, Roger Rees, Michael Richards, Peter Falk, Judd Hirsch, Harry Shearer, Evan Handler, Michael McKean, W.H. Macy, Elaine May, Richard Dreyfuss, Eric McCormak, Helen Slater, Ben Savage

~ For Classes and Private Coaching ~
Call 323-227-8363

"Art, you brought so much magic to the film—joy and magic! Many, many, many thanks for coaching DAKOTA FANNING." —JESSIE NELSON—WRITER-DIRECTOR *"I AM SAM"*

INVEST IN YOUR TALENT

EXPLORE MULTIPLE PERSPECTIVES IN THE CRAFT OF ACTING

All our courses are taught by gifted acting coaches and experienced industry professionals.

Daytime, evening, and weekend courses are held on the UCLA campus and in theaters in and around Los Angeles.

We offer a variety of acting technique courses, as well as courses specializing in:

Acting for the camera

Combat and weaponry

Improvisation

Voice and movement

Stand-up comedy

Voice overs

Accent reduction

Auditioning techniques

Casting procedures

Acting for TV commercials

Stanislavsky, Meisner, Hagen, and Strasberg methods

UCLA EXTENSION
ENTERTAINMENT STUDIES

For more information:
Call: **(310) 825-9064** or **(800) 825-9064**
E-mail: **entertainmentstudies@uclaextension.edu**
uclaextension.edu/entertainmentstudies

EAST WEST PLAYERS, the nation's premier Asian American theatre organization, invites you to take part in our programs designed to develop and nurture the growing community of Asian Pacific American artists.

The Actors Conservatory is designed to challenge actors in various areas of acting and allows artists to continue to hone their craft in a professional environment.

Alliance of Creative Talent Services serves as a conduit to the entertainment industry, introducing Asian American artists to casting directors and executives. It provides a support system for actors and offers numerous special events.

The David Henry Hwang Writers Institute

is designed to foster new writing for the stage and is a nationally recognized force in the creation of plays that embrace the voice of multi-ethnic America.

For more information
contact Arts Education Director Marilyn Tokuda at
mtokuda@eastwestplayers.org
or (213) 625-7000 x15

The Actors Conservatory and ACTS are sponsored in part by the National Endowment for the Arts.
The David Henry Hwang Writers Institute is sponsored in part by the James Irvine Foundation.

EAST WEST PLAYERS
120 Judge John Aiso St., Los Angeles, CA 90012
(213) 625-7000 • www.eastwestplayers.org

THE SANFORD MEISNER CENTER
Founded in 1987
by Sanford Meisner
(818) 509-9651

THE MEISNER TECHNIQUE
65 Years of Tradition Continues
- Five-Week Summer Sessions
- Two-Year Acting Program
- Movement Training
- Screenwriting Program

NOW INTERVIEWING FOR CLASSES.

MARTIN BARTER
Martin Barter was Sanford Meisner's assistant for 14 years and former teacher at The Neighborhood Playhouse, NYC.

WWW.THEMEISNERCENTER.COM

WHEN YOU'RE READY TO DO WHAT YOU CAME HERE FOR.

AARONSPEISER
actingstudio

Will Smith
Jennifer Lopez
LL Cool J
Marlon Wayans
Shawn Wayans
Mandy Moore

BASIC ACTING TECHNIQUES
SCENE STUDY
BUSINESS OF ACTING
COLD READING
PRIVATE COACHING

310-399-4567 • www.aaronspeiser.com

ERIC MORRIS ACTOR'S WORKSHOP

Teaches his own system based on
the "Method" but goes light-years beyond

The Work is Profoundly Life Changing

Author of: "No Acting Please," "Being & Doing," "Irreverent Acting,"
"Acting from the Ultimate Consciousness,"
and "Acting, Imaging & the Unconscious."
Coming Soon: "The Diary of a Professional Experiencer"
Coming Later: "The Actor's Other Selves"

"If you want to be still and full, Eric teaches 'the stuff'" - **Jack Nicholson**

Beginning through Advanced

Also - Weekend Intensive Workshops

323-466-9250

Master Teacher

COMPLIMENTARY AUDIT

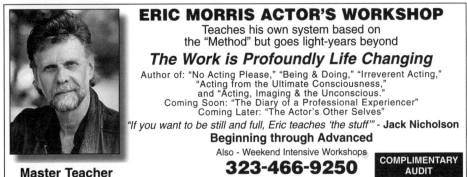

David Mamet   Allison Janney   Kim Basinger   Luis Guzman   Ian Gomez   Matt McCoy

THE WILLIAM ALDERSON ACTING STUDIO

THE MOST EXPERIENCED MEISNER TEACHER IN L.A.

(323) 852-1816 OR (323) 669-1534

For personal quotes of actors pictured above, go to www.aldersonstudio.com

Kimberly Jentzen

AWARD-WINNING DIRECTOR AND COACH

"No other acting coach will help you get results like Kimberly!"

– *Katie Rich , "NYPD Blue,"
"Robbery Homicide Division," "Philly"*

Call for Free Consultation

818.779.7770 www.kimberlyjentzen.net

ALLAN MILLER

Author of *"A PASSION FOR ACTING"*
and the video *"AUDITIONING"*

TEACHER, COACH TO:
***Meryl Streep,Dustin Hoffman, Barbra Streisand,
Lily Tomlin, Peter Boyle, Sigourney Weaver, etc.***

CLASSES IN COLD READING, AUDITIONING, SCENE STUDY

Eves: 7:30 to 10:30 pm   Call: 818.907.6262

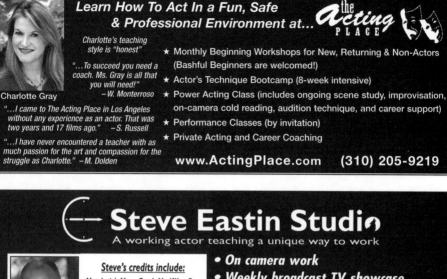

Learn How To Act In a Fun, Safe & Professional Environment at... **the Acting PLACE**

Charlotte's teaching style is "honest"

"...To succeed you need a coach. Ms. Gray is all that you will need!" – W. Monterroso

Charlotte Gray

"...I came to The Acting Place in Los Angeles without any experience as an actor. That was two years and 17 films ago." – S. Russell

"...I have never encountered a teacher with as much passion for the art and compassion for the struggle as Charlotte." – M. Dolden

★ Monthly Beginning Workshops for New, Returning & Non-Actors (Bashful Beginners are welcomed!)

★ Actor's Technique Bootcamp (8-week intensive)

★ Power Acting Class (includes ongoing scene study, improvisation, on-camera cold reading, audition technique, and career support)

★ Performance Classes (by invitation)

★ Private Acting and Career Coaching

www.ActingPlace.com   (310) 205-9219

Steve Eastin Studio
A working actor teaching a unique way to work

Steve's credits include:
Matchstick Men , Catch Me If You Can, A Man Apart, Con Air ,Field of Dreams, Austin Powers, The District, NYPD Blue, X-Files, Seinfeld and over 500 feature films, TV shows & commercials.

• On camera work
• Weekly broadcast TV showcase
• Cold reading technique
• Select casting director seminars
• No Method exercises
• Evening and day classes

VISA MasterCard AMERICAN EXPRESS

IN THE MOMENT

An Acting Class for the Trained Actor

SPECIALIZING IN

ON-CAMERA AUDITION TECHNIQUE

Gerry Cousins has fashioned her studio as a direct segue into the professional world of film and TV—emphasizing craft, focus, relaxation and commitment. "Actors are different, their mechanisms are different." Students needs are met specifically—no single technique. Work in every class! Industry professionals invited.

"allowing the imagination to take you to a place of truth"

(818) 728-6740

TV/Film Workshop & Master Class
AN AUDITION/INTERVIEW REQUIRED

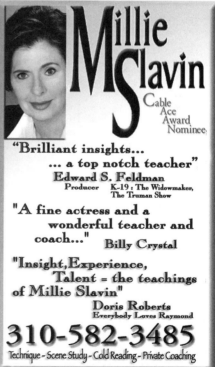

Millie Slavin

Cable Ace Award Nominee

"Brilliant insights... ... a top notch teacher"
Edward S. Feldman
Producer   K-19 : The Widowmaker, The Truman Show

"A fine actress and a wonderful teacher and coach..." **Billy Crystal**

"Insight, Experience, Talent = the teachings of Millie Slavin"
Doris Roberts
Everybody Loves Raymond

310-582-3485
Technique - Scene Study - Cold Reading - Private Coaching

**ACTING
COMMERCIALS
IMPROV
SHOWCASES
SCENE STUDY
MUSICAL THEATRE
COMEDY
ACTOR'S IMAGE
COLD READING**

GAIN AN EDGE!

JUNE·CHANDLER'S
ACTORS
W O R K S H O P

(626) 355.4572   www.junechandler.com

Getting the Readings, but Not Getting the Jobs?
Stop Guessing, and Start Auditioning to Win!

Basil Hoffman

Veteran character actor in more than
30 features and scores of telefilms
and series from "M*A*S*H" to
"The Practice"and "The West Wing."
teaches from his best-selling book–

*Cold Reading
and How to Be
Good at It*

1. Learn to get and hold their
   attention - *the whole time, every time.*

2. Learn to find the seven key
   elements in every scene.

3. Learn the four essential guideposts
   to truthful clarity in every reading.

4. Learn and master the simple
   technique that may get you the job
   before you read.

COLD
READING
AND HOW TO BE
GOOD AT IT

BASIL HOFFMAN

Teaching and Coaching.
Classes/Private Sessions.
(818) 247-0302

Coming soon: New book
Acting and How to Be Good at It

**DIANE
SALINGER**
Leading regular on HBO's new series
CARNIVÀLE

*"The greatest gift you have to offer is
yourself. Bring YOURSELF to the work
and become FEARLESS!"*

TIM BURTON - CLINT EASTWOOD - WOODY ALLEN
– directors who have worked with Ms. Salinger –

ACTING CLASSES
Beginning – Professional
Showcases / On Camera / Auditioning
PRIVATE COACHING
(323) 512-6062

JOEL ASHER

**ACTING
UNLIMITED**
Classes/Private
On-Camera
Scene Study
Cold Reading
Improvisation

818.785.1551

THE ACTORS AT WORK SERIES
Get the Award Winning Video Series, Designed for the Professional Actor!

"Jam-Packed with
REAL, USABLE Information!"
—Back Stage West

"Invaluable Resource
for Actors!"
—Booklist

★ ★ ★ ★
—Video Librarian

1. GETTING THE PART
   Audition with Confidence

2. CASTING DIRECTORS
   "Tell it like it is!"
   Learn what Casting Directors
   are *Really* looking for!

3. AGENTS "Tell it like it is!"
   Get the *Right* Agent to Sign You!

ONLY
$29.95 EA

GET THE SET
($74.85)
& SAVE $15.00!

Joel
Asher
STUDIO

AVAILABLE AT SAMUEL FRENCH, INC. OR CALL 1-800-652-7437

DOUG WARHIT
ACTING WORKSHOPS
310-479-5647

"I wish I could see actors trained by Doug Warhit at every casting session."

JUNIE LOWRY-JOHNSON
Casting Director N.Y.P.D. Blue

"A brilliant coach!" **AMY HECKERLING**
Director of "CLUELESS"

Tom Todoroff
S T U D I O

Acting ~ Directing
Producing ~ Writing
Voice ~ Speech

Classes held Wednesday & Thursday evenings in Santa Monica.

310-281-8688

www.tomtodoroff.com

WHY ARE MOST ACADEMY AWARD WINNERS METHOD ACTORS?
THE METHOD
HULL ACTORS STUDIO
Classes/Private Coaching

Based on **STANISLAVSKI** and **STRASBERG** and **KAZAN**

with Dianne Hull and Lorrie Hull Ph.D.,
author of "Strasberg's Method As Taught by Lorrie Hull"
and "The Method Video."
Also, Private Lessons offered for accent reduction.

Beg.–Adv. (310) 828-0632 www.actors-studio.com/hull

Isn't it time for a reel career?

It would be an absolutely brilliant move on your part if you called **Diane Christiansen** for coaching!

818.523.8283 or 661.263.8252

Diane coaches
KIDS, TEENS, & ADULTS
with high booking ratio.
Reaching the "whole" actor.
Reasonable rates.

Classes and Private Coaching
West Hollywood • Sherman Oaks • Valencia

Acting with
David J. Partington
SAG • AFTRA • AEA

Working Actor and Coach for 25 years

Private Coaching and Classes

Work includes:
• cold reading
• text analysis
• improvisation
• audition preparation
• career guidance

All Sessions on Camera

(818)360-9695

DAVID LeGRANT

STUDIO FOR ACTING

818-506-0717

JANICE KENT PRIVATE COACHING

SPECIALIZING IN SIT-COM
AUDITION TECHNIQUE
ONGOING CLASSES

"A Great Coach! Don't miss an opportunity to train with her!"

JEFF GREENBERG, CASTING DIRECTOR,
Frasier, According to Jim, I'm With Her, etc.

IN 2003, MY STUDENTS APPEARED IN:
One on One, CSI, Scrubs, NYPD Blue, Frasier, Raymond, Reba, ER, Days of Our Lives and more!

818-906-2201

CHRISTIAN ACTORS
ON-CAMERA
FILM ACTING
PERSONAL COACHING
CAREER COUNSELLING
• COLD READING • SCENE STUDY
• RECORDED SCENES • SPIRIT LED

GODWORKS
PRODUCTIONS
323-656-1098
PROVERBS 25:11

STAND-UP COMEDY COACH
Privates   Classes
Sit-Com Auditions
13 Years of Stand-up
100 TV Shows
DANNY WOODBURN
323.376.6317
e-mail ComedyDNA@aol.com
Technique ◆ Voice ◆ Persona

THE YOUNG ACTORS WORKSHOP

ELIZABETH A. BAUMAN
A C T I N G   C O A C H

TEL: 323-656-0552
WEBSITE: http://www.youngactorsworkshop.com

POST OFFICE BOX 241753, LOS ANGELES, CA 90024

ACTION-REACTION ANNOUNCES:
OPENINGS
BY AUDITION ONLY
Michael Holmes
ACTING CLASSES
• RECOMMENDED BY UTA HAGEN AND MICHAEL KEATON!
Enrollment limited!
Serious only call (818) 786-1045

WANTED: 12 ACTORS WITH GOOD ATTITUDES.
-weekly 3-hour class
-reasonable fee
-joyful, nurturing environment
-pro, intermediate, & beginning

Reliable, serious people only.
Kate Randolph **323/882-6669**

Marlon Hoffman
Actors Institute
Classes
•
Private Coach
Professional Studio
Environment
Showcases & Readings
"Marlon Hoffman inspires new levels of trust, confidence and joy in the actors' work."
–Karole Foreman
Credits: Law and Order, Mamma Mia, Becker
Hollywood & Calabasas
Call (818) 878-0242
www.marlonhoffman.com

A NOISE WITHIN CONSERVATORY
• Speaking Shakespeare
• Acting Shakespeare
• Stage Fencing & Combat
• Voice for the Stage
• Young People's Workshop
Class Schedule: 818/240-0910
www.ANoiseWithin.org
ENROLL NOW!
A Noise Within
California's Classical Theatre Company

CASTING DIRECTOR
MELISSA SKOFF, C.S.A.
ADVANCED ONGOING
SCENE STUDY & AUDITION TECHNIQUE CLASSES
PRIVATE COACHING AVAILABLE
CASTING DIRECTOR FOR 100+ FEATURES & TV SHOWS. PROVEN RESULTS!
(818) 760-2058
NO GUARANTEE OF EMPLOYMENT

MICHAEL E. RYAN'S ACTING CLUB
STUDY METHOD/
FILM ACTING
LOS ANGELES AREA
Call (323) 839-5461
Beginners Welcome

COMMERCIAL WORKSHOP
6-Week On-Camera

Learn How To Make 30 Seconds Work For You

TERRY BERLAND, CCDA
Author of "BREAKING INTO COMMERCIALS"
Includes Meeting Agent
www.terryberlandcasting.com
for testimonials and reel.
310-571-4141

VAN MAR ACADEMY
of MOTION PICTURE AND TV ACTING
Since 1967
Hollywood's Top Career School

A TOTAL OF OVER 556 SERIES –
continuing & recurring roles (documented)

*"Ivan Markota is the Guru
of marketing actors toward stardom."*
—JAY BERNSTEIN *(Legendary Starmaker)*

AUDIT FREE – TUITION REASONABLE
(323) 650-8823

---

truth, lies & memory...
Creating the One-Person Show
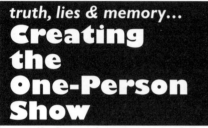
small classes / private coaching
Terrie Silverman 310.281.3175
www.creativerites.com

LOOKING FOR AN AGENT?
It starts here... an extraordinary summer camp for extraordinary young actors in Hollywood. A step-by-step residential program to kick off a career in the film and television industry.

YoungActorsCamp.com

---

*"He is the best example of a teacher
who can give you a technique of acting."*
– Stella Adler

RON BURRUS ACTING STUDIO

www.ronburrus.com

CAROL WEISS
Musical Theatre Workshop

Learn what to say to a pianist
Develop new material
Discover roles that are right for you
Review your work on videotape
Audition for directors, producers

323-460-6006
"You can sing - You can Act - Now put them together!"

BB's Kids
Acting Workshop
On camera with
Belinda Balaski
40 Years Experience

www.BBsKids.com

Commercial/Theatrical/Musical
Theatre/Sitcom/Private Coaching & more
Ages 4 & up/Kids & Teens

(323) 650-KIDS

TO ADVERTISE IN THE NEXT
BACKSTAGE/BACK STAGE WEST
ACTORS HANDBOOK

WEST ■   ■ **EAST**

Back Stage West Advertising	Back StageAdvertising
5055 Wilshire Blvd., 5th floor	770 Broadway, 4th floor
Los Angeles, CA 90036	New York, NY 10003
323.525.2225	646.654.5700

STELLADLER
TUDIO·OF·ACTING

TWO AND A HALF YEAR CONSERVATORY

This full time, 30 hour per week program combines a world class faculty, the highest artistic and theatrical standards and ideals, 2 full rounds of productions and an agent showcase.   Admission by audition.

FULL TIME EVENING PROGRAM

This 35 week, 16 hour per week actor training program is vigorous and thorough. It includes Adler Technique, Scene Study, Voice & Speech, Movement Technique, Shakespeare, Script Interpretation, and Improvisation. The final 5 weeks will be devoted to rehearsal for a performance done for the public. Admission by audition.

SUMMER DAY PROGRAM

An intensive course that introduces the student actor to the fundamentals of the Adler technique and the many different disciplines that go into the training of a well rounded actor. This three day per week, 20 hours per week course is structured along the same lines as our New York University/Tisch School of the Arts BFA Program, allowing the beginning actor an opportunity to work with our world class faculty and gain a solid foundation of craft.   This program is also ideal for the actor who is looking to explore a new technique or approach to acting. Interview required.

SUMMER SHAKESPEARE INTENSIVE

The summer Shakespeare intensive will address Voice, Speech, Language, Movement Techniques, Stage Combat and Scene Study, specifically finding the actor in the character, the character in the scene, the scene in the play and the play in today's world. This full-time program is conducted by a unified team of accomplished faculty. Ends with a presentation. Admission by audition.

SUMMER CHEKHOV INTENSIVE

A unique, 30 hours/week program focusing on the plays of Anton Chekhov towards developing an understanding of and technique for modern realism. Using scenes from Chekhov's plays; the actor will learn to analyze the text and identify the nature of the character, define the character's objectives and activate the character through action. Admission by audition.

WORKSHOPS

Basic, Intermediate, and Advanced classes, held during the evenings – call for complete details.

STELLADLER
TUDIO·OF·ACTING

Larry Rivera

Stella Adler Studio Of Acting   31 West 27th, 3rd FL New York, NY 10001
Phone: 212 689 0087 or 800 270-6775 Fax: 212 689 6110
www.stelladler.com | info@stelladler.com

WILLIAM ESPER STUDIO

DEDICATED TO THE WORK OF SANFORD, MEISNER AND TO THE PROPOSITION THAT ACTING IS A CREATIVE ART AND TRUE EXCELLENCE IN ITS PRACTICE CAN ONLY BE ACHIEVED THROUGH TOTAL MASTERY OF TECHNICAL CRAFT.

ESTABLISHED 1963

INTENSIVE TWO YEAR TRAINING PROGAM
FOR PROFESSIONAL AND
PRE-PROFESSIONAL ACTORS

SIX WEEK SUMMER INTENSIVE

(212) 904-1350
WWW.ESPERSTUDIO.COM

ACTORS! SINGERS! INTIMIDATED BY DANCE CLASS?

"As a teacher/choreographer I believe that dance embellished with feeling and guided by technique and talent will enhance the actor's or singer's ability to develop complete characterizations in performance."

-Haila Strauss

Carol Rosegg Photography

Join The Special Dance Workshop for Actors & Singers
Class Size is Limited. Individual Attention a Priority

To Reserve Your Place Call Haila Strauss
(212) 388-7967

CALL FOR BEGINNER & ADVANCED BEGINNER NEW SCHEDULE

Creation is a Journey of Faith

"Moving from darkness to light... that is why creation is a journey of faith. Through this acting technique you can free the multiplicity of your expressions and find your individual essence. This process reveals your unique creative talent."

"Thurman E. Scott is the inheritor of the Stanislavsky legacy and of my legacy." – Stella Adler

**Study in the Scott Technique
Master Training Program with
Thurman E. Scott**

All experience levels train as an ensemble in a uniquely integrated approach to Technique, Scene Study, Script Analysis and Character Development.

To learn more and receive our newsletter, visit us at www.ActorsTheatreWorkshop.com or call (212) 947-1386

NEW YORK   NEW YORK
THE TED BARDY STUDIO
INTENSE, PERSONALIZED ACTING INSTRUCTION FOR THE DEDICATED ARTIST

*"An amazingly gifted teacher. **Ted Bardy's** students always get very, very serious consideration. They've got it. They've just got it."*
–Lee Rudnick, former V.P., Columbia Pictures Television

*"**Ted Bardy** is an expert on the details that can make each audition count."*
–Show Business Weekly

*"I studied with **Ted Bardy** and I hire actors from **The Ted Bardy Studio**. Why? Because they are the best trained and **Ted Bardy** is the best acting teacher currently teaching in the New York area."*
–Nelson Denis, Actor/Writer/Director of the Tribeca Film Festival Smash Hit "Vote For Me!" ("Scathing Portrayals!" — The New York Times)

Acting Technique & Scene Study – Meisner technique. Establish/re-establish an all-important foundation in basic acting technique. Ongoing classes.

Advanced Workshop –(no beginners please) **Audition technique, film & TV work (on-camera), script analysis & interpretation, cold readings, and character work.** Application of technique is further explored through **advanced scene study** leading to public performance.

Professional Workshop Productions – (Interview/audition required) Presented for **agents, casting directors, managers, filmmakers, and other members of the industry.**

Private Coaching – For: audition preparation (a specialty), actors having problems applying their craft, on-set/on-location coaching also available. Special consults for Directors & Producers.

Motivated Beginners • Working Professionals • Affordable • Small, intimate classes • Actors work multiple times every class

(212) 769-7666   for more info: **(917) 968-4800**
24-hour message center   **www.tedbardy.com**   studio line/coaching appts.

WB The Nations first and most respected school for On-Camera Training since 1956!

Three Great Divisions under one roof offering classes throughout the year in
Film ☆ Soap Opera & Primetime TV ☆ Cold Reading Audition ☆ Speech ☆ Voice-Over
Acting Technique ☆ Improvisation ☆ Musical Theater ☆ Special Summer Courses ☆ Showcases
And of Course the Very Best Commecial Training

WEIST   Adult Division
BARRON
212 840-7025
www.weistbarron.com

ACTeen   Ages 13 to 19
212 391-5915
www.acteen.com

KIDS   Ages 5-6 / 7-9 / 10-12
LOVE ACTING
212 874-1081

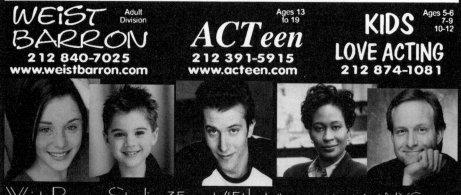

Weist-Barron Studios 35 west 45th st (between 5th & 6th Ave) NYC 10036

MAGGIE FLANIGAN
S T U D I O

917-606.0982 studio
917-606.0983 fax

153 WEST 27th STREET
SUITE 803 NYC 10001

PROFESSIONAL
ACTING CLASSES

2 YEAR PROFESSIONAL ACTOR TRAINING PROGRAM
- *Meisner Technique*

• Master Class - Contemporary Text
• Master Class - Classical Text
• Cold Reading/Audition Class
• Monologue Class
• Private Professional Coaching

Formerly of: The William Esper Studio, Inc. and Mason Gross School of the Arts,
Professional Acting Program, Rutgers University

The Actors Craft
A two year conservatory program
designed to provide a foundation for the actor in the craft and art of acting,
while building an approach to the business of creating a career.

Improvisation • Movement • Voice • Acting Technique • Scene Study •
On Camera Acting • Theatre History • Script Analysis •
Career Coaching • Audition Technique •
The Shakespeare Workshops • The Creative Intensive

NOW AUDITIONING. ONLY 12 STUDENTS ACCEPTED PER SESSION.

"Personal, comprehensive, the way acting training should be."

Entrance by audition and interview.
For more information call **212-924-8888x16**

The Actors Institute
Building Strong Actors Since 1977

159 West 25th Street, 9th Floor
NY, NY 10001
www.tairesources.com

Internationally Acclaimed
Theatre, Concert & Recording Artist

ELLY STONE
Vocal Technique – Coaching

MS. STONE TEACHES Through
Intensive Body/Mind/Breath Work

HOW TO
• Achieve Power without pushing

• Eliminate breaks, and breathiness

• Free The Natural Beauty of the Voice

• Finally reveal the individuality which
is at the heart of performance

Stella Adler – "Elly Stone is a force of nature
onstage, and **a master teacher**"
Show Business – "She is regarded as one of
the best teachers of technique & interpretation
in the U.S. & Canada."
NY Times – "Her voice takes wing and floats
effortlessly-from whispers to triumphant
crescendos."
Newsweek: "She doesn't act her songs-she
becomes their living embodiment."
Time – "Her voice is oracular, like the peal-
ing of bells."

(212) 874-6290

Gregg Goldston

"... a blazing display of physical virtousity."
Anna Kisselgoff - The New York Times

"...among the best I've seen in my long career."
- Marcel Marceau

Mime & Physical Comedy Coach for film and stage

Goldston Studio for Mime & Comedy
Year-round classes in New York City

Goldston School for Mimes
3-Week Summer Intensive
New York City

Call: 212/560-4333
Details at: www.goldmime.com

ACTING FOR CAMERA

• Maria Greco • Tony Greco (Casting Directors)

• Commercial • Film • Soaps • Auditioning Techniques
• "Business of Acting" • Career Guidance And Counseling
• New Saturday Scene Class • Audition Nite: Agents & Casting Dirs.
(for those who have reached professional levels of skills and attitude)
• 10 students or less per class • In Business 30 Years

ARM YOURSELF WITH
KNOWLEDGE OF THE BUSINESS

(212) 247-2011
Dovetail Entertainment Inc. Film Center Building,

www.mariagrecocasting.com

CAC – school for the working actor

Intro to Acting
Scene Study
TV/Film
Advanced Commercial
Comedy

Acting Level 1
Soap Opera
Basic Commercial
Monologue
Improv

AND THE BEST MARKETING FOR ACTORS COURSE IN THE CITY

Call 212.352.2103 to set up a free audit or check out our website www.creativeacting.com

Creative Acting Company 122 West 26th Street Suite 1102 NY

WORK WITH THE MAN WHO WROTE THE BOOK!

THE *Perfect* AUDITION MONOLOGUE

Private Coaching with **Glenn Alterman**

Author of 15 #1 Best Selling Books, including

THE PERFECT AUDITION MONOLOGUE • AN ACTOR'S GUIDE - MAKING IT IN NEW YORK
CREATING YOUR OWN MONOLOGUE • 2 MINUTES & UNDER (VOL. 1 & 2)

PERSONALIZED MONOLOGUES that <u>SELL YOU</u> and <u>WIN AUDITIONS</u>
TOTAL AUDITION PREPARATION from Entrance to Exit
over 5,000 rarely done Theater, Film, TV & Original Monologues

"Those looking for the best ways to create, maintain & strengthen their industry relationships should look no further!" - **Bernard Telsey, casting director**

FLEXIBLE SCHEDULING • REASONABLE RATES • ALL LEVELS

212-769-7928 www.GlennAlterman.com

Three Steps To A Sucessful Career In Acting

1) Read One of the most important books on acting:
Sande Shurin's Transformational Acting

2) Call about a **Free Orientation** seminar to
"The Shurin Technique"

3) Study acting with a **POWERFUL TEACHER**
concerned with **making a difference** in your life.

Ms. Shurin & staff (NYC) **212 262-6848** (Woodstock NY) **845 679-5359**
www.SandeShurin.com

Thomas Vasiliades
Alexander Technique

Group Classes and Individual Lessons
212-726-1569

Actors improve their breathing coordination and vocal production, create the physical life of characters with ease and have greater availability to give expression of their emotions.

ACTING/DIRECTING FOR YOUR CREATIVE LIFE at The Tish School
LONGTERM GOAL TO FORM A COMPANY
Call 212-929-4156

Wanted: (a) Beginners-SERIOUSLY COMMITTED to learning, to your scene partners, to rehearsals. (b) *Intermediate/Experienced* – Wanting to return to Acting. Some previous acting training required. Gentle though detailed approach to discovering a process of acting & directing for theatre/camera emphasizing supportive encouragement, personal expression, relief for those stuck in the corporate business grind, commitment to those with whom you work.   **Call 212-929-4156**

JOAN STEPHENS
presents
THE ONE STOP ACTING WORKSHOP
Commercials • Soaps • Film • Monologues
Taught by well known agents & Casting Directors
Info at: **212-288-0544**
jsstarmaker@aol.com

JEFFREY STOCKER
Director & Professional Acting Coach of
THE FILM ACTING STUDIO
★
ON-CAMERA PRIVATE COACHING • COLD-READING TECHNIQUE
AUDITION/PRE-SHOOT COACHING • CAREER CONSULTATION
SHOWCASE PERFORMANCES
Recommended by leading New York & Los Angeles Casting Directors & Agents
Member of the National Academy of Television & Motion Picture Arts & Sciences
Listed in Who's Who in Entertainment • Member of the National Arts Club
Interview by Appointment Only
WWW.FILMACTINGSTUDIO.com
(212) 725-3437
90 Lexington Avenue, Suite 1 H, NY, NY 10016

ACTING COACH
Matthew Del Negro
of
The Sopranos
(Cousin Brian – Tony's financial advisor)
Classes/Private Coaching
212-330-6941
www.matthewdelnegro.com

Musical Theatre Audition Technique

Paul Harman
-Technique
-Preparation
-Achievement
Studio

Learn the technique to craft any song and give a Great Audition!

Taught by: Paul Harman
–15 Broadway shows and National Tours
–7 original casts including: "Les Miserables," "Chess," and the York's "Merrily We Roll Along."

CURRENT AND FORMER STUDENTS ON BROADWAY AND NATIONAL TOURS.

LIMITED ENROLLMENT
6 CLASSES PER SESSION
Call (212) 252-4767

www.auditionsuccess.com

T. SCHREIBER STUDIO
Acting on the Creative Process since 1969

"There are so many schools for a young actor arriving in New York. For me, finding the T. Schreiber Studio proved to be an enormous blessing."
Edward Norton

CLASSES:
Acting/Scene Study
On-Camera
Audition Technique
Vocal Production
Body Dynamics
Private Coaching

FACULTY:
Terry Schreiber
Betty Buckley
Sally Dunn
Julie Garfield
Peter Jensen
Peter Miner
Carol Reynolds
Pam Scott
Lynn Singer

FULL SEASON OF PRODUCTIONS

212-741-0209
151 West 26th Street ▪ t-s-s.org

STEPHEN ROSENFIELD'S
STAND-UP COMEDY WORKSHOP
With intensive training in classes and private writing sessions conducted by award-winning comedy director Stephen Rosenfield you will create your own stand-up set and perform at
CAROLINES
AMERICAN COMEDY INSTITUTE
Call 212-279-6980
www.comedyinstitute.com

Don't Dream It. Be It.

THE JASON BENNETT ACTOR'S WORKSHOP

Rooted in the theories of all the Master Acting teachers & incorporating advances in psychology, neurology & semiotics: This approach is on the cutting edge.

Workshops, Classes, Coaching
BennettActorsWorkshop.com
212-777-7603

ROBERT HAUFRECHT
Actor, Director, Teacher

- Private Coaching currently available
- Classes forming soon

★ Former Managing Director of Common Basis Theatre

Bob-Smile

★ Former Teacher at NY Acting School (Singapore)

★ Currently teaching at Michael Howard Studios

Coached former student Ian Kirch's first audition in NYC ...and he got the part in "Danny and the Deep Blue Sea"

(917) 294-9833
rhauf55@yahoo.com

Study, Write, and Perform Comedy in NYC in the One Year Program at the American Comedy Institute.

AMERICAN COMEDY INSTITUTE

Call 212-279-6980
www.comedyinstitute.com

ATLANTIC

ACTING CLASSES IN THE TECHNIQUE DEVELOPED BY

DAVID MAMET & WILLIAM H. MACY

FULL TIME 2-YEAR CONSERVATORY

- INTERVIEW NOW!
- Full conservatory training including voice, speech and movement
- Shakespeare classes
- On-camera classes
- Student Productions

6-WEEK SUMMER INTENSIVE IN NYC

- Classes meet 6 days per week
- Full conservatory training including voice and movement
- Script Analysis/ Performance Technique

PART TIME CLASSES ALSO AVAILABLE!
CALL FOR MORE INFO: 212-691-5919
or e-mail **admissions@atlantictheater.org**

INTERVIEW NOW! LIMITED SPACE!
Atlantic Theater Company, 453 W. 16th Street
New York, NY 10011, www.atlantictheater.org

---

unique original monologues

By Actors, For Actors
3 volumes of monologues and scenes

By Kids, For Kids
for ages 6–18

BY KIDS FOR KIDS

"For those searching for material that 'hasn't been done to death'." — BackStage

1-800-729-6423
www.ExcaliburPublishing.com

ZINA JASPER SCENE STUDY

Private Coach & Director
20 years Teaching Experience

Advanced Ongoing Workshop

Contemporary/Classical
Auditors Permitted

212-873-2370

Barbara Kahn
acting coach

* audition techniques
* monologues
* performance
  troubleshooting

212-820-1234

www.barbara-kahn.com
convenient Manhattan location

The Voice Department of
TURTLE BAY MUSIC SCHOOL
244 East 52 Street, New York, NY 10022

- **PRIVATE SINGING LESSONS**
  – All levels, all styles
- **BEGINNING VOICE CLASS**
- **VOICE REHABILITATION**
  – plus–
- **CABARET WORKSHOP**
- **MUSICAL THEATER WORKSHOP**

CALL FOR INFORMATION
Maria Argyros, Chair Voice Dept.
212-753-8811 X20/www.tbms.org

PLAYING SHAKESPEARE

SPEAKING THE TEXT
MONOLOGUE WORKSHOP
STAGING FROM THE TEXT

TAUGHT BY JOHN BASIL

AMERICAN GLOBE THEATRE
www.americanglobe.org

(212) 869-9809

Private Coaching
- V/O, Radio—incl. Demo. CD
- Monologues/Scenes
- Theatre, TV and Film
Call for No Charge Evaluation
212 741 1444
LARRY CONROY
On Camera . . . And off, Inc.
42 West 13th. St. 4D
New York, NY 10011

CAROLINE THOMAS
TOTAL THEATER LAB

Integrated Acting Process • Scene Study
• Monologues • Voice & Speech
• Audition Coaching • Teen & Adult
Private and Group Classes • Showcases

212-799-4224

Acting Coach/Director/On Set
Jim Bonney
Preparing the
Actor to Work
Beginner to Working Actor
Ongoing Workshops & Classes
Private Coaching/Auditions

Studio: 212-713-5277
www.jimbonneyacting.com

Want to "Breakthrough"
and meet NYC's top Casting
Directors and Agents?

Breakthrough Studios. LLC
Industry seminars, Studio rentals and
on-camera classes

212 West 35th Street, 2nd Floor, NYC
212.594.9616

Visit our website for class schedules
www.breakthroughstudios.com

★ Star Map Acting Studio ★
Long Island's Professional Acting School
• *Lil Drama Kids* (ages 6-8) • *Drama Kids* (ages 9-12)
• *Drama Teens* (ages 13-17) • *Adult On-Going Acting
Workshops* (ages 17 & up) • *TV Commercial Training
TV/Film Classes* (ages 6 & up) • *Relaxation/
Meditation Workshops* • *Private Coaching* (all ages)
Sessions available day, evening & weekends.
• *Various Guest Teachers & Seminars.*
**TALENT MANAGER ON THE PREMISES-DREAM-
VISION TALENT, LTD.** Learn all about acting and the
business with qualified teachers who are working
actors!! All children's workshops are kept small (6-10
children per workshop). Two to three teachers are pre-
sent all times. Classes taught by owner/actor Laurie
Ann Davis and actor/teacher Christine Kolenik.
**Call (516) 937-STAR for more information
or to make an appointment!**
102 Woodbury Road, Hicksville, NY 11801
www.Starmapactingschool.com

Thinking of Grad School or Summer Abroad?
Private Coaching:

Monologue Selection and Polishing, Essay and Interview Techniques, Mock Audition Night
My clients have attended **Yale, NYU, ART, UCI, ACT, RADA, U of Wash & UCSD** among others.
Sessions: Jodie Lynne McClintock
(718) 476-2590 • www.jodiemcclintock.com
jlmcclintock@hotmail.com

Elaine Aiken
Lily Lodge
Actors Conservatory

We develop the actor with Sense Memory Techniques

Classes
Monday thru Saturday
Call for Interview
212-764-0543
www.actorsconservatory.org

BACK STAGE® and BACK STAGE WEST®
The #1 weeklies for Performing Artists

SUBSCRIBE TODAY
1.800.745.8922
http://www.backstage.com/backstage/contact/printsub.jsp

3 A Matter of Degrees:

B.A., B.F.A., M.F.A. — Sifting Through the Alphabet Soup of Theatre Programs

BY ESTHER TOLKOFF

Why go to a university to learn to act, dance, sing, design, direct, or write for the theatre, as opposed to simply making the rounds? A slew of faculty members (who are also theatrical artists with extensive credits and ongoing contacts in their areas) all have the same basic answer to this question: You go to school to really learn your craft.

"A university program gives structure and a context to the many skills theatre students have to master," says Dan Carter, head of Pennsylvania State University's School of Theatre Arts and a member of the Commission of Accreditation of the National Association of Schools of Theatre (NAST). "Talent is a must. When we audition potential degree candidates, we look for that and for prior theatre experience, even school theatre. Motivation is also a must. But an artist needs to become an educated person too."

What kinds of university programs are out there? What do they offer? And how do you cross the bridge to the world beyond university theatre?

The most intensive and prestigious university theatre degree is the graduate level M.F.A. (Master of Fine Arts) degree, which generally takes two to three years to earn. Both the M.F.A. and the undergraduate level B.F.A. (Bachelor of Fine Arts) are conservatory-style programs geared toward developing consummate professionals. Both programs are career focused and highly competitive, with hundreds of prospective students often vying for a small number of coveted spots.

Acting, musical theatre, and dance students are selected via auditions, which many schools schedule in several cities around the country. The University/Resident Theatre Association (URTA), headquartered in New York, coordinates many such auditions, so that prospective students can try out for several schools during the course of one visit to a given city.

M.F.A. and B.F.A. programs are also offered for directors, playwrights, and designers, and in such areas as theatre management and technical production. Students in each of these various specialty programs within a school regularly collaborate—under the guidance of faculty members—with the goal of learning about one another's areas. Student actors will often workshop a student playwright's script, working with a student director and student designers.

Many colleges offer undergraduate theatre studies as a major under the umbrella of a B.A. (Bachelor of Arts) liberal arts program. A student generally does not audition to become a theatre major seeking a B.A. "There is some controversy as to whether the B.F.A. or the B.A. is the better approach," notes Sam Leiter, chairman of Brooklyn College's Department of Theatre, which, like many schools, offers both B.F.A. and B.A. theatre degrees, as well as master's degrees. "Some people prefer the concentrated focus of the B.F.A. Others feel an artist needs to acquire a broader education to have a base of cultural knowledge to draw upon."

Brandeis University, in the Boston area, prides itself on the highly personalized conservatory approach of its M.F.A. program. But its undergraduate theatre students also take general liberal arts coursework and earn a B.A. The same faculty members work with both sets of students.

Still other schools, such as Penn State—which offers a B.F.A. in musical theatre, a B.A. acting program, and M.F.A. degrees—feel that a properly planned B.F.A. program can allow a student to acquire the eclectic outlook that Carter speaks of.

For those interested in a scholarly focus, many universities offer Master of Arts (M.A.) and Doctor of Philosophy (Ph.D.) programs in theatre. These generally focus on theatrical history, theatrical criticism, or the study of dramatic works as literature.

It's up to you to take a good look at what each school offers, ask questions, and play an active role in seeking the training and education you will need.

TAKING ONE'S CRAFT TO A HIGHER LEVEL

An increasing number of performers work for a few years after college before deciding to head back to the university world to get an M.F.A.

One reason working performers go back to school is that having an M.F.A. on one's résumé is seen as proof of high-level training. Another reason is to acquire a clearer idea of what one wants or needs to learn or improve upon.

M.F.A. acting students sharpen such skills as text analysis, voice, movement, and stage combat without the distractions of making the rounds and of day-to-day auditions. The goal is to practice your craft. M.F.A. performing programs demand an enormous amount of onstage work, often in connection with professional theatres. Many programs offer financial aid. They also often offer the opportunity to participate in the Actors' Equity Membership Candidate Program.

Are M.F.A. and B.F.A. courses different? Yes, says Lavonia Moyer, head of Wayne State University's acting program in Detroit. "When I work with B.F.A. students, I focus on the foundations: What is the intention? What are the obstacles? What are the personal connections? M.F.A. students have already absorbed those things."

Each university has its own approach and, in some cases, its own specialties, such as classical or musical theatre. Since theatrical work is collaborative by nature, it is important to look over a program and its faculty to see if you feel this is a "match." Study the school's website. Write to people working in areas of interest to you. Visit the school. Contact organizations such as NAST. Some students do best in a large urban environment, others on a small campus.

The personalized nature of theatrical work leads to strong alumni ties, which can be an entrée to important contacts. Professors at each school proudly reel off names of former students who are well-known artists, and stay in touch with them and with graduates doing related work (publicists, agents, etc.)

While Southern California is known as film industry headquarters, it is not the only source of drama students who go on to film work. New York University's Tisch School of the Arts has programs in both theatrical and film work. Most drama programs these days have at least one "Acting for the Camera" course, and possibly a class in voiceover work and "the business of the business" as well.

THE APPRENTICESHIP MODEL

In a theatre center such as New York, the many college theatre programs available offer internships, often paid, with any of a number of well-known theatre companies. Renowned artists regularly give master classes or speak.

Nationwide, university departments cultivate strong ties with top regional theatres. For instance, students at the University of Missouri in Kansas City work with the Missouri Repertory Theatre. All M.F.A. students at the University of California at San Diego work at the La Jolla Playhouse, an excellent credit to have. UCSD undergraduates often audition for, and land, roles at the Playhouse, which works closely with San Diego State University's musical theatre program as well. At the nearby University of San Diego, M.F.A. candidates are involved with the Old Globe Theatre, which specializes in Shakespearean works.

All good theatre departments help students find summer theatre internships or summer study programs overseas, most commonly in London. URTA—found at www.urta.com—offers information about ties that member schools have with theatres throughout the country.

PERFORMING ON CAMPUS

Wayne State University in Detroit is home to the nation's only graduate student repertory theatre, the 532-seat Hilberry, a professional-level regional theatre with a subscription-based audience. The repertory approach allows an actor to play the lead one day and a minor part the next. Wayne State also has the 1,173-seat Bonstelle Theatre, where undergraduates often perform, and a small Studio Theatre for classroom productions. Its Black Theatre Program practices nontraditional casting—choosing African-American themes, while including white, Asian, and Latino actors and characters.

Many campuses offer a similar range of choices. At Brandeis' Spingold Theatre Complex, for instance, M.F.A. students and faculty put on six productions per year in the mainstage theatre—and also work in two smaller theatres. B.A. students put on a mainstage production every year and also perform in an extracurricular Undergraduate Theatre Collective of seven theatre groups.

The University of Washington has three theatres on campus in addition to its ties to Seattle's theatre community. Penn State has three mainstage theatres plus its summer Pennsylvania Centre Stage. At Marymount Manhattan College in Manhattan, where both B.F.A. and B.A. programs are offered, students perform in the college's mainstage productions and in workshops in a black box setting. Each Marymount student must complete an independent project. The school's B.F.A. students have ongoing evaluations by faculty members who are also working professionals.

Brooklyn College's 500-seat Gershwin Theatre presents professional-level student productions to the surrounding, paying community on a regular basis.

SHOWCASING

As students near graduation time, they usually perform in university-arranged showcases for industry professionals, often in New York. Casting directors are also invited to campuses. Some schools—such as UCSD and the Yale School of Drama—cooperate in putting together joint showcases.

URTA holds its National Unified Auditions and Interviews in New York, Chicago, and San Francisco so that college students can try out for summer theatre, internships, and M.F.A. programs. URTA also holds a Master Auditions Program (MAP) for recent M.F.A.s seeking work in the commercial theatre world.

Theatrical work means forever learning and growing—and so do university studies. The two worlds complement one another. They're a natural match for strengthening your career.

AMERICAN CONSERVATORY THEATER

Master of Fine Arts Program

Tony Award®–winning A.C.T. is recognized by *U.S. News & World Report* as a leader in actor training. Enriched by its association with a preeminent regional theater company, the A.C.T. Master of Fine Arts Program graduates men and women of the theater who participate and provide leadership at all levels of the industry.

- Highly selective graduate program offers a rigorous three-year course of training

- Courses are taught by a superb faculty, including members of A.C.T.'s professional acting company

- Students perform alongside veteran actors in A.C.T. workshops and professional productions

- Master classes, seminars, and lectures offered by distinguished guest artists

- Acting showcases presented in New York, Los Angeles, and San Francisco

- School located in the culturally rich theater district of San Francisco

Summer Training Congress

Students, teachers, and professional actors from around the world gather in San Francisco each summer for this rigorous and rewarding nine-week program.

A.C.T.
american conservatory theater

Geary Theater
San Francisco

Carey Perloff, *artistic director*
Heather Kitchen, *managing director*

www.act-sf.org | 415.439.2350

Redford DeVito Cattrall Haysbert Bellows Stickney Sciorra Brody

Join the
ranks of
AADA
alumni.
Act now.

AADA alumni have been nominated for 72 Oscars®, 195 Emmys® and 57 Tonys®.

The American
Academy
of Dramatic
Arts
New York & Hollywood

Audition for

• College Degree
Conservatory Program
(Scholarships available)

New York only:
• Evening Program (Adults) – begins in January
• Saturday Courses (Children, Teens, Adults) – begin in February

Apply Now

120 Madison Avenue, New York, NY 10016
800 463 8990

1336 North La Brea Ave, Hollywood, CA 90028
800 222 2867

www.aada.org

AUDITIONS
FOR THEATRE TRAINING IN
NEW YORK CITY AND LOS ANGELES

- CHOICE OF PROGRAMS OFFERING THE STUDY OF ACTING FOR THE THEATRE, FILM AND TELEVISION, MUSICAL THEATRE AND DANCE
- FACULTY OF PROFESSIONAL ARTISTS
- ACCREDITED BY NAST
- INTERNATIONAL STUDENT BODY
- SCHOLARSHIPS/STUDENT HOUSING PROVIDED

AUDITION LOCATIONS

ATLANTA	LOS ANGELES	SEATTLE
BOSTON	MINNEAPOLIS	ST. LOUIS
CHICAGO	NASHVILLE	TAMPA
CINCINNATI	NEW YORK CITY	WASHINGTON, D.C.
CLEVELAND	PHOENIX	
DALLAS	PORTLAND	CANADA:
DENVER	RALEIGH	CALGARY
HOUSTON	SALT LAKE CITY	MONTREAL
KANSAS CITY	SAN FRANCISCO	TORONTO
LAS VEGAS		VANCOUVER

THE AMERICAN MUSICAL AND DRAMATIC ACADEMY
2109 Broadway, New York, New York 10023
(800) 367-7908   (212) 787-5300
6305 Yucca Street, Los Angeles, California 90028
(866) 374-5300
www.AMDA.edu
AMDA is an equal opportunity institution.

THE SHAKESPEARE THEATRE
ACADEMY FOR CLASSICAL ACTING
AT THE GEORGE WASHINGTON UNIVERSITY

GET THE TRAINING YOU NEED

A ONE-YEAR MFA PROGRAM
IN CLASSICAL ACTING

Spend twelve months studying classical acting with a distinguished professional faculty under the direction of Michael Kahn, one of the country's most respected directors and teachers of classical theatre. Intended for professional actors, this program focuses on the tools needed to handle the texts of Shakespeare and other classical playwrights.

Auditions in:
San Francisco,
Chicago,
New York,
Washington, D.C.

Program runs
August–July

ALEXANDER
CLOWN
MOVEMENT
MASK
VOICE
ACTING

Call 1-800-JOIN GWU
for complete brochure and application

shakespearetheatre.org

GW is an equal opportunity/affirmative action institution.

THEATRE ACADEMY
AT LOS ANGELES CITY COLLEGE

For quality of training and production excellence, location, and low tuition costs, the nationally-recognized Theatre Academy may well be the best professional theatre training program in the country.

Full-time conservatory training begins each Sept. & Feb.

ACTING
TECHNICAL THEATRE
COSTUMING

Evening acting classes taught by Academy faculty also available

For information on the Theatre Academy

(323) 953-4000 x2990

Theatre_Academy.lacitycollege.edu

Interested in the adventure of studying drama abroad?
There's no greater place than The London Academy of Music and Dramatic Art

TRAIN WITH THE BEST

LAMDA
THE LONDON
ACADEMY OF
MUSIC AND
DRAMATIC ART

Double Semester Classical Acting Course
An intensive class and workshop programme ending in a showcase in New York. Entrance by audition only.

Single Semester Classical Acting Course
For people who want to enrich their current university or college courses with an intense burst of conservatoire training from professionals and specialists. Entrance is by arrangement with your university or college.

Two-Year Stage Management & Technical Theatre
A broad-based course providing a high level of training in all aspects of management, stage management and technical theatre.

Actors and stage managers from around the world study on all of LAMDA's courses.

For more information on LAMDA's other courses including Summer Schools, please contact:

Admissions, LAMDA, 155 Talgarth Road, London, United Kingdom W14 9DA
Tel 00 44 20 8834 0500, Fax 00 44 20 8834 0501, enquiries@lamda.org.uk, or visit www.lamda.org.uk

MICHAEL MORIARTY
2002 Emmy

JOHN LITHGOW
2002 Tony

JIM BROADBENT
2002 Academy Award

The Performing Arts at Naropa. Powerful training leading to outrageous presence and innovation. BA, BFA and MFA programs in music, performance and theater.

inward | outward

Photo: Ken Miller

 Naropa
UNIVERSITY
Boulder • London
800-772-6951

The Naropa education comes to life at the intersection of professional training and contemplative practice. The result is compassion made real, fully and joyously engaged in the world. Visit us at www.naropa.edu.

ACTORFEST
A DAY FOR ACTORS

CAREER SEMINARS · CASTING DIRECTORS
AGENTS · FOCUS SESSIONS · MANAGERS
FREE EXHIBIT HALL · AND MUCH MORE

FOR EXHIBIT HALL SPACE CALL

WEST ■   ■ EAST

Back Stage West Advertising   Back Stage Advertising
5055 Wilshire Blvd., 5th fl.   770 Broadway, 4th floor
Los Angeles, CA 90036   New York, NY 10003
323.525.2225   646.654.5700

4 Laughing Matters:

Improving Your Chances with Improv

BY AMELIA DAVID

Honing improvisational skills can be valuable for almost anyone in the entertainment field. That's right: not just stand-up comics, but also actors and singers can reap the rewards. Writers reading from their own work, producers pitching projects, and designers of all kinds giving lectures in front of a group may benefit from the confidence, relaxation, and spontaneity that studying/performing improv can provide.

It's easy, of course, to see why improv classes and performances would be valuable for stand-up comics. They can build up their "crowd work" (i.e., ability to work with/talk to an audience) and their confidence. But improv also gives dramatic and comedic actors and singers the confidence needed for auditions and interviews; it can help them loosen up and go "off the cuff" if they're asked to talk about themselves or to present—even create—new material.

Many performers and directors believe that acting is reacting, and improv teaches how to be more of a team player—by listening to others and building upon others' ideas. It also helps performers explore breaking the fourth wall in order to react to their audience's reactions. It's helpful too, for cold readings, or when you're asked to work with someone you've never met before. It does wonders for your emceeing, hosting, even toasting skills—whether for a benefit, variety show, or your first solo theatre piece or cabaret act.

Many improv performers have become highly sought-after commercial actors because of their ability to be faster on their feet and more creative than their competition. (In commercial auditions, you're often asked to improvise and flesh out the copy.)

And consider those film directors who like to use improvisation as part of their rehearsal process and are looking for actors fluent in that style of work.

You'll find multi-threat performers like Robert Klein who swear by their improv training. Klein went from performing with Second City in Chicago to starring in film, TV, musicals, recording, and theatre. If you look at many of today's popular film/TV comedic actors—including performers from shows like *Saturday Night Live*—you'll likely find improv performance and/or study on their résumés.

One of the most influential improv forms was developed by Viola Spolin and then perfected by the Second City troupe in the 1950s. It used audience suggestions as a basis for scenes, songs, and group games.

Twenty years ago, the improvisation community was a small core of groups. These days the number and variety of performing ensembles have blossomed.

Some of the best-known troupes—and training grounds—that have followed in Second City's footsteps include Chicago City Limits, The Groundlings in Los Angeles, and The Upright Citizens Brigade and Gotham City Improv in New York. (Many of these groups have drawn on the teachings of the late Del Close.) There are also numerous lesser-known but still well-respected companies created for stages, colleges, and clubs across America.

Some groups have even acquired their own theatre spaces and run full-time corporate divisions and schools. It seems that improv can be beneficial to people outside of the entertainment industry too. It's proven to be an effective technique for writers and corporate executives who want to encourage their spontaneous impulses and imagination. These "suits" may find that what they learn in improv class translates into valued business skills.

Choosing an improvisation class can be as personal as choosing your shrink. Tom Soter, a 20-year veteran director, teacher, and producer suggests looking for a supportive environment, where the criticism is constructive.

You can read about classes in ads and get personal recommendations, but eventually you'll have to go to the source to interview (and, hopefully, to audit some sessions) before you audition. Luckily, many companies offering classes also have ongoing mainstage company shows, second/third unit shows, and even traveling tours that you can attend in order to watch their students/graduates work. These will help you gauge whether a class/company might be right for you. Colleges and acting schools have also embraced improv classes, and they book companies to do seminars as well as performances.

Once you get into the loop in New York City, Los Angeles, or Chicago, you'll hear about jam sessions, weekly gatherings, improv Olympics, and an annual twenty-four-hour performance marathon saluting Del Close. These events give students a chance to hone their skills and to network with peers.

You'll find that some groups offer pay-as-you-go, drop-in classes, while others require multi-level programs of study.

All this variety provides something for almost anyone wanting to develop improv techniques. Now all you have to do is find the group that's right for you.

The GROUNDLINGS School

Become Part of the Tradition . . .

The Groundlings School is an
innovative and challenging program that sets
the standard in improvisation and sketch
comedy. For class schedules and registration
information call:

(323) 934-4747

or visit us on the web at:

www.groundlings.com

Day, Evening, and Teen Classes Available

The Groundlings School is located at 7307 Melrose Ave in Los Angeles

---

SCREAMING FROG
PRODUCTIONS

Chicago-style
IMPROV
Classes and workshops
for All Levels

Becoming comfortable with
yourself on stage and in life is
an art form

This year, do something that
scares you!

...slowly taking over LA
www.screamingfrog.com

ACME Company Members have gone on to:
SATURDAY NIGHT LIVE, MAD TV, HBO SKETCH PAD,
FRIENDS, THE SIMPSONS, GROUNDED FOR LIFE,
WARNER BROS. ANIMATION, and more.

ACME
comedy theatre
IMPROV & SKETCH CLASSES

Study and Perform Comedy on the same stage as:
**WAYNE BRADY   RYAN STILES   ADAM CAROLLA
FRED WILLARD   WIL WHEATON   SEAN HAYES**

TO REGISTER,
CALL: 323/525-0233

135 N. La Brea

www.acmecomedy.com

IMPRO THEATRE

Home of Los Angeles Theatresports Since 1988

"Theatresports is the best improv training. Period."
—*Wayne Brady, Star of Whose Line Is It Anyway?*
All levels of improv classes including Character Class, Physical Improv,
Improv for Writers, & Improvising Musicals, Plays & Films

www.theatresports.com   *323.401.6162*

IMPROV OLYMPIC WEST
SHOWS SEVEN NIGHTS A WEEK
FULL BAR!

20 years of honing talents such as Mike Myers, Andy Dick, Jon Favreau, Upright Citizens Brigade, Chris Farley, Tina Fey, Horatio Sanz, Rachel Dratch, Seth Meyers, Tim Meadows, Amy Poehler, and many more. Improv Olympic West offers a creative environment for learning and performing.

CLASSES OFFERED
* 6 levels of Improvisation
* 3 levels of Sketch Writing
* Sitcom Writing
* Electives (one-person, all-women, intensive, teen)

Events at Improv Olympic West include:
- Shows 7 nights a week - featuring improv, sketch, stand-up, and Harold teams.
- Home of the Los Angeles Improv Festival.
- Cagematch every Thursday night (LA's only long-form improv competition).
- Improv Jam every Monday night.

6366 Hollywood Blvd
Hollywood, CA 90028
(323) 962-7560
http://www.iowest.com

The Tradition Continues...
AVERY SCHREIBER'S
IMPROVISATIONAL WORKOUT
Basic, Intermediate & Advanced Performance Level
Classes in Spolin Technique. "Go for the agreement!"

Classes now being taught by
Second City Alumn Karly Rothenberg
(818) 767-5625 email: karfus@aol.com
www.averysimprov.com

Improv and Sketch Performers!
Award-Winning
L.A. CONNECTION COMEDY THEATRE
Weekly Improv & Sketch Shows Since 1977

To Audition, call Kent Skov
(818) 710-1320

Famous Alumni: Matthew Perry, Will Ferrell, Chris Kattan, John Lovitz and Hank Azaria.
www.laconnectioncomedy.com

www.backstage.com

DARE TO BE SPONTANEOUS!

Gotham City Improv Theater & School

Improv & Sketch Comedy Classes • Shows
Corporate Training & Entertainment

FREE Sample Classes Available

WINNER
"Best Improv Group in New York"
The Big Apple Improv Festival 2003

Call 917-558-3549 or visit us on the Internet

www.GothamCityImprov.com

TO ADVERTISE IN THE NEXT

BACKSTAGE/BACK STAGE WEST®

ACTORS HANDBOOK

WEST ■   ■ EAST

Back Stage West Advertising   Back StageAdvertising
5055 Wilshire Blvd., 5th floor   770 Broadway, 4th floor
Los Angeles, CA 90036   New York, NY 10003
323.525.2225   646.654.5700

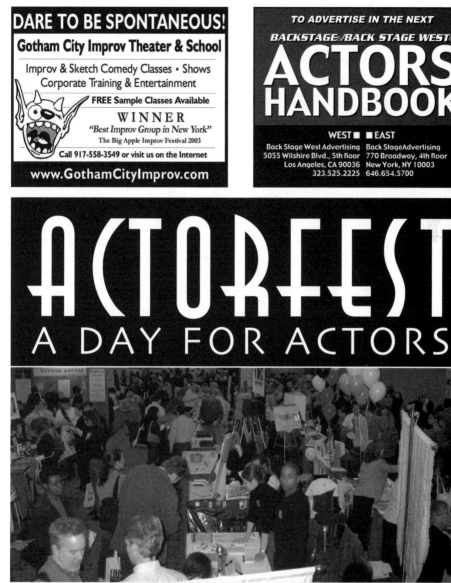

ACTORFEST
A DAY FOR ACTORS

CAREER SEMINARS • CASTING DIRECTORS
AGENTS • FOCUS SESSIONS • MANAGERS
FREE EXHIBIT HALL • AND MUCH MORE

FOR EXHIBIT HALL SPACE CALL

WEST ■   ■ EAST

Back Stage West Advertising   Back Stage Advertising
5055 Wilshire Blvd., 5th fl.   770 Broadway, 4th floor
Los Angeles, CA 90036   New York, NY 10003
323.525.2225   646.654.5700

5 From Noo Yawk to Fur Shur:

American Regionalisms on Stage and Screen

BY MARK DUNDAS WOOD

You're an actor whose agent has just scheduled you for an audition for a major new play: a family drama about wealthy coal barons living in Eastern Tennessee in the late nineteenth century. You're psyched, you're thrilled—it's the break you've been waiting for.

Then your agent drops the bomb: "You'll need to think about the accent."

Hold on. Eastern Tennessee has a mountain dialect, right? Lots of chewed "r" sounds? Or is that Western Tennessee? And does only the working class sound like that? Has the accent changed in the last century? Hey, Elvis lived in Memphis! Maybe a trip to Blockbuster to pick up *Viva Las Vegas* is in order. Wait, Memphis is in *Southwestern* Tennessee . . . .

The linguistic map of the United States can seem like a tangled web of interconnecting sounds. We may think we know a particular accent when we hear it, but reproducing the sound is something else again. Other English-speaking areas— Great Britain, for instance—may well have equally complex systems of accents, but the geographical vastness of North America can make things here seem more daunting somehow.

How many regional American accents are there, anyway? Sam Chwat claims the number is "countless." Chwat is a Manhattan-based accent coach and the founder and director of New York Speech Improvement Services, which has served an impressive array of celebrity clients over the years: everybody from Claire Bloom to Leonardo DiCaprio. Chwat helped Robert De Niro gain an Appalachian sound for the film *Cape Fear,* and he assisted Julia Roberts in eliminating her Smyrna, Georgia, accent.

Chwat explains how the settlement patterns of North America helped create our jigsaw-puzzle linguistic map: "Imagine a world where you lived in the woods of Central Illinois in the mid-1800s; before you could ever hear a national figure speak, all you knew was your local community's way of speaking. Given that communities tended to be homogenous and there was very limited movement, it's been said that an accent changed every 50 miles."

Patterns of conquest, immigration, and migration all affected the way people in a particular American locale spoke—and the way they still speak today. It's widely known, for instance, that the dropped "r's" of Southern England morphed into similar sounds in various colonial settlements: New England, New York, the Deep South.

Even climate may have had an effect on speaking patterns, according to Stephen Gabis—a Manhattan-based dialect coach. Gabis says that during the westward migration connected with construction of the Great Lakes canals, Irish and Slavic elements tweaked the speech pattern. But so, too, perhaps, did those bitter winters, which affected the way people held the muscles of the mouth and jaw. Similarly, says Gabis, the tight-lipped sound that certain Texans emit may be traced back in part to forebears who clenched their mouths to avoid swallowing mouthfuls of hot Southwest-American dust.

"ACCENT" VS. "DIALECT"

Chwat and Gabis both find it useful to make a distinction between the terms "accent" and "dialect." Accent is the shape of the sound, Gabis explains, and dialect is what you do with it. Chwat notes that "dialect" includes particular regional terminologies. He points to an often-cited example: A sandwich of a particular dimension and culinary makeup will be known, in various cities on the Eastern seaboard, as a "hero," an "Italian hero," a "hoagie," or a "torpedo."

That's dialect.

Usually, of course, dialect is the domain of the playwright, while accent belongs to actors—and to the vocal coaches who assist them. However, Chwat notes that he helped director Martin Scorsese find idiomatic expressions from Appalachia to sprinkle into the script of *Cape Fear.*

In helping actors with accents, coaches usually work from a phonetically represented neutral base—the so-called Standard American accent. They then help actors to substitute certain regionally based sounds.

"There are forty-four sounds in general American English," says Chwat. "In New York, of those forty-four, maybe eight to ten are used in such a way that anybody will say, 'That guy's from New York.' Whereas most of the country is saying 'chah-colate' and 'tahk' and 'cah-fee,' in New York, the substitution of that vowel will be a very lip-puckered 'aw': 'chaw-colate' and 'tawk' and 'caw-fee.'

Of course, there are variations within the New York family of accents, mostly ethnic twists: Jewish, Italian, Irish, Spanish, African-American. "You can't talk about borough-specific accents anymore," Chwat says (referring to the five boroughs that make up New York City). "Not when Spike Lee and Andrew Dice Clay come from the same borough—come from Brooklyn. I'm more comfortable talking about ethnically based accents within an accent group than about borough-based accents."

Sometimes, of course, playwrights themselves notate the sounds of speech they want actors to adopt. Elmer Rice in *Street Scene,* for instance, has one Italian-American character say: "Ees no good, da Beethoven. E'es alla time sad." Unfortunately, with some playwrights, these delineations are neither accurate nor consistent. But Gabis suggests that it's helpful for actors to become familiar with exactly which soundscapes major American playwrights had in mind when concocting their masterpieces.

Tennessee Williams, says Gabis, "wrote for the Gulf Coast—he wanted his heroines to sound like himself, basically." Beth Henley writes for "those Mississippi Delta ladies." Lanford Wilson creates mid-Missouri sounds, with "hard r's"—so that "Highway 40" becomes "Highway Farty." As for Sam Shepard's Bakersfield,

California-area characters, "What are those people but Appalachian people that wound up in Oklahoma? The dust bowl drove them to California."

TEACHING METHODS VARY

Although most accent coaches seem to have a pedagogy that pairs phonetic study with listen-and-repeat drills, each expert has his or her own particular instructional track. The late speech-dialect coach Arden Sampson used commercially produced instructional guides and tapes, but if someone needed a more specific accent—say from a particular region of Montana— she would do a cold call to a chamber of commerce and explain her mission. She kept a tape recorder beside her television for years, recording voice patterns—especially from news stories filed from around the country.

The difficulties that students face in mastering a particular American accent seem to vary. What one actor easily mimics may be nearly impossible for another. It depends in part on where the actor himself is from. Chwat claims that sometimes the subtler accents are more difficult to learn "because there aren't that many hooks for the actor to listen for." A Baltimore accent, for instance, has relatively few sound differences to be plugged into that neutral American speech model. Consequently, those few substitutions are sometimes neglected. On the other hand, Chwat finds that speech patterns with a great many substitutions are also difficult—simply because there's so much to keep track of.

FOREVER IN FLUX

Another problem for the actor is that accents are continually evolving. Gabis was surprised to learn that young people in Connecticut have adopted a more western-sounding inflection these days. They say "Flore-ida" now instead of "Flah-rida."

In some cases, identifiable accents and dialects will become obsolete over time. The old-fashioned working-class New York accent—lovingly dubbed "Toidy-toid and Toid"—is virtually dead, although there still may be old-timers in certain bars in Manhattan's Hell's Kitchen who would insist that Popeye's girlfriend is "Olive Earl." Chwat feels that Toidy-Toid and Toid was subjected to such burlesque and ridicule by the greater American public that it eventually became transformed into something else. Fortunately for actors who are trying to recreate this sound, there are plenty of authentic vintage recordings available, as well as such movie series as *The Bowery Boys* and *The Dead End Kids*.

Mass media have certainly helped neutralize particular speech patterns to some degree, but Chwat feels there's a good reason why regional accents will never be completely wiped out. Research, he says, shows that children between the ages of three and seven will pick up speech patterns not from parents or media, but from peers. So the community playground becomes a sort of preservation district for a local accent. When a family immigrates to a particular locale, the younger children will easily assimilate the sound of the new "bedrock" community, while older children will tend to hold on to speech habits from their old home bases.

Chwat acknowledges, however, that teenagers will also change their accents as they consciously choose which groups they wish to identify with. Hence the appearance of "Valley Girl" sound outside of California and the adoption of inner-city hip-hop cadences by middle-class, suburban youth.

The American ear seems to be tuned to subtle differences in accent. Chwat believes that "the public will absolutely notice" that Rosie Perez, Tony Danza, Fran Drescher, and former New York City Mayor Rudolph Giuliani (who has an Irish-based New York accent, despite his Italian surname) speak differently. Those four—New Yorkers all—could never convincingly be cast in a play or film as members of the same family unless some of them modified their speech, Chwat insists.

BEWARE OF BEING TOO SPECIFIC

On the other hand, Gabis thinks that, in some cases, theatre and film people can "get too crazy, too specific" about accent distinctions. Arden Sampson, who hailed from Eastern Tennessee, considered herself to be a "stickler" for authenticity where Southern accents were concerned. But she admitted in a 2001 interview that she had a hard time telling Alabama and Georgia accents apart. Sometimes class distinctions override regional differences, she felt: "If you've got a more upper-class, educated sound, it's the same in Georgia as in Louisiana, as far as I'm concerned. It's a drawl."

Then, too, it's possible to be completely accurate with an accent and be totally unintelligible to an audience. Gabis, who has taught dialect courses for New York University students through the Atlantic Theater School, says: "The first thing I teach is making sure that you split the difference between authenticity and clarity. You've got to keep the tone in the front; you've got to keep it energetic. If you start mumbling, it's gonna be dicey."

Gabis believes that speech patterns can provide "the fire in the belly" of a particular character. He urges actors to start work on an accent early in their preparation of a role. If they commit to an accent—believing in it fully—then the audience will also accept it. He feels that studying the phonetic alphabet is helpful to actors, and he recommends the Edith Skinner approach. Developing what Skinner calls "good theatre speech" will eventually allow actors to riff in a jazz-like way with various accents.

Then again, you can absorb a lot, just by exposing yourself to voices, especially if you live in an urban setting with a robust multicultural mix. "Be listening, listening, listening," Gabis advises. "Be a fly on the wall of humanity."

WANT TO ADD OR REMOVE AN ACCENT?

Laura DiTirro McMillin
M.A. UCLA

Multilingual accent reduction/dialect Professor.

Celebrity Client Coach

For Appointment (310) 430-8733

Vocal Technique

SINGING, SPEECH AND ACCENT REDUCTION

Power • Resonance • Breath Management

Learn valuable techniques that give you a voice that you control!

• American Non-regional Dialect, the Industry Standard.
• Audition Preparation & Performance Coaching.
• Current vocal styles in Theater, Pop, R&B, & Jazz.

Heather Lyle, M.M.

310 454-3078   *vocalyoga.com*

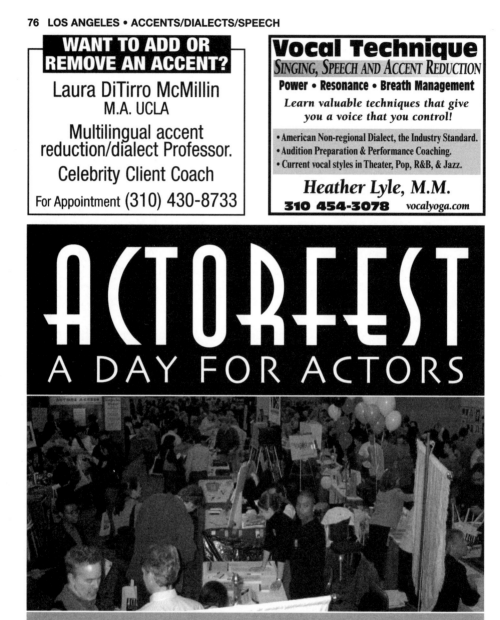

ACTORFEST

A DAY FOR ACTORS

CAREER SEMINARS · CASTING DIRECTORS
AGENTS · FOCUS SESSIONS · MANAGERS
FREE EXHIBIT HALL · AND MUCH MORE

FOR EXHIBIT HALL SPACE CALL

WEST ■	■ EAST
Back Stage West Advertising	Back Stage Advertising
5055 Wilshire Blvd., 5th fl.	770 Broadway, 4th floor
Los Angeles, CA 90036	New York, NY 10003
323.525.2225	646.654.5700

NEW YORK SPEECH IMPROVEMENT SERVICES
Sam Chwat, MS, CCC-SP, Director
1-212-242-8435 – 1 800-SPEAK WELL

• Accent Elimination

- **Regional & Foreign**
- **All Stage Dialects for Acting Roles**
- **Effective Short Term Programs Available**
- **NYS Lic. Speech Pathologists**
- **Reasonable Rates – Flexible Hours**
- **Consultants to Agents & Major Acting Schools**

"He makes it easy and that's what a great teacher does."

Tony Danza
<u>People Magazine</u>

Current & Past Clients:
Robert DeNiro, Leonardo DiCaprio, Julia Roberts, Andie MacDowell, Roberto Begnini, Elle MacPherson, Kathleen Turner, Benjamin Bratt, Joey MacIntire, Naomi Campbell, Cindy Crawford, Jon Bon Jovi, Tony Danza, Willem Dafoe, Olympia Dukakis, Patrick Stewart, Sean Young, Gregory Hines, Matt Dillon, Jude Law, Gloria Gaynor, Joaquin Phoenix, Burt Young, Harry Connick, Jr., West Wing's Dule Hill, John Leguizamo, Roma Downey, Isabella Rossellini, Polly Draper, George Hearn, David McCallum, Charlize Theron, Ally Sheedy, Oz's Eammon Walker, Jason Gedrick, James Gandolfini, Kate Hudson, Aaliyah, Mark Ruffalo, Sarah Gilbert, Molly Sims, Eva Herzigova

VISA *MasterCard*

"Amy is the only person
I call for dialect work."
—Jonathan Bank, Mint Theater Co.

STOLLER SYSTEM
Dialect Coaching & Design
by Amy Stoller

Tired of sitting alone with a tape?
Call: **212-840-1234**

http://www.vasta.org/dir/stollera.html

IMPROVE VOICE PRODUCTION
Reduce Foreign & Regional Accents

Judith A. Pollak M.A., C.C.C.
NY State Licenced Speech Pathologiest,
Faculty Member, Pace University
Adults • Children
FREE CONSULTATION

917-494-2811 • 212-362-6714
Judith.Jae@alo.com

Voice and Speech Training
for students and professionals
Let me help you find your voice, project
with ease, explore texts, and expand
audition opportunities.

Coaching for Specific Roles
Foreign Accent Reduction.
Brian Loxley Speech Studio
New York City
Since 1984
212-682-1445
www.loxleyspeechstudio.com

TO ADVERTISE IN THE NEXT
BACKSTAGE/BACK STAGE WEST
ACTORS
HANDBOOK

WEST ■   ■ EAST
Back Stage West Advertising   Back StageAdvertising
5055 Wilshire Blvd., 5th floor   770 Broadway, 4th floor
Los Angeles, CA 90036   New York, NY 10003
323.525.2225   646.654.5700

PART **2**

The Basic Tools

6 Picture Yourself Working:

Getting the Headshot That's Right for You

BY ELIAS STIMAC

As an actor or an actress, determining and acquiring the ideal headshot for yourself can be simple. All you have to do is act.

Your first assignment: play the role of a busy theatrical agent. Sit in a chair and imagine your current photo has just arrived in the mail. Hold it in front of you and be objective. It's probable the agency has more than enough people in your particular category, so find something in the photo that stands out and makes you want to call yourself in. Is it the sparkle in the eyes, the casual charisma, the confident smile, the no-nonsense demeanor, the inner passion for life, or, hopefully, all of the above?

Next, portray a top casting director, swamped with submissions but seeking that special talent for a high-profile project. Suddenly the envelope is opened and there's your face. Would you consider it inviting, intriguing, mischievous, memorable, direct, and/or different in an indescribable way?

Now adapt a famous director's mindset, and take a closer look at the person behind the picture. Are you looking at someone with star potential, a sturdy sidekick, a winsome ingénue, a comic foil, a fresh face, a crusty character, a solid supporting player—in other words, somebody worth calling in for an audition?

Channel the persona of a successful producer, and review your headshot with an educated eye toward marketability. Do you have universal appeal, or are your looks and attitude better suited to attract a specific group of ticket buyers? Would you pay $10 to see yourself in a movie, or $100 to watch yourself starring in a Broadway show? What do you have that the public wants?

Now switch to the perspective of a photographer. The shot may look great, and garner a lot of industry response, but what adjustments can you make to ensure that the next photo shoot results in even better options? A more-focused point of attention, a clearer expression, an angled pose, a subtle tilt of the head, fewer shadows on the face, no hand on the chin, maybe a brighter background?

Finally, envision yourself as a makeup artist and stylist, and identify all the details that can combine to form a winning look. Study your eyes, teeth, skin, hairstyle, choice of outfits. Can you pinpoint any areas for improvement?

From each point of view, your conclusions should be obvious: the best headshot is a current photo that looks like you, reflects a professional presence, is free of distracting elements, and captures unique aspects of your personality. Above all, it is an essential tool for an actor to have. Along with a résumé (for more on that, see Chapter 7), a headshot is a performer's main calling card; without one, few people will likely be calling you anytime soon.

THE BIG PICTURE

Almost every actor has one, and yet headshots are like snowflakes: no two are exactly alike. That's mainly because no two actors are exactly alike. It also has a lot to do with the photographer's individual style, lighting, mood, and developing and printing methods.

While résumés follow a rather standard format, pictures deviate in everything except size (eight inches wide by ten inches tall) and hue (traditionally black and white, although color versions are becoming popular on the West Coast). Photos can be shot in portrait (vertical) or landscape (horizontal) layouts, with an occasional diagonal composition thrown in for effect. Headshots may also have borders, custom fonts for the performer's name, and matte or glossy finishes. But the thing that varies more than anything else is the actual image. It is that one element that will be most effective in getting you noticed, getting you called in, and getting you work.

There's no one correct way to get a successful headshot—some agents may prefer one style over another, but then again, you can't please everyone.

Different headshots are necessary for different mediums, although all types need to convey confidence and energy. Commercial shots usually feature upbeat emotions. Legit stage and film actors should portray a more serious mood. Soap opera actors can aim for a sexy edge to their image. Character performers can use quirky facial expressions and display their sense of humor.

If you are going to use the same image to submit for both theatrical and commercial jobs, your photos should have an appealing, direct look. Once you become established, you'll be able to afford separate types of headshots for the various kinds of roles for which you are being considered.

A lot of elements involved in a photo session are the work of the photographer; that's why it's important to work with someone who is open to your suggestions and input. Various components of the headshot process can be decided before the shot begins, including what outfits to wear, which makeup to use, and how to style your hair. Will you want to take shots in studio lighting or natural light? Should the focus be a close-up shot on the face and shoulders, or more of a body shot? Should your expression be geared for commercial or dramatic effect? If your photo shoot is going to encompass a wide range of looks, you may be able to cover each of these options.

However, if you choose to do a more limited shoot at a discounted price, you should decide in advance on a few specific setups that will capture both your personality and your performance style, so that the photographer can get exactly the kind of look you desire.

FOCUSING ON PHOTOGRAPHERS

Once you are aware of what to "shoot" for during your headshot session, it's time to find a photographer who will help you achieve the desired effect by providing creative options, sensible feedback, and technical expertise. Before you commit to anything, you'll want to spend some time researching all your options in order to find the right person to work with at the right price. (Of course, cost is a major factor in any decision, but when it comes to headshots, sometimes it's worth a little more to get what you want.) Only then will you be fully prepared to step in front of the camera.

Where to find the right photographer? There are many "headshot-takers" around; you just have to know where to look. You can find examples of their handiwork in newspapers, advertisements, at auditions, and in theatre company lobbies. Trade publications such as *Back Stage* run display ads from photographers showing samples of their work.

Developing and reproduction labs are other places to find potential collaborators. Acting studios and artistic venues will usually have bulletin boards with flyers and comp cards on display. And, of course, there are always your fellow thespians, who will more often than not be eager to share their recommendations (and reservations) with you—as well as anecdotes about their own experiences.

Computers can provide instant access to photographic resources. Now more than ever, surfing the Internet for photography websites that feature headshots is a comprehensive, economical, swift solution to sorting out who's who in the field. Any search engine will lead you to multiple links. As you click through the onscreen images, make mental notes or write down your impressions. Once again, you should be observing the samples as if you were the one doing the hiring, allowing you to skip over photos that might appear too flashy or trendy in favor of strong, sensible, outstanding shots.

Once you make a short list of possible photographers to work with, meeting and interviewing them will help you get a clearer picture of who can offer you the best experience at the best price. Perusing each one's portfolio of sample images will give you a visual clue as to who might be most suitable to capture your unique style. Questions that should be asked at this meeting include: What will the session cost, and what does the shooting fee include? Will clothing changes be possible? What colors work best with each location and the photographer's specific lighting? How many shots will be taken, and in what formats (prints, digital CDs, proof sheets) will you get copies? How many finished prints are included, and who will be responsible for touch-ups to the photos? Who owns the negatives? And if you are not entirely satisfied with the results, is it possible to request reshoots?

BEHIND THE CASTING TABLE

Speaking of those in charge of hiring, most casting experts agree that a striking headshot—along with an impressive résumé—is still the preferred method of introducing yourself to the industry. It can help you secure representation, book an audition, be remembered for future casting calls, and basically get your foot in the showbiz door. Personal letters can't tell the whole story, and phone calls are rarely encouraged.

Reels and videotapes may show you in action, but they can occasionally sit next to an office VCR without ever being viewed. Even a referral from a colleague will be enhanced by a photo and résumé. In this age of technological advances, email submissions may be quicker and save postage, and CDs may hold more information, yet nothing beats having a hard copy of a performer's picture to ponder, peruse, praise, and place in the appropriate pile.

Many agents, casting directors, and managers admit that, while they do concentrate more on a performer's résumé, they tend to look at the photograph first.

Most say "the eyes have it" when pinpointing the feature they notice first in a headshot. New York casting director Bernie Telsey, for one, looks even deeper, hoping to get a visceral response from a person's photo. "I look for shots that pop out, that have a 3-D kind of effect, ones that prompt a live reaction. Shots that say something to me, that look like someone I want to know more about. On certain occasions, I am looking at the photos with a specific job in mind, searching for someone who is right for a specific character. Other times, when I'm going through the general submissions, what I look for will vary with what I am trying to find. But your photo is one of the two most important chances you have to market yourself before you get in the room, so you have to get a great photographer that captures you."

Everyone is happy when the photo actually resembles the person who enters the room. Bob Kale—another Manhattan-based casting director—notes, "What I look for, truly more than anything else, is if the headshot looks like the person. If it is more attractive or less attractive, it doesn't help me, because I need to know what they genuinely look like."

East Coast agent Dave Bennett of the Talent House also tries to assess "the honesty of the presentation, along with the quality of the shot and reproduction." Personal manager Eric Hanson states, "I look at the headshot to see if I have anyone in my talent pool that would compete with them."

Mara McEwin, artistic director and producer of New York City's Treehouse Shakers company, loves when the headshot "reveals the actor's warmth. I also love when you stumble upon a well-taken shot—it always stands out from the crowd. Usually, it has defined contrasts and great lighting that make an actor's features stand out, especially the eyes."

Casting veteran Telsey has the perfect solution for helping actors keep their photos real. "Headshots should look like you look when you're going on a blind date. You want to look your best, and you also want to look like yourself. I think a natural, casual shot that doesn't look overdone is the best way to be represented."

robertkim Studio

Robert Evan, "Jekyll and Hyde"

Barbara Moore, "Playboy Centerfold"

Saycon Sengbloh, "Aida"

George Lopez ABC'S "The George Lopez Show"

"Of all the headshot photographers available in New York, Robert Kim remains my first and only choice. Why? *Simple.* His years of experience in the industry, his quality and professionalism, and most importantly, his proven ability to transform actors' careers."
–Glenn Alterman, Author, "Promoting Your Acting Career,"(Allworth Press) and "The Perfect Audition Monologue" (Smith & Kraus)

Manhattan Location Exclusive "Before & After" Portfolio Viewings
7 days-a-week, 12-6PM By Appointment

101 West 18th Street, Unit 5D (@ Sixth Avenue) **888·KIMFOTO** / www.robertkim.com

LOS ANGELES ▪ NEW YORK

PETER HURLEY

PHOTOGRAPHY | NEW YORK, NY | 917.440.4651

WWW.PETERHURLEY.COM

DISCOVER DIGITAL HEADSHOTS

Try Modernage's "Classic Digital Headshots" and discover a new quality and flexibility.

classic
DIGITAL
headshots

- ⊙ Direct to print process.
- ⊙ Digitally mastered to disk.
- ⊙ Digital archives of your headshots.
- ⊙ Re-order your headshots via email at headshots@modernage.com.
- ⊙ Optional CD with your digital contact sheet allowing you to view, email, resize, print & more.
- ⊙ Email your headshots to agents, friends and family.
- ⊙ Have "Photo Business Cards" or "Photo Post Cards" made.
- ⊙ Digital Retouching - approve your final retouching via our emailed "Online Retouched Proofs."
- ⊙ Printed on real photographic paper.
- ⊙ Turn around time of 2-3 business days.
- ⊙ Costs almost a third less than other labs.
- ⊙ Flexibility to print digitally or from negatives or original prints.

LIMITED TIME SPECIAL OFFER

FREE CLASSIC DIGITAL HEADSHOT CD
a $14.95 value • with this ad only

code: BSAH

COME VISIT OUR NEW
MODERNAGE HEADSHOT RESOURCE CENTER
1150 Sixth Ave., NYC (@44th St.) 2nd Floor

NEW!
2 SIDED COLOR
COMP CARDS

SO WHAT ARE YOU WAITING FOR?
GET OFF LINE AND GET ONLINE.

Digital Printing by

www.**modernage**.com

m⊙dernage
□ CUSTOM DIGITAL IMAGING

<u>Toll Free</u>: 800|997.2510 <u>Midtown</u>: 1150 Sixth Ave. (@45th St.) . 212|997.1800
<u>East Side (open Sat.)</u>: 649 Lexington Ave (@55th St.) . 212|752.3993

HEADSHOTS BY JASON FRIEDMAN FOR

a **adam raphael photography, LLC**

347 Fifth Avenue, #303 (at 34th Street) New York, NY 10016
Tel: (212) 685-6661 Fax: (212) 685-6662 www.adamraphael.com/headshots

PRECISION PHOTOS

Need Headshot Copies?

8x10 Photo & Litho Reproductions

Postcards

Retouching

Digital Output

Modeling Zed Cards

Photo Business Cards

Resume Typesetting

why go anywhere else?

Need New Headshots?
PRECISION PORTRAITS
Digital Headshot Studio
Complete Headshot Session
with 8x10 photo copies
starting at $199

Save 10%
on any order
discount must be mentioned
before placing order...until 12/24/04
One per customer

212.302.2724   800.583.4077
750 8th Ave. @ 46th St.   NYC

Photos by L.A.
SIMMS STUDIO
212-315-9119
www.photosbyla.com

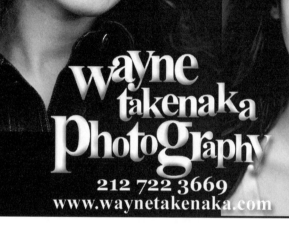

wayne takenaka Photography

212 722 3669
www.waynetakenaka.com

Headshots
Studios & Locations
Dorothy Shi
Appointment Only
$145 per Roll
Shoot 3 Rolls,
Get 2 rolls free
B&W 36 exp

With one
8x10, negs,
and polaroids.

212-924-8282
Cell 917.776.5350
www.shishotme.net
All major credit cards accepted.

ALLURING IMAGES

VISA MasterCard

208 W 29th St. suite 408, NY, Ny 10001, Ph.: 212 967 1610
www.alluringimages.com, e-mail: alluringimages@aol.com

ALL PACKAGES FOR FIRST TIME CLIENTS ONLY

Model CompositeCards **$99**
36 shots, Model Cards (Scan, Name, Info) **$195**
36 shots, **100** 8x10's (copy neg. & name) **$160**
THIS WEEK'S SPECIAL 100 8x10's **call**

We Do Photo Restoration (Specialized in heavy damage)

Artistic Photography, Headshots & Reproductions for Artistic People ...

**Headshot, Photography, Reproductions,
Color & B/W, Model's Card, Printing**

Gil Hagovsky

Call for appointment
7 days a week:
9:00 a.m. - 9:00 p.m.

Heather Van Vleet   *Peter Austin Noto*   MANDIGO   April

---

photos © Bette Marshall

BETTE Marshall PHOTOGRAPHY

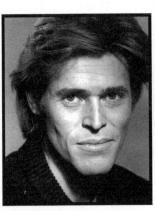

*Bette Marshall's Portraits
of Actors, Dancers, Musicians and
Corporate Leaders have appeared
in International Publications, Exhibitions
and CD Covers*

Phone:
212 947 4267

*Bette is also available
in New York and
Los Angeles for your
headshot, publicity
and modeling photos.*

Visit us at: www.bettemarshallphotography.com

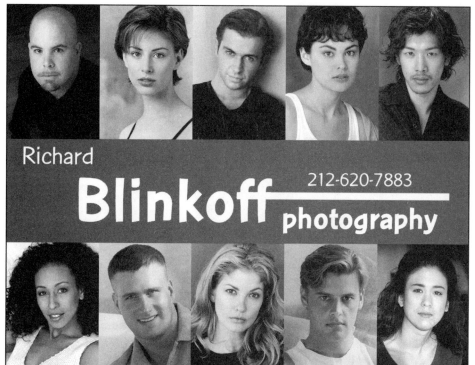

Richard

Blinkoff 212-620-7883 photography

Photography
for
Performing Artists

James J. Kriegsmann Jr.   (212) 247-0553
www.kriegsmann.com

212·876·0275
{etr}
STUDIO
www.etrstudio.com

Publicity Prints

Specializing in high quality, low cost promotional prints for over 35 years

**B&W
8x10's**
500 - $90⁰⁰

**B&W
4x6's**
500 - $75⁰⁰

Elizabeth Wood

**PICTURE
BUSINESS CARDS**
500 - $50⁰⁰

Mail your 8x10
photograph or
order online at
www.abcpictures.com

Prices include typesetting
and ground freight in continental U.S.

Prices subject to change without notice.

Request FREE Catalog & Samples

Toll-Free 1.888.526.5336
www.abcpictures.com

ABC
PICTURES

Dan Wells

John Hart

'Still The Best'

212 • 873 • 6585

Dreams that Come True
Puppydogs and Kittens
Raindrops on Roses
Only Good Times
Warmth and Kindness
Quality Without Compromise

Feel the Happiness

Service Beyond Compare
Only Good Surprises
Every Moments Special
Fond Memories
Lollipops and Rainbows
Fairytale Endings

REPRODUCTIONS
New York & Los Angeles

Quality Printing for Actors and Performing Artists

6 West 37th Street Fourth Floor	3499 Cahuenga Boulevard West
New York, NY 10018	Los Angeles, CA 90068
Tel: 212.967.2568	Tel: 323.845.9595
Fax: 212.629.8304	Fax: 323.845.0188
Toll Free: 800.647.3776	Toll Free: 888.797.7795

www.reproductions.com

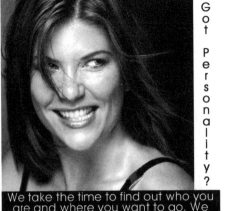

Got personality?

We take the time to find out who you are and where you want to go. We customize every session, location and wardrobe change to your needs. Our digital process allows you to preview the pictures as we take them . You can enjoy **unlimited time and shooting** (Really!). There's no pressure. After all, we believe a great headshot should capture your spirit, not just your face.
www.cain-weidnerstudio.com
212•714•1464

cain-weidner studio

HEADSHOT SPECIAL $199

Austin Pendleton

DAVID BEYDA STUDIO
140 West 32nd St. 2nd Fl. N.Y.C.
(212) 967-6964
www.davidbeyda.com

SCOTT WYNN
P H O T O G R A P H Y

3 ROLLS,
108 SHOTS $400

(212) **874-1449**

S C O T T W Y N N . C O M

BRUCE BENNETTS PHOTOGRAPHY
ACTORS, MODELS, SINGERS & DANCERS

Tired of the "cookie cutter" headshot approach? We offer customized personalized portraits & portfolios. Indoors & outside. Extensive marketing analysis included. Spectacular wardrobe, shoes, jewelry, hats, and prop department. Make-up & stylist available.

212-903-4800

Diane Ingino

headshots

917
834-3124

Spence
Studios

310. 358. 8668

WWW.SPENCESTUDIOS.COM

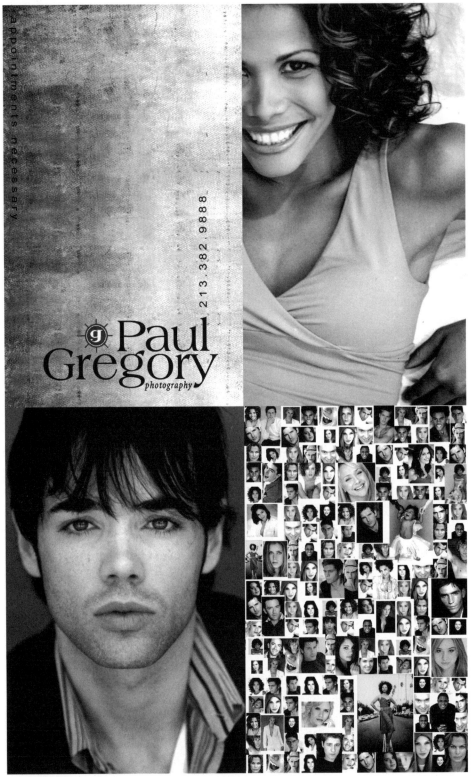

appointments necessary

213.382.9888

Paul Gregory
photography

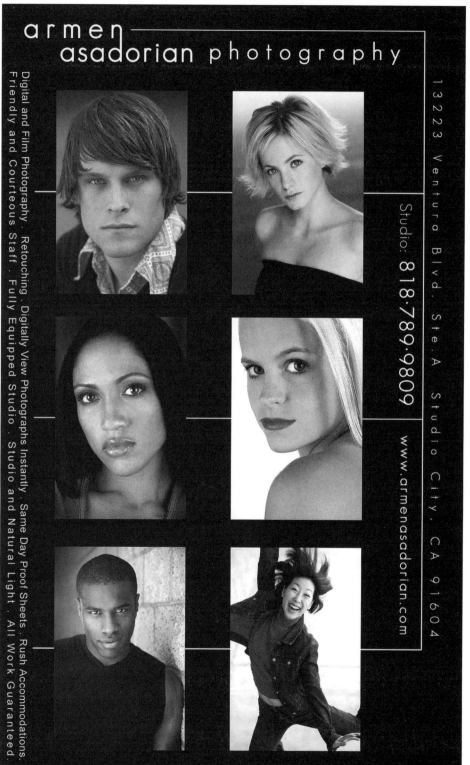

armen asadorian photography

Digital and Film Photography . Retouching . Digitally View Photographs Instantly . Same Day Proof Sheets . Rush Accommodations. Friendly and Courteous Staff . Fully Equipped Studio . Studio and Natural Light . All Work Guaranteed.

13223 Ventura Blvd. Ste.A Studio City, CA 91604

Studio: 818·789·9809

www.armenasadorian.com

WHY PAY MORE?

- AGENCY RECOMMENDED   • INDOOR/OUTDOOR
- SESSION ON CD (ADD'L)
- AFFORDABLE MAKE-UP ARTIST (ADD'L)

SESSIONS START AS LOW AS

$65 36 exp.
includes proof

COLOR OR BLACK & WHITE

ROD GOODMAN
PHOTOGRAPHER

L.A. 818.760.0733
N.Y. 212.252.5364

WWW.PHOTOSBYROD.COM

tim sabatino
photography
818.785.7015

www.timsabatino.com
los angeles

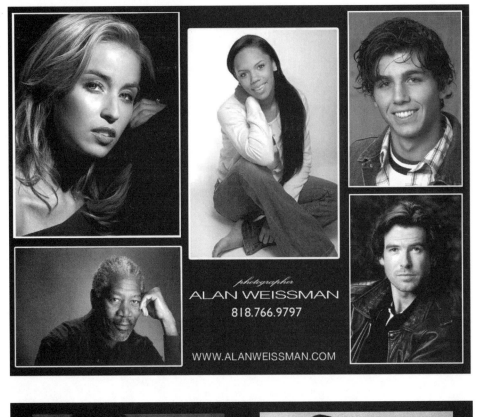

photographer
ALAN WEISSMAN
818.766.9797

WWW.ALANWEISSMAN.COM

Adam Taylor Photography
Ten Years Experience and Published World Wide
Portrait and Headshot Packages Starting at $125
(818) 985-6846   www.adamtaylor.us

GRAPHIC REPRODUCTIONS

Quality Headshot Duplicates for Actors,
Performing Artists & Photographers

Black & White / Color

Toll-Free 1.877.212.6647
323.874.4335

1421 North La Brea Ave.
Hollywood, CA 90028
www.graphicreproductions.com

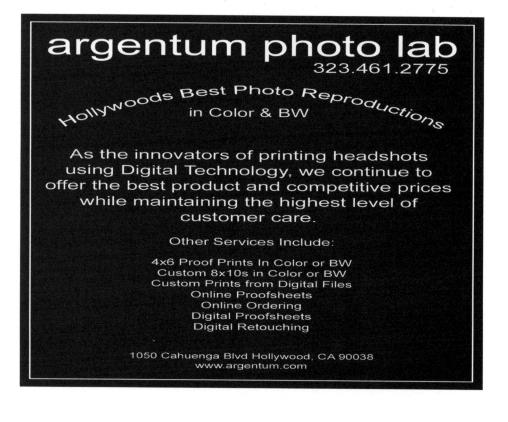

argentum photo lab
323.461.2775

Hollywoods Best Photo Reproductions
in Color & BW

As the innovators of printing headshots
using Digital Technology, we continue to
offer the best product and competitive prices
while maintaining the highest level of
customer care.

Other Services Include:

4x6 Proof Prints In Color or BW
Custom 8x10s in Color or BW
Custom Prints from Digital Files
Online Proofsheets
Online Ordering
Digital Proofsheets
Digital Retouching

1050 Cahuenga Blvd Hollywood, CA 90038
www.argentum.com

PRINTS CHARM'N, INC.

West Los Angeles (310) 312-0904 • **West Hollywood** (310) 288-1786
Studio City (818) 753-9055

Mail Orders: download order forms at www.printscharmn.com

1657 Sawtelle Blvd., West Los Angeles 90025   (310) 312-0904
11020 Ventura Blvd., Studio City 91604   (818) 753-9055
9054 Santa Monica Blvd., West Hollywood 90069   (310) 288-1766

300   *8 x 10 Lithos* as low as Price includes: Name, Specs, Unions and Agency Logo   **49.95** Plus Sales Tax

Lithos B/W - 100 8x 10 as low as $40.95
Next Day $60.95 Same Day* $70.95

100 HEADSHOTS
100 POST CARDS
100 BUSINESS CARDS   **$85.00**   or   **$85.00**   TWO ORDERS OF HEADSHOTS 150 EACH

Photographic Color, B/W or Sepia 100 8 x 10 $69.00
Color Zed Cards - 100 as low as $99.00
Digitally retouch your photos $10.00 for 10 min.
WHILE-U-WATCH   *West LA only

to download order forms **www.printscharmin.com**
Don't drive, call us about emailing your photo

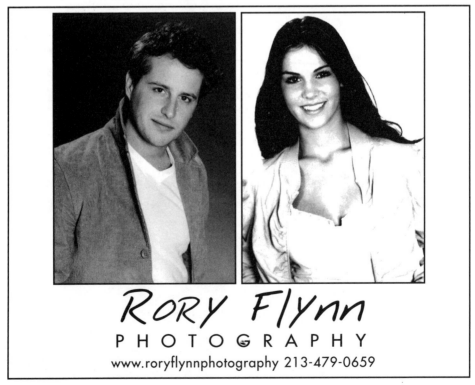

RORY Flynn
P H O T O G R A P H Y
www.roryflynnphotography 213-479-0659

Nancy Jo Gilchrist
www.nancyjophoto.com
818 • 780 • 0803

PRO prints
ray the retoucher

LA's #1 source for Actors

•Retouching
•Headshot Reproductions
•Actor Supplies & Books
•Black & White and Color Printing

Log on for special discounts
www.raytheretoucher.com

Hollywood 1330 N. Highland, LA, CA 90028 **323-463-0555**
Studio City 12345-B Ventura Blvd Studio City, CA 91601 **818-760-3656**

KAREN BYSTEDT
PHOTOGRAPHY
323 993-8558
karenbystedtphotography.com

Johnny Depp   Sandra Bullock   Keanu Reeves
Laurence Fishburne   Courteney Cox   Cuba Gooding Jr.
Brad Pitt   Robert Downey Jr.   Jamie Kennedy

take control of your image
carrie villines
DIGITAL PHOTOGRAPHY
www.digitalheadshots.net
info@digitalheadshots.net
323.422.1284

AJB

PHOTOGRAPHY
909 • 882 • 0656

3 digital rolls • 1-8x10 • Same day proof sheets
• Specializing in Theatrical/Commercial Headshots
• *All-natural* lighting • Digital Processing • Makeup consultation included

michelle
TORIO
photographer
$75
36 EXP
24 HR PROOF
INDOOR/OUTDOOR
AFFORDABLE MAKE-UP
www.michelletorio.com
310.399.0367

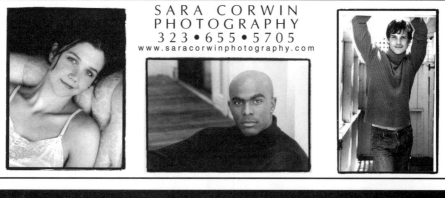

SARA CORWIN
PHOTOGRAPHY
323 • 655 • 5705
www.saracorwinphotography.com

www.**CINEMA PRINTS**.com
7515 Sunset Blvd., Los Angeles, CA 90046 • 323.876.3830

REPRODUCTIONS

Headshots, Postcards, Business Cards, Zed-Cards & Composites
Serving Actors, Agencies and Photographers for the past 16 years!

Mastering Reproductions, here at Cinema Prints we offer Color, 2-tone, and Black & White prints with the best photo reproduction techniques in the industry. We have the ability to fine-tune every detail and contrast from your original print for pure industry perfection. Our new state of the art process eliminates the "grainy", washed-out quality found in many reproductions today. We also specialize in Digital Retouching that results in flawless yet natural-looking headshots.

➤ SAVE MONEY & TIME ◄
GET EVERYTHING DONE HERE
HEADSHOT PHOTOGRAPHY
+ 100-PHOTOGRAPHIC 8X10'S *only* **$149**
With your name, headshots saved on
CD and you keep negs. (Make-up available)

PHOTOGRAPHIC HEADSHOTS
Available in color, b&w, or sepia

25 8x10's *as low as*	$25.00
50 8x10's *as low as*	$45.00
100 8x10's *as low as*	$69.00

Color Zed Cards
100 2-sided Zed Cards
as low as **$99**
up to 4 photos

Postcards
100 - 4x5 Color Postcards
as low as **$49**
Available in color, b&w, or sepia. Includes name &agency logo

Retouching
Additional retouching $15 per 1/4 hour
$15
for 1/4 hour

Other services: Resume Services, Lithos Postcards, Business cards, Web Design.
SUN IMAGING CENTER
8168 W. SUNSET BLVD. (AT CRESCENT HEIGHTS)
323-654-5556

KIM KIMBRO
photography
323.769.5588
www.kimkimbrophotography.com

Headshots by a professional

Headshots By Pierre
323.251.5593

Anderson Graphics, Inc.
since 1968

100 COLOR ZEDS $115.⁰⁰**
100 COLOR 8x10 $85.⁰⁰*'

2 B&W HEADSHOTS
100 of each $88⁰⁰*'

B&W Headshot
100 for $55⁰⁰' / 300 for $70⁰⁰'

400 - B&W
Postcards or Business Cards $52⁵⁰'

400 - COLOR
Postcards or Business Cards $120⁰⁰'

*plus tax &/or shipping where applicable **call for details
"Call for order form or print from our website"

Ship: 6037 Woodman Ave. Van Nuys, CA 91401
Mail: P.O. Box 969, Van Nuys, CA 91408

818-909-9100   800-262-6114
www.andersongraphics.com

VANIE POYEY
PHOTOGRAPHY

www.poyeyphotos.com
323·856·6156

TORY WOLFE
P h o t o g r a p h y

(818) 995-1876

H E A D S H O T
Photography by Jack

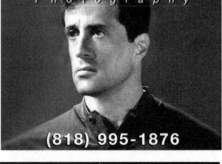

Prices start from $49.95
Film & Digital
(818)887-0549
www.JackShirak.com

Jennifer Johann Photography
(818) 590-0885   jrjohann@pacbell.net

FREE PHOTO SESSIONS
for Actors & Models

International photographer, 15 years experience, works with media make-up artists to build their portfolios.

• Must have great skin.
• We shoot 2-3 different looks. (Prints extra)

Actors say "Best deal in L.A."

View website for details and photos
www.aawd.net
Award Studio   310-395-2779

HEADSHOTS
B/W & Color
Digital
Retouching

SUZANNE ENGLAND
PHOTOGRAPHY
(323)460-6892

TO ADVERTISE IN THE NEXT

BACKSTAGE®/BACK STAGE WEST®

ACTORS HANDBOOK

WEST ■   ■ EAST

Back Stage West Advertising   Back StageAdvertising
5055 Wilshire Blvd., 5th floor   770 Broadway, 4th floor
Los Angeles, CA 90036   New York, NY 10003
323.525.2225   646.654.5700

BACK STAGE® and *BACK STAGE WEST®*
The #1 weeklies for Performing Artists

SUBSCRIBE TODAY
1.800.745.8922
http://www.backstage.com/backstage/contact/printsub.jsp

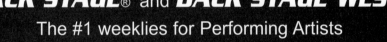

7 Résumé Mucho:

Making Your Credits Count

BY ELIAS STIMAC

We all know what should go on a performer's résumé, right? Name, contact info, credits, training, and those dreaded "special skills." Most of us would love to know how to put all that information together on one 8"x10" page so that it will catch the eye of casting directors, agents, and others in the entertainment industry. But sometimes it seems that everyone and their stage mother has a different opinion about what exactly should go on the back of your headshot, and where exactly it should be placed.

How do you make your résumé stand out while still appearing professional? The answer varies, especially in this technological age. Actors, singers, and dancers need résumés that are designed to highlight their specific strengths. Credits of stage veterans may be listed a lot differently than those of screen newcomers. How-to books, printing services, and casting pros all will have opinions on how to lay out the page. The bottom line is that you have to be satisfied with your résumé, just as you have to be happy with the pose, lighting, and style of your headshot. Only then will you feel confident when mailing your résumé or handing it across a desk in the hope of booking that next big job.

VITAL STATISTICS

Like headshots, résumés are a useful self-promotional tool for anyone trying to get into show business. They help the decision-makers in the industry get a better sense of the individual whose photo is stapled on the other side. A headshot may get an actor noticed, but it is the résumé that will proclaim his experience and more likely prompt the powers that be to schedule an audition. Much information needs to be conveyed in a brief space, so being clear and concise is a top priority.

Whether your résumé will be read by agents, casting directors, managers, producers, or directors, some things must always be included. Your name should be bold and easy to read, and larger than anything else on the page. Usually the name is centered, although off-center placement is becoming more common. Be sure the name on the résumé matches the name on the headshot.

If you are signed with (or freelancing with) an agency, your agents will let you know where to place the company's logo and contact numbers. Usually, they go in the upper-left-hand or upper-right-hand corner. If you don't have representation, make sure your service or voicemail number is current. And, as everyone in the business has probably already told you, never put your home number or address on your résumé.

Performers who are members of one or more professional unions—such as Actors' Equity Association (AEA), Screen Actors Guild (SAG), or the American Federation of Television and Radio Artists (AFTRA)—usually print the abbreviations under their name. If you are not a member, but are eligible for union membership, mention that as well.

Personal statistics also go near the top of the page, including height, weight, and hair and eye color. Singers can add vocal range, while print models may include clothing sizes. Those who feel compelled to fib about height or weight details may want to keep this point in mind: somebody may be looking for your real-life type, but unknowingly pass by your taller, thinner counterpart thanks to a "doctored" résumé.

CREDIT REPORT

The main portion of your résumé will be filled with columns of your film, television, and stage credits—though not necessarily in that order. Credits can be listed beginning with the most prominent or the most recent. Stage actors should start with theatre credits; film and TV performers can highlight those categories first.

The quality and recognizability of particular projects, roles, directors, and venues will figure into the equation. Some of the directors and production companies you have worked for may be better known in one medium than another, and union shows usually take precedence over nonunion.

Remember that agents and casting directors don't always need to read a lot of credits to be impressed. So avoid adding lines, decreasing font size, and reducing the margins to fit in every role in every show you ever did. In fact, having some white space on your résumé isn't a bad thing—it provides a place to write complimentary notes about your audition piece or your cold reading skills.

In addition to stage and screen experience, this area of your résumé is also where you can list commercial, industrial, stand-up comedy, voiceover, and miscellaneous credits. Most of the time, actors will just write "list available upon request" under the commercial heading, as most casting directors are concerned only about conflicts (you can't book a Pepsi ad campaign if you are still under contract with Coca-Cola). Industrial films, voiceover jobs, or stand-up comedy gigs can be listed at your discretion, along with new-media credits such as CD-ROMs and video games. Sometimes the mention of an innovative assignment or production company may rate a second glance.

SKILLFUL WRAP-UP

Don't assume that most people who look at your résumé will stop reading after the experience section. Training and special skills are often where casting experts and talent reps go first when considering a potential client. For example, a lot of younger performers won't have many professional credits, but a good educational background could make a difference. Seasoned performers who've recently studied a different method with an established teacher could open themselves up to a whole new range of roles. And if the part calls for a motorcycle rider who is also a ballet dancer, a quick glance at your "special skills" will instantly let the industry know that you can handle both handlebars and ballet barres.

As with all the other areas on your résumé, the best bet when listing schools and skills is to avoid embellishing. The last thing you need in an interview or audition situation is to have someone asking you about a specific university you attended or unique talent you claim to have, only to discover that you "really didn't go there" or "really can't do that." Honesty is the best policy, even if it means pounding the pavement a little while longer before being discovered.

Nowadays, there are companies with high-tech computers and printers ready to help actors design and print their résumés in a variety of styles. Whether you choose to have your résumé professionally typeset or do it yourself, here are a few other tips that everybody seems to agree on:

1 Don't handwrite any credits on your résumé.
2 Do make sure your résumé is the same size as the headshot.
3 Don't make the type so small that it's hard to read.
4 Do have the résumé attached to the photo, with staples on all four corners.
5 Don't lie.

EXPERT EXAMPLES

It's one thing to speculate on how an effective résumé can be put together. But it's always best to find out what's expected from the people who receive and evaluate résumés on a daily basis.

Shep Pamplin is an agent with the New York-based boutique firm Agents for the Arts, Inc. Countless résumés land on his desk. Says Pamplin: "The headshot is an obvious picture. In my position, I look at the picture that's painted on the back— the résumé. It should say, 'This is what I've done, this is where I'm qualified, this is who I've trained with, and this is why I'm prepared.' To me, the résumé is a better snapshot of the person you're going to meet, which is why you should never lie. I find it a much more interesting portrait of a performer than the actual photograph, which is usually retouched."

Stephen DeAngelis is an in-house commercial casting director for Grey Worldwide, a global advertising agency, and also freelances on theatre and film projects. "I do a little of everything—on-camera, voiceover, radio. I deal with pretty people, character people, little people, children, novelty types, grunge rockers. I'm like a pharmacist— industry people come to me with a prescription, and I fill it." DeAngelis warns actors who are fresh out of college or just starting their careers not to "pad" their résumés. "I'm realistic; I know they just graduated college and just came to town. So I don't expect them to have five Broadway shows. And I don't need them to. At that point, I just want to focus on what kind of experience they've had, if they've done substantial roles or carried a show, and their level of training."

David Caparelliotis is a six-year casting veteran at the Manhattan Theatre Club in New York City. While both union and nonunion actors can submit for MTC projects, the majority of résumés Caparelliotis sees come through agency submissions. "We hire whoever's right for the role. That said, it tends to be experienced actors who have Broadway, Off-Broadway, or, at the very least, regional credits. So, if actors have done mostly showcase work—because they do have to start somewhere— if they just moved here, or just graduated, then it's not going to be experience that is going to make me call this person in; it's going to be something else. Maybe they went to a prominent school or they're studying with someone I've heard of. That lets me know the person takes the craft seriously."

A talent agent for more than thirty-five years, Marv Josephson is currently an independent agent affiliated with Gilla Roos, Ltd. He points out that the world of entertainment is a very "subjective" business. "If an actor sends out a mailing to fifty agents, he or she may get three or four responses. What would appeal to me might not appeal to somebody else. If I see a very extensive résumé, I will perk up and look it over carefully."

Format and readability are two things Josephson looks for. "Most of the time the credits need to be listed in three columns: the play, the role, and the venue. You don't want to read a novel; you want to see it one-two-three. If it's an important director, you should put the name down as well."

Says Ricardo Cordero—chairman of Global Network Pictures, as well as an accomplished director of feature films and theatre productions: "I just received a résumé with a note that read, 'I am interested in being considered for your film. Please contact me. I will do anything, even off-camera work.' That's the right way to make a submission."

But there are certain things that can hurt your submission. Cordero advises actors not to seal the envelope—just clasp the flap in place, so the casting agent or the assistant can open it easier. Also, actors should not put their e-mail address on their résumés if they don't check their e-mails regularly. "A lot of times we will e-mail an actor for an audition, only to have them call back a week later."

Ardelle Striker is the producing artistic director of New York City's Blue Heron Theatre. She doesn't bother looking at film and television credits. "I go directly to their theatre credits and their training. Actors these days usually put their film and TV credits up at the top. The more substantial theatre actor will put Broadway credits, Off-Broadway, and then Off-Off-Broadway, and then film and so on." Blue Heron does most of its casting through a company called Breakdown Services, which sends out casting info to agents and managers on a daily basis. "Actors can submit themselves, but they should look carefully at what the producer and director are looking for. If you are not right for it, don't waste anybody's time by sending in your materials, because they will be set aside immediately."

Now that you know what needs to go on your résumé—and where it should go—you can resume your quest for show biz success, one step ahead of the thundering herd. Again, always remember: As with any résumé, be honest and direct and don't give them any reason not to hire you.

8 The Wonderful World of the Web:

Promoting Yourself on the Internet

BY AMELIA DAVID

You've decided you're ready to publicize yourself on your own website, but what are your options? To begin, of course, you can look at friends' websites or meander through cyberspace for ideas. But to help you learn more about promoting yourself on the Internet, for this chapter we've gathered advice from a diverse mix of Web designers and entertainment professionals.

Some of the services described here can be pricey. But don't let having a "zero" budget get you down: We'll also introduce you to "blogs"(a.k.a. Web logs). They can offer you regularly updated, written Web presentations, sometimes at no cost to start or run.

BUDGETING THE BELLS AND WHISTLES

D. Bruce Stevens of DBS Design Group has an extensive background in graphic design and illustration—with a print and website client list that reads like a who's who of award-winning Broadway and cabaret performers. (Among them are Broadway's first *Aida,* Heather Headley; and the "purrfect" cabaret chanteuse, Eartha Kitt.)

Stevens claims there are advantages to using talented newcomers to the design business. "You can get very good prices for beautiful work," he says. "Keep in mind, however, if you want updates in the future, designers just starting out will seldom offer free or cheap work for a long period of time. Get all the source files for the site, so someone else can work on it."

Sometimes, Stevens acknowledges, using a beginner is not the best bet. He notes that an experienced designer charging $100 can sometimes accomplish in an hour what a newcomer will do for $25 an hour in five hours.

How important are budget-busting extra "bells and whistles"? Stevens explains: "One of the biggest traps designers (and clients) fall into is thinking you need sound and video animation. If a site takes too long to load, you'll lose the viewer. You'll lose them if you incorporate too many gadgets that require a 'plug in' to be loaded that the viewer may not have. Your site is not about animation. It's about you and what you do. A website will look different on different computers. It will load at different speeds. You have to be sure your website works well on all computers."

Music playing in the background on sites can be nice, but it does add more download time and, after a while, can become annoying to your site visitors.

As for content, most performers will want to include a bio, photos, and a roster of press notices. But be careful. You can wind up projecting a questionable image if you have a "quotes and reviews" section that includes only a single rave quotation.

Since it's still a new field, Stevens doesn't feel there are set pricing standards yet. While an experienced designer may be able to help you with the copy (text) for your site, performers traditionally are expected to provide their own. If you don't have your own copy, a designer should always be ready to offer assistance—but you need to be prepared to offer additional compensation. The proposal and contract should cover these matters in advance. A designer should not spring "surprise" charges on a client. As for prices for designing or maintaining a site, it all depends on what you want—and on how much scanning and retouching may be needed. (You can seldom simply scan a photo and put it online without prepping it in some way.)

The least costly submissions to Web designers are digital files, which require no typing or conversion. It's fine to submit photos to designers by e-mail if they're good quality and have sufficiently high resolution. Faxed information can result in typos—hence extra time and costs. When you submit typed and formatted information via e-mail or on disk, you will save time.

Says Stevens, "I seldom quote rock-bottom prices until I've seen the content for a site, because of the variables. But I could say a basic site with a beautiful design, a few photos, reviews, etc., if it's submitted by e-mail, could be designed for as little as $1,200. Some clients have even smaller budgets than that, and there have been times I've been able to create an attractive but modest site for $500. Then, as the client can afford it, we upgrade. Most basic sites can be finished in two to three weeks."

As for selling your CDs and other products via your site, Stevens recommends PayPal or CCNow, which can take customers' orders via credit card. Other companies, such as www.CDStreet.com, can warehouse your CDs and fulfill orders for you. Ticket sales can be handled in similar fashion.

MEETING THE WORLD ON THE WEB

To give you an example of how quickly the Web can generate industry interest, meet singer-songwriter Jill Zutty. She is Mom to three boys. Her oldest, Jason (in his mid-teens), is a self-taught website designer who's happy to explain things like the Hypertext Markup Language Code (which helps turn plain text into interactive Web pages).

Zutty has recorded two original music CDs, which she sells from her website. She's wisely linked her site to other marketing sites, including www.CDBaby.com, which she found just by surfing the Web. Deejays have also found Zutty there, as have an interested record label from Atlanta and a journalist from Germany.

While Zutty has to pay a percentage to the sites selling her CDs (she says that the "new arrivals" category is the best slot for her music), she considers it worth the price, as she has generated sales and radio station airplay as far away as the Netherlands. Zutty also has www.LAmusic.com hosting her site and selling her CDs: They've put all her audio clips on her website and handle the sales of the promotional wear and key chains available through her online store.

Zutty uses the Web to send e-mails about her career progress. She also uses it to network. Whenever she makes new contacts, she adds them to her e-mail list. If she's busy (and what mother of three isn't?), or if she meets people and isn't carrying pictures and music samples, she refers people to her site.

Zutty also uses the Web to generate interest in and work for her middle son, Andrew Blake Zutty—a budding actor. When a show's website features Andrew in production photos or includes his headshot, Mom uses this exposure to help him book new auditions.

BECOMING USER-FRIENDLY

Site designer Tony Montano's expertise was originally in the area of website "usability" (that is, creating websites in a way that makes for an easy and pleasant experience for the site visitor). Montano claims it's very important for a prospective client to look at a designer's portfolio. His or her style may or may not match your personality or express what you want to convey. You should also discuss exactly what you expect technically with your potential designer in order to make sure he or she has the necessary expertise.

Some designers create a new design for each client, while others offer a package where you choose a design from existing templates. The latter is a little cheaper, and there's nothing wrong with using a template.

You should learn as much as you can about search engines. Within six months of your site's being published, most of the major search engines will have found you and added you to their database. You can check for info on getting a listing on Google, one of the more popular sites, at www.google.com/webmasters/1.html. Some search engines charge a fee if you are in a rush, but otherwise they're usually free. You should probably stay away from websites that claim they'll get you listed in hundreds of search engines for a fee. Says Montano: "There are only a handful of major search engines to be concerned about, and it's very easy to submit your site to them yourself."

It's rarely necessary for you to meet your site designer in person.

As you shop around for prices, remember that if a designer in Ohio offers quality sites at a cheap price, there's no reason you can't work with him—no matter where you live.

If your budget is tight, you can start with one page and then add on as your finances permit. On average, Montano says, creating five pages takes about two weeks. This would include ordering the domain name and then getting it hosted with an Internet Service Provider (ISP). If you'd like to find out whether your preferred domain name is still available, go to www.networksolutions.com and enter it at the prompt. When you find a suitable and available name, you can simply order it on the spot.

Your ISP will be a small monthly expense for you. Hundreds of ISPs are out there, and you can see many of them at www.thelist.com. Montano uses and recommends LFC Hosting (www.lfchosting.com). It usually runs about $18 per month.

PUTTING IT TOGETHER

To find what it costs to create and update a website on a shoestring budget, we asked Greg Sullivan, artistic director for the NYC improv group Klaatu, to share what his behind-the-scenes costs have been. To design and update his website, he used Microsoft FrontPage, a Web development software. "It was $125 for the original version and $75 to get the 2000 edition. I got my domain name . . . for $35, and subsequently renewed it for ten years at a cost of $180. It costs $22.45 per month for hosting for the website, and I use Hiway, which I have never had a problem with. Contracts usually run for a year and automatically roll over."

His Website host also provides Sullivan with email. On his home page, he has a "hit counter," which tells how many "hits" (i.e., visits) have been made to the page. Sullivan can use this feature to track whether the ads and promotions he runs during the year have been successful in generating visits to the site. Implementing the initial design took about fifteen to twenty hours. Updating is much simpler: "I am often updating the content on the site, so doing it myself is a great advantage and savings."

One trick to learn from Sullivan: He makes his site's information paragraphs intentionally long, with many "keywords," such as "improv," "improvisation," "New York City," "beginner," "experienced," "acting," "actor," "class," "classes," "inexpensive," "performance," and "show" included in his text, so that search engines can lead people who type these words directly to the site.

All told, Sullivan's first-year costs totaled approximately $500, and he's spent about $290 in each subsequent year. His DSL connection—an added expense—runs $39.95 per month. He also invested in a digital camera.

FREE AND EASY

That subhead could also be the description for keeping a "blog" (a.k.a. Web log). No, you're not reading a typo. The blog is a form of Web communication that *Back Stage* first heard of from comedian Liam McEneaney. Unlike Website owners, "bloggers" are free to offer their writing easily and frequently, because the HTML code is already laid down. Just go to www.blogger.com, for example, and there's a field to enter whatever text you'd like. You type—then you just hit "publish."

McEneaney tells us he found out about blogging from his friend and fellow comedian Adam Felber. The best reason we can see to become a blogger is, of course, that having a blog is free: www.blogger.com puts up the cost of hosting your blog (in exchange, they're allowed to put up banner ads on it). If you don't want the ads and you'd like extra services such as spell check, a $5- or $10-per-month alternate plan is available. McEneaney assures readers that writing a blog is both incredibly easy and, yes, really free. Many other comics and writers are becoming bloggers—and now you can become one too.

Indeed, there are increasingly wonderful worlds to explore on the Web. (By the way—if you haven't already done so, make sure you also visit www.backstage.com!)

9 Promoting Yourself Using CDs

BY DAVID FINKLE

CD or not CD? The answer is, go ahead, if you've got the financing. Make that CD and obtain distribution for it, if you can. But—and it's a big "but"—if you don't take steps to guarantee that your CD receives effective promotion, there's really not much sense bothering in the first place.

Or, as singing LML Music founder (and West Coast industry expert) Lee Lessack puts it, "I always tell artists I can get them on a store shelf, but it's their responsibility to get themselves *off* the store shelf."

In one regard, that's the quintessential CD promo message. The details on how to go about accepting the promotion challenge, however, are many and varied. And they underscore a happy synergistic reality: CDs can sell an artist just as artists can position themselves to sell CDs.

RADIO DAYS

To begin with, pursuing radio play is a solid idea. Yes, at first blush, it looks as if today's play lists are tighter than they've ever been and much harder to crack. (This is due in part to the limiting broadcast policies of such companies as Clear Channel Communications.) But there is reason to take heart. Some 250 deejays across the country feature the music sung by those artists who play concerts and cabarets where the still-expanding "Great American Songbook" is favored. While 250 deejays is, by the way, an approximate number, it should nevertheless cheer nightclub and music hall entertainers.

New York-based cabaret performer Sue Matsuki understands and acts on the need to be aggressive. She says, emphatically: "People just have to do the work." That work involves checking surveys for those 250 deejays on easy-listening and jazz standard stations and then contacting the appropriate people at all of them (or retaining a competent promotion person to do the legwork for you). Then, after making initial contact, you'll need to keep in touch as much as possible—but without becoming too much of a nuisance.

Radio promotion man Len Triola has worked the territory long enough to understand the changes and resulting requirements. He says that a monthly rate of $750—charged by promoters such as himself—is a good ballpark figure, but he adds that most promotion folk aren't averse to negotiation, especially if they believe in you and your product.

When you do use a promoter, the results can be extremely gratifying. Triola, for instance, is friendly with WNYC's longtime quality-music maven Jonathan Schwartz, to whom he regularly recommends discs. For his part, Schwartz responds enthusiastically. An example of the kind of appreciative advocate who is situated in many markets, Schwartz is quick to say he's always listening and hoping to add new names to his playlist of singers interpreting that vaunted Songbook.

Like Schwartz, most accessible jocks are bombarded with CDs, but that's not a worry. More often than not, deejays count on receiving discs. What they might suggest, though is that singers and instrumentalists pursuing airplay carefully consider what they're sending out.

"My main concern," David Kenney at WBAI-New York's "Everything Old Is New Again" explains, "is sometimes they overload their packet." What he means is that it's unnecessary to include all the press releases for all the shows you've ever done. When you dispatch press material, you should include an informational letter of introduction. And keep in mind that material sent from press agents has more weight than that you send yourself.

And be neat about it, or make sure your agent is. Your letter should be typed, not handwritten. "When what is sent is messy," Kenney comments, "when things are folded and shoved into an envelope, that gives the impression this is not a professional package."

Good cover art on the CD itself is essential, as are, if possible, laudatory liner notes from a recognized authority.

What's most important, however, is content. There's no underestimating the importance of having a CD reflect what the artist does on stage.

MAKING THE CONNECTION

Deejays find new artists in myriad ways. The story goes that once Jonathan Schwartz fell in love with the late Nancy LaMott's interpretations, he brought her on his show a number of times. He continues to play her tracks these days. How he was introduced to her is a particularly amusing as well as instructive tale, and underscores the manner by which well-positioned ballyhooers can be reached.

Apparently, a waiter at a midtown Manhattan restaurant overheard Schwartz's accountant/lawyer speaking Schwartz's name. The fast-thinking waiter, who happened to be a friend of LaMott's, produced the singer's Johnny Mercer CD and handed it to the startled but accommodating patron. As luck would have it, the lawyer/accountant was on his way to see Schwartz. Schwartz recalls, "From the first word, 'moon,' on a song I never needed to hear again—'Moon River'— I heard easily the best singer of her generation."

To be sure, the kind of serendipity Schwartz describes can never be counted on, but what can be expected is the luck people make for themselves by having their CDs available wherever they can and in whatever circumstance.

OH, WHAT A TUNEFUL WEB WE WEAVE . . .

The Internet is a useful tool for marketing your CDs. Many cabaret performers sell their releases through CD Baby (at www.cdbaby.com) and are grateful for the check that comes after each copy is sold. (A performer can also add the buyer's name to his or her mailing list.)

New York's Jeanne MacDonald, one of those pleased CD Baby babies, notes, though, that business isn't necessarily gotten through the website. "So much of the time the CDs you sell are through word-of-mouth and people hearing you," MacDonald reports. "I have still found no avenue for selling to unknown audiences."

Sue Matsuki, on the other hand, insists that the cross-referencing policy the CD Baby folks have helps enormously. "I've gotten found on CD Baby," she boasts. She means that anyone looking up, say, Rosemary Clooney or Peggy Lee on cdbaby.com will be referred to Matsuki. When they visit her site, they can also listen to tracks. Matsuki rounds up quotes to include on her CD labels and then features those words of praise in her Cdbaby.com file, which, by no accident, also includes a link to her www.suematsuki.com website.

Incidentally, some artists contended that they were not making enough sales at Amazon.com to cover the e-merchant's annual charges. Subsequently, the aural preview option at Amazon was dropped.

I'LL TELL THE MAN IN THE STREET
To supplement CD radio play and Internet activity, there are innumerable additional marketing stategies. If the budget can handle it, you can help get the word out by giving discs away to the right people—anywhere from 300 to 500 CDs from a 1,500-CD pressing.

Lee Lessack remarks, "There are several other methods of making that CD earn its cost." Among them (and possibly foremost) is hiring a publicist who will get you reviews at *Billboard*, *The New York Times*, *The Los Angeles Times* and similar publications. Such coverage is invaluable.

Don't forget, however, that if you don't yet feel entirely confident about your mastery of the craft, you might be smart to avoid pursuing reviews in major outlets. A well-positioned reviewer may come to hear you once but may not come again anytime soon, if he or she doesn't like what's on view.

Sue Matsuki stresses that visiting individual stores is a must and that CDs should be placed only in geographic areas where the artist is known.

Asked what most helps rivet attention in CD promotion, Jim Caruso, who both performs and boosts other performers, jokingly recommends "prayer." More seriously, he acknowledges that it's a hard row to hoe because "there aren't that many clubs to pitch to." He also advises going to record stores "to get to know the buyer—the shmoozing element."

He adds, "It is do-able. If you keep on it, it's worth it. We know the stuff sells if it's in there."

The idea is that you have to push CDs as you push your shows. Eventually that double push feeds back and forth. New York-based Lisa Dawn Popa, who operates the distribution company The Cabaret Connection, has encouraged artists who are working "out of town" to promote themselves to concierges and other staff at local hotels.

It's also not a bad tactic for any performer to get that CD listed in the catalogue of available product that Popa regularly updates and sends to 400,000 contacts worldwide—something like eight times a year.

One hard truth about stores and cabaret CDs during times when sales are dipping ominously is that to get your CD in major outlets across the country, you must nail down a distributor—and most of them don't want to take independent labels. When, however, an artist does get CDs in stores, it's a savvy move to agree to and even volunteer for signings. David Kenney agrees that signings are a great thing if you can get them. He adds, "I see more and more release parties, which I think is good."

Almost anyone who knows anything about selling CDs will insist that a CD promo "basic" is to sell CDs before and after performances—and, perhaps, to plug them with tongue in cheek during a show. ("That was a number from my new CD, which just *happens* to be for sale on the premises. . . .") Many, if not most, artists, exploit this opportunity. Perhaps the wiliest of them is veteran Blossom Dearie, who divides her set into halves, then sells and signs CDs during the intermission.

And guess what? She doesn't start the second half until she's chatted with every fan who makes a purchase. She knows that the performances promote the CD and, in their turn, the CDs promote the artist and his or her performance.

Momentum inevitably gathers.

10 Promoting Yourself Using Videos

BY AMELIA DAVID

No longer just a visual way to sell a song on cable music channels, videotapes are now used to book auditions and jobs by many entertainers: monologists, stand-up comics, bands, commercial and film performers, cruise ship singers, cabaret artists, and more. Some performers put their complete shows on tape; some include excerpts of past work. Newer entertainment genres—such as talent searches on www.comedycentral.com and TV reality shows—also may require submission of a video.

If you're going to use videotape, one of the most important concepts to grasp is "targeting." Before you spend money on videotapes and postage, you should do some research to make sure the person to whom you're sending an unsolicited tape will actually accept it. You'll also want to make sure that the content of your video matches what the receiver is looking for. You wouldn't want to send a tape of your latest operatic recital to a wedding band looking for pop power belters.

FILM AND THEATRE: NO UNSOLICITED TAPES, PLEASE!

A tape can serve as an important calling card for many jobs, but for others it won't be appropriate. If you're an actor trying to generate interest from an agent or casting director, you'll find that many aren't at all interested in receiving a tape with your initial mailing. Many, in fact, have strict rules about not accepting tapes at all. Aspiring film and TV performers who have gathered professional commercials and film clips for an audition tape—or who've made such a tape in a class—may find that they've wasted money and time by blindly mailing to a big list of offices. It's more likely that recipients will place your video in their "circular files." The best way to do your homework is to look in industry directories such as *Ross Reports*. They may note whether specific talent agencies and casting offices accept unsolicited tapes or not.

Agent Margaret Emory of Dulcina Eisen Associates in New York discourages submission of tapes: "Absolutely 'no' to actors sending me videotapes unsolicited, especially videotapes filled with scenes from an acting class. I don't have the time to see them. I invest my time in seeing live performances."

Jerry Beaver, a casting director in New York City, adds: "Sometimes videos are helpful; sometimes they're not. That's because actors have no standard when it comes to making videotapes. You should see some of the things I get. Some tapes are really bad and undirected. On poor-quality tapes, the whole thing is shot from one angle or just from the head up, which doesn't even let you see what the actor looks like. Besides, you want to meet and see that actor in person. But actors can be working out of town and want to show you what they're doing, so it all depends."

A KEY TO CLUB WORK

For a stand-up comic, musical comedian, comedy songwriter, or comic performer who wants to present something in clubs, a videotape presenting a strong seven- to ten-minute club set is a far more important tool than an 8" x 10" headshot. Club owners, bookers, performers, and managers agree, however, that just because someone is funny, it doesn't mean his or her comedy will work in every room.

Once again, "targeting" is key. You need to visit specific venues, because each has its own type of audience, and the management knows the kinds of acts (and even the language and dress code) that will work best. Also, if you're sending your comedy tapes to venues nationwide, remember that what may work in your local comedy club may not translate geographically: for instance, subway and cab-driver jokes that will "kill 'em" in Manhattan may simply die in Peoria.

Chris Mazzilli, owner of New York City's Gotham Comedy Club, also worked as a performer for seven years. When he watches a tape, he has to consider the performers he's currently booking. Mazzilli observes, "I can't book a show with three comics who all do the same type of material. Even after a great steak, you don't want another steak." He's looking for "comics with their own voice and originality." He also has found that "blue" language doesn't work well for his upscale room.

Mazzilli, who sees at least thirty audition tapes a week, doesn't require an accompanying photo with submissions. (This is true with many other comedy clubs, as well.) He does like to receive a short, personal cover letter that gives a feel for who the person is, rather than a generic form letter. He also likes to know how the performer found out about Gotham, where he or she is performing, and the best time he or she can be reached. Mazzilli notes one big mistake that those submitting videotapes often make: "You have to fully label everything. Things get separated. Make sure your name and phone number are on the tape, as well as on the tape cover."

Mazzilli claims that a professional comic definitely needs a tape. If you don't have one, he says, then you should pay for one or do a "bringer show" (i.e., a show where the comic brings an audience and receives a tape of the set in return). There are clubs that can recommend someone to shoot your videotape, or offer their own club cameras for a fee. You should first look at other tapes the club has done, especially if you're bringing a roomful of customers in return for a tape. And, as many comedy professionals note, a tape of your "SRO" audience—full of friends laughing—won't fool anyone: your material has to be funny to strangers as well.

One final piece of advice that Mazzilli offers applies to singers as well as to stand-up comics: "A tape shouldn't feature clinking glasses in the background, or the waitresses' heads. And it shouldn't be shakily done with a handheld camcorder."

PLANNING A TAPE

One expert who's familiar with the need to target videos is Erv Raible, who's worked as a club booker, coach, director, publicist, and talent representative for cabaret artists. He is executive and artistic director for the Cabaret Conference at Yale University and has viewed many audition videos—good, bad, and awful. He says that if you can produce a decent-quality, one-hour-or-less show tape, you can then break it up into a few smaller, fifteen-minute tapes. You can then target these as audition tapes for different types of bookings. You should keep these target tapes in mind when you're planning your show lineup and thinking about what you'll wear for tapings.

Whether you tape in front of an audience or hire an empty club, Raible advises, you should use a location where you like the light and sound quality and where you feel you can work smoothly with the technician. If you're buying a tape from a club, find out whether they will be using a stationary or a mobile camera (i.e., one able to move with you on songs). Again, a much-overlooked but important factor when planning a tape is how quiet the wait staff can be during your most emotional songs. You might want to see a show at the club first in order to find out.

Once you've got your tape, you have to think further about what you're targeting. For singing jobs on cruise ships or at a hotel, you'll likely want to feature standards from the "Great American Songbook"—recognizable material rather than original songs. A singer's tape needs both serious ballads and some comedy songs—along with a few fast clips with just bits of songs and some patter. With this kind of variety, your prospective boss can assess your personality and how you relate to an audience. Singers should also be sure, Raible says, to include songs that demonstrate their range—from the lowest notes to the highest.

Comics will want to learn whether blue humor is appropriate for the venue. And singers and comedians alike will need to know what kind of apparel is suitable.

Vocalists and comics aren't the only artists who use videos to promote themselves. If you want to book your theatre piece in a club, you might be asked to send a taped excerpt from the show. (Remember to be sure the piece is long enough—but not too long—to allow the establishment to serve its two-drink minimum.)

How important is it to have the added bells and whistles on your video—things like titles and special effects? Raible notes: They're fun to look at, but that's not the work. What's being looked at is your presence, so get who you are in there."

Academy
☐Players
☐Directory

The choice of
the professional actor

"I have used the *Players Directory* on an almost daily basis for the last 15 years. Often, when stuck on a role, I'll just page through each book, making lists as I go along. *The Players Directory* is one of my most important casting tools and I'd be lost without it."

—Ruth Lambert

The *Academy Players Directory* is an invaluable resource to casting professionals in Los Angeles and throughout the world.

The *Players Directory* is the only casting reference to offer actors a biannual printed listing, a searchable Internet listing and inclusion in an electronic submission system.

To find out more visit:
www.playersdirectory.com
or call (310) 247-3058

Breakdown Services
promises accurate information and services

Actors Access
Casting Directors Directory
Agency Guide
Casting Labels
SAG Agency Labels
Flyer Delivery to Casting Directors

Check out all we have to offer at
www.breakdownservices.com
(310) 276-9166

GREAT REELS

"Cinevative creates outstanding actor demo reels that are, unique, professional and fun to watch"
....Michael Donovan - CSA

EDIT and/or SHOOT
Full Production Package

Effective Reels That Get Results
Free Consultation
SPECIAL ACTOR RATES!
Winner - Eleven International Industry Awards

cinevative *productions*
(323) 852-8903
8271 Melrose Suite 203 Los Angeles CA 90046 **www.cinevative.com**

Fade In: Entertainment
Digital Video Production
Complete/Prof. Service Incl.
SCRIPT, SHOOT, EDIT, TITLE,
MUSIC, VOICEOVER, FX, etc.
Actor's Demos (Low Flat Rate)
Performance, Host, Music Videos,
Films & Special Events (Quote)
323-240-9164   www.fade-in.net

MDM
Interactive DVD/Demo Reels
3 2 3 - 7 2 8 - 3 4 5 0
FOR SAMPLES: MDMPS.COM
Production Services

PHANTOM
CASTING.COM

ACTORS GET NOTICED.
Industry Professionals find Talent.
PHANTOM CASTING... The *Premiere* online talent resource.
info@phantomcasting.com
www.phantomcasting.com   323.839.5881

Actors Discount Rates
DEMO REELS
Since 1986
Emmy Award Winner
VIDEO EDITING
VHS & DVD DUPLICATIONS
CUSTOM LABELS
STAGE PRODUCTION
BROADCAST QUALITY
FREE COPIES
with editing purchase
818·843·3188
TVP STUDIOS

digital mechanix
Event Videography
Cinematic 24p Digital Video
"Film Like" Video
DVD DVD Authoring DVD
$50 Demo Reels
digital-mechanix.com
818.377.4422

Monkey Dream Films
DEMO REELS-
REEL AFFORDABLE
Broadcast-quality demo reels on DVD!
Shoot a Monologue,
Edit Existing Reel, Gift Certificates.
*Video production to pound
your chest about.*
(818) 509-8415
*"My reel got me a job with
Miramax sight unseen!"*
—NiCole Robinson
SATISFIED CUSTOMER

DVD DUBS
**Duplications
Demo Reels
Low Rates
Editing**
**323 845 0812
888 DVD DUBS
4 DVD DUBS . COM**

ACT NOW!
LA's most prestigious and exclusive
networking company allows the professional
actor the opportunity to further their
career by meeting and performing with
casting directors, producers and agents.
A thorough prescreening is required.
To schedule an appointment call:
323.790.8200
www.actnownetwork.com

www.backstage.com

Attention all **Actors, Models** and **Performers**:
Place your HEADSHOTS and DEMO REELS
ON-LINE **NOW!**
And we mean RIGHT NOW...**INSTANTLY!**
Announcing the
ONCORentertainment.com
Digital Portfolio

Time to face facts... In this cyber age the World Wide Web has become the fastest growing marketplace available today, and just about every business has their own WEB-SITE, because every smart business owner knows how crucial it is to get maximum exposure at a minimal cost, and the World Wide Web is the place to get that exposure. Isn't it time YOU got into the mix? Isn't it time YOU began to take your career seriously and started treating yourself as a BUSINESS? Isn't it time YOU got the World Wide Web exposure you need to jump start YOUR CAREER? Well...what are you waiting for?   Come On...EXPOSE YOURSELF!

Get your very own Digital Portfolio at
ONCORentertainment.com

Here's what you'll get with ONCOR entertainment:

Personalized Web Address (http://*YourName*.ONCORentertainment.com)

Personal Bio page
Photo Gallery
On Line AUDIO Reels
Private e-mail

Personal Resume page
Calendar of Appearances
On Line VIDEO Reels
On Line Sales of your Merchandise!

Plus, you're in complete controll of your pages for all updates and edits of your portfolio, anytime, 24 hours a day for FREE!

Back Stage Special
Get **50%** off initial membership fee by using the promo code:
B.STAGE-1

Get yourself on the web TODAY!
Rates starting as low as $11.99 per month!

Free Trial Offer
Send us your Headshot & Resume, and we'll put you on our site for a **FREE** six week trial!
(see site for details)

Your Headshot On Line In less than 5 minutes!

ONCOR
entertainment
The digital portfolio source for today's artist.

www.ONCORentertainment.com
1-866- GO ONCOR

ACTORS WANTED

JOIN FREE

www.onemodelplace.com/actor

- Free online portfolio includes 5 images
- Worlds largest talent community
- Access to 25,000 agents, managers, and photographers
- Over 2 million visitors monthly
- Free access to message boards

Portfolios easily upgraded to include

- Demo real including audio & video
- 21 to 41 images
- Access to daily casting calls
- Listings and directories distributed to agents

Be Seen!
Be Heard!
Make an Impact!

The newest and most powerful technology to promote acting careers is now available in N.Y.

Your video clips, headshots, curriculum vitae, web site link and more! All integratedin high impact style on a unique business card size CD-ROM or DVD.

Stop by our new TRIBECA office for a demo, or call us for more information.

Impact Showreels   212-334-2441

www.ImpactShowreels.com

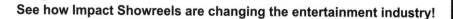

See how Impact Showreels are changing the entertainment industry!

need an agent? help with your career? advice on marketing tools?
one-on-one career coaching * personal referrals to agents

www.actormarketing.biz

"understanding the biz of showbiz...the way to a successful acting career!'
*FREE information seminars -soaps, comm'l's, agents, primetime, films, sitcoms
* network receptions to meet agents *actormarathons to audition for agents

888-889-9009

oMYmedia

Custom

DVD

917.6807700

TO ADVERTISE IN THE NEXT

BACKSTAGE®/BACK STAGE WEST®

ACTORS HANDBOOK

WEST ■   ■ EAST

Back Stage West Advertising	Back StageAdvertising
5055 Wilshire Blvd., 5th floor	770 Broadway, 4th floor
Los Angeles, CA 90036	New York, NY 10003
323.525.2225	646.654.5700

BACK STAGE® and BACK STAGE WEST®

The #1 weeklies for Performing Artists

SUBSCRIBE TODAY
1.800.745.8922

http://www.backstage.com/backstage/contact/printsub.jsp

11 Money Matters:

Financial Advice for Beginning Actors

BY MARC BERNSTEIN

Some wise old soul once remarked, "The person who doesn't know where his next dollar is coming from usually doesn't know where his last dollar went."

Managing money is a challenge for anyone. It's especially challenging for actors who frequently fluctuate between temporary employment and acting gigs. Here are three areas of financial management that are crucial to any beginning actor.

REPORTING INCOME

When it's time to file your tax return, this is the area in which you will have to be most precise—to the dollar! There are different types of income that are to be reported on your return. The most common is the income itemized on Form W-2. This is the document you receive to report your wages or salary from employers that withhold taxes and social security. Many people outside of the business have but one or two W-2s. It is not uncommon, however, for an actor to have ten, twenty, or more of these forms to include with their filing.

Box 1 on Form W-2 is wages, tips, and other compensation. This indicates the amount you should report as income. Box 2 is the amount of Federal Income Tax that your employer withheld on your behalf and sent on to the government. Boxes 17 and 19 indicate the amount of State and City taxes withheld. Those are the most important of the twenty boxes on this form. Each box, however, should be examined and checked for accuracy. W-2s should be in the mail to you by January 31.

Suppose you worked for someone who didn't withhold anything—you just did your job, supervised yourself, and they sent you a check or paid you cash. You probably would call this income that was earned as an "independent contractor" or "freelance worker." The titles are pretty much interchangeable. For most amounts $600 or over that are earned this way, you will receive Form 1099. These forms should be in the mail by February 28.

How many times over the years I've heard about income being "off the books," "under the table," and "tax free"? Let us set the record straight. These concepts are false. Every dollar you earn for payment of a job you had or a service you rendered is taxable and reportable. It doesn't matter if you were paid by check, cash, or beads. Whether or not you receive a Form 1099 is irrelevant. You should report all such income, starting with dollar one.

The most important thing to remember with this freelance income is that you are responsible for paying both the tax and social security. You see, when you are a salaried employee who gets paid with a W-2, your employer withholds the tax and social security on your behalf. You pay 7.65 percent for social security and your employer pays 7.65 percent. The total, 15.3 percent, is sent to the Social Security Administration to be placed into your personal social security account.

As an independent contractor, you must pay both halves of your Social Security, totaling 15.3 percent. That extra 7.65 percent comes directly out of your pocket, not your employer's. If your employer does not withhold these taxes and Social Security, how does the government receive the money?

You, as an independent contractor, are obligated to send the taxes to the government on a "timely basis." This means that you are responsible for sending your payments to the government four times a year. This is call paying "Estimated Taxes." The dates for these payments are April 15, 2003; June 16, 2003; September 15, 2003; and January 15, 2004. Being obligated to make these payments means that if you don't, you may be liable for a penalty to be assessed. In simple terms, the government has the right to earn the interest on your money. That is why payments must be sent in on a timely basis. If your taxes were withheld, you paid them as you went. Being an independent contractor, you must adhere to the prescribed schedule. Of course, exceptions to these rules apply, so make sure you read the instructions regarding Estimated Taxes.

Some less common types of income that are taxable include, bonuses and commissions, prizes and awards, jury pay, honoraria, royalties, tips, and vacation pay. In addition, interest earnings and dividends are taxable, as are unemployment compensation, pensions, some state refunds, rental income, and some social security benefits. Make sure, if any of these apply, that you include them on the proper place on your tax return. This is an important point that some taxpayers are careless about. If a certain type of income is not in the correct place on the return—is on an incorrect schedule or line number, for example—the government will not know to look in another place. They will simply think that this income was omitted from the return.

What I'm stressing, therefore, is that if you plan to prepare your own taxes, do your homework. Read the instructions for each line and schedule, and go over the return more than once before you submit it. If you seek help with the preparation, make sure you go to someone with the experience and credentials necessary to make your return as accurate and complete as possible. Going to someone simply because the fee they charge is the cheapest, is the best way to pay more in the end. You know the adage. . .

ITEMIZING DEDUCTIONS

The most important itemized deduction for theatrical professionals is this: theatrical expenses incurred in order to earn income. If you itemize deductions, these would be considered miscellaneous business expenses. There are over eighty such deductions. The more obvious ones—photos; resumes and duplications; drama, voice, and dance lessons; and agents' commissions—are self-explanatory. You can also deduct materials used for research, such as tapes and CDs, scripts, scores, and plays. The portion of your cell phone and pager that is used for business purposes is deductible, as is the portion of your home phone that is used for business-related long-distance calls. Basic union dues are also deductible. Don't forget to include the two percent assessment to AEA if you worked through that union. If you buy trade papers such as *Back Stage,* the cost is deductible, as are special costumes required for roles, and stage makeup.

The following deductions require a special explanation: You may deduct the cost of a gift given to a person with whom you have a business relationship. This gift is limited to $25. The limit is $25 per gift and $25 per person. Therefore, if you buy a gift that is $50 and give it to an individual with whom you have a business relationship, you may only deduct $25 of the $50. You may not deduct another gift given to that individual in the same year.

Business dinners are limited to a 50 percent deduction. They must be ordinary and necessary to your business. In addition, business must be discussed at the meal. You may include taxes and tip as part of the total cost. So let's say you take a director out and the bill comes to $100. You can only deduct $50 as a business expense. As with almost anything you use as a deduction, you must be able to provide a receipt. For these business meals, the receipt must include the restaurant name, the amount spent, your business relationship to your guest, and what was discussed. The receipt must also include a full date: month, day, and year.

The cost of looking for work is definitely deductible. This means the use of public transportation such as subway, bus, and taxi. It is difficult to obtain receipts for these. The thing to do is to jot down your business travels in your date book or diary. A simple notation will do, explaining the business nature of the trip (audition, meeting with your agent, visiting the photographer for new 8x10s, etc.) and the amount.

If you use your own automobile, you can use the standard mileage allowance while looking for work. This allowance is in lieu of all operating costs. For tax year 2003, the standard mileage allowance was 36 cents per mile. In addition, you may deduct the cost of parking and tolls for business. Keep an accurate record of your business miles in your date book. And, remember, it must be your own car.

Many more deductions are available to you as an actor. Simply put, an item is deductible if its cost is incurred in the production of your income. In other words, if you needed to spend money in order to make the money you are paying taxes on, it is generally deductible. Remember: if you can get a receipt, keep it. No receipt is too small. Make sure the receipt is complete with a description of the item, the place where it was purchased, the price, and a full date. If a receipt is not obtainable, use your diary.

DEDUCTING BUSINESS-RELATED EXPENSES

Most of us know the difference between standard deduction and itemized deductions. There is, however, one other way that actors may deduct their expenses. Under a category called "Qualifying Performing Artist," actors, if they meet certain criteria, can deduct business-related expenses, dollar for dollar, from their income. In addition, they can use the standard deduction. Since 1986, "Q.P.A." has proved to be a real lifesaver and money saver to the struggling actor with regard to tax savings.

The criteria for meeting the "Q.P.A." requirements are as follows: 1) Your adjusted gross income must be $16,000 or less; 2) You must have performed service in the performing arts as an employee (this means income received on a W-2 form) with at least two employers during the tax year, and received at least $200 from each of these employers (in other words, you must receive at least two W-2s with two different employers of at least $200 each—I must stress again that to qualify for this category, the compensation you received must have been reported on a W-2 and not on a 1099); and 3) You must have had allowable business expenses attributable to the performing arts of more than 10 percent of gross income in the performing arts. If you meet these criteria and fall into the category of "Q.P.A.," make sure you take advantage of it. It usually ends up being a tremendous savings to people who need it most.

The cost of hunting for a new job is deductible, even if you don't land the job. This ruling is not just for actors; it's for anyone who is unemployed. It is designed to encourage people to look for work in other states or cities if they cannot find work in their home areas. (Years ago, job hunting was deductible only if you got the job. However, be careful on this: in order to avail yourself of this deduction, you must be seeking employment in your present line of work. If you are just coming into a profession or looking for that first acting job, that expense is not deductible. You must already have had a job in the business.)

So if you are not working and hear of something in another part of the country, regardless of where, and you decide to look into it, whether you go by plane, train, or whatever, keep your ticket stubs, as well as a record of the dates on which you left and returned. Make a note of the people you saw. Of course, your food and lodging expenses are deductible, too, so make certain that you keep receipts for meals and hotels.

Your food expenses can be documented in one of two ways. You may either deduct the actual cost of your meals while away from home on business, as supported by receipts, or you may use the standard meal allowance. This allowance is referred to as the "M&IE" rate (meals and incidental expenses). The allowance covers, in addition to meals and tips for servers, incidental expenses, such as laundry and tips for baggage handlers.

The size of the meal allowance depends on the city that you visited—there are five different allowances. In order to find out what the allowance is for each city, you should go online to the General Services Administration (GSA) website at www.policyworks.gov/perdiem. Contained therein you will find a complete listing of most large cities or counties in the U.S. and the daily dollar allowance for each (either $30, $34, $38, $42, or $46). If the city you visited is not on the list, you can assume that $30 per day is allowed.

One more thing concerning food: the percentage of deductibility is 50 percent. So, for instance, if you went to Chicago for an audition and were there for three days, you could take the standard meal allowance for Chicago—$46 per day, which equals $138. You would then be able to deduct 50% for a meal deduction of $69 for the three days. You should also keep a record of all your travel-related expenses—a diary, a little book, whatever—to support your receipts.

If you drive to that interview or audition, be aware that when an automobile is used for business purposes, you may deduct the actual cost of operating that vehicle while on business. This deduction can be used whether you drove your own car or leased one. If you drove your own auto, you may elect instead to use the standard mileage allowance for operating your automobile for business, as noted on page 133. This standard amount covers all operating expenses except for parking and tolls, which you'll deduct separately.

Not much we can
do about death.

**BUT WE CAN MAKE
A _BIG_ DIFFERENCE
ON YOUR TAXES.**

- *Free Consultation*
- *Electronic Filing*
- *Extensive Experience*
- *Anytime Availability*
- *Offers In Compromise*
- *Mortgage Originators*

**ActorsTaxPrep, LLC
(800) 316-3755
www.actorstaxprep.com**

**ALL ACTORS AND
ACTRESSES WELCOME!**

You may benefit from
special tax treatment due
to total income of less than
16K. Affordable rates!

*JRT International, Inc.,
Tax & Bookkeeping, Los Angeles*
(818) 501-0965

TO ADVERTISE IN THE NEXT

BACKSTAGE®/BACK STAGE WEST®

ACTORS
HANDBOOK

WEST ■   ■ EAST

Back Stage West Advertising   Back StageAdvertising
5055 Wilshire Blvd., 5th floor   770 Broadway, 4th floor
Los Angeles, CA 90036   New York, NY 10003
323.525.2225   646.654.5700

The monthly Who To Contact Guide
For Casting, Agents & Production

***ROSS
REPORTS®***
TELEVISION & FILM

To Subscribe call
800.745.8922

ACTORTAX™

Reasonable Tax Prep Services for the
Performing Arts Community Since 1985

1-800-366-2829
FAX: 1-518-587-7809

www.actortax.com
actortax@ix.netcom.com
available 7/365

TO ADVERTISE IN THE NEXT
BACKSTAGE®/BACK STAGE WEST®

ACTORS
HANDBOOK

WEST ■ ■ EAST

Back Stage West Advertising   Back Stage Advertising
5055 Wilshire Blvd., 5th floor   770 Broadway, 4th floor
Los Angeles, CA 90036   New York, NY 10003
323.525.2225   646.654.5700

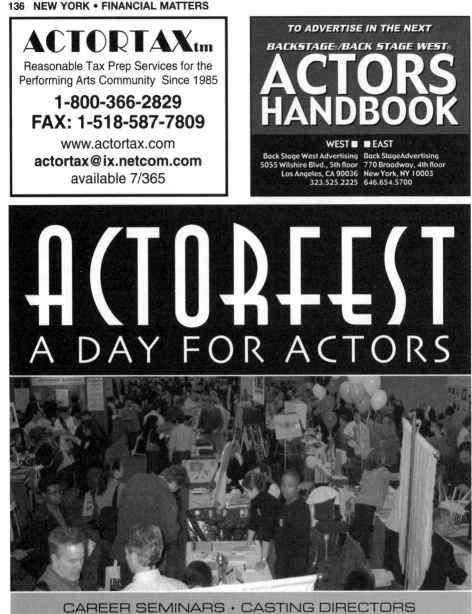

ACTORFEST
A DAY FOR ACTORS

CAREER SEMINARS · CASTING DIRECTORS
AGENTS · FOCUS SESSIONS · MANAGERS
FREE EXHIBIT HALL · AND MUCH MORE

FOR EXHIBIT HALL SPACE CALL

WEST ■   ■ EAST
Back Stage West Advertising   Back Stage Advertising
5055 Wilshire Blvd., 5th fl.   770 Broadway, 4th floor
Los Angeles, CA 90036   New York, NY 10003
323.525.2225   646.654.5700

12 Dealer's Choice:

How to Negotiate Your Contract

BY MICHAEL LAZAN

After all the years of effort that most actors put into getting work, you would think that they'd have some salient ideas about what to do once they actually get a contract to read and sign.

But, perhaps because the acting field requires an especially narrow and singular focus, or perhaps because actors shy away from the pyrotechnics involved in contract negotiations, many performers do not know even the basics of a deal. Worse, they may be so very eager to get a job that they tread very delicately in negotiations, barely skimming the surface of what they can get.

Some actors may even direct their agents to ask for very little so as not to jeopardize the job, as Teresa Wolf, a New York agent with Schiowitz/Clay/Rose relates. "When some actors give me a contract to negotiate, they say, 'Don't lose this for me!' and that ties my hands. I'm really unable to do much when they say that."

Where to start, then, if you're an actor with a fresh contract on your lap? The first place for a theatre actor, without question, is Actors' Equity Association, which has rule books explaining each and every contract that falls within its wide jurisdiction. Every actor in the midst of a negotiation should consult with the union, since a union contract is not a "standard agreement" that all actors sign onto. The union is there to provide you with a minimum; you can (and should) negotiate for any extras that you can get. In many instances there is more to be had than the minimum, especially if you know how to ask for it.

THE MAJOR ISSUES

1. MONEY

Naturally, salary is going to be on the top of anyone's list of issues. The question for most is, when can salary be effectively negotiated, and how do you conduct that negotiation?

The answer—as with answers to most questions surrounding negotiation—is a bit diffuse. The key is understanding how to figure your bargaining power, using your intuitive sense of the situation. Donald Farber, an entertainment law attorney in New York, explains that you must simply "trust your instinct and what you're doing."

But what if instinct isn't telling you enough? It's then a good idea to get professional help to see whether you have any leverage—and that means possibly getting an agent or lawyer involved. Performers may not realize that many agents will be happy to represent you on a particular deal even if they don't represent you generally, especially if the deal in question is a union job or a job that pays well. Shep

Pamplin, an agent with Agents for the Arts in New York City, says flatly: "If it's a union job, by all means call an agent—they will negotiate it for you." This arrangement might also allow the actor to retain the services of the agent on a permanent basis should the relationship blossom.

In the theatre, regardless of who represents you, one clause that's worth thinking about is the so-called "favored nations" clause, which can protect the actor if someone else in a comparable role is able to negotiate better terms. "You must be specific and request it for salary, terms, and conditions," says Rich Cole, a New York casting director. The "favored nations" concept tends to be more useful in negotiations where an actor has some clout, and especially where an actor is involved in a commercial production. In the not-for-profit world, producers may use the term "favored nations" as part of an offensive strategy—calling for an actor to agree to "favored nations," but often having in mind a low salary that all of the performers are persuaded to accept.

Note that in television and film you may see clauses that are analogous to "favored nations" clauses only in those independent films that have tighter budgets, according to Carole J. Russo, another agent with Agents for the Arts.

Another means of enhancing salary (again, in the theatre) is by securing additional money for understudying. Ordinarily, performers get a minimum of an additional one-eighth of their weekly salary for each time they're "on," but you can try to negotiate for more than that (it's still far less than the star is getting, so often producers will be agreeable). Whether in theatre, television, or film, bonuses are also possible, including built-in raises for an award nomination, or for when the show itself does well.

Residuals are, of course, very important in television and film. Most of the terms for them, however, are spelled out in basic agreements.

2. OUTS

Among the most important terms and conditions in the theatre is the question of when an actor can happily and legally leave a production. These terms, called "outs" in the business, are cherished by many and received by, well, less than many.

It's always important to focus on the length of the deal itself. Most producers will want to retain actors for as long as possible, and even veteran performers might have trouble negotiating an adjustment. It's also important to focus on terms and conditions for leaving a show before the contract has elapsed. Equity rules will ordinarily specify that a member give notice of four weeks or so before leaving, but you might want to leave with notice of two weeks or less. You also might want to leave a show temporarily, perhaps for a single date that is particularly lucrative or rewarding.

Particularly desirable (though difficult to negotiate, and not really applicable to film or TV contracts) is an "MRE" or "more remunerative employment" clause. This clause allows actors to leave the run of a play for a short period of time, perhaps to benefit from a high-paying commercial or film shoot.

3. OTHER TERMS AND CONDITIONS

Additional issues you may raise in contract negotiations depend, again, on your bargaining power, but there are quite a few to consider should you have some leverage.

Billing (*i.e.*, where an actor's name is located on programs and flyers) tends to be "a particularly big issue in television and film negotiation," says Stephen Burrow, executive director of the New York local of the American Federation of Television and Radio Artists (AFTRA).

Billing is often important psychologically, especially when actors are playing roles with similar amounts of dialogue. It is often relatively easy to adjust billing, especially if an actor has creative suggestions on how his or her name might be displayed.

When on a film shoot or on a theatre tour, there is a wide range of practical issues to consider, such as cost of travel, the intensity of schedule, housing, per diem, food, and laundry.

Believe it or not, pets can also be an issue. Many places will not accommodate them—so if you're really attached to your dog, you may have to choose between forgoing the job and getting someone to dog sit.

Transportation is another issue (if, say, you live in a town remote from the performance venue). There are also questions concerning hair (you might not have to cut it, if you don't want to), makeup, and wardrobe. (Dancers, for instance, may negotiate to have a new pair of shoes every week.)

NEGOTIATION PROTOCOL

It's essential in negotiation to take full notice of whom you are dealing with. Commercial producers are ordinarily focused on the show, while producers in the nonprofit sector are burdened with financial and time issues. If you're joining a show that has been running a fairly long time, there will be an established protocol concerning contractual rules. Find out about these rules before you get involved in talks with the producers. Some terms may be available that you didn't think possible—while others might not be worth demanding or even suggesting.

For touring shows and location shoots, the question of working conditions may be at the forefront. Some tour operators work without a union contract. Be sure the operator has money enough to pay you up front. Also, make sure you have some kind of roundtrip ticket, and try to secure reasonable housing arrangements. Things to focus on include how many people share a room, whether there is a private bath, and whether smoking is or is not allowed. It's also important to know exactly what kind of technical requirements will be made of you—from building and/or moving the set to cleaning out the bathroom.

What about mastering the art of negotiation itself? How do you get what you want from a producer who is vastly more experienced than you at negotiating and who very likely has more leverage?

It's called "show *business*" for a reason, explains Carole Russo. She believes that actors have to start thinking like business people. That means be "slick" even if you are one who tends to dissolve into tears at the slightest shove. On the other hand, coming out aggressively and with an "attitude" can work against you.

Creating a poor impression might suggest to a producer that you'll be difficult to deal with during the show itself. Says Donald Farber, "Actors do push themselves out of jobs; it's not common, but—if you start with an offer that's outrageous, forget it. We all have different styles, but be in the ballpark."

Rather than take a hard-edged approach to negotiations, be cordial and respectful, even if (perhaps *especially* if) your counterpart is being less than gracious. New York entertainment attorney Bruce Lazarus says: "Be nice. Everybody who's in this business—chances are they started as an actor. To some extent, everyone who's not an actor is really doing a support role because they don't have the courage to do the other."

As far as your demands go, respectful and thorough questioning is always in order. If a producer is wary of all your questioning, don't worry. Comprehensive negotiation must be distinguished, however, from negotiating with an utter lack of perspective. The effective negotiator must know what's suitable to give up. Indeed, you should consider having some "dummy demands" to be conceded during the negotiations.

THE SAVVY NEGOTIATOR

It's also important to understand each and every clause in a contract. Many contracts are written in language that is turgid, cryptic, or just plain incomprehensible. Ask questions if the contract is written in "legalese," and insist on a rewrite if the language is open to two or three interpretations.

What if your agent wants you to sign something that you don't want to sign? Usually the actor should listen to the agent, keeping in mind that agents usually have a symbiotic relationship with actors. Note, however, that there are some unusual situations (say, when the pay is low, but the actor wants to take the job for the aesthetic value) in which agents may want you to turn a job down because it's not in their financial interest.

It's also important to understand that agents are not lawyers, even though they are negotiating a legal document. If you think the agent is ignoring a legal point, you might well want a lawyer to look into it.

Whatever you do, remember to have everything that is promised to you set in writing—preferably word-processed—and signed by both parties.

13 Bells Are Ringing— and Beepers and Cell Phones:

Using New Technology to Keep in Touch

BY ELIAS STIMAC

If you've ever missed an audition because you weren't home to get the call from your agent; if your time on the pay phone ran out before you could confirm your callback; or if you've ever passed up a golden opportunity for fame and fortune because you just didn't know about it in time—you're in luck. Because now, more than ever, technology has made it incredibly easy to keep in touch with agents, managers, casting directors, and anyone else who can put you under the spotlight or in front of the camera.

Cell phones are everywhere, and provide instant access between you and the industry—that is, if you're not out of range and your battery's not dead. And voice mail is still the most convenient way of getting incoming messages. The technology is constantly being upgraded with services such as caller I.D., toll saving, fax capabilities, and wake-up calls. That's a long way from the old days when the only option for receiving and retrieving messages was live operator service. Now, since so many companies are providing voice mail service, a smart actor will do his or her research and compare the many features each one delivers to get the right services at the right price.

What's the 411 on all the other latest communications options? We called or paged a few industry professionals, e-mailed some experts, and received lots of text messages giving us the lowdown on this high-priority issue.

SEARCHING FOR SERVICE

Trying to connect—and getting connected—to the industry means always being reachable when a job offer comes in. This has never been easier than with the advent of cell phones. Now you can get a call from your agent or make a call to your manager almost anywhere (excluding subways, airplanes, and other out-of-range places).

Cellular phones have been available in the United States since 1983, but only in recent years have they reached widespread popularity. Many performers who go from a classroom to an audition or from rehearsals to a set (and consequently are hardly ever home) now consider these once-luxury items practically indispensable.

Various types of services are available—including analog, digital cellular, and digital PCS—all of which have their pros and cons. A website devoted to defining these systems and comparing the wide range of billing options is www.point.com. There are seemingly countless choices for service plans, with different combinations of service providers, monthly fees, number of minutes, lengths of contracts, and roaming charges (charges for airtime and long distance calls made outside your carrier's area), not to mention the prices and features of the cell phones themselves. Enhanced services—including text messaging, roadside assistance, and three-way calling—are also available. Cost, contracts, and call quality seem to be the most important aspects you will want to inquire about.

AGENT ADVICE

So how do agents prefer to keep in touch with performers? Eileen Haves is a New York City talent agent who represents performers for commercials, industrials, and voiceovers. She explains, "The easiest way is if the actors have a cell phone, so we can talk to them right away—although some cell phone services are terrible; it's a problem sometimes. When cell phones are out of service areas, it's frustrating, and if actors always use their cell phone or their pager and it doesn't work, they really have to have an alternative number. That's when voice mail is recommended."

Although most actors get back to Haves quickly when responding to audition, callback, or booking messages, she does know how disappointing it can be when a performer is temporarily out of touch. "I've had cases where actors did not get back in time. I paged somebody once, paged him time after time, and put the message on his machine. But the person was so involved in doing something, he didn't have his pager on, and never checked the other messages. The actor never realized the pager was off, and he lost a booking."

CASTING CALLS

Casting directors sometimes contact actors directly for auditions and job bookings, and need to be in touch with performers just as much as agents and managers do. New York-based Jimmy Floyd has cast television series and shows for Food Network, Oxygen, and PBS. He prefers not to have all those phone calls going back and forth. "I like to talk directly to an actor, explain what's going on, and then have them come in for either an audition or an interview, or come to a show and see if they want to be a part of it. I don't like dealing with anybody except for person I'm booking."

Floyd thinks the cell phone is an actor's very best tool. "In this day and age, it's the easiest way to reach an actor any time. If I have a dropout on a job, and I want to find somebody right away, I may have literally two or three hours to notify someone and get them to the location. So I love seeing a cell phone number on résumés. I know I'm going to get a hold of them very fast. Pagers are fine; they would be my next pick. I also love e-mails. I can send out a mass e-mail to a cast, reminding them what to wear or what to bring, rather than making twenty-five phone calls."

New York-based casting director Ross Mondschain stresses that actors should always be reachable when somebody wants to get in touch with them, whether it's via a pager or voice mail. "If you don't have an agent, then you are your own agent.

So if somebody wants to get in touch with you, or book you, or has a question about you professionally, you should literally be able to be back in touch with that person fifteen to twenty minutes later."

Mondschain also has some pertinent advice about what to say on your outgoing message, whatever system you use. "Make sure that the message you leave on the voice mail is clear and up to date, letting people know if you're available. You should change the message every day, so if I call and you're inaccessible or going out of town, I don't just get a beep, and wonder where you are. You can communicate with me and let me know you will be checking in, or if you'll be at another number. Be specific—it can be a way of having a dialogue with me before I've even reached you on the phone."

ACTIVE ACTORS

Most performers either own a cell phone, are planning to get one, or have vowed never to use one. Ted Zurkowski, artistic director and co-founder of the Frog & Peach Theatre Company in New York, went through all three stages of cell phone commitment. "I resisted having a cell phone for a long, long time. But between trying to run my life as an actor and running a theatre company, I finally had to break down and get modernized." Nowadays, Zurkowski also uses a cell phone in his office, instead of a regular phone connection. "When in history have you been able to move into your office, whip something out of the pocket of your sport jacket, sit down and go to work? Everyone should have a cell phone—God, I never thought I would say that!"

Of course, the convenience of cell phones still does not excuse anyone from leaving them on while attending other people's performances. Zurkowski says that most theatre groups make an announcement before each show: "Please turn off anything that beeps or goes bump in the night," and most audience members comply. "But I was on stage once doing *Much Ado About Nothing,* and while Beatrice and Benedick are alone trying to profess their love for each other, somebody's phone went off. When I got to the line, 'Oh, that was in the time of good neighbors, Beatrice,' I simply ad-libbed, 'before we had cell phones.' It got a huge ovation. When things happen like that, you have to deal with them."

Lisa Bayer has worked as an actress in independent films, theatre, and television. She swears by her cell phone and voice mail service. "I check my messages frequently. If I know it's going to be difficult to be at an audition at a certain time, I may ask the agent if the time is flexible, so I can somehow rearrange my schedule and get everywhere I need to be. As long as I ask, and it's within a reasonable amount of time, they are usually understanding about switching times. I've never really experienced any missed auditions or other catastrophes."

When she is called with details about an upcoming audition or booking, Bayer prefers having it all recorded. "Even if I've written something down, I always save the message in the event that I'm somewhere else, and the piece of paper with the audition information is inaccessible to me. I think you need to know exactly where you need to be, what you're going for, and how you're supposed to be dressed. When I'm called in, I want to be really clear about how to present myself. The more information I have, the better."

PERSONAL CONNECTIONS

As you can tell, plenty of options are available to performers when it comes to staying in constant contact with their agents, managers, casting directors, and other industry contacts. And each person's method is unique. With all these choices to consider—along with the arrival of hands-free cell phones, two-way interactive message devices, and two-way "walkie-talkie" radios—you can be pretty sure that "playing phone tag" with your agents and others will soon be a thing of the past. If you still have questions, just ask around. Most people will be happy to share their opinions—if they're not on the phone.

NEW YORK'S PREMIER ANSWERING & MAIL SERVICE FOR MODELS & ACTORS.

VOICEMAIL

$5.95 Per Month

GET YOUR OWN (212) PHONE NUMBER!

Voicemail Service

- Free Instant Set-Up
- Private Phone Number
- Your Own Personal Greeting
- One Number/Multiple Boxes
- Get Voice Messages by Phone & by E-mail

Your (212) Voice mail Number Can Ring On Any Phone! Anywhere!

Receive Your Voice Messages By Phone And By E-mail!

New York City, Long Island, Westchester And New Jersey Area Codes Available.

Fax Mailbox

- Get your own fax number
- Receive faxes by e-mail & by phone
  Your faxes go directly into your e-mail, you can store, delete, print or forward them

Postal Mail Receiving

- Use our prestigious Fifth Avenue address as your own
- Receive your packages and mail from all carriers
- Mail Forwarding available

Call Today! **212.679.0000**

AEROBEEP & VOICEMAIL SERVICE, INC.
244 Fifth Avenue (corner of 28st.)

Visit us on the web @ www.nymail.com

THIS YEAR GET ORGANIZED

REACH THAT STAR, the one year day planner/calendar for actors, is the perfect tool to organize personal industry contacts, drop offs and submissions, target lists, audition tracking, measurements, mileage and more.

Including:
- Weekly Scheduling Calendars
- Career Tips
- Goal Setting Recommendations
- Protective Pocket for Headshots & Sides
- Tax Receipt Bag

It's the only day planner you'll need in 2004 and beyond!
www.reachthatstar.com or 310.920.1175

TO ADVERTISE IN THE NEXT
BACKSTAGE®/BACK STAGE WEST®
ACTORS HANDBOOK

WEST ■   ■ EAST

Back Stage West Advertising   Back StageAdvertising
5055 Wilshire Blvd., 5th floor   770 Broadway, 4th floor
Los Angeles, CA 90036   New York, NY 10003
323.525.2225   646.654.5700

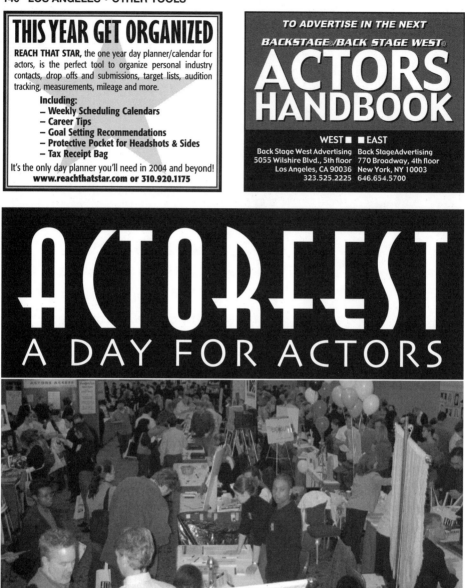

ACTORFEST
A DAY FOR ACTORS

CAREER SEMINARS • CASTING DIRECTORS
AGENTS • FOCUS SESSIONS • MANAGERS
FREE EXHIBIT HALL • AND MUCH MORE

FOR EXHIBIT HALL SPACE CALL

WEST ■

Back Stage West Advertising
5055 Wilshire Blvd., 5th fl.
Los Angeles, CA 90036
323.525.2225

■ EAST

Back Stage Advertising
770 Broadway, 4th floor
New York, NY 10003
646.654.5700

PART 3

Finding the Work

14 Theatrical Agents:

What Do They Do, and When Are You Ready for One?

BY MARGARET EMORY

Agents are among the top industry players, serving as gatekeepers to career advancement. The services of an agent are needed for three reasons: 1) To submit performers for projects; 2) To negotiate offers of employment; and 3) To offer career advice. Many actors can and do lead successful lives as artists without the help of an agent. They work as company members at any of the fine repertory theatres across the country, infiltrate the scene in theatre hubs like Seattle or Chicago, or compile credits in the Off-Off-Broadway houses of New York City. Many nonunion actors, in fact, are encouraged to build their résumés and gain experience before joining the ranks of the union-affiliated so they may attract the attention of an agent at a time that is mutually beneficial for making business together.

If the silver screen, the little screen, or the Great White Way beckons you, however, you must face the music and get yourself an agent. Some wiggle room exists in New York City for actors to obtain employment through Equity Principal Auditions (EPAs), open auditions, and exposure gained from appearing in show-cases. But if you are serious about making a living in Los Angeles, you need an agent. The density of the business on the West Coast forces casting directors to adhere to a strict policy of soliciting agent/manager submissions only. And casting directors on the East Coast are beginning to follow that policy too. There isn't enough time or manpower to process submissions from actors, so the quest for an agent becomes paramount in an actor's rise in the business.

Because there are so many more actors than there are roles, casting directors (who are responsible for choosing which actors to bring in for auditions) must draw the line somewhere in making their selections. The most natural demarcation line seems to be drawn between actors that have agent representation and those that don't. Presumably, an actor submitted by an agent has already passed a favor-able evaluation, and a casting director feels safe selecting that talent because of the agent's reputation.

Certainly an actor can get jobs through personal contacts with directors, writers, and theatres. However, there is a whole range of projects that an actor would never be "up for" without an agent's submission: projects that don't get cast through the breakdown service or the trade newspaper or magazine; projects that don't even surface on the Internet; projects that get cast purely through a phone conversation between an agent and a casting director. These can include Broadway shows, television shows, films, and commercials.

Casting directors call agents with audition appointments for their clients, giving out pertinent information—time, date, place, and type of material required for the audition. The agents then calls his or her clients with this information, instructing them to call back to confirm the appointment. Commercial auditions are set up on a very fast turnaround, sometimes less than twenty-four hours, and the information given out is very brief and requires little preparation. Legit auditions can ask for more complex preparation involving coordination of audition material and suggestions for coaching sessions. Many factors influence the setup and preparation of an audition. Agents do their utmost to help clients prepare the best audition possible.

NEGOTIATING AND DECISION MAKING

An actor needs an agent to negotiate offers of employment. No matter how savvy you are at business, negotiating for yourself can be problematic. For example, demanding a larger salary, an extra round-trip airplane ticket for your girlfriend, or housing for your pet can be daunting when, each time you ask for something, you're afraid (either consciously or subconsciously) that the job offer will be pulled because you're being "difficult." It helps to have a business representative speak for you, make specific requests, and possibly fight some battles with the folks who are hiring you. Also, no matter how much sleuthing an actor does to discover details regarding an offer, the objectivity and know-how of an agent can uncover key points and provide valuable ammunition at the negotiation table. Having an agent do business frees the actor up to be the creative artist he or she was meant to be.

An actor needs a business rep to help make important decisions, especially when the career gets rolling. For example, who's going to help you decide between those multiple job offers on your plate? Or what to negotiate for in a particular deal? Who's going to fight for your interests when the Off-Off-Broadway showcase you're in moves to Broadway? Every actor, at various times in his or her career, needs advice. The student turning professional, the regional actor breaking into the New York scene, the New York actor taking a stab at pilot season in Los Angeles—each circumstance calls for the expertise and experience of an agent.

WHEN ARE YOU READY FOR AN AGENT?

When your career is fertile, and you can offer the promise of booking jobs and making money, that's the time to start looking for an agent. Many actors seek the services of an agent too soon in their careers and are frustrated by their lack of success in landing one. They do endless mailings of photos and résumés and follow up with postcards sent monthly like clockwork, without accepting the fact that an agent will represent an actor only when it's clear they can do business together.

Specific agents in the specific areas of the industry look for different things when prospecting for new talent. For example, legit theatre agents place the emphasis on training and experience. (Legit representation covers all areas of theatre, TV, and film, excluding commercials. That includes Broadway, Off-Broadway, and regional theatre; high-profile but low-paying New York showcases, workshops, and readings; episodic TV series, daytime series, movies of the week, and pilots; and studio and independent films, plus the occasional student film.) Because the competition for legit jobs is so fierce, and the demand for A-list actors so high, the selection of new clients requires a careful, in-depth approach, not to be taken lightly. How could an agent push an actor against a television personality with box office pull if he didn't have the actor's fine training and exhaustive experience to back up his "push"? An actor can build the components of training and experience into his résumé. The third component—luck (being at the right place at the right time)—comes from consistent perseverance.

LEGIT AND COMMERCIAL AGENTS: WHAT EACH LOOKS FOR

To get a legit agent, an actor needs a headshot (preferably one that looks like him or her and is captivating in some way) and a résumé that clearly states personal statistics, experience, training, and contact information. The agent might respond to a photo and résumé and call the actor in for an interview. But the real answer comes after the agent has seen the actor in action in some kind of live performance. Seminars providing this opportunity are good beginnings, but any worthwhile legit agent will opt to see more than two monologues before deciding to represent an actor.

Commercial agents dealing in on-camera commercials, voiceovers, and industrials spark to a talent's "look," personality, and special abilities. They are more likely to respond to a headshot and résumé received in the mail than are legit agents, simply because they deal in specific types and age ranges and work in volume. When it comes to headshots, they look for "something in the eyes," personality, honesty, and sincerity. If they sense commercial potential, they will call an actor in for an interview, provide some copy to read in the office, and decide then and there whether to start sending him or her out on calls. Depending on advertising trends, a talent is either hot or not. Referrals from casting directors, directors, and clients can get you in the door. It also helps to show what you can do in showcases. The ability to handle commercial copy, do improvs, give consistent reads ten to twenty times for a single take, shave five seconds off a thirty-second spot to get it in on time—all these factors help determine whether an agent will freelance or sign an actor. The higher the skill level and the more experienced the actor, the more likely the agent will want to sign.

Photos, résumés, cover letters, phone calls, invitations to showcases, and recommendations from friends and family, along with classes, seminars, and networking of any variety: these are all proven methods for securing an agent in New York. The terrain changes in Los Angeles, however, where the market tends to be driven more by youth and physical attractiveness. Someone just starting out or someone new to L.A. can try the customary route of sending out photos and résumés. Those who have been around and worked a bit may use industry referrals. Rule of thumb is always to use any contacts you may have—and that goes for both coasts. L.A. agents tend to focus primarily (or even exclusively) on film and TV and don't concern themselves much with theatre. The efforts of an actor to get an agent to see his work in a showcase can come to no avail. It's sometimes even difficult for signed clients to get their agents to see them in theatre projects.

THE ACTOR-AGENT RELATIONSHIP: VARIOUS STAGES

The metaphor most often used to describe the three stages of agent representation is one of romantic progression whereby "freelancing" is likened to dating, "going exclusive" to getting engaged, and "signing" to marriage. Depending on skill level and agency needs, agents will offer to freelance, go exclusive, or sign an actor. Factors such as age, experience, and specific skills influence the kind of representation an actor needs and how an agent chooses to represent him or her.

Freelancing enables an actor to work with several agents at one time. In this arrangement, the agent must call the actor to get clearance for each submission. This eliminates double submissions to casting directors. The actor generally gives clearance to the agent who calls first.

CHOOSING AN AGENT WHO'S RIGHT FOR YOU

After freelancing for several months with a few agencies, an actor may evaluate these relationships by reviewing submissions. How do the various agents see the actor in regard to type and skill level? Which agents submit him or her for comedy, drama, musicals, theatre, TV, or film, respectively? Which submit the actor for jobs like national tours—which make money (including commissions for the agent), but don't necessarily build careers? Which agents submit the actor for jobs that are noncommissioned but high profile? What is the rate of audition per submission?

The actor also sees how each agency functions. Is the client-agent interface warm and pleasant? Impersonal and abrupt? Which agent returns calls? Which has lost interest because of no callbacks? At the same time, agents get a sense of the actor's business etiquette and professionalism.

Freelancers should remember two things: 1) Keep very clear records of clearance calls on projects to avoid "miniwars" between agents and casting directors; 2) An agent's first priority is to the signed client. Whenever there's a choice between signed and freelance talent, the signed client will always come first. That's what it means to be signed.

Many legit agents refuse to work with freelancers. The exclusive relationship they have with their clients signifies a real awareness of the serious responsibility they have for their actors' livelihoods. They don't wish to share their actors with other agents, and they certainly want to protect their good efforts through a formal agreement of exclusivity. They feel that freelancing dilutes the nature of that representation. Like a marriage contract, agency papers legalize the representation and protect each party: the actor for the agent submissions on his or her behalf, and the agent for collecting commissions.

It's important to remember that agents are not forced to represent actors. They have the freedom to choose whom they represent. The selection process levels the playing field to a matter of subjective taste. On that evened field, however, lie opportunities for agents and actors to make business together—building and maintaining careers, the longevity of which depends on the good efforts of each party.

New York Area Agents

The following talent agencies are franchised with Actors' Equity Association, the Screen Actors Guild, and/or the American Federation of Television and Radio Artists. They have been compiled from union lists with additional information updated from *Ross Reports,* and are indicated (E) for Equity, (S) for SAG, and (A) for AFTRA. Unless otherwise stated, pix & resumes are accepted by mail only. No drop-offs. Note the age range represented by the agencies. If the agency represents children, that information will be stated.

ABOUT ARTISTS AGENCY
1650 Broadway, #1406
New York, NY 10019
(212) 581-1857
(S) (A) (E)
Represents stand-up comics, comedic character actors, and other types. Late teens and up.

ABRAMS ARTISTS AGENCY
275 Seventh Avenue, 26th fl.
New York, NY 10001
(646) 486-4600
(S) (A) (E)
All types for all areas. Literary department. Also has L.A. office.

ACCESS TALENT
37 E. 28 Street, Suite 500
New York, NY 10016
(212) 684-7795
(S) (A)
Actors/actresses & narrators (adults 18 and over) for voiceovers only. Accepts demos by mail only. No unsolicited tapes.

ACME TALENT & LITERARY
875 Sixth Avenue, Suite #2108
New York, NY 10001
(212) 328-0388
(S) (A) (E)
Represents mainly adults and some children; all areas including musical theatre. Literary department. Also has L.A. office.

BRET ADAMS, LTD.
448 W. 44 Street
New York, NY 10036
(212) 765-5630
(S) (A) (E)
Adults (16 and up); legit only. No unsolicited tapes. No commercials. Also has literary department.

AGENTS FOR THE ARTS, INC.
203 W. 23 Street, 3rd fl.
New York, NY 10011
(212) 229-2562
(S) (A) (E)
Adults and children; accepts pix & resumes. All areas. Interview by appointment only. Don't phone or visit. Voiceover tapes and reels by request only.

MICHAEL AMATO AGENCY
1650 Broadway, Rm. 307
New York, NY 10019
(212) 247-4456
(212) 247-4457
(S) (A) (E)
All types for all areas including celebrities, athletes, ethnics, teens, character actors, and models. Also maintains a Latin file. Literary department. No phone calls.

AMERICAN INTERNATIONAL TALENT AGENCY
303 W. 42 Street, Suite 608
New York, NY 10036
(212) 245-8888
(S) (A) (E)
All types for all areas, including children 5 and up; no voiceovers; not accepting photos & resumes or new clients until further notice. By appointment only.

BEVERLY ANDERSON
1501 Broadway, Suite 2008
New York, NY 10036
(212) 944-7773
(S) (A) (E)
Adults (late teens and up); mostly legit; specialty is musical theatre. Also film & T.V.

ANDREADIS TALENT AGENCY, INC.
119 W. 57 Street, Suite 711
New York, NY 10019
(212) 315-0303
(S) (A) (E)
All types for all areas, including children, 10 and up. Interviews by appointment only.

ARCIERI & ASSOCIATES, INC.
305 Madison Avenue, Suite 2315
New York, NY 10165
(212) 286-1700
(S) (A)
Adults (18 and up); commercial; voiceovers; and hand, leg, and body-part models for commercials.

THE ARTISTS GROUP EAST
1650 Broadway, Suite 610
New York, NY 10019
(212) 586-1452
(S) (A) (E)
All types for legit only (16 and up). Also has L.A. office.

ASSOCIATED BOOKING CORPORATION
1995 Broadway, Suite 501
New York, NY 10023
(212) 874-2400
(S) (A) (E)
Represents adults and teens (no actors); singers, musicians, and musicals for major recording artists. Accepts only bio & CDs from artists on major record labels.

THE RICHARD ASTOR AGENCY
250 W. 57 Street, #2014
New York, NY 10107
(212) 581-1970
(S) (A) (E)
Adults and teens; all types for legit, film & T.V.

ATLAS TALENT AGENCY, INC.
36 W. 44 Street, Suite 1000
New York, NY 10036
(212) 730-4500
(S) (A) (E)
Commercials, industrials, voiceovers, promos, narration, animation, and broadcasting.

BARRY-HAFT-BROWN ARTISTS AGENCY
165 W. 46 Street, Suite 908
New York, NY 10036
(212) 869-9310
(S) (A) (E)
All types for all areas. No children.

BAUMAN, REDANTY & SHAUL
250 W. 57 Street, Suite 2223
New York, NY 10107
(212) 757-0098
(S) (A) (E)
Adults, legit only; all types for all areas except print and commercials. Also has L.A. office.

PETER BEILIN AGENCY, INC.
230 Park Avenue, Suite 200
New York, NY 10169
(212) 949-9119
(S) (A)
Adults; commercial.

THE BETHEL AGENCY
311 W. 43 Street, Suite 602
New York, NY 10036
(212) 664-0455
(S) (A) (E)
Adults, 18 and up; legit and commercial. Also represents writers.

BLOC NYC
41 E. 11 Street, 11th fl.
New York, NY 10003
(212) 905-6236
(S) (E)
Dancers and choreographers only, 20s and up, all areas including film and theatre.

JUDY BOALS, INC.
208 W. 30 Street, #401
New York, NY 10001
(212) 868-0924
(E)
Adults; legit.

DON BUCHWALD &
ASSOCIATES
10 E. 44 Street
New York, NY 10017
(212) 867-1200
(212) 867-1070
(S) (A) (E)
Adults; children (4–19); legit and commercial including voiceovers; literary and broad-casting departments. Also has L.A. office.

CARRY COMPANY
49 W. 46 Street, 4th fl.
New York, NY 10036
(212) 768-2793
(S) (A) (E)
All types for all areas, including ethnics, athletes, stand-up come-dians, character types, musical theatre performers, and choreog-raphers. Not accepting scripts for film & T.V. Interviews by appoint-ment only.

CARSON-ADLER AGENCY, INC.
250 W. 57 Street, Suite 2030
New York, NY 10107
(212) 307-1882
(S) (A) (E)
Infants through young adults; legit and commercial; no print.

THE CARSON-KOLKER
ORGANIZATION, LTD.
The Sardi Bldg.
234 W. 44. Street, Suite 902
New York, NY 10036
(212) 221-1517
(S) (A) (E)
Infants to adults; all types for all areas; legit and commercial including print.

MARY ANNE CLARO TALENT
AGENCY, INC.
1513 W. Passyunk Avenue
Philadelphia, PA 19145
(215) 465-7788
(S) (A) (E)
Adults; children (3 and up); legit and commercial.

CLASSIC MODEL & TALENT
MANAGEMENT
213 W. 35 Street, 2nd fl.
New York, NY 10001
(212) 947-8080
(S)
Adults; children (2 and up); accepting pix & resumes; no walk-ins accepted; legit, commercial, and voiceovers.

COLEMAN-ROSENBERG
155 E. 55 Street, Suite 5D
New York, NY 10022
(212) 838-0734
(S) (E)
Adults (18 and up); not accepting pix & resumes at this time; legit.

COLUMBIA ARTISTS
MANAGEMENT, INC.
165 W. 57 Street
New York, NY 10019
(212) 841-9500
(A)
Adults; classical music, musicians only; accepts audiotapes and pix & resumes.

CORNERSTONE TALENT
AGENCY
37 W. 20 Street, Suite 1108
New York, NY 10011
(212) 807-8344
(S) (A) (E)
Adults (18 and up); legit.

CUNNINGHAM, ESCOTT,
DIPENE & ASSOCIATES
257 Park Avenue S., Suite 900
New York, NY 10010
(212) 477-1666
(S) (A) (E)
Adults; children; represents adults only in commercial and

children both in legit and commercial. Also has L.A. office.

GINGER DICCE TALENT AGENCY
56 W. 45 Street, Suite 1100
New York, NY 10036
(212) 869-9650
(S) (A) (E)
Adults; represents children through managers only; legit and commercial.

DOUGLAS, GORMAN,
ROTHACKER & WILHELM, INC.
(DGRW)
1501 Broadway, Suite 703
New York, NY 10036
(212) 382-2000
(S) (A) (E)
Adults; legit.

DULCINA EISEN ASSOCIATES
154 E. 61 Street
New York, NY 10021
(212) 355-6617
(S) (A) (E)
Adults; legit.

EASTERN TALENT ALLIANCE,
INC.
1501 Broadway, Suite 404
New York, NY 10036
(212) 220-9888
(S) (A) (E)
Adults; legit.

ELECTRIC TALENT, INC.
172-13 Hillside Avenue, Suite 202
Jamaica Estates, NY 11432
(718) 883-1940
(A)
Ages 12 and up; all types; both union and nonunion performers; T.V., film, and commercials & print. Accepts pix & resumes by mail only.

EWCR & ASSOCIATES
311 W. 43 Street, Suite 304
New York, NY 10036
(212) 586-9110
(S) (A) (E)
Represents adults; children through managers only. Accepts pix & resumes by mail only; no unsolicited tapes; legit. Also has L.A. office.

FLAUNT MODEL & TALENT, INC.
114 E. 32 Street, #501
New York, NY 10016
(212) 679-9011
(S) (A)
Adults (18 and up); all types in all areas, legit and commercial. No voiceovers.

THE JIM FLYNN AGENCY
208 W. 30 Street, Suite 401
New York, NY 10001
(212) 868-1068
(S) (A) (E)
Adults; legit.

FRESH FACES AGENCY, INC.
2911 Carnation Avenue
Baldwin, NY 11510-4402
(516) 223-0034
(S) (A) (E)
Adults; children; legit.

FRONTIER BOOKING
INTERNATIONAL, INC.
1560 Broadway, Suite 1110
New York, NY 10036
(212) 221-0220
(S) (A) (E)
Children; all types, from babies to mid-20s; for all areas including legit, commercial, and print.

G. WILLIAMS AGENCY (GWA)
525 S. 4th Street, Suite 365
Philadelphia, PA 19147
(215) 627-9533
(S) (A) (E)
All types including children (children must be musical-theatre trained).

THE GAGE GROUP
315 W. 57 Street, Suite 408
New York, NY 10019
(212) 541-5250
(S) (A) (E)
Adults; legit and commercial. Also has L.A. office.

GARBER TALENT AGENCY
2 Pennsylvania Plz., Suite 1910
New York, NY 10121
(212) 292-4910
(S) (A) (E)
Adults (18–70s); legit, film & T.V., and commercial. No voiceovers. Don't phone.

GENERATION TV
20 W. 20 Street, #1008
New York, NY 10011
(646) 230-9491
(S) (A)
Children only (babies to 18); commercial.

THE GERSH AGENCY NEW
YORK, INC.
41 Madison Avenue, 33rd fl.
New York, NY 10010
(212) 997-1818
(S) (A) (E)

Adults; early teens, 12 and up; legit and commercial. Literary department.

VERONICA GOODMAN AGENCY
34 North Black Horse Pike
Runnemede, NJ 08078
(856) 795-3133
(S) (A) (E)
Adults; children; legit, including special projects for film & T.V., and game shows.

H.W.A. TALENT
REPRESENTATIVES
220 E. 23 Street, #400
New York, NY 10010
(212) 889-0800
(S) (A) (E)
Adults (18 and up); legit; and commercial (all ages, including children). Also has L.A. office.

PEGGY HADLEY ENTERPRISES
LTD.
250 W. 57 Street, Suite 2317
New York, NY 10107
(212) 246-2166
(S) (A) (E)
All types for all areas except commercials. No models or children.

HARDEN-CURTIS ASSOCIATES
850 Seventh Avenue, Suite 903
New York, NY 10019
(212) 977-8502
(S) (A) (E)
Represents adults; legit. Literary department.

HARTIG HILEPO AGENCY, LTD.
156 Fifth Avenue, Suite 1018
New York, NY 10010
(212) 929-1772
(S) (A) (E)
Adults (18 and up); no phone calls or drop-ins; legit, film & T.V.

HENDERSON-HOGAN AGENCY,
INC.
850 Seventh Avenue, Suite 1003
New York, NY 10019
(212) 765-5190
(S) (A) (E)
Adults (16 and up); legit.

IDMODELS.COM
137 Varick Street, 4th fl.
New York, NY 10013
(212) 206-1818
(S)
Adults (18 and up); legit and commercial; represents female models only, 5'9" and up.

INDEPENDENT ARTISTS AGENCY
(formerly Carlson-Menashe Artists)
159 W. 25 Street, Suite 1011
New York, NY 10001
(646) 486-3332
(S) (A) (E)
Adults; legit, film, and T.V. No phone calls.

INGBER & ASSOCIATES
274 Madison Avenue, Suite 1104
New York, NY 10016
(212) 889-9450
(S) (A) (E)
Adults (20 and up); commercial on-camera, voiceover, industrial, and print; attends showcases.

INNOVATIVE ARTISTS TALENT &
LITERARY AGENCY
235 Park Avenue S., 7th fl.
New York, NY 10003
(212) 253-6900
(S) (A) (E)
Adults; children; legit and commercial. Also has L.A. office.

INTERNATIONAL CREATIVE
MANAGEMENT
40 W. 57 Street
New York, NY 10019
(212) 556-5600
(S) (A) (E)
Adults; legit and commercial. Literary department. Also has L.A. office.

JORDAN, GILL & DORNBAUM
AGENCY, INC.
1133 Broadway, Suite 623
New York, NY 10010
(212) 463-8455
(S) (A) (E)
Children; legit and commercial. Also represents commercial talent from 4 years old to 30, and specialties.

KMA ASSOCIATES
11 Broadway, Suite 1101
New York, NY 10004
(212) 366-9577; (212) 581-4610
(S)
Adults; children (8 and up); legit and commercial. Literary department.

STANLEY KAPLAN TALENT
139 Fulton Street, Rm. 503
New York, NY 10038
(212) 385-4400
(S) (A) (E)
Adults, babies, children, and teens; send multiple pix & resumes; all areas, legit and commercial.

KAZARIAN/SPENCER &
ASSOCIATES, INC.
162 W. 56 Street, Suite 307
New York, NY 10019
(212) 582-7572
(S) (A) (E)
Adults; legit, T.V. & film, theatre.

KERIN-GOLDBERG &
ASSOCIATES
155 E. 55 Street, Suite 5D
New York, NY 10022
(212) 838-7373
(S) (A) (E)
Adults, late teens and up; legit.

ARCHER KING LTD.
317 W. 46 Street, Suite 3A
New York, NY 10036
(212) 765-3103
(S) (A) (E)
*Adults; legit (film & T.V.). Literary
department (screenplays & plays).*

KOLSTEIN TALENT AGENCY
85 C Lafayette Avenue
Suffern, NY 10901
(845) 357-8301
(S) (A) (E)
*All ages, all ethnicities; commer-
cials, film & T.V., theatre, and
voiceovers.*

THE KRASNY OFFICE, INC.
1501 Broadway, Suite 1303
New York, NY 10036
(212) 730-8160
(S) (A) (E)
*Adults (18 and up); legit and
commercial.*

LALLY TALENT AGENCY (LTA)
630 Ninth Avenue, #800
New York, NY 10036
(212) 974-8718
(S) (A) (E)
*Adults; no unsolicited tapes; no
phone calls; legit. By recommendation only.*

GREER LANGE TALENT
AGENCY
3 Bala Plaza West, Suite 201
Bala Cynwyd, PA 19004
(610) 747-0300
(S) (A) (E)
*Adults only. All types. Legit and
commercial.*

LIONEL LARNER, LTD.
119 W. 57 Street, Suite 1412
New York, NY 10019
(212) 246-3105
(S) (A) (E)
Adults; legit.

LEADING ARTISTS, INC.
(formerly Silver, Massetti &
   Szatmary/East Ltd.)
145 W. 45 Street, Suite 1204
New York, NY 10036
(212) 391-4545
(S) (A) (E)
Adults; legit.

BRUCE LEVY AGENCY
311 W. 43 Street, Suite 602
New York, NY 10036
(212) 262-6845
(S) (A) (E)
*Adults, late teens and up; legit
and commercial.*

BERNARD LIEBHABER AGENCY
352 Seventh Avenue
New York, NY 10001
(212) 631-7561
(S) (A) (E)
*Adults; no phone calls or drop-
ins; legit.*

THE LUEDTKE AGENCY
1674 Broadway, Suite 7A
New York, NY 10019
(212) 765-9564
(S) (A) (E)
Adults; legit. Literary department.

MODELS ON THE MOVE MODEL
AND TALENT AGENCY
1200 Rt. 70, Barclay Towers,
   Suite 6
PO Box 4037
Cherry Hill, NJ 08034
(856) 667-1060 or (212) 946-1347
(S) (A)
*All ages, all ethnicities, babies
through mature adults.
Represents actors, voiceover
talent, models, dancers, enter-
tainers, and character actors for
all areas. Will accept demos,
headshots, and resumes. Send
SASE for response.*

WILLIAM MORRIS AGENCY, INC.
1325 Avenue of the Americas
New York, NY 10019
(212) 586-5100
(S) (A) (E)
*Adults; not accepting pix &
resumes at this time; legit and
commercial. Literary department.*

NICOLOSI & CO., INC.
150 W. 25 Street, Suite 1200
New York, NY 10001
(212) 633-1010
(S) (A) (E)
*All ages; legit. No commercials,
no print.*

OMNIPOP INC. TALENT
AGENCY
55 W. Old Country Road
Hicksville, NY 11801
(516) 937-6011
(S) (A) (E)
*Adults (17 and up); legit and
commercial. Also has L.A. office.*

FIFI OSCARD AGENCY INC.
110 W. 40 Street, Suite 1601
New York, NY 10018
(212) 764-1100
(A) (E)
*Adults; children (8 and up); legit
and commercial. Literary department.*

DOROTHY PALMER TALENT
AGENCY, INC.
235 W. 56 Street, Suite 24K
New York, NY 10019
(212) 765-4280
(S)
*All types, all ethnicities, all ages;
all areas except theatre; legit and
commercial & print. Also packages independent films. Literary
department.*

MEG PANTERA, THE AGENCY
INC.
1501 Broadway, Suite 1508
New York, NY 10036
(212) 278-8366
(S) (A) (E)
*Adults (17 and up); legit (film &
T.V. and theatre).*

PARADIGM
500 Fifth Avenue, 37th fl.
New York, NY 10110
(212) 703-7540
(S) (A) (E)
*Adults; legit and commercial.
Also has L.A. office.*

PLAZA-7
160 North Gulph Rd.
King of Prussia, PA 19406
(610) 337-2693
*Adults and children (from 6
months and up); legit and
commercial.*

PROFESSIONAL ARTISTS
321 W. 44 Street, Suite 605
New York, NY 10036
(212) 247-8770
(S) (A) (E)
*Adults (18 and up); all types; also
represents hosts, directors, and
choreographers; legit.*

RADIOACTIVE TALENT, INC.
(R.T.I.)
(mailing address only)
350 Third Avenue, Box 400
New York, NY 10010
(917) 733-4700
(S) (A)
*Adults; children; for broadcast,
commercial, music, screen, and
stage.*

REINHARD TALENT AGENCY,
INC.
2021 Arch Street, Suite 400
Philadelphia, PA 19103
(215) 567-2000
(S) (A) (E)
*All types for legit (film & T.V.),
commercials, industrials, print,
runway, and makeup artists;
interviews by appointment only.*

GILLA ROOS LTD.
16 W. 22 Street, 3rd fl.
New York, NY 10010
(212) 727-7820
(S) (A)
*Adults; children; legit, commercial,
and print.*

S.E.M. TALENT, INC.
(212) 330-9146
(S) (A) (E)
*Adults; children (5 and up); legit
and commercial. Not taking any
new clients at this time.*

SCHIOWITZ/CLAY/ROSE, INC.
165 W. 46 Street, Suite 1210
New York, NY 10036
(212) 840-6787
(S) (A) (E)
*Legit. Represents adults.
Looks for well-trained actors.*

SCHULLER TALENT/NEW
YORK KIDS
276 Fifth Avenue, #204
New York, NY 10001
(212) 532-6005
(S) (A) (E)
*Children, teenagers and
young adults, all ethnicities,
for modeling and T.V. Also
beauty division. Pictures,
video/audio tapes are not
returnable.*

ANN STEELE AGENCY
330 W. 42 Street, 18th fl.
New York, NY 10036
(212) 629-9112
(S) (A) (E)
*Adults; union performers only;
legit and commerical.*

STONE-MANNERS AGENCY
900 Broadway, Suite 803
New York, NY 10003
(212) 505-1400
(S) (A) (E)
*Adults; legit. Also has L.A.
office.*

PETER STRAIN & ASSOCIATES
INC.
1501 Broadway, Suite 2900
New York, NY 10036
(212) 391-0380
(S) (A) (E)
*Adults (18 and up); legit. Also
has L.A. office.*

TALENT HOUSE AGENCY
311 W. 43 Street, Suite 602
New York, NY 10036
(212) 957-5220
(E)
*Adults (18 and up); legit; union
only; referrals only.*

TALENT NETWORK GROUP
111 E. 22 Street, 3rd fl.
New York, NY 10010
(212) 995-7325
(A)
Adults; legit and commercial.

TALENT REPRESENTATIVES,
INC.
20 E. 53 Street, #2A
New York, NY 10022
(212) 752-1835
(S) (A) (E)
Adults (18 and up); legit.

TAMAR WOLBROM, INC.
130 W. 42 Street, Suite 707
New York, NY 10036
(212) 398-4595
(S) (A)
*Adults (late teens and up);
accepts CDs only; voiceover
talent and on-camera; commercial—all areas.*

TOP CAT TALENT AGENCY, INC.
1140 Broadway, Suite #701
New York, NY 10001
(212) 447-4504
(S)
*Adults; children (six months and
up); commercial.*

HANNS WOLTERS
INTERNATIONAL, INC.
10 W. 37 Street, 3rd fl.
New York, NY 10018
(212) 714-0100
(S) (E)
*Adults (18 and up); accepts pix &
resumes by mail only; legit and
commercial. Has language department, specializing in languages of
every ethnic group and New York
character types. Also represents
writers, producers, and directors.*

ANN WRIGHT
REPRESENTATIVES
165 W. 46 Street, Suite 1105
New York, NY 10036
(212) 764-6770
(S) (A) (E)
*Adults (late teens and up); legit;
commercial; voiceovers; and
literary department.*

WRITERS & ARTISTS GROUP
INTERNATIONAL
19 W. 44 Street, Suite 1410
New York, NY 10036
(212) 391-1112
(S) (A) (E)
*Adults; legit, film, T.V., & theatre;
and commercial. Literary department. Also has L.A. office.*

BABS ZIMMERMAN
PRODUCTIONS, INC. (AGENCY)
305 E. 86 Street, Suite 17 FW
New York, NY 10028
(212) 348-7203
(E)
*All types for all areas except
children or models. Interviews
by appointment only. Accepts
professional singing voices on
audiotapes or CDs.*

*(For a list of Los Angeles-based
agents, see page 406)*

Showcase Your Portfolio Online!

With Star Caster GO! your complete portfolio is available instantly to the nations leading agents and directors.

The Star Caster Go! Portfolio

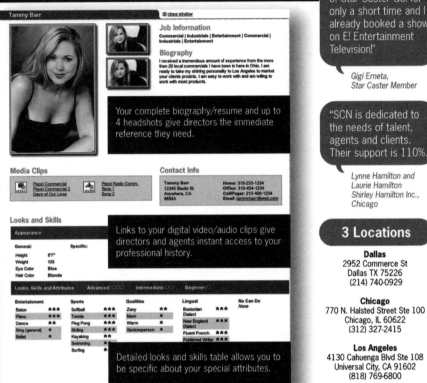

"I have been a member of Star Caster Go! for only a short time and I already booked a show on E! Entertainment Television!"

Gigi Erneta,
Star Caster Member

"SCN is dedicated to the needs of talent, agents and clients. Their support is 110%."

Lynne Hamilton and
Laurie Hamilton
Shirley Hamilton Inc.,
Chicago

Your complete biography/resume and up to 4 headshots give directors the immediate reference they need.

Links to your digital video/audio clips give directors and agents instant access to your professional history.

Detailed looks and skills table allows you to be specific about your special attributes.

3 Locations

Dallas
2952 Commerce St
Dallas TX 75226
(214) 740-0929

Chicago
770 N. Halsted Street Ste 100
Chicago, IL 60622
(312) 327-2415

Los Angeles
4130 Cahuenga Blvd Ste 108
Universal City, CA 91602
(818) 769-6800

Who uses our software?

Agents

5 Star Talent Agency • Abrams Artists Agency
Access Talent • Actors Etc. • Agency 2000 Management
Amsel, Eisenstadt & Frazier • Arcieri & Associates • Arlene Wilson Talent
Art House Management • Atlas Talent Agency
Baker & Rowley Talent Agency, Inc. • Barbara Gray Talent
Baron Entertainment, Inc. • The Beddingfield Company • Big Mouth Talent
Bret Adams, Ltd. • Buffalo Casting • Champagne Trott Agency
Ciao Talent Agency • Cindy Osbrink Talent Agency Inc.
Circle Talent Associates • Click Model Management
Click Model Management - LA • Commercial Talent • Company Management
Cool Films • Cunningham Escott Dipene • Cunningham, Escott, Dipene, LA
Diverse Talent • Don Buchwald & Associates • Dragon Talent, LLC
D VA Talent & Models • Encore Talent Agency • Encore! Talent Management
Epstein, Wyckoff, Corsa, Ross & Associates • Evolution Entertainment
Fifi Oscard Agency • Frontier Booking International • Funnyface Today
Gage Group • Geddes Talent Agency • Gold/Marshak/Liedtke & Associates
Good Karma Management • Harden-Curtis Associates
Henderson/Hogan Agency • Hollander Talent Group
HWA Talent Representatives • Images Model Management
Ingber & Associates • Innovative Artists • Intermedia Model & Talent
Iota Productions • Ivett Stone Agency • Jack Lippman Agency
... and hundreds more.

Casting Directors

Al Guarino • AMS • Barbara Brinkley Casting • Big Bad Wolf Creative
Bottom Line Productions • Boy Scouts of America
Brock & Company Casting • Buffalo Casting • Caryn Gorme Casting
CFB Casting • CFM Communications • Chelsea Studios Chicago Casting
Circle R Group • Claire Simon Casting
Claymation Digital Video/Film Production • Crystal Video Production
Custom Comedy Capers • Dallas Casting • Disney Feature Films
Dolores Jackson Casting • Frames Per Second
Iota Productions • J C Penny, Co. • Jo Edna Boldin Casting
Kevin Howard Casting • Lien-Cowan Casting • Locke Bryan Productions
Lori Cobe-Ross Casting • Lynn Ambrose Casting
Media By Design • O'Connor Casting • Richard Shavzin Casting
Ricki G. Maslar Casting • Rona Lamont Casting • Rosemary Weldon
See Pictures • Service Corporate International
Steppenwolf Theatre Company • TBA Corp Communications
Tenner Paskal Rudnicke Casting • Texas Video & Post • The Call
The Casting Company • Tracey Roswell Casting
Ulrich-Dawson-Kritzer • Warner Brothers Television

www.scnetwork.com

The entertainment industry standard for electronic casting

Smart Girls

the leader in marketing actors and screenwriters to Hollywood
phone: 818.907.6511   *website:* smartg.com

GET AN AGENT OR MANAGER NOW!
80% Success Rate since 1992
— ask about monthly mailings to casting directors —

Call (818) 907-6511 for information on how our cover letter mailings and career marketing solutions work.

"It works! I did my mailing and the agents started calling the very next day. I went to my first meeting and found the agent to be exactly what I wanted."
— *Jane Lemon*

"Thank you so much. I had 13 agents call right away. After interviewing them, I ended up with agents for both commercials and theatrical work!"
— *Timothy Jayson Travers*

TERRY LICHTMAN
ACTOR'S CAREER CONSULTANT

FORMER TALENT AGENT with 30 years experience in film, TV & theatre now available for private consultation.

ph 818-990-3533 • fx 818-905-5627
e-mail: Terrylichtman@aol.com

TO ADVERTISE IN THE NEXT

BACKSTAGE/BACK STAGE WEST

ACTORS HANDBOOK

WEST ■ ■ EAST

Back Stage West Advertising
5055 Wilshire Blvd., 5th floor
Los Angeles, CA 90036
323.525.2225

Back StageAdvertising
770 Broadway, 4th floor
New York, NY 10003
646.654.5700

www.backstage.com

15 Personal Managers:

To Sign or Not to Sign?

BY ESTHER TOLKOFF

Tossing around the expression "my manager" sounds impressive. But just what does a personal manager do? How can he or she help your career? What's the difference between a manager and an agent? And how can you spot good managers, sorting them out from the bad ones?

A personal manager's job is to provide "advice and counsel," to use the expression found in the National Conference of Personal Managers' Code of Ethics.

That means career guidance. "Advice and counsel" can include helping a client select classes, coaches, monologues, or songs; working with the performer to rehearse for auditions; and pinpointing skills that need strengthening. Managers also spread the word about the client's strengths, and, most importantly, help plan what directions a performer should be heading.

Working with a personal manager is very much a joint venture, ideally a close partnership. Managers often help a client get an agent. This is a key reason why performers at early stages in their careers seek a manager. A more well-established performer often turns to his or her manager to coordinate busy schedules that span several genres: theatre bookings, films, singing engagements, voiceover work, tours. These performers may be signed to several specialized agents. The manager has the overview and ties it all together.

Talent agents are legally regulated, but anyone can call him- or herself a manager. So it is important to know whom you are dealing with, what to expect from a true professional, and how to protect yourself from people who seek to take advantage of you or who are too inept to carry out their promises.

In show business there are many highly respected personal managers whose clients have worked with them for years and are thrilled with their positive effects on the clients' performing careers. Other performers believe managers are not necessary. Some actors describe having met up with shady individuals who claim to be personal managers—who sign actors to contracts, then provide little or no assistance to their careers.

First, on the brighter side, let's take a look at what a legitimate, hardworking manager can do for a performer. Then we'll talk about how to avoid the bad apples.

Respected managers have strong relationships with agents and great credibility when they recommend clients. This is often why actors seek a manager to begin with. Managers will discuss with agents the direction they'd like to see the client take, or they'll point out opportunities they may have heard about. Of course, agents give their clients career advice, too. Many managers started out as agents. But agents have very large rosters and cannot talk to every client at length every day.

A manager keeps a small roster—usually anywhere from ten to fifteen clients. That allows for a more intense focus on the artist's career—hence the term "personal manager."

"ADVICE AND COUNSEL"

New York-based manager Michael Katz explains, "The actor is the product, the agent is the salesperson, the casting director is the customer, and the manager is 'R&D.' I research and develop the actor's career."

"It's not about the immediate booking," agrees actress-singer Christiane Noll. "My manager, Matthew Sullivan, and I work on my long-term goals. I do classical concert appearances, theatre, corporate performances, cabaret, and recordings. Matthew coordinates my schedule and is the go-between with the different worlds I deal with. Agents organize auditions, but Matthew helps me decide where I want to spend my time. I'm not the same person as before, or as I will be. He helps me with my presentation, films me when I practice for auditions."

Sullivan, based in New York, says that one of the key things managers do is to help a client turn down work that's not in the best long-term career interest. "Let's say he or she wants to work in film and is always offered regional theatre jobs. It's not easy for actors to turn anything down after having gone through so much rejection, but it may be the only way to move forward. It's hard for agents to do it all for a performer. It is better for the client if there is a team at work."

Manager John Essay, also based in New York, says one example of efforts on his clients' behalf is his fostering relationships with writers and directors who may think of a client for a project. "It's all about networking in this business." Actress Neva Small, a longtime client of Essay's, says, "Working with a manager requires commitment and continuity." She adds that her manager gives her "perspective" and that she turns to him for "what to sing, what to wear, whether I should go on the road, planning business trips, optioning material, producing original work, and choosing collaborators."

"Agents and managers both want to see a client work," stresses New York agent Barry Katz. Managers may point out that a client is interested in specific types of auditions. They may also ensure there are no conflicts with commercial auditions. Many agents, pressed for time, dislike managers calling them too often. "But," notes Katz, "if a manager we respect really believes in you, it brings your skills to our attention and helps us find the right kinds of bookings for you."

Managers mention finding clients through word-of-mouth—through a casting director's or another client's recommendation. Some managers look at pictures and résumés. Others do not.

Among those performers who do not feel it necessary to have a manager is actor Eric Michael Gillett. "Most actors can do for themselves what a manager can do," he believes. "The first couple of years you need entrées, but after that you know people on your own. A casting director may get you an agent as readily as a manager can. I have seen dissatisfied people who couldn't get out of contracts. I think actors can need a manager if they're bicoastal, or if they've become a hot property. Then it can help."

Personal manager Lynn Rawlins, who's based in Los Angeles, agrees. "Managers are most useful to highly successful performers who face choices like deciding which of several scripts sent to them is worth looking into."

Clearly, people differ as to how important it may be to have a manager. But if you do decide you want to find one, what do you need to know?

LOOK BEFORE YOU LEAP—GROUND RULES

In general, agents are regulated by state business law. In some cases, states have specific provisions for entertainment agents (for instance, the New York State General Business Law, Section 171 (8), and California's Talent Agencies Act). Only agents can book and negotiate a job. The agent's commission cannot exceed 10 percent of a performer's earnings from jobs the agent has booked, and franchised agents can only sign performers for a specified amount of time. If an agent doesn't get the performer any work over a specified period, the client can terminate the contract.

Managers are not governed in this strict fashion, other than being limited to "incidental" work toward procuring employment (career planning, referrals to contacts). This is often a blurry line.

Because anyone can claim to be a manager, it is essential to ask around and see whether the manager you're considering has a good reputation. It is a good sign if he or she is a member of either the New York-headquartered National Conference of Personal Managers or the Los Angeles-based Talent Managers Association, though there are perfectly reputable managers who have never joined either organization.

A manager's customary fee is 15 percent of the client's earnings, but since this is not fixed by regulation, some take less—and others, especially those representing a celebrity, may have an agreement for more.

Putting things in writing is a must. A contract with a manager counts as an agreement between two individuals, so if you've signed it, you've agreed to the terms. Jean Frost of AFTRA Los Angeles' Agency Department says that because unions do not have jurisdiction over managers, "We advise our members to show any contract they sign to an attorney and to be sure there is an 'exit clause,' in the event a given manager doesn't make an appropriate effort to guide the performers' careers." It is wise not to sign an overly lengthy contract. Horror stories abound of actors signing away more than they should and then being stuck with the situation.

Legitimate managers will never ask for money up front. Since their fees are commissions based on clients' getting work, they want to see the performer work and will do their best to see this happen.

A legitimate manager will not insist that a performer use a specific photographer—a common scam that bad apples use to get kickbacks. Another practice that some see as questionable and others defend is a manager doubling as producer or casting director. Some believe this puts undue pressure on the client. Others see it as creating opportunities. Situations vary.

Check who the manager's client roster consists of. Are these people working? Specific types of performers may want a manager who specializes in their area. Comedians, for instance—who are often also writers, and who, like some singers or actors, are often on tour—may have different needs than actors who are chiefly based in one city. Child performers will generally have personal managers, as their parents often aren't entertainment professionals and need someone to serve as a liaison to agents and to help in planning the many changes encountered as children change from year to year.

The performer-manager relationship can indeed be like a marriage, and it therefore requires careful decision making. The wrong decision can lead to strife, while the right decision can lead to a close partnership that improves the performer's working life.

Personal Managers

The following, from *Ross Reports,* is a list of personal managers and management companies on both coasts. Those listed may be contacted by mail, but please respect their wishes if they request that you DO NOT PHONE, FAX or VISIT. "NCOPM" after company names indicates that they are members of the National Conference of Personal Managers (www.ncopm.com). Companies with "TMA" after their names are members of the Talent Managers Association (www.talentmanagers.org). For more information on these organizations, visit their websites.

Arizona

WATERFRONT MANAGEMENT (NCOPM)
Henry Isaac Neuman
6221 East Huntress Drive
Paradise Valley, AZ 85253
(480) 551-1010
Clients: Actors, Actresses, Musical Talent.

California

THE MICHAEL ABRAMS GROUP (TMA)
Michael Abrams
2934 1/2 Beverly Glen Circle
Bel Air, CA 90077
Developing young talent, 18–22, to play younger.

ANGEL FLIGHT ENTERTAINMENT (TMA)
Paul Duran
312 South Glendora Avenue
West Covina, CA 91790
(626) 917-9639
Clients: Actors, Dancers, Singers, Writers.

ARTIST'S WAY MANAGEMENT (TMA)
Leslie Ann Perlow
6 Northstar Street, Suite 305
Marina Del Rey, CA 90292
(310) 305-1106
Clients: Actors, Actresses.

ARTS AND LETTERS MANAGEMENT (TMA)
Steven Nash, President,
Talent Managers Association
7715 Sunset Blvd., Suite 208
Los Angeles, CA 90046
(323) 883-1070
Clients: Actors (ages 15–24), with exceptional credits. May send pictures, resumes & tapes by mail only. Writers by referral only. Also attends showcases. Don't phone or visit. Will call if interested.

ASSOCIATED ARTISTS MANAGEMENT
Melisa Birnstein
6399 Wilshire Blvd., #211
Los Angeles, CA 90048
(323) 852-1972
www.associatedartistmngt.com
Clients: Actors, Actresses, Teenagers. Also does public relations.

AVALON BAY ARTIST MANAGEMENT (TMA)
Kathi Mallec
P.O. Box 2512
Toluca Lake, CA 91610
(818) 623-0055
Clients: Actors, Actresses, Comic Actors.

DAVID BELENZON MANAGEMENT, INC. (TMA)
David Belenzon
P.O. Box 3819
La Mesa, CA 91944-3819
(619) 462-6400
Clients: Actors, Variety/Comedy Performers, Musical Performers, Producers.

CARL BELFOR ENTERTAINMENT MANAGMENT (TMA)
Carl Belfor
3556 Locust Drive
Calabasas, CA 91302
(818) 224-3036
Clients: Actors, Actresses, Writers, Directors, Producers.

BIEDERMAN & ASSOCIATES (TMA)
Sharon Biederman
330 Main Street, Suite 203C
Seal Beach, CA 90740
(562) 598-3700
Clients: Children, Teenagers.

BETWIXT TALENT MANAGEMENT (TMA)
Daniel Wojack
12655 Washington Blvd., Suite 204
Los Angeles, CA 90066
(310) 313-6442
Clients: Actors, Actresses (14 and up). Will accept talented nonunion actors. Demo tapes preferred.

BLACK ORCHID ENTERTAINMENT (TMA)
James Ward
7095 Hollywood Blvd., #675
Hollywood, CA 90028
(323) 962-9501
Clients: Actors, Actresses, Writers, Music Performers.

BLACKWOOD ENTERTAINMENT (TMA)
Horacio Blackwood
15030 Ventura Blvd., Suite 19464
Sherman Oaks, CA 91403
(818) 264-1932
Clients: Actors, Actresses (union talent), Teenagers, Comedians, Models, Writers, Directors, Young Male/Female Singers & Singing Groups. Management & Production.

ROBIN BROOKS MANAGEMENT (TMA)
Robin Brooks
5619 Lankershim, #1104
North Hollywood , CA 91601
(949) 460-0858
Clients: Actors, Actresses, Children, Teenagers, Newscasters, Media Personalities, Sports Personalities, Music Performers, Recording Artists, Orchestras, Bands. Specializing in babies, kids, teens, and young adults. In business for 10 years. Accepts submissions and inquiries from actors regarding representation by U.S. mail only. Absolutely no phone calls.

CMC MANAGEMENT (TMA)
Chelsea Cameron
625 East Palm Avenue, Suite 202
Burbank, CA 91501
(818) 843-4882
Clients: Actors, Actresses. Seeking all ethnic types for management.

CP & ASSOCIATES (TMA)
Cindy Perry
P.O. Box 2405
Toluca Lake, CA 91610
(818) 207-4033
Clients: Actors, Actresses,
Variety/Comedy Performers,
Recording Artists.

CENTRAL ARTISTS INC.
(TMA)
Jean-Marc Carre (Print &
Commercials); Laura Walsh
(Theatrical Division)
269 West Alameda Avenue,
  Suite A
Burbank, CA 91502
(818) 557-8284
www.centralartists.com
Clients: Actors, Actresses,
Children, Teenagers
(all races five yrs. old to 100+).

CHANCELLOR
ENTERTAINMENT
(TMA)
Robert P. Marcucci
10600 Holman Avenue, #1
Los Angeles, CA 90024
(310) 474-4521
Clients: Actors, Actresses,
Dancers, Musical Performers,
Composers, Recording Artists,
Orchestras, Bands.

THE COPPAGE
COMPANY
Judy Coppage
5411 Camellia Avenue
North Hollywood, CA 91601
(818) 980-8806
Clients: Actors, Actresses,
Directors, Producers,
Writers, Artists, Authors,
Choreographers, Photogra-
phers, Set Designers,
Costume Designers.

CREATIVE MANAGEMENT
GROUP
Rodney Omanoff, Graham Kaye,
Edward Horowitz
9465 Wilshire Blvd., Suite 335
Beverly Hills, CA 90212
(310) 888-0082
Clients: Actors, Actresses,
Children, Teenagers,
Directors, Producers, Writers.
Accepts photos-resumes by
mail only. Do Not Phone or
Visit. (See also listing under
New York.)

CUZZINS MANAGEMENT
(NCOPM)
(a division of Sokol-Frankmano
Entertainment Enterprises)
Helene Sokol, Victoria
Frankmano, Marion Falk
499 North Canon Drive
Beverly Hills, CA 90210
(310) 887-7044
Clients: Actors, Actresses,
including Children and
Teenagers, Musical Performers.
(See also listing under New York.)

DINER ENTERTAINMENT (TMA)
Diane L. Williams
(661) 250-3006, ext. 3
www.dinerentertainment.com
Clients: Actors, Bands, Directors,
Writers by referral only. Prefers
submissions on website.

DOWN RIGHT TALENTED
ENTERTAINMENT
MANAGEMENT (TMA)
Doyle Ray Taylor
2901 South Sepulveda Blvd.,
  Suite 306
West Los Angeles, CA 90064
(310) 281-6199
Clients: Actors, Actresses,
Directors, Writers.

DRAMA 3/4 MANAGEMENT
(TMA)
Josh Uranga
6762 West Lexington Avenue,
  Suite B
Los Angeles, CA 90038
(323) 556-5060
Clients: Actors, Actresses,
Music Performers, Composers,
Recording Artists, Orchestras,
Bands.

DUCK-LIT PRODUCTIONS
(TMA)
Donnice Wilson
8285 Sunset Blvd.
  Suite #9
Los Angeles, CA 90046
(323) 656-1759
Clients: Actors, Actresses
(SAG only). Partial to strong
stage credits.

JOEY EDMONDS
MANAGEMENT (TMA)
Joey Edmonds
4165 Sarah Street
Burbank, CA 91505
(818) 955-8710
Clients: Actors, Actresses,
Variety/Comedy Performers.

ENCORE! MANAGEMENT
AND CONSULTING
(TMA)
Lin Bickelmann
2219 West Olive, #100-51
Burbank, CA 91506
(818) 955-8821
Clients: Actors, Actresses,
Children, Teenagers. Prefers
submissions by website.

ENDURE MANAGEMENT
TAMINIKA OUTLAW
12335 Santa Monica Blvd.,
  Suite 106
Los Angeles, CA 90025
(310) 281-6859
Clients: Directors, Producers,
Writers. No unsolicited material.
No phone calls.

LISA ESSARY
MANAGEMENT (TMA)
Lisa Essary
c/o Cole Avenue Studios
1006 North Cole Avenue
Hollywood, CA 90038
(323) 610-1345
Clients: Actors, Writers.

EVANS MANAGEMENT
Los Angeles, CA
(818) 766-0114
(See also listing under Florida.)

KAREN EVANS
MANAGEMENT
Karen Evans
(323) 933-9218
Clients: Writers, Producers.
Not accepting unsolicited
materials at this time.

EXCEED ENTERTAINMENT, INC.
(TMA)
David Weber
11601 Wilshire Blvd.,
  Suite 500
Los Angeles, CA 90025
(310) 575-4842
www.exceedentertainment.com
Clients: Actors, Actresses,
Variety/Comedy Performers.

DOROTHY FINDLATER
MANAGEMENT (TMA)
Dorothy Findlater
7095 Hollywood Blvd., #574
Hollywood, CA 90028
(818) 281-0468
Clients: Actors, Actresses.

FOURTEENTH COLONY
MANAGEMENT (TMA)
Margaret Gottfried
10 Universal City Plaza, Suite
    2000
Universal City, CA 91608
(818) 753-2350
*Clients: Actors, Actresses,
Children, Teenagers.*

GLO ENTERPRISES (TMA)
Gloria Burke
9931 Melvin Avenue
Northridge, CA 91324
(818) 907-7776
Clients: Music Performers.

GLOBAL ONE LTD. (TMA)
Sunny Chae
3530 Wilshire Blvd., #1860
Los Angeles, CA 90010
(213) 380-9206
www.globaloneltd.com
*Clients: Actors, Actresses,
Children, Teenagers, Recording
Artists, Bands, Photographers,
Models, Singers, Dancers.*

GREEN KEY MANAGEMENT
(NCOPM)
www.GreenKeyManagement.com
*(Refer to above website for
temporary Los Angeles address
during pilot season, main office
listing under New York.)*

GUARDIAN ANGEL
MANAGEMENT (TMA)
Kate Romero-Hibbard
11271 Ventura Blvd., Suite 271
Studio City, CA 91604
(323) 874-4051
*Clients: Actors, Actresses, Music
Performers, Dancers. Demo
tapes are accepted by mail only.
No phone calls please.*

HHR MANAGEMENT (TMA)
Adam Lewis
8306 Wilshire Blvd., #533
Beverly Hills, CA 90211
(310) 474-3305
www.hhrmanagement.com
*Clients: Actors, Actresses,
Writers, Teenagers, Sports
Personalities.*

HAND N' HAND
MANAGEMENT (TMA)
Shanti Olcese Brook
P.O. Box 5741
Sherman Oaks, CA 91413
(818) 980-4354
*Clients: Actors, Actresses,
Stunt Performers.*

HAZEN TALENT
MANAGEMENT (TMA)
Nan Hazen, Melinda Bassett
3500 West Olive Avenue,
    Suite 300
Burbank, CA 91505
(818) 558-4072
Clients: Actors, Models.

HOLLYWOOD
MANAGEMENT COMPANY
(TMA)
Jake Azhar
8275 Fountain Avenue, #1
West Hollywood, CA 90046
(310) 999-4747
*Clients: Actors, Actresses,
Teenagers.*

HYPE ENTERTAINMENT
(TMA)
Stacey Pokluda
1784 North Sycamore Avenue,
    #207
Los Angeles, CA 90028
(323) 876-7642
Clients: Actors, Actresses.

IMT (TMA)
Leif Soderling
Sunset-Gower Studios
1438 North Gower Street,
    Box 22
Hollywood, CA 90028
(323) 468-7900
*Clients: Actors, actresses,
models.*

ISM MANAGEMENT (NCOPM)
Janelle Starr
8500 Wilshire Blvd.,
    Suite 527
Beverly Hills, CA 90211
(310) 360-6992
*Clients: Actors, Actresses,
Children, Teenagers,
Variety/Comedy Performers.*

INCOGNITO MANAGEMENT
Andrew Howard
9440 Santa Monica Blvd., #302
Beverly Hills, CA 90210
(310) 246-1500
*Clients: Actors, Actresses,
Directors, Producers, Writers.*

(JME) JEROME MARTIN
ENTERTAINMENT (TMA)
Jerome Martin
8300 Yuma Place, 2nd Floor
Los Angeles, CA 90046
(323) 822-1604
*Clients: Actors, Writers,
Directors.*

THE LAB MANAGEMENT
GROUP (TMA)
Allan Marks, Brett Carella
5540 Hollywood Blvd., 2nd Floor
Hollywood, CA 90028
(323) 960-2850
*Not accepting any submissions
at this time.*

LANDIS-SIMON PRODUCTIONS
& TALENT MANAGEMENT (TMA)
Judy Landis, Steve Simon
2410 East Oakshore Drive
Westlake Village, CA 91361
(805) 370-6387
*Clients: Children/Teenagers,
Young Adults (five–21). No
babies. No print work. (See also
listing under Steve Simon.)*

LANE MANAGEMENT GROUP
(TMA)
Sharon Lane
13331 Moorpark Street,
    Suite 118
Sherman Oaks, CA 91423
(818) 501-6051
*Clients: Actors, Actresses,
Writers, Children, Teenagers.*

LEVITON MANAGEMENT
(NCOPM)
Abbe Leviton
1008 Indiana Avenue
Venice, CA 90291
(310) 452-7400
*Clients: Actors, Actresses,
Comedy Performers.*

MYRNA LIEBERMAN
MANAGEMENT (TMA)
Myrna Lieberman
3001 Hollywood Drive
Hollywood, CA 90068
(323) 463-8092
*Clients: Actors, Actresses,
Children/Teenagers (up to 21).*

THE LLITERAS GROUP, LLC.
(TMA)
Ralph Angel Lliteras
2432 Butler Avenue
Los Angeles, CA 90064
(310) 478-8398
*Clients: Actors, Actresses,
Writers, Models.*

JEFFREY LOSEFF
MANAGEMENT (NCOPM)
Jeffrey Loseff
4521 Colfax Avenue,
    Suite 205
North Hollywood, CA 91602
(818) 505-9468

TAMI LYNN PRODUCTION AND
MANAGEMENT (TMA)
Tami Lynn
20411 Chapter Drive
Woodland Hills, CA 91364
(818) 888-8264

MM GERTZ ENTERTAINMENT
(TMA)
Mathius Mack Gertz
3940 Laurel Canyon Blvd., #222
Studio City, CA 91604
(310) 497-7212
*Clients: Below-the-line; Make-up
Artists, Hair Stylists, Wardrobe
Designers, Producers, Directors,
Writers, Classically-trained
actors, comedians, def poets.*

MGC CUSHMAN
ENTERTAINMENT GROUP (TMA)
Micheal Cushman
11127 La Maida Street, Unit #15
North Hollywood, CA 91601
(818) 980-6215
*Clients: Actors & Actresses
(extremely good-looking), Writers,
Teenagers, Adults. Age range for
actors (14–22) M/F; Age range for
singers/recording artists (16–22)
M/F. Currently seeking African-
American/Hispanic, Latin
Actors–M/F.*

MANAGEMENT ONE (TMA)
Robert Lee
13226 Aetna Street
Valley Glen, CA 91401
(818) 787 6239
*Clients: Actors, Actresses (all ages,
ethnics, SAG preferred), commercial and theatrical. Interested in
young, beautiful, and character
actors, actresses and seniors.*

MANAGE THIS! (TMA)
Valerie O'Brien
2973 Harbor Blvd., #657
Costa Mesa, CA 92626
(714) 545-6889
*Clients: Actors, Actresses,
Directors, Writers, Children,
Comedy Performers, Composers,
Bands.*

THE MARSHAK/ZACHARY
COMPANY (TMA)
Darryl Marshak, Susan Zachary,
Alan Mills, Mitch Clem
8840 Wilshire Blvd. First Floor
Beverly Hills, CA 90211
(310) 358-3191
*Clients: Actors, Writer-Directors,
Comedians.*

MATRIX MANAGEMENT
(TMA)
Celia Z. Kahn
5903 Fallbrook Avenue
Woodland Hills, CA 91367
(818) 999-9941
*Clients: Actors, Actresses,
Choreographers, Producers.*

MATTIE MANAGEMENT
(TMA)
Mattie Semradek
3327 Sumac Ridge Drive
Malibu, CA 90265
(310) 317-0028
*Clients: Actors, Actresses,
Directors, Producers,
Writers, Newscasters,
Media Personalities, Sports
Personalities, Comedy
Performers.*

PAT MCQUEENEY
MANAGEMENT (TMA)
Patricia McQueeney
10279 Century Woods Drive
Los Angeles, CA 90067
(310) 277-1882
*Not taking on new clients at
this time.*

MIDWEST TALENT
MANAGEMENT, INC.
(TMA)
Betty McCormick Aggas;
Mark Blake (Associate Manager)
4821 Lankershim Blvd.
Suite F, PMB 149
North Hollywood, CA 91601
(818) 765-3785
*Clients: Actors, Actresses,
Children, Teenagers.*

MILLENNIUM ARTIST
MANAGEMENT
Joann Henrich & Keith Zarin
777 Silver Spur Road,
Suite 225
Rolling Hills Estates, CA 90274
(310) 377-4854
*Clients: Actors, Actresses,
Directors, Producers,
Writers, Children, Teenagers,
Variety/Comedy Performers,
Music Performers, Recording
Artists. Accepts photos and
demo reels by mail only.
Newcomers welcome.
Phone calls accepted after
2 P.M. Currently seeking
experienced actors/actresses
ages 16–65.*

MONKEY DREAM
MANAGEMENT (TMA)
Jay Caputo
P.O. Box 2446
Toluca Lake, CA 91610
(818) 752-4275
*Clients: Actors, directors,
producers, Stunt Performers.*

MOORE STAR TALENT
MANAGEMENT
(TMA)
London Moore
10 Universal City Plaza,
Suite 2000
Universal City, CA 91608
(818) 753-2313
*Clients: Actors, Actresses,
Directors, Producers, Writers,
Teenagers, Newscasters,
Media Personalities, Sports
Personalities, Variety/Comedy
Performers, Music Performers,
Composers, Recording Artists,
Orchestras, Bands, Artists,
Authors, Choreographers,
Photographers, Set Designers,
Costume Designers.*

CAROL MORRIS
MANAGEMENT
Carol Morris
9660 Marilla Drive,
Suite 16
Lakeside, CA 92040
(619) 390-6710
*Clients: Actors, Actresses,
Directors, Writers, Comedy
Performers. Only "union
talent"! Extremely well-trained.
Personal Manager in Los
Angeles for over 28 years.
Works both coasts.*

NEBULA MANAGEMENT
(TMA)
Kevin R. Carr
P.O. Box 29490
Los Angeles, CA 90029-0490
(323) 664-8244
Clients: Actors, actresses.

PB MANAGEMENT
(TMA)
Paul Bennett
6449 West 6th Street
Los Angeles, CA 90048
(323) 653-7284
*Clients: Established Actors
(Male and Female), Writers,
and developing young talent
(18–21).*

PALISADES PARTNERS
ENTERTAINMENT
(TMA)
Ryan Akins
956 Jacon Way
Pacific Palisades, CA 90272
(310) 454-5292
*Will accept submissions
from actors with reels.
Will accept USPS talent
submissions.*

PARK PLACE
MANAGEMENT (TMA)
Eric W. Parkinson
922 South Barrington Avenue,
   #305
Los Angeles, CA 90049
(310) 826-8126
*Clients: Actors, Actresses,
Writers, Children,
Teenagers, Newscasters,
Media Personalities,
Sports Personalities,
Variety/Comedy Performers.
Also literary department.*

PERSONA MANAGEMENT
(NCOPM)
Bill Civitella
14271 Dickens Street
Sherman Oaks, CA 91423
(818) 528-7773
*Clients: Children, five to
25 years. Actors, Actresses,
including teenagers and
models. No Phone calls.
(See NY listing under
Personal Management.)*

PLAIN JANE
ENTERTAINMENT
(TMA)
Crystal Young
P.O. Box 3324
Santa Monica, CA 90408
(310) 226-7016
www.plainj.com
*Clients: Actors, Actresses.
Accepts mailed submissions,
but is not actively seeking
talent now.*

PLATINUM
MANAGEMENT SPORTS
& ENTERTAINMENT
(TMA)
Paul N. Philips
655 North Central Avenue,
   17th Floor
Glendale, CA 91203
(818) 649-7510

PRINCIPATO-YOUNG
ENTERTAINMENT (TMA)
Peter Principato, Paul Young,
E. Brian Dobbins, Ted Bender,
Allen Fischer, David Gardner
(Managers); Dave Rosenthal,
John Chung, Dana Horlick,
Daniel Ortega, Regan Frisby
(Assistants).
9665 Wilshire Blvd., Suite 500
Beverly Hills, CA 90212
(310) 274-4474
*Clients: Actors, Actresses,
Directors, Producers, Writers,
Variety/Comedy Performers.
(See also listing under New York.)*

REACH FOR THE STARS
(TMA)
Rose Frohlich
3686 Barham Blvd., #H-302
Los Angeles, CA 90068
(323) 850-7523
*Clients: Actors, Actresses
(all ages, ethnicities and types).
Will consider talented nonunion people. Demo tapes
accepted, but if you would
like them back please include
a self-addressed stamped
envelope. Will accept e-mail
talent submissions.*

RED BARON
MANAGEMENT (TMA)
Robert Enriquez
2022 A Broadway
Santa Monica, CA 90404
(310) 828-8866
Clients: Actors, Actresses.

LINDA REITMAN
MANAGEMENT (TMA)
Linda Reitman
820 North San Vicente Blvd.,
   Box 691736
Los Angeles, CA 90069-9736
(323) 852-9091
*Clients: Actors: with film/T.V.
credits and reel; Writers,
Directors, Producers, Musical
Talent & Comedian submissions
(all must be experienced, with
resumes).*

RICHESON MANAGEMENT
(TMA)
Elaine Richeson
P.O. Box 93552
Palmdale, CA 93590
(661) 533-1063
*Clients: Actors, Actresses,
Children, Teenagers.*

PATRICIA RILE MODELS &
TALENT MANAGEMENT
Patricia Rile
4716 Foulger Drive
Santa Rosa, CA 95405
(707) 537-8247
*Not accepting submissions at
this time.*

MARK ROBERT MANAGEMENT
(TMA)
Mark Robert
14014 Moorpark Street, #316
Sherman Oaks, CA 91423
(818) 907-9178
www.markrobertmgmt.com
Clients: Actors, Actresses.

SAFFRON MANAGEMENT
(NCOPM)
Alan Saffron, Jerald Silverhardt,
Nyle Brenner
8899 Beverly Blvd., Suite 401
West Hollywood, CA 90211
(310) 271-8704
*Clients: Actors, Actresses,
Directors, Producers, Writers.
Written submissions only.*

SAXON ASSOCIATES
MANAGEMENT (TMA)
Daniel Saxon
552 Norwich Drive
West Hollywood, CA 90048
(310) 657-6033
*Clients: Actors only for T.V., film,
stage.*

SEFTON PRODUCTIONS
(NCOPM)
Daniel Sefton
Hollywood Taft Building
1680 North Vine Street,
   Suite 727
Hollywood, CA 90028
(213) 917-7874

SERENDIPITY ENTERTAINMENT
& MANAGEMENT
Mark Papp (Designated Manager)
VP West Coast Talent
510 South Ardmore Avenue,
   Suite 231
Los Angeles, CA 90020
(213) 487-0610
*Clients: Actors/Actresses,
Directors, Producers, Writers,
Children, Teenagers, Music
Performers, Composers,
Recording Artists, Orchestras,
Bands. Boutique management
company. Interviews by appoint-
ment only. Currently seeking
teens (17–22)/young adults for
film/T.V./theatre/commercials.*

Strong theatrical training preferred. Photos/tape/resume by mail only. Attends showcases. Also represents celebrity look-a-likes. Please do not visit. (See also listing under New York.)

SEVEN SUMMITS PICTURES
& MANAGEMENT
(NCOPM)
Sarah Jackson
8447 Wilshire Blvd.,
    Suite 200
Beverly Hills, CA 90211
(323) 655-0101
Clients: Actors, Actresses, Directors, Producers, Writers.

SHALLON STAR
MANAGEMENT GROUP
(TMA)
Hazel Shallon
15030 Ventura Blvd., #911
Sherman Oaks, CA 91403
(818) 990-9881
Clients: Actors, Actresses.

EARL SHANK PERSONAL
MANAGEMENT (NCOPM)
Earl Shank
520 North Kings Road,
    Suite 316
West Hollywood, CA 90048
(323) 651-5241
Clients: Actors, Actresses, Writers, Children, Teenagers.

SHARK ARTISTS, INC.
Debbie DeStefano, Carolyn
Derek, Sam Boyd
P.O. Box 88225
Los Angeles, CA 90009
(310) 503-2121
Clients: Actors, Actresses, Directors, Producers, Writers, Children, Teenagers, Media Personalities, Music Performers, Composers, Recording Artists, Bands, Artists, Authors, Innovative drive . . . caring and creative leadership, intensely focused boutique firm. No unsolicited submissions. Industry referrals only.

SILVER EPIC
ENTERTAINMENT (TMA)
Nolayan O. Herdegen
2820 South Vermont Avenue,
    Suite 17
Los Angeles, CA 90007
(323) 732-2159

SIMONÉ TALENT AGENCY &
MANAGEMENT COMPANY
Mary Taylor
9701 West Pico Blvd.,
    Suite 115
Los Angeles, CA 90035
(310) 377-1587
(310) 277-7275
Clients: Actors/Actresses, Children/Teenagers, Media Personalities, Comedy Performers, Dancers.

SKYE MANAGEMENT (TMA)
David O. Thompson
20450 Pacific Coast Highway
Malibu, CA 90265
(310) 456-1230
Clients: Actors, Actresses, Children, Teenagers, Writers.

STEVE SIMON TALENT
MANAGEMENT (TMA)
Steve Simon
8899 Beverly Blvd.,
    Suite 815
West Hollywood, CA 90048
(310) 281-0944
(See also listing under Landis-Simon Productions & Talent Management.)

STEIN ENTERTAINMENT (TMA)
T.J. Stein
11271 Ventura Blvd.,
    Suite #477
Studio City, CA 91604-3136
(818) 766-6525
Clients: Actors, Actresses.

STUDIO TALENT GROUP (TMA)
Phil Brock
1328 12th Street
Santa Monica, CA 90401
(310) 393-8004
www.studiotalentgroup.com
Clients: Actors, Actresses, Children, Teenagers. Also handles literary for screenplays. Accepts queries by mail only.

THE SUCHIN COMPANY (TMA)
Milton B. Suchin
12747 Riverside Drive,
    Suite 208
Valley Village, CA 91607
(818) 505 0044
Clients: Actors, Actresses, Children, Teenagers, Newscasters, Media Personalities, Sports Personalities, Variety/Comedy Performers, Music Performers, Recording Artists, Authors, Photographers.

THE SUSAN SMITH COMPANY
Susan Smith
121 A North San Vicente Blvd.
Beverly Hills, CA 90211
(323) 852-4777
Clients: Actors, Actresses. No submissions. Existing clients only.

STUDIO TALENT GROUP (TMA)
Phil Brock
1328 12th Street, Suite 3
Santa Monica, CA 90401
(310) 393-8004
Clients: Actors, Actresses, Writers, Children, Teenagers. Past Director Talent Managers Association. Also licensed as a talent agency by State of California. STG is full service MP/T.V./theatre/ commercial representation.

3:33 ENTERTAINMENT (TMA)
Sheila True
7033 West Sunset Blvd.,
    Suite 201
Hollywood, CA 90028
(323) 468-3500
Clients: Children, Commercials, Models, Music, Print, Theatrical.

TALENTINK LA-NY (TMA)
Terrie W. Snell
P.O. Box 2583
Toluca Lake, CA 91610
(818) 846-5540
Clients: Actors, Actresses, Children, Teenagers, Variety/Comedy Performers.

TEMPTATION MANAGEMENT
(TMA)
Brandon Ross
8306 Wilshire Blvd., Suite 232
Beverly Hills, CA 90211
(323) 281-9918
www.tptalent.com
Clients: Actors, Actresses, Models, Music Performers, Composers, Recording Artists, Orchestras, Bands, Photographers.

ROZ TILLMAN MANAGEMENT
(TMA)
Roz Tillman
11054 Ventura Blvd., Suite 289
Studio City, CA 91604
(818) 985-3514
Clients: Actors, Actresses, Children, Teenagers (all ethnicities and types). Will consider talented nonunion people as well. No unsolicited drop-offs, faxes, or tapes accepted.

VERVE MANAGEMENT
(TMA)
Didgie Blain-Rozgay
4261 Caledonia Way
Los Angeles, CA 90065
(323) 259-8479
*Clients: Committed and
focused Actors, Writers.*

WQ TALENT MANAGEMENT
(TMA)
Ric Williams
5225 Blakeslee Avenue, #154
North Hollywood, CA 91601
(818) 634-8494
Clients: Actors, actresses.

MICHAEL WALLACH
MANAGEMENT (TMA)
Michael Wallach
11033 Massachusetts Avenue,
   Suite 500
Los Angeles, CA 90025
(310) 268-8450
*Clients: Actors, Actresses,
Producers, Children, Teenagers,
Newscasters, Media Personalities.
California licensed talent agent.
Also teaches UCLA extension
course The Business of Acting.
Admitted to bar in New York
State.*

WARNER MANAGEMENT (TMA)
Pamela Warner
9171 Wilshire Blvd., #541
Los Angeles, CA 90210
(818) 385-1641
*Clients: Actors, Actresses (must
have solid T.V. & film credits and
current demo reel). Must sign
both commercially and theatrically. Not accepting submissions
at this time.*

WARNING MANAGEMENT
Kim Matuka
9440 Santa Monica Blvd.,
   Suite 400
Beverly Hills, CA 90210
(310) 860-9033
*Warning Management is the
Los Angeles office of Online
Talent Group in New York.
We are a boutique bicoastal
management company. Clients
include established actors,
young adults, comediannes and
recording artists. Just opened
selected beauty department.
(See also Online Talent Group
under New York.)*

MIMI WEBER MANAGEMENT
LTD. (NCOPM)
Mimi Weber
10717 Wilshire Blvd., PH3
Los Angeles, CA 90024
(310) 470-5224
Clients: Established Actors only.

MARTIN WEISS MANAGEMENT
(TMA)
Martin Weiss
P.O. Box 5656
Santa Monica, CA 90409-5656
(310) 399-7658
www.martinweissmanagement.com
*Clients: Actors, Actresses,
Children/Teenagers. Will take
over 18 years of age if they can
play 18.*

WIZARDS ENTERTAINMENT
(TMA)
Margaret O'Neal
150 South Glenoaks Blvd., #9191
Burbank, CA 91502
(310) 460-6909
*Clients: Actors, Actresses,
Dancers, Singers, Producers,
Directors, Writers.*

Connecticut

FASTBREAK MANAGEMENT
(NCOPM)
Bud Mitchell
70 Clay Hill Road
Stamford, CT 06905
(203) 329-7335
*Clients: Actors, Actresses,
Directors, Producers, Writers,
Variety, Comedy Performers,
Musical Performers, Composers,
Recording Artists, Orchestras,
Bands.*

GMS MANAGEMENT
(NCOPM)
Dick Grass, Danny Scarpone
585 Ellsworth Street, Suite 2G
Bridgeport, CT 06605
(203) 334-9285
*Clients: Comedy/Variety
Performers, Directors, Producers,
Writers, Musical Performers.*

RICK MARTIN PRODUCTIONS
(NCOPM)
Rick Martin
125 Fieldpoint Road
Greenwich, CT 06830
(203) 661-1615, ext. 5
*Clients: Recording Artists, Actors,
Actresses, Musical Performers,
Composers.*

CHERYL SCOTT
MANAGEMENT (NCOPM)
Cheryl Scott
25 Breezy Hill Road
Canton, CT 06019
(860) 693-0891
*Clients: Musical Performers,
Orchestras, Bands only.*

STEINER TALENT
MANAGEMENT (NCOPM)
Mark Steiner
P.O. Box 1005
Southport, CT 06890
(203) 319-0050
www.steinertalent.com
*Clients: Actors, Actresses,
Directors, Producers,
Writers, Newscasters,
Media Personalities, Sports
Personalities, Variety/Comedy
Performers, Music Performers,
Composers, Recording Artists,
Orchestras, Bands.*

Florida

BURRIS MANAGEMENT
GROUP
Michael J. Burris
3127 Fort Jackson Drive
Jacksonville, FL 32246
(904) 998-8469
*Clients: Actors, Actresses,
Variety/Comedy Performers,
Musical Performers, Composers,
Recording Artists, Orchestras,
Bands.*

CFB PRODUCTIONS, INC.
(NCOPM)
Wanda Kilman
19148 Seneca Avenue
Weston, FL 33332
(954) 389-5674
*Clients: Singers & Christian
Performers, Media Personalities,
Actors, Actresses.*

EVANS MANAGEMENT
(NCOPM)
Stanley Evans
2808 60th Avenue West,
   Suite 1601
Bradenton, FL 34207
(941) 756-1756
*Clients: Actors, Actresses,
Directors, Producers,
Writers, Newscasters,
Media Personalities, Sports
Personalities, Variety/Comedy
Performers, Musical Performers,
Composers, Recording Artists,
Authors. Currently National*

Vice President, National
Conference of Personal
Managers. Formerly four-time
Executive Director, Western
Division, National Conference
of Personal Managers. (See
also information for Los Angeles
office under California.)

F.J.M. PRODUCTIONS, INC.
(NCOPM)
Fred Montilla, Jr.
7305 West Sample Road,
    Suite 101
Coral Springs, FL 33065
(954) 753-8591
Clients: Musicians only.
Submissions from musicians are
accepted.

LANE MANAGEMENT
GROUP (TMA)
Sharon Lane
Greenwich Studios
12100 NE 16th Avenue,
    Suite 210
North Miami Beach , FL 33161
(305) 891-2213
Clients: Children, Young Adults.

WALLS ENTERTAINMENT
GROUP/
The L.A. Connection (NCOPM)
4237 Henderson Blvd., Suite A
Tampa, FL 33629
(813) 639-0922
Nashville Office: (615) 664-1660

Maryland

DAZZLING STARS TALENT
MANAGEMENT, INC.
Sandy Kolar
1726 Reisterstown Road,
    Suite 210
Baltimore, MD 21208
(410) 486-7766
www.dazzlingstars.com
Clients: Actors, models on the
East Coast (babies thru seniors)
for print, films, and commercials.

Massachusetts

MIXED MEDIA ENTERTAINMENT
CO. (NCOPM)
Michael Glynn
26 Arrowhead Road
Weston, MA 02493
(781) 647-3400
Clients: Writers, Musicians,
Directors. No Actors.
Submissions from established
talent only. No phone calls.

MTM/MODELS & TALENT
MANAGEMENT
Kathryn Ryan
P.O. Box 646
Newtonville, MA 02460
(617) 969-3555
Clients: Actors, Actresses,
Models, Children.

Nevada

CFB PRODUCTIONS, INC.
(NCOPM)
Clinton Ford Billups, Jr.
P.O. Box 50008
Henderson, NV 89016
(702) 837-1170
Clients: Newscasters, Media
Personalities, Sports
Personalities, Variety/Comedy
Performers, Musical Performers,
Composers, Recording Artists,
Orchestras, Bands.

New Jersey

ALPHA-CENTAURI
MANAGEMENT (NCOPM)
Al Caz
6 Ocean Blvd.
Keyport, NJ 07735
(732) 583-4441
Clients: Actors, Actresses,
Directors, Producers, Writers,
Variety/Comedy Performers.

THE ENTERTAINMENT GROUP
(NCOPM)
Ms. Bobbie Merritt,
Marc Zimbardi
28 Alana Drive
Hawthorne, NJ 07506
(973) 238-0056
Clients: Actors, Actresses,
Children, Dancers, Comedians.
(See also listing under New York.)

SHIRLEY GRANT
MANAGEMENT
Shirley Grant (Owner); Laura
Van Winkle (Associate); Dave
McKeown (Associate)
P.O. Box 866
Teaneck, NJ 07666
New Jersey: (201) 692-1653
New York: (212) 926-9082
www.shirleygrant.com
Clients: Actors, Actresses,
Children, Teenagers, Young
Adults, Infants, Comedians,
Dancers, Singers, Models
(male & female) for commercials,
theatre, feature films, T.V.,
voiceovers, industrials, and

print advertising. Accepts
photos-resumes by mail.
Interviews by appointment only.
Attends showcases. No phone
calls.

JAMISON COMMUNICATIONS
Harlan Jamison
1225 River Road, Suite 10D
Edgewater, NJ 07020
(201) 886-0234
Clients: Actors, Actresses,
Directors, Producers, Writers,
Variety/Comedy Performers.

LILLIAN KERR TALENT
MANAGEMENT OF NEW
JERSEY
Lillian Kerr
130 Romaine Avenue
Jersey City, NJ 07306
(201) 451-8276
Clients: Actors, Actresses,
Babies, Children, Teenagers,
Variety/Comedy Performers,
Music Performers, Composers.
Adults and Seniors.

MILLER PRODUCTIONS &
MANAGEMENT, LLC
Joe Miller
3145 Bordentown Avenue,
    Suite C-4
Parlin, NJ 08859
(732) 727-4621
Clients: Variety/Comedy
Performers. Books comedians
in comedy clubs nationwide.

NEW TALENT MANAGEMENT
Bill Perlman
590 Route 70
Brick, NJ 08723
(732) 477-3355
Clients: Actors/Actresses,
Children/Teenagers. Newborns
through young adults. Bicoastal
NY & LA clients. All areas, all
ethnicities.

NOBLE TALENT
MANAGEMENT (NCOPM)
Eileen DeNobile (Owner);
Heather Morris (Associate)
P.O. Box 66095
Lawrenceville, NJ 08648
(609) 896-5928
Clients: Actors, Actresses,
Children, Teenagers/Young
Adults, Variety/Comedy
Performers. Specializes in film,
T.V., theatre, commercials, and
voiceovers. Accepts photos
& resumes by mail.

CATHY PARKER
MANAGEMENT
(See listing under New York.)

PARKSIDE TALENT INC.
(NCOPM)
Judith A. Battista
105 Braidburn Road
Florham Park, NJ 07932
(973) 822-1318
*Clients: Children (four to 12),
Commercials, Voiceovers,
Print and Musical Performers.
Primarily interested in boys
(six–12) for musical theatre.
Accepts photos & resumes.
Attends showcases & local
theatre productions. No phone
calls please.*

RYBIN TALENT
MANAGEMENT, LTD.
Susan Rybin
74 Raritan Road
Linden, NJ 07036
(908) 486-8841
*Clients: Actors, Actresses.
Children, Teenagers. Specializing
in Latino talent for the past
20 years. Not accepting new
clients at this time.*

SAM'S KIDS & ADULTS
MANAGEMENT
Shari Sussman
901 Old Marlton Pike
Marlton, NJ 08053
(856) 596-7401
*Clients: Actors, Actresses,
Children, Teenagers (birth to
adults). Specializes in film,
T.V., commercials, and print.*

SOIREE FAIR, INC. (NCOPM)
Karen L. Gunn
133 Midland Avenue, Suite 10
Montclair, NJ 07042
(973) 783-9051
*Clients: Actors, Actresses,
Children/Teenagers, Writers.
Especially seeking musical
theatre children, ages seven–11.*

TM TALENT MANAGEMENT, INC.
Tamara Markowitz
P.O. Box 72
Marlboro, NJ 07746
(732) 972-4957
*Clients: Management specializes
in newborns to 18 years old and
twins, of all ethnicities, for all
areas, including T.V., movies,
print, and voiceovers. No phone
calls please.*

VIOLA TALENT GROUP
Viola Perrowe, Robin
Gresham Chin
811 Church Road, Suite 105
Cherry Hill, NJ 08002
(609) 239-3607
*Clients: Children (four and up),
Actors. Performers with
specialized skills.*

VIVO ARTISTS MANAGEMENT
CO. (NCOPM)
Robert Gatollari
70 West Passiac Street
Rochelle Park, NJ 07662
(201) 845-8333
*Clients: Actors, Actresses,
Directors, Producers, Writers,
Children, Teenagers, Newscasters,
Media Personalities, Sports
Personalities, Variety/Comedy
Performers, Music Performers,
Composers, Recording Artists,
Orchestras, Bands, Artists,
Authors, Choreographers,
Photographers, Set Designers,
Costume Designers.*

New York

A.M. AMBROSINO
MANAGEMENT (NCOPM)
Amy Ambrosino
P.O. Box 307
New York, NY 10044
(212) 317-8511
*Clients: Actors, Actresses,
Voiceover Talent, Directors,
Producers, Writers, Variety
Performers, Stand-up Comedians.
Videotape, CDs and treatments
received weekly.*

THE ACTORS CLUB TALENT &
MANAGEMENT (NCOPM)
Sal Di Bella
P.O. Box 36
Oyster Bay, NY 11771
(516) 250-4152
*Clients: Actors, Actresses,
Children, Teenagers, Newscasters,
Media Personalities, Sports
Personalities, Variety/Comedy
Performers, Music Performers,
Composers, Recording Artists,
Orchestras, Bands.*

ALLIED ARTISTS MANAGEMENT
John R. Sanchez
244 Fifth Avenue, Suite E273
New York, NY 10001
(212) 726-3125
*Clients: Actors, Actresses, Children,
Teenagers, Comedy Performers.*

AMERICAN TALENT
MANAGEMENT (NCOPM)
Herb Rothman
244 Fifth Avenue, Suite 503
New York, NY 10001
(212) 686-6547
*Clients: Actors, Actresses, chil-
dren. No drop-ins. Potential new
clients only seen by appointment.
Mail submissions of headshots &
resumes accepted. Audio/video
demo reels accepted by mail only.*

BAKER MANAGEMENT
Jaime Baker
311 West 43rd Street, Suite 1106
New York, NY 10036
(212) 262-4234
*Clients: Actors, Actresses,
Directors, Producers, Writers,
Variety/Comedy Performers.*

HARRY BELLOVIN (NCOPM)
410 East 64th Street
New York, NY 10021
(212) 752-5181
*Clients: Actors, actresses, come-
dians, composers, songwriters.*

THE BLACK DRAGON GROUP
Leland Hardy
257 West 137th Street, Suite 4
New York, NY 10030
(212) 694-4324
www.newyork.com
*Clients: Actors, Actresses,
Directors, Producers, Writers,
Children, Teenagers, Newscasters,
Media Personalities, Sports
Personalities, Variety/Comedy
Performers, Musical Performers,
Composers, Recording Artists,
Orchestras, Bands.*

BOOKED
Rita Powers
9 Desbrosses Street, Room 513
New York, NY 10013
(212) 965-1683
*Clients: Actors, Actresses,
Children, Teenagers. Non-
exclusive, newborn thru adult for
T.V., film, commercials, Videos,
Industrials, soaps, commercial
print.*

THE BRITTO AGENCY (NCOPM)
Marvet Britto
234 West 56th Street, PH
New York, NY 10019
(212) 977-6772
*Clients: Actors, Actresses,
Athletes, Musicians, and all areas
of entertainment.*

CTM ARTISTS
Charlene Turney
484 West 43rd Street,
Suite 11-S
New York, NY 10036
(212) 564-3536
*Clients: Actors, Actresses,
Directors, Computer
Animators.*

CAROLINE'S
MANAGEMENT
(NCOPM)
Caroline Hirsch
1626 Broadway
New York, NY 10019
(212) 956-0101
Clients: Comedic Performers.

JOYCE CHASE
MANAGEMENT
(NCOPM)
Joyce Chase
2 Fifth Avenue
New York, NY 10011
(212) 473-1234
*Clients: Actors, Actresses.
Resumes & headshots
accepted from SAG and
EQUITY members only.*

THE TORY CHRISTOPHER
GROUP (TMA)
Robbyn Navatto
8264 A Austin Street
Kew Gardens, NY 11415
(718) 850-1553
www.torychristopher.com
*Clients: Actors, Actresses,
Children, Teenagers and
Musical Performers.*

COASTAL
ENTERTAINMENT
PRODUCTIONS
Linda Rohe
32-31 35th Street
Astoria, NY 11106
(718) 728-8581
*Clients: Actors, Actresses,
Variety/Comedy Performers.
Comunicados.*

JUAN DAVILA
29 Broadway,
Suite 1825
New York, NY 10006
(212) 514-6990
www.comunicados-usa.com
*Clients: Hispanic Actors &
Actresses, Directors, Writers,
Children, Teenagers, Musical
Performers, Authors.*

CREATIVE MANAGEMENT
GROUP
Edie Robb, Edward Lefferson
301 West 53rd Street, Suite 4K
New York, NY 10019
(212) 245-3250
*Clients: Actors, Actresses,
Children, Teenagers. Accepts
photos-resumes by mail only.
Do not phone or visit. (See also
listing under California.)*

CREATIVE TALENT
MANAGEMENT (NCOPM)
Tanden R. Heyes
91-08 172nd Street
Jamaica, New York 11432
(718) 658-0443
*Clients: Actors, Actresses,
Directors, Producers, Writers,
Comedy/Variety Performers.*

CUZZINS MANAGEMENT
(NCOPM)
(a division of Sokol-Frankmano
Entertainment Enterprises)
Victoria Frankmano, Helene
Sokol, Marion Falk
250 West 57th Street, Suite 1500
New York, NY 10107
(212) 765-6559
*Clients: Actors, Actresses,
including Children and Teenagers,
Musical Performers. (See also
listing under under California.)*

DCA PRODUCTIONS (NCOPM)
Daniel Abrahamsen,
Geraldine Abrahamsen
330 West 38th Street, # 904
New York, NY 10018
(212) 245-2063
*Clients: Variety/Comedy
Performers, Actors, Actresses,
Writers, Musical Performers,
Recording Artists, Bands. Pictures
& resumes are accepted by mail
only. Tapes are accepted but not
returnable.*

DEE MURA ENTERPRISES, INC.
(NCOPM)
Dee Mura
269 West Shore Drive
Massapequa, NY 11758
(516) 795-1616
*Clients: Actors, Actresses,
Directors, Producers, Writers,
Children, Teenagers, Newscasters,
Media Personalities, Sports
Personalities, Variety/Comedy
Performers, Musical Performers,
Composers, Recording Artists,
Orchestras, Bands, Artists, Authors.*

WINTER DONALDSON
MANAGEMENT/
WINTER'S KIDS (NCOPM)
Ms. Winter Donaldson
33 Cedar Lane
Ossining, NY 10562
(914) 941-6063
*Clients: Actors, Actresses,
Children, Teenagers.*

MICHELE DONAY TALENT
MANAGEMENT
Michele Donay
76 West 86th Street
New York, NY 10024
(212) 769-0924
*Clients: Children. Management
for T.V. commercials, feature
films, television, soaps, series,
and movies.*

DONELAN MANAGEMENT
Paul Donelan
440 9th Avenue, 8th Floor,
Suite 15
New York, NY 10001
(212) 404-3226
www.donelanmanagement.com
*Clients: Actors, Actresses,
Children, Teenagers. Accepts
8x10's, resumes, model comp
cards and voiceover CDs. No
phone calls. Never drop-offs.
Attends showcases. Demo
tapes will not be returned
without a SASE.*

ROBERT DUVA, INC.
Robert Duva
277 West 10th Street,
Suite 9-F
New York, NY 10014
(212) 243-7845
*Clients: Directors, Writers,
Composers, Choreographers,
Set Designers, Costume
Designers, Lighting Designers.
Not accepting any new actor
clients at this time.*

THE ENTERTAINMENT
GROUP (NCOPM)
Ms. Bobbie Merritt, Marc
Zimbardi
292 Fifth Avenue,
Suite 509
New York, NY 10001
(212) 714-3562
*Clients: Actors, Actresses,
Children, Dancers, Comedians.
(See also listing under New
Jersey.)*

ESTELLE FUSCO TALENT
MANAGEMENT
Estelle Fusco
72 Moriches Road
Lake Grove, NY 11755
(631) 467-7574
Clients: Actors, Actresses,
Children, Teenagers.

FOX-ALBERT
MANAGEMENT, INC.
(NCOPM)
Jean Fox (President)
88 Central Park West
New York, NY 10023
(212) 799-9090
Clients: Actors, Actresses
(all ages). Not accepting new
clients at this time.

FOX ENTERTAINMENT
COMPANY, INC.
(NCOPM)
Dick Fox
1650 Broadway, #503
New York, NY 10019
(212) 582-9072
Clients: Actors, Actresses.

INGRID FRENCH
MANAGEMENT
Ingrid French
928 Broadway, Suite 302
New York, NY 10010
(646) 602-0653
Clients: Actors, Actresses,
Children, Teenagers. Photos
and resumes are accepted
by mail. Absolutely no
walk-ins.

FRETLESS PRODUCTIONS,
MANAGEMENT LLC
(NCOPM)
Andree Kaminsky
70-A Greenwich Avenue,
    PMB #212
New York, NY 10011
(212) 243-7549
Clients: Children, Musical
Performers, Recording Artists.
Singers (adult & children)
ONLY. Must write ref. via Ross
Reports on all submissions.

G.M.I. ENTERTAINMENT
(NCOPM)
Diane Gibson, Heather Moore
1285 Avenue of the Americas,
    35th Floor
New York, NY 10019
Clients: Musical Performers,
Actors, Actresses.

GENUINE ARTIST
MANAGEMENT (NCOPM)
Philip Cassese
P.O. Box 470
Midtown Station
New York, NY 10018
(646) 335-8692
www.genuineartist.com
Clients: Actors, actresses, singers.

GOLDSTAR TALENT
MANAGEMENT (NCOPM)
Sidney Gold
850 7th Avenue, #904
New York, NY 10019
(212) 315-4429
Clients: Actors, Actresses,
Children, Teenagers.

GOODWIN & MCGOVERN
Theatrical Management (NCOPM)
Arlene McGovern, Lois Goodwin
8 Franklin Avenue
New Hyde Park, NY 11040
(516) 932-5310
Clients: Actors, Actresses,
Children, Teenagers (up to 18).
Specializing in identical twins.

SHIRLEY GRANT
MANAGEMENT
(See listing under New Jersey.)

GREEN KEY MANAGEMENT
(NCOPM)
Seth R. Greenky; Boni Mollins
(Associate); Nicole Valentin
(Associate); Susan Chia (Office
Manager)
251 West 89th Street, Suite 4-A
New York, NY 10024
(212) 874-7373
www.GreenKeyManagement.com
Clients: Actors, Actresses,
Teenagers, Newscasters, Media
Personalities, Sports Personalities,
Variety/Comedy Performers,
Musical Performers, Composers,
Recording Artists, Bands.
Accepts headshots & resumes by
mail. No videos unless requested.
(Please also refer to website for
temporary Los Angeles Address
during pilot season.)

HH TALENT & ENTERTAINMENT
386 Park Avenue South,
    Suite 315
New York, NY 10016
(212) 251-0900
Clients: Actors/Actresses,
Variety/Comedy Performers.
Please call for an appointment.
Headshots, tapes, demos
accepted by mail.

ERIC HANSON MANAGEMENT
Eric Hanson
89 Fifth Avenue, Suite 306
New York, NY 10003
(212) 366-9149
Clients: Actors, Actresses,
Newscasters, Media Personalities,
Sports Personalities, Variety/
Comedy Performers. Submissions
are accepted by mail only.

HARVEST TALENT
MANAGEMENT (NCOPM)
Donnalyn Carfi
132 West 80th Street, #3F
New York, NY 10024
(212) 721-5756
Clients: Children, Teenagers,
Young Adults. Absolutely no
drop-offs. Do not phone.

HERBOSCH MANAGEMENT
Jano Herbosch
1035 Park Avenue, Suite 4B
New York, NY 10028
(212) 534-6558
Clients: Actors, Actresses,
Teenagers. Only accepts
mail submissions. No phone
calls please.

JOSSELYNE HERMAN &
ASSOCIATES (NCOPM)
(formerly Reve Entertainment
Group, LLC.)
Josselyne Herman-Saccio;
Eric Jacobs (Company
Manager); Don Rodgers
(Music Division Manager);
Sonya Kolba (Assistant
Manager); Donovan Green
(Development Assistant)
244 West 54th Street,
    12th Floor
New York, NY 10019
(212) 974-3300
Clients: Actors, Actresses,
Directors, Producers, Writers.

CARY HOFFMAN
MANAGEMENT
Cary Hoffman
236 West 78th Street
New York, NY 10024
(212) 873-4840
Clients: Actors, Actresses,
Directors, Producers, Writers,
Variety/Comedy Performers.

THE HOLDING COMPANY
Lucien A. Hold III
230 West End Avenue, Suite 1A
New York, NY 10023
(212) 362-1788

Clients: Comedy performers. Not seeking new clients at this time. Does not look at tapes. Will arrange audition for comic strip.

DONALD P. JACKSON TALENT
MANAGEMENT OF USA
142 East 23rd Street,
    P.O. Box 1961
New York, NY 10159
(212) 683-4417
Clients: Actors, Actresses, Children, Teenagers, Newscasters, Media Personalities, Sports Personalities, Variety/Comedy Performers, Music Performers, Composers, Recording Artists, Orchestras, Bands, Artists, Authors, Choreographers, Photographers, Set Designers, Costume Designers.

KANNER ENTERTAINMENT
Cathy Kanner
30 West 74th Street, Penthouse 1
New York, NY 10023
(212) 496-8175
Clients: Actors, Actresses, Directors, Producers, Writers, Comedy/Variety Performers.

MICHAEL KATZ TALENT
MANAGEMENT
Michael Katz
P.O. Box 1925
Cathedral Station
New York, NY 10025
(212) 316-2492
Clients: Actors, Actresses. Represents all types in all areas. Accepts materials. No phone calls.

LLOYD KOLMER
MANAGEMENT CO.
Lloyd Kolmer
65 West 55th Street
New York, NY 10019
(212) 582-4735
Clients: Actors, Actresses, Newscasters, Media Personalities, Sports Personalities.

SHARON KUTNER
P.O. Box 728
Tenafly, NJ 07670
(212) 252-4997
Clients: Actors/Actresses, Children, Teenagers, Variety/Comedy Performers, Offbeat Types, Twins, Triplets (babies–adults) Photos & resumes accepted. No phone calls.

JENNIFER LAMBERT
22 East 49th Street, 7th Floor
New York, NY 10017
(212) 315-0754

Clients: Actors, Actresses, Children, Teenagers, Musical Performers, Composers, Recording Artists, Orchestras, Bands.

THE LYONS GROUP
Michael Lyons
505 8th Avenue, Suite 12A
New York, NY 10018
(212) 239-3539
www.lyonsgroupny.com
Clients: Actors, Actresses, Children, Teenagers, Sports Personalities (Athletes), Models (Fashion & Commercial).

M.A.P. (MANAGEMENT
FOR ARTISTS AND
PRODUCTION, LLC)
Ted Alexander, Hans Jent
127 Fulton Street, Penthouse
New York, NY 10038
(212) 571-6644
mappenthouse.com;
mapmodels.com; mapmen.com
Clients: Actors/Actresses, Artists, Authors, Choreographers, Photographers, Set Designers, Costume Designers.

MJC ENTERTAINMENT
Michael J. Cohen
443 Greenwich Street, 5th Floor
New York, NY 10013
(212) 965-8432
Clients: Actors, Actresses, Children, Teenagers, Variety/Comedy Performers.

MM MANAGEMENT (NCOPM)
Melanie McLaughlin
331 West 57th Street,
    Box 233
New York, NY 10019
(212) 830-0347

J. MITCHELL MANAGEMENT
(NCOPM)
Jeff Mitchell
440 Park Avenue South,
    11th Floor
New York, NY 10016
(212) 679-3550
www.jmmtalent.com
Clients: Actors, Actresses, Children, Teenagers. Phone calls for appointments are welcome for kids, ages five–18. Others please mail picture & resume.

MORGIT MANAGEMENT
(NCOPM)
Margaret Karaszek
(516) 358-7056

Clients: Actors, Actresses, Children/Teenagers. Contact by e-mail or phone.

NEZOD MANAGEMENT GROUP
Reginald Murray
1006 Caton Avenue, Suite D3
Brooklyn, NY 11218
(718) 287-8140
www.nezod.com
Clients: Actors, Actresses, Directors, Producers, Writers, Newscasters, Media Personalities, Sports Personalities. Music Performers, Composers, Recording Artists, Orchestras, Bands.

ONLINE TALENT GROUP
Kim Matuka
276 Fifth Avenue, Suite 204
New York, NY 10001
(212) 532-5923
The New York Office of Warning Management in Los Angeles. A boutique bicoastal management company, with clients that include established actors, young adults, comediennes and recording artists. Also beauty department and selected kids department. (See also Warning Management under California.)

RICHARD ORNSTEIN &
ASSOCIATES
Richard Ornstein
P.O. Box 1
Freeport, New York 11520
(516) 623-8888
Clients: Actors, Actresses, Newscasters, Media Personalities, Sports Personalities, Musical Performers, Composers, Recording Artists, Orchestras, Bands. Representing Joe Franklin, Jack LaLanne, Captain Lou Albano, Freddie Scott, Whitey Ford, "Wildman" Jack Armstrong, and other celebrities, including police officers and fire fighters.

KEN PARK MANAGEMENT
(TMA)
Ken Park
401 Washington Street,
    2nd Floor
New York, NY 10013
(212) 226-3731
Clients: Actors, Actresses, Children, Teenagers, Variety/Comedy Performers, Music Performers, Composers, Recording Artists, Orchestras, Bands.

CATHY PARKER MANAGEMENT,
INC. (NCOPM)
Cathy Parker
P.O. Box 716
Voorhees, NJ 08043
(856) 309-7087
*Clients: Actors, Actresses,
Children, Teenagers, Musical
Performers. Please do not call.
Will accept headshots & post-
cards only. No reels or CDs.*

ROGER PAUL MANAGEMENT
*(See Spellman-Paul
Management.)*

PEARL MANAGEMENT
(NCOPM)
Marvin Pearl
1650 Broadway, Suite 508
New York, NY 10019
(212) 399-7224
*Clients: Actors, Actresses.
Looking for experienced serious
actors with credits and/or
younger (18–24) actors with a
great look—very talented actors,
a prerequisite. Work in T.V.,
film, theatre, commercials,
voiceovers, etc.*

PERSONA MANAGEMENT
(NCOPM)
Lori Danziger
40 East 9th Street, Suite 11J
New York, NY 10003
(212) 674-7078
*Clients: Actors, Actresses
(five–young adults). Photo
submission accepted only. (See
also listing under California.)*

PRINCIPATO-YOUNG
ENTERTAINMENT (TMA)
Brian Steinberg
100 West 57th Street, Suite 21E
New York, NY 10019
(212) 582-4255
*Clients: Actors, Actresses,
Directors, Producers, Writers,
Variety/Comedy Performers.
(See also listing under California.)*

RKS MANAGEMENT, LTD.
(NCOPM)
Rochelle Kishner Shulman
975 Park Avenue, Suite 10C
New York, NY 10028
(212) 717-2716
*Clients: Actors, Actresses
(up to age 25), Children,
Teenagers, for print, stage,
feature films, T.V., commercials,
voiceovers. Accepts clients
from all parts of the country.*

RAMOS MANAGEMENT
(NCOPM)
Vic Ramos, Sandy Erickson
49 West 9th Street, 5B
New York, NY 10011
(212) 473-2610
Clients: Actors, Actresses.

CHARLES RAPP ENTERPRISES,
INC. (NCOPM)
Howard Rapp
1650 Broadway, Suite 1410
New York, NY 10019
(212) 247-6646
*Clients: Actors, Actresses,
Directors, Producers, Writers,
Variety/Comedy Performers,
Musical Performers, Composers,
Recording Artists, Orchestras,
Bands.*

ROSALEE PRODUCTIONS
(NCOPM)
Philip Rose
137 West 78th Street,
   Garden Suite
New York, NY 10024
(212) 877-5538
*Clients: Actors, Actresses,
including Teenagers.*

ROSENBERG & ASSOCIATES
LTD. (NCOPM)
Joan M. Rosenberg
3 Adam Street
Floral Park, NY 11001
(212) 534-0045
Cell: (516) 647-4766
LA: (323) 656-5822
*Clients: Actors, Actresses,
Writers. Interested in young talent
(15–22) willing to work in NY & LA.*

RICHARD ROSENWALD
ASSOCIATES
Richard S. Rosenwald
300 West 55th Street, Suite 5Y
New York, NY 10019
(212) 245-4515
*Clients: Actors, Actresses,
including Teenagers, Directors,
Producers, Writers.*

SERENDIPITY ENTERTAINMENT
& MANAGEMENT
Gabriella Messina (Owner,
VP East Coast Talent)
P.O. Box 4019
Wantagh, NY 11793
(516) 221-4825
*Clients: Actors/Actresses,
Directors, Producers,
Writers, Children, Teenagers,
Variety/ Comedy Performers.
Boutique management*

*company. Interviews by appoint-
ment only. Currently seeking
teens/young adults (17–22) for
film/T.V./theatre/commercials.
Strong theatrical training preferred.
Photos/tape/resume by mail only.
Attends showcases. Also represents celebrity look-a-likes. (See
also listing under California.)*

SINCLAIR MANAGEMENT
Judith Lesley
95 Christopher Street, Suite 6F
New York, NY 10014
(212) 366-9400
*Clients: Actors, Actresses
(ages four–seniors). Prefer union
actors. May send pictures &
resumes. Do not stop by.*

SPELLMAN-PAUL
MANAGEMENT
Roger Paul, Chris Spellman
1650 Broadway, Suite 705
New York, NY 10019
New York: (212) 262-0008
Los Angeles: (323) 871-1011
*Clients: Actors, Actresses,
Writers, Variety/Comedy
Performers. Interested in clients
who are driven and easy to work
with. No divas. Company goal is
to develop talent, seeking
teenagers/young adults.*

STEINBERG TALENT
MANAGEMENT GROUP
Jason Steinberg
1560 Broadway, Suite 405
New York, NY 10036
(212) 843-3200
www.steinbergtalent.com
*Clients: Actors, Actresses,
Directors, Producers, Writers,
Newscasters, Media Personalities,
Sports Personalities, Variety/
Comedy Performers, Animators.
Specializes in comedic talent
for film, T.V., and commercials.*

SUNDANCE PRODUCTIONS,
INC. (NCOPM)
Roseanne Kirk
165 West 46th Street, Suite 412
New York, NY 10036-2501
(212) 489-2203

SUZELLE ENTERPRISES
(NCOPM)
Suzanne Schachter
853 7th Avenue, #8D
New York, NY 10019
(212) 397-2047
*Clients: Actors, Actresses,
Directors, Producers, Writers,*

Children, Teenagers, Newscasters, Media Personalities, Sports Personalities, Variety/Comedy Performers, Music Performers, Composers, Recording Artists, Orchestras, Bands. Office in Los Angeles (818) 995-6000; Office in Mexico City 011-5255-5523-3604.

THJ MANAGEMENT
T. Harding Jones
405 East 54th Street
New York, NY 10022
(212) 758-9093
Clients: Actors, Actresses, including Teenagers, Directors, Producers with credits, Newcasters and Media Personalities. Prefer at least one industry referral. Seeking established actors, particularly those with Meisner backgrounds, who wish to make career changes and adjustments, television/movie actors who seek a return to theatre or want to redirect their careers, and successful theatre actors who wish to do movies and television. Clients on both coasts.

TMT ENTERTAINMENT GROUP
(NCOPM)
Tina Thor
648 Broadway, Suite 1002
New York, NY 10012
(212) 477-6047
Clients: Actors, Actresses, Directors, Producers, Writers.

TANNEN'S TALENT AND MODEL MANAGEMENT
Lynne Tannen
77 Tarrytown Road
White Plains, NY 10607
(914) 946-0900
www.tannenstalent.com
Clients: Actors, Actresses, Children, Teenagers, (infants to young adults).

TERRIFIC TALENT ASSOCIATES, INC. (NCOPM)
Marianne Leone
419 Park Avenue South, Suite 1009
New York, NY 10016
(212) 689-2800
Clients: Actors, Actresses (ages three to young adults).

TSU TSU UNLIMITED
Tsu Tsu Stanton
145 West 12th Street, Suite #1-4
New York, NY 10011
(212) 989-3424
Clients: Actors/Actresses, Directors, Producers, Writers, Children/Teenagers, Variety/Comedy Performers, Music Performers/Composers/Recording Artists Orchestras/Bands, Artists/Choreographers.

VESTA TALENT SERVICES
(NCOPM)
Jacqueline Tellalian
460 Second Avenue, Suite 11F
New York, NY 10016
(212) 685-7151
Clients: Actors, Actresses, ages 17 and up. Specializes in actors with disabilities.

W.S. MANAGEMENT
William Schill
302A West 12th Street, #183
New York, NY 10014
(212) 924-4982
Clients: Actors/Actresses, Children/Teenagers. Accepts photos/resumes by mail only

WILHELMINA KIDS & TEENS TALENT MANAGEMENT
Marlene Wallach (President),
Teri Bader-Bostaji (Manager);
Kim Dargenio (Manager);
Melissa Farnum (Assistant)
300 Park Avenue South, 2nd Floor
New York, NY 10010
(212) 473-0700
Clients: Babies, Children, Teenagers for Print, T.V., Film, Voiceovers, Commercials. Accepts photos, resumes by mail only. Do not phone, fax, or visit. Attends showcases.

YOUNG TALENT, INC. (NCOPM)
Tobe Gibson
P.O. Box 792
Hartsdale, NY 10530
(914) 948-4744
1 (800) 947-4950
Clients: Actors, Actresses, Children, Teenagers, Young Adults. Specializes in commercials, prime time T.V., films, soap operas, print ads, Broadway theatre.

ZIEMBA TALENT & ASSOCIATES
244 West 54th Street, #1201A
New York, NY 10019
(212) 707-8500
Clients: Actors, Actresses, Children, Teenagers, Variety/Comedy Performers. Please do not phone or visit. We accept referrals through casting directors. Do not send demo reels without a request.

MARILYN ZITNER MANAGEMENT
Marilyn Zitner
240 West 35th Street
New York, NY 10001
(212) 643-0111
Clients: Actors, Actresses, Children, Teenagers for T.V., Film, Theatre, Voiceovers, Commercials.

Pennsylvania

STAR TALENT MANAGEMENT
(NCOPM)
Lois Miller
682 North Brookside Road
Allentown, PA 18106
(610) 366-1700
Clients: Actors, Actresses, Children, Teenagers. Please send photos & resumes with S.A.S.E. or call for interview—works with NY & CA agencies and Philadelphia Casting Directors.

South Carolina

METEOR GROUP
(NCOPM)
James L. Dooley
266 West Coleman Blvd., Suite 102
Mount Pleasant, SC 29464
(843) 856-0544
Clients: Actors, Actresses, Children, Teenagers.

16 Joining the Unions:

The Why, When, and How

BY MICHÈLE LaRUE

For many performers, "being union" means being professional. But getting your membership card *does not* automatically make you a mature pro, and it certainly doesn't guarantee you work. Like any important career move, joining a performers' union requires careful research and deliberation—and it also helps to be the right person in the right place at the right time. Certainly, "How do you get in the union?" is a critical question. But before you tackle that "how," you should very carefully study the "why" and "when."

We interviewed representatives from the largest of the several performers' unions: Actors' Equity Association (AEA, which protects principals, chorus, and stage managers in live theatre), Screen Actors Guild (SAG, whose jurisdiction is film as well as many television programs and commercials), and the American Federation of Television and Radio Artists (AFTRA, which represents performers on radio and TV, audio and video tape, and sound recordings).

Two other major unions are the American Guild of Musical Artists (AGMA, for performers in opera, dance, oratorios, concerts, and recitals) and the American Guild of Variety Artists (AGVA, for singers, dancers, and comedians in revue or variety productions or venues). SAG, AFTRA, and Equity have for many years been discussing mergers, but until these complicated proceedings have been negotiated, each union will continue to abide by its own membership rules.

THE "WHY"

The first reason to join a union is professionalism. Equity membership assures your potential employers and co-workers that you are serious about the theatre, that acting or stage managing is not interim employment—it's your profession. Second, union contracts set salary minimums that are usually higher than those volunteered by nonunion producers. They include benefits almost never offered outside the union, like health insurance coverage and pension points.

As collective bargaining agencies, unions exist to promote and protect their members' welfare. They monitor employers to ensure that agreed-upon monies and benefits are received on time; that performers work in safe, sanitary environments and get ample rest; that they are compensated for extra rehearsal and performance time; and that they are respected by producers, directors, and fellow members.

For the health of the unions and the profession as a whole, unions discipline their members, too. Thereby unions guarantee employers that their investment in union performers will secure professional behavior—no unlearned lines, no late arrivals or no-shows for rehearsals or performances, no physical, drug, or alcohol abuse on the job.

Each union has its own membership "perks" as well. Equity, SAG, and AFTRA communicate with their members via newspapers, magazines, and websites, and arrange professional seminars throughout the year. The three jointly manage the Actors' Federal Credit Union, which is sympathetic to performers' needs and provides banking services and some shopper discount plans.

Unions support the welfare of the theatre community by contributing to national organizations like the Actors' Fund of America and Broadway Cares/Equity Fights AIDS. Equity members frequently are "comped" for live shows. In New York and Los Angeles, SAG's Film Society offers sizeable discounts on screenings of new features, and SAG and AFTRA offer equipment and instruction in on-camera and film performance. Additional services may be available in your area's union offices.

THE "WHEN"

If you're right out of college or conservatory, you may dream of quick validation of your talent through union membership. But even if you're precocious—or lucky— enough to get an immediate offer, think twice before taking it.

If you join Equity at too young an age, for example, you can price yourself out of the market. The number of young performers far exceeds the number of suitable roles for them, and those roles are generally easy to fill cheaply with young non-Equity actors. Nonunion companies offer a great deal of work, and the more experience you have before you "go union," the better your chances of employment as a union member.

Because joining the unions is an expensive process and a long-term commitment, you should also be certain that acting is what *you*—not your mother or great uncle—really want for yourself. Before you rush to join a union, experience the business in as many ways as you can—through classes, live showcases, and student films, and by speaking to more seasoned actors about the reality of what they face by trying to make a living in this business. You should have no doubt whatsoever that acting is your career choice and not just a hobby. And make sure that you develop some "civilian" skills, too, so that you'll have another source of income to fall back on.

THE "HOW"

Each union has its own membership qualifications and procedures. We'll begin with the least complex:

AFTRA

Founded in 1937, AFTRA represents nearly 80,000 members, including actors, newscasters, announcers, disk jockeys, sportscasters, talk show hosts, and recording artists. They work in radio, on sound recordings, and on live and taped television. These performers are served by a national board of 125 members from every geographic area and every category of membership, and by approximately thirty local offices across the nation.

New members pay a one-time initiation fee, plus dues covering the first dues period. As of November 1, 2003, the initiation fee was $1,300 and minimum dues for the first six-month dues period were $60.90. After joining, a member's dues are based on his or her earnings in AFTRA's jurisdiction during the prior

year. Dues are billed each May 1 and November 1, but may vary throughout the country. It's important to contact your local office for specific rates.

A performer may join AFTRA, with or without a job offer, by applying to his or her local office.

SAG

Founded in 1933, SAG is a national union representing 120,000 performers working in films (including theatrical, TV, industrial, educational, and experimental), commercials, and music videos. In some cases, TV shows on tape go to SAG as well. Upon joining, the eligible performer pays SAG's initiation fee of $1,356 (as of February 2004), plus the first semi-annual basic dues payment of $50.00. Additional dues are assessed at a rate of 1.5 percent of SAG income up to $250,000.

An actor satisfying any of the following qualifications may join SAG by making an appointment with its membership department:

1 Entering SAG via employment as a principal performer requires proof of employment or prospective employment by a SAG signatory company in a principal or speaking role in a SAG film, videotape, TV program, or commercial. You may apply as soon as you have your contract in hand or, if you prefer, after you have completed the work. Your proof of employment will be a signed contract, a payroll check or check stub, or a letter from the company. This document must include your name and Social Security number, the name of the production or commercial, the salary, and the date(s) of employment.

2 Entering via employment as a background performer requires proof of employment as a SAG-covered background player at full SAG rates and conditions for a minimum of three workdays. The employer must be signed to a SAG Background Players Agreement for a SAG film, videotape, TV program, or commercial. Proof of employment must be in the form of a signed employment voucher, plus a payroll check or check stub. (SAG's background entry requirements were being revised at the time this book went to press, so be sure to contact the union's membership department for the current guidelines.)

3 If you are already a paid-up member of an affiliated performers' union for a period of at least one year and have worked at least once as a principal in that union's jurisdiction, you are eligible for SAG membership. Affiliates are Equity, AFTRA, AGMA, AGVA, the Hebrew Actors' Union (HAU), the Guild of Italian American Actors (GIAA), the former Screen Extras Guild (SEG), and Canada's ACTRA.

ACTORS' EQUITY

The oldest of the three major U.S. actors' unions, Actors' Equity Association was founded in 1913. A national organization, it represents 45,000 legitimate principals, chorus members, and stage managers. Equity's initiation fee, $1,100 (as of April 1, 2004), must be paid within a maximum two-year period. The amount may be reduced by up to 50 percent, however, for those who are already members of AGMA, HAU, GIAA, or Canadian Equity. Dues consist of two components: basic dues, payable in $59 installments each May and November, and working dues (a small percentage of salary), which are deducted from weekly gross earnings.

You can "go Equity" in three ways:

1 If you are offered an Equity contract, you are eligible to join the union upon its signing. Membership applications are valid only during the term of the contract, however. Some contract types also have a length-of-employment requirement before an application becomes valid.

2 Participation in Equity's Membership Candidate Program allows nonprofessionals to credit their work in an Equity theatre toward eventual Equity membership. After securing a position at a participating Equity theatre, you may register as a candidate by completing the registration form and submitting it to Equity with the registration fee, which will be deducted from your initiation fee when you join the union. After a total of fifty weeks of work at one or more participating theatres, a registered candidate may join Equity.

3 Finally, Equity accepts membership applications from those who are members of a sister performing-arts union, such as AFTRA or SAG. You must prove yourself to have been a member in good standing of the sister union for at least one year, and you must have worked as a performer under that union's jurisdiction.

LEAVING THE UNIONS

If, after all, you decide that professional performance is not for you, there are mechanisms for temporary or permanent withdrawal.

Actors who have been AFTRA members in good standing for at least a year—and who don't intend to work or seek work in AFTRA's jurisdiction for at least one year—can request Honorable Withdrawal status in writing. You will not be charged dues during your period of withdrawal, although if you work or seek work in AFTRA's jurisdiction, your membership will be reactivated and current dues will be charged. You can reactivate your membership at any time, but if you do so before the one-year period is up, you will be responsible for any unbilled dues.

SAG has two means of going on inactive status: Honorable Withdrawal and Suspended Payment. Each must be requested by applying in writing to the membership department prior to either dues period (May 1 or November 1). The applicant must have been a SAG member for at least eighteen consecutive months, an active member for at least one year, and after becoming inactive, must remain so for at least one year. Inactive members may *not* seek employment under SAG's jurisdiction and therefore are precluded from attending open calls and auditioning.

Honorable Withdrawal from SAG is granted to those whose dues are paid in full. Upon returning to active status, the member pays only the dues owed for the current period. Suspended Payment permits withdrawal by those whose dues are not paid up (but no more than two periods behind) at the time they apply. When they return to active membership, they must pay the outstanding dues, plus the current period's dues.

Similarly, Equity offers Temporary Withdrawal status for paid-up members in good standing, and Suspended Payment status for members who cannot pay their dues. Each is granted to members who request it in writing and each can extend to any length of time—although after five years, the member loses first rights to his or her professional name. A return to active status requires a $25 reinstatement fee, plus the payment of dues for the current period and any previously unpaid dues. Equity members are forbidden to work in non-Equity productions while on Temporary Withdrawal or Suspended Payment.

Equity members under the age of fourteen, however, may request juvenile withdrawal status. This allows young performers to participate in school and community theatre projects, although they are not allowed to work in a non-Equity venue or as a nonprofessional at an Equity theatre.

SUMMING UP

If performing is to be your career—and if you're a capable performer—someday the unions will be an important part of your life. In preparing for that time, you should understand what membership will require of you and do for you.

Unions, Guilds & Associations

Los Angeles Based

ACTORS' EQUITY
ASSOCIATION (AEA)
5757 Wilshire Blvd., Suite 1
Los Angeles, CA 90036
(323) 634-1750
www.actorsequity.com
John Holly, Western Regional
    Director

AMERICAN FEDERATION OF
MUSICIANS (AFM)
3550 Wilshire Blvd., #1900
Los Angeles, CA 90010
(213) 251-4510
www.afm.com

AMERICAN FEDERATION
OF TELEVISION & RADIO
ARTISTS (AFTRA)
5757 Wilshire Blvd., Suite 900
Los Angeles, CA 90036
(323) 634-8100
www.aftra.com
John Russum, LA Executive
    Director

AMERICAN GUILD OF VARIETY
ARTISTS (AGVA)
4741 Laurel Canyon Blvd.,
    Suite 208
North Hollywood, CA 91607
(818) 508-9984

AMERICAN SOCIETY OF
COMPOSERS, AUTHORS
AND PUBLISHERS (ASCAP)
7920 West Sunset Blvd.,
    Third Floor
Los Angeles, CA 90046
(323) 883-1000
(800) 95-ASCAP
www.ascap.com

ASSOCIATION OF TALENT
AGENTS (ATA)
9255 Sunset Blvd., Suite 930
Los Angeles, CA 90069
(310) 274-0628
www.agentassociation.com
Karen Stuart, Executive Director

BROADCAST MUSIC INC. (BMI)
8730 Sunset Blvd.,
    Third Floor West
West Hollywood, CA 90069
(310) 659-9109

CASTING SOCIETY OF
AMERICA (CSA)
606 North Larchmont Blvd.,
    Suite 4-B
Los Angeles, CA 90004
(323) 463-1925
www.castingsociety.com
Gary M. Zuckerbrod, President

COMMERCIAL CASTING
DIRECTOR'S ASSOCIATION
(CCDA)
Big House Studios
4420 Lankershim Blvd.
North Hollywood, CA 91602
(818) 752-7100
Jeff Gerrard, President

DIRECTORS GUILD OF
AMERICA, INC. (DGA)
7920 Sunset Blvd.
Los Angeles, CA 90046
(310) 289-2000
www.dga.com

IATSE WEST COAST OFFICE
10045 Riverside Drive
Toluca Lake, CA 91602
(818) 980-3499

INTERNATIONAL
CINEMATOGRAPHERS GUILD
7715 Sunset Blvd.
Los Angeles, CA 90046
(323) 876-0160

NATIONAL CONFERENCE
OF PERSONAL
MANAGERS
P.O. Box 609
Palm Desert, CA 92261-0609
(760) 341-1565
Candee Barshop, Western
    Executive Director

PRODUCERS GUILD OF
AMERICA (PGA)
8530 Wilshire Blvd.,
    Suite 450
Beverly Hills, CA 90211
(310) 358-9020
info@producersguild.org

SCREEN ACTORS GUILD
(SAG)
5757 Wilshire Blvd.
Los Angeles, CA 90036-3600
(323) 954-1600

SESAC
501 Santa Monica Blvd.,
    Suite 450
Santa Monica, CA 90401
(310) 393-9679

STUNTWOMEN'S
ASSOCIATION OF MOTION
PICTURES
12457 Ventura Blvd., #208
Studio City, CA 91604-2411
(818) 762-0907
www.stuntwomen.com
Jane Austin, President

WRITERS GUILD OF
AMERICA WEST, INC.
(WGAW)
7000 West Third Street
Los Angeles, CA 90048
(323) 951-4000
(800) 548-4532
www.wga.com

New York Based

ACTORS' EQUITY
ASSOCIATION (AEA)
165 West 46th Street
New York, NY 10036
(212) 869-8530
www.actorsequity.com
Alan Eisenberg, Executive
    Director

AMERICAN FEDERATION
OF MUSICIANS (AFM)
NEW YORK—NATIONAL
1501 Broadway, Suite 600
New York, NY 10036
(212) 869-1330
www.afm.org

AMERICAN FEDERATION
OF TELEVISION & RADIO
ARTISTS (AFTRA)
260 Madison Avenue,
    Seventh Floor
New York, NY 10016
(212) 532-0800
www.aftra.com
Stephen Burrow, NY Executive
    Director

AMERICAN GUILD OF
MUSICAL ARTISTS
(AGMA)
1430 Broadway,
    14th Floor
New York, NY 10018
(212) 265-3687
www.musicalartists.org
Alan S. Gordon, Executive
    Director

AMERICAN GUILD OF
VARIETY ARTISTS (AGVA)
363 Seventh Avenue, 1
    7th Floor
New York, NY 10001
(212) 675-1003

AMERICAN SOCIETY OF
COMPOSERS, AUTHORS AND
PUBLISHERS (ASCAP)
One Lincoln Plaza
New York, NY 10023
(212) 621-6000
(800) 95-ASCAP
www.ascap.com

ASSOCIATED ACTORS AND
ARTISTS OF AMERICA (4 A'S)
165 West 46th Street, Room 500
New York, NY 10036
(212) 869-0358

BMI FOUNDATION, INC.
320 West 57th Street
New York, NY 10019
(212) 586-2000

CASTING SOCIETY OF
AMERICA (CSA)
 (212) 868-1260
Bernard Telsey, NY Vice
    President, C.S.A.

DIRECTORS GUILD OF
AMERICA, INC. (DGA)
110 West 57th Street
New York, NY 10019
(212) 581-0370
www.dga.org

GUILD OF ITALIAN
AMERICAN ACTORS (GIAA)
(ITALIAN ACTORS UNION)
31 East 32nd Street, 12th Floor
New York, NY 10016-5509
(212) 420-6590
www.nygiaa.org
Lea Serra, President
Guy Palumbo, Vice President

HISPANIC ORGANIZATION OF
LATIN ACTORS (HOLA)
107 Suffolk Street, Suite 302
New York, NY 10002
(212) 253-1015
www.hellohola.org

INTERNATIONAL ALLIANCE
OF THEATRICAL STAGE
EMPLOYEES (IATSE)
1430 Broadway, 20th Floor
New York, NY 10018
(212) 730-1770

INTERNATIONAL
CINEMATOGRAPHERS GUILD
80 Eighth Avenue, 14th Floor
New York, NY 10011
(212) 647-7300

NATIONAL ASSOCIATION OF
TALENT REPRESENTATIVES
(NATR)
315 West 57th Street, #408
New York, NY 10019
(212) 541-5250
Philip Adelman, President

SCREEN ACTORS GUILD (SAG)
360 Madison Avenue,
    12th Floor
New York, NY 10017
(212) 944-1030
Jae Je Simmons, NY Executive
    Director

SESAC
152 West 57th Street, 57th Floor
New York, NY 10019
(212) 586-3450

SOCIETY OF STAGE
DIRECTORS &
CHOREOGRAPHERS
1501 Broadway, Suite 1701
New York, NY 10036
(212) 391-1070

WRITERS GUILD OF AMERICA
EAST, INC. (WGAEAST)
555 West 57th Street,
    Suite 1230
New York, NY 10019
(212) 767-7800
www.wgaeast.org

AFTRA-SAG Federal Credit Union

www.aftrasagfcu.org 818-562-3400 or 800-826-6946

WE UNDERSTAND PERFORMERS NEEDS:

- Coogan and Personal Service Corporation Accounts
- Loan Qualification for Unusual Income Patterns
- Residual Direct Deposit

Savings and Checking Accounts, Consumer and Real Estate Loans for AFTRA, SAG and AGVA members and their families.

EQUAL HOUSING LENDER

NCUA

Financial Performance to Build a Career

ACTORS: Not happy with the roles you're getting?
Make your own movie.

Do you know that

SAGINDIE

offers

Signatory Workshops

2nd Wednesday of every month from 6 – 8 p.m. at **SAG LA Branch,** 5757 Wilshire Blvd., 8th Floor
SAG NY Branch, 360 Madison Ave., 12th Floor

SAG Theatrical representatives will walk you through the signatory process of SAG Low Budget Agreements from start to finish.

LEARN WHICH AGREEMENT IS RIGHT FOR YOUR FILM

Don't miss this opportunity to have all your questions answered.

How can we you make your movie?

Space is limited and workshops fill up quickly so

RSVP NOW: online at
www.sagindie.org
or
LA: 323.549.6064
NY: 212.827.1481

TO ADVERTISE IN THE NEXT

BACKSTAGE®/BACK STAGE WEST®

ACTORS HANDBOOK

PLEASE CALL

WEST ■   ■ EAST
Back Stage West   Back Stage
Advertising   Advertising
5055 Wilshire Blvd., 5th fl.   770 Broadway, 4th floor
Los Angeles, CA 90036   New York, NY 10003
323.525.2225   646.654.5700

17 Making Monologues Matter:

Choosing the Right Material for Your Audition

BY LEONARD JACOBS

Imagine the perfectly prepared actor at an audition: quality pictures and résumés in hand, knowledge of unions, contracts, and the business of "the business" clearly in mind.

While that's great, having a well-researched, well-rehearsed, highly varied portfolio of strong, attention-grabbing monologues that are deliverable on demand is vitally important.

Finding standout monologues that really work can drive the most driven of actors to distraction. Knowing who might ask to see a monologue—casting directors? directors? producers?—when and why they might ask for one, and what they glean from witnessing one are complex questions that have long bedeviled the actor.

Once, at least, there were ground rules: Always have a few one- to two-minute monologues—a comedic and a dramatic piece—ready. Always do your monologue at the top of the audition. Always deliver your monologue toward a fixed spot in the room. And just *do* the monologue—don't explain it, excuse it, or defend it.

Alas, only that last maxim still holds true. Beyond that, there's not one correct way to go anymore, because every auditor works differently. Some directors will request a monologue mid-audition; others may ask for one at the end in order to sense your range or to gauge how you cope with being given an adjustment. Many casting people will never ask for one—many despise them—and while you can always offer one, whether this results in something positive for you is about as certain as next week's weather.

So just know, from the outset, that all the work you'll put into finding, rehearsing, and polishing your monologues may matter little when it comes to getting the roles you want. Still, getting caught without the right monologue is to be umbrella-less in the rain. New guidelines are needed—up-to-date hints and clues for moving through monologue mania.

MINING FOR MONOLOGUES: READ, READ, READ

The most difficult part of making it through the monologue morass is finding a selection that displays your acting chops. Even if you think this is a cliché, it's true:

reading plays (and screenplays) on a constant basis is the most reliable way to discover effective monologues, and all the shortcuts—such as dashing into your local bookstore and snatching up anthologies of plays you haven't read—are short-term solutions, doomed to failure. Directors and casting directors are smart: they can tell who has done their "monologue homework" and who has merely memorized and moved on.

Directors and casting directors, in fact, are looking for context—a sense that you understand why the monologue you have chosen was written, which play and scene it came from, and what the emotional journey was that led up to it. As Jordan Thaler, head of casting for The Joseph Papp Public Theater in New York, says, "When the actor is learning a monologue, they function as their own director." It's true! So ask yourself these questions: How does the monologue fit into the play? How does the monologue work when extracted from the play? What are the differences in the rhythm of the monologue when it stands alone?

Most important of all, get into the world of the play—don't stand outside of it. If you emotionally "check out," what's to compel the director or casting director who's watching you to emotionally "check in"?

MISSIONARY MONOLOGUES: AIM FOR APPROPRIATENESS

Many actors learn new monologues right before auditioning for specific roles, industry folk, or companies. One might assume that such monologues are always appropriate, right?

Yes and no. Appropriateness varies from audition to audition in terms of what a director or casting director will want to see. Some might be open to seeing a monologue from the show that's being cast. Some will immediately knock you out of contention if you try this. And you won't always know ahead of time which key will open the magic door to success.

How, then, to have the best shot? Vary your monologue diet. Director Russell Treyz says he knows an actor from the regional theatre circuit with "six monologues in his pocket, ready to go at any time, from Shakespeare to contemporary," and he's now trying to get his menu up to twelve. Why so many? "Because when a director says, 'Can you give me another color?' he can."

Now, getting a dozen monologues ready involves more than mere memorization—indeed, if you really want to make sure you can enter the world of your monologue every time you present it, you'll have to make sure to invest some emotional time with the piece.

You may want to do some additional research to determine whether a particular monologue is "appropriate."

For example, if you're auditioning for a theatre company, find its mission statement. Every not-for-profit theatre group has one—a written proclamation outlining artistic beliefs, a rationale for why the company does the shows it does. If you're auditioning for a group that specializes in the classics, chances are that barging in with your *Glengarry Glen Ross* monologue won't likely work.

If your audition is for a specific production, you can also try familiarizing yourself with the director's work—and if the play is published, read it! Imagine the character(s) you'd be appropriate for, and then pick a monologue that comes closest, in terms of tone and style, to the part you'd like to play. You want every opportunity to show that you genuinely desire the role.

A final tip: find out which monologues your fellow actors are auditioning with. If you can discern a trend—say, monologues from the same play, playwright, or even on one thematic subject—steer clear. And be savvy about subject matter. A piece about rape, murder, and incest is more likely to bruise your audition than burnish it, especially if it's the first time you're being seen. The exception might be when you're auditioning for something requiring brutality—a play like *Extremities,* for example. But even then, directors or casting directors will probably want to see range more than rage. Give an "educated" audition.

CLASSIFYING THE CLASSICS, CAPTURING THE CONTEMPORARY

So now you've read every American play since Clyde Fitch, and you've selected some monologues—maybe four or more—that you've memorized, burrowed into, rehearsed, and can deliver on command. But you realize that all of them are modern.

Don't forget the classics! While the old adage that actors should always have a classical as well as a contemporary monologue isn't hard and fast anymore, let's face it: It's one thing to ace a David Mamet aria with the right scatological staccato; it's quite another thing to put iambic pentameter to the pavement.

But here again, make your creativity work for you. If your *Measure for Measure* monologue is mediocre, don't do it. "Classic" means many things to many people. Take the time to read some T.S. Eliot; give Shaw or Somerset Maugham a chance. Above all, don't be adverse to verse.

If you're an experienced classicist, meanwhile, and if you truly believe your "Tomorrow and tomorrow and tomorrow" speech is insightful, rich, and galvanizing, don't avoid it, particularly if you've actually done *Macbeth.* Says Jeffrey Horowitz, artistic director of the Manhattan-based Theatre for a New Audience, "The monologue seen many times before is not necessarily going to act as a strike against the actor if done well. It's how well the monologue is done—not *which* monologue is done—that's crucial."

MONOLOGUE MÉLANGE: PUTTING PEN TO PERSONALITY

More and more actors are creating their own monologues. These come in two basic forms. First, there are monologues cobbled together from dialogue bits in which the other characters are "stripped out" of the text (which is then radically restructured). Second, there are monologues conjured from whole cloth, about a minute long and structured like a one-act—perhaps even developed through the techniques employed by performance artists.

If your experience as a writer is limited, you may want to test out your first original monologues on trusted friends and colleagues rather than barreling into an audition with your first creation. And remember, monologues are often held in high regard because there's a true art to writing them. If you're going to create one, take steps to ensure that you have the skills to do so.

Finally, if you're going to craft your own monologue, don't forget to think twice about subject matter. While waxing lyrical about the birds and the trees may be old hat, complaining ruefully about your past failed relationships is perhaps even worse. Providing that thing called TMI—Too Much Information—takes the focus away from your talent. So while it's true that you should write what you know, keep in mind that some of what you write might be wrong.

TO LOOK OR NOT TO LOOK, THAT IS THE QUESTION

Okay, so you're in the door, your monologues are at the ready, and the clock is ticking. The floor is yours; the attention is on you. Where should *your* attention go?

Again, it depends on whom you're auditioning for. One director known for producing outdoor Shakespeare might look directly at you—and want you to look directly back—since doing environmental theatre often means that performer-spectator interaction is key to the action. Other directors will refuse to engage even slightly in your audition process. That means you can look high, low, east, or west, but don't look at them while delivering your monologue. Simply ask what's preferred before you begin.

And you should understand why in either case. New York-based film and television casting director Todd Thaler, for example, notes, "some casting directors say 'don't use me' because it puts a layer of added responsibility on them to act appropriately and to respond to what the actor is doing." At the same time, ordering the actor to look out into nothingness runs the risk of generating an audition that's presentational, too broad, and too theatrical. So for an audition for an on-screen role, the goal may be to force you to be as natural as possible. If the audition is for a legit role, the director or casting director may want you to focus elsewhere.

MANO A MONOLOGUE

In the end, remember that your monologue must not only illuminate your talent, but impart something about you: the artist and the individual.

In fact, consider this amusing anecdote from Jeffrey Horowitz: "I used to be an actor, and the one Broadway show I did was a play called *The Merchant*. It was directed by John Dexter and starred Zero Mostel—a rewritten version of *The Merchant of Venice*—and I was asked to fly in from California on the red-eye to audition. So there I am, it's 10 a.m. on this Broadway stage, and I did my audition, and they said, 'Thank you.' I said, 'May I please do a monologue?' They hadn't asked for one, but they let me do it. And I did an Arnold Wesker monologue—Arnold Wesker, the playwright, had done the adaptation.

"Actors who have monologues they really like, and who feel there's been a warm feeling in the audition room, should never hesitate to say—if there's time—'May I do a monologue for you?' It's really a tool to help the actor make an impression. I know, because I got the job."

18 Finding and Choosing the Right Songs for Your Audition

BY ERIK HAAGENSEN

Choosing audition songs that are right for you may possibly be the single most crucial challenge facing a musical performer. Once the rules were simple and clear. If you were auditioning for an actual role in a musical, you needed an "uptempo" and a "ballad," which meant one song that was fast (and usually funny) and one that was slow (and usually sad). If you were at a chorus call, you used your sixteen bars to show off your voice and hit your money note. Singers didn't have to dance much, dancers didn't have to sing much, and neither really had to act all that much. Today, that world is as vanished as vaudeville.

Increasingly, there are few hard-and-fast rules. So the more informed you are—about your material, your own strengths and weaknesses, as well as what's expected of you out there in the cold, cruel world—the more chance you'll have of nailing that role that lets you show 'em all you've got what it takes.

THERE ARE A HELLUVA LOT OF STARS IN THE SKY

There's now virtually a century's worth of musical theatre material to choose from. So first, you've got to learn the repertoire. Many of those earlier shows still get produced, and you are sure to end up auditioning for them. But musical and performance styles have evolved over the years. A great rendition of "And I'm Telling You I'm Not Going" from *Dreamgirls* is unlikely to win you the role of Adelaide in *Guys and Dolls*, though you could easily be right for both. You need versatility and flexibility. Vocal coach Michael Lavine tells his students to "get at least one or two songs from every decade: turn-of-the-century ragtime, '20s Charleston, '30s MGM movie song, '40s big band number, gospel, doo-wop, right up through '90s pop and rock. There's always going to be something different coming up, so get as many different categories as you can."

Don't rely solely upon a good vocal coach with an encyclopedic knowledge to give you what you need. Book writer-lyricist-composer Douglas J. Cohen warns, "A vocal coach can certainly make good suggestions. But you are limiting yourself to that person's perspective. You have to find that personal joy, that when you hear a song you just go, 'I gotta sing that!'"

Start by going to a sheet music store and looking at composer songbooks. Or go to the library and listen to a number of CDs featuring a composer's work. Check out the recordings of cabaret performers such as Michael Feinstein, who often devotes a CD to the songs of one theatre composer. Director-actor Gabriel Barre recommends that you "set yourself a personal goal to do it one song at a time, one show at a time. You're not going to appreciate and learn the whole catalogue at once. Learn a song a week, or a song every two weeks, or a song every month. Twelve songs in a year is a lot of material if you're careful—with each song—to do something new, explore new directions."

IT'S ME! IT'S ME! IT'S ME!

But what criteria determine which songs you actually choose to use for an audition?

It isn't enough for you to feel a personal affinity for the songs; they also need to fit your strengths as a performer. Obviously, you should make sure the song is in your vocal range and shows off your voice to good effect. Musical director Kristen Blodgette recommends performing show material in the key in which it is performed in the theatre. "If somebody is transposing standard material in a known key, it says to me that they can't sing it in the key that it's written in."

For "actors who sing," casting director Stuart Howard has a particular suggestion: "Try picking songs that were written for dancers. Gwen Verdon wasn't really a singer. Neither were Fred Astaire and Gene Kelly. There are so many great songs they did, often tailored specifically for them."

Lavine advises choosing songs that are geared to the role you think you're right for. At the same time, he notes that although you may be auditioning for a character, "you don't want to become too much of a character in an audition." Letting them see who you are and your essence as a performer is a main concern of any audition. So the content has to help you do that. For example, you might be absolutely crazy about Stephen Sondheim's "Could I Leave You?" but if you're a dewy-eyed twenty-something just out of school, singing a bitter song about middle-aged divorce is probably not a good idea.

PUT IT IN THE BOOK

The songs that you prepare for auditioning are what constitute your "book." Generally, you'll be asked for two contrasting numbers in any principal audition. But today, that contrast should be more than just slow/fast. Try finding two pieces of music that show a range—an emotional contrast, something that shows different colors.

Make sure you have material prepared in the musical style of the show for which you are auditioning. At the same time, always have something available that's not in the style of the show, just in case. Even a rock show might have one character who sings in "legit." Also, directors and casting directors often work on many shows at once; they might suddenly think of you for something else—in another, different show.

How big should your book be? Blodgette suggests that a basic book is made up of seven songs: "A traditional uptempo and ballad, a contemporary uptempo and ballad, and then three others that I call 'and I also have,' which are numbers that can't be placed in any particular category."

Lavine recounts, "A lot of students of mine have three or four books, and each one of them is really thick. If you know your auditions for the day, you can have a book for that day that's fairly light."

Do make sure that you are prepared to perform—and perform well—every song that you include in your book. Nothing upsets auditioners more than choosing a song from your book only to be told you don't know it well enough. If it's in the book, you should be ready to do it.

ANYTHING THAT'S FRESH'LL EARN YOU A BIG FAT CIGAR

Auditions are all about standing out from the crowd. You can start by avoiding songs currently overexposed on the audition circuit. So talk to voice teachers, coaches, and also to your peers and find out what they're performing. If a show is playing on Broadway long enough to audition replacements, it's likely that songs from that show will be overused. As Cohen says, "The best thing is just to have an ear to the ground—or to the door."

You should have some "standard" songs in your book. As acting teacher-director Jeffrey Dunn points out, "There are some producers and directors who only want to hear standard repertoire. I worked with one summer stock producer who says, 'I only want to hear something I know.'" Howard notes, "A casting person can listen to songs like 'I Could Have Danced All Night' or 'On the Street Where You Live' *ad infinitum*. They're brilliant songs. I'd rather hear them sung well than some obscure thing."

But the burden of singing a standard is the history behind it. Great performers have indelibly placed their stamps on the material, and there's a lot to live up to. It's incumbent upon the auditionee to make the song as fresh as the day it was written. Or to provide an entirely new take that surprises without offending. Lavine has a student who sings "I'm Flying" from *Peter Pan* as an extreme ballad, making it about being deeply in love rather than physically flying. Says Lavine, "People say to her, 'I've heard that song a million times; I've never thought about it being done like that. You're smart.'"

But be careful in rethinking a song. A new arrangement is one thing; rewriting, however, is a bad idea. The occasional pronoun change can work, but altering words or notes is far too disrespectful and sends a bad signal.

Always make sure that you know a song's original dramatic intention and context. Who is the character who sings it? Where does it come in the show? What dramatic action is it written to achieve? This means that you should always try to read the script of the musical from which it comes, or see a production or rent the movie. When you don't have such information, you can't achieve the song's dramatic intent. And if you are attempting to reinterpret it, you are likely to do something completely inappropriate.

What about singing pop songs? The problem, as Cohen puts it, is "there's nowhere to go with them. They're not written as if there's a beginning, middle, and end. Once you establish a sound, you just riff on it. It's all about the vocal gymnastics." The trick is to find something that's actable as well as singable. Which means avoiding pop songs that depend upon their musical arrangement for effect, or rely extensively upon a repeated "hook." If you're going to use a pop song, you have to create an actable dramatic context for it.

Another way to stand out is to perform a song by the author(s) of the piece for which you are auditioning. This demonstrates nerve and will almost certainly gain you undivided attention. But the risks are high, warns Howard. "Some composers hate to hear their own stuff except the way they want to hear it, which means the way they taught it to you." Always ask in advance what the author(s) would prefer.

THIS IS ALL VERY NEW TO ME

Another way to stand out from the crowd is to choose obscure songs. These can be from Broadway shows that flopped, have fallen out of favor, or never got recorded, or from new shows that have only had regional productions or readings and workshops. A wealth of songs out there would make excellent and surprising audition material. In Dunn's opinion, "Almost every single score of a Broadway musical that has flopped usually has at least one terrific song in it." And why not? Often those scores are by Broadway's best writers. It only stands to reason that, even if the show itself didn't work, the writers would be likely to turn out a number or two that matched their best work.

Make sure, however, that the material suits you. Don't fall into the trap of choosing a song simply because it's obscure. And avoid distracting the auditioners. If they are trying to figure out where the song came from and who wrote it, they are not concentrating on your performance. Lavine suggests finessing this problem by announcing the song before you sing it. "During the introduction of the song, say in the same energy of your song, 'Leonard Bernstein and Alan Jay Lerner wrote this for *1600 Pennsylvania Avenue*.' Then we know everything we need to know about it and we can concentrate on you."

USE YOUR IMAGINATION

A final method for standing out from the crowd is to put together an audition tailored specifically for a show. In a chorus call, Lavine had one of his students audition for *The Producers* dressed up as "Edna," a little old lady. In character, she sang a medley that included the lyrics "If you think I'm sexy/And you like my body" and "Tonight's the night we're gonna make it happen." She was cast for Broadway as the "hold me, touch me" woman.

Barre offers a final tip. "Confidence is what matters. And if you don't have confidence, just pretend you do. Because it's the same thing. No one will ever know the difference."

19 Demo Reels:

A Trailer for the Feature That Is You

BY BONNIE GILLESPIE

One of an actor's most essential marketing tools is the demo reel. Yet no one element of the actor's marketing arsenal seems to have so many variables: How long should it be? Can a theatrical reel include commercials? Should it include a montage? How can I get the footage promised to me? Does scene work produced just for reel "count"? How much should I be prepared to spend? And, after all of that, will anyone really watch it?

A demo reel is basically a trailer for the feature that is *you.* As you make your decisions about content, length, and distribution, make sure you advertise yourself accurately and in a way that leaves the viewer wanting more. Like any good advertising or marketing, it's all about giving the viewer a call to action—and in the case of a demo reel, the goal is to get the viewer to want to cast or represent you, and to *know* what parts you're right for. Make that clear, from start to finish.

COMMON SENSE

Before we plunge into the nitty-gritty, here are some basic rules of the road:

1 **Unsolicited demo reels are generally discouraged.** Make contact with the producer, director, casting director, agent, or manager you hope will view your demo reel and *ask* whether it would be okay to drop off or mail in a demo reel.

   When mailing a reel, package it securely so that it doesn't get too banged up in transit, and take it to the post office to ensure that you've included enough postage. Enclose a self-addressed, stamped envelope for the reel's return. Industry execs who do accept unsolicited demo reels—and that's not the majority of them, by any means—prefer to receive reels with packaging for the tapes' safe return. If you can help them get your reel back to you, they'll usually return it and perhaps even share feedback.

2 **Don't highlight someone else's performance in your reel.** There are many tales of actors who have been cast from *other* actors' demo reels. Make sure, when selecting material to include, that you choose scenes in which your performance is the focus. If your partner's work is stellar and cannot be edited out without compromising the scene, make sure your partner is not someone of your *type* or category. Why should your reel put you out of a job?

3 **Generally commercials do not belong on a theatrical reel.** However, if a combination is the only way for you to fill two or three minutes on a reel, put your theatrical material up front, then fade to black to clearly separate the two types of footage, and then include your commercial footage. Do not try to break up your theatrical work with your commercials. That transition is jarring and generally considered unprofessional by commercial and theatrical casting directors and agents.

4 Lead off with your best material and include work that shows your range.
Highlight your specialty and never use material more than two years old. Just like a headshot, your demo reel footage should be updated regularly.

WHAT EDITORS SAY

Rob Ashe, with five years of demo reel editing to his credit, began editing reels when he moved to Los Angeles after having worked extensively as an actor in Orlando.

"In my first three meetings [in L.A.], people asked for my demo reel," recalls Ashe. "I wasn't required to have tape in Orlando, so I knew I needed to know what tape *was,* first of all. I started going around town to see what I liked and what I didn't like. I picked up *Back Stage West* and called around to find out what services editors were providing. Then I figured out what I could do differently."

With an eye for what would best serve the actor, Ashe developed a successful editing business. He explains that filmmakers are far more patient when watching reels than are agents or casting directors. "Your reel can be a little longer if you're sending it out to directors," he says.

Other tips from Ashe include the following: "Open with your highest-paid gig. If you have a scene with a name actor, include it, no matter what. If all you have are student films or DV [digital video] work, keep the reel under three minutes, total."

As for what raw material you should bring to your editor, preference seems to skew toward Beta SP-versions of the work, although it can become grainy during transfer. Digibeta, while higher priced, holds the best depth of color and lasts longer than other media. The half-inch VHS copy that talent usually receives in "copy, credit, meals" arrangements is already a second-generation copy of the work. When that is edited onto a reel, it becomes third-generation. Dubbing takes it down to fourth, and so on. While it may take quite a bit of follow-up and persistence—and perhaps cost—to get a copy from the master, the final product will be far superior in quality.

According to Allen Fawcett, twelve-year veteran demo reel producer and editor, "An actor needs a reel to prove he can do what he says he can do. In TV land, a reel gets you an agent. There is no time for TV [casting] people to cast from a reel. In the film world, the reel is everything. Film people have more time to watch reels, and more interest in seeing them."

Fawcett, who teaches on-camera technique and produces demo reels from his Los Angeles studio, describes being on-camera as golden time. "It is impossible to spend too much time in front of a camera doing dialogue and calibrating yourself to being inside of frame, hitting your mark, learning that you cannot do the things you do onstage, when you're on camera," says Fawcett. "You'll learn that you blink excessively, lick your lips too much—things that make you say, 'Oh, my God, I'm not watchable!' Those are things you should learn as early as possible, so you can begin to eradicate bad habits. A set is not a school. A set is somewhere that money is being burned by the second."

It is important, when producing a demo reel, to know your goals. Are you trying to land an agent or a manager? Are you hoping to move up to another level in your career? Are you trying to get from co-star to lead?

"If your goal is to get an agent, student films are fine," Ashe notes. "Agents just want to see if you are castable." Fawcett concurs, adding, "Agents are looking at your reel, asking, 'Could I have made any money off this person in the past thirty days, based on what I've been seeing in the Breakdowns and what I'm seeing on this reel?' A reel shows your potential for booking, even if it's a reel made up of produced scenes. It's about risk assessment."

As for montages—those little clips of the actor in various roles, set to music and edited together in rapid succession—opinions vary widely.

"Agents like montages. Casting directors hate them," states Fawcett. "Agents can see right away if there's a conflict in their stable and can get rid of the tape after ten seconds. Montages are not as useful for casting directors and are seen as a waste of their time."

Indeed, some casting directors I have interviewed suggest placing a montage at the end of your reel so that they can see your work first and your looks last. Ashe agrees that montages are a matter of taste, and his taste is pro-montage. "A lot of people say it's a no-no, but I feel that a ten-second montage psychologically gives people a second to sit down, breathe, get an emotional feel for what they're going to get. I like to put music down that matches the personality of the actor."

So how long should that demo reel be? My research shows that actors have found success with reels as short as two minutes and as long as eight minutes. Industry preference tends to run in the three- to five-minute range. Still, most industry experts would agree that less is always more when it comes to the length of a demo reel. Says Fawcett, "I have never heard a casting director, a manager, or an agent say that a demo reel was too short."

And how much should demo reel editing run? "If you're doing a basic reel with your name and your scenes, and you've come in with your tapes all cued up and ready to go, more than $80 for editing is a rip-off," Ashe insists. "If I'm doing some major rearranging of clips and spending more than ten hours on it, editing will go into the $200 range. A redo—for adding a clip or taking one out—I'll do for $30."

As for fully produced scenes, with direction, lighting, sound, sets, props, and editing—the type of full-service reel production Fawcett provides—the cost for four original scenes (forty to fifty seconds each) is $1,500. This includes consultation, instruction, and editing of the finished product.

Is there value to a demo reel comprising produced scenes? "Tape is a marketing piece," Fawcett explains. Says Ashe, "The main purpose of a reel is for people to know how to hire you, how you are cast. Even if your reel is one [produced] scene and one student film, if it's great footage, it says, 'This is how I look, this is how I act, and this is how I am on camera.'"

WHAT CASTING DIRECTORS SAY

Some casting directors welcome unsolicited demo reels; most abhor them. It is important to do research before going to the expense of sending tapes out. For example, do *not* send an unsolicited demo reel to Donna Ekholdt, Big Ticket TV's vice president of Talent Development and Casting. "It's like crashing an audition," says the L.A.-based CD. "It's an unscheduled appointment with me. Send your headshot and résumé with a request to send me tape. If I'm interested, I'll ask to see it."

At the other end of the spectrum are feature film casting directors Donald Paul Pemrick and Dean E. Fronk, both of whom work out of L.A. "We'll put our feet up and watch a bunch of them at a time," reports Pemrick. "But don't send a scene from acting class, or a performance at your sister's bat mitzvah. Include three to four scenes, and tell me what show I'm about to see. Also include some credits, especially the directors' names. If you've worked with someone I know, I'd like to ask them about your work."

"It's a very small town," Fronk adds. "We know those indie directors. And, if you want, send over a work-in-progress and let us tell your manager or agent how to help you make it a better reel."

Casting directors who do *not* want to see unsolicited demo reels include indie film caster Adrienne Stern, casting director for the ABC hit *Alias* April Webster, *The Young and the Restless* casting exec Marnie Saitta, and award-winning feature casting legend Debra Zane, each of whom works in Hollywood. "An unsolicited tape is a little tricky, especially if it's not sent for a specific role," says Zane. "We're so busy looking at tapes we've requested and then editing together tapes of actors to send to directors and producers, there's just no time to look at an unsolicited demo. It's not a top priority."

Los Angeles-based casting directors who specifically note that they welcome demo reels include Michael Donovan (films, commercials, theatre), Patrick Baca (films, MOWs, pilots), and feature film casting partners Mike Fenton and Allison Cowitt. Fenton underscors the importance of having a demo reel, noting that it must be made up of work you list on your résumé.

"Don't go to a corner production house and have a demo tape made," Fenton says. "You're just throwing money away." Adds Cowitt, "If you have to include a commercial on your demo reel, that's better than nothing. Documentaries are fine. Industrials are okay. We need to see you on film."

The West Coast-based head honchos at CBS and NBC enjoy watching actors' demo reels. Peter Golden, senior vice president of Talent and Casting for CBS, explains that a demo reel is more representative of what to expect from an actor.

"I don't judge an actor on just their experience in the room [during a casting session]," observes Golden. "That's such an uncomfortable setting for so many actors. That's why you *must* have tape. If you don't audition well, your most valuable tool becomes one great scene, even from a student film."

Marc Hirschfeld, NBC's executive vice president of Talent and Casting, agrees, adding a note about the importance of timing and variety. "I want nice, tight, short pieces that show the different things you can do, not three scenes of you being a hooker or a cop or a nurse."

L.A. casting-director-turned-director Ellie Kanner emphasizes the value of *good* tape. "You must have a demo reel," she insists. "However, bad tape is worse than no tape. So, unless your tape is of broadcast quality—with good writing and talented actors playing with you—don't use it. Remember that the tape could be the last thing a producer sees on you."

TIPS FOR HAPPY REELING

While it can take some effort to get copies of your on-camera work, it's worth the effort. Build relationships with the people most likely to be able to provide copies while you're on the set: the director, the producers. If you're working on a commercial, speak with a representative from the ad agency. Exchange business cards and make sure to stay in touch, asking for a copy of the spot even if it never airs. If you're working on a student film, try to get the name of the student's professor.

Many times a request from the professor will aid your quest to get a copy of the student film when your requests of the student filmmaker have gone ignored. With film, work with the production company. With episodic television, if you haven't been able to get an advance copy of your footage, have a video service record the episode as it airs. At the very least, set up your VCR and make your tape on your own. Having copies of your work is your right as a performer.

Show up to your reel-editing appointment with all of your tapes cued and ready to go. Review the clips with the editor to make sure you have a shared vision of the image you are trying to market with your reel. Plan the flow of the reel, from segment to segment, and decide on stylistic elements such as title cards and credit, music, and whether you will use a montage. Decide on the number of copies you will need; if you need more than a few, you may find that it is more cost effective to use a dubbing facility than to use your reel's editor for that part of the process.

Make sure the material you use in your reel is good—technically and artistically. Although we hope that agents, managers, and casting directors will add the impression your demo reel leaves on them to information they already have about you—from your stage performances, your résumé, and any prior auditions you've had with them—many times the last and best impression you'll make on industry professionals is the only one they'll retain. If you are providing a demo reel, it should be at least as impressive as your last personal encounter, if not far superior.

Finally, remember that everyone was a beginner at some point. Don't rush to get a demo reel together if what you need to be building up is a résumé of strong parts. It's a bit of a Catch-22: You need great on-camera work to put on a reel, and you need a reel to get more great on-camera work. Everyone has to start somewhere, though—and here's a hint: Student and independent films place a lot of casting notices in *Back Stage* and *Back Stage West.*

ACTORS WANTED

JOIN FREE

THE OMP ADVANTAGE

* FREE ONLINE PORTFOLIO INCLUDES 5 IMAGES *

* WORLDS LARGEST TALENT COMMUNITY *

* ACCESS TO 25,000 AGENTS, MANAGERS, AND PHOTOGRAPHERS *

* OVER 2 MILLION VISITORS MONTHLY *

* FREE ACCESS TO MESSAGE BOARDS *

PORTFOLIOS EASILY UPGRADED TO INCLUDE

* DEMO REAL INCLUDING AUDIO AND VIDEO *

* 21 TO 41 IMAGES *

* ACCESS TO DAILY CASTING CALLS *

* LISTINGS AND DIRECTORIES DISTRIBUTED TO AGENTS *

www.onemodelplace.com/actors

ACT WITH PASSION, LIVE WITH LOVE
IT'S TIME TO BECOME THE ACTOR
YOU DREAM OF BEING

ELIZABETH BROWNING STUDIO

Training and inspiring actors in film,
television, and theater for 18 years

♦ AUDITION SKILLS

♦ ACTING FOR ALL LEVELS

♦ DEVELOPMENT OF ORIGINAL MATERIAL

♦ INSTRUMENTALS TO DISSOLVE
PERSONAL BLOCKS

Elizabeth Browning, one of New York's most respected acting coaches has been teaching acting to working professionals for 18 years. Formerly on faculty at N.Y.U./Circle in the Square and Director of The Studio of The Actors' Space, Ms. Browning is featured in *The Actor's Guide to Qualified Acting Coaches.* She's also appeared on ABC and NBC.

CALL NOW: 212 946-1702

www.ElizabethBrowningStudio.com

A DAY FOR ACTORS

CAREER SEMINARS

CASTING DIRECTORS

AGENTS

FOCUS SESSIONS

MANAGERS

FREE EXHIBIT HALL

AND MUCH MORE

FOR EXHIBIT HALL SPACE CALL

WEST ■	■ EAST
Back Stage West	Back Stage
Advertising	Advertising
5055 Wilshire Blvd., 5th fl.	770 Broadway, 4th floor
Los Angeles, CA 90036	New York, NY 10003
323.525.2225	646.654.5700

Look what's new from

Showfax and Actors Access

(310) 385-6920

Now you can submit yourself via the Internet and update the information your agent uses to submit you too!

You've always been able to mail your picture
and resume for projects listed in Actors Access
from Breakdown Services.

1. Now submit yourself Electronically
via the Internet for projects listed in Actor Access.

2. Up-load and Up-date your
Picture, Resume and Profile
information your representatives use when they
submit Electronically!

With our database of over 69,000 pictures and resumes,
we may already have your picture and resume submitted
by your agent or manager. You can use your picture and resume
already on file to submit yourself for projects listed
in Actors Access.

To view or update your picture and resume, contact your
agent or manager for your Actors Access code or call
Showfax to verify that we have your picture and resume.
If you aren't represented, get your picture and
resume to Showfax so you can submit yourself via Actors Access.

PART 4

The Work

20 Getting In:

Breaking into Film and Television

BY ANNE KELLY-SAXENMEYER

Late one evening, Los Angeles-based casting director Bonnie Zane got a call from the writer's room of *The Drew Carey Show:* "We need a beautiful twenty-one- or twenty-two-year-old girl to do a couple of lines, and she works tomorrow at 7 a.m."

Zane had one actress in mind but couldn't get her on the phone, so she called her sister, feature film casting director Debra Zane. Debra suggested her intern, Jaime Ray Newman. Newman showed up on-set the next day, happily did her few lines, talked shop with the cast—many of whom came from Chicago theatre backgrounds like herself—and walked away with her SAG card.

From that first job, Newman got an agent, then a year's contract on *General Hospital* and a small role in the popular film *Catch Me if You Can.* Later Bonnie Zane was casting the play *Turnaround,* which would star David Schwimmer and Jonathan Silverman. Newman was cast in the production's only female role.

Like many actors who have succeeded at breaking into television or films, Newman had years of preparation and familiarity with a few casting directors. She also had a good dose of serendipity on her side.

But how do you take luck out of the equation? For starters, you have to be an excellent actor. That means you need to continue practicing your craft, whether in class, on the local stage, in small films, or all of the above. Casting directors need to find you in the places where they look for talent—if not in their agent submission piles, then in critically acclaimed plays, in film festivals, in the graduating class of a good training program, or, for some, in casting director workshops. Finally, after they've seen your work or even called you in once or twice, casting directors may occasionally need to be reminded of your existence, reassured that you are still hard at work and ready to be cast.

SHOWCASE ZEN

Whether you're seeking representation or looking to make a fan of a particular casting director, the most important thing to remember is that people have to see you act. That doesn't mean you should do mass mailings of your reel (though that tape will eventually become an essential tool) or that you should pester offices to let you come in and read. The best place for decision makers to get familiar with your work is in a professional venue.

Los Angeles-based casting director Mali Finn explains: "You want people coming after you, not you chasing them. When you chase agents and managers by sending out mailing after mailing or postcards, you are really asking them to get excited about something that is an unknown. What you want them to do is see your work. You want them to see you in theatre. If an agent sees you in a piece of theatre, they think they've discovered you, which is exactly what you want, because then they have a vested interest. They get excited about bringing you into the agency and saying, 'Look what I found!'"

While actors who aspire to film and TV work do get exposure by working in live theatre, they should avoid looking at it simply as a stepping stone. Hep Jamieson and writing partner Andrea Fears, now members of the Open Fist Theatre Company in Los Angeles, learned that lesson.

"I think the trap people can fall into when they first start doing theatre in L.A. is that they do it solely to get a casting director or an agent," said Jamieson. "We went through years of doing that, and finally we said, 'Let's just have a good time and write our own show.'"

They formed their own production company and wrote *The Andrea and Hep Show* for the EdgeFest theatre festival; it poked fun at what actors go through to put up a show in the hope that it will lead to instant stardom. After a successful run they found out that executives from Warner Bros. and Fox, people they hadn't even invited, had seen the show and loved it. Soon they were taking development meetings, and Jamieson got a shot at a series regular role.

"I think we let go of the pressure of trying to get television gigs from it and just had a really great time," said Jamieson. "When you do it out of desperation, like, *I gotta book television work,* people can feel it, and I think that's a real turnoff. I was doing theatre for the wrong reasons when I first came out here. Now I pick my pieces really carefully."

What exactly are your chances of getting casting directors to attend your theatrical showcases in the first place?

Los Angeles casting director Sandi Logan says she loves to go to the theatre, but cautions, "If you don't think the production is good, if you're doing good work in it but it's not a great play, don't invite people to see it. Do it for the joy of acting, do it for the experience of being in the theatre. We remember the bad theatre a lot more than the good. But if you have a small part in a great piece of theatre and there are some fantastic actors in it, invite us. Chances are we're going to make it to those big productions, and we'll get to know you as a co-star or supporting actor."

Logan also advises actors to give casting directors plenty of advance notice when sending out invitations, and to be sure the entire cast is listed on the postcard: "If there are two other actors whom I know, I've read, or I'm interested in getting to know, I have more of a chance of going to that play, because now it's not just about getting to know you; there are two, three, or four actors I can get to know better by attending this play."

One thing to remember: many, if not most, casting directors are adamant about not taking unsolicited calls. You can do research to find out which casting directors are willing to have phone contact. But it's always safer to send showcase invitations via postcard only.

AUTEURS OF TOMORROW

Another L.A. casting director, Dori Zuckerman, very rarely has time to go to the theatre. But if you've been in an independent film, she may get to see you.

That's how she was first introduced to actor Brian Sites, whose role in the 2002 indie *Real Women Have Curves* propelled him to the next level in his film career.

Sites leapt from high school into the business after being signed by a manager at an IMTA (International Modeling and Talent Association) convention. He remembers walking onto the set of his first job, an American Film Institute senior project called *Destiny Stalled.*

"It was kind of intense to step onto an actual film set for your first time and to be doing a lead role," remembers Sites. "That definitely jump-started me into doing a lot of independent movies."

For any actor looking to break into film or TV, working on student projects can be a great way to build a reel, learn about the filmmaking process, and begin to build a professional network. Getting your pictures to film schools is essential for the relatively unknown actor. Says Finn: "You will be working with the filmmakers of tomorrow if you are in those student films. Instead of doing three to five lines on television, you can usually get a good supporting role or a lead role in an AFI film, and you don't get paid but you ask for that copy. You'll have better footage and probably a role with some emotional range that'll be much more interesting, eventually, for an agent to see. And those directors, if you're good, are going to be loyal to you in the future, so you're building really, really good connections for future work."

(For more details on getting involved in student films, see chapter 23, "Shooting for Success: An Actor's Guide to the Student-Filmmaking Experience.")

POST-GRAD BUZZ

If there are any shortcuts to breaking into film and television—and outside of nepotism, there may not be—doing an M.F.A. program is certainly not one, as such programs require a huge investment of energy, time, and money. With that investment, however, can come invaluable experience and instant credibility in the job market. Many casting directors say they scout talent from graduating classes not only of M.F.A. but also of B.F.A. programs. Los Angeles casting director Pam Dixon says she goes to all of the presentations done by the graduating classes of universities presenting in Los Angeles.

Sandi Logan also attends the round of university showcases. One of the new faces she saw among the UC San Diego graduating class in 2001 was Chane't Johnson, an actress who found herself suddenly in demand after appearing in her school's New York and Los Angeles M.F.A. showcases.

While she was still deciding on an agent, Johnson was already having meetings with casting directors and executives, which contradicted what she'd been told about the business—that you couldn't meet anybody without representation.

The thing about the post-grad buzz—or, for that matter, any momentum you create in your career—is that it can dissipate quickly. While Johnson racked up a good list of TV credits during her first couple of years on the market, she has also learned how to steer through the slow times.

"Get out there and find out what you can do now instead of sitting at home waiting," she suggests. "Find out which organizations have free seminars, like Women in Film and SAG Conservatory. Find a theatre company in town that you're passionate about. And make phone calls—literally make phone calls to your friends, because the support system you have now is the one you'll have later, and the hope is that everyone you're in touch with will eventually be working and you can all help each other."

As important as maintaining your personal network is nurturing those relationships with casting directors who have seen your work. Johnson has found that the best way to stay in touch is with thank-you cards and postcards.

"Especially after they've brought you in, send them a sincere thank-you card that doesn't have your headshot in it," she advises. "After that, whenever you've got a gig or you're doing something, send them a postcard with an update. Write a little note on it: 'Hey, Sandi. I'm doing this episode of this show. It'll be on this date at this time. Hope you can watch it.' It's not obtrusive, because it's not you in their face, trying to get into their office. It's just a way of letting them know that you appreciate their hard work, but that you're working hard, too."

HOMEWORK ASSIGNMENT

One controversial way to research casting offices is through casting director workshops. The argument against them is that actors end up paying for what they mistakenly believe are auditions. Dixon told us she never has and never will do a workshop because, simply put, she doesn't believe that actors should have to pay to be seen by her.

That said, many casting directors and their associates participate in workshops and attest that, if you choose them carefully and approach them in the right way, they can be a great way to learn and be introduced.

"It's a lot like theatre—you have to do your homework," says Wright. "Talk to other actors, do some research, find out which ones are reputable and which ones seem to have more of an audition process. It's a business like anything else, and in order for any of those places to stay alive they have to accept a lot more people than are probably ready to be in front of casting directors."

Logan advises actors to approach workshops with the appropriate expectations: "Don't go in with the hope that they will see you, know your talent, and cast you. You should go in with your own sense of getting to know casting directors, what they're looking for, what they like and don't like in an audition."

Adds casting director G. Charles Wright of Los Angeles: "If you have an opportunity to have even two minutes of one-on-one time with a casting director, you should take advantage of that. That means when you go to these workshops, have two or three questions in your bag. If you can ask a valid question that will not only move you forward as an actor and give you the knowledge you need to better prepare for your next job, but also give you that one-on-one time, so much the better. We're very willing to share our information; that's why we're there."

Another research method that deserves brief mention is doing an internship in a casting office. While it isn't for everyone and some casting directors are hesitant to take on actors, Jaime Ray Newman says that observing all the factors that go into choosing a cast—not simply the strength of actors' auditions, but the myriad considerations that go into creating an ensemble—help put things into perspective for her on the other side of the desk.

"I think it's an invaluable experience," states Newman, who cautions interns not to discuss their acting careers while on the job. "If they ask you, that's one thing. If not, you're just there to do your job and soak up information."

HARD REALITY

So, with all the things you can do to take charge of your career, how hard is it, really, to break into television and films? Look at the numbers: thousands and thousands of actors, hundreds of roles. It's not just hard to break in—it's hard to stay in.

Logan offers this assessment of the market: "I think reality television has taken away a lot of jobs from actors in Los Angeles. Every hour of reality television represents about fifteen to seventeen co-star and guest-star roles in episodic TV. So there are a lot fewer roles available and there are a lot more actors than were out here, say, ten years ago.

"However, if an actor is talented, if that actor has abilities and the confidence in those abilities, the work is available."

Showfax

www.showfax.com

The acting community's first and #1 resource for audition material and Actors Access!

SIDES ONLINE -	get all the sides you need - online or via fax.
ACTORS ACCESS	Showfax members submit electronically for roles
ACTORS 101	free quarterly seminars with industry professionals
INSIDE TRACK	weekly newsletter from an insider's viewpoint

BACK STAGE® and BACK STAGE WEST®

The #1 weeklies for Performing Artists

SUBSCRIBE TODAY
1.800.745.8922

http://www.backstage.com/backstage/contact/printsub.jsp

21 Working on the Spot:

Opportunities in Commercial Casting

BY MARK DUNDAS WOOD

Those who've spent any time working in the world of television commercials know that the business is in a perpetual state of flux. The one thing you can depend on is change.

Back in the late 1970s, the majority of casting for national TV spots was done inside the casting departments of advertising agencies (many of which were located in Manhattan, clustered on Madison Avenue between 38th and 59th streets).

"There were commercial stars back in those days," recalls talent agent Doug Kesten, of the Paradigm Agency. "We had clients who had twenty-five, thirty active commercials at any time. It wasn't a big issue. If you were good at talking into the camera and selling something, or being that sort of Donna Reed mom or that 'Father Knows Best' dad, and everyone knew you were good at it, that was valuable. That technique was employable."

Nowadays, few ad agencies have their own casting departments, and it's rare for an actor to have as many as eight or nine active commercials on the air at any given time. The varieties of opportunity have changed as well. In fact, in some ways ad work seems to have become more akin to modeling than to stage or feature film acting.

"The pool of actors we have to have at our disposal has widened," remarks Kesten. "If they want a Hell's Angel in a commercial these days, they're gonna get the real thing. Back in 1979, they would have taken the guy who sometimes was the plumber in a commercial and sometimes the soccer coach and sometimes the longshoreman. They would have dressed him up in leather and put on fake tattoos. But they don't do that anymore."

The "up" side of this demand for authenticity is that it's opened up doors for people of different ethnicities and body types. And performers with an offbeat appearance, personality, and demeanor likewise have greater opportunities, according to New York actor Liam Mitchell. "They're looking for quirky people now," he says. "If you're quirky, you've got an edge."

Other trends aren't so welcoming. In the last few years, one unfortunate practice for actors has been to shoot commercial spots overseas, where they're cheaper to produce. Meanwhile, advertisers here at home rely increasingly on talent from sources unaffiliated with labor unions—the Screen Actors Guild (SAG) and the American Federation of Television and Radio Artists (AFTRA). However, as New

York casting director Elsie Stark puts it, "The problem with nonunion work is still that it's not organized, and it's not covered very well by a representative like a manager or agent."

THE "LOOK" VS. THE "CHOPS"

If directors and casting teams are on the prowl for "the real thing," does that mean there's any need for acting technique at all in commercials? You may ask yourself, "Why should I even bother with formal acting training if I'm going to just show up and 'be myself'?"

Hold on a minute. While "the right look" is certainly a primary consideration in the casting of television commercials, insiders agree that the need to develop "acting chops" remains.

Of course, actors with considerable training for stage work may find they'll need to tone down their emoting for the more naturalistic style called for in many commercials. You may even consider taking an "acting for the camera" course to learn how to work in this very different medium.

But you needn't toss out your copy of *An Actor Prepares* with the bath water! You can still rely on the basic strategies: character development techniques, sense memory, subtext, inner monologue, and the like.

Stephen DeAngelis, an in-house casting director with the ad agency Grey Worldwide, says that contemporary TV commercials tend to focus on selling products by showing how they can make consumers' lives simpler, so that they consequently have time for the things that really matter in life: family and other interpersonal relationships. Highly valued are actors who can give the impression—in a matter of seconds—that the characters they're portraying have rich, full lives. The ability to invent an inner life for a character may be as valid for a thirty-second Advil spot depicting a family crisis as it is for the most complex sequences of *Uncle Vanya*.

Training in voice and speech can be very beneficial to actors who seek commercial work. So is movement training: an actor with strong background in dance can easily (and quickly) "hit the marks" in the almost-choreographed movements dictated by a director of commercials.

MOVE IT OR LOSE IT

Business acumen and flexibility are essential for actors of any stripe. But they're especially important when you work in the world of TV ads.

Unlike feature films, commercials move fast, fast, fast. "Sometimes they book you, you shoot it, and within a week the commercial's running," says Liam Mitchell. And the spot may disappear nearly as quickly as it arrived: Mitchell notes that most national commercials are slated to run thirteen weeks. Local and regional ads may play somewhat longer.

The speed with which commercials are produced necessitates actors who can pick up and fly to a location at a moment's notice, and who can absorb direction quickly and with good humor. Unlike in the theatre, in commercials directors often give line readings to actors. One New York-based director says he does it all the time. If he gets what he wants in the first three to five takes, he'll sometimes allow the actor to experiment with a take or two. But his eye is always on the clock.

As is commonly assumed, you *can* make good money in commercials—especially in nationally broadcast ones. The amount you can collect depends on various factors, including, of course, the number of times the spot airs and whether or not it's a union job. For further details on established rates for work in TV spots, consult AFTRA at www.aftra.com or call SAG at 1-800-SAG-0767.

AGENTS AND COMMERCIAL WORK

Actors will sometimes sign with a single agent for their theatrical, film and/or television bookings, but will utilize several agents for commercials. Mitchell says he's worked with five different agencies for his ad work. Another New York-based actor, Lisa Gorlitsky, also "freelances" when it comes to commercials.

Some casting directors in New York may seek new talent on their own—going to Equity showcases, for instance, to scope out promising performers. If you book a handful of commercials directly through a casting director, without having an agent, there's a possibility that the CD will eventually steer you to a flourishing commercial agent.

If you freelance for a while and later decide to sign with one agent for your commercial work, your decision will be made based on a solid, shared history. You may take notes and discover that the agency with the nicest office and the friendliest attitude also was the one that proved least effective in getting you in to see casting directors—and securing those high-paying gigs.

It's essential, when you do get an agent, that you view him or her clearly as someone who works for you. New York casting director Elsie Stark's mantra is "90 percent rules 10":

"If you're the person bringing in the paycheck, you give your agent 10 percent and keep 90. That means you're the boss. Well, the boss has to lead by example. The mathematics alone makes you the person in charge—the decision maker."

THE MOMENT OF TRUTH: THE AUDITION

Usually, an actor arrives at a preliminary audition with little more than knowledge of the product name and some notion of the character he or she will be reading for. (This allows one to adopt something in the nature of a costume—or at any rate to avoid pinstripes if the audition is for the part of a cattle rancher. Casting directors may call literally hundreds of actors for this first round of auditions.

Unlike in other acting genres, in ad work the 8"x10" glossy is not always an essential part of the casting process. Actors may instead have a Polaroid snapshot taken of them at the audition, which the casting team will use for reference. Callbacks may be taped or shot on 35mm film, and are usually attended by directors, ad agency personnel, and representatives of the product or service being marketed.

Most often, one gets the sides for the first audition only a matter of minutes before the process begins. But actors can do themselves a favor if they manage to get a look at the storyboard for the commercial ahead of time.

Lisa Gorlitsky once volunteered to be a reader for various casting directors (i.e., to read opposite auditionees); this proved to be an invaluable stint. She experienced what casting directors experience: hearing a script repeatedly—sometimes six hours a day for three straight days. The auditionees who stood out for the casting team she was a part of were those who exuded unwavering confidence, even if they weren't quite right for the part.

It's hard to be confident all the time. But in auditions, you should avoid blatant self-deprecation, which is definitely *not* considered an endearing trait. Liam Mitchell remembers seeing an actress cap her reading with the pronouncement: "Ah, I stink. That was awful." Obviously, any interest the casting director harbored for this performer quickly evaporated.

Sometimes it pays to take a risk and put an unusual spin on the material. Playfulness is not necessarily a bad thing in auditions. Says Stephen DeAngelis: "I don't think anyone's ever had a great audition where they've said, 'Oh, my God, I had the best audition in my life—I played it safe.'"

FROM GERBERS TO GERITOL

As with any performing endeavor, commercial work is fraught with the potential for brush-offs and disappointment. But veterans from the ad business remind actors not to take rejection personally. Sometimes, they say, the director may have loved your work, but the advertiser somehow didn't feel you had the right look or manner for that particular product. You shouldn't be hard on yourself—unless you've not done your homework or you've allowed yourself to become intimidated during the audition process. If casting directors were impressed with you, they may remember you when something else comes along.

Even in the worst economy, there are fresh opportunities waiting around the next bend in the commercial business. And there is endless potential for virtually everyone in the acting pool. You can, after all, find a possible slot for yourself at any stage of life—as a child, a teenager, a parent, or a grandparent.

AT LAST! THE QUICKEST, MOST COST EFFECTIVE WAY TO BREAK INTO COMMERCIALS!

They know the commercial industry better than anyone else. They're simply the best!
booked: Del Taco,Kia
Melissa Smith

Their awesome camera techniques turned my callbacks into bookings! I owe my first national to them.
booked: McDonald's
Al Bayon

My confidence levels soared after just 1 class! If you want success in commercials start here!
booked: KFC, Bolle'Vodka, ESPN Promo
Heidi Wanser

I was trapped in sales for 20 years. After 4 weeks with them, I got a great agent and a new life!
signed with: Kazarian, Spencer & Assoc.
Jun Tanisaki

- TOP AGENT SHOWCASE – New!
- Easy Payment Options
- Lifetime Career Counseling
- Free Working Audit
- Agency Recommended
- Free Seminars Every Month!

$200
(4-week course)

Hey, I Saw Your Commercial.com
Casting Director Commercial Workshops

Classes begin every first Tuesday, Thursday, & Saturday of the month.

These classes fill quickly! Call NOW!
TOLL FREE: 877-835-9809

Sign up online NOW!

The monthly Who To Contact Guide For Casting, Agents & Production

To Subscribe call
800.745.8922

22 Industrial-Strength Performing:

Opportunities in Non-broadcast Media Projects

BY MARK DUNDAS WOOD

They're still looked on by some people as grunt jobs—as the slightly dorky cousins of broadcast commercials. They're seen as a way for an actor to break into the business, but probably not as something he wants to do forever—certainly not exclusively.

They're industrials. Or call them "non-broadcast," if you must: short for "non-broadcast media" projects. Whatever you call them—or think of them—they'll probably always be around. Indeed, technological advances in the 1980s and 1990s have created multitudes of new possibilities. Training and corporate films, point-of-purchase videos, voiceovers for CD-ROM-based outlets, recordings for companies' phone-prompt systems, books on tape, computer games, product demo videos—all of these and more fall into the non-broadcast media category. If it's not sent out on the airwaves or shown in your local cinema, it will likely be tagged as an industrial, whether it's a film/video or an audio-only presentation.

Even in months (or years) when the economy is sluggish, new opportunities present themselves. "With the slowdown, there is need for stimulus," says New Yorker Carol Nadell, casting director for Selective Casting by Carol Nadell and a specialist in non-broadcast. "That includes stimulating customers, as well as sales-people—giving them direction."

So what are the trends in industrials in the 21st century? There's definitely more sophistication—and far less innate nerdiness—in the look and feel of many of today's non-broadcast projects.

"The way they're written has improved," industrials actor Bob Goodman (who's worked in both New York and Florida) says of today's non-broadcast scripts. "Before, it was cookie-cutter dialogue: 'Jim, don't you think Nancy needs a little work? Maybe she should stay a little bit late.' It's more in the vernacular now—more like an independent film."

Agent Ellen Manning of Manhattan's Gilla Roos, Ltd. talent agency concurs: "You still have your narrators and announcers and people that are giving informa-tion. But I'm finding a lot of 'real people' requests for actors, to play the patient or the customer or the victim. Which is sort of nice for the actors—they get to play more of a scene."

While it may be useful to have an agent or manager to help you get jobs in industrials, it's not mandatory. A common assumption is that agents don't represent actors for non-broadcast because such limited money is involved. And there's some truth in this. Unlike broadcast commercials, non-broadcast doesn't provide actors with use fees ("residuals"); performers are paid on a flat-fee basis, so if an agent gets 10 percent of that fee and nothing more, it does sometimes amount to much ado for little return.

Some agents, such as Manning, do concentrate on non-broadcast work. But you can certainly seek jobs on your own by directly contacting companies that produce industrials. And in some cases you can go right to the corporate client itself (because some corporations have their own in-house production companies). As is the case with all commercial work, it's a smart idea to begin putting together a compilation reel showing clips of your work.

"INDUSTRIALS" ANATOMY 101

So what's it like, exactly, to work in an industrial?

To begin, you should know that union and nonunion work is available, with union jobs falling under SAG/AFTRA jurisdiction. For information on the basic pay scale, go to www.aftra.com and consult the "Industrials and New Technologies" section.

Because there's such diversity in the area of non-broadcast, it's impossible to make generalizations about what will be involved in any given project. Still, it may be useful to look at a handful of representative examples:

- One major project completed by New York producer Gary Giudice was a demo video for a piece of equipment known as the "Smart Mirror," manufactured by a company called ABS. The machine is used by customers trying on different eyeglass frames in opticians' offices. The video Giudice made was meant to serve both as a Smart Mirror marketing tool and a training film for opticians and their staff. It ran about twenty minutes and took two days to shoot. Computer graphics that illustrated the various steps used to operate the Smart Mirror were overlaid on live-action footage, shot by Giudice. Actors portrayed both customers and opticians, and the video was shot on location in an actual optician's office.

- Brevity is the soul of point-of-purchase (or "point-of-sale") videos—which are short, looped films to be viewed by customers in retail settings. Giudice produced one of these for an Italian line of men's clothing. Although the project was shot in Times Square, it was only shown overseas. For this video, a single model was seen wearing three different outfits. There were no spoken words on the soundtrack. Cameras circled around the actor, creating a whirling effect.

- New York actress Annette Jenkins took on the role of onscreen narrator-instructor for one portion of an industrial project—it involved the application of makeup for male models. In this case, Jenkins was hired partly because of her own expertise: "It was something I was good at. I was a makeup artist and that's why I was asked to do it. That doesn't happen often." Because of her knowledge and experience, Jenkins was also requested to help develop the script. Working from a general outline, she spoke the narration in her own words, giving the video a spontaneous, off-the-cuff feel.

- One of the best gigs Bob Goodman ever had in a non-broadcast was a series of videos for Princess Cruises. The company sent him to places like Alaska and the Caribbean with a good-humored, friendly crew. He was seeing the world and being paid good money. On the flip side, perhaps his worst assignment was a pharmaceuticals project: chock-full of unpronounceable words. Goodman played a technician, dressed in a lab coat: "Doctor Jorgenssen," he says of his "mad scientist" persona for the project. "I'm there with 'Igor' mixing these things. . . ."

It's easy to see that the genre runs the gamut from costly and elite to bargain-basement basic. Says low-budget freelance producer Graham Suorsa, who has worked in both Boston and New York: "A lot of companies have really small budgets, so they come to companies like mine with low overhead. And we're able to put something really simple together for them."

MARSHALING YOUR NON-BROADCAST SKILLS

Exactly what does it take to work as a performer in non-broadcast media, as opposed to, say, broadcast commercials? Here are some things to keep in mind.

1 Develop sharp vocal skills. Industrials can pose more daunting acting challenges than other genres, especially when it comes to vocal stamina and concentration. Says Carol Nadell: "Whereas a commercial is thirty seconds—or a tag line, or three words—a non-broadcast voiceover tends to be longer. And therefore, the ability, the technique is much more apparent. So actors need to be able to breathe properly, have proper mike techniques. 'Voiceovers' is a technique: It's not just having a specific kind of voice."

2 Know your own image. Particular types of voices—and appearances—have special appeal to corporations and producers of industrials. It's important to know what you, as an actor, project. Annette Jenkins believes that she is often hired because of her assertive, authoritative sound. "My voice is a sort of strong, almost masculine, female voice. I think that's what they look for in me." She claims her appearance is also right for businesswoman roles—a staple of corporate videos. (Roles for "young mother" types, however, can turn up in videos for pharmaceutical companies, Jenkins adds.) Bob Goodman tells that his first paying job in South Florida came about because of his look: the producer wanted a tall, red-haired guy. Like Jenkins, Goodman these days often "plays corporate," and he keeps Wall Street-worthy clothes on hand to wear for corporate shoots. As he ages, Goodman allows his image to keep evolving.

3 Invest in your memory bank. Because there are often very long stretches of monologue (or dialogue) in non-broadcast projects, on-camera actors should polish their memorization skills. Says Goodman: "It's not too different from soaps. You can be dumped ten pages, and you get there in the morning and there are nine pages of revisions. You float or sink."

4 Get with the technology. Performers in industrials should be adept at using teleprompters and/or ear-prompters. Many actors who do non-broadcast projects now own the latter. Reportedly the gizmos—flesh-colored for camouflage purposes—are especially popular in the Midwest and South.

Gerry Gartenberg, a performer based in New Rochelle, New York, has had considerable experience in non-broadcast: some on-camera work, but mostly voiceovers.

He outlines a three-pronged strategy for narrators to successfully maneuver through lengthy scripts riddled with elaborate syntax and tongue-twisting medical or other technical jargon.

First, readers should concentrate on grasping the essence of the material. They should focus less on "how" they're going to perform it and more on the message they're conveying. Skills in script analysis are invaluable: "Where do the transitions in the copy occur? Where are the new ideas occurring? And because [audiences for the projects] are only listening to it and not reading it over again, how can you put all of the vocal grammar into the read? Developing that skill is very important."

Next, readers should find the right emotional attitude (or attitudes) that permeates the script. "For example," Gartenberg says, "you might have a medical story that's very objective—but certain aspects of the story might deal with a child who's been affected by a new treatment, maybe very positively. Where are the places within the copy where the emotions change? How do you make those adjustments in a real way?"

Finally, readers for industrials should work on their timing. Gartenberg: "Sometimes the copy is overwritten, so you need to speak faster. Sometimes the copy is sparse, and you need to be able to space it out." A producer might say after a take: 'That was fine, but this next time trim off two seconds.'"

But exactly how important is it for actors to have a real grasp of the jargon they're spouting in a voiceover—or to understand the intricacies of a piece of machinery they're demonstrating on camera? "I don't think you're going to get a medical degree," Gartenberg says. "But, having said that, I think it is important to understand a lot of it." Gartenberg has medical doctors in his family, so when he's cast in a pharmaceutical project, he'll occasionally run concepts or words past them.

Annette Jenkins recommends an exercise for coping with difficult medical text. It's useful, she says, to practice for such assignments by reading aloud the ingredients and directions from prescriptions and over-the-counter drugs.

Carol Nadell is impressed with actors who have a medical dictionary at their disposal. As a casting director looking at résumés, she wants to know about an actor's theatrical training and experience, but for industrials, she's also interested in knowledge they can bring from other disciplines. "Seeing that they might have had a financial background or a background in law or a medical background is always very good, because usually they bring a broader understanding of the material. But I find actors to be very smart. And the interesting thing about acting is the ability to learn about other areas. So it's more the willingness to learn than anything else."

23 Shooting for Success:

An Actor's Guide to the Student-filmmaking Experience

BY LUKE THOMAS CROWE

In the early 1960s, an unknown actor by the name of Robert De Niro was auditioning for every possible production he could find—for both stage and screen, paid and "un." "If you don't go, you'll never know," he explained later, to *The New York Times Magazine*. The auditioning process was arduous and didn't lead to much work at first. However, he said, "You have to *not* look at it like a rejection. There are so many reasons you're not picked that you can't even worry about it."

One role De Niro did manage to land was a small part in a New York University (NYU) student film called "The Wedding Party." That project's co-director, Brian De Palma, would later give De Niro his first leading role in a professional film— De Palma's debut feature, *Greetings*. De Palma and De Niro remained friends and, in the early '70s, they went to a party where De Palma introduced De Niro to another NYU film-school alumnus, Martin Scorsese. This meeting would lead to Scorsese's casting De Niro opposite Harvey Keitel in *Mean Streets,* the film that would jumpstart the careers of everyone involved. (Keitel, incidentally, met Scorsese while acting in a student film.)

Beginning with these student productions, Keitel, De Niro, Scorsese, and De Palma inaugurated highly esteemed actor-filmmaker relationships that have now spanned over thirty years, making clear at least one important lesson: An actor must not only impress the filmmakers he works with right from the get-go—exhibiting the full range of his talent and passion even on the smallest of projects—he must also make use of his networking skills, because, while not every film student is going to become wildly successful, the student-director of today might one day introduce his actor friends to fellow filmmakers who will provide them with the biggest breaks of their careers. Remember: for every film student an actor works with, a hundred more are lurking in the walls. When a performer ties himself into the network of one student filmmaker, he will link himself to a multitude of others. As these students graduate, making their way into the film industry, the actor's network will grow and expand with theirs.

FINDING THE GIG

In the majority of film programs, students are encouraged to explore a variety of talent-finding methods, and each filmmaker has his own unique casting preferences—

from using friends to casting individuals off the street. David Irving, undergraduate chairman of New York University's Department of Film and Television, says he always encourages his students to seek out professionally trained performers, but notes that casting novice actors can have its own creative and educational rewards.

Many student filmmakers attend plays to find talent, while some even hire professional casting directors; most place casting notices in *Back Stage,* or, in smaller college towns, in the local newspaper. Mike Titus, who studied film at The Cooper Union for the Advancement of Science and Art (in New York City), cast most of his student films while working on his fellow classmates' projects, where he could observe actors in the midst of their performances and see how they responded to being on set. "You can just tell if they have what you need, if you'll enjoy working with them," he says.

This variety of casting techniques offers up a truly unique experience on set, where actors might be coming from completely divergent backgrounds, with levels of skill and training varying wildly. Novices must be prepared to work alongside experienced actors, and vice-versa. Ideally, it's a learning and exploratory process for everyone involved, with the added benefit that the finished project might just end up being a work of art.

WORKING WITH STUDENT DIRECTORS

Regardless of an actor's level of professional experience, "he should react to a student director the way he reacts to any director," suggests actor-director Joe Paradise, a professor at New York's School of Visual Arts (SVA). "He should keep in mind the youth of the director, but still be prepared to take direction. At any age, if a director is impressed with an actor and they develop a good working relationship and rapport, then of course they'll continue to work together for a long time to come."

And, says Emmy-winner Iris Cahn, director of the State University of New York's Purchase College Film Department (SUNY Purchase), actors need to have faith that even though some students are beginners, they wouldn't be directing if they weren't qualified or talented or driven in some way.

A SUNY Purchase graduate, critically acclaimed filmmaker Hal Hartley (*Simple Men, Trust, Henry Fool,* etc.), who is currently teaching at the Visual and Environmental Studies department at Harvard, adds, "With a student project, I would caution the actor to be patient. In the best circumstances, the student film-maker is making it in order to learn, and so different kinds of attempts—revisions—are encouraged. At least this is how I teach my students. I don't urge them to make 'calling card' films." (A "calling card" film is intended strictly as a showcase of professional talent, as opposed to a project where a director is free to take risks, experiment, and learn.)

THE PERFORMER'S PERSPECTIVE

"I'm working on a pretty big independent film right now," says actress Chelsea Varano, "and it's made me realize how all these student projects I've acted in throughout the years have helped prepare me to feel more natural and comfortable with the technical aspects of the filmmaking process—allowing me to concentrate more on my performance and less on the camera and crew."

Student directors can become so encumbered with the technical aspects of film-making that, in some cases, the actors may feel they're secondary to the camera, lights, or location. Performers might even find themselves with no structured rehearsals before the shoot and little or no direction being offered on set. On the other hand, some directors may care *only* about the acting, and might try directing actors down to the slightest minutiae. In either of these circumstances, advises Hartley, actors need to trust in the director, but they should also protect their own craft. For instance, if actors don't feel like the director has scheduled enough rehearsal time, they should consider scheduling time among themselves. In the long run the director will appreciate the extra effort, and the film will be better for it.

Artist-actress Alice Rose Hurwitz doesn't have any such complaints—however, she notes, "Whether or not a student director graduates and 'makes it' in the film industry *and* remembers me as a talented actor is yet to be seen."

THE JUICE

Brigitte Bourdeau, a French-Canadian actress, has found some monetary success acting in films and commercials, but with professional gigs in the U.S., she finds herself continually cast as "The French Girl" and "The Model." To break away from this typecasting, Bourdeau seeks out roles in the theatre and student films, where she's less likely to be cast as two-dimensional window dressing. "Money we all think about, somehow, in the end," she laments, "but when you're in character, you forget about that, because if the character is good, well, that's the juice you're looking for as an actor."

Student films have given her that juice, but she does have some caveats about the process: Some film schools offer "crash courses, so as an actor you're crashed into them," she cautions, noting that when an actor decides to audition for a project, he should take into account the sort of program the student is in, what medium the project is being shot on, and what year the student is at within his course of study. As film students move from their first to their fourth year of film school, and then—in some cases—on to grad school, they are typically given increasing access to higher-end equipment, additional lights, dollies, cranes, and specialized lenses. They also become more experienced with the equipment they're using and more assured of their ability to work with actors.

Actress Emily Grace starred as the title character in *What Alice Found,* an independent film costarring two-time Tony-winner Judith Ivey. The film debuted to critical and audience acclaim at the 2003 Sundance and Tribeca film festivals, but even with this recent success, Grace hasn't stopped auditioning for student projects. "I'd definitely advocate for the process," she says. "Student films still help me grow as an actor, and learn and do what I love. I believe that the more you work, well, the more you work." If nothing else, she says, trying out for these projects "helps me hone my auditioning skills, keeping them fresh."

SECURING YOUR COPY, WATCHING YOUR BACK

Outside of the learning experience itself, there are few tangible benefits to working on a student film. Depending on the filmmaker's situation, some travel costs may be covered and meals might be provided on set, but the most important thing the film student has to offer the actor is a copy of the finished project—because, for a performer lacking professional representation, clips from these films can be used to build a reel of work for submission to agents. Also, with the director's permission, an actress can publicize herself by submitting her copy of the film to festivals, organizing a large screening of the film, or distributing copies to video stores.

But here's the rub: for endless reasons, many film students never actually give the actors a copy of the finished film. "It *is* a big problem," says SUNY Purchase's Iris Cahn, but if an actress is promised a video or DVD copy at the beginning of a production, she should be provided with one by the end of the semester. Even if all the filmmaker has available is an incomplete film, the student needs to deliver what he can. To ensure this, insists Cahn, "Everybody should have a contract when they work on *any* film," even a student production.

Nonunion actors should consider drawing up a contract based on the Screen Actors Guild (SAG) student agreement, which provides SAG actors with a certain amount of protection. By the same token, SAG actors should make sure they understand the details of the contract (often referred to as a "SAG waiver") before they agree to work on a project—and, more importantly, they should guarantee that the filmmaker has the contract available, without which a union actor cannot participate. The details of the contract, officially titled *The SAG Student Film Letter Agreement,* can be obtained by visiting the union's website at www.sag.org.

COMPETITION, STARDOM, AND REALITY

A number of successful actors got their start in student films, and even some well-known professionals occasionally still act in student productions, but for an unknown performer, landing a role is not always easy. In fact, the competition for these roles can rank in the tens of thousands, and rejection is frequent.

On a positive note, however: most film students share the headshots and résumés they receive from actors. Many submissions are filed away in the film schools' resource centers (especially headshots submitted to "general calls," which are casting calls run by the school itself, or by a particular class, as opposed to those run by individual students), and can be accessed for years to come. So it's quite possible that three years down the road a film student will discover your old submission tucked away in his school's resource database, inspiring him to offer you a brilliant lead role.

Of course, by then you may already be famous. But if not, then with hard work, perseverance, and professionalism, you might just find your very own Scorsese, beginning a career the way De Niro and Keitel did—through the world of student cinema.

24 Giving Full Voice to Your Talents:

Finding Voice and Voiceover Work

BY MARK DUNDAS WOOD

"Voice" and "voiceover" work seems to be one area of the entertainment/advertising industry that has remained healthy, even during times of economic downturn.

Developments in technology have a lot to do with this vitality. While the traditional avenues in voice are still there (television and radio commercials, industrial films, animated cartoons), there's a wide array of new paths to take as well. CD-ROMs and audio books require just the right vocal stamp. And the continuing importance of cable television provides even more opportunities for voice talent, especially in outlets like Discovery and The Learning Channel that are programmed heavily with narrated documentaries.

According to one New York-based voiceover producer, some television stations (along with networks like CNBC) will pay $100 per hour for a "voice talent" to come in as a staff announcer. He or she will spend a few hours per week recording short promo blurbs for upcoming programming—along with other assorted "bumpers" or "tags."

But the opportunities don't stop there. There's need for actors to record prompts for telephone systems (the voices you hear when you call your physician's office after hours) and for computer games. One company producing an interactive astronomy game decided to use a very soothing, high-tech-sounding female voice. The company recorded the vocals in both English and French.

Such multilingual gigs are also a part of the growth in the voice biz. In particular, the proliferation of Spanish-language TV and radio provides plenty of work for fluent speakers, especially in parts of the country with a large Hispanic population.

Most of these new opportunities are covered by union contracts, of course. But sorting out the union jurisdiction for the new technologies can be complicated. In fact, Ralph Braun, assistant executive director of the American Federation of Television and Radio Artists (AFTRA), explains that getting a handle on the intricate rules regarding contracts requires real patience and attention to detail. Generally speaking, voices used in television commercials are considered true "voiceovers" and are covered by Screen Actors Guild (SAG) contracts. AFTRA, meanwhile, handles radio-broadcast commercials and nonbroadcast recordings such as audio books and CD-ROMs.

"People tend to use the term 'voiceover' when they're talking about a radio commercial," says Braun. "It sort of doesn't make sense, because 'voiceover' comes from 'voice over picture'—meaning you're watching something and listening to something else."

Although union-affiliated actors may be reluctant to talk about it, there has also been a boom in nonunion voice work in recent years. The prolonged SAG strike of 2000 clearly changed the industry. Producers of national spots employed nonunion talent during the strike—and doors were opened for a lot of people who wouldn't otherwise have had a chance to audition.

Generally the voice business has been spared one piece of bad fortune that has afflicted on-camera work in recent years: while cost-conscious advertisers have tended to use on-camera work produced outside of the country, they've not relied heavily on such "runaway" product when it comes to vocal spots.

WHAT'S WITH YOUR VOICE?

According to one producer, there are three basic voice categories in commercial spots. There's the Announcer Voiceover (AVO), which is anyone who speaks about the product and comments on the action without offering a personal point of view. Then there's the Voiceover (VO): similar to the AVO, but offering a personal point of view. Finally there are the voices of characters, either on or off camera.

What constitutes an "announcer" voice has changed fairly drastically over the years. For one thing, female announcers have many more opportunities these days. And there's less distinction between announcer and character voices than in decades past. Announcers now tend to be natural and relaxed, perhaps with a kind of "textured" (but not damaged-sounding) vocal edge.

When it comes to character voices, quirkiness may always be in vogue. Many years ago, actress Alice Playten became nationally famous for Alka-Seltzer commercials in which she played a young bride with a distinctively baby-doll-ish voice. More recently, a pitch woman for Glad Bags demonstrated a similar cutesy affect.

Big advertisers may angle for a celebrity voice to sell their products. Richard Dreyfuss has been heard on Honda spots, and Donald Sutherland has pitched for Volvo. And we've all heard Lauren Bacall touting the virtues of a certain delectable brand of cat food. But sometimes the celeb goes unrecognized. Barbara Feldman (from TV's *Get Smart*) has reportedly done booming business for herself in voiceovers through the years, although her voice is seldom identified.

Some celebrities are paid big-time simply to audition for voiceovers. In fact, some won't audition for anything less than $200,000. However, when the deal falls through, a noncelebrity can rush in and reap the benefits. AT&T reportedly wanted Meryl Streep for a major campaign, but signed an unknown voice instead—in a $600,000 contract.

Versatility—even within a fairly narrow vocal range—is a good thing for voice talent to develop. "There's different intonations," says New York-based producer Steve Garrin. "You work the mike a little closer. You come in a little low and tight on the mike and it gives you a different sound. Or you move back a little bit."

Those who want to master these particular techniques may decide to seek formal instruction. But it's important to research the reputability of a particular teacher or course. Classes taught by producers and other business professionals—as opposed to those led by former or working voice talent—are probably the best bet. Courses offered at sound studios will probably be reputable, because studio owners won't risk putting their reputations on the line by hiring teachers who don't know what they're doing.

VOCAL INFLECTIONS: SOME CASE STUDIES

It's difficult to recommend one particular path for those interested in pursuing voice work. Of those who've made it in the business, each seems to have taken a unique route.

Take the case of Preston Trombly, whose voice has been featured in commercials for clients as diverse as UBS PaineWebber and Ricola throat lozenges. Trombly, who's also a musician, began working as a radio announcer and deejay when he was still in school. For several years, he concentrated on being a composer—but a few years ago he took some classes, put together a demo reel, and began actively seeking spoken voice work once again.

In addition to his work in commercials, Trombly has served as a staff announcer at New York's WOR radio and has hosted a classical music program for Sirius Satellite Radio. His live voice work in these venues has been an important complement to his taped voice work in commercials. It's helped him gauge, for instance, how to deliver a sixty-second spot in precisely sixty seconds.

Trombly's musical background has been beneficial, too: "If you're improvising a solo on the saxophone, you're telling a story in the same way you're telling a story with words. It's all about timing and breathing and phrasing."

Voice work was the very first avenue in the business that Rita Rehn pursued— several years ago, in Los Angeles. Later, when she took on jobs in regional theatre, she made it a point to contact nearby agents, who helped her land jobs in local commercials.

Actor Ernie Sabella was rehearsing for Broadway's revival of *Guys and Dolls* when he and *Guys* co-star Nathan Lane auditioned for the roles of two of the hyenas in a planned Disney animated feature, then called *The King of the Jungle*. Eventually the roles of Pumbaa the warthog and Timon the meerkat in *The Lion King* were penned especially for Sabella and Lane, based on their freewheeling improvisations during that initial audition.

Ronnie Farer was always interested in doing vocal work, but it wasn't until about 1995 that she decided to concentrate on voice instead of live theatre. Farer has since found a niche for herself as narrator of television documentaries—from *Diana: Death of a Princess* to *Women Behind Bars*.

When she arrived in Washington, D.C., to read for her first documentary booking—a program on the African savannah for Discovery—she found that the script she'd studied had been revised considerably. Initially, she was cued in by bar codes on the screen, which matched codes on her script. But she found she was a bit distracted by the onscreen animal behavior she was describing (what she refers to laughingly as "My Friends Were Eating Each Other"). So the engineers decided it would be best to have her follow a cue light instead.

Besides documentaries, Farer has read TV promos for Turner Classic movies. Promo reading is a whole different voiceover arena, she says, though it, too, calls for vocal variety. Big networks often request rapid, high-energy promos, while cable stations prefer a more leisurely delivery.

For those interested in pursuing narration, Farer recommends trying to break first into the world of industrials: training or informational films produced by companies such as the pharmaceutical giant Pfizer. (See chapter 22, "Industrial-Strength Peforming.")

GETTING NOTICED: THE DEMO REEL

Having a demo reel is essential for anyone pursuing work in the area of voice and voiceover. The reels should be concise—probably no more than one to two minutes for those desiring work in commercials. Several clips of commercials (not full commercials) should be included. One casting director admits that you need to "grab her" with your voice during the first seven seconds of demo—otherwise, that's all she'll listen to.

Whether or not aspiring voice talent should spend big for the production of a demo is something on which the experts disagree. One casting director cautions against having a CD produced on the cheap, because producers will recognize the work as unprofessional. But another casting director advises beginners not to spend "thousands of dollars worth of sound studio." The range in terms of cost is big. There are people who will produce your tape for $95, though these may be "cookie-cutter" operations, where each talent's demo is basically the same as the next. In some markets, studios will charge up to $1,200.

As much as possible show variety in your reel, as different spots show different aspects of your personality. Rehn says that "if you're selling Gerber baby formula as opposed to Snickers, it's just going to be different."

But even while providing variety, you should concentrate on presenting the real you—demonstrating what it is you do best, right off the bat. Unless you're preparing a cartoon reel, you probably shouldn't include a whole zoo-full of funny voices.

Demos for work in industrials or documentaries can run a bit longer than those for commercials—perhaps three and a half minutes. You'll need that extra time to show that you can tie ideas together and tell a story.

Remember that while you may attract the notice of an agent based on the content of your demo reel, you'll inevitably need to audition in person for jobs. Also, before you start mailing tapes, you should consult with a publication such as *Ross Reports* to determine which talent agencies have voice/voiceover divisions. While the primary people you'll want to target with your demos are agents, it's not unusual to send tapes directly to casting directors, or even, producers.

THE FRUIT BOWL

Angling for work in the area of voice/voiceover is not entirely a matter of luck. Skills and talent are certainly essential ingredients. But if you're an above-competent reader and still aren't getting gigs, it may just be a matter of pounding that proverbial pavement . . . and waiting.

Ronnie Farer, who always wanted to do voice work but only had a breakthrough in the last few years, explains: "I always compare this business to a bowl of fruit. You bring in the bowl . . . and on any given day, the people in charge decide whether they want an orange or an apple or a kiwi. It's taste, and it's dictated by styles of the moment."

TALKING FUNNY FOR MONEY
An Introduction to the Cartoon/Character/Looping
Area of Voice-Overs

by Pamela Lewis

First time ever! The acclaimed *Talking Funny for Money* workshop on two CDs, accompanied by exercise manual and companion text.

Curious about entering the exciting and lucrative world of "talking funny for money"?

Available at bookstores and www.talkingfunnyformoney.com
or
Order directly from Music Dispatch (Item #314627):
1-800-637-2852 or www.musicdispatch.com
$22.95 + tax + shipping
Published by Applause Theatre & Cinema Books

LIZ CAPLAN VOCAL STUDIOS
CONGRATULATES....

Amy Spanger (*Hope*) • *Urinetown* • Broadway
Michael C. Hall (*Billy*) • *Chicago* • Broadway
Molly Ringwald (*Sally Bowles*) • *Cabaret* • Broadway
Lisa Datz (*Pam*) • *The Full Monty* • Broadway
Kerry Butler (*Audrey*) • *Little Shop* • Broadway
Hunter Foster (*Seymour*) • *Little Shop* • Broadway
Jo Ann Hunter (*Gloria*) • *Thoroughly Modern Millie* • Broadway
Luther Creek (*Bobby*) • *Urinetown* • Broadway
Deven May (*Bat Boy*) • *Bat Boy* • Off-Broadway
Kathy Brier (*Tracy*) • *Hairspray* • Broadway
Isabelle Flachsmann • *42nd Street* • Broadway
Michael Holmes (*Bloom u/s*) • *Producers* • National Tour
Victoria Matlock (*The Full Monty*) • National Tour
Ana Gasteyer (*Fanny*) • *Funny Girl* • Pittsburgh CLO
Cathy Trien (*Rose u/s*) • *Gypsy* • Broadway
Kate Reinders (*June*) • *Gypsy* • Broadway
Peter Scolari (*Wilbur*) • *Hairspray* • Broadway
Aymee Garcia • *Avenue Q* • Broadway
Adrienne Franz (*Amber*) • *Bold and The Beautiful* • CBS Daytime
Willa Ford • *Atlantic/Lava Records*
John Rzeznik (*Goo Goo Dolls*) • *Warner Records*
The Donnas • *Atlantic Records*

1 (866) SING OUT (746-4688) or **212-645-9369**
Phone/fax: 212-645-9369 toll free: 1 (866) SING OUT
email: LizVocal@aol.com   web: www.LizCaplan.com

TO ADVERTISE
IN THE NEXT

BACKSTAGE®/BACK STAGE WEST®

ACTORS
HANDBOOK

PLEASE CALL

WEST ■   ■ EAST
Back Stage West Back Stage
Advertising   Advertising
5055 Wilshire Blvd., 5th fl. 770 Broadway, 4th floor
Los Angeles, CA 90036 New York, NY 10003
323.525.2225   646.654.5700

VOICEOVER WORKSHOPS

LEARN FROM THE BEST
SUSAN BLU

RENOWNED ACTOR, DIRECTOR, CASTING DIRECTOR, AUTHOR OF
"WORD OF MOUTH"

CLASSES IN COMMERCIAL & ANIMATION
ALL LEVELS
(818) 509-1483
FOR FINEST PROFESSIONAL DEMOS
(818) 501-1258
www.blupka.com

THE VOICECASTER

Voiceover Workshops   All Levels + Animation
Study with Huck Liggett, Owner
818-218-2342
CASTING VOICEOVERS FOR OVER 27 YEARS...

VOICEOVER WORKSHOPS

IN ORANGE COUNTY & SAN DIEGO
• Bootcamp • Advanced Workout
• Accent Reduction • Singing
Also available - Demo Production & Private Coaching
BEVERLY BREMERS (949) 874-0616
www.voicercise.net

Leigh Gilbert
Privates, Group Classes,
Demo Tapes
Improve Technique
& Booking Ratio's
(323) 692-5704
leeleethevoguru@aol.com

25 Jingles All the Way:

Singing Opportunities in the
Commercial Industry

BY MARK DUNDAS WOOD

A key point for an aspiring jingle singer to keep in mind is that—in today's corporate world—the word "jingle" itself tends to be frowned on.

"Nobody likes to refer to anything as a jingle anymore," explains Joey Levine of Crushing Enterprises—one of the biggest Manhattan commercial music houses. "It's 'an original song' or 'a short-form song' or a song that's contemporary and sounds like something else. . . . Nobody really wants that word used alongside their brand."

Levine should know. He's essentially America's "J-word king." He segued from a career as a writer of bubblegum pop songs ("Chewy Chewy," "Yummy Yummy Yummy (I Got Love in My Tummy)") to a life writing such classic commercial spots as "Sometimes You Feel Like a Nut" (for Almond Joy/Mounds) and "Just for the Taste of It—Diet Coke."

Yes, the term "jingle" is quaint—conjuring up an old-fashioned, lilting, heavily harmonic sound—perhaps best epitomized by the merry old Roto-Rooter ad that whisked the consumer's troubles gently down the drain. Nevertheless, some commercial music insiders still use the term "jingle" unapologetically—even fondly.

SNUGGLE UP TO YOUR CASH REGISTER

The conventional wisdom about jingle singing on the national level is that it's a field that's practically impossible to break into—a business dominated by a circle of twenty to twenty-five New York-based vocalists who work regularly and rake in thousands and thousands of dollars a year.

And to some degree, conventional wisdom is correct.

That jingle singing can be lucrative is unquestionably the case. True, the basic payment scale for a jingle recording session under union contracts—The American Federation of Television and Radio Artists (AFTRA) for radio spots; the Screen Actors Guild (SAG) for filmed commercials; both unions for videotaped commercials—is unimpressive. A singer hired for a single recording session earns a session fee, the size of which depends on whether he or she is hired as a choral singer or a soloist, and whether he or she appears on or off camera. (For a current fee schedule, go to www.aftra.com.)

The real money can be made from the use fees (commonly called "residuals"). If the vocal from a session is selected for airing as part of a nationally televised campaign, the original session fee covers the first airing of the recording. Then the singer is compensated on a payment schedule that decreases with each subsequent airing—but eventually levels off. The numbers can add up, depending on the relentlessness of the tele-campaign.

Commercials may also be distributed as locally aired "wild spots"—running on time purchased by the advertiser at each station in each local market. Radio commercials involve a flat-use fee that is paid to singers for a broadcasting period of one, four, eight, or thirteen weeks. When singers perform for the initial session, they usually have no idea how—or even whether—their work will be distributed. Perhaps the session will be made for demonstration purposes only, i.e., to sell the tune. A client may love the jingle, but not the voice singing it.

So it's impossible to tell how much you may eventually make in a studio session. As one veteran singer explains, "In one afternoon, you can make seventy grand—or you can make $145. You never know; it's like a lottery." Some jingles may air for two months; others may be around for three years—or even longer.

There's also no guarantee that a single successful spot will necessarily lead to future work in the jingle field. As Levine tells it, there used to be cliques of singers that would be hired regularly. "Nowadays," he explains, "you really look for originality and fresh sounds. . . . You're on a talent search to find someone who hasn't been used a lot."

This is terrific for a singer who hopes to make some money on the side, but it's not great news for those who want to make a whole career out of singing the praises of soft drinks, paper towels, and automobiles.

THE RIGHT (VOCAL) STUFF

What kind of voice do you need for jingle singing? Versatility and a gift for mimicry are key. Newcomers should listen to the pop charts—or follow shows like *American Idol*—to become aware of which sounds are currently in vogue. In fact, producers often keep their eyes on those singers who are close to landing recording contracts of their own.

According to Valerie Wilson Morris of Val's Artist Management in New York, "Fifteen or twenty years ago, jingles were jingles. They didn't sound like songs on the radio. Now the jingle business imitates the record business."

Those classic jingles were often closely aligned with a Broadway sound. Some may remember that, years ago, Frank Loesser's "Fugue for Tinhorns" from *Guys and Dolls* was recast as a commercial for Pillsbury Flour: "Create a chocolate cake/ create a cherry pie/Create a stack of golden biscuits ten feet high./Can do, can do/ With Pillsbury, you can do."

More recently, Stephen Sondheim's "Putting It Together" was used in a Xerox spot. And the Gershwin classic "Our Love Is Here to Stay" has been heard on Chrysler ads. These instances prove that there are opportunities in jingle singing for all kinds of music makers. But those who want steadier work need to have a fairly broad range.

One successful New York jingle singer, Elaine Caswell, describes her own usual singing style as soulful in a Linda Ronstadt kind of way: But for jingle work, she has been called on to modify her voice—twisting it to sound like Cyndi Lauper, for instance.

"It was really fun . . . to do these characters or turn on a certain sound: 'Oh, you want that really kind of pinched nasally sound? If we put it in a lower key, I can give you a warmer, richer, more naive sound.'"

This knack for on-the-spot modulating proves useful for group-sung jingles as well as for solo work. Choral singers need to know how to cooperate with one another and how to experiment to get just the right flavor. Part of that means knowing how to turn off your own "solo" sound and become part of the blend. Do you need to sing stronger on certain notes? Should you be singing the highest part? The melody? The tenor or the baritone line? "There's all these little subtleties that you become hip to through experience," Caswell explains.

Choral groups for jingles have grown smaller in recent years. This is partly attributable to musical trends: The public wants to hear a Backstreet Boys or Blink-182 sound, not the Ray Conniff Singers. But the trend also has to do with economic realities. Why should producers pay for eight or more voices when three or four will suffice?

Composers themselves often sing at their own jingle demo sessions these days—and some go on to sing in the final broadcast product. Technology has made all of this possible. It's now much easier for independent producers to create a finished-sounding product in the privacy of their own apartments than it was fifteen years ago.

The ability to sight-read is a plus—but not essential according to veteran singer Russell Velazquez. "If you can sing in pitch and have a good ear and can learn quickly, then you certainly can work in the business. . . . Basically you go to the session and they're gonna play it down for you a couple of times and you're gonna sing it. That's it."

SELLING IT

Knowing how to market yourself is a big part of success in the jingle field. Certainly you will want to create a demo reel—a tape or, more likely these days, a CD.

Biz insiders cite the following tips for creating an outstanding jingle reel:

1 Keep it short and sweet—no more than five minutes altogether. Put your best stuff right at the top of the reel.

2 Don't try to predict what it is producers are looking for. Include the musical clips you like best, and the ones you take pride in.

3 Avoid inclusion of original material. Sometimes it's easier for producers to "locate" a new singer if they're hearing him or her sing familiar material.

4 When packaging the demo, don't just slap a handwritten label on it. Give some thought to the presentation of the package.

There are differences of opinion about whether or not jingle artists need professional representation. While actors and commercial voiceover artists have tended to work through agents, jingle singers customarily have marketed themselves. Agents are legal for jingle singers under union rules, but they've not traditionally been utilized. As a spokesman from AFTRA puts it: "Jingle singers usually get their jobs through contractors, or the producer knows them personally. It's a field in which you build a reputation from doing the work and then you're called back and back and back again."

In recent years, however, there's been a growth in "personal managers" for jingle singers. While these people won't book jobs for you, they can help in other phases of your career: advising, marketing, recommending vocal coaches, etc.

The utilization of personal managers by jingle singers is controversial. If you're thinking of pursuing a career in this area, try to find out whether most of the performers in your geographical market utilize personal managers to help promote their careers.

THE EAR KNOWS

Jingle singing is certainly not something to pursue with a lackadaisical attitude. According to one writer-producer, Chris McHale of the McHale Barone music house in Manhattan, the consumer's aural mechanism is finely tuned:

"The psychology of the ear is really subtle," he explains. "The eye is nothing. You take it in and you delight in it. That's why I think people can sit in front of the TV for hours and look at junk. Because the eye is being entertained—'Oh, pretty colors!'—you know? But the ear is very discerning. And the ear will see the crap and go, 'That's crap, that's false, that's not true.'"

McHale is always on the lookout for new talent. He's unperturbed by here-today-gone-tomorrow trends—such as the phenomenon of "needle drops": the use of vintage and not-so-vintage pop recordings in commercials (in lieu of new vocal recordings). Thirty advertisers may use such a gimmick, McHale notes, but the thirty-first will say, "I want something fresh."

Which should come as welcome news to fresh new voices who are trying to machete their way through the jingle jungle.

Studio & Jingle Singing Prep

Study sight-reading, sight-singing,
ear-training, pitch control, rhythm
training, performance
anxiety, how to sing harmony,
self-accompanying, song writing,
piano skills.
Howard Richman
818.344.3306
www.soundfeelings.com
(search: sight-singing)

ACTORFEST
A DAY FOR ACTORS

CAREER SEMINARS • CASTING DIRECTORS
AGENTS • FOCUS SESSIONS • MANAGERS
FREE EXHIBIT HALL • AND MUCH MORE

FOR EXHIBIT HALL SPACE CALL

WEST ■　　**■ EAST**

Back Stage West Advertising	Back Stage Advertising
5055 Wilshire Blvd., 5th fl.	770 Broadway, 4th floor
Los Angeles, CA 90036	New York, NY 10003
323.525.2225	646.654.5700

26 Daytime Drama:
Don't Be Left in the Dark

BY ESTHER TOLKOFF

True love, illicit lust, family ties, family conflicts, lifelong friendships, scheming betrayals.

Kidnappings, murders, weddings, royal coronations, amnesia.

Laughter, tears, envy, anger, youthful rebellion.

The cascade of emotions and of crisscrossing plots and characters to be found on daytime television drama call for actors who have access to the complete spectrum of emotions.

And they must do so quickly.

Speed is the one consistent theme that emerges when speaking with those involved with "soap operas," as daytime dramas are, of course, informally referred to. The nickname springs from Procter & Gamble, which originated the genre to keep radio listeners so interested in the programming that they would "stay tuned" and hear the commercials for P&G's many soap-related products.

THE SUDSY "SKINNY"

Most of the soaps that broadcast regularly—some from New York, some from Los Angeles—have been on the air for years. These programs are avidly followed by huge numbers of fans. To keep viewers watching, the programs come up with new cliffhanger plots day after day. That adds up to plenty of work for actors.

But it's very hard work. "Every day is opening night," says New York-based agent Honey Raider. In theatre, rehearsals are held for weeks or months. Feature films are shot over long periods of time. Even in the high-pressure world of prime-time sitcoms or episodic television series, the team works on a single show per week. Soaps churn out a show per day.

Daytime drama principals handle a vast amount of rapid memorization—anywhere from twenty to sixty pages per day, according to Susan Pratt, who has played principal roles on *Guiding Light, General Hospital, All My Children,* and *Loving.*

Actors with speaking roles report to the set at seven or eight in the morning. They go through a "dry rehearsal," which consists of running their lines, going through their scenes, and receiving initial blocking instructions off the set, with the director and the producers. There may be script changes even at that late point. The actors then break for makeup and wardrobe and next head to the set, where their blocking instructions may be adjusted somewhat for the camera. Then there is a combination tech and dress rehearsal, followed by the actual taping of the show. Occasionally, more than one show is taped on a given day.

Rebecca Budig, known for her portrayal of Greenlee Smythe on New York-based *All My Children,* points out, "Many times your scene is the climactic moment on one day's show, and you start the next day picking it up right there, leaping directly into an intense scene, like a long-term romance breaking up. My scene-study training proved to be important."

There is very little rehearsal time to establish these quickly memorized scenes. Teleprompters are rarely used. So agents and casting directors say that while good looks are important when filling most soap roles, topnotch acting skills, reliability, and a willingness to work very hard are also musts.

Every series employs "contract players": the ongoing principals. But throughout the season, other actors are cast in principal-level "day player" roles. These can be recurring parts or may be one-time stints.

"Under-fives" are actors who literally have five lines or fewer.

Many background actors ("extras") are also cast in soaps. These performers get their blocking direction from the stage manager. They do not attend the "dry rehearsal," but are there for all other aspects of the day's work.

Sometimes a background actor can become an under-five without even speaking a word. According to the office of the American Federation of Television and Radio Artists (AFTRA), if a principal character addresses a background actor, and that line moves the story plot along, the actor spoken to then counts as an under-five.

Contract players' schedules vary but are intense. When a character's storyline is on "the front burner," the actor is there every day for long hours. If the plot moves that character to "the back burner," the actor may be called in only two or three days a week for shorter scenes.

LANDING THE ROLES

Each series has its own casting director, who consults with the producers when seeking contract players. The casting director also selects day players. Each series also has an associate or assistant casting director who hires the under-fives and background actors.

At the contract player level, the search is a major endeavor, with auditions held in both New York and Los Angeles. "I'll see well over 300 actors for most of those roles," says Rob Decina, casting director for New York's *The Guiding Light.* "They'll get four to seven pages of sides to learn." After the field is narrowed, those under consideration will undergo screen tests, playing a scene from the show opposite a cast member. The tests are shot on a set, using three cameras. The executive producer then views the tests. Actors may be called back several times.

Julie Madison, casting director for New York's *One Life to Live,* says the actors she sees for contract role auditions are either sent by agents or recommended by someone she knows professionally.

When casting day players, casting directors see roughly seventy-five actors for a recurring role and five or six for a one-time day-player part.

Casting directors look for actors who make strong choices and quickly establish their characters. This ability is a must in view of the high speed and ensemble nature of daytime dramatic work. For the same reasons, casting directors also look for flexibility and an ability to take direction. On the set, performers must respond rapidly to the director's notes or sudden script changes.

Casting directors say they have called back actors who did not seem right for the initial role they auditioned for but did seem suitable for another part later.

Contrary to widespread belief, the actors sought for soaps are not necessarily young. Extended family storylines span generations. There is also more ethnic diversity in today's daytime dramas than past years'.

Plot lines determine what sorts of performers are sought. Some scripts stick to the ongoing principal characters. Others may use several day players. A new story-line may require new contract players. Or an actor may leave, creating the need for a replacement. So openings do occur.

UNDER-FIVES AND BACKGROUND

A good way to break into daytime drama can be through under-five roles and background work. And while networking, word-of-mouth referrals, and agents are the most likely routes to getting cast, daytime drama is one area where sending in headshots and résumés may bring results. Casting directors for these roles receive enormous numbers of photos, but they do make an effort to look at as many as possible.

Lamont Craig, who casts under-fives and background players for New York's *As the World Turns,* observes, "There are people who look down on doing extra work. I think they're wrong. When you're on the set, you learn firsthand how it all works. You can establish yourself as a reliable professional and acquire valuable informa-tion from others about auditions and contacts."

Daytime dramas often call background actors back for additional episodes. Since the plots often take place in small towns, the same waiters, for instance, are likely to work at a local restaurant. The background actors' role is to create a real-istic atmosphere for the principals' scenes.

Background players who work on a show regularly are often upgraded to under-five spots. There are also cases—though this is far less likely—in which extras are upgraded to the principal level.

Rebecca Budig's first soap role was as a day player on Los Angeles' *The Bold and the Beautiful.* Her manager used this tape to get her an agent and auditions, which led to later contract roles on other soaps.

Punctuality and a spirit of cooperation are crucial to an actor's being rehired. The casts of these shows work together regularly as well-honed ensembles. If a background performer gives the job less than full attention, or doesn't show up without giving prior notice, those in charge will remember. If you don't want a job, don't take it. But if you take it, do it properly.

THE JOB ITSELF

Daytime performers have a knack for processing the enormous amount of memo-rization required. Though they get their scripts about a week in advance, many wait until shortly before taping to learn their lines, so as not to get confused. This also leaves them alert for changes. They often run lines with fellow actors while other scenes are being shot.

As in film, all of the scenes on a given set are shot in a block before the work moves on to another set. These scenes are later interspersed throughout the episode. An effort is made to tape the scenes in sequence on each specific set.

Because time is at such a premium, reactions are as important as actions and words. A facial expression telegraphs those emotional reactions. The "tags" at the end of a scene (those intense takes!) sum up for the viewer exactly how the character is affected.

The time factor also means that making too many mistakes becomes a real problem. Of course, some flubs (and certainly technical glitches) are inevitable. Sometimes, as in a theatrical production, another actor comes through with a quick "save" and the tape keeps rolling. Other times, taping stops, and the action picks up where it left off.

Casting directors mention theatre training as good preparation for daytime dramas. Actors agree, but add that a class in acting for the camera is also useful. A major difference from theatre is that you can't let a performance grow by refining it over time with each evening's performance. You have to deliver it once, let go of it emotionally, and move right on to your next scene.

As in real life, every day is a new episode.

Daytime Soaps
(FROM *ROSS REPORTS*)

New York Based

ALL MY CHILDREN
ABC, Monday–Friday, 1–2PM NYT - Tape
Prod. Co: ABC-TV, 320 West 66th Street, New York 10023. Executive Producer: Jean Dadario Burke. Supervising Producer: Ginger Smith. Producer: Casey Childs. Associate Producer: Nadine Aronson. Assistant Producer: Enza Dolce. Directors: Conal O'Brien, Bob Scinto, Angela Tessinari, Jim Baffico. Creator: Agnes Nixon. Writers: Megan McTavish (Head); Jeff Beldner, Lisa Conor, Addie Walsh, Victor Miller, Mimi Leahey, Bettina F. Bradbury, John Piroman, Karen Lewis, Rebecca Taylor, David A. Levinson (Breakdown Writers). Casting: Judy Blye Wilson (Casting Director); Robert Lambert (Associate - Under 5's & Extras); Anthony Volastro (Casting Assistant). Send photos, resumes, postcards to above address. DON'T PHONE.

AS THE WORLD TURNS
CBS, Monday–Friday, 2–3PM NYT - Tape
Prod. Co: TeleVest Daytime Programming for Procter & Gamble. Executive Producer: Chris Goutman. Senior Producer: Carole Shure. Producers: Vivian Gundaker. Coordinating Producer: Kelsey Bay. Associate Producer: Jennifer Maloney. Directors: Maria Wagner, Michael Eilbaum, Ellen Wheeler, Steven Williford. Writers: Hogan Sheffer (Head); Jean Passanante (Co-Head Writer), Christopher Whitesell (Associate Head Writer); Susan Dansby (Associate Head Writer), Lynn Martin, Courtney Simon, Judy Donato, Susan Dansby, Judy Tate, Meg Kelly, Tom Reilly, Elizabeth Page, Craig Heller, Charlotte Gibson. Casting: Mary Clay Boland (Principals); LaMont Craig (Under 5's); Kate Martineau (Extras), 1268 East 14th Street, Brooklyn, NY 11230. Send photos-resumes. DON'T PHONE OR VISIT.

GUIDING LIGHT
CBS, Monday–Friday, 10–11AM NYT - Tape
Sponsor: Procter & Gamble. Prod. Co: TeleVest Daytime Programming for Procter & Gamble. Executive Producer: John Conboy. Senior Producer: Robert D. Kochman. Producer: Alexandra Johnson. Directors: Bruce S. Barry, Jo Anne Sedwick, Susan Strickler, Brian Mertes. Writers: Ellen Weston (Head Writer) Carolyn Culliton (Co-Head Writer), Christopher Dunn, Lucky Gold, Jill Lorie Hurst, Penelope Koechl, David Kreizman, Eleanor Labine, Melissa Salmons, David Smilow, Danielle Paige, Kimberly Hamilton. Coordinating Producer: Maria Macina. Casting: Rob Decina (Casting Director), Melanie Haseltine (Associate Casting Director), 222 East 44th Street, New York 10017. Accepts postcards/showcase invitations. DON'T PHONE OR VISIT.

ONE LIFE TO LIVE
ABC, Monday–Friday, 2–3PM NYT - Tape
Prod. Co: ABC-TV, 56 West 66th Street, New York 10023. Executive Producer: Frank Valentini. Producer: Suzanne Flynn. Coordinating Producer: Sonia Ann Blangiardo. Assistant Producer: Jennifer Margulis. Directors: Larry Carpenter, Bruce Cooperman, Gary Donatelli, Jill Mitwell. Creator: Agnes Nixon. Writers: Josh Griffith (Head Writer), Michael Malone (Head Writer), Lorraine Broderick (Head Writer), Shelly Altman (Breakdown), Richard Backus (Breakdown), Ron Carlivati (Breakdown), Anna Theresa Cascio (Breakdown), David Cherrill, Michelle Poteet Lisanti, Leslie Nipkow, Becky Cole, Ginger Redmon, Daniel S. Griffin. Casting: Julie Madison (Director); Victoria Visgilio (Associate), Sheryl Baker-Fisher (Assistant). Send photos-resumes or postcards only to: 157 Columbus Avenue, 2nd Floor, New York 10023. NO PHONE CALLS OR VIDEO TAPES.

Los Angeles Based

THE BOLD AND THE BEAUTIFUL
CBS, Monday–Friday, 1:30–2PM NYT - Tape
Prod. Co: Bell-Phillip Television Prods, Inc.
at CBS Television City, 7800 Beverly Blvd.,
Suite 3371, Los Angeles, CA 90036.
(323) 575-4138. Executive Producer: Bradley
Bell. Supervising Producer: Rhonda Friedman.
Senior Producer: Ron Weaver. Producer:
Cynthia J. Popp. Associate Producer: Erin E.
Stewart. Directors: Michael Stich, Deveney
Kelly, Cynthia J. Popp. Creators: William J.
Bell, Lee Phillip Bell. Writers: Bradley Bell
(Head Writer), Meg Bennett (Executive Story
Consultants), Teresa Zimmerman, Tracey Kelly,
Beth Milstein, Michael Minnis, Rex Best,
Candace Kirby. Executive Story Consultant:
William J. Bell. Casting: Christy Dooley at
above address.

DAYS OF OUR LIVES
NBC, Monday–Friday, 1–2PM NYT - Tape
Prod. Co: Corday Productions, Inc. with
Columbia Pictures TV, NBC Studios 2 & 4,
3000 West Alameda Avenue, Burbank,
CA 91523. (818) 295-2831. Executive
Producers: Ken Corday, Stephen Wyman.
Senior Coordinating Producers: Janet
Spellman-Rider, Tom Walker. Coordinating
Producer: Debbie Ware Barrows. Directors:
Herb Stein, Phil Sogard, Randy Robbins,
Roger Inman. Headwriters: Paula Cwikly,
Peter Brash. Casting: Fran Bascom (Director);
Linda Poindexter (Atmosphere) at Corday
Productions, The Pinnacle, 3400 West Olive
Avenue, #315, Burbank, CA 91505.

GENERAL HOSPITAL
ABC, Monday–Friday, 3–4PM NYT - Tape
Prod. Co: ABC-TV, The Prospect Studios,
4151 Prospect Avenue, Los Angeles, CA 90027.
Executive Producer: Jill Farren Phelps. Producers:
Carol Scott, Mary O'Leary, Mercer Barrows.
Associate Producer: Michele Henry. Coordinating
Producer: Deborah Genovese. Directors: Bill
Ludel, Scott McKinsey, Owen Renfroe, Joe Behar,

Grant Johnson. Writers: Bob Guza, Jr., Charles
Pratt, Jr. (Head Writers); Garin Wolf, Michael
Conforti, Michelle Patrick, Elizabeth Korte,
Susan Wald, Mary Sue Price, Michelle Val Jean.
Creators: Frank & Doris Hursley. Casting: Mark
Teschner at above address. Publicity: Mitch
Messinger.

PASSIONS
NBC, Monday–Friday, 2–3PM NYT - Tape
Prod. Co: NBC Studios, 4024 Radford Avenue,
Studio City, CA 91604. Creator: James E. Reilly.
Executive Producer: Lisa de Cazotte. Supervising
Producer: Richard Schilling. Producer: Mary-Kelly
Weir. Coordinating Producer: Jeanne Haney.
Associate Producer: Denise Mark. Writers: James
E. Reilly (Head), Darrell Ray Thomas, Jr., Nancy
Williams Watt, Maralyn Thoma, Roger Newman,
N. Gail Lawrence, Marlene Clark Poulter, Pete
Rich. Directors: James Sayegh, Karen Wilkens,
Peter Brinckerhoff, Phideaux Xavier, Gary Tomlin.
Casting Director (Principals Only): Jackie Briskey;
Under 5's & Extras: Don Philip Smith (Associate).
NO PHONE CALLS. Publicity: Eva Demirjian.

THE YOUNG AND THE RESTLESS
CBS, Monday–Friday, 12:30–1:30PM NYT - Tape
Prod. Co: Bell Dramatic Serial Co./Corday
Prods, Inc./Sony Pictures Domestic Television,
7800 Beverly Blvd., Suite 3305, Los Angeles,
CA 90036. (323) 575-2532. Senior Executive
Producer: William J. Bell. Co-Executive Producer:
John F. Smith. Supervising Producer: Edward J.
Scott. Producer: Kathy Foster. Associate Producer:
Josh O'Connell. Directors: Mike Denney, Kathy
Foster, Sally McDonald, Noel Maxam. Creators:
William J. Bell, Lee Phillip Bell. Writers: William J.
Bell (Head), Kay Alden,
(Head), Jack F. Smith (Co-Head), Trent Jones
(Co-Head Writer), Jerry Birn, Janice Ferri,
Jim Houghton, Eric Freiwald, Natalie Minardi.
Executive Vice President, Marketing, Sony
Pictures Domestic Television: Robert Oswaks.
Director of Publicity, The Young and the
Restless: Elise Bromberg. Casting: Marnie
Saitta (Casting Director) at above address.

27 Promoting Business with Show Biz:

The State of Live Industrials Today

BY SIMI HORWITZ

"I was playing a tough Philip Marlowe-type gumshoe, hired by a floozy who was having trouble with her computer," recalls actor Steve Friedman. "After I tracked down the computer problem—there was a lack of security, and important material from her computer had been stolen—the floozy and I realized we knew each other. . . ."

Undoubtedly, romance was in the air, but, no, this was not a scene from a foolish play or sitcom. It was business theatre—also known as a "live industrial"—and Friedman was using his considerable acting skill to demonstrate the virtues of a new security system designed for computers. He was performing at a convention center, and his audience was made up of corporate salespeople in the computer world.

Business theatre is, of course, not new. It has been around in one form or another for half a century or more and reached its heyday in the 1960s with the now-legendary Milliken extravaganzas, which touted the beauty of Milliken textiles. These lavish shows—not unlike mini-Broadway musical productions—boasted large singing and dancing casts, awash in costumes and sets.

Admittedly, such large-scale offerings are rare today. The big consideration, of course, is economic. "How can a corporation justify spending large sums of money for entertainment when it's downsizing its staff?" asks Bob Pushkin, who has been a stage manager at these events for twenty-two years.

For the most part, when these shows are mounted—say, for the launching of a pricey car or computer—they're on a smaller scale these days, with fewer performers on hand. But live industrials are by no means dead.

In this chapter we will take a look at this unusual genre to find out what's happening now: who's doing what, the opportunities, the do's and don'ts, the caveats.

WHO'S DOING WHAT?

Three corporate-event categories include an element of entertainment, says Pushkin: "For starters, there are trade shows, which may be open to the public or only open to industry insiders. Then there are corporate internal meetings, where, for example, the national sales staff has gathered to learn about a new product or service. And, finally, there are the 'recognition events' that pay tribute to special employees."

At the recognition events (which often evoke a "roast"), the entertainment component is probably the most pronounced. There is also a strong inspirational and instructional element at play. Indeed, at all of these gatherings, training and motivation are none too subtly couched in the entertainment. In many instances, the performances are peppered with videos and/or skits that train employees, as well as straightforward speeches that promote team spirit.

Very few of these events are exclusively entertainment based. And even within the parameters of entertainment, an evolution has occurred. There's an effort at being current, not hokey or excessively "show-biz." And state-of-the-art technology in lighting, sound, and multimedia effects is standard fare.

In an attempt to reflect the sensibilities—indeed, the demographics—of those in attendance, the producers of these events hire a diverse group of performers—ethnically, racially, and sociologically speaking. There's more of an effort to mirror reality these days. In the old days, the "hot babe" might promote a car. Today, the "soccer mom" is a more likely candidate.

The quirky has an appeal. So do celebrities and celebrity look-alikes. And it's not uncommon today for executives—or other nonactors who are nonetheless authorities in their fields—to perform alongside the actors in order to give the event the necessary authenticity.

Peter Scott, a vice president of New York City-based Drury Design Dynamics (a company that creates industrial theatre, among other things) describes one of the more colorful productions for a pharmaceutical company's sales staff. The presentation promoted a once-a-month injectable birth-control device.

"We wanted to motivate the salespeople to sell the new product," says Scott. "So we set up a mock trial—the pill vs. the injection—with a judge sitting at the dais, prosecutors, and witnesses, including real doctors, testifying on both sides. The judge, prosecutors, and bailiff were all actors. The salespeople were the jury. At the end of the trial, we asked the salespeople to cast their vote."

Guess which side won?

There are more traditional productions. Bob Penola, a creative director at Jack Morton Worldwide (one of the heavy hitters in special events, including live industrials) talks about a full-scale musical show he helmed for the Philadelphia-based fundraisers for the Salvation Army.

"The ninety-minute show, which employed seven actors and a six-piece band led by Broadway conductor Joe Baker, brought together the music of Broadway shows, gospel, and pop. . . . The production, which was called 'Four Freedoms'—freedom from fear, freedom from want, freedom of faith, and freedom to express oneself—had sets and costumes. We rehearsed for three weeks and, at the end of the show, we got five ovations."

THE NATURE OF THE WORK AND PAY

Some gigs, like the aforementioned, are one-shots, running ninety minutes or two hours. More commonly, however, shows run fifteen or twenty minutes and are offered as repeat performances over a period of days—up to nine times a day over three or four days.

"The actor who works in industrial theatre has to be able to pace himself," notes actor Friedman. "He always has to sound like he cares about what he's doing and the product he is promoting. But he can't give it all away, especially when he has to repeat the performance many times in the course of the day."

Audiences may be as small as several hundred, or 1,500, or all the way up to 150,000—for computer or car product launches.

Scripts may be twenty pages or more, and there may be only one rehearsal. "I use an ear prompter," says Friedman. "I think it's a good idea for actors who do this kind of work to be comfortable with one."

An ear prompter is not unlike a hearing aid with a volume control and, in some devices, a hand-held pause button. All of the equipment is discreetly connected to a small tape recorder worn under the clothes. It is custom-made, pricey—and it is only suggested for the most seasoned actor.

Whether you memorize the copy or use an ear prompter, you need to sound as though you know what you're talking about, says Pushkin. Mark Hider, CEO at Imagination USA (one of the major players in corporate theatre), agrees: "Actors have to be very well versed in the product and company. They are comprehensively briefed by the client."

Because the expense is sizeable and the stakes are high, clients are usually hands-on participants, notes Andrew Feigin, a stage manager who specializes in industrial theatre. "The atmosphere is not like a theatre. Actors have to be very aware of the corporate hierarchy and be careful about what they say and to whom. Even at the rehearsal, you don't wear sweatpants. You wear your good stuff. You take your habits, like smoking or even eating, outside. And you never mock the product or process. Some clients have a sense of humor. But many don't."

Adds Peter Scott: "Working in industrial theatre often means working unusual hours. You may start at seven in the morning and work well into the night."

And there are acting challenges that are peculiar to the field. Carol Nadell heads Selective Casting, a company that specializes in casting industrials—live and on video. "The purpose of the industrial is to get information out there," she says, "whether it's targeting sales reps at a pharmaceutical company or patients suffering from tuberculosis." Nadell casts many educational industrials.

"Acting for industrials is hard because the characters are not organic," she continues. "The words are neutered; they can come out of anybody's mouth. So it's really up to the actor to create the character."

Despite some of these pressures—and others (such as using a cubicle alongside a kitchen as a dressing room)—business theatre has a very good reputation among performers. According to most of those we interviewed, it is fun to do. Part of the deal often includes travel to the posh resorts where the events take place. And, most important, the participants are well paid.

A fair number of those who are employed in live industrials are union members (though many are not). Members of Actors' Equity Association work under the LCCC (Live Corporate Communications Contract) and earn, according to an Equity spokesperson, a minimum of $1,398 for seven days; $1,133 a week for two weeks or more (numbers based on the 2001 contract). On a daily basis, Equity actors will get a minimum of $518 for the first day and $298 for each subsequent day.

As mentioned, a live industrial run is short; two- or three-week gigs are considered very long (and rare). Again, the hours may be trying, with rehearsals possibly taking place at night and repeat performances occurring during the course of seven-hour days.

GETTING THE JOB

Not unexpectedly, landing these jobs is not easy. For the most part, the clients and/or creative teams employ actors they've used in the past. Or they'll rely on recommendations, or go to agents or casting directors with whom they've had successful relationships in the past. Yet it is rare for agents to represent corporate performers exclusively. By all accounts, fewer and fewer jobs are available these days for seasoned industrial actors.

Plus, more actors than ever are trying to get into this end of the business, in part because the stigma attached to doing industrial theatre—like the once-negative attitude toward actors who make TV commercials—no longer exists. A large pool of talented actors is available, eager, and willing. And thus the competition is keener than ever.

So, what are the creative teams looking for in their actors?

"Talent—and that hasn't changed," says Peter Scott. "Warmth and connection."

Adds Doug Bernstein, a freelance creative writer and director who has pulled together many corporate theatrical events: "We need actors who are good natured and flexible, willing to travel, and not afraid of hard work or of spending a lot of time just sitting around."

The ability to sing and dance is obviously a plus. So are comic timing and improvisational skills (especially for those shows that are not fully scripted). Actors who are hired to play the "Vaseline smiling" emcees (as one actor dubbed them) certainly need to be able to ad-lib quickly, interact with the talker or heckler in the crowd, and always sound positive.

That said, Penola notes that he'd rather hire an actor who is "terrific in one thing—a great singer or acrobat"—as opposed to the more generic talent he'd hire for an old-fashioned book musical.

THE FUTURE

As for the future of industrial theatre—what it will look like, who will be employed— that's anyone's guess, although most of the players we interviewed suggest that the genre's evolution is a function of the economy more than anything else. And a show's particular aesthetic—not to mention its audience—will reflect what's going on in the culture at large.

28 Landing a Job at Sea:

Is Working on a Cruise Right for You?

BY CATHERINE CASTELLANI

Cruise vacations lure thousands of passengers every year with the promise of tropical paradise, arctic majesty, or exotic ports of call. But between those glamorous harbors the ship is out to sea, with as many as 1,500 people aboard. In these isolated conditions, the cruise line is responsible for keeping its passengers entertained. Cruise lines employ more than one hundred performers per ship every year, including bands, orchestras, pianists, magicians, cabaret performers, dancers, singers, actors, and comedians. Want a job?

WHO'S HIRING?

There's more than one way to land a job at sea. Do you want a job singing and dancing in the shipboard revue? Have your own cabaret act you want to book? Play the piano? Cruise lines hire performers in all these capacities, but it's not always the same department that's doing the hiring. For example, on Norwegian Cruise Lines (NCL), musical entertainers are hired directly by the manager of music, Michael Suman.

But what about singer-dancers? NCL is very proud to present full-scale, Equity-level book musicals on board, usually recent Broadway hits. But Suman doesn't cast them. They are cast, produced, and delivered by Jean Ann Ryan Productions, an independent producing organization based in Fort Lauderdale, Florida. Like other production companies of this type, Jean Ann Ryan Productions is contracted by the cruise line to put together the onboard revues and musicals, which is done by holding auditions around the country (some producers cast around the world), rehearsing the show on land, and preparing the performers for cruise life.

Cabaret acts are hired through booking agents connected to the cruise industry, such as New York- and Fort Lauderdale-based Bramson Entertainment. Agencies typically maintain relationships with a host of cruise lines, connecting independent acts with particular ships, and sometimes representing production companies hoping to book entire shows onboard.

Decide where you fit in the hiring picture and take the time to determine where your headshot, résumé, or video should go. If a line's guidelines tell you they don't hire dancers or singers individually for their revues, believe it and find out who produces for the line. Too many actors take the "no stone unturned" approach, pursuing work where there's no work to be had.

OPEN CALLS

Of course, cruise lines and production companies aren't out to make a mystery of casting. The lines and producers run frequent advertisements (often in *Back Stage*) seeking performers, and they often hold their auditions in multiple cities, making it easy for performers to connect with producers. If you miss one round of auditions, you won't have long to wait. Cruise producers tend to cast on a quarterly basis.

Stiletto Entertainment, based in Los Angeles, is one of these producing organizations. Stiletto provides musical revues for Holland America. General Manager of Cruise Ship Operations Douglas Senecal describes the open casting call as "the most effective way to make contact with us, so we can get a feel for your personality."

Stiletto hires 160 performers every year, rotating them onto ships on a biannual schedule, which means they are constantly busy casting, rehearsing, and preparing the next cast to take over for the last. As in any casting situation, producers and directors are looking for talent and skill, suitability for the roles to be cast, and chemistry among potential cast members. But in casting for cruise ships, there is another crucial element: personality.

OPEN, FRIENDLY, AND PERSONABLE

Senecal describes sitting with the casting panel at a Stiletto Entertainment open call as intensely observational. Not only does the casting group listen to the quality of singing voices and watch the grace and power of the dancers, but they also observe every interaction a performer has with staff or other performers, from the time he or she arrives until the call ends. Panel members are looking for the intangibles that spell success or disaster onboard. As shipboard veterans themselves, they look for people they'd like to be in close quarters with for the typical six-month contract offered to revue performers. Because, as Senecal says, once you sign on, "there's no getting off." Clean, friendly, considerate, and upbeat count for as much as perfect pitch and great extensions.

LIFE AT SEA

Once hired, revue performers generally rehearse on land. They're then flown (at company expense) to a port where they will connect with their vessel. This is home for the next six months for most revue performers. Headliners may be flown in by the cruise line for as short a stint as one week or as long as two months or more. While the company will fly performers in at the start of the job and out again at completion, if you quit halfway through, you will be on your own financially to get home.

Performers on cruise lines generally work a lighter performance schedule than they would on land. The revue may have only five or six performances a week. Sometimes performers will do an early, then a late show, on one or two nights, then have a couple of nights off. Many lines, though not all, also require revue performers to assume some light duties in addition to performing—typically helping out in the library, teaching dance classes, and assisting with disembarkation. These additional duties might add up to an extra eight hours a week. Extra duties never include cleaning tasks or food service chores. Headliners do not take on any extra duties and may only perform two to four times a week. All performers are encouraged to mingle with the guests.

PLUSES AND MINUSES

"Shipboard life is confining," says Suman, "but there's no commute, there's no worrying about what to eat, even your bed is made for you by a cabin steward—although your room is very small." Those who have lived the life mention the same pluses and minuses over and over. Because the conditions are the same for everyone, it's really the individual's attitude that determines whether the trip is good or bad.

Actress Melissa Hartman spent six months at sea in a revue with Holland America. She thoroughly enjoyed her cruise experience and is still close to the people she performed with onboard, but she describes a certain up-and-down quality to cruise life. "It was a challenge because, in a sense, you are repeating your life over and over again. It was great, but every ten days you were doing the same speeches, the same jobs, the same shows. Yet it was wonderful. I'd be on the beach in Barbados saying, 'Wow! They're paying me for this!' The next day, I'd be on disembarkation duty telling 1,250 people to have a nice day, one after the other."

Tom Postilio, a cabaret performer who starred in New York's long-running revue *Our Sinatra,* did headlining cabaret gigs on cruise lines for nearly five years, spending about half his time during that period at sea, the other half at home in New York. As a headliner, Postilio played mostly under short-term contracts, although once he accepted a six-month world tour, because the lure of an around-the-world cruise was just irresistible. He made contact with the industry through Bramson Entertainment.

Cruise lines emphasize to potential headliners the importance of familiar material, and that can get tiring. "The show I'd do at the Algonquin is not what I'd do on a cruise," says Postilio. "This is not the place to try out an act full of the obscure songs of Mabel Mercer. You don't have to sing 'New York, New York' or 'Mack the Knife' every night, but the more familiar, the better."

EVERYONE'S A CRITIC

Each and every passenger who chooses to fill out the comment sheet submitted by the cruise director will rate your work as a performer. On this form, passengers grade the accommodations, the food, the entertainment, and any other aspect of the trip. The cruise lines take these forms very seriously. Performers who rate above a certain point standard will be asked back. Those who fall below that standard will not.

Be prepared for direct commentary from your audience as well. You are all floating along together for the duration, and many passengers will offer their comments, praise, and criticism poolside or in the lounge. Most people will be positive, but the occasional severe critic is out there, so leave your thin skin on shore.

FINANCES

Headliner salaries are extremely variable, depending on all the showbiz factors that affect a headliner's salary on land. Revue performers, however, will find comparable salaries and benefits from line to line. At the present time, weekly performance salary for a singer-dancer in a revue ranges from $500 to $650 a week, depending on the employer, the contract specifications, and the role, with featured performers earning more than those who are strictly chorus. Rehearsal pay is usually half performance pay.

As mentioned, accommodations and food are provided, as is basic cleaning service for the room. Onboard health benefits may merely consist of the right to see the ship's doctor free of charge. Check out your prospective employer's situation in this regard—some lines offer higher quality service than others. On many lines, guests of the performers may board the cruise—in some cases, free of charge; in others, at half price. Guests are always responsible for their own airfares.

What expenses might you have on a cruise? They typically include shopping, customs duties on goods, charges from the onboard restaurant (if meals there are not covered by your contract), any bar tab, and tips for your cabin steward and other crew personnel. (The cruise director can provide guidelines if you're not sure how much to tip or whom.)

Hartman found cruise work a great way to save money. By subletting her New York apartment, she eliminated her "on land" expenses, and was able to bank most of her pay. Her cast mates had similar experiences. While the base pay is not outstanding, the low overhead of most performers onboard compensates.

Some lines offer bonuses to valued cast members. Stiletto Entertainment employs cast members as company manager/liaison, dance captain, and wardrobe supervisor for each show. These jobs entail higher pay. Stiletto also offers what amounts to a signing bonus for cast members who agree to extend their contracts. Three months into a six-month contract, cast members are offered a bonus equal to their rehearsal pay in exchange for extending the contract to nine months. In this way, Stiletto saves money and reduces its risk by extending the contract of a known and liked employee rather than hiring a new and untried one. Bonuses and incentives vary from line to line among production companies, but the basic idea is to reward good work and happy personalities.

IS IT FOR YOU?
The wonderful/difficult world of cruise line performing offers some real rewards and some real headaches. A careful and honest self-assessment is necessary before you audition. Do you honestly think you'd enjoy the work and the living conditions? Do you think your personality and predominant attitude would be a plus onboard ship? Are you free to go? If your answer to each of these questions is "yes," a real performing challenge/travel adventure/vacation might be in your future.

Production Companies & Bookers

COMPILED BY ERIK HAAGENSEN,
WITH DAVID FAIRHURST

Cruise line websites will give you a feel for the style and tone on different lines. Read descriptions of the type of entertainment featured. Many sites have links to employment listings and offer detailed information regarding what kind of talent is needed and the best way to apply. Some of these lines hire talent directly and produce their own shows; others contract these responsibilities out. (See Outside Production Companies & Bookers listings later in this section.)

CARNIVAL CRUISE LINES
3655 NW 87th Avenue
Miami, FL 33178-2428
Attn: Entertainment Dept.
(305) 599-2600 or (800) 438-6744
fax: (305) 406-4905
www.carnival.com
Hires singers and dancers for Las Vegas and Broadway-style musical revues, instrumentalists, mainstream music bands with soloists (R&B, Top 40, Country, Standards, Classic Rock), comics, jugglers, variety or specialty acts, and disc jockeys. Send audition package that includes audio or video demo tape of your work, current photo, and resume. Go to above website for more detailed info and to send an e-mail indicating your employment opportunity interest.

CELEBRITY CRUISES, INC.
1050 Caribbean Way
Miami, FL 33132
Attn: Shipboard Human Resources
(305) 262-6677
www.celebritycruises.com
Hires a wide spectrum of variety acts, including vocalists, comedians, magicians, jugglers, hypnotists, and ventriloquists. Also hires singers and dancers for musical revues produced in-house. Musical revue hiring also outsourced to Nederlander Worldwide Entertainment in New York, Molyneux Entertainment and Gary Musick Productions in Nashville, Dick Foster Productions in Las Vegas, and F.J.M. Productions in Florida (see listings for preceding companies). Pro-Ship Entertainment in Canada hires orchestra musicians only. Send demo tape, current photo, and resume to Rob Waterfield (comedians, variety acts, and musicians) or Leigh-Ann Thomasson (singers and dancers).

COSTA CRUISE LINES
Venture Corporate Center II
200 South Park Rd., Suite 200
Hollywood, FL 33021-8541
Job Hotline: (954) 266-5645
www.costacruise.com
Italian cruise line sailing worldwide hires dancers, choreographers, magicians, novelty acts, and vocalists. Send videotape, current photo, and resume to above address.

CRYSTAL CRUISES
2049 Century Park East, Suite 1400
Los Angeles, CA 90067
Attn: Artistic Directors - Production Office [for ensemble talent]
Attn: David Stewardson, Manager - Guest Programs [for cabaret acts and solo artists]
www.crystalcruises.com
ProdOps@crystalcruises.com
Produces lavish Broadway-style shows in-house. Most recent show, "Excalibur!," received the 2000 "Diamond Award for Onboard Entertainment" from Onboard Services Magazine. Looking to hire singers, dancers, singer-dancers, and lead vocalists. Accepts promotional packages by mail only at above address. E-mailed pictures/attachments will not be viewed. Package should include videotape, current photo and resume; are reviewed upon receipt, and, should a suitable position be available, you will be contacted for a live audition. Website has more detailed information on specific types and talents currently being sought.

CUNARD LINE
Entertainment Dept.
6100 Blue Lagoon Drive, Suite 400
Miami, FL 33126
Attn: Entertainers
(305) 463-3000
www.cunardline.com
All entertainment currently supplied by outside companies like Bramson Entertainment, Morag Productions, and Broadway Bound Inc. (see listings). May start in-house production/booking in the near future.

DELTA QUEEN STEAMBOAT COMPANY, INC.
Robin Street Wharf
1380 Port of New Orleans Place
New Orleans, LA 70130-1890
Attn: Entertainment Dept.
(504) 586-0631
www.deltaqueen.com
Hires performers directly, including musicians (especially banjo, ragtime, and piano) and singers who dance (these positions perform staff and managerial duties as well). Contract is usually one year with rotation. Send video or audio demo tapes, current picture, and resume to above address.

DISNEY CRUISE LINE
Jobline: (407) 566-SHIP
Audition Hotline: (407) 397-3299
fax: (407) 566-7575, Attn: Entertainment
[include source code JLEN]
www.disney.go.com/disneycruise/jobs/
For auditions: www.disneyauditions.com
*Hires musicians, singers, dancers, and
comedians to perform in three original
Broadway-scale Disney musicals in fully
equipped, onboard 975-seat theatre, plus
a Junkanoo-style, audience-participation,
original production celebrating the rich heritage
of the Bahamas. An online job application
system is currently "under construction" at the
above website. In the meantime, you must call
the jobline above to make an application.*

HOLLAND AMERICA LINE
300 Elliott Avenue West
Seattle, WA 98119
Attn: Entertainment Manager - Talent
[for variety entertainers and musicians
only; singers and dancers are hired
through Stiletto Entertainment]
Entertainment Jobline: (206) 286-3499
www.hollandamericaentertainment.com
*An online job application system is at the
above website. Hires singers, magicians,
jugglers, and other specialty acts directly.
Family-appropriate material only. Videotape
or agent submissions only. Musical revues are
cast and produced by Stiletto Entertainment
(see listing). "Dick Clark's Rocking New Year's
Eve®" is cast and produced by Anita Mann
Productions (see listing).*

IMPERIAL MAJESTY CRUISE LINE
2950 Gateway Drive
Pompano Beach, FL 33069
(954) 956-9505
fax: (954) 971-6678
www.imperialmajesty.com
employ@imperialmajesty.com
*All entertainment hiring is outsourced to
production companies, but performers of all
kinds may submit a resume to Imperial by fax
only at the above number.*

NORWEGIAN CRUISE LINE
NCL Corporate Office
7665 NW 19th Street
Miami, FL 33126
Attn: Michael Suman [musicians]
Attn: Sue Carper [nonmusicians]
www.ncl.com
*Musicians and music groups send video
or audio demo tape, photo, and resume to
above address or e-mail Michael Suman at
msuman@ncl.com. Revues are cast by Jean
Ann Ryan Productions (see listing).*

PRINCESS CRUISES
Fleet Personnel Department
24844 Avenue Rockefeller
Santa Clarita, CA 91355-4999
www.princesscruises.com
careersatsea@princesscruises.com
*Hires dancers with professional experience in
jazz, tap, and ballet. Acrobatic, stunt, and acting
skills are also a plus. Also have opportunities
for dancer/cruise staff to conduct onboard
activities in addition to performing in their
production shows. Send video or audio demo
tape, photo, and resume to above address.
No phone calls will be accepted.*

RADISSON SEVEN SEAS CRUISES
Paul McEvoy, director of onboard
programming
600 Corporate Drive, Suite 410
Fort Lauderdale, FL 33334
(800) 477-7500, ext. 311
www.rssc.com
*Books upscale acts such as classical performers,
instrumentalists, strong vocalists, comedians
(must be clean and classy), and some classic
magic. All acts must have at least two 45-minute
headlining shows, be capable of socially inter-
acting with guests, and host a dinner table when
asked. To apply, submit a video, biography, and
current photo to the director of entertainment
at above address. No phone calls regarding
employment, or follow-up calls accepted.
Will contact the act if it qualifies. At this time,
booked one year in advance. Peter Grey Terhune
Presents hires singer-dancers for musical revues
(see listing). Occasionally some acts are booked
through Spotlight Entertainment, Elaine Avon
Agency, Bramson Entertainment, and Blackburn
International (see listings).*

ROYAL CARIBBEAN INTERNATIONAL
CRUISE LINES
2700 Hollywood Blvd.
Hollywood, FL 33020
Attn: Shipboard Human Resources
(305) 262-6677
www.royalcaribbeanproductions.com
*All shows produced in-house (see Celebrity
Cruises above for details).*

ROYAL OLYMPIA CRUISES, INC.
805 Third Avenue
New York, NY 10022-7513
(800) 872-6400
fax: (888) 662-6237
www.royalolympiacruises.com
rocruises@rocusa.com
*Employment opportunities outsourced to
production companies. Does not accept
promotional packages.*

SEAESCAPE ENTERTAINMENT, INC.
3045 North Federal Highway, Landmark Bldg. #7
Fort Lauderdale, FL 33306
Attn: Entertainment Dept.
www.seaescape.com
smcaleer@seaescape.com
*Hiring of singers and dancers for musical revues
currently outsourced, but will become in-house
production shortly. Also looking for musical acts
and bands, plus specialty/novelty acts, such as
magicians, impersonators, acrobats, and ventriloquists. Particularly interested in the different,
fresh, and unusual. Promotional packages should
include video or audio demo tape, current photo,
and resume. Please send to above address.*

SILVERSEA CRUISES
Corporate Headquarters
110 East Broward Blvd.
Fort Lauderdale, FL 33301
Attn: Entertainment Dept.
(954) 522-4477
fax: (954) 522-4499
www.silverseacruises.com
*Jean Ann Ryan Productions and The Walter
Painter Company (see listings) produce musical
revues for the line. Individual acts booked in-
house. Looking for magicians; classical pianists,
violinists, and guitarists; comedians; vocalists who
can sing in different languages; variety/specialty
acts. International flavor to entertainment in
general. Promotional packages should include
videotape, CD or CD-Rom, current photo, and
biography. Previous cruise experience important.
Send packages to above address.*

Outside Production
Companies & Bookers

Much of the onboard entertainment for
cruise lines is provided by outside production companies who put together musical
shows or agencies that book individual acts.
In such cases, these companies and agencies provide the performing talent, so it's a
good idea to approach them about employment opportunities in addition to contacting
the cruise lines directly.

ELAINE AVON ARTISTE
MANAGEMENT & AGENCY
Montage
127 Westhall Road
Warlingham, Surrey CR6 9HJ
England
011-44-188-362-2317
fax: 011-44-188-362-7478
www.elaineavon.com
avon07@aol.com
*One of the longest-established cruise bookers in
the business, specializing in the top end of the
market. Clients include Crystal Cruises and*

*Radisson. Sophisticated and polished artists
are required. Books performers from the
United States, Europe, and South America,
as well as the United Kingdom. Looking for
singers, magicians, jugglers, classical pianists,
instrumentalists, variety/specialty acts.
Biography, current photo, videotape (U.S.
and Canadian video recorder NTSC format
acceptable), or CD-Rom should be sent to
above address.*

BIG BEAT PRODUCTIONS, INC.
1515 University Drive, Suite 108
Coral Springs, FL 33071
(954) 755-7759
fax: (954) 755-8733
www.bigbeatproductions.com
talent@bigbeatproductions.com
*Books musical groups, bands, and comedians
for a number of cruise lines, including Carnival,
Norwegian, and Royal Caribbean. Send demo
tape (audio or video), current picture, resume,
and playlist to above address.*

BLACKBURN INTERNATIONAL UK LTD.
Allen Blackburn
Le Montaigne
7 Avenue de Grande Bretagne
Monte Carlo, 98000 Monaco
(377) 93-30-67-98
or
Jonathan Blackburn
Suite B, 26 Craven Court
Stanhope Road
Camberley, Surrey GU15 3BS
England
011-44-127-668-6661
www.jblackburn.com
jonathan@jblackburn.com
*One of the oldest established cruise booking
agencies, with over 50 specialized cabaret
acts plus bands and groups working on top
cruise ships. The company also provides
production shows, most recently on Holland
America's flagship Rotterdam, when seven
different productions were mounted for the
world cruise. Books all sorts of specialty and
variety acts: magicians, jugglers, ventriloquists,
comedians, musicians, and singers. Also hires
singers and dancers for musical productions.
(The Monte Carlo office specializes in productions, the Surrey office in individual acts, but
there is an overlap.) Promotional package
should include videotape (NTSC acceptable)
or CD-Rom, current photo, and biography, and
can be sent to either of the above addresses.*

BRAMSON ENTERTAINMENT BUREAU, INC.
630 Ninth Avenue, Suite 203
New York, NY 10036
(212) 265-3500
Attn: Linda Raff, president
or

1541 West Oak Knoll Circle
Fort Lauderdale, FL 33324
(954) 423-8853
www.bramson.com
info@bramson.com
Books novelty acts, singers, musicians, instrumentalists, comedians, and "big name" headliners in cabaret and comedy for Cunard and a host of major cruise lines. Send videotape (preferably of a live performance), current photo, resume, and any promotional literature to Linda Raff at New York address.

BROADWAY BOUND, INC.
830 Broadway, 3rd Floor
New York, NY 10003
Attn: Alice Scarpinato
(212) 674-8631
fax: (212) 475-1567
www.broadwayboundinc.com
castingcoordinator@broadwayboundinc.com
Hires singers, dancers, and actors for musical revues on the QE II, among other ships. Holds auditions in various cities around the world, including NYC, between two to three times annually. Check Back Stage for notices. Also accepts promotional package by mail at above address. Include videotape or CD-Rom (preferably of a live performance), current photo, and resume.

GARRY BROWN ASSOCIATES
27 Downs Side
Cheam, Surrey, U.K. SM2 7EH
011-44-208-643-3991/8375
fax: 011-44-208-770-7241
gbaltd@compuserve.com
This is a long-established agency run by a former musician and bandleader. Books internationally for all major shipping lines; also books Rhine River cruises in Germany. Looking for variety/specialty acts of all sorts, headliners, stars, singers, and dancers for musical revues and other entertainment. Holds showcases in New York and other major cities seeking talent. Check Back Stage for notices. Promotional package should include videotape (NTSC acceptable) or CD-Rom, current picture, and biography, and can be sent to above address.

DON CASINO PRODUCTIONS
20880 W. Dixie Highway, Suite 105
Miami, FL 33180
(305) 931-7552
fax: (305) 931-7553
www.doncasino.com
info@doncasino.com
Booking mostly comics, also some singers, musicians, novelty acts, novelty impressionists, and magicians for most major cruise lines. Send videotape, current headshot, and bio to above address. No phone calls, please.

FJM PRODUCTIONS, INC.
7305 West Sample Rd., Suite #101
Coral Springs, FL 33065
(954) 753-8591
fax: (954) 753-5146
www.fjmproductions.com
fjm@fjmproductions.com
Hires singer-dancers for song and dance spectacle shows "Made in Italy" and "Metamorphosis" for Costa Cruise Lines, as well as shows for Celebrity Cruises, Inc. Holds auditions twice yearly in New York and other major American cities, look for the ads placed in Back Stage. Accepts videotapes, current photo, and resume at above address. No phone calls, please.

DICK FOSTER PRODUCTIONS
6260 Stevenson Way
Las Vegas, NV 89120
(702) 434-9782
fax: (702) 434-9784
www.dickfosterproductions.com
dfpco@aol.com
Hires singer-dancers for four musical productions, each with a cast of 20, for Celebrity Cruises. DFP accepts video submissions, but it is very rare that a dancer will be hired without being seen in person. It does help if your video comes with an industry recommendation. Send videotape, current photo, and resume to above address.

GARY MUSICK PRODUCTIONS, INC.
885 Elm Hill Pike
Nashville, TN 37210-2852
Attn: Auditions
(615) 259-2400
fax: (615) 259-2457
www.garymusick.com
auditions@garymusick.com
Hires singers and dancers for musical revues for Celebrity Cruises. Holds live auditions at least once a year in various cities in the U.S. and in London. Check Back Stage for ads. Send videotape, current photo, and resume to above address.

KENNEDY ENTERTAINMENT
244 S. Academy Street
Moorseville, NC 28115
Attn: Bonnie Brown
(704) 662-3501
Hires singers, dancers, and actors for musical revues, plus individual performers and variety/specialty acts such as magicians, comedians, jugglers, ventriloquists, and a jazz trio. Also hires for a children's theatre on one cruise line. Holds live auditions in NYC, West Palm Beach, Fla., and Wilmington, N.C. twice a year. Check notices in Back Stage. Send promotional packages containing videotape or CD-Rom (audio demo tapes for singers acceptable), current photo, and resume to above address.

ANITA MANN PRODUCTIONS
Casting Department
405 North Foothill Rd.
Beverly Hills, CA 90210
(310) 274-6111
www.anitamannproductions.com
info@anitamannproductions.com
Produces the "Dick Clark's Rocking New Year's Eve®" for Holland America. To be considered for an audition, send your resume/bio, headshot, and video to the address above.

MATRIX ENTERTAINMENTS LTD.
Al Radcliffe, president
P.O. Box 222
Esher, Surrey KT10 9YB
United Kingdom
011-44-137-246-4829
Agents/producers specializing in the cruise industry. In-house production company produces musical revues for cruise ships. Also books individual performers and variety/specialty acts of all sorts. Looking for experienced performers only. Promotional package should include videotape (NTSC acceptable) or CD-Rom, current photo, and biography, and can be sent to above address.

MORAG PRODUCTIONS, INC.
P.O. Box 80-1736
Aventura, FL 33280
(305) 937-2586
fax: (305) 937-1492
www.moragproductions.com
moragprd@bellsouth.net
Hires singers, dancers, and actors for Broadway-style musical revues on Cunard and other top-end lines. Singers must be able to read music, dancers must have training. Also hires individual performers and variety acts, such as adagio dancers, acrobats, and vocalists, plus tech staff and musical directors. Particularly interested in new, innovative talent. Live auditions held at least once a year in London, New York, Paris, Los Angeles, Chicago, and Eastern Europe. Check Back Stage for notices. Promotional packages should include a videotape or CD-Rom (audiotape acceptable for singers), clean, current photo and resume, and be sent to above address.

MOLYNEUX ENTERTAINMENT
312 9th Avenue South
Nashville, TN 37203
Attn: Auditions
(615) 254-5411
www.molyneux.org
questions@molyneux.org
Hires singers and dancers for Broadway-style musical shows produced for Celebrity Cruises and Royal Caribbean Cruises and actors for

shows aboard Crystal Cruises. Holds regular auditions year-round and highly recommends an audition in person. Accepts promotional material from new talent. Send a non-returnable NTSC videotape, current picture, and resume to the above address. Detailed information regarding talent needed for upcoming shows posted on website.

NEDERLANDER WORLDWIDE ENTERTAINMENT
1450 Broadway, 20th Floor
New York, NY 10018
(212) 822-4200
www.nederlanderdigital.com
Produces musical revues for Celebrity Cruises, Inc. No further information available as of press time.

HANNA OWEN PRODUCTIONS
22600 Bella Rita Circle
Boca Raton, FL 33433
(561) 394-3798
fax: (561) 393-7098
www.hannaowen.com
Owner/Producer: Hanna Owen;
    hannadat@hannaowen.com
Company Manager: Danny Leone;
    (954) 972-0594,
    dleoneme@hannaowen.com
New York Manager: Sherry Overholt;
    (212) 316-0770,
    soverholt@hannaowen.com
This agency books entertainers for Cunard, Norwegian America, Celebrity Cruises, and other top cruise lines, specializing in musical specialty acts, such as classical singers, concert pianists, and dancers, either as soloists or in especially created ensembles. Send video or audio demo tape, current photo, and resume to above address.

THE WALTER PAINTER COMPANY
P.O. Box 496
11684 Ventura Blvd.
Studio City, CA 91604
(818) 763-8026
www.walterpainter.com
walterpainter@walterpainter.com
Produces shows for Silversea Cruises. Looking for singers, dancers, and singer-dancers for five-person cast musical revues. Also books individual acts such as concert pianists, magicians, celebrity lecturers, and headline singers. Prefer late 20s to 40s age group. Also sometimes books star names. Auditions held in New York, Chicago, Toronto, and Los Angeles on a periodic basis, at least once a year. Check Back Stage for notices. Promotional packages should be sent to above address and include video or audio demo tape, current photo, and resume.

PROSHIP ENTERTAINMENT
5253 Decarie Blvd., Suite 308
Montreal, Quebec
Canada H3W 3C2
(514) 485-8823 or (888) 4-PROSHIP
fax: (514) 485-2675
www.proship.com
info@proship.com
Hiring singers, dancers, musicians, comedians, variety acts, acrobats, ventriloquists, magicians, hypnotists, jugglers, and more. No one is hired without a live audition, but promotional packages are accepted by mail at the above address. They should include uncut live videotape in front of an audience and printed show sequence, audiotape and songlist (if applicable), current photo and resume, biography, and letters of reference. Must complete a preliminary registration form on the website before sending in a promotional package. Also see detailed info on required content for promotional packages on website.

JEAN ANN RYAN PRODUCTIONS
308 SE 14th Street
Fort Lauderdale, FL 33316
Attn: Casting
Audition Hotline: (954) 523-6399, ext. 2
www.jeanannryanproductions.com
jarjobs@aol.com
Casts principals and singer-dancers for the Broadway Program for Norwegian Cruise Lines. Current shows include "42nd Street" and "Smokey Joe's Café," plus "Hey, Mr. Producer" and "Music of the Night" in conjunction with Cameron Mackintosh Productions and the Really Useful Group, respectively. Hires crew for these shows as well. Hold auditions around the U.S. and abroad. Look for advertisements in Back Stage. Accepts videotaped auditions along with current picture and resume at above address (call audition hotline for full submission instructions).

SPOTLIGHT ENTERTAINMENT
Barry Ball
2121 N. Bayshore Drive, Suite 909
Miami, FL 33137-5135
(305) 576-8626
spotent@aol.com
Books comedians, jugglers, magicians, singers, ventriloquists, acrobats, instrumentalists, and novelty acts for all the major cruise lines. Submit videotape and publicity package, including current photo and biography, to above address.

STILETTO ENTERTAINMENT
8295 S. La Cienega Blvd.
Inglewood, CA 90301
Attn: Cruise Ship Casting
(310) 957-5757, ext. 218
fax: (310) 957-5771
www.stilettoentertainment.com
Casts and produces revues for Holland America. Stiletto hires over 100 singers and dancers each year to cast for five ships. They perform in a variety of shows including Broadway, Las Vegas and contemporary pop, and Stiletto's cruise ship production of "Barry Manilow's Copacabana," which received the 1999 Entertainment Award from Onboard Services Magazine. Auditions are held several times a year at Stiletto's studios in Los Angeles and at studios and musical theatre departments at schools throughout the country. Look for audition notices in Back Stage and Back Stage West. You can also receive e-mail or direct mail audition notices by signing up on a mailing list on their website, which features comprehensive audition information, as well as a wealth of information for potential performers. Detailed instructions for submissions of promotional packages containing video auditions (what a videotape should include and more) and necessary submission forms are also on the website.

PGT ENTERTAINMENT
1353 N. Courtenay Parkway, Suite Y
Merritt Island, FL 32953
Attn: Submissions
(321) 453-2313
Hires singers, dancers, and singer-dancers for musical shows for a wide range of cruise lines. Auditions held periodically in NY, Los Angeles, London, Chicago, Williamsburg, Va., and Cocoa, Fla. May also send videotape, current photo, and resume to above address.

Job Services on the Web

The following free websites offer information about and links to various available entertainment-related jobs on cruise lines.

WWW.JOBSINPARADISE.COM
Site featuring "adventure" employment. Convenient links to major, and some smaller, cruise lines.

WWW.CRUISEJOBLINK.COM
Offers free postings of a variety of entertainment jobs available.

Casting Call for Submissions

Production Show Ensemble Talent

Crystal Cruises ranks as the top luxury cruise line at sea, voted the "World's Best Large-Ship Line" by readers of both *Condé Nast Traveler* and *Travel + Leisure*. Our lavish, Broadway-style productions have earned title of the "best production shows afloat." While we do hold live auditions periodically (advertising in advance via trade publications), we gladly accept submissions from talent 21 years and older. A résumé, photograph and video tape may be sent to: **Crystal Cruises, 2049 Century Park East, Suite 1400, Los Angeles, CA 90067**, ATTN: Artistic Directors. Audition packets must be mailed via the postal system; submissions sent via e-mail will not be reviewed.

Female Dancers and Male Dancers and Male Singer-Dancers   Video tapes should highlight strong ballet technique, along with jazz and tap. We also look for any adagio and acrobatic experience. Female dancers are needed 5'6" to 5'9"; male dancers and male dancer-singers are needed 5'9" to 6'1". *Male Dancer-Singers should include in their tapes two musical selections: one up-tempo and one ballad.*

Female Vocalist Lead   We look for females 5'6" to 5'9" in height, with dress sizes of 6 to 10. You must have dance ability for set choreography. Legit Soprano range: E-3 to F-4; Belt range: A-2 to C-4. Age Range: 23-40. *Please submit a video tape showcasing the stated registers, along with a traditional musical theatre (or opera) piece in your head voice and a big Broadway-style belt. We also need to see movement on your video.*

Male Vocalist Lead   We look for males 5'10" to 6'2", with jacket sizes 38R-42L. You must have movement ability for set choreography. Baritone range: F-1 to C-3; occasional G-3. Age Range: 25-40.

Please submit a video tape showcasing a big Baritone voice. We are looking for legitimate musical theatre voices, able to sing several styles of music, including opera, musical theatre, '40s Jazz and '50s Rock & Roll. Please submit a big ballad and an up-tempo. We also need to see movement on your video.

EMPLOYMENT BENEFITS FOR ENSEMBLE TALENT:

Yearly contracts and salaries; paid rehearsals and vacations; medical benefits; onboard officer status with single cabin; elegant Six-Star cruising aboard "the most glorious ships at sea." As cruise lines are not governed by any union jurisdiction, union and non-union talent may work at sea without threat to their status. Initial rehearsal period is 8-10 weeks in Los Angeles; lodging and transportation are provided.

FOR MORE INFORMATION ABOUT PERFORMING AS ENSEMBLE TALENT:
Visit www.CrystalCruises.com or email ProdOps@CrystalCruises.com

CRYSTAL 🦋 CRUISES®

29 Adventure of a Lifetime:

Theme Park Performance Opportunities

BY LEONARD JACOBS

Performing at theme parks takes commitment, endurance, strength, and craft. And, like any performing arts endeavor, it has its pluses and minuses. On the plus side are the steady pay and welcome perks; on the minus side are arduous hours, foreshortened rehearsals, a grueling thirty to forty performances per week, and stretches of time away from home that will run for months.

Still, theme park performing remains a popular way for young artists to hone their craft and get a résumé-building boost. Peruse *Playbills* from Broadway shows, particularly musicals, and you may well see theme parks listed in the performer biographies. There are no shortcuts that take you from theme park performing to Broadway, but the former can provide a fine preparation for the latter.

You'll likely be playing to larger audiences than on Broadway: Most theme parks sport at least one venue holding several thousand people, in which you'll perform four to eight shows daily, each lasting twenty to forty minutes. A huge number of job opportunities arise as performers' contracts expire, new shows get mounted, and seasons come and go. Theme parks may employ thousands of performers; even the modest ones keep a few dozen performers on the payroll.

The bottom line: If you're high energy, given to projecting a positive outlook, and have no qualms about giving 110 percent of yourself, theme park opportunities may be for you.

GETTING STARTED: DO YOUR RESEARCH

Auditioning to be a cast member at a theme park isn't like auditioning for Shakespeare—casting directors and talent recruiters are less interested in watching you plumb a character's depths than in assessing your energy level and range of skills. Families go to theme parks for a happy diversion, which you must provide. Thus, possessing multiple skills—say, singing and dancing, but also juggling, stilt walking, doing voices, or working with animals—is paramount. The key to getting going is research.

First, familiarize yourself with how theme parks recruit talent. Such events as the New England Theatre Conference (NETC) and the Southeastern Theatre Conference (SETC), both typically late-winter occurrences, are good places to start. (See the list of Regional Combined Auditions, page 347.) Smaller conferences are held in the West, too, and most theme parks maintain a presence at those combined-audition events.

Additionally, most theme park casting directors will organize auditions specifically for themselves—some monthly, some semi-monthly—and will travel extensively to find the talent they want. A good rule of thumb: the larger the venue, the more auditions a theme park will hold. Many theme parks maintain toll-free, 24/7 hotlines that disseminate call times, talent needs, and other general information.

Once in the door, you ought to ask as many questions of the theme park reps as they will likely ask about you: What is the pay? Is there health insurance? Are relocation costs paid? And what are the accommodations—are they paid by you or *for* you? Are there "friends and family" discounts to the park?

Consider, too, your own long-term thinking. Since most theme park jobs are nonunion, is getting an Equity card a priority for you or something you're willing to put off for the time being? Once employed at the theme park, do you wish to take any master classes that are offered? What about developing and performing your own work? (That's something that can be arranged informally at some, though not all, theme parks.) Indeed, being clear about your long-range goals as a performer is perhaps more important than the here-and-now questions that come with accepting a position at a theme park. If you know you can't commit to more than six months, audition only for parks where the season lasts for the summertime. If you prefer putting down roots, focus on parks that operate year-round or that offer special performance opportunities at various times of the year, such as Labor Day, Halloween, Thanksgiving, and Christmas.

THE DISNEY DISTINCTION

With more than 50,000 employees, Walt Disney Entertainment is one of the world's biggest theme park operators. From Disneyland's two theme parks in California, to the multi-park complex at Walt Disney World in Florida, to the company's new international venues—Tokyo Disney World Resort, Tokyo Disney Sea, Disneyland Paris, and Hong Kong Disneyland (slated to open in 2005)—there are 2,000–3,500 performing spots available. (That job tally also includes performers working for Disney Cruise Line.) All jobs are highly prized.

But that's not to say that getting cast is easy. Weekly salaries are high by industry standards—$500 and up—so jobs are much sought after. A job at Walt Disney World is also a bit of a trophy because performers there become eligible for their Equity cards upon contract signing.

Contracts vary in length according to the location, but typically run six months to a year. Full-time cast members have two days off weekly and work an eight-hour shift, depending on the number of daily shows they do. Perks vary from park to park, but the company benefits are relatively generous. Also, relocation assistance and housing are available for performers who work at the Tokyo Disney Resort (and for the Disney Cruise Line).

Casting directors look for strong technical skill, charisma, and the ability to connect with an audience. "Personality, personality, personality," is how Kenneth Green, casting director for Walt Disney Entertainment, recently put it.

Green, who works with a year-round auditioning team, says that open-call auditions are held monthly in New York, Toronto, Chicago, Atlanta, and Orlando, with an average of 200 performers seen each time. International casting "tours" are conducted multiple times throughout the year and often cover fifteen or more cities at a time.

Disney's casting people know what it's like to audition.

"We've *all* been on the other side—we're all performers to one degree or another—and we have empathy for the performer," states Ron Rodriguez, talent casting director and leader of the Disney casting team's efforts. "Performers should relax and do the best they can, because we want to give you work."

HERSHEY HIRING

Another enormously popular theme park is Hersheypark, located in Hershey, Pennsylvania. More than the national home of chocolate, it's where Allan Albert Productions has cast hundreds of performing artists over the last quarter century, and where Senior Producer Kathy Carney has become an expert on the talent required for theme park performing.

"I see hundreds of kids at open calls," Carney reports, "and you pretty much know when you say 'learn the combination' whether they are going to be the right fit or not . . . sometimes it's even in the first thirty seconds that you know. . . . I may be looking for something totally different than what a summer stock casting person may be looking for, but I need to know that someone can last thirty-five shows a week for seventeen weeks—because at Hersheypark, that's the season."

Sound terrifying? Not quite—shows are typically a half-hour long, which means that doing five daily shows is less about excess than about building up your stamina. In both the audition and in practice, it's where your technique will serve you most, for you will have to ensure that your voice and body can hold out for the length of your contract.

There's another reason why doing well at Hersheypark may be in your interest: Allan Albert Productions not only does all the casting for the venue, but produces Christmas shows both inside the park and at nearby Hershey Lodge and Convention Center. And it casts shows for Atlantic City, overseas venues, and industrials, as well.

One final Hersheypark perk: while it's a non-Equity producer, Allan Albert Productions treats performers as if they're union members. Rehearsals, for instance, are never more than eight hours daily. By day, performers may work in a 500-seat indoor auditorium or a 2,000-seat outdoor amphitheatre; by night, they thrive in any of several well-appointed apartment complexes just miles from the park.

LIFE AT LAGOON

Only in the world of theme parks can Lagoon Amusement Park, a 121-acre venue found fifteen minutes north of Salt Lake City, be considered small, even with 1.2 million visitors a year. Yet it's a good example of a more modest venue.

Equally modest is the entertainment the visitors want to see. Shows are less "button-pushing" than in other parks—whether it's an all-Top 50 pop show or a "Flower Power" revue that pays homage to the hippie movement. Another popular event is the Signature Show—a paean to a particular performer, such as Aretha Franklin.

Adding to the Lagoon allure is the park's reputation for stellar perks, from above-average compensation to top-drawer insurance to beautiful accommodations. And the surroundings aren't bad: the park was created in 1886 along the shores of the Great Salt Lake, eventually moving inland where the exceptional scenery of the Rocky Mountain area is a sight to behold. The Lagoon is especially alluring for those unable to make a year-round commitment: the park opens in mid-April, runs weekends-only through June, then full-time in July and August, then back to week-ends-only through the end of October.

BELLE OF THE BUSCH

An interesting contrast to the Disney model is Busch Gardens, located in Tampa Bay, Florida. It's part of a group of properties owned by beer manufacturer Anheuser-Busch that includes Sea World in San Diego, California, Sesame Place in Langhorne, Pennsylvania, and Busch Gardens Williamsburg and Water Country U.S.A. in Williamsburg, Virginia. Busch runs a fairly decentralized operation—instead of having one set of casting directors hire talent for the entire operation, each park shares info but maintains its own rigorous audition schedule.

For example, in addition to holding monthly auditions in Tampa, Busch Gardens casting personnel go to the SETC auditions. Unlike many theme parks, Busch also accepts videos from prospective performers, since casters believe that valuable talent sources may not, for whatever reason, be able to make it to the auditions. Be judicious and savvy when you submit a video: casting teams would much rather see you in a clear picture singing contemporary songs than in a fuzzy opera or musical-theatre video. Give a call to the person you're submitting to and double-check as to what's appropriate.

Because Busch Gardens runs year-round, the performer roster tends to fluctuate; you can assume the payroll will include 300 to 700 people at any given time, including technicians and staff. Most shows run about twenty-five minutes, and if you're hired to step in for someone who is finishing a contract, being willing to learn a show quickly is perhaps your biggest asset. After being put through your paces by a show's captain, the final test is getting through an "onstage approval rehearsal" in which a cast must perform an entire show for the casting directors, musical directors, and senior artistic personnel.

Fortunately, not only are the performing standards high at Busch Gardens, but the perks are superb. It's arguably one of the best benefit packages offered to theme park performers: The advantages go way beyond the weekly compensation of $400 to $500 and up. There are medical benefits (including optical and dental), tuition reimbursement after six months of employment, and vacation time. While housing isn't included in the package, the park's proximity to the surrounding college community makes the area quite affordable. Friends and family are encouraged to come see you perform, as deep discounts and season passes are available. From time to time, Busch performers can take master classes and get an inside track when industrials are being made.

ENDGAME

Whichever theme park opportunity you pursue, remember that this is a cyclical industry, so outside-the-box thinking and smart research will be required to land employment.

Remember, too, that theme parks can benefit from both boom and bust times—in boom times because disposable income allows families to vacation more, and in bust times because everyone needs a diversion from daily life. It's then that your performances not only pay your bills, but bring joy to the hearts and minds of your captive, captivated audience.

Major Theme Parks & Production Companies

Below is a selected listing of key information for the major theme parks, and production companies (the latter denoted by an asterisk *) that employ live entertainers throughout the country. Performers are advised to call and confirm audition locations and times.

*ALLAN ALBERT PRODUCTIONS
665 Broadway, Suite 402
New York, NY 10012
Attn: Kathy Carney, Senior Producer
(800) 966-8881 (actors toll-free)
(212) 388-9500
fax (212) 388-9848
kc@allan-albert.com
www.allan-albert.com
Season: May through Labor Day, plus two Christmas shows. Both shows run from November through the end of December.
Hiring: Dancers, singers who dance well, dancers who sing well, and high-energy physical comedy and improv performers.
Pay Scale: Minimum of $435/week.
Shows: Allan Albert Productions does the casting for Hersheypark, including summer and winter productions. Also produces Christmas shows inside Hersheypark and at the Hershey Lodge & Convention Center. Also casts for casino shows, overseas shows, and industrials.

BUSCH GARDENS TAMPA
P.O. Box 9158
Tampa Bay, FL 33674-9158
Attn: Entertainment Dept.
(813) 987-5164
fax (813) 987-5180
www.tampatalent.com
Season: The park is open 365 days a year.
Hiring: Dancers, singers who move well, actors/costumed characters, musicians, and technicians.
Pay Scale (average): Musicians, $11.70/hr.; performers, $11.25/hr.; costumed characters, $9.43/hr.; technicians, $9.75/hr. Full time is 32–40 hours per week; overtime is time and a half. Benefits include master classes, medical, dental, and vision care; company-paid holidays; time off with pay; complimentary tickets; tuition reimbursement; and a 30% discount on merchandise.
Shows: "International Celebration," "Captain Kangaroo's Roo Crew Live," "Moroccan Roll," "Jungle of Dreams," costumed characters, strolling actors and musicians, and atmosphere entertainment.

BUSCH GARDENS WILLIAMSBURG
AND WATER COUNTRY USA
One Busch Gardens Blvd.
Williamsburg, VA 23187-8785
Attn: Carrie Morgan, Special Events Manager
(757) 253-3302
fax (757) 253-3320
(800) 253-3302 (audition hotline)
Carrie.Morgan@anheuser-busch.com
www.talentsearchbgw.com
Season: March 23 through October 27.
Hiring: Singers, dancers, actors/character actors, musicians, variety artists, costumed characters, puppeteers, technician-stage managers, stage managers, dressers.
Shows: Nine mainstage shows during the summer season, four mainstage productions during the Howl-O-Scream October season. Musical revues (some with live bands), strolling actors, puppeteers, musicians, variety artists, and children's characters.
Pay Scale: Average per week:
Performers/Musicians: $460; Technicians: $400; Stage Managers: $560.
Additional Info: Cast members work five to six days per week with four to six shows per day. Benefits include relocation reimbursement; a housing coordinator; mileage per diem for Spring Weekend commuting performers; a health program; a sports medicine program, including a Pilates studio; free classes in dance and vocals; free music clinics and seminars given by professional guest artists; special after-hours events produced by the cast members themselves; free park admission.

CEDAR POINT
c/o Cedar Point Live Entertainment
One Cedar Point Drive
Sandusky, OH 44870-5259
(419) 627-2390
fax (419) 627-2389
Attn: Herbe Donald, Manager
liveshows@cedarpoint.com
www.cedarpoint.com
Season: Various reporting dates in May and June. Contracts run late August to early September. Some contract extensions for weekends through October.
Hiring: Singers, musicians, dancers, singer-musicians, singer-actors, singer-dancers, costumed characters, stage managers, backstage technicians, lighting technicians, sound engineers, dressers, costume shop personnel, party-style DJs, karaoke DJs, assistant choreographer, music supervisors, technical assistants, and theatre usher/escorts.
Pay Scale: $360–$450/wk, plus $48/wk bonus. Benefits include: (for a minimal fee) multiple occupancy housing on grounds, free dance and performance-related classes, employee park privileges, and special events.
Shows/Projects: Variety of musical revues offering styles of Rock, Pop, Country, and Musical Theatre, plus Peanuts(tm) Character Sidewalk Theatre.

DISNEYLAND, DISNEY WORLD, TOKYO DISNEY, AND DISNEY CRUISE LINE (SEE WALT DISNEY ENTERTAINMENT).

DOLLYWOOD
1020 Dollywood Lane
Pigeon Forge, TN 37863
Attn: Auditions Director
(865) 428-9433
www.dollywood.com
Season: March 30 to late December.
Hiring: Singers, dancers, technicians, and stage managers.
Pay Scale: Average $400–$500/wk. Benefits include profit-sharing plan, relocation package, workers' compensation, on-park discounts, on-park employee medical center, discounts, and exchange program with area businesses.
Shows: Three original musicals, plus contract acts.

DORNEY PARK AND WILDWATER KINGDOM
3830 Dorney Park Rd.
Allentown, PA 18104
Attn: Live Entertainment Manager
(610) 391-7730
www.dorneypark.com
Season: May through Labor Day, plus bonus weekends.
Hiring: Singers, dancers, costumed characters, musicians, and costumers.
Pay Scale: $450–$750/wk.
Shows: Features a variety of musical styles from Top 40, swing, country, rock 'n' roll oldies, and Motown.

*ENCORE INTERNATIONAL, INC.
4918 Temple Avenue, Suite G
Evansville, IN 47715
Attn: Maria A. Rivers, Senior Vice President
(812) 473-0880
Season: Contracts are seasonal in the summer months, but the company is now doing extensive work in the "off" months. There are lots of opportunities in the fall, winter, and early spring. Can offer some contracts for seasonal summer work and then change over in the fall and winter, so an entertainer can possibly be working year-round.
Hiring: Singers, dancers, actors, musicians, puppeteers, stunt performers, and unique specialty acts. Submit promotional material to the office address above.
Pay Scale: $360–$450/wk. depending on contract, facility, and experience. Many contracts include bonuses and housing assistance.
Shows: Musical revues, in styles from Broadway to pop to country, patriotic, and specialty themes such as swing, movie themes, rock 'n' roll, etc.
Additional Info: Encore International Inc. is an independent production company specializing in live performance opportunities: Theme and amusement parks, resorts, hotels, restaurants, cruise lines, and corporate and industrial events in several different venues, including Arizona, Indiana, Maine, New Hampshire, Ohio, and Pennsylvania. Over 350 performers are employed each year.

*HEARTBEAT PRODUCTIONS, INC.
Melinda Grable, casting director
832 South Cooper Street
Memphis, TN 38104
(901) 278-0138
fax (901) 278-0139
mgrable@heartbeatproductions.com
www.heartbeatproductions.com
Auditions: Heartbeat accepts resumes, headshots, and video/audio tapes year-round. Call for specific details on future auditions. Currently casting park shows for the 2004 season.
Season: Heartbeat casts year-round for corporate events, and seasonally for the amusement park industry.
Hiring: Stage managers, singers, dancers, specialty acts, directors, choreographers, scenic designers, art directors. Some creative staff positions are open on a per-project basis.
Pay Scale: Varies greatly, based on experience and role. Housing allowance and per diem available on some contracts.
Shows: Heartbeat Productions offers live theatrical productions for the amusement park and special events industries, from musical production shows to theatrically presented sports and stunt spectaculars, galas, and concert series.

HERSHEYPARK
100 West Hersheypark Drive
Hershey, PA 17033
(717) 534-3177
fax (717) 534-3336
audition@hersheyPA.com
www.hersheyPA.com.
Season: Mid-May through Labor Day.
Hiring: Dancer-only, singers/dancers, and specialty performers (e.g., jugglers).
Pay Scale: $450–$500/wk.
Shows/Projects: Dance show, rock 'n' roll show, country show, variety show.
NOTE: See also Allan Albert Productions for submission information.

KNOTT'S BERRY FARM
Entertainment Division
8039 Beach Blvd.
P.O. Box 5002
Buena Park, CA 90620
(714) 220-5386
www.knotts.com
Season: Open 364 days a year, with peak operations during spring break, summer, Halloween, and Christmas.
Pay Scale: Various rates and methods of pay commensurate with type of performances, length of run, and time of year. Performers hired directly onto payroll, rather than by contract, are eligible for a variety of benefits.
Shows: Range in form and styles from stunt, musical, cultural, and seasonal shows to variety and environmental performers.

LAGOON AMUSEMENT PARK, INC.
PO Box 696
Farmington, UT 84025
or
375 North Lagoon Drive
Farmington, UT 84025
Attn: Mark Huffman, Entertainment Director
(801) 451-8059 or (800) 748-5246
fax (801) 451-8015
www.lagoonpark.com
Season: Summer season is from April–September,
with rehearsals beginning in March. Halloween
"Frightmares" season is in October, with
rehearsals beginning in late August.
Hiring: Singers (all styles), dancers (all styles),
comedic actors, specialty performers, stage
managers, sound technicians, lighting technicians,
and wardrobe personnel. Also looking for "teen"
singers and dancers for a pop/top 40 show called
"Rock U2 the Top."
Contract dates and salary: Rehearsal and performance dates may vary depending on the position
and the specific production. For the summer
season, some shows will begin rehearsal as early
as mid-March, while other shows may begin
rehearsing as late as April 30. Performers and
technicians are paid hourly for rehearsal and the
season. Hours vary depending on the specific
production and range from 24–40 hours/wk. Some
shows will only play weekends in the spring and
fall, with hours adjusted accordingly. Average pay
rate is $10–$15/hr., but varies according to position, experience, and training.

*OSBORNE SHOWS
5118 Goodwin Avenue
Dallas, TX 75206
Attn: Paul Osborne
(214) 631-8414 (audition hotline)
Season: Typically May 30 through Sept. 5;
contracts finalized in January and February.
Hiring: Singers, dancers, actors, musicians, and
technicians.
Pay Scale: Varies, depends on ability. Often
housing and bonus provided.
Shows: Musical, magic, comedy, stunt shows,
and dance.

PARAMOUNT PARKS
5555 Melrose Avenue
Hollywood, CA 90038
Attn: Mr. Stan Morrell
(704) 561-8100
Hiring: Singers, dancers, actors, variety and
performing artists, show characters, comedians,
technicians, stage managers, and escorts/ushers
(non-performers). Paramount Parks are non-Equity
parks.
*NOTE: Paramount's five North American theme
parks are located across the U.S. and Canada and
provide the opportunity to work with nationally
recognized producers, designers and directors.*

*Paramount Parks is a division of Viacom
International Inc., one of the world's largest
entertainment and publishing companies.
Viacom's other operations include Nickelodeon®,
Paramount Pictures, MTV, and CBS Television.
Paramount Parks' theme parks are located
throughout the United States and Canada:*

Paramount's Carowinds
Charlotte, NC 28241
(704) 587-9011

Paramount's Great America
Santa Clara, CA
(408) 986-5941

Paramount's Kings Dominion
Doswell, VA 23047
(804) 876-5134

Paramount's Kings Island
Kings Island, OH
(513) 573-5740

Paramount's Canada's Wonderland
Vaughan, Ontario, Canada
(905) 832-7454

SEAWORLD ORLANDO
SeaWorld Staffing Center
7007 Sea Harbor Drive
Orlando, FL 32821
(407) 363-2600/ fax (407) 363-2615
(407) 370-1JOB (job line)
www.becjobs.com

SEAWORLD ADVENTURE PARK
SAN ANTONIO
10500 Sea World Drive
San Antonio, TX 78251-3002
Attn: Entertainment, Lynne Chapman
(210) 523-3328
Season: The season lasts from early March
through the last weekend in November.
Hiring: Announcers, performers, and pre-show
performers, strolling costume characters,
musicians, dancers, stage managers, and
lighting, audio, and special effects technicians
and operators.
Pay Scale: $7–$13/hr.

SEAWORLD SAN DIEGO
500 SeaWorld Drive
San Diego, CA 92109
(619) 226-3842
(619) 226-3861 (job line)
(619) 226-3607 (audition hotline)
www.seaworld.com or www.seaworldjobs.com.
Auditions, Hiring, Shows: SeaWorld's hiring
season begins in February. SeaWorld looks for
many types of talent including character actors,
host announcers, physical comedians, specialty
acts, and musicians. Check audition hotline for
upcoming dates and other information.
Season: Year round; peak-schedule Memorial Day
to Labor Day.

SESAME PLACE
100 Sesame Rd.
Langhorne, PA 19047
(215) 752-7070 ext. 298/ fax (215) 741-5307
Attn: Entertainment Dept.
Entertainment@SesamePlace.com
www.sesameplace.com
Auditions: Early January—usually first or second weekend on site. Call (215) 752-7070 ext. 298 during mid-December for more information.
Season: Mid-May through end of October. September and October are weekends only.
Hiring: Dancers (jazz and tap), actors (two different kinds: physical comedians and singer/dancers), musicians (trombone, trumpet, sousaphone, percussion—snare and bass), and costumed-character performers.
Pay Scale: Dancers, $7.30–$7.85/hr; actors, $7.30–$7.85/hr.; musicians, $7.30–$7.85/hr; costumed-character performers, $6.20–$7.85/hr.; technicians, $6.35–$7.35/hr.; seasonal supervisory, $7.90–$10.00/hr.
Shows/Projects: Big Bird Musical Revue, Sesame Brass Band, "Rock Around the Block Parade," "Gotta Dance," "Oscar's Big Game Show," "Elmo's World, Live!"

SHOW BIZ INTERNATIONAL (*SEE* ENCORE INTERNATIONAL INC.)

SILVER DOLLAR CITY AND SHOWBOAT BRANSON BELLE
399 Indian Point Rd.
Branson, MO 65616
Attn: Audition/Talent Coordinator
(417) 338-8084 (audition hotline)
Hiring: Singers, dancers, actors, and variety artists with stage experience.
Shows: Ten mainstage productions on seven stages. Performance styles include classic and contemporary country, bluegrass, gospel, western swing, Broadway, and family-oriented comedy.

SIX FLAGS PARKS CORPORATE HEADQUARTERS
11501 Northeast Expressway
Oklahoma City, OK 73131
906 N. Ann Arbor
Oklahoma City, OK 73127
Attn: Angie Stephens
(405) 942-0308 ext. 3016
(405) 475-2500 (for info on overseas parks)
AStephens@SilvertreeProductions.com
www.SixFlags.com
Season: Mainly March–October (actual commitments vary with each park).
Hiring: Singers, dancers, actors, stunt persons, costume characters, musicians, and technicians.
Pay Scale: $300–$500/wk. Varies with each show and park.
Auditions: Six Flags has periodic auditions throughout the year; call individual parks for details. It also accepts videotapes, headshots, and resumes by mail, to Angie Stephens at the above address, or directly to the individual parks listed below.

Atlanta: *Six Flags Over Georgia*, 275 Riverside Parkway, Austell, GA 30168; (770) 948-9290 ext. 3711

Buffalo: *Six Flags Darien Lake*, 9993 Allegheny Road, Darien Center, NY 14040; (585) 599-5352

Chicago: *Six Flags Great America*, 542 N. Route 21, Gurnee, IL 60031; (847) 249-2133 ext. 4606 *(further details below)*

Cleveland: *Six Flags Worlds of Adventure*, 1060 N. Aurora Rd,, Aurora, OH 44202; (330) 995-2095 *(further details below)*

Columbus: *Wyandot Lake (Six Flags Family)*, 10101 Riverside Drive, Powell, OH 43065; (614) 889-9283

Dallas: *Six Flags Over Texas*, PO Box 90191, Arlington, TX 76004-0191; (817) 640-8900 ext. 4547

Denver: *Six Flags Elitch Gardens*, 299 Walnut Street, Denver, CO 80204; (303) 595-4386 ext. 231

Houston: *Six Flags AstroWorld & Waterworld*, 9001 Kirby Drive, Houston, TX 77054; (713) 799-8404 ext. 3240 *(further details below)*

Lake George: *The Great Escape (Six Flags Family)*, P.O. Box 511, Lake George, NY 12845; (518) 792-3500

Los Angeles: *Six Flags Magic Mountain*, 26101 Magic Mountain Parkway, Valencia, CA 91355; (661) 255-4100 ext. 4810

Louisville: *Six Flags Kentucky Kingdom*, P.O. Box 9287, Louisville, KY 40209-0287; (502) 366-2231

New England: *Six Flags New England*, P.O. Box 307, 1623 Main Street, Agawam, MA 01001; (413) 786-9300 ext. 3322

New Jersey: *Six Flags Great Adventure*, Route 537, P.O. Box 120, Jackson, NJ 08527-0120; (732) 928-2000 ext. 2822

New Orleans: *Six Flags New Orleans*, 12301 Lake Forest Blvd., New Orleans, LA 70129, (504) 253-8126

Oklahoma City: *Frontier City (Six Flags Family)*, 11501 Northeast Expressway, Oklahoma City, OK 73131; (405)-478-2140 ext. 396

San Antonio: *Six Flags Fiesta Texas*, 17000 IH-10 West, San Antonio, TX 78257; (210) 697-5000 (Main); (210)-697-5482 (Entertainment Dept.)

Seattle: *Enchanted Parks (Six Flags Family)*, 36201 Enchanted Parkway South, Federal Way, WA 98003; (253) 661-8000

St. Louis: *Six Flags St. Louis*, 4900 Six Flags Rd., Eureka, MO 63025; (636) 938-5300 ext. 368

Washington D.C.: *Six Flags America*, 13710 Central Avenue, Largo, MD 20721; (301) 249-1500 ext. 3090

Mexico: *Six Flags Mexico*, Carretera Picacho al Ajusco #1500, Col. Heroes de Padierna, Mexico, D.F.C.P. 14200; (252) 728-7200 ext. 1442

Montreal, Canada: *La Ronde (Six Flags Family)*, Ile Notre-Dame, Montreal (Quebec), Canada H3C 1A9; (514) 397-2000

SIX FLAGS ASTROWORLD
9001 Kirby Drive
Houston, TX 77054
Attn: Terry Overstreet, Entertainment Manager
(713) 799-8404
toverstr@sftp.com
www.sixflags.com.
Season: March–October.
Hiring: Singers, dancers, actors, costume characters, musicians, magicians, and technicians.
Pay Scale: Varies.
Shows/Projects: Country, high-energy dance, rockabilly, kids' show, jazz band, Fright Fest.

SIX FLAGS WORLDS OF ADVENTURE
1060 North Aurora Rd.
Aurora, Ohio 44202
Attn: Clint Huber, Entertainment Manager
(330) 995-2095
chuber@sftp.com
www.sixflags.com
Season: May–October.
Hiring: Theatre technicians, singer/dancers, Costume Character performers, stunt performers, and more. Halloween Haunted House performers in fall. (Note: All positions are seasonal.)

SIX FLAGS GREAT AMERICA
542 North Route 21
Gurnee, IL 60031
Attn: Todd Stickney, Manager of Entertainment
(847) 249-1776 ext. 4606 (entertainment ofc.)
Fax (847) 249-2392
tstickne@sftp.com
www.sixflags.com
Season: May 1 through October. Actual commitment varies with each show.
Hiring: Singers, dancers, actors, costumed characters, theatre and TV technicians, IMAX projectionists, stage managers, and wardrobe personnel.
Pay Scale: Average $280–$410/wk. Varies with position.
Shows: TBD

UNIVERSAL STUDIOS HOLLYWOOD
100 Universal City Drive, Bldg. 5511-4
Universal City, CA 91608
(818) 866-4021 (audition hotline)
www.universalstudios.com
Hiring: If the show is an action-based or stunt show (like "T-2" or "Waterworld"), then professional stunt men and women are encouraged to attend auditions. Stunt coordinators are at each of the auditions and will test the abilities of the performers. After they get past the stunt coordinator, they go on to the director who will audition them as an actor for whatever role is right. If the show is musical, then actors and actresses with very strong singing and dancing are encouraged to audition. Walk-around characters that wear covered costumes are usually based on height and improv. ability. If the role requires a star look-a-like, then a series of auditions is needed to see if the actor can look, act, and sound like the star s/he is impersonating.

Improv. work is extremely important in these roles. Sometimes the actor must, also be approved by the family or estate that has the rights to the movie or TV star. Universal Studios Hollywood has employees (and former employees) represented on film, television, and the Broadway stage. USH hires some of the best actors, actresses, singers, dancers, stunt people, and improv. actors in the country.
Pay Scale: Ranges from $7.25/hr. to $60.00+/show, depending on the part and the contract for that part or show.
Shows: "Blues Brothers R&B Revue," "Waterworld," "Terminator 2," "Animal Planet Live," and a variety of walk-around cartoon and face characters based on television shows and films.

UNIVERSAL ORLANDO
1000 Universal Studios Plz.
Orlando, FL 32819-9610
(407) 224-7622 (audition hotline)
www.universalstudios.com
Season: Year-round.
Hiring: Actors, singer/dancers, stunt performers, animated character performers, celebrity look-a-likes.
Pay Scale: $6.95–$12.85/hour depending on role to start.
Shows/Skills: Live shows requiring actors with improvisational and audience interactive skills; musical requiring talent who sing and dance well in a high-energy show; stunt shows requiring actors who are skilled stunt performers—stage combat, staff and sword fighting, high and low falls, slide for life, rope swings, bungee, fire diving. Animated characters and character shows.

UNIVERSAL STUDIOS JAPAN
2-1-33 Sakurajima, Konohana-ku
Osaka, Japan 554-0031
Attn: Gregg Birkhimer, Senior Show Director, Show Development
011.81.6.6465.3086 (dial 011 only if calling from the U.S.)
www.usj.co.jp
Hiring (in four separate categories):
PRINCIPAL STUNT ROLES (i.e., "WaterWorld," "T2-3D," "Wild West," "Rumble by the Bay"): For "WaterWorld": expert stand-up jet skier, high divers, 45' fire divers, jet skiers, boat drivers, water skiers. For "Wild West": 30' high fall, fight choreography, slide for life or flying fox. For "T2-3D": look-a-likes for Arnold Schwarzenegger, Linda Hamilton, Edward Furlong who have rappelling and weapons experience. For "Rumble by the Bay": martial artist, physical comedian.
ATMOSPHERE ACTING ROLES (i.e., "High Noon West," "Celebrity Look-a-Likes," "5th Avenue Players"): For "High Noon West": improvisational "Freeze Frame" actors, theatrical stage combat. For "Celebrity Look-a-Likes": Marilyn Monroe, Doc Brown, Charlie Chaplin, and impersonators with character integrity. For "5th Avenue Players": improvisational actors with strong comedic skills.

MUSICAL PERFORMANCE ROLES (i.e., "Blues Brothers," "MonsterFest," "Miami Spice," "The Flo Show"): For "Blues Brothers": look-a-likes for John Belushi and Dan Ackroyd who possess strong singing and movement ability. For "MonsterFest": Dracula, Wolfman, Frankenstein, The Bride, and strong singers with excellent dance ability. For "Miami Spice": Latin male singer with movement skills to host live show with today's latest hits. For "The Flo Show": a '50s roller-skating romp with adagio lifts and swing and sock hop skills.

CONTRACTED ACTS: Various skills and acts ranging from street magicians and steel drums to balancing acts and country western guitarists.
Pay Scale: Check with HR for accurate pay scale.

VALLEYFAIR!
One Valleyfair Drive
Shakopee, MN 55379
Attn: Kris Stauffer, Live Entertainment Manager
(952) 496-5341
(877) 438-6562 (toll-free)
liveentertainment@valleyfair.com
www.valleyfair.com
Season: Performance season varies by show. Full-time schedules begin between Memorial Day and mid-June, and end between mid-August and Labor Day. Some shows might also do May and/or September weekends.
Hiring: 13 singer/dancers, 19 instrumentalists, 11 costumed characters, one house manager, three sound engineers, one master electrician, two stage technicians, five Imax theatre projectionist/ushers.
Pay Scale: $436/wk. for singer/dancers and instrumentalists; $427/wk. for costumed charac-ters; $418/wk. for sound engineers and master electrician; $404/wk. for stage technicians; and $420/wk. for Imax theatre projectionist/ushers. Housing coordination and accommodations for a minimal fee. Free park access and workshops and employee events provided.

WALT DISNEY ENTERTAINMENT
Walt Disney Entertainment Auditions
P.O. Box 10,000
Lake Buena Vista, FL 32830
(407) 397-3299 (hotline)
www.disney.com or
disney.go.disneycareers/events.html
Season: Ongoing—365 days a year.
Hiring: Singers, dancers, actors, stunt performers, and characters for Walt Disney World® Resort, Tokyo Disney Resort, and Disney Cruise Line.

Pay Scale: WDW—Contracts start at $500 a week and are negotiable based on experience and ability; TDR—Salaries range from $590–$840, round trip airfare, per diem, and single housing is provided. Contracts range from six to eight months; DCL—Contracts are eight months, with two months of rehearsal in Toronto. Housing is provided.
Shows/Projects: WDW—Shows range in musical styles from a cappella to gospel rock, acting styles from book shows to improv, and dance style from classical to hip-hop; TDR—Singers and dancers for shows such as "Encore," a Broadway-style show; "Sail Away," a fun-filled revue with Mickey and the gang; "Adventureland Show"; and "Pecos Bill and Goofy Revue." "Once Upon a Mouse" requires dancers and singers are needed for "Dockside Porters." The "Under the Sea" show requires female aerialists, and the "Mystic Rhythms" show utilizes dancers and aerialists. In addition, looking for actor atmosphere groups; DCL—The Disney Wonder three- or four-day cruise is Jamaica and Castaway Cay. The Disney Magic has a seven-day cruise itinerary that includes St. Thomas, St. Marteen, and Castaway Cay. For the ships, Disney is seeking singers, dancers, actors, and character performers for its "Disney Dreams," "Hercules: The Musical," and "Morty the Magnificent" shows.

DISNEYLAND TALENT CASTING AND BOOKING
P.O. Box 3232
Anaheim, CA 92803
Mail Code: TDA329R
Attn: Talent Casting and Booking Manager
(714) 781-0111 (audition hotline)
www.disney.com or
disney.go.disneycareers/events.html
Season: Year-round.

WORLDS OF FUN
4545 Worlds of Fun Avenue
Kansas City, MO 64161
Attn: Brent Barr and Dawna Welborn, Mgrs. of Live
    Entertainment
(816) 303-5114
barr@worldsoffun.com, wellborn@worldsoffun.com
www.worldsoffun.com
Season: April to October, most shows run from the end of May to August.
Hiring: Singers, dancers, costumed characters, musicians, and technicians.
Shows: Contemporary/pop, country, and '60s–'70s rock revues, big-band swing, Motown, disco, rhythm & blues.

30 Theatre for Young Audiences:

More Adult Than Ever

BY SIMI HORWITZ

If you think theatre for young audiences is kid's stuff, guess again. There's nothing childish about it—certainly not in its production values. Remember, boosting future audiences is a collective goal of the theatrical community, so creating high-quality theatre is of the essence. And there's surely nothing childish about the demands placed on actors appearing in children's theatre. Before you dismiss it as unimportant, consider this:

Today children's theatre is big industry, with budgets for some theatres soaring as high as $9 million per year. The number of children who are served by these theatres is in the millions (4.6 million entertained by the New York City-based Theatreworks/USA alone), and certain companies that are committed to theatre for children and/or teenagers are doing booming business.

Some of these theatres are affiliated with parent theatres or cultural institutions; others are independent. Some have permanent homes (and may or may not do tours), while others are exclusively touring operations. Some are Equity companies employing a Theatre for Young Audiences (TYA) contract; others are non-Equity.

The bottom line: theatre that entertains children and young adults provides a terrific outlet for actors interested in honing their craft and working with top professionals in a very adult environment. And working in an Equity theatre may also serve as a steppingstone, allowing you to earn points toward union membership.

NO LONGER CHILD'S PLAY

Perhaps what's most striking about today's theatre scene for youngsters is the caliber of artist (not to mention project) it's attracting. Check this out: the 2003 Broadway show *A Year with Frog and Toad* was launched at The Children's Theatre Company of Minneapolis.

Among the writers, choreographers, and performers who have worked at the New York State Theatre Institute in Troy, New York (and not necessarily at the beginnings of their careers, by the way), are William Gibson, Charles Strouse, Sheldon Harnick, Patricia Birch, Zoe Caldwell, Carolee Carmello, Allison Janney, Piper Laurie, Tony Lo Bianco, Darren McGavin, Jane Powell, Jonathan Pryce, and James Whitmore.

At Theatreworks/USA—a venerable children's theatre company specializing in children's musicals—directors Christopher Ashley and Michael Mayer, and actor Brian d'Arcy James have stretched their artistic muscles.

The Seattle (Washington) Children's Theatre has showcased the work of such writers as David Henry Hwang, John Oliver, and Robert Schenkkan.

And not too long ago, the 2003 Pulitzer Prize-winning playwright Nilo Cruz dramatized Gabriel García Márquez's short story "A Very Old Man with Enormous Wings" for the Children's Theatre of Minneapolis. Tony-nominated director Graciela Daniele helmed the piece.

Cruz insists that working in children's theatre fulfills a mission for him that is, at least in part, cultural-political in nature. "I love children's theatre, but I don't love 'cute.' I think it's very important for plays to touch children so that they laugh and cry. Being entertained is not enough. I want to reach out to children."

"A Very Old Man with Enormous Wings" is an allegorical fable about an angel who has fallen from the sky into the home of an impoverished family, none of whose members recognize his divinity. Instead, they display him like a freak to bring in some desperately needed money. The townspeople come to pluck the feathers from his wings and mockingly ask him for miracles.

In the original story, children play no role. Cruz's adaptation, however, places children at center. They discover the angel, know he's an angel, communicate with him (without words), and ultimately save him—thus making it truly possible for him to create miracles.

"It is only when the angel can fly again—when he is whole, and the children, not the adults, make him whole—that he can perform miracles," says Cruz. "Children in the audience identify with children on stage, and I hope that they can recognize the angels inside them."

He adds, "To see children in a theatre, completely taken with what's happening on stage, is better than winning a Pulitzer Prize. I can't wait to do more children's theatre."

WHERE IT'S ALL BEEN AND WHERE IT'S ALL GOING

Clearly, children's theatre is not a recent phenomenon, although after World War II, there was a major increase in theatre for youngsters, says Linda Hartzell, artistic director of the Seattle Children's Theatre. There was an outpouring of fairy tales on stage. The zeitgeist was right. "Following the Depression and the war, you can see why people wanted archetypical representations of good and bad," Hartzell explains.

In the late 1960s and into the 1970s—in the wake of cultural upheavals—there was a move away from fairy tales to more realistic plays for children, often focusing on heavy-duty problems in their lives. A groundbreaking piece called *Step on a Crack,* written by Suzan Zeder in 1975, dealt with the traumatizing experience of a child whose father remarries, and, her troubled relationship with her stepmom.

Step on a Crack opened the floodgates to a wave of age-appropriate social issue plays and to historical dramas that taught important and/or inspiring lessons. These included Mary Hall Surface's *Most Valuable Player,* a play about Jackie Robinson, the first black baseball player to be admitted to the major leagues. Novels became springboards for children's shows, and many of these were turned into musicals.

Musicals for children are, of course, not new. Theatreworks/USA, for example, has been mounting musicals for forty years. Still, there's been a change. "Years ago, we did lots of historical musicals with simple, linear plots," says Barbara Pasternack, artistic director of Theatreworks. "Now they've become more sophisticated. For example, in *The Mystery of King Tut,* a musical about King Tut and Howard Carter [the English archeologist who discovered the Egyptian ruler's tomb in 1922], we show how each of the two men in some way created the other."

And not all pieces have happy endings. For example, there's *The Great Gilly Hopkins,* a work that began at Stage One: The Louisville Children's Theatre and ran at the New Victory in New York. *Gilly* tells the story of a young girl who moves from foster home to foster home, one worse than the next. When she finally finds herself in a good one, she sabotages herself—because of her bad experiences, she can't help it—and ultimately lands in the care of a relative she has never met.

"Still, the play ends on a note of hope," notes J. Daniel Herring, artistic director at Stage One. "You're left with the sense that maybe things will work out. But we don't sugarcoat."

PICKING, STAGING, AND PERFORMING

The challenge in selecting a show for kids is several fold. Besides ensuring its entertainment value—and gauging its age-appropriateness—one of the goals is making kids think. Topicality and relevance are sought. There are also time constraints: Children's plays generally don't run more than ninety minutes. And, most central, the plays must have at least one character the kids can identify with.

So what about the staging and acting? Are there different demands when performing for kids as opposed to adults? Yes and no.

All agree that everyone in a theatre—and that includes kids—wants clarity, truth, presence, and generosity of spirit from the actors on stage.

Hartzell spells it out: "You want to keep the actors in the moment and the action moving, just as you would for adult theatre."

That said, some distinctions should be considered. "I believe actors in children's shows have to bring an added sense of wonder and innocence," comments Joseph T. Annese, Jr., executive director of New York City's Gingerbread Players and Jack. "But that doesn't mean they should sound patronizing. That's a very real danger."

Overacting and engaging in cutesy posturing were repeatedly cited as common pitfalls for actors in children's shows. Nevertheless, there are those who feel that acting for children requires a willingness on the actor's part to add a sort of "extra layer" to the performance, while, of course, remaining truthful.

"Language is only one way for kids to understand what's happening on stage," says Janet Stanford, artistic director of Imagination Stage in Bethesda, Maryland. "I believe actors who perform for kids should be able to physicalize their actions. The space should be open and accessible."

Notes Carrie Libling, director of children's theatre at Vital Theatre Company in New York City, "I think actors in children's theatre should be quirky, comic, and be able to sing. They should be open and free and, most of all, love children and be willing to spend time after a show talking with them."

It's not that actor-audience interaction never happened in the past. But today, the interaction is conscious and deliberate, with philosophical underpinnings.

"Years ago, you'd put on a show for the kids, they'd see it, and leave," recalls Annese. "Today, we want the experience of going to the theatre to have application to other aspects of their lives. We're all wondering and addressing the questions:

What is the child taking away from the theatre? What is his economic and family situation? What kind of neighborhood does he come from?"

Annese describes the workshops that Vital sometimes conducts with the kids after the show: "We introduce them to the actors and the idea that actors are playing roles. We then ask the kids to think about people who play roles in life."

FROM THE ACTOR'S POINT OF VIEW

The actors interviewed here concurred that love of kids is a must for performers who want to do children's theatre well. By all accounts, kids are a tough audience, if for no other reason than lack of sophistication and, in many instances, lack of theatre etiquette. Kids react loudly, sometimes talk to each other during the show. And then there are occasional untoward events—e.g., a baby starts howling. Actors have to be able to improvise, ad-lib, and speak loudly over the noise.

Undoubtedly, special challenges come with the job. But interestingly, these challenges are a source of pleasure, too.

Actress Katie Blockerby, a resident member of Louisville's Stage One, says this: "I'm a thirty-seven-year-old woman who frequently plays fifteen-year-old kids before an audience of fifteen-year-old kids. So I'd better be dead on. If I'm not, the kids will let me know it. Younger kids may chuck pennies at you. They are completely honest and will keep you on your toes. But if they're really with you, they're the best audience."

Dean Holt, an actor who has been with Minneapolis' Children's Theatre Company for nine years, describes his task in these terms: "When an adult audience member goes into a theatre, he brings his life's experience. A child's life experience is obviously not as great and therefore he has no parameters on his imagination. So the actor performing for children has to be bigger and, at the same time, more realistic in his acting."

Holt adds that he loves performing in children's theatre and so far hasn't been offered anything else that intrigues him as much. "My only frustration is that the work is enormous. We do ten to eleven shows a week, and they are large-scale shows."

A LAUNCHING PAD

Still, for most actors, theatre for younger audiences is perceived as a launching pad. And although it is hard to track down precise numbers, many, many actors have done theatre for youngsters and teens at some point in their careers. Some, as noted, return to it from time to time.

Actor Herndon Lackey, who has created original roles on Broadway in such shows as *Parade* and *Kiss of the Spider Woman*, starred in Theatreworks' *Sarah, Plain and Tall* not too long ago. "I did it because I loved the material," he recalls. "It was one of the best scripts I had seen anywhere in years. It also gave me the chance to play a good guy. I always play the villain. And, of course, at the end, when I get to kiss the girl, the kids screamed. Where else would you get a vocal response like that?"

Actor Rick Long, a longtime member of Louisville's Stage One, emphasizes, "We're not folks who couldn't hack it in a LORT theatre, and we don't hop around in bunny suits. Since I've been here, I've played a range of roles, including Benjamin Franklin, Frankenstein, Charlie Brown, and the Giant in *Jack and the Beanstalk*. In a profession where only two percent work steadily, I'd say I'm doing all right. I know where I'll be next week and where my paycheck is coming from."

Equity Theatre for Young Audiences Companies

The following is a list of companies with Theatre for Young Audiences (TYA) contracts in the Eastern, Central, and Western regions of the United States. They are listed alphabetically in their appropriate regions followed by an address, phone number, fax, e-mail address, and website (if available), and the names of the head(s) of the company's children's theatre program. Note that the TYA may not be the only Equity contract under which a company operates.

Eastern Region

ABRONS ARTS CENTER
HENRY STREET
SETTLEMENT
466 Grand Street
New York, NY 10002
(212) 598-0400
www.henrystreet.org
Jane Delgado, chief
    administrator

ALHAMBRA DINNER THEATRE
12000 Beach Blvd.
Jacksonville, FL 32246-6706
(904) 641-1212 or
    (800) 688-SHOW
fax (904) 642-4199
Tod Booth, Jr., general manager

ALLIANCE THEATRE
COMPANY
1280 Peachtree Street N.E.
Atlanta, GA 30309-3502
(404) 733-4650
fax (404) 733-4625
www.alliancetheatre.org
Max Leventhal, general
    manager
Rosemary Newcott, artistic
    director for theatre for youth

ARDEN THEATRE COMPANY
40 North Second Street
Philadelphia, PA 19106
(215) 922-8900
fax (215) 922-7011
Amy L. Murphy, producer

ARTSPOWER INC.
39 South Fullerton Avenue
Montclair, NJ 07042-3354
(973) 744-0909 or
    (888) 278-7769
Fax (973) 744-3609
www.artspower.org
Gary and Mark A. Blackman,
    co-directors/founders

CREST THEATRE AT OLD
SCHOOL SQUARE
51 North Swinton Avenue
Delray Beach, FL 33444
(561) 243-7922
fax (561) 243-7018
Joe Gillie, executive director
Jerilyn Brown, director of
    education

FANFARE THEATRE
ENSEMBLE
100 E. Fourth Street
New York, NY 10003-9001
(212) 674-8181
fanfare71@aol.com
Joan Shepard, producer

FORUM THEATRE
314 Main Street
Metuchen, NJ 08840-2430
(732) 548-4670
fax (732) 548-4230
Paul Whelihan, producer

GINGERBREAD PLAYERS &
JACK
PO Box 750296
Forest Hills, NY 11375
(718) 263-4078
www.gingerbread.org
Joseph T. Annese Jr., executive
    director

GROWING STAGE THEATRE
PO Box 36
Netcong, NJ 07857
(973) 347-4946
fax (973) 691-7069
www.growingstage.com
Stephen Fredericks, executive
    director

HIPPODROME STATE
THEATRE
25 Southeast Second Place
Gainesville, FL 32601-6567
(352) 373-5968
fax (352) 371-9130
hipp@gru.net
http://hipp.gru.net
Mark Sexton, general
    manager
Lauren Caldwell, artistic
    director

IMAGINATION STAGE
4908 Auburn Avenue
Bethesda, MD 20814
(301) 961-6060
www.imaginationstage.org
Janet Stanford, artistic director

INSIDE BROADWAY
630 Ninth Avenue, Suite 802
New York, NY 10036
(212) 245-0710
fax (212) 245-3018
www.insidebroadway.org
Michael Presser, executive
    director

KENNEDY CENTER YOUTH &
FAMILY EDUCATION
DEPARTMENT
2700 F Street N.W.
Washington, DC 20566-0001
(202) 416-8837
Kim Peter Kovac, senior
    program director for youth
    & family programs

LONG WHARF THEATRE
222 Sargent Drive
New Haven, CT 06511-5919
(203) 787-4284
fax (203) 776-2287
www.longwharf.org
Michael Stotts, managing
    director

MCCARTER THEATRE
EDUCATION DEPARTMENT
91 University Place
Princeton, NJ 08540-5121
(609) 258-6513
Christopher Parks, education
    director

NASHVILLE CHILDREN'S
THEATRE
724 Second Avenue South
Nashville, TN 37210
(615) 254-9103
fax (615) 254-3255
www.nashvillechildrenstheatre.org
Scot E. Copeland, producing
    director

NASHVILLE SHAKESPEARE
FESTIVAL
800 Fourth Avenue South
Nashville, TN 37210
(615) 255-2273
fax (615) 248-2273
nashshake@aol.com
Steve Cardamone, producing
    artistic director
Shellie Fossick, managing
    director

NEW YORK STATE THEATRE
INSTITUTE
37 First Street
Troy, NY 12180
(518) 274-3200
fax (518) 274-3815
www.nysti.org
Patricia Di Benedetto Snyder,
    producing artistic director
Christine Saplin, education
    director

PUSHCART PLAYERS
197 Bloomfield Avenue
Verona, NJ 07044-2702
(973) 857-1115
fax (973) 857-4366
www.pushcartplayers.org
Ruth Fost, executive director
Geoffrey Morris, general
    manager

SLIM GOODBODY CORP.
POB 242
Lincolnville Center, ME 04850
(800) 962-7546 or
    (207) 763-2820
fax (207) 763-4804
www.slimgoodbody.com
James Bradney, general
    manager
Regina Sainio, event
    coordinator

STORYBOOK MUSICAL
THEATRE INC.
PO Box 473
Abington, PA 19001
(215) 659-8550
fax (215) 659-2775
sbmt@libertynet.org
www.storybookmusical.org
Marc Goldberg, producer

SYNAPSE PRODUCTIONS, INC.
220 E. Fourth Street
New York, NY 10009
(212) 674-2716
fax (212) 674-8012
info@synapseproductions.org
www.synapseproductions.org
Ginevra Bull, artistic director
David Travis, producer

THEATREWORKS USA
151 W. 26 Street
New York, NY 10001
(212) 647-1100
info@theatreworksusa.org
www.theatreworksusa.org
Barbara Pasternack, artistic
    director
Ken Arthur, managing director

UNDERGROUND RAILWAY
THEATRE
41 Foster Street
Arlington, MA 02474
(781) 643-6916
fax (781) 643-7539
Debra Wise, artistic director
Catherine Carr-Kelly, managing
    director

VICE OMAHA PRODUCTIONS
275 Monmouth Street
Jersey City, NJ 07302
(201) 200-9087
Terrance M. Hendrickson Jr.,
    producer

YATES MUSICAL THEATRE
19 Morse Avenue
East Orange, NJ 07017-2115
(973) 677-0936
fax (973) 677-0631
www.yatesmusicaltheatre.com
Peggy Yates, general manager

YOUNG PLAYWRIGHTS INC.
306 W. 38 Street, #300
New York, NY 10018
(212) 594-5440
writeaplay@aol.com
www.youngplaywrights.org
Sheri M. Goldhirsch, artistic
    director
Brett Reynolds, managing
    director

Central Region

ACCESSIBLE ARTS INC.
1100 State Avenue
Kansas City, KS 66102
(913) 281-1133
fax (913) 281-1515
accarts@accessiblearts.org
www.accessiblearts.org
Martin English, executive director

CHICAGO SHAKESPEARE
THEATER
800 E. Grand Avenue
Chicago, IL 60611
(312) 595-5656
fax (312) 595-5607
www.chicagoshakes.com
Barbara Gaines, artistic director

DRAMARAMA THEATRE CO.
7627 Mission Valley Drive
St. Louis, MO 63123
(314) 605-7788
trueman@dramaramatheatre.com
www.dramaramatheatre.com
Nicole Trueman, artistic
    director/producer

DRURY LANE THEATRE
2500 W. 95th Street
Evergreen Park, IL 60805
(708) 422-8000
fax (708) 422-4329
www.drurylane.com

DRURY LANE OAKBROOK
THEATRE
100 Drury Lane
Oakbrook Terrace, IL 60181
(630) 530-8300
fax (630) 530-0456
www.drurylaneoakbrook.com
Diane Van Lente, producer

FIRST STAGE CHILDREN'S
THEATER
929 N. Water Street
Milwaukee, WI 53202-3122
(414) 273-2314
ageyser@firststage.org
www.firststage.org
Jeff Frank, artistic director
Amy Geyser, company manager

HISTORYONICS THEATRE CO.
PO Box 2938
St. Louis, MO 63130
(314) 361-5858
hist@historyonics.org
www.historyonics.org
Lee Patton Chiles, artistic director

ILLUSION THEATER
528 Hennepin ave.
Suite 704
Minneapolis, MN 55403-1814
(612) 339-4944
fax (612) 337-8042
info@illusiontheater.org
www.illusiontheater.org
Michael Robins, executive
    producing director

IMAGINARY THEATRE
COMPANY
c/o Rep. Theatre of St. Louis
PO Box 191730
130 Edgar Rd.
St. Louis, MO 63119-7730
(314) 968-7340
fax (314) 968-9638
www.repstl.org
Jeffrey Matthews, ITC artistic
    supervisor

INDIANA REPERTORY THEATRE
140 W. Washington Street
Indianapolis, IN 46204-3403
(317) 635-5277
fax (317) 236-0767
www.indianarep.com
Janet Allen, artistic director

JEWISH ENSEMBLE THEATRE
6600 W. Maple Rd.
West Bloomfield, MI 48322-3003
(248) 788-2900
fax (248) 788-5160
www.comnet.org/jet/
Evelyn Orbach, artistic director

MARRIOTT THEATRE IN
LINCOLNSHIRE
10 Marriott Drive
Lincolnshire, IL 60069-3700
(847) 634-0204
fax (847) 634-7358
producer@MariottTheatre.com
www.marriotttheatre.com
Terry James, executive producer

MEADOW BROOK THEATRE
Oakland University
Rochester, MI 48309-4448
(248) 370-3310
fax (248) 370-3108
mbtkthea@oaland.edu
www.oaland.edu/mbt/
Gregg R. Bloomfield, managing
director

MINNESOTA SHAKESPEARE
PROJECT
4253 Newton Avenue N.
Minneapolis, MN 55412-1643
(612) 871-5168
mnshakespeare@aol.com
www.mnshakespeare.org
Diane Mountford, artistic
director

MIXED BLOOD THEATRE CO.
1501 S. Fourth Street
Minneapolis, MN 55454
(612) 338-0937
fax (612) 338-1851
audition@mixedblood.com
www.mixedblood.com
Raúl Ramos, associate
producer

NEW AMERICAN THEATER
118 N. Main Street
Rockford, IL 61110-1102
(815) 963-9454
fax (815) 963-7215
www.newamericantheater.com
Richard Raether, artistic
director

OLD LOG THEATER
PO Box 250
Excelsior, MN 55531-0250
(52) 474-5951
fax (952) 1290
oldlog@qwest.net
www.oldlog.com

PERFORMANCE NETWORK
120 E. Huron
Ann Arbor, MI 48104
(734) 663-1430
fax (734) 663-7367
www.comnet.org/PNetwork/
Daniel C. Walker, artistic
director

RIDGEWOOD ARTS
FOUNDATION INC.
907 Ridge Rd.
Munster, IN 46321-1721
(219) 836-0422
fax (219) 836-0159
www.theatreathecenter.com
Michael Weber, artistic
director

STAGE ONE: THE
LOUISVILLE CHILDREN'S
THEATRE
501 W. Main
Louisville, KY 40202-2957
(502) 589-5946
fax (502) 588-5910
www.stageone.org
J. Daniel Herring, artistic
director

THEATRE FOR YOUNG
AMERICA
4881 Johnson Drive
Mission, KS 66205-2924
(913) 831-2131
fax (913) 831-7717
www.tya.org
Gene Mackey, artistic
director

Western Region

BERKELEY REPERTORY
THEATRE
2025 Addison Street
Berkeley, CA 94704-1103
(510) 647-2900
www.berkeleyrep.org
Rachel Fink, director of The
School of Theatre

CASA MAÑANA
MUSICALS INC.
300 W. Third Street
Suite 1715
Fort Worth, TX 76102
(817) 332-9319
fax (817) 332-5711
www.casamanana.org
Denton Yockey, executive
producer
Cindy Honeycutt, instructor
of education & outreach

EAST L.A. CLASSIC
THEATRE
2168 S. Atlantic Blvd.
PMB #378
Monterey Park, CA 91754
(323) 260-8166
fax (323) 260-8153
Tony Plana, producer

FALCON THEATRE
4252 Riverside Drive
Burbank, CA 91505
(818) 955-8004
fax (818) 955-7732
www.falcontheatre.com
Kathleen Marshall,
producer

KINGSMEN SHAKESPEARE
COMPANY
PO Box 1772
Thousand Oaks, CA 91358
(818) 985-8231
www.kingsmenshakespeare.org
Sue Marrone, producer

L.A. TROUPE THEATRE IN
EDUCATION
9991 Maude Avenue
Shadowhills, CA 91040
(818) 951-6882
tietroupe@aol.com
Koni McCurdy, producer

LAGUNA PLAYHOUSE
PO Box 1747
Laguna Beach, CA 92652-1747
(949) 497-5900
fax (949) 376-8185
www.lagunaplayhouse.com
Donna Inglim, education
director

MUSICAL THEATRE GUILD
PO Box 2612
Toluca Lake, CA 91610
(818) 848-6844
www.musicaltheatreguild.com
Alan Weston, producer
Kevin McMahon, artistic
program coordinator

SEATTLE CHILDREN'S
THEATRE
201 Thomas Street
Seattle, WA 98109
(206) 443-0807
fax (206) 443-0442
sctpr@sct.org
www.sct.org
Kevin Maifeld, managing
director
Linda Hartzell, artistic
director

SHAKESPEARE AND
FRIENDS
11824 Dorothy Street
Los Angeles, CA 90049
(310) 820-2292
fax (310) 820-2292
Dee M. Neito, producer

SOUTH COAST REPERTORY
THEATRE
PO Box 2197
Costa Mesa, CA 92628
(714) 708-5500
fax (714) 545-0391
www.scr.org
David Emmes, producing
    artistic director

THEATRE WEST
3333 Cahuenga Blvd. West
Los Angeles, CA 90068
(323) 851-4839
fax (323) 851-5286
theatrewest@theatrewest.org
John Gallogly, executive
    director

THEATREWORKS
PO Box 50458
Palo Alto, CA 94303
(650) 463-1950
fax (650) 463-1963
www.theatreworks.org
Randy Adams, producer

WILL & COMPANY
514 South Spring Street
Los Angeles, CA 90013
(213) 239-8777
fax (213) 489-3481
office@willandcompany.com
www.willandcompany.com
Sam Robinson, managing
    director

WORD FOR WORD
c/o Z Space Studio
131 Tenth Street, Third fl.
San Francisco, CA 94103
(415) 626-0453
fax (415) 626-1138
www.zspace.org
Laura Bergman, executive
    director

The following children's
theatre companies are
mentioned in the feature
article, and have either an
Equity contract other than
TYA or are non-Equity.

THE CHILDREN'S THEATRE
COMPANY
2400 Third Avenue South
Minneapolis, MN 55404-3597
(612) 874-0500
info@childrenstheatre.org
www.childrenstheatre.org
Peter C. Brosius, artistic director
Equity Special Agreement.

VITAL THEATRE COMPANY
CHILDREN'S THEATRE
432 W. 42 Street, Third fl.
New York, NY 10036
(212) 268-2040
www.vitaltheatre.org
Carrie Libling, director of
    children's theatre
Non-Equity.

PART 5

The Life

31 Welcome to New York:

The Performer's A to Z Guide to Getting Started in the Big Apple

EDITED BY DAVID FAIRHURST

FINDING AN APARTMENT

"**A** matchbox of our own" goes the line from *Little Shop of Horrors,* and it's no exaggeration. Expect the rent on a closet-size apartment to consume 50 percent of your income if you decide to live "in the City" (as natives call Manhattan). And even that can be hard to find in the world's tightest housing market. You can pick up *The Village Voice* when it hits the newsstands on Tuesday night, but the best deals are often hidden in small neighborhood newspapers and on community bulletin boards. Explore the outer boroughs and nearby New Jersey for bargains. If you choose to use a broker, expect to pay a hefty fee and be prepared to answer prying questions about your finances. Be wary of services offering to sell you a list of "no fee" apartments—many of them are outright scams. Consider splitting the rent with roommates with whom you don't mind sharing already cramped quarters. Finally, keep your ears open—many New York apartments are never listed anywhere, passing from tenant to tenant via word-of-mouth—and be prepared to plunk down a deposit the moment you find your new home, or risk losing it to someone else.

ORGANIZING YOUR SPACE

"**B**usinessperson" is a word not often used to describe actors, but that's what they are: entrepreneurs whose product is themselves. And like every entrepreneur, you'll need a home office: a computer for storing your customer list (casting directors and producers). A printer for creating your marketing materials (cover letters and résumés). A phone for scheduling appointments, and an Internet connection for hunting down leads. But mostly, you'll need a quiet, well-organized space, free from the noise and distractions of the city, where you can dedicate a part of each day to being your own manager, agent, and publicist, and focus on the business of building a career.

LANDING A DAY JOB

Careers in the performing arts are difficult enough without having to rely on them as your sole source of income. That's why nearly every actor new to the city also needs a "day job" (though it's often, in fact, a "night job"). Given the vagaries of an actor's schedule—from daytime auditions to evening performances—flexibility is key. For those with up-to-date computer skills, temporary agencies are a boon: they keep offices all over New York humming into the wee hours with actors working the graveyard shift. If you're better with people than with computers, waiting tables and working the phones are two traditional actor-friendly sources of income. Better yet, if you've got a special skill—from accounting to Pilates to teaching guitar—working as a freelancer or starting up a small business allows you to be your own boss while supplementing your acting dollars.

OPENING A BANK ACCOUNT

Dollars are what you're hoping to make, and when you do, you'll need a place to put them. All it takes to open a bank account in New York is two forms of ID. But don't settle for the first bank on the block—shop around for perks like no-fee checking, no minimum monthly balance, and free ATMs. Or consider a credit union, where interest rates are often better. The Artists Community Federal Credit Union and the Actors' Federal Credit Union are two founded by and for performers.

PAYING FOR HEALTH CARE

Echinacea may help with the common cold, but you'll need more than that to cover accidents and serious illnesses. Some actors receive health insurance through their day jobs. More-established performers whose acting income has reached a minimum level are eligible for health insurance through SAG, AFTRA, or Equity. For everyone else, go to the Artists' Health Insurance Resource Center at www.actorsfund.org for a comprehensive database of health insurance alternatives and a list of free and low-cost health clinics in New York.

KEEPING HEALTHY AND FIT

Fitness and health are key to sustaining a long-term performing career, and those who stay in top shape will have a decided advantage. Acting can be physically as well as emotionally exhausting, and the stresses and strains of life in New York can prove taxing to the system. Though fitness fads may come and go, the basic principles stay the same: a balanced diet, plenty of fluids, and regular exercise. But don't forget your mental health: whether yoga, music, meditation, or communing with nature is your outlet of choice, we all need a way to replenish our psychic energy.

SETTING GOALS

Goals—long-term and short-term—are essential for maintaining your focus. The "business of show" is fraught with peril, and the temptation to give up the fight and find an easier way to make a living can be overwhelming at times, even for seasoned performers. But by setting reasonable career goals, writing them down, and resolving to do at least one thing for your career every single day, the satisfaction of being able to check off those goals one at a time will be a powerful incentive to keep up the struggle.

STAYING CONNECTED

"**H**ow can I reach you?" is a question every performer needs to be able to answer readily. Show business moves at a breakneck pace, and accessibility can mean the difference between landing an important audition and missing out. A cell phone offers immediate access everywhere—provided you're not stuck in a subway tunnel. Pagers provide instant notification to call your agent, e-mail and voice mail are convenient for receiving messages, and a fax machine is vital for getting sides. New options are added almost daily, so make "phone tag" a thing of the past and never again find yourself apologizing for missing a call.

TAPPING INTO TECHNOLOGY

Internet technology, PDAs, digital cameras, home editing systems, and other modern gadgets are more than just expensive toys for technophiles—they can be valuable tools for your career. On the Internet, you can research theatre companies, classes, and upcoming productions, as well as respond to online casting calls. With a PDA, you can keep track of your auditions and contacts. A digital camera is convenient when a director requests a "recent snapshot," and with a home editing system you can create your own reel. None of these tools are cheap, but in this most competitive of all businesses, they may give you a technological edge.

FINDING SUPPORT

Joining a clan of like-minded performers—whether the informal chat of an e-mail list or the formal meetings of a structured support group—can provide a valuable network of news and encouragement for novice and experienced actors alike. By exchanging information and sharing the everyday frustrations and disappointments of the performer's lot, newcomers to New York can remotivate themselves, learn from their more experienced peers, and find reassurance that they're not alone.

KNOWING YOUR TYPE

"Know thyself" was the fabled inscription of the Oracle at Delphi; equally valuable wisdom for actors is "know thy type." Typecasting is a word that makes actors cringe, but you can't change the way casting is done: by first impressions and physical characteristics. So don't take it personally; instead, use it to your advantage. Ask people who know you well what qualities and personality traits are suggested by your face, your body language, the sound of your voice. Think about how you've been cast in the past. Once you recognize your type, you'll know the essence you want to convey in headshots and audition material—as well as the initial impressions you may want to play against.

GETTING HEADSHOTS

Look in the eyes of any great headshot and you'll see something that's hard to describe—a vitality, a sense of purpose, perhaps an air of mystery—qualities guaranteed to catch the eye of a casting director. New York is filled with photographers, but finding one who can capture your essence, and with who, you're comfortable working, will take research. Ask actors whose shots you admire, who took their pictures; peruse the portfolios of various photographers before settling on one. Good headshots are not cheap, and having a variety of prints to choose from (for commercial and theatrical submissions) will only increase the price, but a good photo is one of the most valuable investments you can make for your career.

DESIGNING A RÉSUMÉ

Marketing your talent also means letting people know what you've done in the past, and a résumé listing your credits, accomplishments, skills, and training is how you do it. A great headshot will get you noticed, but it's the résumé stapled to the back that validates your experience and gets you the call to audition. Make it clean, well organized, and easy to read, with your name, contact numbers, and union affiliations clearly visible. In New York, stage experience is usually listed first, with your most impressive or best-known credits at the top. Above all, never, ever lie—it could come back to haunt you.

ACQUIRING SPECIAL SKILLS

Niche marketing is the goal of the special skills section of your résumé: a list of your unique abilities that could land you a role requiring a particular talent or characteristic. Athletic skills, musical instruments, foreign languages and dialects, dancing ability, a knack for comedy, circus talents, stage combat, full-body tattoos, a license to operate heavy machinery—just about anything goes here, provided you can do it well and at the drop of a hat.

TAKING CLASSES

On-the-job training is a valuable asset, but if you're a performer new to the industry, a casting director will most likely look at your classroom training before he or she is willing to trust you with a professional job. Even experienced performers keep themselves fresh by taking classes when they're between gigs—as well as fill the holes in their résumés to make themselves more castable. If a lack of training in Shakespeare, Meisner, musical theatre, tap dancing, or any number of performance specialties is holding you back, you'll find an abundance of classes to choose from in New York: Taking advantage of them will show the industry you're serious about improving your craft and add one more weapon to your actor's arsenal.

TRAINING BEYOND THE CLASSROOM

Performers learn by doing; but watching great performers at work can be a powerful learning tool as well, and in New York there's no shortage of opportunities. Discount theatre tickets are available at the TKTS booth in Times Square, and through TDF and other programs; some theatres look for volunteer ushers. Movies and TV shows are a laboratory for studying on-camera acting. And don't forget museums, parks, and the streets of the city itself—your observations of how people behave and interact will inform your choices as an actor.

AUDITIONING

Queuing up for auditions is the actor's lot in life, but you should never treat it as routine. Always arrive on time (anticipate traffic and subway delays) and know what you're auditioning for. Always have at least two contrasting classical and contemporary monologues at your disposal. Singers should bring a selection of songs with sheet music in their key. The single biggest complaint of casting directors is actors who show up for an audition unprepared, but don't be rigid in your preparation. If the director gives you an adjustment, go with it. Be flexible, spontaneous, upbeat, and professional. And go to every audition you can: Auditioning is a skill, and the more you do it, the better and more confident you'll be.

DRESSING FOR SUCCESS

Remembered is what you'll be if you arrive at a Shakespeare audition in full Renaissance regalia, but it probably won't get you the role. The rule of thumb when dressing for auditions is to keep it simple and comfortable—dress in a way to suggest the character, but without putting on a fashion show or making a spectacle of yourself. Let your talent do the talking, not your costume. And if you get a callback, wear the same thing you wore to the first audition: it'll help them remember you.

GETTING AN AGENT OR MANAGER

Securing the representation of an agent or manager is a prerequisite for landing most commercial and many legit (theatre, film, and TV) auditions in New York, not to mention the priceless career guidance an experienced rep can offer. Agents and managers work with actors on a freelance or contract basis and collect commissions on the money earned from jobs they help to procure. Agents are licensed by law; make sure that any agent you sign with is franchised by the talent unions. Personal managers are not licensed, so be careful about signing with a manager who makes promises that sound too good to be true. Mailings serve as a good introduction, but most legit agents will want to see you in a live performance before committing to taking you on as a client.

JOINING THE UNIONS

Toiling for little or no money in NYU student films and Off-Off-Broadway showcases is known as paying your dues, but to make any kind of significant money—by working on Broadway, in feature films, on TV, and in commercials—you'll need to pay your dues to a union. Actors' Equity, SAG, and AFTRA are the three major performers' unions, and each has specific eligibility requirements; in general, once you've been hired to work in a production covered by a union contract, you're eligible to join that union. Novice performers, however, should be wary of signing up before they're ready, and shutting themselves out of the learning opportunities provided by nonunion work—once you join the union, there's no legal going back.

DOING MAILINGS

Unemployment is a nearly perpetual state for performers, and mailings are what they do when they're looking for work—as well as being a way to promote the work they're doing at the moment. Mailings consisting of a headshot, résumé, and cover letter (and a reel, too, if it's been requested) are sent to casting directors in the hope of landing an audition, and to agents and managers in the quest for representation. Postcards are a quick and convenient way to follow up; flyers are used to invite industry pros to your show. Do your research and target your mailings wisely. (Don't sell yourself as a Toyota spokesman to an agent who only handles legit.) Keep your mailings upbeat, personable, and with a specific purpose, and don't get discouraged by a lack of response—a rate of one percent is considered normal.

PROMOTING YOURSELF

Video isn't just for selling bands on MTV. Nowadays actors, comedians, cabaret artists—performers of nearly every variety—are expected to have a "reel": a brief, professional-quality videotape or DVD featuring performance highlights. For singers and voiceover artists, an audiotape or CD is an essential marketing tool. While the Internet hasn't yet lived up to its potential as a casting mechanism, it remains the great equalizer in terms of marketing, with websites available for every budget—star and novice alike—featuring photos, résumés, and show information.

NETWORKING

"Work leads to work" is an old actor's adage, and this is the essence of networking. Entertainment is the ultimate "people" business, and every class you take, every audition you attend, every show you do—no matter how small—is another source of contacts that could lead to your next job. Your teacher could hear of a role that's perfect for you; that bit part you did in a no-budget student film could be helmed by the next Martin Scorsese. And remember that today's intern or receptionist is tomorrow's agent or casting director. So be nice to everyone, and remember their names—you never know where your next job may come from.

AVOIDING SCAMS

Xanthippe, the shrewish wife of Socrates, might make for a juicy role, but if the ad says "no experience necessary," that may be a tipoff that the producer is after more than your talent. Young, ambitious, and often inexperienced performers new to New York make the perfect target for scam artists. Never pay money for the chance to audition. Never pay a fee to anyone as a condition of representation. And if an agent or manager urges you to choose a particular photographer, take classes with a certain teacher, or have your photo published in a "book," you can be certain that he's making his money from kickbacks, *not* by getting work for his clients.

READING *BACK STAGE*

You'll be part of a tradition that goes back more than forty years when you head to the newsstand on Thursday morning to pick up your copy of *Back Stage*. For generations, performers new to the city have landed their first gigs in New York from one of the thousands of casting notices published in *Back Stage* every year. And now you can get them online as well, at www.backstage.com, along with the weekly features, news stories, contact lists, and reviews that'll soon have you navigating the city—and the industry—like a pro.

HAVING A LIFE

Zest for life is the last essential ingredient every performer needs. The relentless, single-minded pursuit of your dream may be the only way to succeed in the world's most competitive business—but it's also the fastest way to burn out the passion that brought you here in the first place. So don't forget to have a life away from "the industry": go shopping in Chinatown, ride the roller coaster at Coney Island, stroll through the Brooklyn Botanical Gardens—experience everything the city has to offer. Not only will it restore your spiritual, emotional, and creative energies, but by living life to the fullest, it'll make you a more fully alive performer onstage.

32 Prepping for L.A.:
The Business of Showbiz on the West Coast

BY ESTHER TOLKOFF

"Hollywood" brings to mind the glamour of "the movies." But conversations with agents, casting directors, managers, and performers who have taken the voyage make it clear that the tremendous amount of ongoing television production—especially the weekly shows calling for lots of one-time featured and principal roles entailing a week's worth of shooting—is what provides most of the working actor's bread and butter.

The key word there, of course, is "working."

Los Angeles draws a huge number of hopefuls, precisely because of this extensive television production—plus commercials, voiceover work, and films (though these are not necessarily shot in Los Angeles, and casting may also take place in New York and other cities). Newcomers range from starry-eyed beginners to people with solid credits elsewhere. If you make it, the money can be far higher than for theatre work, and that's why so many actors head for "the Coast."

But getting into the loop requires carefully thought-out hard work and planning. Ideally, that means establishing contacts and making introductions.

"If you don't educate yourself first as to the market here and what you will do when you get here, then you can spend a lot of time floundering," says Mark Measures, head of the voiceover and television commercials department at Abrams Artists Agency's L.A division.

Lots of hopefuls arriving in L.A. are extremely good looking and extremely young. Actors, agents and casting directors repeatedly mention the advantage of youth and the fact that the competition is overwhelming.

But not everyone who books work falls into the drop-dead-gorgeous or super-young category. As Eileen Haves, a New York-based commercials agent at Acme Talent & Literary, points out, "They are casting far more diverse types of people than they did years ago, including more character types." So there are many exceptions to the "rules" one hears.

And while a good-looking young performer can readily get an agent and be sent on many auditions, the professional tie will only last if the young actor books work steadily.

SPRAWL

In view of Los Angeles' famed "sprawl," you must drive to get anyplace, and that affects your professional life. *The Thomas Guide,* which contains detailed street maps of the Los Angeles area, is often recommended to newcomers. Auditions must be scheduled to allow for extensive traveling—meaning fewer calls per day than in a place like New York where casting directors, agents, and rehearsal locations are near enough to one another that the expression "pounding the pavement" can be taken literally.

Very few open calls are held in L.A. for film and TV work, and they are sparsely attended. Open calls do exist at times for stage work. So networking plays a central role: word-of-mouth referrals and prearranged appointments are needed to get an agent and/or auditions.

Of course, it helps in any market to be able to say "so-and-so sent me." But the geographic setup and the sheer number of actors seeking their big break make this a must in Los Angeles.

Even so, there are quite a few successful working actors who initially arrived in L.A. with no connections. They talk about networking from a different perspective—working intensively to establish contacts. This can be done by taking part in classes, workshops, and cold readings.

Fellow actors are a goldmine of information about upcoming auditions and about contacts. Actors also share information through websites such as www.actorsnetwork.com and www.actorsite.com. Professional gatherings—panel discussions, screenings—are often frequented by industry members other than actors, and give you a chance to meet these people and to ask questions. The Samuel French Bookstore (7623 West Sunset Boulevard) is a source of lists of agents, managers, and casting directors. And union offices often post casting notices and other professional advice on their bulletin boards.

Reading "the trades"—publications such as *Back Stage West* and *The Hollywood Reporter*—provides information about specific casting calls, classes, and projects slated for production down the road—a "heads up" about roles you might be suited for and with whom you should get in touch.

Actor Peter Allas, who works regularly in television and films, arrived in L.A. knowing nobody. He learned the names of whomever cast for studios and production houses, and drove to see them. "Casting directors can recommend you to agents," he found.

BE PREPARED—AND HAVE A REEL

As for auditions, Los Angeles-based casting director Mark Paladini notes, "Casting directors hate it if an actor shows up unprepared. Good training, experience, and professional behavior count a lot. That's true anywhere. Many actors believe that you have to do something odd to stand out at an audition. Good acting and being right for the part are what make you stand out."

Headshots are basically the same in L.A. as anywhere else, though some people have observed a trend toward more "outdoorsy" shots. "Pretty" shots are often more associated with L.A. as opposed to an "edgy," "real people" look associated with New York photos. Many people suggest having multiple headshots with different looks, and urge their agents to send the photo with the look closest to that of the role being cast. Others in the industry lean more toward having one or two standard headshots.

Color photos are becoming increasingly popular. According to actor Peter Allas, "Color is rapidly becoming the 'in' way. I think that soon it will be necessary for all actors to have a color shot too. The price is becoming much more affordable."

Agents and casting directors also expect actors to have a reel showing about five minutes of their best work. "If you don't have clips from a film, television program, or commercial," advises actress Whitney Hall, "include a tape of a theatrical showcase you were in—whatever you can show on tape." See also, Chapter 10, "Promoting Yourself Using Videos," page 122.

GETTING AN AGENT

Eileen Haves says, "The ideal way to arrive is if you're represented by a bicoastal agency and have an appointment set up for you with the L.A. agent in advance, especially in the theatrical area."

If you have appeared in a production with name recognition, or in anything featuring a well-known performer, you will have a better chance of being seen.

Getting an agent is essential. Performers do not freelance in Los Angeles. Actors often have more than one agent—for theatrical projects, for commercials, possibly for voiceovers—but the actor is signed to each one.

Many actors have both an agent and a personal manager. Many managers are hired to help actors get an agent. Opinions vary as to whether having a manager is necessary (see Chapter 15, "Personal Managers: To Sign or Not to Sign," page 161). To find an agent or a manager, former Talent Managers Association President Paul Bennett says, simply "send a headshot, résumé, and a reel, and write, 'I'm new here and I'm seeking representation.'"

Casting directors can be a good source of referral to agents. Once again, networking is the key. Mark Paladini suggests checking casting credits in films and television shows to see what types certain casting directors work with, so you can better target your mailings.

PILOT SEASON

Many actors come to L.A. for "pilot season"—mid-January through April—when sample episodes of potential television series are cast and shot. These roles are coveted. Actors who do not have representation are unlikely to land auditions.

Since producers want a pilot to be "picked up," casting is done with great care. Of course, having a steady role in a series is an excellent thing, but being cast in a pilot doesn't mean being cast in the actual series if it does get picked up; an established star may get the role. Still, listing pilots on one's résumé is impressive.

Television episodics are shot from July up till the December holidays. Next there's a hiatus, then comes pilot season. Actors and agents alike agree that it is wiser to make your first trip to Los Angeles at a time of year when the competition is less frenetic and you may be more likely to be seen.

THEATRE

Los Angeles is not thought of as a theatre town, and doubtless television and film production command most of the entertainment industry's energy and attention. But there is a thriving theatre community (which *Back Stage West* covers in depth). Even performers who are primarily interested in film and television find that theatrical roles can showcase their work to producers.

Actor Robert Mobley's experience was mostly theatrical. He was cast in a play, *Names,* which featured some well-known actors and was reviewed in L.A. "I got an agent as a result of that play and was cast in principal roles in two films," he says.

On the other hand, F. William Parker only lists his extensive television and film credits on the Web, omitting his work with top Southern California theatres. "People don't care about that as much here," he finds.

RÉSUMÉS, BACKGROUND WORK, AND SURVIVAL JOBS

Several industry people recommend that if you land a small part, even a one-liner in an episodic program, you should take it—even if your prior experience is at a higher level. With this credit on your résumé, you are more likely to be considered for another such show.

Small roles are one thing, but when it comes to background (or "extra") work, many actors say that once you are seen as an extra, you are always seen as an extra. They advise never to put extra work on your résumé.

Others see positive sides to background work and feel it deserves more respect. Bill Kalatsky signed up with the famed Central Casting agency (www.central-casting.com), which lists available extra work for member actors, both union and nonunion. "You see up close just how films are made." And, he adds, you swap information with fellow actors. Those who join Central Casting have their head-shot and stats posted on a data base used by casting directors.

SAG extra work "counts" toward qualifying for health insurance and toward your pension. If you are not a SAG member, you might get an upgrade and/or a voucher that leads to SAG eligibility. So background work can be an important way to supplement income.

Many actors seek out stand-in work, viewed as an excellent "gig." Stand-ins are considered part of the crew. A stand-in bears a resemblance to a principal actor and performs his or her role while the crew sets up the lighting, sound, etc. Once the technical setup is ready, the principal comes onto the set and the stand-in steps back.

WEIGHING THE ODDS

When heading for Los Angeles, it's best to educate yourself and have a careful plan while remaining aware of the odds and keeping your options open. But then, that's true when taking any chance in show business—or, for that matter, pretty much anywhere in life.

33 Welcome to L.A.:

Neighborhood by Neighborhood

BY JENELLE RILEY

For many newcomers intimidated by the big bad city the first question is, Do I really need to live in L.A.? Can't I just get a place in one of the many "bedroom" communities ringing the city and commute into town when I have an audition/job/ meeting/rehearsal? After all, I'll have to drive everywhere, anyway.

But not all commutes are created equal. And the simple reality is, if you want to seek work as an actor in film and television, you will have to commit to being in Los Angeles for the majority of your working day, and often long into the night. (Bear in mind that "working" includes going to auditions, rehearsals, and classes, as well as to actual shooting or recording gigs.) That's the simple truth, no matter how many industrials a San Diego agent can land you, or how great your part is in that play at South Coast Rep.

Once you've acclimated—or once you've established yourself as a working actor in the business—you might make the decision to put a little distance between yourself and the bustle and smog. Many do. If you crave a pleasant, slower-paced, relatively homogeneous community to come home to after a hard day's work, you'll have to go far afield, to the beaches or the canyons (where it will cost you), or to pockets of Orange, Ventura, or Riverside counties. But when you first arrive in L.A., it's best to stay near the action. For those just starting out, extensive freeway time can add just one more stress factor to an already stressful and uncertain career.

Wherever you live, it's essential that you have voice mail or a cell phone with an L.A. area code (323, 213, 310, or 818), as the industry implicitly prefers actors it can rely on to arrive on time at short notice. How you get there is always up to you, but why give them a reason to doubt your immediate availability? Remember: here, image is everything.

The following, then, is our highly subjective guide to those areas we feel are closest to the industry hubs while still offering a standard of living reasonable and safe enough for an actor just off the bus.

Downtown L.A., Boyle Heights, City Terrace, and East Los Angeles offer apartments for reasonable rent, good highway access to anywhere you need to go, and a cultural oasis or two: the East L.A. Classic Theatre, the theatre departments of East Los Angeles City College and Cal State Los Angeles, and the Plaza de la Raza Cultural and Educational Center. There is also the vast, diverse area known as South Central Los Angeles, where the neighborhoods differ widely—from the low-income Compton to the family community of Hyde Park. The San Fernando Valley includes a number of cities actors call home but are in no way considered particularly accessible from industry hubs: Tarzana, Topanga, Woodland Hills, Reseda, Canoga Park, Northridge, North Hills, Panorama City, Sun Valley, and

Mission Hills. Also low on the accessibility scale are such San Gabriel Valley neighborhoods as Alhambra, San Gabriel, and Monterey Park.

Then there are those coastal areas: great for visiting but not an option if you're not rich and famous, or very good friends with someone who is rich or famous. These include Malibu and Pacific Palisades, for example.

And, of course, to the south there is the often maligned but admittedly comfortable Orange County. It has plenty of well-lit two-way streets, practically no potholes, and all the protected left-hand turn lanes you could ever want, but it's accessible from L.A. primarily via two of the Southland's most congested freeways: the gargantuan 405 and the less scenic 5, which is perpetually under construction, often attempting to funnel four lanes of traffic through a mere two.

More picturesque parts of Orange County include the surfer-haven beaches of Newport and Huntington, and the quaint, artsy Laguna Beach—home to several yearly arts festivals and the Laguna Playhouse, one of the area's best theatres. Rent for a one-bedroom starts at around $900, a two-bedroom around $1,075. Orange County is also home to the Orange County Performing Arts Center—which brings in everything from large Broadway musicals and world-class symphonies to cabaret artists—and South Coast Repertory, a nationally renowned LORT theatre with acting conservatories for adults and for children.

But enough about the also-rans. On to the best places for apartment-hunters new to the City of Angels.

LOS ANGELES

DOWNTOWN
The famous Downtown L.A. skyline is near the city's original Mexican settlement, now memorialized in the tourist destination of Olvera Street, and Downtown is still headquarters for federal and state courthouses and other government agencies, City Hall, two locations of the Museum of Contemporary Art, an excellent Central Library, the *Los Angeles Times,* the LAPD, the Staples Center, the city-run Los Angeles Theatre Company, and L.A.'s answer to Lincoln Center: the Music Center, which includes the Ahmanson Theatre, the Mark Taper Forum, and the Dorothy Chandler Pavilion. The newest addition is Frank Gehry's stunning new concert venue, Disney Hall, a glistening construction of metal and elegance that includes two outdoor amphitheatres.

Downtown L.A. is very much like other American downtowns in that it has a confounding one-way street layout, finding reasonable parking is tough anywhere, and take a wrong turn and you'll end up in an unsettling skid row. Downtown is also crammed with memorable neighborhoods, such as the bustling (if touristy) Chinatown; the vibrant and well-maintained Little Tokyo (home to the nationally renowned Asian-American theatre company East West Players). Bargain hunters will want to check out Santee Alley in the fashion district, an always-packed hub of cheap clothing, accessories, and children's toys.

Also included are the jewelry and flower districts, both of which contain varieties to make your head spin. Beautiful historic movie palaces, on the vibrant shopping boulevard Broadway, are still worth a visit for special screenings or on historic tours of the area, available through the L.A. Conservancy, www.laconservancy.org.

Downtown is a packed place to work and visit, but does anyone live there? More and more lately. Downtown L.A. has hit a remarkable resurgence. The Downtown Center Business Improvement District (BID) and the Los Angeles Economic Development Corporation (LAEDC) have worked diligently to improve the status of Downtown as an ideal place to live and work. By working to combat the rampant homeless problem in the area, boosting cleanliness and safety, and increasing the transportation options, it won't be long before Downtown becomes a better place to visit and live. Further boosting the resurgence of the area is the 12.5-acre Los Angeles Center Studios, the first new studio in L.A. in more than fifty years. The center offers state-of-the-art production facilities for the film, television, and commercial industries.

Since the mid-1980s, young artists have been flocking to the gigantic New York-style loft apartments for relatively low prices. Traction Avenue has been coined the Artists District. (Expect to pay about $1,000 a month for a 585-square-foot loft to $3,000 for a 2,200-square-foot unit.) Also look for the recent revitalization of the Old Bank District, the area between Fourth and Main streets that is walking distance to City Hall, Little Tokyo, and the Music Center. Three major loft-apartment buildings have recently opened in this area: the San Fernando, The Hellman, and Continental—all offer Soho-style exposed brick walls, concrete floors, stripped wood, and high ceilings.

Some high-rise apartment dwellers live near that skyline—mostly senior citizens at Angelus Plaza or young professionals at Bunker Hill Towers or Grand Tower (rentals ranging from $965 to $2,450). There is also Pico-Union/Westlake to the southwest, where the ethnically specific neighborhoods can give visitors the feeling of being in another country altogether. South of that is University Park, around the campus of the University of Southern California, where the student life and college-related amenities make it an affordable and relatively dynamic place to live. This neighborhood boasts the scrappy 24th Street Theatre.

MT. WASHINGTON, EAGLE ROCK, HIGHLAND PARK

Once called Northeast L.A., this historic cluster of neighborhoods is more or less tucked between the 5, 134, and 110 freeways. Lately the area has experienced a revival that's been compared hopefully to the Silverlake renaissance of the 1990s. The area boasts a wide mix of incomes and ethnicities, reflecting its proximity to East L.A., Chinatown, and Echo Park.

The height, in many senses, is Mt. Washington, a round knob of a hill with great views and winding streets, with an emphasis on Craftsman-style and stucco houses and bungalows. There are plenty of rentals, with two-bedroom homes going for $1,500 a month and up. Ringing the base of Mt. Washington are lower-income families and thus cheaper rentals.

Eagle Rock, which takes its name from a bird-like rock formation in the hills over-looking Colorado Boulevard, is best known as the home of the venerable Occidental College; at its best this quiet tree-lined community has the feel of a small college town. It also has the best pizza restaurant in L.A., Casa Bianca Pizza Pie. Houses rent for less than $900; one-bedroom apartments can rent for about that.

Southeast of Eagle Rock, abutting the 110 Freeway, is Highland Park, an area of historical and architectural interest. Noted poet, writer, and L.A. *Times* editor

Charles Lummis lived here. The neighborhoods are hit-and-miss, but the cheap rent (deals as low as $550) still attracts artists and bohemians. At the south end, near Lincoln Heights, is the Brewery Arts Complex, a loft-style artists' colony in a former brewery that boasts some of the best square-foot deals in town.

One drawback: actor-related services are minimal, apart from the Lincoln Heights-located Bilingual Foundation of the Arts, which stages plays in Spanish and English. These remain good neighborhoods to look at if you have roommates or you wish to get away from the hustle and bustle of the city. But that's also the downside: despite its proximity to the 110, 134, 5, and 2, and hence the relatively easy commute to Hollywood, Downtown, and the Valley, Northeast L.A. can feel a bit removed from the center of action, industry-wise.

ECHO PARK, SILVERLAKE, LOS FELIZ

If West Hollywood is comparable to New York's West Village, the hilly Silverlake area, east of Hollywood and west of Downtown, is L.A.'s answer to the East Village (or to San Francisco Bay Area's Mission District). That's due not only to its eclectic, Latino-rooted ethnic mix and thriving gay community, but also to its perennial attractiveness to left-of-center artists—or young industry types who still fancy themselves left-of-center artists—which dates back to the 1930s when the hilly Echo Park neighborhood was nicknamed "Red Hill" after the number of communists and fellow travelers holed up there.

Silverlake—named after the boulevard that winds north-south from Glendale Boulevard to Beverly Boulevard—has become increasingly desirable since the early 1990s, managing to resist wholesale gentrification or blight (despite the inevitable Starbucks), holding on to its low-key blend of suburban kitsch and post-punk practicality, as well as its reassuring blend of Latino, Anglo, Asian, and African-American gays, straights, singles, and families.

This mix extends to housing types and architecture: up in the heights of the area's verdant hills, secluded homes (some Neutra originals) can sell for between $300,000 and $500,000, while down the hill, closer to the boulevards, rentals range from 1950s-era apartment complexes to Spanish-style '30s single-family homes. These homes can also be split into fourplexes or duplexes, with rents that can range from $600 to $1,500.

Los Feliz, west of Silverlake, is a venerable L.A. neighborhood dominated by Craftsman-style houses. The area's well-kept rentals tend to run higher than in Silverlake: studios and one-bedrooms rent for $700 and up. Nearby is Griffith Park, L.A.'s answer to Central Park. A major landmark with great jogging paths, Griffith Park also contains lots of diversions, including horseback riding, the Los Angeles Zoo, and the Greek Theatre. (Not what it sounds like—it books mostly rock and pop acts.) The neighborhood also has attractive pedestrian and dining corridors along Vermont and Hillhurst avenues between Sunset and Franklin, and Barnsdall Art Park and its theatre is nearby.

Echo Park, nestled between Silverlake and Dodger Stadium's Elysian Park, is the lowest-profile of this trendy troika; rents are accordingly lower, and the neighborhood's demographic is more mixed. Landmarks include Aimee Semple McPherson's famous Angelus Temple and the pleasant park that gives the neighborhood its name.

With close proximity to the 101, 110, 2, and 5 freeways, the area is extremely accessible to Hollywood and Downtown, pretty good to the Valleys, but something of a haul to the Westside. And though it boasts no film studios or major theatres, small performance spaces like Company of Angels and the Skylight Theatre seem a natural part of the area's funky nightlife, which ranges from rock clubs like Spaceland to dance clubs like The Echo, to one-of-a-kind watering holes like the Dresden Room, The Silverlake Lounge, the Tiki Ti, Akbar, Good Luck Bar, The Short Stop, and the Red Lion.

HOLLYWOOD

Hollywood has become the entertainment industry's unofficial brand name, but the name comes from the actual region of L.A. overseen by the famous hillside sign (formerly "Hollywoodland") that just celebrated its eightieth birthday. While people may think of Hollywood as a endless view of studios and starlets, the actual Hollywood area is made up of several cheap tourist storefronts and sex shops. Still, in many ways, this remains the heart of Los Angeles. And, in a series of bold civic/commercial moves that have been as rapid as they have been massive, the neighborhood and the industry are, to a large extent, coming together again. The Hollywood/Highland complex (Hi-Ho as some call it) sports stores such as the Gap and Banana Republic, combined with the renovated and expanded Mann's Chinese Theatre; and the neighborhood looks cleaner and safer than it's been in years. There's always a premiere or an event happening in the area, especially now that Jimmy Kimmel tapes his live talk show, which features frequent outdoor musical performances, right across from the Hi-Ho complex. The Kodak Theatre, now the home of the Academy Awards, is a classy new edition. And one should never overlook the Hollywood Bowl, which has housed just about every famous act known to man in its spacious amphitheatre.

Of course all this night-life can make traffic in this already-choked region a real trial. Highland Avenue was bad enough thanks to drivers trying to hop on the 101 freeway, but the new complex has only added to the gridlock. This influx of people and cars in a tightly gridded old neighborhood has made living in Hollywood begin to seem a little like living in Manhattan: residents pay a big mark-up in rent, but they're able to walk to a lot of amenities, and the excitement on the streets often has that intoxicating urban mixture of conviviality and danger.

The area does boast, however, a glut of small theatres, from Santa Monica Boulevard's so-called "Theatre Row" to Theatre of NOTE, the Tamarind, the Stella Adler Theatre, etc., and many acting and rehearsal studios, as well. Many of L.A.'s best restaurants and clubs are here too—for your employment, as well as your entertainment, needs—even on streets where you wouldn't want to live. Off the main drag of Hollywood Boulevard such venues as Beauty Bar and Vinyl are the latest ultra-trendy nightspots. And for a distinctly New York feel, slip into the peerless, and pricey, jazz club Catalina Bar & Grill for a cocktail after browsing at the bustling, open-all-night World Book & News on Cahuenga.

Among the most village-like and thus popular places to live in Hollywood is the Beachwood Canyon area, just below the Hollywood sign, where young working actors congregate at the Hollywood 101 coffee shop or on a nearby block of shops and restaurants on Franklin Avenue. The farther south you go down from the hills, the more likely you are to find one-bedrooms as low as $700, in duplexes and in apartment complexes. But with another nearby area of entrenched trendiness, Los Feliz, on the east and south, rents are climbing: Two-bedrooms can run from $1,800 to $2,500. As you go up into the hills, you're talking serious-money houses. A good place to look for rental info is the bulletin board at the Beachwood Market on Beachwood Canyon Drive.

Another popular cluster is a few hills west, in the blocks north of Hollywood and Sunset boulevards, west of Highland and La Brea but south of Mulholland Drive. Following the trend of much of L.A., rental prices steepen along with the ground elevation, so the farther you get into the hills, the less likely you are to find anything under $1,000 (even a one-bedroom), if you can find rentals at all. In this area, though, is Runyon Canyon, which offers a good hike (for dog-lovers, no leashes required) and arguably the best free view of the city in town.

KOREATOWN, WESTLAKE, MID-CITY

This area stretches from Hancock Park to Downtown L.A., between Washington and Beverly boulevards. Though much of it is considered Koreatown, this area is quite ethnically diverse, with a larger Latino population the closer one gets to Downtown, especially around Lafayette and MacArthur parks. Ethnically specific restaurants and clubs abound in this area, particularly with some of the finest Asian cuisine to be had in L.A. Housing is a mix of small homes and apartment houses. Fairly cheap apartments can be found ($600 and up), some surprisingly large.

Young people are moving into these neighborhoods, attracted to the spacious apartments, many with hardwood floors and an older East Coast feel to them. There's very little in this area in terms of theatres and studios, and much of it tends to be more economically impoverished. However, bounded by the 101 to the north and the 10 to the south, this area is centrally located and offers short commutes to most places to which an actor needs access.

Koreatown houses a plethora of interesting Korean barbecue restaurants, karaoke bars, and Asian-inspired clubs. Hancock Park and Westlake Village offer a more suburban feel, but you'll pay for it with steeper rent prices. (Expect to pay around $1,200 for a one-bedroom.)

PARK LA BREA, HANCOCK PARK, FAIRFAX DISTRICT, MID-WILSHIRE

This area of Los Angeles encompasses the range of wealth and ethnicities that make up the city. For actors, especially, this is a prime area to call home because it is central to so much going on in entertainment and culture—particularly the Fairfax district.

Park La Brea is a group of apartment complexes in a planned community, which houses many retirees, most of Eastern European Jewish background. There are many young families and singles in Park La Brea, as well, and the place seems to fill up every pilot season, as it has an inordinate number of furnished apartments for short-term rent. Parking is virtually non-existent, to non-residents at least. Rent tends to be high, $900-plus for one-bedrooms.

The surrounding Fairfax District, bordered by CBS Studios and Farmers Market to the south and trendy Melrose Avenue to the north, is made up of high-priced modest homes and fourplex apartments in a range of styles from

Spanish to Tudor. This is a dog-walkers' neighborhood with an interesting mix of young Hollywood types and older Jewish residents, along with a large pocket of Orthodox Jewish families to the east, near Hancock Park. Recently, The Grove, a Vegas-like outdoor shopping center, has taken over the land surrounding Farmers Market—and wreaked havoc with local traffic. The movie theatres in the Grove are pretty great, though because of the heavy traffic shows tend to sell out with alarming frequency.

Melrose is the place for outrageous fashion, from leather dresses to tattoos and body piercings. It is packed with pedestrians on the weekends. Fairfax, on the other hand, combines small Jewish-owned stores and the famous Canter's Deli with hip smaller clubs such as the Kibitz Room and Largo. Third Street, west of Farmers Market, offers low-priced but trendy restaurants and little parking. Rents in the Fairfax District for one-bedrooms a few years ago were in the $750–850 range, but recently they have moved into the $1,000–1,300 range, comparable to West Hollywood. Nearby theatres include the Matrix, the Zephyr, the Third Street Theatre, and the Greenway Court Theatre.

Hancock Park, to the east of La Brea Avenue, is one of the wealthier communities in Los Angeles. Big yards and estates with lots of trees give this neighborhood an old-money, East Coast feel. Apartments are few and far between, and typically quite expensive. Hancock Park is purely residential, with no theatres or audition spaces to speak of.

Mid-Wilshire (also called the Miracle Mile—also, rather spuriously, called "Beverly Hills adjacent") is south of the Fairfax District and is the most densely populated area in L.A. On Wilshire Boulevard are numerous high-rise buildings, including the VNU building, home to *Back Stage West.* South of Wilshire are block after block of apartment houses and single-family homes. Rents seem to get lower the farther one goes south of Wilshire. One-bedrooms generally start at $800–900 in the nicer areas.

Centrally located between Downtown and the beach, these four areas are typically reached by the 10 Freeway to the south or the 101 to the north. However, most locals use surface streets to get wherever they need to go, avoiding the freeways altogether.

LONG BEACH AREA

This area is quite affordable compared with other coastal cities and their beachfront apartments, like Santa Monica and Venice. However, it boarders on being too far a drive to the industry focal points, considering that the ever-congested stretch of the 405 Freeway is the main route to the Westside, Hollywood, and the Valley. One-bedrooms start as low as $500–600. Long Beach, the busiest cargo port on the West Coast, has a diverse ethnic mix, including a large Spanish-speaking population. About sixty percent of Long Beach is apartment dwellings. Although it's a schlep to the center of industry activity, the Long Beach Airport services three airlines with frequent flights—including the popular, affordable New York carrier Jet Blue. The MetroLink Blue Line connects Long Beach to Downtown L.A. by train. L.A. International Airport is also 17 miles north. In addition to the 405, this area is connected by the 710, 605, and 110 freeways. International City Theatre, the Long Beach Playhouse, and the Edison Theatre are located here.

SAN FERNANDO VALLEY

For some reason the San Fernando Valley, or "the Valley," as locals refer to it, often gets a bad rap. True, it does not have nearly as many cultural/historical landmarks as "the city" (Hollywood, Downtown, etc.). The Valley is also not as architecturally diverse, as it is made up mostly of one-story suburban homes built in the 1940s and '50s, a lot of nondescript stucco apartment buildings, and too many mini-malls.

The Valley is just not as hip as other spots in L.A., such as Silverlake, West Hollywood, Fairfax, Venice, or Santa Monica. And, yes, the Valley tends to get about ten to twenty degrees hotter than the Westside and beach areas during the summertime, leading to rolling blackouts. Not only is it not as hip, it sometimes lacks in the beauty department, with clouds of smog, and street after street of graffiti. In addition, as it is always under construction, traffic can be overwhelming and parking problematic.

So what's the draw? While we often think of film and television as happening in Hollywood, much of the entertainment business takes place on the other side of the hill, in the Valley. Many of the film/television studios, casting offices, and acting workshops are rooted here. Another plus is that the Valley tends to be a more affordable place to live in than other parts of Los Angeles—with some exceptions, of course. Although prices have gone up quite a bit, in comparison the Valley is still cheaper than many L.A. areas, and you get a lot more for your money. Along with housing, gas prices are slightly lower in the Valley.

There's plenty going on here, especially on Ventura Boulevard, which is the pulse of the Valley—running through Universal City and traveling west through Studio City, Sherman Oaks, Encino, Tarzana, and Woodland Hills. There are tons of good restaurants, movie theatres, coffeehouses, and shops along this popular boulevard. And just north of the fault line (Nordhoff Street), we enter the earthquake cities—more commonly known as Northridge, Sylmar, and San Fernando—where the attractions are shopping centers and affordable housing.

BURBANK, GLENDALE, TOLUCA LAKE

Like much of the Valley, the ambience here is suburban, except for downtown Burbank and the studios. Burbank is home to Disney Studios, NBC, and Warner Bros. In other words, this is a prime area, close to the 134 and 5.

Glendale tends to be more affordable than Burbank or Toluca Lake, offering a full array of apartment buildings, from the large and modern to 1930s and '40s duplexes and fourplexes. Singles start at $650, one-bedrooms at $900. Two-bedrooms go for $1,200 and up. Small single-family houses are available for rent in the southern part of Glendale, usually in the moderate price range of $1,400 and up. The northern area of Glendale is more affluent, and rent is generally more expensive. Notable points of interest include the Glendale Galleria, the Alex Theatre, and the historic Brand Library. The noted classical repertory theatre troupe A Noise Within is back in its historic Masonic Temple building in downtown Glendale. There are also many temporary agencies, a large number of them catering to the entertainment industry. For a coffee break or quick lunch, Porto's Bakery on Brand Boulevard is worthy of a visit.

In Burbank most of the single-family houses were built in the 1940s and '50s. Most of the apartment buildings were built in the 1940s through the '80s. The most notable theatres in this area are Burbank Center Stage, home of the first-class Colony Theatre Company, and the Falcon Theatre, owned by film/television producer Gary Marshall. There's also the Third Stage and the Victory Theatre, as well as other smaller theatres and many workshops and acting classes in the area. The Burbank Airport is nearby too, as are the popular Oakwood Apartments—month-to-month temporary housing that's a favorite of pilot-season visitors. Lake Hollywood off Barham Boulevard offers an oasis in the city: great for walking, jogging, or just taking in the beauty. Star sightings are common, as many make their homes in the surrounding hills. For make-up needs, there is Cinema Secrets, where you can find almost anything imaginable and take advantage of its ten percent discount if you can show a union card or proof of employment at a studio. There are also numerous thrift shops for props and costumes.

Toluca Lake, referred to as the jewel of the Valley, tends to be an even more affluent area than Burbank. Despite popular legend, there is a lake, although it's not easy to see, as it's surrounded by large homes. The streets are wide, safe, and clean—ideal for walking, bike riding, or just sightseeing. Popular hangouts include one of the first Bob's Big Boy restaurants, home to classic car club meetings on weekends.

NORTH HOLLYWOOD, STUDIO CITY

North Hollywood covers a vast span of the Valley and, like many parts of Los Angeles, has its good and bad areas. Apartment buildings date from the 1960s to the present. Rental costs are less expensive in the north end of the area and more expensive closer to Studio City, which is populated mostly by middle- to upper-income residents. Rentals start at $800 for a one-bedroom and $1,200 for two-bedrooms.

Expect to pay more in Studio City, which is a little cozier and more centrally located to Ventura Boulevard, close to the 170, 101, and 134 freeways. Points of interest include Universal Studios and CityWalk, the Academy of Television Arts & Sciences, MTM Studios, CBS Studio Center, the NoHo Arts District—an area on and near Lankershim Boulevard populated with a number of theatres and coffee-houses—and the El Portal, the Valley's only mid-size Equity theatre. Woodbridge Park, the neighborhood between the Los Angeles River and the 101, is particularly bucolic. It sits adjacent to Woodbridge Park, and many homes are within walking distance to Tujunga Village—a quaint single block of coffeehouses, restaurants, a gourmet food store, and a bookstore.

VAN NUYS, SHERMAN OAKS, ENCINO

Childhood Van Nuys resident Robert Redford was once quoted as saying, "Van Nuys is just this furnace that could easily destroy any creative thought that managed to creep into your mind." But how can you hate the city that housed one of California's first Krispy Kreme donut shops? The rent is also considerably cheaper than in the neighboring Sherman Oaks and Encino, though it's not as well located for shopping and eating. Still, with studios and one-bedrooms beginning at $650 and homes as low as $1,200, what difference does a few blocks make? Sherman Oaks is less industrial and boasts two megaplex shopping malls: Sherman Oaks Fashion Square and the renovated Galleria. A desirable area for all ages, Sherman Oaks is mainly populated by middle- and upper-class homes and townhouses. The crème de la crème of the area is Encino, with its million-dollar homes and tree-lined streets. Of course this also means higher rent—don't be surprised to find a one-bedroom apartment charging more than a house in Van Nuys.

These three areas are located near the 101 and 405 freeways and are close to a wide variety of theatres and acting schools in the Valley.

SAN GABRIEL VALLEY

ALTADENA, PASADENA, SOUTH PASADENA, SAN MARINO
Pasadena, with its wide tree-lined boulevards and stately homes, offers a taste of the East Coast to those who miss it. Old Town Pasadena is a hot spot among young people for shopping, drinking, and eating, and has a decidedly yuppie feel. Apartments are few and far between in Pasadena and are therefore not cheap—$900 and upwards for one-bedrooms. However, things get less expensive north of the 210, and some homes are also available for rent at fairly affordable prices.

Pasadena is accessible; the 110 dead-ends here from Downtown, the 134/210 runs through the north side, and the 2 is not far away. The area offers peace and quiet, but it's by no means close by. A commute from Downtown L.A. is only fifteen to thirty minutes, but from Hollywood it is thirty minutes to an hour, depending on traffic. One of the original irrigation colonies, Pasadena is home to the Rose Bowl, the Rose Parade, and some of the finest homes in the Southland, designed by such architects as Frank Lloyd Wright and the Greene brothers. Theatre companies in Pasadena include the venerable Pasadena Playhouse, as well as the Pasadena Shakespeare Company, the Knightsbridge Theatre, Arroyo Repertory Company, Furious Theatre Company, and Fremont Centre Theatre.

Altadena to the north and South Pasadena to the south are farther from freeways and offer fewer apartments, though both are very attractive suburbs. But those subdivisions in Altadena and South Pasadena that do exist are often cheaper than in Pasadena and worth a look. One-bedrooms are often available for $600 and up. Every winter, Altadena lights up its thoroughfare, dubbed Christmas Tree Lane. Then there is San Marino, a very expensive city to live in, not easily reached by any major freeways, home of the Huntington Library. Unless you've suddenly come into some money and don't need to get to auditions often, San Marino is probably not the place for you. It's great to visit, however.

COASTAL

SANTA MONICA, VENICE
While no major studios are to be found here, a number of production companies and casting offices make their home on the Westside. Most importantly, the easy, breezy feel of ocean-living embodies California culture at its best.

The colorful, funky Venice, known for its strong community of resident artists, was first constructed in 1904 under the direction of Abbot Kinney, for whom one of the more popular streets in Venice is named. Indeed it was originally conceived as a city built along water canals, like the Italian original, but many of the canals were eventually replaced by concrete to make way for cars. In the 1960s, the remaining canals became a hangout for artists and hippies, including Jim Morrison of The Doors.

As property values skyrocketed, the longhairs and struggling artists were chased out of these areas, and many of the homes have since been remodeled; the canals were restored by the city six years ago. Even if you can't afford to live along the canals, it's a beautiful place for walking if you live nearby.

There are many other areas within Venice, which is a mix of Craftsman-style bungalows, modest duplexes, and ultra-modern apartment buildings and homes. An element of ultra-cool still remains in this place; Dennis Hopper lives nearby "the 'hood," the notorious Oakwood area of Venice (between Rose Avenue and Abbot Kinney and west of Lincoln Boulevard), where some serious gang activity occurs. Even "the 'hood" has seen some improvements, and residents there have noticed that some of their blocks have cleaned up significantly in recent years.

Affordable rentals are still to be found, but you have to look hard or be willing to live with roommates. The farther away you live from the beach, the more affordable rent gets. For the most part, the cost of living has gone up over the years because of this neighborhood's popularity—the main draw being Venice Beach. A one-bedroom cottage in the heart of Venice went for $800 just a few years ago. Now it's renting for around $1,200 and up. Keep in mind that parking can be a problem if you live near the beach and do not have an assigned parking space, especially on the weekends when thousands flock to watch the festivities along the Venice boardwalk.

Likewise, Santa Monica has long been a favorite neighborhood, although it has a more toned-down reputation compared with its neighbor Venice. There are many apartment buildings, dating from the 1940s to the present, as well as Craftsman-style and 1950s suburban homes, which now sell for outrageous sums. Rent varies depending on the quality of the building and the proximity to the beaches or major shopping areas, which include Montana Avenue, Third Street Promenade, and Main Street.

Santa Monica and Venice are close to Pacific Coast Highway and the 10 and 405 freeways. Rent starts at $775 for a studio, $795 for a one-bedroom, $1,250 for a two-bedroom, and $1,050 for a house. Theatres include Pacific Resident Theatre in Venice and, in Santa Monica, Highways Performance Space, the Powerhouse Theatre, and Santa Monica Playhouse.

MARINA DEL REY, PLAYA DEL REY
Playa del Rey is probably best known as the land even DreamWorks couldn't afford, as the studio originally hoped to build offices on the property. Concerns about preserving the coastal wetlands prevented this move, but now agreements to conserve the natural environment have allowed several condominum complexes to pop up seemingly overnight. Its proximity to the airport, the harbor, and major freeways make this area a convenient, if pricey, place to live. Having lost to San Pedro in a battle to become Los Angeles' main commercial port, Marina del Rey turned from an estuary filled with duck hunters into what its chamber of commerce calls "a pleasure-craft harbor," with more than 6,000 recreational boat slips and a lot of moderate to expensive restaurants.

Rent starts around $750 for a studio, $800 for a single bedroom, or $1,195 for a double. Residents tend to be somewhat well established, active, and over the age of 35. Actor-related resources are limited in these areas, though the ever-bohemian Venice Beach lies a few miles north.

SOUTH BAY CITIES

MANHATTAN BEACH, HERMOSA BEACH, REDONDO BEACH
With plenty of great surfing, volleyball tournaments, long flat bike paths ideal for
biking—when not occupied by rollerbladers—and an abundance of sports bars
where microbrews flow freely, these beachside cities attract lots of single, sun-loving
twentysomethings. Once an area covered with sheep and barley, as these cities grew
and became more easily accessible via the Pacific Electric Railroad, they began to
attract day-tripping Angelenos who sought to escape the heat of the Greater Los
Angeles basin. The place became a vacation refuge for such legendary figures as
Errol Flynn and the Charlie Chaplin family.

This is also where the Beach Boys came of age—in Manhattan Beach—and
where, in nearby Hermosa Beach and Redondo Beach, Southern California's surf
culture got its biggest sendoff in the 1950s and '60s.

Housing ranges from the well-kept lawns and luxury apartments of the south
Redondo ultra-rich to boxy beachfront apartments where young groups of friends
rent pads to clutter with beer cans and members of the opposite sex. Rent is not
cheap, with studio and one-bedroom apartments starting at $850 and quickly
going up from there. There are also plenty of beautiful Spanish-style homes on
winding streets where more family-oriented residents can nest.

The main theatrical attraction is the Redondo Beach Performing Arts Center,
a modern, 1,425-seat proscenium-type theatre, home to the Civic Light Opera
of South Bay Cities, the largest producing civic light opera in Southern California.
Keep in mind that commuting to these areas from Hollywood can turn into an
hour-long drag if undertaken at the wrong time of day.

EL SEGUNDO
Although sports enthusiasts may favor El Segundo for being home to the Los Angeles
Kings' and Lakers' practice facility, it doesn't offer much for those interested in the
performing arts. In general, it is a higher-rent area with few or no notable theatres,
audition spaces, or acting schools. On average, one- to two-bedroom apartments start
at $1,000 to $1,500. This small industrial town hugs the beach and is just south
of LAX, so those who often travel for out-of-state auditions may want to consider
living here. However, it suffers from continually high levels of traffic noise.

WESTSIDE

WEST HOLLYWOOD
Considered by most to be L.A.'s equivalent of NYC's West Village, West Hollywood
(or "WeHo" as it is sometimes called) comprises the largest gay community in
L.A. The two main WeHo boulevards are Sunset and Santa Monica. Santa Monica
is known for its bistros and theatres—of the legit and the porn variety. Sunset is
known for its chic, expensive restaurants, its neon signs, and its clubs. These include
the ever-trendy the Whisky, the Viper Room, and the Roxy. Both boulevards typically find more pedestrians out at all hours than do most other areas of Los Angeles.
The late-night scene throughout the week is very much alive.

In addition to a number of casting directors and agents who have offices in West Hollywood, there are theatres such as the Court, the Coast Playhouse, the Coronet, the Globe Playhouse, the Celebration; and comedy clubs the Laugh Factory, the Comedy Store, and the Improv. West Hollywood also offers some excellent bookstores, art galleries, and the Laemmle Sunset-5 movie theatre complex, which screens arthouse fare.

Many new apartment complexes are in West Hollywood, though most typically date from the 1930s and '40s. Rents are high in this area. Studios are typically $800-plus, one-bedrooms $1,000-plus, and two-bedrooms $1,400-plus. To the north of West Hollywood, making their way up to the Hollywood Hills, are more homes than apartments. These are quite pricey as well and cater more to young people in the industry than to families. As in surrounding areas, parking can be a nightmare here unless you have a permit. Urban, exciting, and always hopping, West Hollywood caters to the young—for a price, of course.

WESTWOOD, BRENTWOOD, WEST LOS ANGELES

This is a very widespread area of Los Angeles that includes modest to upscale neighborhoods and a large variety of apartment buildings. Brentwood tends to have the most expensive homes, townhouses, and apartments because it is such a desirable neighborhood, with many shops and restaurants within walking distance, relative safety, and close proximity by car to the beaches.

Most of the apartment buildings in Brentwood date back to the 1950s. Studios tend to run $850. One-bedrooms go for $1,200 and up, two-bedrooms are above $1,450. San Vicente and Wilshire boulevards are the main arteries through Brentwood, connecting it to Santa Monica, West Los Angeles, and Westwood.

Westwood, an area first developed in the 1920s, is a mix of upscale traditional homes, million-dollar modern high-rise condos along Wilshire Boulevard, and apartments, many of which are occupied by students at UCLA.

Westwood Village, where a number of restaurants and shops are located, has seen better days, but it remains a walking area with many movie theatres, including two 1950s movie palaces: the Bruin and the Village.

West Los Angeles covers the widest area of these three neighborhoods and seems to have the most affordable rent. There are many nondescript stucco apartment buildings from the 1950s to the present, as well as modest but very nice homes. Apartment rentals begin at $750 for a studio, $900 for a one-bedroom, $1,200 for a two-bedroom. This area is close to the 405. Points of interest for actors include the Geffen Playhouse and UCLA (home to the Freud Playhouse), as well as a multitude of tiny black-box theatres.

BEVERLY HILLS, BEL AIR

If you imagined Beverly Hills as the pinnacle of wealth and glitz, you won't be disappointed. Both Beverly Hills and Bel Air are home to some of the richest folks in L.A.—movie stars, studio executives, and business tycoons settle here. Bel Air is set in the hills north of Sunset Boulevard and consists entirely of expensive homes. There are also wealthy areas of Beverly Hills that extend into the canyons.

The area between Sunset and Santa Monica boulevards, with homes dating back to the 1920s, is probably what you picture when you think of Beverly Hills—wide streets lined by trees such as tall palms. There are no apartments in this area—only million-dollar-and-up homes.

However, if you drive south, to the area south of Wilshire and Olympic boulevards, you'll find many apartment buildings, dating back to the 1930s and '40s. They start at $800 for singles, $1,000 for one-bedrooms, and $1,500 for two-bedrooms—although rent tends to be higher for most apartments. You'll find the more affordable apartments are often in areas called "Beverly Adjacent," which technically fall into Los Angeles zip codes but border Beverly Hills.

Beverly Hills and Bel Air are within easy driving distance of many areas, including Santa Monica and Hollywood. Several routes through the canyons, such as Beverly Glen and Coldwater, provide street access to the San Fernando Valley. It is a relatively safe area in which to live and offers many restaurants and shops close by, including those on the ritzy Rodeo Drive. Many agents and casting offices are here. Theatres include the Beverly Hills Playhouse and the Canon Theatre.

CULVER CITY, MAR VISTA, PALMS, WESTCHESTER, SAWTELLE

The Culver City area is a great place to get away from it all but still maintain easy access to more bustling parts of the city. With easy access to the 405 and 10, residents are only minutes away from the coastline or Downtown. The freeways are usually easy to navigate, although you might not want to make a trip to the Valley in rush-hour traffic. The spacious Sony Studios, where many game shows like *Wheel of Fortune* are taped, make up the heart of Culver City and lend a retro Hollywood feel to the area. Best of all, rent can be surprisingly cheap for West L.A. Clean, safe apartments can be found in the $1,000 range for two bedrooms, and as low as $700 for a one-bedroom. The surrounding areas can also be fairly affordable, especially with all the new luxury condos and apartments constantly popping up nearby.

Palms houses many UCLA students who can't afford the pricier neighborhoods north of the area. For frequent travelers, the L.A. airport is literally minutes away, and you'll never have to bug a friend for a ride again. Thanks to the elaborate new Promenade at the Howard Hughes Center in Westchester, residents no longer have to trudge to Westwood or Santa Monica for all their shopping and movie needs. While you may want to expand your search for acting schools or theatres to Santa Monica, nearby theatres include Gascon Center Theatre and the Ivy Substation. If you think you're too hip to live in Culver City, you can always tell people you're "Marina-adjacent."

The Sawtelle area includes a mini-Little Tokyo, with its cozy cluster of noodle houses, Japanese groceries, and nurseries. It's also within whistling distance of the West Los Angeles Police Department—for safety, excitement, or to report that your issues of *Back Stage West* are being stolen from your mailbox. The YMCA provides a low-key place to exercise for those unhappy with the snooty, image-conscious gyms around town.

On the east end of the Sawtelle area is The Odyssey Theatre: It tends to run three simultaneous productions, and classes are taught on weekends by members of Circus Theatricals.

CENTURY CITY, CHEVIOT HILLS, RANCHO PARK

Work in the business area of Century City or live in one of its snazzy apartments—to rent or buy—and know you're on what was the back lot of Fox studios as recently as the 1960s. Indeed the 20th Century Fox lot still calls Century City its home.

Century City, with its skyscrapers and pristine streets, is quite pricey for the working-class actor. But you'll be within walking distance of umpteen movies at two multiplexes, as well as the great fresh-air shopping mall.

Rent becomes more affordable south of Pico Boulevard. Near the 10, with easy access to the 405, the areas of Cheviot Hills and Rancho Park are host to many working-class families. These areas feature single-family homes, with some apartment buildings interspersed. Pico Boulevard is a restaurant row, boasting nearly every cuisine at moderate prices for those who want to take a meeting on the Westside. (We've spotted Drew Barrymore, Billy Baldwin, Charles Martin Smith, John Lithgow, Adam Arkin, and Denzel Washington at coffees and lunches within a one-block area.)

To work off those meals, Rancho Park is, indeed, a park, with one of the finest public golf courses in town. The park also includes a parcourse fitness circuit, tennis courts, basketball courts, a swimming pool, and an outdoor amphitheatre for those impromptu rehearsals.

Adjacent to the park is the Century City Playhouse—which allows a glimpse of the towers of Century City but is not in its zip code. And near restaurant row is The Empty Stage, for improv classes and theatre rentals during the week, improv and sketch comedy shows weekend evenings.

And for those weekly headshot mailings: the Rancho Park Post Office branch, while nearly always busy, provides ample free parking.

Look for a single-room studio to start renting for $750 and up, with Century City at the high end ($1,000-plus) for a one-bedroom high-rise apartment. Parking is difficult in the business districts and restricted throughout most of the residential areas.

AND ASSOCIATES, INC

blaine

NEVER A FEE!!!
TEMPORARY AND FULL-TIME
POSITIONS AVAILABLE

CALL FOR AN APPOINTMENT
(310) 785-0560

IVY WEST

EDUCATIONAL SERVICES, INC.

PRIVATE
TUTORS
WANTED

Since 1989 Ivy West has offered rewarding part-time work to hundreds of talented actors and writers. Ivy West instructors receive:

- comprehensive training on the industry's most respected curriculum
- autonomous and flexible scheduling
- competitive pay and aggressive merit increases
- the support and dedication of a professional staff
- the opportunity to mentor and impact the lives of high school students

Ivy West has become CA's most popular provider of SAT prep, primarily due to the legendary reputation of our team of tutors. If this opportunity interests you and you share our commitment to student success, we would like to hear from you.

Learn more at *www.tutorjobs.com*
then call
310-301-7189 (Southern CA), 650-524-2711 (Northern CA)

Where do Hollywood Stars shape up and train for Action Movies?

Cynthia Rothrock's

United Studios Of Self Defense

Now Open! 12147 Ventura Blvd., Studio City
For more information call (800) 288-4249
www.CynthiaRothrock.info

• 5 time Undefeated World Karate Champion • Inducted into the Black Belt and Inside Kung Fu Hall of Fame
• Star in over 40 International Action Movies • Fight/Stunt Choreographer in over 100 TV/ Movie Productions
• More than 40 Magazine Covers in 13 languages.

**Exclusive One-on-One Private Lessons/ In House Stage Combat/Stunt Choreography
Stage Combat & Stunt Certification Available**

WOMEN'S CLINIC
& Family Counseling Center

Quality Health Care Since 1972

Low-Cost Sliding Scale Fees

• Birth Control
• Cancer Screenings
• Pregnancy Testing
• STD Testing/Treatment
• HIV Testing-Same Day Results
• Hormone Replacement Therapy
• Mammograms
• Exams For Men
• Same Day Appts.

Counseling Services Available
• Individuals
• Couples
• Families

9911 W. Pico Blvd.,
Suite 500
Los Angeles

(minutes from Fox Studios & West Hollywood)

310-203-8899

www.womens-clinic.org

INTERNS NEEDED

Learn what Casting Directors, Agents and Managers do. Empower yourself with Industry contacts and knowledge. Unpaid internship

**CALL (323) 852-1972
FOR MORE DETAILS**

Auto Insurance Pros.com

• Auto
• Health
• Life
• Home

**AUTO INSURANCE
800-664-8044**
john@autoinsurancepros.com
Lic.#OC50475

MODELS OPEN-CALL!
(Females & Males)

More info at:
www.ottomodels.com
or call Otto Models at:
(323) 650-2200 TA 3637

TO ADVERTISE IN THE NEXT
BACKSTAGE/BACK STAGE WEST
ACTORS HANDBOOK

WEST ■   ■ EAST
Back Stage West Advertising   Back StageAdvertising
5055 Wilshire Blvd., 5th floor   770 Broadway, 4th floor
Los Angeles, CA 90036   New York, NY 10003
323.525.2225   646.654.5700

34 Moving Out:

Relocating Your Acting Career

EDITED BY RICK PENDER

For the actor who is thinking about stepping off the treadmill in New York City or Los Angeles, what's the next choice? What are the options for the performer who wants to leave his small home town, but is not quite ready to engage with New York or Hollywood? The United States has many cities with thriving theatre scenes. They offer Equity stages that produce a broad array of work in small houses specializing in new, creative material; nor are the classics overlooked. Chicago, for instance, offers a scene almost as broad and deep as that of New York. If you prefer a laid-back lifestyle on the West Coast, San Francisco and Seattle offer appealing choices. Warmer climates and supportive audiences are waiting in Atlanta and South Florida. And don't rule out Minnesota: there's a lot of snow in the Twin Cities, but area residents flock to theatre productions there.

Small theatres operating on lean budgets may find out-of-town casting an expensive proposition, perhaps enhancing chances for local talent. On the other hand, reduced finances mean that many theatres will be doing shows with smaller casts or co-productions with theatres in one or more other cities. So getting steady work in some places might be a challenge. One reporter cited an actress who, after saying her city had more than one hundred theatres, quickly added that fewer than fifty actors locally made a living primarily from theatre.

So why relocate? Living a more balanced life in a significant American city is appealing to many actors. Stepping away from the hyperactive pace of New York and L.A. to become part of a less-frenetic urban center's arts scene can be a satisfying life choice. Here are some cities worth considering:

CHICAGO
(reported by Jonathan Abarbanel, WBEZ-FM, *Windy City Times;*
Back Stage regional correspondent)

Many observers maintain that Chicago is the best theatre scene in America after New York City. Some say it's the best, period. Regardless, Chicago credits are worth their weight in gold for actors who move on to New York or Los Angeles. Doors open for actors who score improv training at The Second City or work at one of three Tony Award-winning theatres: the Goodman, Steppenwolf, or Victory Gardens. More opportunities can be found at Shattered Globe, Famous Door, and Lookingglass, all of which cast outside their ensembles. There's occasionally the chance to work with renowned directors, including Robert Falls, Mary Zimmerman, and Frank Galati. And drama programs at Northwestern, Columbia College, or DePaul University enrich the scene.

Chicago and its collar counties boast some 200 theatre companies producing 900 shows a year. Many are new works, although the classical repertory remains well represented. In addition, many sit-down tours hold Chicago casting calls, and many national touring companies originate here. Chicago has a healthy—and growing—number of African-American and Latino theatre companies, although the Asian theatre community remains miniscule.

There is also a long-established commercial industry (both on-camera and voiceover) and an irregular but frequent flow of TV/film production. Actors don't usually become rich and famous working *in* Chicago, but they can become rich and famous working *from* Chicago.

Chicago is home for the Central Region of Actors' Equity Association, with about 7 percent of the union's membership. Many leading regional theatres hold calls in Chicago, including the Guthrie Theater in Minneapolis, Milwaukee Repertory Theater, the Muni in St. Louis, Kansas City's Missouri Repertory, and the Indiana Repertory Theatre in Indianapolis. Dinner theatres and substantial summer stock opportunities provide further options.

Chicago boasts about fifty Equity companies, most using the extremely flexible Chicago Area Theatre contract (CAT), with weekly salaries ranging from about $150 (three performances in a low-tier theatre) to over $600 (seven-performance week in a high-tier company, such as Steppenwolf). In addition to CAT, the most-used pacts are the LORT and dinner theatre agreements. Non-Equity theatre— beyond church, school and community groups—frequently is paid and regarded as fully professional by local critics. Theatre casting in Chicago does not require participation by an agent, although commercials, TV, film, and modeling work usually do.

Compared to other major theatre centers, rents for performance space and living space are cheap and stable, audiences are strong, and the political climate is very pro-arts. Studio apartments in good neighborhoods start at $500/month; one-bedrooms from $600/month. Public transportation—rapid transit and buses—runs 24/7.

Best of all, Chicago offers a caring and healthy theatrical community, without the cutthroat competitiveness of New York or Los Angeles, perhaps because there are no stars. There is an exceptionally strong professional association (the League of Chicago Theatres, www.chicagoplays.com), a trade paper (*PerformInk*, www.performink.com), and a healthy entertainment press, with a wide range of critical opinions and features. No single paper has *The New York Times'* power to make or break shows.

SAN FRANCISCO
(reported by Richard Dodds, *Bay Area Reporter; Back Stage* regional correspondent)

The city of San Francisco is a compact place. But the Bay Area theatres providing work for professional actors stretch across one hundred miles, from the wine country of Sonoma to the silicon centers near San Jose.

An essential meeting place is the annual general auditions organized by Theatre Bay Area (TBA, www.bayareatheatre.org). TBA is a membership organization serving 300 companies, and most of these theatres, including the major players, send representatives to scout talent at the February event. Equity actors new to the area who are seeking full-time work should also contact casting directors at the area's LORT theatres; casting is not handled by agents.

Theatre Bay Area also publishes *Callboard,* a monthly theatre news magazine that contains an extensive list of local auditions. The individual listings include information on salary and on whether an Actors' Equity contract is possible for the approximately 900 Equity actors in the region. *Callboard* also operates an audition hotline for late-breaking updates.

The main opportunities for Equity actors are at fifteen or so area theatres operating under either a LORT (League of Resident Theatres) or BAT (Bay Area Theatres) contract, including American Conservatory Theater, Berkeley Repertory Theatre, San Jose Repertory Theatre, and Marin Theatre Company. Most theatres have seasons running September through May or June; however, summer-only theatres, including the various Shakespeare festivals, offset any seasonal dip in acting opportunities.

Numerous other theatres operate under Letters of Agreement with Equity. The Bay Area also has its own version of the Equity Showcase or ninety-nine-seat production. The Bay Area Project Policy permits Equity actors to work without the benefit of a contract under certain conditions; the arrangement is frequently employed at smaller theatres.

San Francisco is a famously expensive place to live, and because of that, and the spread-out nature of the theatre scene, no affordable artistic "enclaves" have developed. The Bay Area can't match a city like, say, Seattle, in terms of offering a close-knit theatrical community.

A complaint heard in most communities with major regional theatres—that too many out-of-towners are jobbed in—is also true in the Bay Area. But for the local actor, some good news has been emerging from the hard economic times. The big theatres have been using more and more Bay Area-based actors, avoiding the per diem and housing expenses needed when hiring from out of town.

While the economic downturn hasn't significantly diminished traditional stage work, it has taken its toll on other opportunities. Several big ad agencies that were either based in San Francisco or had major offices here have departed, and while voiceover work remains a viable income source, work in locally shot commercials has been shrinking. While most theatre actors stay abreast of casting opportunities themselves, there are several franchised agents working on SAG and AFTRA projects.

Vancouver and Toronto have become cheaper stand-ins for San Francisco in feature films, but the city still draws several major movie productions each year. The natural beauty and distinctive look of San Francisco will always be a lure.

SEATTLE
(reported by John Longenbaugh, *Back Stage* regional correspondent)

Seattle has a surprising number of professional theatres for a city its size: Seattle Repertory Theatre, A Contemporary Theatre, Intiman Theatre, the 5th Avenue Theatre Association, and the Seattle Children's Theatre; two mid-sized houses with regular Equity contracts (The Empty Space and Taproot theatres); and smaller fringe groups, a few of which have their own spaces.

In the early 1990s, Seattle had more theatre. But the economic downturn, compounded locally by the bursting dot.com bubble and steady lay-offs from Boeing, took its toll. At the time of this writing, it's harder for actors to support their art. But Seattle is still a varied and interesting community and, despite some scares (the venerable ACT theatre weathered a near-closing in late 2002), there's an under-lying support for live theatre and a civic pride in what it brings to the local culture.

Seattle actors have ruefully joked that to work on one of the town's Equity stages, an actor should move to New York or Los Angeles. The hiring practices of Intiman, the Seattle Rep, and ACT have not favored locals. The Seattle Children's Theatre and theatres with fewer Equity contracts (such as The Empty Space, Seattle Shakespeare Company, and Taproot) tend to hire Seattle actors almost exclusively.

The main theatres hold general auditions at different times during the year; most also attend the twice-yearly general auditions held by the local theatre organization, Theatre Puget Sound (TPS). Casting directors at theatres are somewhat approach-able, although they prefer to see actors on stage. It's recommended that actors who've been cast in local productions contact casting directors with an invitation to come and observe.

TPS (www.tpsonline.org) is surprisingly young (formed in 1997) and still in many ways finding its way, though it does offer member discounts on tickets, general audi-tions, an on-line headshot and acting résumé resource, and a lively listserv (electronic mailing-list server). Individual memberships are $50.

The Canadian economy has enticed much film and TV production to Vancouver. The Washington State Film Commission is under funded, but still manages to recruit a few feature films annually. Student and independent efforts dominate the local film scene. Often this work is unpaid, but it's not unrewarding or uninteresting; local short films earn critical acclaim at film festivals.

There is regular industrial work, particularly via the high-tech industry, dominated by Adobe and Microsoft. Microsoft, Nintendo, Sierra, and a clutch of smaller game companies often use actors for video games and multimedia products.

Urban redevelopment has sterilized some of Seattle's artsy neighborhoods, including Belltown and once-funky Fremont. Capitol Hill overlooking Downtown still supports small fringe theatres and a lot of local artists, and Ballard is filling up with young artists and live-music venues.

Some Seattle actors concentrate on their craft, working with local troupes, perhaps finding opportunities with a local Equity company, before moving to New York or Los Angeles. Others choose to balance careers with a high quality of life, enjoying a rich cultural scene, a laidback lifestyle, and spectacular natural scenery.

SOUTH FLORIDA
(reported by Jack Zink, *Fort Lauderdale Sun-Sentinel*)
South Florida encompasses Miami, Fort Lauderdale, and West Palm Beach, a one-hundred-mile strip sandwiched between the Atlantic Ocean and the Everglades. No single area offers enough work to support many acting careers, but the region's theatre community includes a trio of LORT theatres and a half-dozen other Equity houses at the top of a pyramid that numbers thirty or more theatres. The economy has reduced the ranks of smaller non-Equity troupes.

Greater Miami has the most theatres, spread around a twenty-five-mile diameter. The largest LORT house is the Coconut Grove Playhouse, which casts nationally. It occasionally serves as a tryout house for shows with New York aspirations, and frequently co-produces with New Jersey's Paper Mill Playhouse and Philadelphia's Walnut Street Theatre. Coral Gables has The Actor's Playhouse at the Miracle

Theatre. Nearby is the GableStage and the small New Theatre, which commissioned Nilo Cruz's 2003 Pulitzer Prize-winner, *Anna in the Tropics*.

Greater Fort Lauderdale has smaller, mostly non-Equity operations. And the suburban Broward Stage Door Theatre has dropped its Equity contract.

To the north are several front-rank Equity houses and a smattering of non-Equity companies. The Caldwell Theatre Company (Boca Raton) and Florida Stage (Lake Worth) are respected LORT theatres. The Maltz Jupiter Theatre (the former Burt Reynolds Theatre) in Jupiter was recently renovated for a 2004 opening with a LORT contract.

Most managing and artistic directors or company managers will take the time to meet briefly with newcomers. Calling ahead is advised, as is bringing a headshot and résumé. Auditions are announced weekly in listings in area newspapers. The Theatre League of South Florida (www.theatreleague.net) is the best place to start. The 700-member league has regular networking forums, an annual audition for South Florida theatres in February, and a weekly e-mail newsletter listing auditions and job openings. Individual membership is open to all for a modest fee. Equity also provides a regional hotline that lists opportunities.

The Florida Professional Theatres Association (www.fpta.net) is a statewide network of the larger regional theatres. FPTA offers an annual audition in August for twenty or more theatres, open to Equity and non-Equity performers.

Film and commercial work is concentrated in Miami. Agents are unnecessary for stage work, but needed for film, TV, and commercial work. Florida might not be the "Hollywood East" that its film community has long dreamed of becoming, but it is one of the nation's top five film markets.

Theatre, film, and most of show business are seasonal in South Florida, dropping off in summer. The cruise ship sector is constantly busy, though, and the producers and production houses for most lines' entertainment are based in Miami and Fort Lauderdale.

Actors, technicians, and designers have to be flexible and mobile to find work in South Florida. Public transportation isn't convenient; I-95 and Florida's Turnpike are the arteries through which all successful careers must pass. Many actors live around Fort Lauderdale and adjacent Hollywood, keeping commutes in any direction to an hour or less in off-hour traffic.

ATLANTA
(reported by Dave Hayward, *Back Stage* regional correspondent)

Atlanta touts itself as "The City Too Busy to Hate" and, in terms of colorblind casting, that's pretty true. Myriad opportunities are here for everyone. Atlanta hosts the National Black Arts Festival every year, as well as provides a home for True Colors, the professional theatre troupe that operates under former Alliance Theatre Artistic Director Kenny Leon.

There are two Equity houses: the Alliance Theatre Company, at the expansive Woodruff Arts Center complex, and Theatre in the Square, in the bedroom community of Marietta (a half-hour north on I-75). Three in-town theatre groups operate under Equity agreements: the politically correct 7 Stages and the eclectic Horizon Theare Company (both in Little Five Points), and the mainstream Theatrical Outfit (Downtown). Suburban Stone Mountain's Art Station Theatre also has an Equity agreement. Actor's Express is a prime showcase for actors, and the Atlanta Shakespeare Tavern keeps many artists busy with its series of rotating contracts.

Film and TV work fluctuates, but about six features a year are shot in the region. Atlanta is a day's drive or less from cities where considerable film work is available, including Nashville, Tennessee; Asheville, North Carolina; and the mega-studio complex in Wilmington, North Carolina.

Many actors find employment in commercials (including clever spots for the Georgia Lottery) and in voice work. Industrials are an easier market to crack; Atlanta is a convention Valhalla, so there are many opportunities for live work at the auto shows and computer showcases constantly booked into Downtown's World Congress Center.

Atlanta Performs, formerly the Atlanta Coalition of Theatres, operates a website (www.atlantaperforms.com), a source of job postings, auditions, and survival information. Talent agencies include the Genesis Agency, Houghton Talent, the Talent Group, and Atlanta Models and Talent.

Theatrical work falls off during the summer, and many local actors head for the hills to do outdoor dramas in North Georgia and the Carolinas. Atlanta summers are hot and steamy, but not unbearable, thanks to the city's high altitude in the foothills of the Appalachian Mountains.

News media include the big daily, *The Atlanta Journal-Constitution,* and the weekly *Creative Loafing.* Atlanta is quick to embrace new work, and is enthusiastic, if not overly sophisticated, in its tastes. The in-town communities of Little Five Points, the East Atlanta Village, Ponce de Leon, Virginia Highlands, and Midtown are artist-friendly and reasonably priced places to live. A car is not needed in many of these areas, but getting around the widespread metropolitan area without your own transportation can be daunting.

MINNEAPOLIS-ST. PAUL
(reported by Michael Sander, *Back Stage* regional correspondent)

The Twin Cities of Minneapolis and St. Paul offer a thriving theatrical region that boasts of selling more tickets per capita than any other location in the United States outside of New York City. Actors will find an entrenched community of performers, numbering some 450 Equity members, and an approximately equal number of nonunion professionals (whose numbers are more difficult to track).

Theatres range from those whose casts are virtually all-Equity (such as the Guthrie Theater, the Ordway Center for the Performing Arts in St. Paul, and the suburban Chanhassen Dinner Theatre), through a number of mid-sized theatres that work under Small Professional Theatre (SPT) contracts (including The Jungle, Illusion, Penumbra, Great American History, Eye of the Storm, Park Square and Mixed Blood theatres), to non-Equity houses (including the massive Theatre de la Jeune Lune, which functions as a collective). The SPT houses apply a ratio of Equity to nonunion personnel that, along with salaries, can shift depending on length of run and size of venue.

Additionally, graduates from the University of Minnesota's theatre department have started several theatres. Some mount a production or two and then drift away; others become part of the theatrical landscape. Most theatres offer productions year-round, although the choices thin out in the summer until the popular Fringe Festival arrives in August.

No central body coordinates general auditions: The theatres are left to their own devices. Some—like the Guthrie, Jungle, Children's Theatre, and Chanhassen—hold auditions regularly, with ample notice given to actors. Others operate more casually, or neglect to provide timely information to the acting community. Much Twin Cities casting is director driven: a director finds a group of actors with whom he or she feels comfortable, and reuses them from show to show, or chooses productions with their specific skills in mind.

The prime source of casting information is *The Minneapolis-St. Paul Star-Tribune;* the daily newspaper runs notices from all theatres on all levels. Equity's telephone hot line and website are dependent on the theatres' taking responsibility for posting notices. Word-of-mouth is a valuable resource. Agents play practically no role in theatrical casting in the Twin Cities, although they are vital to finding work in local commercials and print advertising. The commercial business is active, largely because of the numerous advertising agencies in the area. Few films are shot locally, and budget cuts to the Minnesota Film Board suggest that studios will find little incentive to travel to the state.

The Uptown area of South Minneapolis has a reputation as the city's "artsy" neighborhood. Artists, musicians, and dancers help make up the diverse local arts community. In terms of opportunities for newcomers, sometimes a "hot new face" will find work almost immediately. Others will have a difficult time breaking into the ranks of "directors' choices." Actors are generally supportive and encouraging, but finding the first opportunity can be a struggle.

We Always Have Room for Talent!

Oakwood, the Entertainment Housing Specialists

- All-inclusive rates on fully furnished apartment homes with kitchens, housewares, utilities and more.
- Custom packages for large group move-ins.
- We are only minutes from most major studios and centrally located to dance studios, acting workshops and photographers.
- Locations available throughout Los Angeles, New York, nationwide and select worldwide destinations.

Oakwood

The Most Trusted Name in Temporary Housing Worldwide.[SM]

866.327.3077

oakwood.com

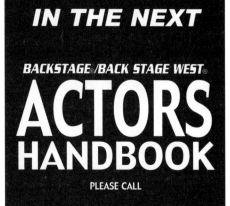

TO ADVERTISE IN THE NEXT

BACKSTAGE/BACK STAGE WEST

ACTORS HANDBOOK

PLEASE CALL

WEST ■	■ EAST
Back Stage West	Back Stage
Advertising	Advertising
5055 Wilshire Blvd., 5th fl.	770 Broadway, 4th floor
Los Angeles, CA 90036	New York, NY 10003
323.525.2225	646.654.5700

BACK STAGE® and BACK STAGE WEST®

The #1 weeklies for Performing Artists

SUBSCRIBE TODAY

1.800.745.8922

http://www.backstage.com/backstage/contact/printsub.jsp

35 It's Only Temporary:

Working Non-legit Jobs While Waiting for Your Big Break

BY CATHERINE CASTELLANI

If your acting career isn't providing you with the financial support you need, the temporary employment field is open for business and placing actors in a wide variety of jobs. It may take a little patience and determination to get the work you want, but actors have always rated high in patience and determination.

ATTITUDES TOWARD THE ACTOR-TEMP

When the phenomenon of hiring temps was new, temporary employees in general and actors in particular were all too frequently regarded with disdain. As suspicions about temps in general have melted away over the years, so have prejudices against actors and other artists on the job. Experience has taught even the most buttoned-down executive that his phone system is safe with a voiceover actress, his PowerPoint presentation well done by the guy who just returned from a national tour.

"People from the performing arts make great temps," says Sal Bordonaro of Merlin Temps in New York City. "They're literate, they have the charisma, and most clients will be flexible to get someone like that. The ones who won't—well, we don't send them performers. That's the service's job."

Of course, you are still expected to do the job at hand. Some actors are understandably frightened that by committing to any job, even on a temporary basis, they will hurt their acting careers. "Fear of Day Job" may not be a category recognized by the psychiatric community, but it's well known in the theatrical profession.

GETTING STARTED

Most services screen and interview prospective employees in standard ways, so your introduction to one service will prepare you to register with others. While some services welcome walk-ins at any time, others require an appointment. Always call the service first.

Dress for your interview as you would for a conservative corporate client. You can't make a bad impression by being too formal, but can easily ruin your chances by erring too far in the casual direction. Even if you are eventually placed in an entertainment company with no discernible dress code, you should appear at the offices of a temporary staffing service dressed like a banker.

If you have a résumé of job experience, bring it. Even if it lists only college work-study jobs and catering gigs, it is a record of gainful employment, and it counts. Also be prepared with several professional references—a former supervisor, boss, or even a theatre director you have worked for in the past. If you truly have no prior job experience, you may use former teachers as references.

Be honest about your level of experience and skills. The service screeners have seen lots of job seekers come and go, and have heard every excuse, scam, and embellishment imaginable. Don't insult their intelligence and sink your chances by trying to inflate your credentials.

In general, a service will ask you to fill out an application, take a series of tests, and interview with a staff member. Testing usually includes a selection of the following: typing speed, software proficiency, basic English grammar, basic arithmetic, a filing or matching test (designed to determine whether you can alphabetize material and recognize matching information), and an office etiquette test (usually multiple choice). At services placing bilingual temps, you will also be tested in your second language.

Treat the tests seriously, even those that appear insultingly basic or hilariously absurd. Behave as you would before a suspicious customs agent. Remember, there are people seeking jobs who can't alphabetize a list, match zip codes, or differentiate a socially acceptable answer from a wildly inappropriate response. It is the staffing service's job to weed out these people before they show up at a client's office and prove just how incompetent and offensive they can be. If you clown around on your etiquette test, you may be taken for a clown, and promptly and politely shown the door.

Allot at least two hours per service for the whole intake process. If you plan to tackle more than one service a day, be kind and give yourself at least an hour between appointments to eat, unwind, and relax. Although a good portion of those two hours might be spent waiting, the whole job search process can be stressful. Don't make it harder by cramming your schedule.

Before leaving the office, take a minute to orient yourself. It's tempting after hours of testing and interviewing to stumble out the door in search of lunch without a backward glance. Before you flee, ask the person you have tested or interviewed with if he or she will be your main contact with the service, and if not, ask whom you should report to with your availability or with any questions. Get a stack of time sheets, and clarify when they must be received and what day you will be paid. Take a business card for your wallet. These few extra minutes will help you establish a good relationship with your new service.

HOW FLEXIBLE IS FLEXIBLE?

Nine-to-five is not the only shift available, and Monday through Friday is not the only schedule being booked. In New York and other big cities, the work goes on twenty-four hours a day, seven days a week; you can work whatever shift works for you, and change that at any time.

Great flexibility is often possible with clients who have come to know and value your work. If you've been a reliable, professional worker, and the company has a variety of work available, an offbeat arrangement that suits you both is possible.

Actor and director Steven McElroy has held a long-term temp job at *The New York Times* that has consistently offered a huge degree of flexibility. McElroy has appeared in and directed showcases; performed in Russia with the Laboratory for International Theatre Exchange; gone to Charleston, South Carolina, with his company, The New Ensemble Theatre; and, in between, he is at the *Times*. For him, his long-term status has meant leeway. "It goes the other way, too," says McElroy. "The week of the [September 11, 2001] attack, I worked eighty-five hours. If I'm not busy, I can give more. Give a little, get a little." Those long hours in the crunch are rewarded when McElroy hits the road—he's confident he can come back to his temp job when he needs to.

LONG-TERM VS. SHORT-TERM

In addition to allowing actors freedom to work inside or outside the nine-to-five structure, temporary employment can offer jobs that range from open-ended, long-term positions to jobs that last only one shift and are over. Both have advantages and disadvantages for the actor.

A long-term assignment is one way to have the best of both worlds. By committing to a particular job, you eliminate at least some of the uncertainty in your earning life. It can be stressful dealing with new people and new procedures on a constant basis at your bread-and-butter job while doing the same in your acting career. Many staffing services now offer benefits such as health care, and even paid vacation, to temps who log enough hours with the service to qualify. It's easier to log those hours in a long-term spot than it is when you hop from assignment to assignment.

However, there is a real pitfall in the long-term world. The longer you stay in one stable spot, the more your co-workers and supervisors come to think of you as one of the gang. The company depends on a good employee, temporary or otherwise. It's easy for a firm to begin to expect behavior of a long-term temp that it would naturally expect of a staff member, even though the temp usually has no job status, isn't paid for sick days or holidays, and usually works with no benefit package or with one substantially less than that of a full-time staff member. That flexibility—so precious to the actor-temp—begins to quietly erode.

Short-term jobs are just that—as short as a single shift, as long as a week. Short-term work is ideal for the actor who has a heavy audition schedule or commercial work at unpredictable hours, but who still needs to pull in extra cash. Most services welcome a call early in the morning (that means long before 9 a.m.) to let them know you'd be ready and able to work that day if something comes in. It's a gamble, but in flu season and on Mondays, "standby" is a good bet.

On a one-day job, the temp's responsibility is to get to the office as soon after booking the job as he or she can, and to be a good sport. On short-term assignments, there often isn't time to get oriented, much less comfortable. It may sound stressful, but most companies are so happy to see someone show up to help that they'll do all they can to be friendly, even if no one has time to train a temp. To do short-term work, you need a good attitude and common sense. The reward: a quick check in the mail.

EARNING TOP DOLLAR

If you've got top-notch computer skills, graphics and Web design capabilities, type at lightning speed, and have glowing references from a roster of satisfied past employers, you will pull top dollar rather easily. But what if you don't have any of those assets? You can get them and, in most cases, you can get them for free.

Even while working as a low-paid receptionist, you can often find opportunities to learn on the job. Ask if you can use your downtime to study a computer program. Corporations usually have the latest software, complete with tutorial, and most supervisors will be happy to let you use it if you ask.

If the opportunity isn't available, or if the phone calls are so heavy that you couldn't take the time to do a tutorial anyway, ask your service what kind of training it offers. Many services offer free, no-strings-attached training to their temps. That means no fee, no minimum hours to work—no strings. They do it because it improves the skills of their employees, which is their greatest professional asset. Improving your skills not only raises your hourly rate, it raises theirs.

Keep in mind that your first job for a service will probably pay less than future jobs. They don't know you yet, and they're taking a risk. Sometimes it pays to accept a lower rate at the beginning of a relationship, but by all means speak up. Let them know how much you'd like to be making. Be willing to audition, so to speak, to prove your reliability and skills. Then don't be shy about asking for a raise on your next job—or, if you're on a long-term job, a few weeks into it.

CHOOSING A SERVICE—OR, RATHER, SERVICES

So how do you choose from the many services available? Talk to your friends. Talk to other actors and artists with a primary passion who do "side work" of any kind. Happy temps would love to recommend you to their services, as most get a bonus when they refer a good employee.

Most veterans suggest that you sign up with at least three services initially. One service may not be able to get you work exactly when you want it. The more patchy your schedule is, the more you'll benefit from using multiple services.

Trust your gut when you meet the staff. Pay attention to how you're treated and how staff members treat each other. If you're insulted, ignored, or otherwise made to feel uncomfortable, go elsewhere. It's a big world.

A LITTLE PERSPECTIVE

It's only a job, and it's only temporary. It may not be part of your vision for your life, but it will fit right in if that's what you need. Don't despair of your acting career just because you need to spend part of your time faxing and filing. Very few are the performers who never worked a day job.

Your Future's Bright! Want to Share It?

compensation:
$5,000 – $10,000
(and up)

Exceptional Women Needed for Egg Donation

FERTILITY
⊖FUTURES
INTERNATIONAL

323.965.9200   www.FertilityFutures.com
(Conveniently located in Museum Square, 5757 Wilshire Boulevard, Suite 601)

blaine AND ASSOCIATES, INC

NEVER A FEE!!!
TEMPORARY AND FULL-TIME
POSITIONS AVAILABLE

HOLLYWOOD

CALL FOR AN APPOINTMENT
(310) 785-0560

Calling All Angels

The Egg Donor Program
$5,000 to $10,000
Compensation

*"You are in a truly unique position of bringing
healing and a new beginning to a pair of broken hearts."*
"This is one of the most rewarding things I have and will ever do."

*Let us make your experience safe and rewarding.
Learn about your couple and receive the most personalized
attention from the oldest donor program in L.A.*

Shelley Smith M.A., M.F.C.C.

323-933-0414

SSmithMFCC@AOL.COM   www.eggdonation.com

ACTORS! NO SELLING!

INDIE FILM CO. SEEKS LA-BASED
PHONE SURVEYORS
800-562-1999 EXT. 269 OR 336
rich@alpinepix.com
Great $$$ while waiting for big break!!

TO ADVERTISE IN THE NEXT
BACKSTAGE/BACK STAGE WEST

ACTORS HANDBOOK

WEST ■   ■ EAST

Back Stage West Advertising	Back Stage Advertising
5055 Wilshire Blvd., 5th floor	770 Broadway, 4th floor
Los Angeles, CA 90036	New York, NY 10003
323.525.2225	646.654.5700

www.backstage.com

Temporary Staffing

When Industry Knowledge Matters

Wall Street Services' commitment is to create win-win
situations. We take the time to get to know YOU –
your schedule requirements, your interests—and use
that information to match you with a
perfect placement.

Current openings for:
· *Administrative/Executive assistants, Excel & PowerPoint
  professionals*
· *Analysts, trade support and other financial professionals*
· *Word Processors and Proofreaders*
· *Graphics: Presentation specialists, Web Development and
  Multimedia*

Clients include New York's top investment banks
and major law firms.

Excellent hourly rates and weekly pay. Benefits are unmatched
in the industry. For immediate placement, send resume to:
resume@wallstreetservices

Send your resume to:
Wall Street Services
11 Broadway, Suite 930, New York, N.Y. 10004
Phone: 212-509-7200
Fax: 212-943-1597
resume@wallstreetservices.com

TRUTH...
SOUL...JOBS

The
TUTTLE
AGENCY
NEW YORK

• **FASHION**
• **ADVERTISING**
• **FINANCE**
• **ENTERTAINMENT**
• **PUBLISHING**
• **MEDIA**
• **MEDICAL**
• **LEGAL**

(212) 499-0759
www.tuttleagency.com

Segue Legal Staffing

24 Hours/7 Days
Short Term – Long Term
Temp-to-Perm
...we've got them all...

• **Legal Secretaries**
• **Word Processors**
• **Proofreaders • Receptionists**

212-696-5913
resume@seguestaffing.com

295 Madison Avenue, 12th Floor

For Permanent Opportunities
Entry-Level, Administrative &
Executive Assistants & Legal

Please call 212-878-2000
jrs@seguestaffing.com

TO ADVERTISE
IN THE NEXT

BACKSTAGE®/BACK STAGE WEST®

ACTORS
HANDBOOK

PLEASE CALL

WEST ■   ■ EAST
Back Stage West   Back Stage
Advertising   Advertising
5055 Wilshire Blvd., 5th fl.   770 Broadway, 4th floor
Los Angeles, CA 90036   New York, NY 10003
323.525.2225   646.654.5700

36 Freeing Yourself from Fear:

Strategies for Coping with Stage Fright and Stress

BY AMELIA DAVID

The Book of Lists rates fear of public speaking as the number one fear among Americans (higher even than the fear of death). Many people would rather be six feet under than speak in front of a group! And "show folk," who *choose* to be in the spotlight, don't necessarily have it easier than "civilians." One of the confusing things about stage fright is that years of "fearless" success don't inoculate you from future episodes of the malady.

TAMING TENSION

The ramifications of a particular performer's stage fright may seem illogical. You might feel great when performing/speaking before hundreds, but troubled when you have to audition/interview for one person. Or your stage fright may develop later in life. Some people can find coping mechanisms (being well prepared, rested, and rehearsed) to control their fright, while others experience emotional and even physical terror—sometimes from things they've done effortlessly before.

Even if you know your fear is irrational, stress can make you take shorter, shallower breaths—causing your diaphragm to become rigid. You trigger your sympathetic nervous system to feel threatened, releasing chemicals (including adrenaline), which tell your body to feel afraid (and to flush, sweat, and make your heart race). This is known as the "fight or flight" response (important for potential danger when hunting lions, but difficult to cope with when all you want to do is audition for *The Lion King*). To switch off your sympathetic nervous system, you must switch on what your body uses to soothe itself—your parasympathetic system. You do this by slowing down your breathing, which can lower your heart rate and help you feel more relaxed.

TRIUMPH OVER FEAR

Jerilyn Ross, M.A., L.I.C.S.W., is the president of the Anxiety Disorders Association of America (ADAA) and director of The Ross Center for Anxiety and Related Disorders in Washington, D.C. Ross is one of the country's leading authorities on fear. "For business people, public speaking is part of their job," Ross explains. "Actors love their work, but it's still the same treatment approach. A little performance anxiety is healthy. It's fear of the fear that one day might trigger panic. We use cognitive therapy to explore what's the worst people think will happen and then modify that. Many of my clients fear that as anxiety increases, their blood pressure will rise and they'll pass out. It's important for them to understand what's happening. When you pass out, your blood pressure goes down, not up. We must challenge catastrophic *what if* thinking, one thought at a time."

Ross also does what she calls "in vivo" (real life) work to help people desensitize. Social phobia is an extreme fear of public embarrassment and of being judged. The condition can affect thirteen out of every one hundred Americans. Ross' clients' privacy is always protected, but many clients/performers openly credit her for their recovery. Donny Osmond wrote about his experiences in *Life Is Just What You Make It,* and Ross offers his case as an example. When Osmond experienced the ultimate actor's nightmare of forgetting lines, Ross went with him backstage while he performed. Because of his fear of being judged, he also had her go with him when he went shopping.

Ross believes that many people who suffer from stage fright can achieve significant relief by following a self-help program. Her experience from twenty-two years of working with patients is presented in *Triumph over Fear.* The book includes a self-help manual offering the same tools she uses in her twelve-week therapy groups.

We asked Ross for tools that our readers could use. For example, how do her performing clients deal with dry mouth? Ross asked one singer, "What makes you salivate?" The client thought of lemons, so Ross suggested visualizing lemons.

She also offers an eight-point plan "as a portable tool box to manage panic attacks." These are featured in Ross's audio/video program and workbook.

THE EIGHT POINTS—FREEDOM FROM ANXIETY
1 Expect, allow, and accept that fear will arise.
2 When fear comes, stop, wait, and let it be.
3 Focus on the present and do manageable things in the present.
4 Label your level of fear from zero to ten. (Watch it go up and down.)
5 Ask yourself, "What am I really afraid of?"
6 Ask yourself, "What is actually happening?" (Compare it to your fear.)
7 Function with fear—be proud of your achievement.
8 Expect, allow, and accept that fear will reappear.

LEARNING BY DOING—GRADUALLY
Anxiety almost ended the career of Jordan Knight, former lead singer for New Kids on the Block. Knight credits his use of a piano bar to desensitize himself. "I would go incognito at first and watch, and then got enough courage to sing a song. The next week, I took off my glasses, then my hat." In this way, Knight desensitized himself in a less pressured environment.

GIVING FEAR CENTER STAGE
Connecticut-based Janet E. Esposito, M.S.W, is the author of the book *In the Spotlight—Overcome Your Fear of Public Speaking and Performing,* from the national organization Freedom From Fear. Esposito observes, "[Stage fright] is especially hard for performers who feel a strong need for perfection. In an audition, they

have to again be themselves. The layperson thinks it's a lack of self-confidence, but it has nothing to do with that. I called my book *In the Spotlight* because that's what it feels like—all eyes on you."

How do you know if your symptoms are manageable and self-treatable, or if it's better to seek professional help? Esposito offers, "Some of the clues are, developing avoidance behaviors where you avoid performing or avoid being prepared so you won't be able to audition; self-medicating with food, drugs, alcohol; preoccupation; and lack of sleep. Avoidance, although it relieves immediate stress, actually reinforces the fear cycle and makes things worse over time."

Esposito advises that if you are experiencing feelings that have graduated to panic, it's best to seek professional help. From her list of "Top 10 Tips for Reducing Stage Fright," Esposito offers, "People with this fear get self-absorbed. Take the focus off yourself and put it on your true purpose, which is to contribute something of value to your audience. Focus on contribution, and it's not about you anymore. . . ."

HEALING FROM WITHIN

To better understand creating mind/body support, we enlisted the help of Dr. Lawrence B. Palevsky. His success using an integrative medicine approach in his New York City medical practice has been featured in the pages of *Self, New Age,* the *New York Daily News,* and on NBC's *Live at Five* and *The CBS Evening News with Dan Rather.* Since Palevsky also has a performance background and continues to perform while in practice, "he knows whereof he speaks." His relaxation prescription includes yoga, meditation, aromatherapy, reflexology, massage, exercise, and healthy nutrition. He especially advises skipping caffeine, alcohol, white sugar, and foods naturally high in sugar (which produce mucus and raise insulin, causing mood swings).

Palevsky observes, "There is an amazing restorative power in us that goes untapped. Using yoga and meditation lowers stress and creates a world of new information we can use. The mere power of being aware of how we're breathing can change the production of nerve chemicals, slow heart rate, reduce inflammatory chemicals, and relax the diaphragm."

Breath work is an important component of yoga, which, while it may seem a current media buzz word, is actually an ancient Eastern concept whose name means "unity" or "oneness." Palevsky explains, "For centuries, adults have reaped the physical and mental benefits of yoga. It encourages a person to stay more connected to their breathing, provides specific movements to relax the diaphragm, and opens the rib cage and lungs. Besides providing relaxation, this helps maximize your speaking and singing potential. When you are anxious and tense, you can forget to breathe. The very act of being frightened means you are no longer in touch with how you're breathing. Yoga encourages you to stay connected to what's happening with your body and your breath. Yoga positions help you discover where you have restriction and tightness, and how you can open those areas. Being able to do that gives a great sense of strength and freedom, which carries over into all areas of your life and performing."

Yoga is now being acknowledged as a powerful treatment in many areas of the medical community, including the *Journal of the American Medical Association.* You can learn just the basics, or seek out more challenging skill levels. One respected resource is *Yoga Journal Magazine*, which also produces videos. If you have access to the Internet, try www.yogaeverywhere.com, created by Megan Lurie McCarver, M.A., CMT. McCarver is a certified yoga instructor, who also provides information for the ivillage web site. Her no-cost site features an introduction to yoga and breathing, and her "Keyboard Yoga" lets you explore positions at your desk. This type of chair yoga can come in especially handy when you're in a cramped dressing room, waiting in the wings, or dealing with little personal space in an audition hallway.

Yoga, meditation, and de-stressing go hand in hand. As early as 1968, a Harvard Medical School study by Dr. Herbert Benson showed that the physical effects meditation produces on the body were the exact opposite of those produced by stress. Another doctor who sees the benefits of breath work as a foundation of wellness is Dr. Andrew Weil. His many books detail his prescription for learning the "relaxing breath," which he offers for managing stress and its related health problems. See also his no-cost website at www.drweil.com.

CAN YOU SAY "AH"?

Dr. Palevsky has had especially successful results using essential oils and aromatherapy for stress reduction. "Essential oils are concentrations of the foods and herbs we already eat. They are also much easier to use than medicines." Palevsky has found "many of the citrus oils—including tangerine, orange, and mandarin—are very relaxing to the nervous system, and sometimes just inhaling their aroma (even just the peel) is enough to bring relaxation." Since each person's response is unique, give your new coping strategy a trial run before using it at an audition or in a performance situation. The doctor also reminds readers, "Essential oils should never be taken internally." Since oils are concentrated, he also suggests, "Always mix them with a carrier oil, like almond or avocado oil." Applying oils to the feet is a good way to start (but be careful not to use oils on broken or irritated/sensitive skin without the guidance of a professional). The back of the neck is another area to try.

Essential oils can also be used with massage. (Palevsky finds shiatsu especially helpful for anxiety issues.) Learning about foot and hand reflexology and acupressure will also give you more options. Many health bookstores carry books and tapes on this subject—along with laminated wallet-size diagrams for doing foot and hand reflexology. If getting regular massages is out of your price range, check to see whether massage schools in your area have student training nights.

As all of our experts will tell you, it's important to remember that general reference information like that in this chapter is not intended as a substitute for consulting with a healthcare professional or physician. Still, there are numerous inexpensive ways for you to start making your time in or around the spotlight as stress free as possible—ensuring that you break a leg without breaking the bank.

37 Method, Madness, Meditation:

Advice and Insights on What Actors Go Through Before They Go On

BY ELIAS STIMAC

It's minutes before showtime. You are in your dressing room—or the converted storage space that passes for one. You're nervous, excited, joking with cast mates, flirting with crew members, hoping your agent has shown up, and wondering where everyone's going for the after-party.

Then you hear the stage manager call, "Places!" You suddenly realize your makeup's not done, your costume's missing, and you can't remember your first line. What is your motivation? What show are you doing? What will you do to keep panic away so you can get on with the play?

A lot goes into putting on a theatrical production before the curtain rises, and yet the final product has to come across as effortless in order for audiences to get drawn in. Whether gossiping in the green room or concentrating behind the backdrop, performers anticipate the moment the show begins with a mixture of euphoria and fear. That is why entertainers of all types and talent levels have to learn to be relaxed, warmed up, and focused before a performance.

Dancers stretch, singers vocalize, actors run lines. Models and mimes paint their faces; stand-up comics and circus performers say a prayer. Some people sit quietly by themselves, some meet for group circles, some peek out at the audience, some put on their lucky socks. Broadway ensembles go so far as to pass along a decorated "Gypsy Robe" that chorus members all touch on opening night in a tradition started more than fifty years ago.

Pre-show preparation techniques are necessary between the time that actors sign the call sheet and the moment they step into the spotlight. Physical, vocal, and mental warm-ups are only a part of the picture. The rituals and exercises that players employ as they take the stage are always intriguing and oftentimes integral to a successful production. Professional players and up-and-coming ingénues alike need to plan out their strategy, so they can control what they go through in the hours before they go on.

DAY OF SHOW

Each person has his or her individual approach to acting, and the same holds true for patterns of preparation. One universal rule, however, is always to arrive at the theatre early enough to get ready. Whether an actor's call is an hour or half-hour, it's wise to get there ahead of time, so you don't feel rushed. If you are running late for any reason—your day job, rush-hour traffic, or a broken alarm clock—you upset your cast members, the director, and the stage manager, who may have to notify your understudy or start finding someone else who fits your costume.

Michelle Lynn Bates, who played Abigail Adams in a recent national tour of *1776*, has a specific pre-show timeline. She likes to arrive at least one hour before performance to give herself time to relax, check her costume and props, and get any notes from the director. "Then I have a full half-hour to apply makeup and costumes. So by showtime, I can get the butterflies in 'flying formation.'"

But preparing your mind and your body for a show shouldn't just start when you step into the theatre. Most actors begin the minute they wake up in the morning (or mid-afternoon). Some take it a step further. Daria Hardeman, whose credits include Broadway's *The Full Monty* and Off-Broadway's *Bat Boy*, suggests that the real preparation should be done the day before each show. "If your body is tired, your voice is tired. So getting to bed on time is very important, especially if you have to sing high notes. Also, make sure to drink lots of water—someone once said the water you drink twenty-four hours beforehand is what hydrates your body for the next day."

Many performers have to juggle their passion for acting with the reality of a day job. Actor-singer Jenny Greeman says, "Often I have to work on show days, so I try to keep my mind clear and not let any work issues or other anxieties stick to me."

Even while traveling to the theatre by car, train, cab, bike, or on foot, you can be getting into a frame of mind that will help you pull off a stellar performance. Olinda Turturro, familiar to audiences from her work on TV, film, and theatrical projects, says, "On my way to the theatre, I simply try to think positive thoughts and anticipate a good show."

Dawn Vicknair—who has done everything from film and theatre to voiceovers and industrials—practices deep, controlled breathing and some relaxation exercises to help her concentrate. "I try to remain focused and 'in the moment,' so that whatever emotions I need to tap into are near the surface."

MAKE UP, DRESS UP, WARM UP

Getting into the mindset of creating an entire characterization and keeping a clear head while a hundred other things are happening around you is crucial to pulling off a live show. Backstage activity can include technicians checking equipment while the talent checks props, directors giving notes while singers hit notes, and musicians tuning their instruments while actors tune themselves up for another great performance.

Once you've checked in with the stage manager or signed the callboard (which can be a ritual in itself), the next step is to situate yourself in your dressing room or a quiet corner. Placing personal items in your area and around your mirror can help bring a sense of calm to your mind and body. Putting on your own makeup is another longstanding backstage tradition. If you've never taken a makeup class, it is a good idea to enroll in one and discover all the possibilities.

Also on the agenda for all actors is some type of warm-up. Many performers prefer to spend time alone, running lines in their heads or doing meditation techniques. Richard Todd Adams, who has portrayed Raoul in the road company of

The Phantom of the Opera, states, "It depends on the show—sometimes I'll do sit-ups or stretching exercises, other times I'll read a magazine with my feet propped up. If I'm doing a play, I'll do a pretty typical vocal routine, limbering up my tongue, palate, and lips."

Performer Adrienne Pisoni usually does pushups and sit-ups to get her body energized, and a vocal warm-up for ten to fifteen minutes. "Backstage, I focus on centering myself. I try to get in touch with my character through breathing and meditating quietly. I also find that hearing the sound of the audience can help center me and bring my thoughts to the immediate moment."

Group warm-ups for musical shows happen closer to curtain time, and include stretching and breathing exercises, neck rolls and body twists, dance combinations, and singing scales around the rehearsal piano.

METHOD MENTALITY
Countless procedures have been developed over the years to help actors and other performers get their heads together before a show. Renowned teacher Lee Strasberg created "The Method" after being inspired by the work of Konstantin Stanislavski and his "System." It was a breakthrough approach that utilized relaxation and concentration exercises to help actors tap into their sensory and emotional memories.

Contemporary actors continue to incorporate this process into their pre-show routines. Method actor Ricardo Cordero worked extensively in cabaret and theatre before forming his own film company, Global Network Pictures. "The Method prepares you for the realities of the stage. On the day of a show, my dialogue, actions, and movements begin to go through my mind in the morning. I do meditation and 'sense memory' exercises at home. You focus on all your senses—sight, smell, hearing, tasting, feeling. Getting in touch with your senses is very important for any actor who's going to walk on a stage."

Leslie Hopps is a Canadian performer who has found much success in the U.S. "I recommend the famous 'chair relaxation' taught at Strasberg," she says. "You sit in a straight-backed, armless chair, and slowly begin exploring the body for tension—keeping relaxed as possible, almost falling asleep, but still active. When tension is discovered, you use the mind to ask the muscles to simply 'let go.' Unwanted tension must be released in order to not block expression during the work on stage."

New York-based actor Luan Begetti utilizes the Method when trying to keep calm and concentrate on his role. "When I'm backstage, I focus on an object of attention to keep myself from freaking out. It's scary back there right before you go on stage."

Other useful approaches have been applied to the art of acting, including the Loyd Williamson technique, which helps actors create a character's physical presence, and the Sanford Meisner technique, by which you use imagination skills to develop a circumstance similar to the one your character is going through. (See Chapter 2, "Training, Technique, and the Acting Workplace.")

Besides formal techniques, there are plenty of things you can do to block out the disruptions of daily life and put your mind solely on the task at hand. Actor Anthony Go always listens to whatever music he thinks his character would "be into," and during group circle he believes in "breathing out yourself and breathing in your character."

An actress who's working in both film and theatre, Samantha Gutterman recalls, "Before some of my shows, we would sing and dance around like idiots to get our blood flowing."

SHOW TIME

As the stage manager counts down from "half-hour" to "fifteen minutes" to "places," actors must learn to pace themselves and their routines so they don't leave everything to the last minute. You'll need to allow even more time if the role requires specialized dancing, acrobatics, or stunts, as each of these requires its own separate warm-up routine.

Once the show has begun, when an actor is offstage between scenes, his or her concentration must remain high. Otherwise, he or she might disturb the proceedings—or worse, miss an entrance. Whether you can shift in and out of character, or have to stay quietly focused, your habits during the show depend on the type of show—comedy, drama, musical, etc.—and how demanding your role is.

Cordero makes a habit of not talking very much backstage: "If I do talk, I talk in character." Greeman admits, "I've been known to joke around and gossip backstage, but I stay out of the way of other actors if they're preparing to enter for a scene." Hopps finds that she is really quiet while a show is going on. "I tend to keep to myself, and watch—and learn—from the wings."

While some performers can't even think about eating while a performance is going on, Hardeman finds herself snacking during shows. "I guess it relaxes me. There's always food around, and the bigger the show budget, the better the food. I always gain weight doing a show. That's something I have to work on."

NERVE ENDINGS

Whether or not you can control anxieties during a show can affect your believability on stage. Stage and screen veteran Enzo Carlino suggests, "To avoid getting nervous, each time you make an entrance, remember what your objective is and what happened right before the scene."

Vicknair puts a positive spin on being on edge. "I always have nervous energy before a performance—for which I am thankful. Of course, nervousness needs to be distinguished from panic. For me, nervous energy is a function of preparedness and being in the moment. It's your body's way of saying, 'Let's go!' I think adrenaline serves as a catalyst for delivering a fresh performance, particularly night after night."

Whatever your particular performance venue and level of expertise, Hopps reminds all performers to simply have fun. "It's easy to forget how lucky we are as artists to be allowed to live our dream. Enjoy, delight, and surrender to all possibilities!"

Success is not a secret...It's a system!

Hypnotherapist Cheryl O'Neil knows how much stress and anxiety can lead to personal problems. She has helped thousands of people, and chances are she can help you too.

- *Release bad habits*
- *Overcome fears*
- *Increase confidence*
- *Create positive change*
- *Conquer performance anxiety*
- *Metaphysical Hypnotherapy*

Cheryl O'Neil, C.Ht. **(310) 274-5998**

PERFORMING ARTISTS THERAPIST
Dr. Heide Hamelberg,
License# PSY 15284

Clinical Psychologist/Professional Dancer
❖Consultations/Psychotherapy
❖Performing Artists Personal Growth Program
❖Individuals/Groups
Affordable Rates for Performers

Call (310) 660-8176

ACTORFEST
A DAY FOR ACTORS

CAREER SEMINARS · CASTING DIRECTORS
AGENTS · FOCUS SESSIONS · MANAGERS
FREE EXHIBIT HALL · AND MUCH MORE

FOR EXHIBIT HALL SPACE CALL

WEST ■   **■ EAST**

Back Stage West Advertising
5055 Wilshire Blvd., 5th fl.
Los Angeles, CA 90036
323.525.2225

Back Stage Advertising
770 Broadway, 4th floor
New York, NY 10003
646.654.5700

In New York,
e v e r y   a r t i s t'
needs a
place to call
home.

real **COMMUNITY** in the heart of the city

www.nyjourney.com

Journey-Upper West
Promenade Theatre*
2162 Broadway (@76th St.)
Sundays @ 10:30am

Journey-Village
PS 41 Auditorium*
116 W. 11th St. (@6th Ave.)
Sundays @ 6:00pm

The Journey Church of the City
Whether you live in New York, or frequently visit,
The Journey is a church for the performing arts.
The Journey is a casual, contemporary, Christian church that places
a high value on relationships, authentic growth, media, and the creative arts.

The Journey

* Locations and times subject to change. Please visit www.nyjourney.com for current information.

1

38 Welcome to the Jungle:

Actors Too Often Fall Prey to the Unholiest of Scams

BY LAURA WEINERT

Your typical scam goes something like this: An actress reads an ad or flyer stating that a company is "casting" or holding "auditions" for people who want to "break into the business." Great, she thinks. So she calls the number, gets an appointment, and heads down to the office for her audition. The office is in a nice area and looks professional enough: headshots all around, other actors waiting in the lobby, perhaps even a "Better Business Bureau" sign on the wall. There are forms to fill out. The staff members seem fairly organized, and they conduct a fairly typical interview, asking questions, perhaps having the actress read copy. They thank her and tell her they'll call.

Inevitably, the actress gets called back in for a meeting. She's told how talented she is, how much money she can make in commercials and TV. She'll hear stories of the company's successes. *Then* comes the scam: the sales pitch. "This is usually the first time they will tell you there are costs involved," says Los Angeles Deputy City Attorney Mark Lambert, a prosecutor in the Consumer Protection Unit. The company may try to sell you any number of services: photographers, overpriced drama lessons, cold-reading lessons, personal websites. They might claim these services are "optional" or strongly recommended, but in many cases, if you don't agree to pay, you don't hear from them ever again.

"Usually they will say that you have to decide right then and there," continues Lambert, "that it's a take-it-or-leave-it deal. They'll say, 'If you don't want it, that's fine. We have somebody else who we're going to sign instead.'"

But as a matter of law, under the Advance Fee Talent Service Act of the California Labor Code, it is illegal to charge any kind of upfront fees to represent an actor as an agent or manager. This means that potential agencies or managers cannot force you to spend money on their acting classes, or to hand over cash to their photographer buddy for new headshots. (In most scams, they take a kickback for this kind of "referral.") They cannot force you to buy a website from them—or anything else, for that matter. The only thing they are allowed to charge you is a commission—usually ten percent to twenty percent—on the money you make from jobs they get you. This means that until they get you work, you don't pay them a cent.

The relatively new Advance Fee Talent Service Act—written by California state Senator Sheila Kuehl and effective in California since January 2000—has already seen its first day in court. In September, Lambert used it to sue the L.A.-based Malibu Talent, which had been charging fees of $290–340 for mandatory photos with one of the company's photographers. The company had placed ads in *The Penny Saver* and *LA Weekly* as well—ads that the city also claimed made false statements. Malibu Talent owner Simone McCue and employees Donald John Cherry and Michael Pasby were ordered to pay fines and restitution, and were forbidden to work in the talent business for the next three years.

The good news is, the clients who made complaints got their money back. "This is why it's important to make complaints," says Lambert. Obviously those who didn't complain did not get their money back.

BAD EXAMPLES

Indeed, since the passage of the act, Los Angeles' consumer protection unit seems to be going after talent scammers as never before. Scam companies can be charged with more crimes than just violating the talent agency act, and sentencing can go well beyond merely having to pay a few fines. In 2001 L.A.-based talent manager Christopher Valentino received a jail sentence after pleading no contest to one count of criminal conspiracy and two counts of grand theft for conspiring with photographer Svetlana Kraft of Beverly Hills' Lana Kraft Photography. They had been swindling clients by charging them for photographic sessions and promising them acting work that was never provided.

Valentino also told clients that he represented former Miss America Ali Landry, that he had appeared in numerous soap operas—including a sixteen-year stint on *All My Children*—and that he was represented by the William Morris Agency, according to investigators. Unfortunately none of this was true. Neither were his alleged promises to find these actors work.

What he did find them, however, were headshots from a "highly recommended" photographer, who, he said, was a "former European model" who had done a lot of work for Jennifer Aniston. But Aniston had never heard of Kraft, investigators determined.

Another all-too-common scam is simply a bad management contract—which is why any and all contracts should be taken home and examined carefully before signing. Agent Ryan Glasgow of the L.A.-based Gold-Marshak-Liedtke described his shock at seeing a contract in which a manager had written in that at any time, should he feel it necessary, he wanted the client to be responsible for postage, travel expenses occurred on his behalf, long-distance phone calls, and cell phone bills. "Unethical didn't even come close to describing what this was," declares Glasgow.

Actors should also remember that if they do agree to pay their management company upfront money for any services, they should at least make sure the services they pay for are rendered as promised. In some cases they are not. When actor Casey Reidling agreed to pay his new management company $195 to place his photo and résumé on its website, the check was cashed, he reports, but the photo never appeared online. Actress Deborah Ramaglia claims to have faced a similar situation: after the company cashed her check, it placed her photo on a separate website— a website that, she said, she never knew existed. When their attempts to get a refund failed, the actors took the Van Nuys-based International Actors Management

Company to court. While company owner Keith Kaminsky denied all the allegations, a Small Claims Court judge ordered IAMG to pay the actors restitution.

The problem with so many of these scams is that they work, and often they work on people who view themselves as smart, streetwise adults. In a 1998 case against the L.A.-based West Coast Talent—a scam "management" operation that was charging parents thousands of dollars for promotional materials and acting classes for their kids—the victims were educated adults. These were lawyers, university professors; one worked for the fire department. And they bought it hook, line, and sinker.

"I've seen very savvy people lured into these things," says Lambert. "These places have nice buildings, they have nice offices, they're well decorated. They have photographs everywhere, posters, all the trappings of what people think a legitimate management or talent office would look like. They can talk a good talk, and they fool people."

PROTECTION PLAN
You can do a number of specific things to avoid being duped:

1 **Pay attention to how people approach you.** Scam artists rely on a whole slew of tactics to draw you in, including setting up seductive websites, cold calling, and handing out cards in shopping malls.
2 **Listen to what the businesses are saying.** "They might tell you they 'submit' to different companies for commercials," notes Lambert. "To me, that's a big difference from saying they actually get work for people. Anyone can submit. Are they telling you they personally manage someone into a successful career? Or are they just showing you pictures of people?"
3 **Ask questions and get references.** Whom do they do business with around town? Where are their clients placed?
4 **Research.** Once you get the information, check it out. When you get a list of clients or projects they've worked on, call around and verify them. Call the Better Business Bureau; call the Department of Consumer Affairs. Find out how many showcases this person has held in this particular space that you're going to. Is it one of those fly-by-night, traveling-circus things where they do one night here and then disappear?
5 **Take any and all contracts home, read them, carefully, and perhaps call a lawyer to have a look, as well.** "It's a big decision you're making," says Lambert. "You at least ought to look at the law and see if the contract follows the law. If the business won't let somebody take home a contract to look at, then, personally, I think they should run away. Why wouldn't they let you look at a contract?"
6 **Last, if you feel you've been scammed, complain.** "Complain, complain, complain," urges Lambert. "That's the most important thing. I can't stress it enough. People don't seem to do this, but people need to make complaints when they think they've been ripped off, even if it's a small amount of money—because it's the only way these dishonest people get stopped. Call the Department of Consumer Affairs and the Better Business Bureau."

39 A Dozen Ways to Score Big at Musical Auditions

BY SHERRY EAKER

"The most important thing about a musical theatre audition—or any audition—is that *you* be the answer to the needs of the auditioner. That is the way you stop the conveyor belt—on you. And, in order to be that answer, you need to know what is wanted and needed in the space," states stage and film actress-singer Tovah Feldshuh.

In other words, you need to be one hundred percent prepared at the audition, and not only with the right number of songs and kinds of songs. Taken from interviews with New York-based directors, casting directors, and musical directors and musical supervisors of over three dozen Broadway and Off-Broadway shows from a recent season, here are a number of things you need to keep in mind before heading for your next musical audition:

1 **Audition with material that's familiar to you.** Your selection should be in the style of the show, but not from the show. Never go to an audition with a song that you just learned the night before. It takes a while to really understand a song and make it your own. In addition, it's more important that the song you select reveal something about you, even more important than showing off your range.

2 **Always have more songs along with you, all ready to sing, in case you're asked to sing additional songs.** You should have at least five or six songs in your repertoire: a traditional musical-theatre ballad and up-tempo; a rock or pop ballad and up-tempo; a standard, perhaps from Gershwin, Porter, or Rodgers and Hart; and one song that can show off your creativity and sense of humor. Again, they should all reveal something about you as an actor—your type and personality. Which leads to . . .

3 **Develop a sense of self.** Know who you are. Try to see where you fit in terms of type, and which roles you feel most comfortable in. Once you get an understanding of this, you can select audition material that will show you off best, and you can . . .

4 **Be who you are.** Never try to be other than that, guessing what would please the casting director. As mentioned previously, the accent seems to be on personality; make sure that comes through in your audition. It will allow you to be distinctive and stand out. Being honest with yourself allows for the honesty to come through in your performance.

5 Triple threats . . . plus! Being able to sing, dance, and act is the norm. You now need to go one step further: Quadruple threats are in demand. One might need to play a musical instrument *(Cabaret)*, have a great comic sensibility *(The Producers)*, speak comfortably with a foreign accent, or be a master of the art of stage combat.

6 Be familiar with the show, and figure out which role you might be right for. It gives you an idea of the style of acting, singing, and movement that the show calls for, and helps you to understand what the casting director is looking for. Once you "know yourself," you'll know if you're right. If you can't afford to see the show, then at least buy the cast album. See the movie that it's based on. If it's a brand-new show, research the period that it takes place in.

7 Be prepared. Casting directors complain all the time that many actors are simply not prepared at auditions. Know your material; don't sing more than what was asked; make sure your headshot and résumé look professional. Says casting director Howie Cherpakov, "You'd be surprised how many people waste so much audition time with the technicalities of auditioning, which are things they should be fluent with. If you have people who are not confident in their auditioning skills, it makes you nervous about hiring them. It reflects back on their discipline and work ethic."

8 Be nice to the piano man. How you relate to other people in the room can help the auditioner determine how you might fit in with the company. For associate musical supervisor Kristen Blodgette, the relationship between audi- tionee and accompanist is crucial. "It gives us a window into what you are like to work with." Also, make sure your music is clean and legible, so that it's easy on the eyes of the accompanist who's sight-reading it. Another point to consider, if you can afford it: bring your own accompanist to the audition. You can then rehearse in advance and leave much less to chance under already pressured circumstances.

9 Dress character-appropriate. "This does not mean wear a costume," says casting director Bernard Telsey. "I still want to see you as an individual." Adds caster Dave Clemmons, "Never wear anything to an audition that you wouldn't wear out in public." Wear clothes from your everyday wardrobe that may be appropriate for that particular show or role, something that will help give you a sense of the show or a feel for the part without being too literal. If you don't know how you want to show up, Tovah Feldshuh suggests that you wear "all black, or something with a neutral palette onto which the auditioners can read whatever they want."

10 Think twice before choosing obscure material. Not only might the accompa- nist have trouble playing it, but, notes musical director Kevin Stites, "it tends to upstage the singer—distracting the music director, who may be tuning you out while thinking about who wrote the number and what show it came from." On the other hand, some auditioners perk up at unusual material. They like the care put into choosing it and find it makes you stand out from the pack.

11 Don't apologize for your audition. Musical director David Chase's advice: "Don't tell me you're sick. Don't tell me you're . . . whatever. Just come in and do it."

12 **Note a specific role** when you're sending out your picture/résumé to the casting director. Especially when you're dealing with casting directors who are handling many shows at a time. Knowing what you're right for makes it that much easier for the caster. Also, advises Bernard Telsey, send a picture/résumé for each show you're submitting for if handled by the same office. Different sets of files are kept for each production.

13 Might as well make it a baker's dozen. One more piece of advice: **Be persistent!** If you don't get a callback or win a role, keep trying. This was mentioned by so many of the auditioners. There could be any number of reasons why you weren't picked the first time around.

Working as a performer is all about building a career. As stage and film director and choreographer Rob Marshall once remarked: "You work your way up. It's a natural progression. Look at it as building blocks. All of your experiences are important, and they will lead to something. But, absolutely, the most important thing is to keep working and keep trying to be better at the craft."

Think!

When was the last time you really felt GREAT about your Singing?

Steven Memel's clients experience dramatic growth in their comfort, their control, their confidence, and their performance.

Steven's unique training style will help you build the range and power you desire or reclaim and surpass what you once had.

(Client list and bio on website)

"Steven starts with the essence of "who you are" and cultivates your natural ability until you become your best possible self as a singer and a performer. Steven Memel is the most gifted vocal coach I have ever encountered."

Marty Jabara, Producer, Musical director - World Tour - "Wild Women Blues" with Linda Hopkins

"Stunning results! Steven accomplishes wonders without ever squashing the personality or talent of the performer he is guiding."

Jeffrey Silverman, Broadway conductor "Les Miserables", 3 multiplatinum CD's

"Wow! I couldn't believe it. Steven took a non-singer and had him singing well enough in three weeks to join our show in Europe!".

Jim Lenny, Producer, Wolfgang Bocksch Concerts

"He's a genius! "

Anika Paris, EAR Recording Artist, Faculty - Musicians Institute

Contemporary - Musicals - Speech

(818) 789-0474
steven@stevenmemel.com
Visit Steven's website at: www.stevenmemel.com

DEBORAH SHULMAN

Specialist in the Art of Selling a Song from the Musical Theatre Repertoire
Recording Consultation
Vocal Technique and Coaching

Whether one needs to extend and improve one's vocal range, eliminate a stubborn vocal break, strengthen the voice, improve resonance in the speaking voice as well as singing voice, or learn how to sell a song, there are practical solutions for each specific problem. Along with vocal technique, one learns performing strategies, finds one's performance personality, and most importantly, builds and increases one's self-confidence as a complete performer.

RECCOMENDATIONS

"Deborah Shulman has given me solid technique and greatly increased my range."

Larry Raben
(Original assistant director and star of FOREVER PLAID nationally.)

"Deborah Shulman, you've brought back my voice, and you've brought me back to life. Deborah Shulman is a singer's singing teacher."

Brooks Arthur
(Producer for *Bette Miller, Michael Feinstein, John Pizzarelli, Liza Minelli* and others.)

"Deborah has tremendous understanding of the vocal process. She has the uncanny ability to identify and correct vocal problems."

Gary Bachlund
(Metropolitan Opera artist)

"Deborah quickly gets me in shape for those last minute auditions. Her technique is to the point, strong and centered."

Annette Cardona
(Cha-Cha from the movie, **GREASE**, and the original Acid Queen in **TOMMY**.)

Private instruction/Group Classes Available (Small Classes with Individual Attention)
DEBORAH SHULMAN
323.851.7344

Elisabeth Howard's
Vocal Power
Academy Original Since 1980

For 20 years the best training in all styles of singing, including:
Musical Theater•Blues•Jazz•Rock•Pop•Country•Classical

Private Lessons•Performance Workshops
Showcases • Seminars

Los Angeles•Hollywood•Glendale•Silver Lake•Santa Monica•Topanga•West S.F. Valley

CALL NOW (800) 829-7664   www.vocalpowerinc.com

Announcing the West Coast Opening of

THE THOMAS SHEPARD SINGERS STUDIO

THOMAS SHEPARD, M.A., private singing coach to the BROADWAY THEATRICAL COMMUNITY and instructor at New York City's major training institutions, including NEW YORK UNIVERSITY and the AMERICAN ACADEMY OF DRAMATIC ARTS, is now teaching in L.A.

- Find your singing voice
- Belt effortlessly
- Select the right material
- Styles from B'way to Rock
- Work through vocal challenges
- Increase your range
- Set the action of the character
- Understands dancers

call: (323) 953-0027
or visit: www.thomasshepardsingersstudio.com

Carol Tingle
Vocal Technique

(310) 828-3100

Singers: All Ages · Levels · Styles
30 Years Experience · Private Instruction
Workshops · Audition Preparation
Merging Inner & Outer Resources to:
Reduce Stress · Performance Anxiety

Resolve Blocks

Voice Studio

www.caroltingle.com

FREE YOUR VOICE
STEVEN DAHLKE
Master of Music
Manhattan School of Music

A Holistic Approach to singing which will free your voice, mind, and soul.

Awesome Results with all Levels
Great W. Hollywood/Beverly Hills Location

- Singing Teacher
- Vocal Coach
- Accompanist

310-995-9659

The monthly Who To Contact Guide
For Casting, Agents & Production

ROSS REPORTS®
TELEVISION & FILM

To Subscribe call 800.745.8922

Learn How to Sing...BETTER!
R&B, Jazz, Gospel, Hip-Hop
The Right Way!

Singing Classes and Workshops
Every Saturday
at the **Nola Studios**
250 West 54th Street – 11th Floor
between Bway & 8th Ave.
New York City
            3pm - 6pm
• **LEARN**
  How to interpret and perform a song
  Effective Breathing Techniques!
  Song Writing/reducing/Auditioning Secrets
  How to properly record a CD!
  Improvement Guaranteed!

  Guest Speakers
  Isaac Hayes - LL Cool J, Ashanti
  Roberta Flack – Mary Wilson, Me'lisa Morgan
  Hezekiah Walker – Leon, Blue Magic
  Ray, Goodman & Brown and others

  4 Weeks of 3 hour weekly
  sessions for only $160

Call **(212) 978-3640**
web-site www.soyouwanttobeastar.org
to register for our next session

BRUCE KOLB VOICE STUDIOS

BRUCE KOLB, D.M.A.

126 West 73rd Street • Apt. LB
New York, NY 10023
(212) 595-5564 • kolbstudio@earthlink.net

SIGHT-SINGING with **Liz Fleischer**
ear-training • music theory

"One of New York's great teachers."
—*New York Magazine*

"A teacher who gets results..."
—*The New York Times*

3o years and still humming!

Call **212 501 3362** or e-mail
adultdivision@kaufman-center.org
for FREE placement schedule or class information

Lucy Moses School at Kaufman Center • 129 W. 67th St., NYC

BACK STAGE® and **BACK STAGE WEST®**
The #1 weeklies for Performing Artists

SUBSCRIBE TODAY
1.800.745.8922
http://www.backstage.com/backstage/contact/printsub.jsp

40 5-6-7-8! Tips for Terps Auditioning for Musicals

BY LISA JO SAGOLLA, WITH PHYLLIS GOLDMAN

Dancers who work in musicals are often kidded about not being able to count higher than eight. But regardless of what is said about their mathematical abilities, these dancers perform one of the most rigorous jobs in the theatre. The hard-working dancing ensemble is often the lifeblood of big musical shows. And the excitement of being a part of such an electrifying team of dancers is unparalleled.

How then do you, the dancer, go about getting a job performing in a musical? Well, clearly, after you have acquired the requisite training—a firm grounding in ballet technique plus a mastery of modern, jazz, and tap—you peruse the casting notices in *Back Stage* and venture out to auditions. But what exactly is expected of you at an audition? What are musical theatre choreographers really looking for when they hold dance auditions?

To find out more about this, we spoke with several choreographers (and some of their assistants) who cast dancers in Broadway musicals. They explained to us how they go about casting dancers. They told us what it is they want to see at auditions, and offered heartfelt words of advice for dancers seeking work in musical theatre. It really doesn't matter whether or not there is any truth to that "mathematically challenged" characterization of Broadway dancers, as all the wisdom we collected about getting work dancing in musical theatre productions can be found in the following "count of eight" tips.

1 Know the requirements of the show. The first thing you must do, before even deciding whether or not to attend a dance audition for a particular musical, is to determine, as best you can, exactly what that show's dance needs are. Musical theatre dance is perhaps the world's most eclectic form of choreography. A Broadway musical can incorporate virtually any and all kinds of dance and dancers, depending on its setting and storyline. Find out if the show you're auditioning for requires dancers with specific kinds of technical training—pointe work, rhythm tap, acrobatics, ballroom dance, world dance forms—and if it has particular physical requirements in terms of gender, height, ethnicity, or body type. No matter how well you dance, if you do not "fit" the needs of the show, you will not be cast. Learn as much as possible ahead of time and go, well-prepared, to those auditions appropriate for you.

2 Acting counts. In most musicals you will be playing a character. In addition to capturing the formal designs of the choreography with your body, you must also be able to convincingly act a role and help tell the story of the show as you dance. "The most important thing dancers can bring into an audition," says choreographer Jerry Mitchell, "is their ability to tell a story with their steps."

3 Learn to sing. Gone are the days when Broadway musicals featured a dancing ensemble and a separate singing ensemble. It's too expensive nowadays to employ all those people. So the dancers who are cast in musical theatre productions today are generally expected to carry the show's ensemble singing responsibilities as well. And not only are they expected to do this double-duty as part of an ensemble, but often they also serve as the individual understudies for many of the show's supporting roles. At a dance audition, if a choreographer must choose between two similar performers whose dancing he or she likes equally well, chances are the stronger singer will win out. But if you really want to dance in musicals, don't let the fact that you think of yourself as a non-singer deter you. *Aida*'s associate choreographer, Tracey Langran Corea, says, "We never want to discourage those who are amazing dancers and don't *think* they can sing, because oftentimes you will find out you *can* sing, but you just don't know it yet because you haven't gone out and tried to learn."

4 Get the style. Musical theatre choreographers are extremely concerned with style. It's the all-important element that makes choreography succeed in creating the time period, place, or mood necessary for a show. "It's not just about getting the steps," says Jerry Mitchell. "It's about getting the steps *in the style* in which the step is choreographed." Before auditioning for shows set in historic periods or foreign locales, visit a major library (such as the Library of the Performing Arts at Lincoln Center in New York City), or rent videotapes of authentic performances so you can become familiar with the choreographic style you will be asked to emulate. For example, for *42nd Street,* the dancers need to be able to pick up an "Astaire" style. "This is a period piece," explains its dance captain, Kelli Barclay. "If a dancer shows up with superb tap technique, but has a contemporary look, I can't take him." For auditions, choreographers will usually create several combinations for you to do that represent the style of the particular show they're casting. "I like to see if the dancers can pick up the style I'm playing around with," explains choreographer Wayne Cilento. "Even if they're amazing technical dancers, if performers cannot get the stylistic quirkiness I'm after, I do not pick them."

5 Be brave, adventurous, and energetic. Choreographers like to work with dancers who are fearless. "You look for a dancer who will try whatever you ask of them, without judging it first," says choreographer Ann Reinking. "I want people with a real sense of adventure." The dancers who have the greatest success at musical theatre auditions are those who show a courageous commitment to animating the choreographer's vision. *The Lion King*'s associate choreographer, Aubrey Lynch, states, "I look for a fearlessness that says to me, 'I can tackle the job and keep this energy going eight times a week.'"

6 Individuality is key. "I can't stress enough how important individuality is in casting," says *Movin' Out*'s dance supervisor, Stacy Caddell. "We really want to see who you are as a dancer." And the secret is confidence—that's what enables you to display your individuality at a dance audition. You must be so sure of your technique that you can perform the steps perfectly while imbuing them with a special quality that is uniquely your own. This is what draws the choreographer's eye to you and makes you stand out among the others. It is important to develop your individuality, however, in an intelligent and honest fashion. "People on the other side of the table will know immediately if you are trying to be something you are not," claims Denny Berry, the dance supervisor for *The Phantom of the Opera*. Choose your dance audition attire, makeup, and hairstyle wisely. "If someone comes into an audition dressed up in a really outrageous kind of a look, but it matches how they perform, then it's great," says Wayne Cilento. "But if they come in with an outrageous look and it has nothing to do with who they are, then they just look ridiculous."

7 Behave yourself! "The audition begins the minute you enter the waiting room," warns Aubrey Lynch. "If I see you outside, or in the back, waiting your turn to audition, I am aware of your attitude, your energy, what you are wearing—your demeanor." Musical theatre is a highly collaborative art form with lots of close interaction between all kinds of performers, designers, and directors. Choreographers are always mindful of the fact that when they hire a dancer, they (and many others) are going to have to work closely with that person in an intense environment over an extended period of time. "I'm always watching for people's behavior," says choreographer John Carrafa. "If somebody comes into an audition late, or if they're pushy, or if I see them give another person a hard time, that becomes a problem." Choreographers want to hire dancers who are fun to work with. "The way you behave yourself in an audition," stresses choreographer Luis Perez, "is, for me, a very important part of the casting process."

8 Make sure you're committed. Dancing in a musical is a big responsibility. To perform the same show eight times a week requires great endurance, both physically and mentally. If you start to tire, or lose interest, and you find yourself missing performances, you will quickly develop a negative reputation that may hinder your future career. Do not audition for a show or for a choreographer whose work you are not prepared to commit to one hundred percent. "I pick dancers who want to be there eight times a week," declares Jerry Mitchell. "It's a commitment, and those who give one hundred percent are those who will be cast again and again and again." As a dancer, you must never forget how important you are to the choreographer's work. "You are the person I put my heart and soul into," states John Carrafa. "You're the person who is showing my work. You're representing me."

All of this advice notwithstanding, it is perhaps most important to remember that you must really enjoy yourself at dance auditions. If you're genuinely having a good time, you will undoubtedly dance better and your individual personality will shine through in a true and appealing manner. Although choreographers tend to re-hire dancers they have worked with successfully in the past, they are also always looking for new talent, and when you walk into an audition, they want very much to like you. "We're always looking for somebody new, somebody cool, somebody we're really going to like and get excited about," says Luis Perez, "so try to look at the auditioning process as just a way to meet new people. And simply enjoy letting us get to know you."

41 The Big Chill:

Experts Offer Tips for a Better Cold Reading

BY DANY MARGOLIES

You will at some point in your career be called upon to pick up a script and read for one or more auditors—casting directors, directors, producers—looking to cast a role. Sometimes you will have been given the script the night before, sometimes it will be handed to you on the spot and you will be allowed perhaps five minutes to prepare. This is known as cold reading. What makes it cold is the sweat pouring from your shaking body.

On the other hand, you may find you enjoy the process. A substantial number of actors say they like the freedom that cold reading allows them, the chance to create on the spot, the opportunity to practice "risk and concentration," the feeling of collaborating in shaping the product.

Or you may never overcome the fear. In that case you'll need to function on willpower and any or all of the following techniques.

How cold are they?

Theatrical auditions are almost never cold. Occasionally, once they see you, the auditors may realize you're better suited to another role and ask you for a quick cold reading. Say "yes" without hesitation, but ask for some time: it shows you're flexible but savvy.

Film and television technology allow actors to see their sides at least a day before auditions. Commercial copy is probably the coldest, but it seldom requires intense preparation.

Reduce some of the agony of cold reading by researching the full play and the theatre's season, the television series, the product's other commercials, a film director's other projects, before you audition.

HOW CAN I POSSIBLY PREPARE?

There's no one right way to prepare for a cold reading, so how can you know what to do? Try everything. Eventually you'll learn what's right for you.

Everyone agrees: you can't create a complete, fully realized character for a cold reading, so just commit to your choices. Let the text tell you what to say and how to say it, then make the most interesting, dynamic choices possible.

Here's where everyone disagrees: some say read the script only once; this way you remain loose, relaxed, malleable. Others suggest that you read as much of the script as you can and do a solid analysis: your character's age, health, state of mind; where you are; what's happening to you . . . you know the drill. Some suggest doing something distinctive that will make the auditors remember you. But everyone agrees that no one should ever try for shock at a cold reading.

Finally, remember: cold reading is usually used to test your acting, not your reading. It gives the auditors a glimpse of your working method as a performer and allows them a rough sense of how you fit a specific role.

Here are other pointers:

- If you receive sides for several scenes, check the page numbers to get a feeling for when in the chronology your scenes take place; that will help you better understand the evolving relationships.
- Don't overcomplicate the character or reach for big emotions.
- Don't try to play the whole play or screenplay at once; find the central action of the side you have, and play that.
- Make one strong choice, focusing on what your character wants from the other character(s).
- Find a way to make an emotional change so that you end the scene differently from the way you began.
- Read stage directions for clues, but don't follow them mindlessly.
- Don't revert to the last character you played. It's comfortable, but it's dangerous. Let it indicate to you that you are not "in the moment."
- Understand dictionary meanings and pronunciations, as well as the character's usage, of every word.
- Mark your beats in pencil, because you may change your mind as you rehearse.
- If you can, practice with a partner.
- Memorize the first two or three sentences without looking back on the page— if you can't do this, you're in the wrong business.
- Practice walking across a room, shaking hands, and saying "hello." First and sometimes lasting impressions are being formed. Make sure you don't have a wet-fish handshake.
- Some suggest dressing appropriately for your character but not necessarily for the specific scene you're reading; others say avoid this. If possible, check the preference of your auditors before you arrive.
- Finally, remember: The auditors look to you to show them something the other actors haven't shown them. And they would rather say, "You're hired!" than "Thank you. Next."

CAN I HELP MYSELF RIGHT BEFORE MY AUDITION?

You bet you can. Your demeanor, even your confidence are within your control. Your preparation has helped. Now it's show time. Experiment with any or all of these pointers:

- You may be under scrutiny even before you enter the building. Sometimes cameras are trained on you as you drive onto the lot or casting director's office. Get into "presentation mode" as you near the audition venue.
- Don't socialize, even in a room full of acquaintances. Instead find a private space where you can prepare.
- Physicalize in the hallway, in a restroom, or outside the building.
- Turn the reception area into a warm, familiar place by connecting with something there that reminds you of a place you know and like. Or view the reception area through the eyes of your character.
- Some actors read their lines while waiting; try reading the other character's lines instead.

WHAT SHOULD I DO DURING MY AUDITION?

Anything can and will happen in that room. Be in an alert state. Remember, your auditors are looking to fill the role, but they're also looking for someone with whom they will want to spend hours, days, weeks. Try these helpful hints:

- Arrive with as little as possible in your hands. Try to leave your belongings outside the audition room, but if you can't, leave them just inside the door so you can gracefully gather them up on your way out.
- Unless they call you by name, slate (clearly state your name). If you're being taped, and if you're represented, include the name of your agent.
- Be prepared to be asked a few questions; the auditors may want to know how you come across when you're not acting. It's not your answers that are important; it's your general demeanor.
- Enter the room as yourself, not the character, even though legends have done otherwise (but see below, under ". . . commercials").
- If you are dyslexic or a slow study, try to negotiate more time with the script: "May I go last today?" or "May I come back tomorrow?" are legitimate questions, but don't demand—or necessarily expect—any accommodation.
- Check possibly strange pronunciations with the auditors.
- Don't try to second-guess what casting people are looking for. If you must, ask a few carefully considered questions about what is going on in the scene—unless you already have this information at hand. Certainly never ask, "What are you looking for?"
- Some experts suggest that you remain seated, facing forward. Try not to sit in a comfortable chair. Others suggest moving if you want, but beware of aimless pacing. Also avoid aimless hand gestures that will dilute your work.
- Try to break away from the script for the first few and last few lines for strong eye contact.
- When reading the rest, don't hide your face.
- Mark your place with your free hand.
- If you lose your place in the script, don't drop the character. Stay with it until you find your line, or improvise the line.
- Otherwise, try not to paraphrase the script, particularly if the writer is in the room; note, however, that some auditors prefer paraphrasing to awkward fumbles for the line or requests for redos (but, again, see below, under ". . . commercials").
- Avoid breathy or whispered speech (unless specifically asked for it).
- Use available stimulus as much as you can.
- By the same token, don't touch (certainly don't kiss) the casting director or other reader, unless you've prearranged the mechanics.
- If you're getting a flat, bored, rushed line reading from your scene partner, use it to fuel your actions, as long as it's appropriate for the character.
- Use an accent if indicated by the script—and only if you're sure it's flawless.
- Don't bring props. Don't mime props.
- Breathe. Don't rush. Control the pace of the reading, but be very sparing with dramatic pauses.
- Listen to your partner, even if he or she is a poor actor or uninterested hired reader.
- If an auditor offers specific direction after your first read-through, and if that direction is result oriented, you must reinterpret and justify that direction—

in other words, instantly come up with an appropriate and specific motivation for being "bigger" or having "more energy." Here's where all those acting classes come in handy.

- If the auditor gives you a suggestion, don't throw out everything you've done and try something completely new. Incorporate his or her adjustments into your preparation. But always listen to the suggestion.
- Remember: Casting people are not always directors, so they may not know how to speak in the language of directing. Cut them some slack, too.
- If you feel self-conscious, focus on the person reading with you and connect with him or her when your eyes are not on the page. Are you getting what you want? How do they make you feel? Use these stimuli.
- If your character leaves at the end of the scene, don't use the real door.

IS THERE ANYTHING SPECIAL I SHOULD KNOW ABOUT COMMERCIALS?

Commercial casting directors say they can usually tell within the first five seconds after an actor has entered the room whether he or she is right for the part. Again, auditors have differing opinions on what actors should do at the casting session:

- Most agree that actors should wear appropriate clothes, but not necessarily a costume.
- Some suggest being in character as much as you can when you first walk in the door; others hate that. Ask before you walk into the room.
- Here more than in other areas, if you are playing a tough or angry character, walk in with some of those characteristics in evidence, but still try to show that you are a likeable actor underneath.
- These days most of the reads the clients want are low-key, natural, and easy. Come into the room with that easy manner (if it fits the character, of course).
- If you are having trouble with the copy, ask if you may paraphrase.

SHOULD I DO ANYTHING AS I'M LEAVING?

- Thank the person you read with and say goodbye to everyone pleasantly but quickly. Don't ask follow-up questions.
- If you think you did poorly, never show it. No one wants to hire a temperamental artist.
- Never discuss your audition in the hallway; certainly don't let the auditors overhear your parting comments.

WHAT SKILLS SHOULD I BE WORKING ON BETWEEN AUDITIONS?

- Nothing replaces a good acting class, appearing onstage at every opportunity, or otherwise polishing your skills.
- Practice cold reading every day. Download scripts off the Internet, or cold-read a new book every week.

HOW CAN I BE OF GOOD CHEER NO MATTER WHAT HAPPENS?

- Promise yourself a treat within your budget after your cold reading.
- Use your spiritual resources—from strong religious faith to stuffed toys—to ground you after your audition.
- Have a good friend waiting by the phone to hear your report. Complain as much as you need. Or call to share the good news that you got the role.

chelsea**eye** associatesLLP

157 West 19th Street
Tel: 212·727·3717
Fax: 212·727·3789
www.ChelseaEye.com

Are you ready for your Close Up?

When the camera moves in
what do you want them to
see? **Your Eyes!**

Not your contacts or wrinkles.

**Come in now for a
FREE LASIK Screening!**

15% off LASIK
& Cosmetic
procedures
with this ad!

Offer expires January 31, 2005

The Most Advanced Custom LASIK Treatments

Improve your appearance with:
Laser Hair Removal
Botox/Fillers
Cosmetic Facial & Eyelid Surgery
Liposuction

Board Certified LASIK & Cosmetic Specialists

Christopher T. Coad, M.D., F.A.C.S.   Joseph A. Eviatar, M.D., F.A.C.S.

Carl D. Corrow, O.D.   ■   Robert A. Guida, M.D., F.A.C.S.   ■   Carole Lea Burns, Aesthetician

---

YOUR CHANCE
TO MAKE A DIFFERENCE

BECOME AN EGG DONOR.

$7,000

You're healthy, compas-
sionate and generous.
Through egg donation you
can give a couple one of the
greatest gifts — the chance for
them to fulfill their dream of parent-
hood. Donors will receive $7,000 in compen-
sation as well as a free, comprehensive
medical evaluation. All applicants must be in
good health and between the ages of 21 and
32. All treatment will be administered by
board certified physicians at Reproductive
Medicine Associates of New York, a division
of Mount Sinai Medical Center. Anonymity
and confidentiality guaranteed. Please
call **(212) 756-5775**. Or, visit us at
www.rmany.com/donor_app.asp

RMA *of New York*   Mount Sinai

TO ADVERTISE
IN THE NEXT

BACKSTAGE®/BACK STAGE WEST®

ACTORS
HANDBOOK

PLEASE CALL

WEST ■   ■ EAST
Back Stage West   Back Stage
Advertising   Advertising
5055 Wilshire Blvd., 5th fl.   770 Broadway, 4th floor
Los Angeles, CA 90036   New York, NY 10003
323.525.2225   646.654.5700

LOWEST PRICES FOR
PORCELAIN LAMINATES,

WHITENING AND BRITE✦SMILE.

COSMETIC CENTER OF NORTHERN NJ

Serving NY and NJ Actors for over 22 years.
Financing Available. No Charge Consultation Recommended.

General and Cosmetic Dentistry
1509 Palisade Ave., (2 Blocks from G.W. Bridge)
Fort Lee, NJ 07024
Call 201-944-5550

DR. PAULA S. GOULD
Graduate of Univ. of Pennsylvania
Northwestern University Dental School,
West Virginia Medical Residency
Member of the American Academy of
Cosmetic Dentistry

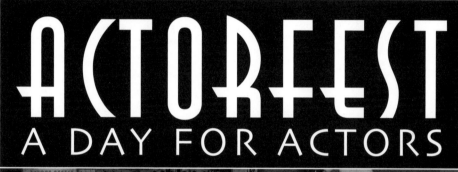

ACTORFEST
A DAY FOR ACTORS

CAREER SEMINARS · CASTING DIRECTORS
AGENTS · FOCUS SESSIONS · MANAGERS
FREE EXHIBIT HALL · AND MUCH MORE

FOR EXHIBIT HALL SPACE CALL

WEST ■   ■ EAST

Back Stage West Advertising   Back Stage Advertising
5055 Wilshire Blvd., 5th fl.   770 Broadway, 4th floor
Los Angeles, CA 90036   New York, NY 10003
            323.525.2225   646.654.5700

Resource Listings

Regional Combined Audition Sites

BY DAVID FAIRHURST

Summertime offers a wealth of opportunities for beginning and seasoned performers alike, and the regional combined auditions are where actors can start taking advantage of them. From January through the end of March, representatives from hundreds of theatre companies—both summer-only and year-round—will congregate at nearly two dozen audition sites from coast to coast, searching for actors to fill thousands of roles. It's a valuable chance to be seen by a host of top regional and summer theatres all at once.

There's a lot of work to go around. For many Equity actors, these are the jobs that keep the wolf from the door during the fallow months between theatre seasons. Non-Equity actors have no reason to feel left out: most of the regional combined auditions welcome nonunion performers—even college students—with open arms, sometimes to the exclusion of their Equity brethren.

In addition, there is work to be found in a variety of nonperforming jobs: for technicians, designers, stage managers, musical directors, administrators, box office staff, and other behind-the-scenes positions.

What follows is a quick overview of the major regional combined auditions across the country, moving geographically from East Coast to West Coast. If information is missing from a particular listing, it's because the details of some auditions change from one year to the next. So be sure to contact the organizer or visit its website for the latest news and updates.

New England Theatre Conference

Audition Dates: Mid-March
Place: Natick, Massachusetts
Eligibility: Non-Equity and Equity Membership Candidates, at least 18 years old and no longer in high school
Fees: $30 for NETC members; for nonmembers, $45 for students, $55 for nonstudents
Format: Two minutes to present two contrasting selections—two monologues, two songs, or one of each (accompanist provided), plus dance auditions
Application Deadline: Early February
Info/Contact: NETC Auditions, New England Theatre Conference, PMB 502, 198 Tremont Street, Boston, MA 02116-4750; www.netconline.org; call (617) 851-8535, or e-mail mail@netconline.org

Vermont Association of Theatres & Theatre Artists

Audition Dates: Mid-March
Place: Colchester, Vermont
Eligibility: Equity and non-Equity
Fees: $20 for Vermont residents and students, $30 for non-Vermonters
Format: Three minutes to present two monologues and an optional song (no accompanist)
Application Deadline: Varies
Info/Contact: www.vermonttheatre.com

StrawHat Auditions

Audition Dates: Mid-late March
Place: New York, New York
Eligibility: Non-Equity, at least 18 years old
Fees: $28, plus an additional $40 if you receive an audition slot
Format: Ninety seconds to present two pieces (monologues, songs, or both; accompanist provided), plus dance auditions
Application Deadline: Mid-late February
Info/Contact: StrawHat Auditions, 1771 Post Road East, #315, Westport, CT 06880; www.strawhat-auditions.com; info@strawhat-auditions.com

New Jersey Theatre Alliance

Audition Dates: Late August
Place: New Brunswick, New Jersey
Eligibility: Equity and non-Equity (with preference given to New Jersey residents)
Info/Contact: New Jersey Theatre Alliance, 163 Madison Avenue, Suite 500, Morristown, NJ 07960; www.njtheatrealliance.org; info@njtheatrealliance.org

Theatre Alliance of Greater Philadelphia

Audition Dates: Early June
Place: Philadelphia, Pennsylvania
Eligibility: Equity and non-Equity performers who live within 50 miles of downtown Philadelphia
Format: Three minutes to present two contrasting monologues or one monologue and a song
Application Deadline: Mid-March
Info/Contact: www.theatrealliance.org/auditions

Institute of Outdoor Drama

Audition Dates: Mid-March
Place: Chapel Hill, North Carolina
Eligibility: Equity and non-Equity (though most of the available roles are non-Equity), at least 18 years old
Fees: $30
Format: One-minute monologue or one-minute song (accompanist provided), plus dance auditions
Application Deadline: Early March
Info/Contact: Auditions Coordinator, Institute of Outdoor Drama, CB #3240, UNC-CH, Chapel Hill, NC 27599-3240; www.unc.edu/depts/outdoor/auditions; call (919) 962-1328, or e-mail outdoor@unc.edu

Southeastern Theatre Conference

Audition Dates: Early March
Place: Varies throughout the Southeast
Eligibility: Equity and non-Equity, at least 18 years old, not currently enrolled in school, available for full-time employment, having worked in at least two paid professional jobs, with the recommendation of a professional director
Fees: $135
Format: One minute for a monologue or song, or one and a half minutes for one of each (accompanist provided), plus dance auditions
Application Deadline: Mid-January
Info/Contact: SETC, P.O. Box 9868, Greensboro, NC 27429-0868; www.setc.org; call (336) 272-3645, or e-mail april@setc.org

Unified Professional Theatre Auditions

Audition Dates: Early February
Place: Memphis, Tennessee
Eligibility: Equity and Equity Membership Candidates, as well as non-Equity performers who either have a postgraduate degree in theatre, have the approval of a current or former UPTA theatre or a current TCG theatre, or have attended a previous UPTA
Fees: $25 before December 31; $40 afterwards
Format: Ninety seconds to present material, including at least one monologue (accompanist provided), plus dance auditions
Application Deadline: Late January
Info/Contact: Unified Professional Theatre Auditions, 51 South Cooper Street, Memphis, TN 38104; www.upta.org; call (901) 725-0776, or e-mail upta@upta.org

Ohio Theatre Alliance

Audition Dates: Late January–early February
Place: Springfield, Ohio
Eligibility: Equity and non-Equity, at least 18 years old (non-Equity requires the qualifying signature of a director or educator)
Fees: $40
Format: Ninety seconds for a monologue, song, or both (accompanist provided), plus dance auditions
Application Deadline: Mid-January
Info/Contact: www.ohiotheatrealliance.org

Indiana Theatre Association

Audition Dates: Early February
Place: Indianapolis, Indiana
Fees: $20
Format: Two minutes for a monologue or two and a half minutes for a song
Application Deadline: Late January
Info/Contact: ITAP, Office 227, 1035 Sanders Street, Indianapolis, IN 46203; www.intheatre.org; call (317) 634-4670, or e-mail itap@intheatre.org

Illinois Theatre Association

Audition Dates: Late February
Place: Chicago, Illinois
Eligibility: Students currently enrolled in an Illinois college, college students intending to move to Chicago, and non-Equity performers
Fees: $25 for ITA members, $30 for nonmembers
Format: Three minutes for two contrasting monologues or four minutes for two monologues and 16 bars of a song (accompanist provided)
Application Deadline: Mid-February
Info/Contact: www.iltheassoc.org; call (773) 929-7288, ext. 219, or e-mail iltheassoc@aol.com

National Dinner Theatre Association

Audition Dates: Mid-March
Place: Rock Island, Illinois
Eligibility: At least 18 years old with the endorsement of a professional director or producer
Fees: $35 (though the fee increases as the day of the event approaches)
Format: One-minute monologue and 16 bars of music
Application Deadline: None
Info/Contact: NDTA Audition Office, P.O. Box 726, Marshall, MI 49068; www.ndta.com; call (517) 857-3851, or e-mail KathyKopulos@aol.com

Theatre Auditions in Wisconsin

Audition Dates: Mid-February
Place: Madison, Wisconsin
Eligibility: Non-Equity
Fees: $18 for one performance category (actor, actor-singer, or dancer), $30 for two or more
Format: Two minutes for a monologue, two and a half minutes for a monologue and song (accompanist provided), plus dance auditions
Application Deadline: None
Info/Contact: www.dcs.wisc.edu/lsa/theatre/auditions.htm

Midwest Theatre Auditions

Audition Dates: Mid-late February
Place: St. Louis, Missouri
Eligibility: Equity and non-Equity, with the
signature of a professional director or theatre
educator
Fees: $30
Format: Ninety seconds for a monologue
and/or song (accompanist provided), plus
optional dance auditions
Application Deadline: Early December
Info/Contact:
www.webster.edu/depts/finearts/theatre/mwta04;
call (314) 968-6937, or e-mail
mwta@pop.webster.edu

Southwest Theatre Association

Audition Dates: Early November
Place: Plano, Texas
Info/Contact: www.southwest-theater.com

Rocky Mountain Theatre Association

Audition Dates: Early March
Place: Colorado
Eligibility: Equity and non-Equity actors no
longer in high school
Fees: $55–85
Format: Two minutes to present two contrasting
monologues, plus another 30 seconds for an
optional song (no accompanist)
Application Deadline: early February
Info/Contact: www.rmta.net

Northwest Drama Conference

Audition Dates: Mid-February
Place: Varies throughout the Northwest
Fees: $90–105; $60–75 for students
Format: Four minutes to present two contrasting
monologues, or five minutes for either two mono-
logues and a song or two songs and a monologue
(no accompanist)
Application Deadline: Late January
Info/Contact: www.cwu.edu/~nwdc/

Theatre Bay Area

Audition Dates: Late January
Place: San Francisco, California
Eligibility: Equity, as well as non-Equity performers
with at least one year of full-time training or eight
nonschool productions on their resume
Format: Three minutes for Equity performers or
two minutes for non-Equity to present whatever
they wish
Application Deadline: Early December
Info/Contact: www.theatrebayarea.org;
call (415) 430-1140, ext. 14, or e-mail
dale@theatrebayarea.org

Kennedy Center American College Theater Festival (Region VIII)

Audition Dates: Early–mid-February
Place: Varies throughout the West
Eligibility: Non-Equity
Fees: $20 (plus additional KCACTF fees)
Format: Three minutes to present monologues
and/or songs, plus dance auditions
Info/Contact: www.kcactf.org/nextstep/index.htm

League of Resident Theatres

The following is a list of theatres operating under Equity's LORT (League of Resident Theatres) contract. They are listed alphabetically according to state, by city within each state, and by theatre within each city. The letter that follows the name of each theatre (A, A+, B, B+, C, D, or Experimental) indicates the LORT category in which that theatre operates. Category is based on the certified actual weekly gross receipts averaged over the theatre's three fiscal years of 1999, 2000, and 2001. In some instances, theatre companies have two or more theatres, so therefore each theatre is categorized, which is why you might read two or more letters next to a company's name. Following the name of the company is its address, phone number, and the name of its key artistic or administrative personnel.

These are not the only Equity regional theatres. The 50 states are filled with Equity theatres that operate under Letters of Agreement (LOA) and Small Professional Theatre contracts (SPT). An all-inclusive list of those theatres would be too extensive to include here.

Alabama

ALABAMA SHAKESPEARE
FESTIVAL (C) (D)
1 Festival Drive
Montgomery, AL 36117
(334) 271-5300
Kent Thompson, artistic director
Alan Harrison, managing director
Mark Peoples, general manager

Arizona

ARIZONA THEATRE COMPANY
(B) (B)
40 E. 14 Street
Tucson, AZ 85701
(520) 884-8210
David Ira Goldstein, artistic director
Jessica L. Andrews, managing
  director

California

AMERICAN CONSERVATORY
THEATER (A)
30 Grant Avenue
San Francisco, CA 94108-5800
(415) 834-3200
Carey Perloff, artistic director
Heather Kitchen, managing
  director
James Haire, producing director

BERKELEY REPERTORY
THEATRE (B) (B)
2025 Addison Street
Berkeley, CA 94704
(510) 647-2900
box office (510) 647-2949
Tony Taccone, artistic director
Susie Medak, managing
  director

CALIFORNIA SHAKESPEARE
FESTIVAL (D)
701 Heinz Street
Berkeley, CA 94710
(510) 548-3422
Jonathan Mascone, artistic
  director
Debbie Chinn, managing
  director

CENTER THEATRE GROUP
(A) (EXP.)
MARK TAPER FORUM AND
THE AHMANSON THEATRE,
LOS ANGELES MUSIC
CENTER
601 W. Temple Street
Los Angeles, CA 90012
(213) 972-7353
Gordon Davidson, artistic
  director
Charles Dillingham, managing
  director

GEFFEN PLAYHOUSE (B)
10886 Le Conte Avenue
Los Angeles, CA 90024
(310) 208-6500
Gilbert Cates, producing director
Randall Arney, artistic director
Stephen Eich, managing director

LA JOLLA PLAYHOUSE (B) (B)
PO Box 12039
La Jolla, CA 92039
(858) 550-1070
Des McAnuff, artistic director
Terrence Dwyer, managing director

LAGUNA PLAYHOUSE (B)
PO Box 1747
Laguna Beach, CA 92652
(949) 497-5900
Andrew Barnicle, artistic
  director
Richard Stein, executive
  director

THE OLD GLOBE (B) (B) (D)
THE OLD GLOBE THEATRE,
CASSIUS CARTER CENTER
STAGE, AND THE LOWELL
DAVIES FESTIVAL THEATRE
PO Box 122171
San Diego, CA 92112-2171
(619) 231-1941
Jack O'Brien, artistic director
Lou Spisto, executive director

PASADENA PLAYHOUSE
(B) (D)
39 South El Molino
Pasadena, CA 91101-5220
Mailing Address:
80 S. Lake Avenue, Suite 500
Pasadena, CA 91101-2023
(626) 792-8672
Sheldon Epps, artistic director
Lyla White, executive director

SAN JOSE REPERTORY
THEATRE (C)
101 Paseo de San Antonio
San Jose, CA 95113
(408) 367-7266
Timothy Near, artistic director
Alexandra Urbanowski, managing
  director

SHAKESPEARE
FESTIVAL/LA (D)
1238 West First Street
Los Angeles, CA 90026
(213) 481-2273
Ben Donenberg, artistic director
Sara Adelman, director of
  operations

SOUTH COAST REPERTORY
THEATRE (B) (D)
PO Box 2197
Costa Mesa, CA 92628
(714) 708-5500
David Emmes, producing
  artistic director
Martin Benson, artistic
  director
Paula Tomei, managing
  director

Colorado

ARVADA CENTER FOR THE
ARTS (C)
6901 Wadsworth Blvd.
Arvada, CO 80003-3499
(270) 898-7286
Deborah Elerman, producer
Rod Lansberry, associate
producer

DENVER CENTER THEATRE
COMPANY (B) (C) (D)
1050 13 Street
Denver, CO 80204
(303) 893-4000
Donovan Marley, artistic director

Connecticut

EUGENE O'NEILL MEMORIAL
THEATRE CENTER (D)
(Includes: The O'Neill Playwrights
Conference; The O'Neill Music
Theater Conference; and the
O'Neill Puppetry Conference)
305 Great Neck Rd.
Waterford, CT 06385
(860) 443-5378
Amy Sullivan, executive director
Thomas Viertel, chairman
J Ranelli, artistic director of
the O'Neill Playwrights
Conference
Paulette Haupt, artistic director
of the O'Neill Music
Conference
Pam Arciero, artistic director of
the O'Neill Puppetry
Conference
George White, founder

GOODSPEED MUSICALS (B) (D)
GOODSPEED OPERA HOUSE
Box A
East Haddam, CT 06423
(860) 873-8664
and
GOODSPEED-AT-CHESTER/THE
NORMA TERRIS THEATRE
200 N. Main Street
Chester, CT
Michael Price, executive and
artistic director
Sue Frost, associate producer

HARTFORD STAGE
COMPANY (B)
50 Church Street
Hartford, CT 06103
(860) 525-5601
Michael Wilson, artistic director
James D. Ireland, managing
director

LONG WHARF THEATRE (B) (C)
222 Sargent Drive
New Haven, CT 06511
(203) 787-4284
Gordon Edelstein, artistic director
Michael Stotts, managing
director

YALE REPERTORY
THEATRE (D) (D)
PO Box 208244
New Haven, CT 06520-8244
(203) 432-1234
James Bundy, artistic director
Victoria Nolan, managing director

Delaware

DELAWARE THEATRE
COMPANY (D)
200 Water Street
Wilmington, DE 19801
(302) 594-1104
(Ms.) Fontaine Syer, artistic
director
John Grassilli, associate
artistic director
Rebecca Frederick, managing
director

District Of Columbia

ARENA STAGE (B+) (B) (D)
1101 6th Street S.W.
Washington, DC 20024
(202) 554-9066
www.arenastage.org
Molly Smith, artistic director
Stephen Richard, executive
director
Guy Bergquist, managing
director

THE SHAKESPEARE
THEATRE (B+)
516 8th Street, S.E.
Washington, DC 20003-2834
(202) 547-3230
Michael Kahn, artistic director
Nicholas T. Goldsborough,
managing director
Mike Curry, director of
production

Florida

ASOLO THEATRE
COMPANY (C) (D)
5555 North Tamiami Trail
Sarasota, FL 34243
(941) 351-9010
Howard Millman, producing
artistic director
Linda Di Gabriele, managing
director

CALDWELL THEATRE
COMPANY (C)
7873 N. Federal Hwy.
Boca Raton, FL 33429-0277
(561) 241-7380
Michael Hall, artistic director
Patricia Burdett, company
manager

COCONUT GROVE
PLAYHOUSE (B) (D)
3500 Main Hwy.
Miami, FL 33133
(305) 442-2662
Arnold Mittelman, producing
artistic director

FLORIDA STAGE (C)
262 S. Ocean Blvd.
Manalapan, FL 33462
(561) 585-3404
Louis Tyrell, producing
director
Nancy Barnett, managing
director

RIVERSIDE THEATRE (D)
3250 Riverside Park Drive
Vero Beach, FL 32963
(772) 231-5860
Allen D. Cornell, artistic
director
Chuck Still, executive
director

Georgia

ALLIANCE THEATRE
COMPANY (B) (D)
1280 Peachtree Street N.E.
Atlanta, GA 30309
(404) 733-4650
Susan V. Booth, artistic
director
Thomas Pechar, managing
director

GEORGIA SHAKESPEARE
FESTIVAL (D)
4484 Peachtree Rd. N.E.
Atlanta, GA 30319
(404) 264-0020
Richard Garner, producing
artistic director
Robert Fass, managing director

Illinois

COURT THEATRE (D)
5535 S. Ellis
Chicago, IL 60637
(773) 702-7005
Charles Newell, artistic director
Diane Claussen, executive
director

GOODMAN THEATRE
COMPANY (B+) (C)
170 N. Dearborn
Chicago, IL 60601
(312) 443-3811
Robert Falls, artistic director
Roche Schulfer, executive
    director
Katherine Murphy, general
    manager

THE NORTHLIGHT
THEATRE, INC. (C)
NORTH SHORE CENTER
FOR THE PERFORMING
ARTS
9501 N. Skokie Blvd.
Skokie, IL 60077
(847) 679-9501
B.J. Jones, artistic director
Phil Santora, managing
    director

Indiana

INDIANA REPERTORY
THEATRE (C)
140 W. Washington Street
Indianapolis, IN 46204-3465
(317) 635-5277
Janet Allen, artistic director
Daniel Baker, managing
    director

Kentucky

ACTORS THEATRE OF
LOUISVILLE (B) (D) (D)
316 W. Main Street
Louisville, KY 40202
(502) 584-1265
Marc Masterson, artistic
    director
Sandy Speer, executive
    director

Maine

PORTLAND STAGE
COMPANY (D)
PO Box 1458
Portland, ME 04104
(207) 774-1043
Anita Stewart, artistic director

Maryland

CENTER STAGE (B) (D)
700 N. Calvert Street
Baltimore, MD 21202
(410) 685-3200
Irene Lewis, artistic director
Michael Ross, managing
    director

Massachusetts

AMERICAN REPERTORY
THEATRE CO. (B) (D)
LOEB DRAMA CENTER
64 Brattle Street
Cambridge, MA 02138
(617) 495-2668
Robert Orchard, executive
    director
Robert Woodruff, artistic
    director
Robert Brustein, founder &
    creative consultant

BERKSHIRE THEATRE
FESTIVAL (B)
PO Box 797
Stockbridge, MA 01262
(413) 298-5536
Kate Maguire, executive
    director

HUNTINGTON THEATRE
COMPANY (B+)
BOSTON UNIVERSITY
    THEATRE
264 Huntington Avenue
Boston, MA 02115
(617) 266-7900
Nicholas Martin, artistic
    director
Michael Maso, managing
    director

MERRIMACK REPERTORY
THEATRE (D)
132 Warren Street
Lowell, MA 01852
(978) 654-7550
Charles Towers, artistic
    director
Lisa Merrill-Burzak, managing
    director
Edgar Cyrus, general manager

Michigan

MEADOW BROOK
THEATRE (D)
OAKLAND UNIVERSITY
Rochester, MI 48309-4448
(248) 370-3310
David Regal, artistic director
Gregg Bloomfield, managing
    director

Minnesota

THE GUTHRIE THEATER (A) (D)
725 Vineland Place
Minneapolis, MN 55403
(612) 347-1100
Joe Dowling, artistic director
Tom Proehl, managing director

ORDWAY CENTER FOR
PERFORMING ARTS (C)
345 Washington Street
St. Paul, MN 55102-1495
(651) 282-3000
www.ordway.org
David M. Galligan, president &
    CEO
Lynn A. Von Eschen, vice
    president of programming &
    marketing
Mary McColl, vice president &
    general manager

Missouri

MISSOURI REPERTORY
THEATRE (B)
4949 Cherry Street
Kansas City, MO 64110
(816) 235-2727
Peter Altman, artistic director
Bill Prenevost, managing
    director
Laurie Jarrett, business
    manager

THE REPERTORY THEATRE
OF ST. LOUIS (B+) (D)
PO Box 191730
130 Edgar Rd.
St. Louis, MO 63119
(314) 968-7340
Steven Woolf, artistic director
Mark Bernstein, managing
    director

New Jersey

GEORGE STREET
PLAYHOUSE (C)
9 Livingston Avenue
New Brunswick, NJ 08901
(732) 846-2895
David Saint, artistic director
Mitchell Krieger, managing
    director
George Ryan, producing director

McCARTER THEATRE
COMPANY (B+) (D)
91 University Place
Princeton, NJ 08540
(609) 258-6500
Emily Mann, artistic director
Jeffrey Woodward, managing
    director

SHAKESPEARE THEATRE OF
NEW JERSEY (C) (D) (D)
36 Madison Avenue
Madison, NJ 07940
(973) 408-3278
Bonnie J. Monte, artistic director

New Mexico

SANTA FE STAGES (D)
422 West San Francisco Street
Santa Fe, NM 87501
(505) 982-6680
Craig Strong, producing
    director

New York

THE ACTING COMPANY (C) (D)
Mailing address:
PO Box 898
Times Square Station
New York, NY 10108
And offices at:
690 Eighth Avenue, Third fl.
New York, NY 10036
(212) 258-3111
www.theactingcompany.org
Margot Harley, producing
    artistic director
Jared Hammond, general
    manager

BAY STREET THEATRE (C)
PO Box 810
Sag Harbor, NY 11963
(631) 725-0818
Sybil Christopher & Emma
    Walton, co-artistic
    directors

CAPITAL REPERTORY
THEATRE (D)
111 N. Pearl Street
Albany, NY 12207
(518) 462-4531
Maggie Mancinelli-Cahill,
    artistic director
Jeff Dannick, managing
    director

GEVA THEATRE (B) (D)
75 Woodbury Blvd.
Rochester, NY 14607
(716) 232-1366
Mark Cuddy, artistic director
Nan Hildebrandt, executive
    director
John Quinlivan, managing
    director

HELEN HAYES ARTS
CENTER (D)
117 Main Street, Suite 13
Nyack, NY 10960
(845) 358-2847
Mary Oleniczak, executive
    director
Tony Stimac, artistic
    director
Marilyn Stimac, associate
    producer

LINCOLN CENTER THEATER
COMPANY (A) (B)
150 W. 65th Street
New York, NY 10023
(212) 362-7600
Bernard Gersten, executive
    producer
Andre Bishop, artistic director
Adam Siegel, general manager

MANHATTAN THEATRE
CLUB (B) (D)
311 W. 43 Street, Eighth fl.
New York, NY 10036
(212) 399-3000
www.manhattantheatreclub.com
Barry Grove, executive producer
Lynne Meadow, artistic director

NATIONAL ACTORS
THEATRE (B)
c/o Pace University
1 Pace Plaza
New York, NY 10038
(212) 748-3490
info@nationalactorstheatre.com
Tony Randall, founder & artistic
    director
Fred Walker, managing director
Manny Kladitis, general
    manager

PEARL THEATRE
COMPANY, INC. (D)
80 St. Marks Place
New York, NY 10003
(212) 505-3401
Shepard Sobel, artistic director

THE PUBLIC THEATER (B)
425 Lafayette Street
New York, NY 10003
(212) 539-8500
George C. Wolfe, producer
Mara Manus, executive director
Michael Hurst, managing
    director

ROUNDABOUT THEATRE
COMPANY (A+)
231 W. 39 Street, Suite 1200
New York, NY 10018
(212) 719-9393
Todd Haimes, artistic director
Ellen Richard, managing director
Julia Levy, director of external
    affairs

STUDIO ARENA THEATRE (B)
710 Main Street
Buffalo, NY 14202-1990
(716) 856-8025
Gavin Cameron-Webb, artistic
    director
Ken Neufeld, executive director

SYRACUSE STAGE (C)
JOHN D. ARCHBOLD THEATRE
820 E. Genesee Street
Syracuse, NY 13210-1508
(315) 443-4008
Robert Moss, artistic director
James A. Clark, producing director
Diana Coles, administative
    director

THEATRE FOR A NEW
AUDIENCE (D)
154 Christopher Street, Suite 3D
New York, NY 10014
(212) 229-2819
Jeffrey Horowitz, artistic director
Jessica Niebanck, general
    manager

North Carolina

CHARLOTTE REPERTORY
THEATRE (D)
129 W. Trade Street, Suite 401
Charlotte, NC 28202
(704) 333-8587
Michael Bush, producing artistic
    director
Matt Olin, managing director

NORTH CAROLINA
SHAKESPEARE FESTIVAL (D)
PO Box 6066
High Point, NC 27262
(336) 841-2273
Pedro Silva, managing director &
    interim artistic director

PLAYMAKERS REPERTORY
COMPANY (D)
Campus Box 3235
Center for Dramatic Art
UNC Campus
Chapel Hill, NC 27599
(919) 962-1122
David Hammond, artistic director
Donna Heins, managing director

Ohio

CINCINNATI PLAYHOUSE IN
THE PARK (B+) (C)
PO Box 6537
Cincinnati, OH 45206
(513) 345-2242
Edward Stern, artistic director
Buzz Ward, producing director

CLEVELAND PLAY HOUSE
(C) (C) (D) (C)
8500 Euclid Avenue
Cleveland, OH 44106
(216) 795-7000
Peter Hackett, artistic director
Dean Gladden, managing director

GREAT LAKES THEATER
FESTIVAL (B)
1501 Euclid Avenue,
   Suite 423
Cleveland, OH 44115
(216) 241-5490
Charles Fee, producing artistic
   director
Greg Quinlan, production
   manager

Oregon

OREGON SHAKESPEARE
FESTIVAL (B+) (B+) (D)
15 S. Pioneer Street
PO Box 158
Ashland, OR 97520
(541) 482-2111
www.osfashland.org
Libby Appel, artistic director
Paul E. Nicholson, executive
   director
*(Contract negotiated inde-
pendently with Equity, not
with LORT.)*

PORTLAND CENTER
STAGE (B)
PORTLAND CENTER FOR
THE PERFORMING ARTS
1111 Southwest Broadway
Portland, OR 97205
(503) 248-6309
Chris Coleman, artistic director

Pennsylvania

ARDEN THEATRE
COMPANY (D) (D)
40 N. Second Street
Philadelphia, PA 19106
(215) 922-8900
Terrence J. Nolen, producing
   artistic director
Amy L. Murphy, managing
   director

CITY THEATRE (D)
1300 Bingham Street
Pittsburgh, PA 15203
(412) 431-4400
Tracy Brigden, artistic director
David Jobin, managing
   director

THE PEOPLES LIGHT &
THEATRE COMPANY (D) (D)
39 Conestoga Rd.
Malvern, PA 19355
(610) 647-1900
Abigail Adams, artistic director
Grace Grillet, managing
   director

PHILADELPHIA THEATRE
COMPANY (D)
Mailing Address:
230 S. 15 Street, Fourth fl.
Philadelphia, PA 19102
And theatre at:
1714 Delancey Street
(215) 985-1400
Sara Garonzik, producing
   artistic director
Ada G. Coppock, general
   manager

PITTSBURGH
PUBLIC THEATRE
ST THE O'REILLY
THEATRE (B)
621 Penn Avenue
Pittsburgh, PA 15222
(412) 316-8200
Ted Pappas, artistic &
   executive director

PRINCE MUSIC THEATER (D)
100 S. Broad Street,
   Suite 650
Philadelphia, PA 19110
(215) 972-1000
Marjorie Samoff, producing
   artistic director
Joseph Farina, managing
   director

WALNUT STREET
THEATRE (A) (D)
825 Walnut Street
Philadelphia, PA 19107-5107
(215) 574-3550
Bernard Havard, producing
   artistic director
Mark Sylvester, managing
   director

WILMA THEATRE (C)
265 South Broad Street
Philadelphia, PA 19107
(215) 893-9456
Blanka Zizka, Jiri Zizka,
   co-artistic/producing
   directors
Lynn Landis, managing director

Rhode Island

TRINITY REPERTORY
COMPANY (B) (D)
201 Washington Street
Providence, RI 02903
(401) 521-1100
Oskar Eustis, artistic director
Edgar Dobie, managing
   director
Ruth Sternberg, production
   director

Tennessee

CLARENCE BROWN
THEATRE (D) (D)
University of Tennessee
Dept. of Theatre
206 McClung Tower
Knoxville, TN 37996-0420
(865) 974-6011
Blake Robison, producing
   artistic director
Tom Cervone, managing
   director

TENNESSEE REPERTORY
THEATRE (C) (D)
PO Box 198768
Nashville, TN 37219
(615) 782-4000
www.tnrep.org
David Grapes, producing
   artistic director

Texas

ALLEY THEATRE (B) (C)
615 Texas Avenue
Houston, TX 77002
(713) 228-9341
Gregory Boyd, artistic
   director
Paul R. Tetreault, managing
   director

DALLAS THEATER
CENTER (C) (C) (D)
3636 Turtle Creek Blvd.
Dallas, TX 75219
(214) 526-8210
Richard Hamburger, artistic
   director

Utah

PIONEER THEATRE
COMPANY (B)
University of Utah
300 S. 1400 E., Rm. 325
Salt Lake City, UT 84112-0660
(801) 581-6356
Charles Morey, artistic
   director
Christopher Lino, managing
   director

UTAH SHAKESPEAREAN
FESTIVAL (B+) (B+)
351 West Center
Cedar City, UT 84720-2498
Admin. (435) 586-7880
Fred C. Adams, founder &
   executive producer
R. Scott Philips, managing
   director

Virginia

BARTER THEATRE (D) (D)
PO Box 867
Abingdon, VA 24212
(276) 628-2281
Richard Rose, artistic
director
Joan Ballou, business
manager

VIRGINIA STAGE
COMPANY (D)
Mailing Address:
PO Box 3770
Norfolk, VA 23514
And offices at:
254 Granby Street
Norfolk, VA 23510
(757) 627-6988
Charlie Hensley, producing
director
Robert Chelimsky, managing
director
Catherine Pritchard, company
manager

Washington

ACT THEATRE (C) (B)
*(formerly A Contemporary
Theatre)*
Kreielsheimer Place
700 Union Street
Seattle, WA 98101
(206) 292-7660
Kurt Beattie, artistic director

INTIMAN THEATRE (C)
PO Box 19760
Seattle, WA 98109
(206) 269-1901
Bartlett Sher, artistic director
Laura Penn, managing director

SEATTLE REPERTORY
THEATRE (B+) (C)
BAGLEY WRIGHT THEATRE &
LEO KREIELSHEIMER THEATRE
155 Mercer Street
PO Box 900923
Seattle, WA 98109
(206) 443-2210
Sharon Ott, artistic director
Benjamin Moore, managing
director

West Virginia

CONTEMPORARY
AMERICAN THEATER
FESTIVAL (D) (D)
PO Box 429
Shepherdstown, WV 25443
(304) 876-3473
(800) 999-2283
Ed Herendeen, founding and
producing director
Catherine Irwin, managing
director

Wisconsin

MILWAUKEE REPERTORY
THEATER (B) (D) (D) (A)
108 E. Wells Street
Milwaukee, WI 53202
(414) 224-1761
Joseph Hanreddy, artistic
director
Tim Shields, managing
director
Diane Dalton, general
manager

Off- & Off-Off-Broadway Theatre Companies

COMPILED BY B.L. RICE

Following is a list of Off- and Off-Off-Broadway theatre companies in New York City. Each listing contains the name of the company and its contact information and, if available, (1) name(s) of company staff members (2) photo & resume acceptance policy, and (3) Equity affiliation(s).

Back Stage sent out questionnaires to theatre companies in order to update its list. An asterisk (*) indicates that the company did not respond to either the questionnaire and/or follow-up phone calls.

ABINGDON THEATRE COMPANY, INC.
312 W. 36 Street, First fl.
New York, NY 10018
(212) 868-2055
fax (212) 868-2056
ATCNYC@aol.com
www.abingdon-nyc.org
Jan Buttram and Pamela Paul, artistic directors
Samuel J. Bellinger, managing director
Kim T. Sharp, associate artistic director
Send pix & resumes directly to co.?: Yes
Usually casts/accepts pix & resumes: Year-round and at EPAs.
Equity Showcase or Tiered Showcase

THE ABSINTHE-MINDED THEATRE COMPANY
1484 Stadium Avenue
Bronx, NY 10465
(212) 714-4696
fax (914) 779-7494
rscarp@aol.com
Ralph Scarpato, founder & managing director
Send pix & resumes directly to co.?: Yes
Usually casts/accepts pix & resumes: Year-round.
Manhattan performances.
Equity Showcase
Non-Equity

ACCESS THEATER
380 Broadway, Fourth fl.
New York, NY 10013
(212) 966-1047
fax (212) 966-9790
theater@Accesstheater.com
www.accesstheater.com
Margarett Perry, producing director
Jacqueline Christy, artistic director
Send pix & resume directly to co.?: No
Usually casts/accepts pix & resumes: Prior to show, during casting session.
Equity Showcase

THE ACTING COMPANY
PO Box 898
Times Square Station
New York, NY 10108
Office address:
630 Ninth Avenue, #214
New York, NY 10036
(212) 258-3111
fax (212) 258-3299
mail@theactingcompany.org
www.theactingcompany.org
Margot Harley, producing artistic director
Send pix & resumes directly to co.?: Yes
Usually casts/accepts pix & resumes: Year-round.
Equity Off-Broadway contract
Equity Letter of Agreement

THE ACTORS COLLECTIVE
447 W. 48 Street, Suite 1E
New York, NY 10036
(212) 956-9456
Catherine Russell, managing director
Send pix & resumes directly to co.?: No
Usually casts/accepts pix & resumes: Several times a year as needed.
Equity Off-Broadway contract
Equity Showcase or Tiered Showcase

(TACT) THE ACTORS' COMPANY THEATRE
at The Field
161 Sixth Avenue, 14th fl.
New York, NY 10013
(212) 645-TACT (8228)
fax (212) 462-2678
INFO@TACTNYC.ORG
www.tactnyc.org
Scott Alan Evans, Cynthia Harris, Simon Jones, co-artistic directors
Kate Ross, general manager
Send pix & resumes directly to co.?: Yes
Usually casts/accepts pix & resumes: As needed.
Company works under Equity agreement similar to the Equity Showcase Code.

ACTORS OF THE WORLD
128 W. 70 Street, #8
New York, NY 10023
(212) 721-3576
actorsoftheworld@cs.com
Marco Aponte, artistic director
Lance Lattig, managing director
Send pix & resumes directly to co.? Yes
Usually casts: Spring, summer, and fall
Non-Equity

THE ACTORS THEATRE WORKSHOP
145 W. 28 Street, Third fl.
New York, NY 10001
(212) 947-1386
fax (212) 947-0642
info@actorstheatreworkshop
www.ActorsTheatreWorkshop.com
Thurman E. Scott, artistic director and founder
Janet Marie Scott, general manager
Send pix & resumes directly to co.?: Yes
Usually casts/accepts pix & resumes:
    Anytime.
Equity Off-Broadway contract
Equity Letter of Agreement
Equity Showcase or Tiered Showcase
Non-Equity

*ADOBE THEATRE COMPANY
138 South Oxford Street
Brooklyn, NY 11217
(212) 477-3661
Jeremy@adobe.org
www.adobe.org
Jeremy Dobrish, artistic director
Christopher Roberts, producing director
Send pix & resumes directly to co.?: No
Usually casts: Year-round.
Equity Showcase or Tiered Showcase

AGRIPPINA PRODUCTIONS
101-68 105 Street
Ozone Park, NY 11416-2709
(212) 229-7672
Bernard Lucchesi, artistic director
Arlean Fackina, managing director
Send pix & resumes directly to co.?: Yes
Usually casts/accepts pix & resumes: Anytime;
    also accepts all types of scripts and resumes
    from directors and tech people.
Casting director: Bernard Lucchesi
Equity Showcase or Tiered Showcase
Non-Equity

AMAS MUSICAL THEATRE INC.
450 W. 42 Street, Suite 2J
New York, NY 10036
(212) 563-2565
fax (212) 268-5501
amas@amasmusical.org
www.amasmusical.org
Also has Teen Performance Program
Rosetta LeNoire, founder
Donna Trinkoff, producing director
Send pix & resumes directly to co.?: Yes
Usually casts/accepts pix & resumes: Yes
Equity Letter of Agreement

AMERICAN GLOBE THEATRE
145 W. 46 Street, Third fl.
New York, NY 10036
(212) 869-9809
fax (212) 869-9807
John@americanglobe.org
www.americanglobe.org

John Basil, producing artistic director
Elizabeth Keefe, executive director
Send pix & resumes directly to co.?: Yes
Equity Showcase or Tiered Showcase

AMERICAN INDIAN
COMMUNITY HOUSE
Office address:
708 Broadway, Eighth fl.
New York, NY 10003
Theatre space at The Circle (not a mailing
    address):
404 Lafayette Street, Eighth fl.
New York, NY
(212) 598-0100
fax (212) 598-4909
peraaich@aol.com
www.aich.org
Jim Cyrus, director of performing arts
Rosemary Richmond, executive director
Send pix & resumes directly to co.?: Yes
Usually casts/accepts pix & resumes:
    Year-round.
Equity Showcase or Tiered Showcase
Non-Equity

THE AMERICAN PLACE THEATRE
266 W. 37 Street, 22nd fl.
New York, NY 10018
(212) 594-4482 ext. 10
fax (212) 594-4208
vsparling@americanplacetheatre.org
www.americanplacetheatre.org
Wynn Handman, founder & artistic director
David Kener, executive director
Send pix & resumes directly to co.?: No
Equity Off-Broadway contract

AMERICAN PLAYWRIGHTS THEATRE
Attn: Dr. Ronni Aramowitz
c/o English Dept.
New York City College of Technology
300 Jay Street
Brooklyn, NY 11201
Amerplath@juno.com
www.americanplaywrightstheatre.org
Send pix & resumes directly to co.?: No
Usually casts/accept pix & resumes: When
    advertised.
Equity Showcase or Tiered Showcase
Non-Equity

AMERICAN THEATRE OF
ACTORS, INC.
314 W. 54 Street
New York, NY 10019
(212) 581-3044
James Jennings, artistic director
Send pix & resumes directly to co.?: Yes
Usually casts/accepts pix & resumes: Anytime
    (casts twice a month).
Casting: James Jennings
Equity Letter of Agreement
Non-Equity

AMERICAN THEATRE OF HARLEM
PO Box 1618
Morningside Station
New York, NY 10026
(212) 414-5144
info@americantheatreofharlem.org
www.americantheatreofharlem.org
Dawn Bennett, president
Bill Johnson, vice president
Keith Johnston, artistic director
Send pix & resumes directly to co.?: Yes
Usually casts/accepts pix & resumes:
    Winter/spring productions.
Equity Letter of Agreement
Equity Showcase or Tiered Showcase
Non-Equity

AMERICAN THYMELE THEATRE (ATT)
1202 Lexington Avenue, #138
New York, NY 10028
(212) 781-3631 (also fax)
compphilus@aol.com
Stephen Diacrussi, founder
Michael Roche, managing director
Send pix & resumes directly to co.?: Yes
Usually casts: Around Oct. 15.
Equity Off-Broadway contract
Equity Letter of Agreement
Equity Showcase or Tiered Showcase
Non-Equity

ANIMATED THEATERWORKS, INC.
240 Central Park South
New York, NY 10019
(212) 757-5085
fax (212) 247-3826
Elysabeth Kleinhans, director
ek@animatedtheaterworks.org
www.animatedtheaterworks.org
Send pix & resumes directly to co.?: Yes
Usually casts/accepts pix & resumes: Cast
    per production; accept pix & resumes
    anytime.
Equity Showcase or Tiered Showcase
Non-Equity

AQUILA THEATRE COMPANY
58 W. 10 Street
New York, NY 10011
aquilausa6@aol.com
www.aquilatheatre.com
Peter Meineck, producing artistic director
Robert Richmond, associate artistic director
Nate Terracio, general manager
Send pix & resumes directly to co.?: Yes
Usually casts/accepts pix & resumes:
    Ongoing.
Note: Also has an Equity/AGMA Agreement.
Equity Off-Broadway contract
Equity Letter of Agreement
Equity Showcase or Tiered Showcase
Non-Equity

ARTGROUP (A REGIONAL THEATRE
GROUP, INC.)
PO Box 1751
Murray Hill Station
New York, NY 10156-1751
(212) 229-7556
AnArtgroup@aol.com
www.ARTGroupNewYork.cjb.net
Ray L'Dera, executive director
Gordona L'Dera, artistic director
Tracy Walsch, literary manager
Send pix & resumes directly to co.?: No.
    No headshot file.
Usually casts/accepts pix & resumes:
    Auditions only. Throughout the year.
    See website for casting policies.
Non-Equity

ATLANTIC THEATER COMPANY
336 W. 20 Street
New York, NY 10011
(212) 691-5919
fax (212) 645-8755
www.atlantictheater.org
Neil Pepe, artistic director
Send pix & resumes directly to co.?: No
Equity Off-Broadway contract
Equity Letter of Agreement

THE BARROW GROUP
312 W. 36 Street, 4 West
New York, NY 10018
(212) 760-2615
fax (212) 760-2962
barrowgroup@earthlink.net
www.barrowgroup.org
Seth Barrish & Lee Brock, artistic
    directors
Eric Paeper, managing director
Send pix & resumes directly co.?: No
Usually casts/accepts pix & resumes:
    Show by show.
Equity Showcase or Tiered
    Showcase

THE BAT THEATER COMPANY
c/o The Flea Theater
41 White Street
New York, NY 10013
(212) 226-0051
fax (212) 965-1808
katyas@theflea.org
www.theflea.org
Jim Simpson, artistic director
Carol Ostrow, producing director
Send pix & resumes directly to co.?: No
Usually casts/accept pix & resumes:
    At time of audition.
Equity Off-Broadway contract
Equity Letter of Agreement
Equity Showcase or Tiered Showcase
Non-Equity

*BLACK SPECTRUM THEATRE
COMPANY, INC.
177 Street and Baisley Blvd.
Jamaica, NY 11434
(718) 723-1800
Carl Clay, executive producer
Non-Equity

BLUE HERON THEATRE, INC.
123 E. 24 Street
New York, NY 10010
(212) 979-5000
fax (212) 979-8144
ardelle@blueheron-nyc.org
www.blueheron-nyc.org
Ardelle Striker, artistic director
Send pix & resumes directly to co.?: Yes
Usually casts/accepts pix & resumes:
    Ongoing.
Equity Showcase or Tiered Showcase

*BLUNT THEATER COMPANY
232 Meserole Street, #25
Brooklyn, NY 11206
(212) 330-7702
blunttheater@go.com
Kenneth Garson, executive producing
    director
Sheila Morgan, artistic director
Send pix & resumes directly to co.?: No
Usually casts/accepts pix & resumes:
    Show-by-show basis.
Equity Showcase or Tiered Showcase
Non-Equity

BOND STREET THEATRE
2 Bond Street
New York, NY 10012
(212) 254-4614
info@bondst.org
www.bondst.org
Joanna Sherman, artistic director
Michael McGuigan, managing director
Send pix & resumes directly to co.?: Yes
Usually casts/accepts pix & resumes: All year.
Casting: Artistic director casts for ensemble
    members.
Equity Showcase or Tiered Showcase
Non-Equity

BOOMERANG THEATER COMPANY
PO Box 237166
Ansonia Station
New York, NY 10023
(212) 501-4069
info@boomerangtheatre.org
www.boomerangtheatre.org
Tim Errickson, artistic director
Rachel Wood, associate artistic director
Send pix & resumes directly to co.? Yes
Usually casts/accepts pix & resumes: In
    April/May each year.
Equity Showcase or Tiered Showcase

BREAK A LEG PRODUCTIONS
PO Box 20503
Dag Hammarskjold Convenience Center
New York, NY 10017
(212) 330-0406
fax (212) 750-8341
www.breakalegproductions.com
Teri Black, founder/artistic director
Peter Blaxill, associate artistic director
Send pix & resumes directly to co.?: Yes
Usually casts/accepts pix & resumes: Ongoing.
Equity Showcase or Tiered Showcase

BROADWAY TOMORROW
191 Claremont Avenue, Suite 53
New York, NY 10027
(212) 531-2447
btomorrow@juno.com
www.solministry.com
Elyse Curtis, artistic director
Send pix & resumes directly to co.?: No
Usually casts: At auditions.
Equity Showcase or Tiered Showcase
Non-Equity

BROKEN WATCH PRODUCTIONS, INC.
201 E. 30 Street, Suite #61
New York, NY 10016
(212) 496-3743
fax (775) 263-6024
contact@brokenwatch.org
www.brokenwatch.org
Drew DeCorleto, artistic director
Send pix & resumes directly to co.?:
    No unsolicited pix & resumes.
Usually casts: Summer/winter.
Equity Mini Contract
Equity Letter of Agreement

CARIBBEAN AMERICAN REPERTORY
THEATRE, INC.
114-13 Ovid Place
St. Albans, NY 11412
(718) 454-3180
shawcart@aol.com
www.offbroadwayonline.com
Pat Bevan, artistic director
Send pix & resumes directly to co.?
    Send to above office address.
Equity Contract
Equity Showcase

CASTILLO THEATRE
543 W. 42 Street
New York, NY 10036
(212) 941-5800
fax (212) 941-8340
castilloth@aol.com
www.castillo.org
Fred Newman, artistic director
Gabrielle Kurlander, producing director
Diane Stiles, managing director
Kenneth Hughes, casting director

Dan Friedman, dramaturg
Send pix & resumes directly to co.?: Yes
Usually casts/accepts pix & resumes:
    1–2 times/year.
Casting director: Kenneth Hughes,
    c/o Castillo Theatre at above address.
Non-Equity

**CENTER STAGE COMMUNITY
PLAYHOUSE, INC.**
Mailing address:
PO Box 138
Westchester Square Station
Bronx, NY 10461
Theatre address:
2474 Westchester Avenue
Bronx, NY 10461
(212) 823-6434
info@centerstageplayhouse.org
www.centerstageplayhouse.org
Donna Bellone, president
Send pix & resumes directly to co.?: No
Non-Equity
*Membership organization; $20 yearly
membership dues.*

CHAMELEON THEATRE CO., LTD.
English Rose Theatricals
25-26 42 Street, Suite #3B
Astoria, NY 11103
(718) 204-9763
Robert D. Carver, artistic director/dramaturg
Philip Langer, producer/development
    director
Michael Foutch, producer
Cash Tilton, associate artistic director
Send pix & resumes directly to co.? Yes
Usually casts: Year-round.
Equity Special Agreement contract

CHEKHOV THEATRE ENSEMBLE
138 South Oxford Street, #1-B
Brooklyn, NY 11217
(718) 398-2494
www.stagesoflearning.org
Floyd Rumohr, artistic director
Send pix & resumes directly to co.?: Yes;
    send to Attn: Casting.
Usually casts/accepts pix & resumes: Only
    when casting project. Pix sent at other
    times will not be kept on file.
Equity Showcase Code

**THE MICHAEL CHEKHOV THEATRE &
COMPANY**
70 University Place, #5
New York, NY 10033
(212) 505-8068
Michael Horn, managing director
Ann Bowen, artistic director
Send pix & resumes directly to co.?: Yes
Usually casts/accepts pix & resumes:
    Quarterly; accepts pix & resumes always.

Equity Showcase or Tiered Showcase
Non-Equity
*This is a membership company; dues
are $50 per month to cover production
costs.*

CHICAGO CITY LIMITS
1105 First Avenue
New York, NY 10021
(212) 888-5233
info@chicagocitylimits.com
www.chicagocitylimits.com
Paul Zuckerman, executive producer and
    artistic director
Send pix & resumes directly to co.?: Yes
*Note that the company will notify via email
about upcoming auditions, if performers
go to website, sign up for mailing list,
and list auditioning as one of their areas
of interest.*
Non-Equity

CHINESE THEATRE WORKS
34-23 Steinway Street, #241
Long Island City, NY 11101
(718) 392-3493
chinesethtrwks@aol.com
Kuang-Yu Fong, executive artistic director
Send pix & resumes directly to co.?: Yes
Usually casts/accepts pix & resumes: Show
    by show.
Non-Equity

CITIZEN PELL THEATER GROUP
30 The Hamlet
Pelham, NY 10803
(914) 738-4556/ fax (Attn: Jeff Menaker)
    (212) 545-1656
citizenpell@yahoo.com
Jeffrey A. Menaker, artistic director
Joseph Cohen, managing director
Send pix & resumes directly to co.?: Yes,
    to the following address:
    PO Box 471
    Pelham, NY 10803
Usually casts/accepts pix & resumes:
    Oct.–Jan.
Equity Showcase or Tiered Code

CLASSIC STAGE COMPANY
136 E. 13 Street
New York, NY 10003
(212) 677-4210
fax (212) 477-7504
www.classicstage.org
Barry Kulick, artistic director
Anne Tanaka, general manager
Liebhart Alberg Casting, casting
Send pix & resumes directly to co.?: No
Usually casts/accept pix & resumes:
    Agent submissions only
Equity Contract
Equity Letter of Agreement

THE CLASSICAL THEATRE OF HARLEM
PO Box 1222
New York, NY 10027
(212) 539-8828
CTHarlem@aol.com
www.CTHarlem.org
Christopher McElroen, co-founder &
     executive director
Alfred Preisser, co-founder and artistic
     director
Send pix & resumes directly to co.?: Yes
Usually casts/accepts pix & resumes:
     Year-round.
Equity Showcase or Tiered Showcase

THE COLLEAGUES THEATRE COMPANY
321 W. 76 Street, #2B
New York, NY 10023
magnicath@juno.com
www.americantheaterweb.com/colleaguestheatreco
Catherine Wolf, executive producer
Send pix & resumes directly to co.?: Yes
Usually casts/accepts pix & resumes: As
     announced
Equity Showcase or Tiered Showcase

CREATIVE VOICES THEATRE COMPANY
750 Eighth Avenue, Suite 602
New York, NY 10036
(212) 388-2772
Kathy Towson, managing producer
Send pix & resumes directly to co.?: Yes
Usually casts/accepts pix & resumes:
     All year.
Equity Showcase

THE CULTURE PROJECT
Theatre: 45 Bleecker Street
Office: 49 Bleecker Street
New York, NY 10012
(212) 253-7017
fax (212) 529-4497
Box Ofc. (212) 253-9983
bleeckertheater@aol.com
www.cultureproject.com
Allan Buchman, founder/executive director
Send pix & resumes directly to co.?: No
Usually casts/accepts pix & resumes:
     At audition.
Equity Contract

THE CURAN REPERTORY COMPANY
561 Hudson Street, Suite 88
New York, NY 10014
(212) 388-2508
fax (212) 645-7495
kenatcuran@hotmail.com
www.curanrep.com
Ken Terrell, artistic director
Tom Berdik, treasurer
Send pix & resumes directly to co.?: Yes
Usually casts/accepts pix & resumes:
     Year-round.
Non-Equity

DAP ENSEMBLE LTD.
330 E. 46 Street, #1D
New York, NY 10017
Phone, fax (212) 922-0031
khigginsdap@nyc.rr.com
www.daponline.org
Ken Higgins, artistic director
Lorraine Higgins, business manager
Rene Poplaski, producing director
Send pix & resumes directly to co.?: Yes
Usually casts/accepts pix & resumes:
     Year-round.
Equity Showcase
Non-Equity

THE DEPTFORD PLAYERS
552 Riverside Drive, Suite 2G
New York, NY 10027
Phone, fax (212) 666-6509
marlowe@deptfordplayers.org
www.deptfordplayers.org
Lorree True and Jeff Berry, co-directors
Send pix & resumes directly to co.?: Yes
Usually casts/accepts pix & resumes:
     All year-round.
Equity Showcase or Tiered Showcase

DEVELOPING ARTISTS THEATRE CO.
48 W. 21 Street, Fourth fl.
New York, NY 10010
(212) 929-2228
fax (212) 929-2722
info@developingartists.com
www.developingartists.com
Jill DeArmon, artistic director
Jinn S. Kim, managing director
Send pix & resumes directly to co.?: Yes
Usually casts/accepts pix & resumes:
     Year-round.
Non-Equity
Youth theatre co., 13–21 years old.

DICAPO OPERA THEATRE
184 E. 76 Street
New York, NY 10021
(212) 288-9438
Michael Capasso, general director
Non-Equity

THE DIRECTORS COMPANY
311 W. 43 Street, Suite 307
New York, NY 10036
(212) 246-5877
directorscompany@aol.com
www.thedirectorscompany.org
Michael Parva, artistic/producing
     director
Veronica Bainbridge, business manager
Send pix & resumes directly to co.?: Yes
Usually casts/accepts pix & resumes:
     Ongoing.
Equity Off-Broadway contract
Equity Showcase
Non-Equity

*DIRECTOR'S PROJECT/THE
DRAMA LEAGUE
520 Eighth Avenue, Suite 320
New York, NY 10018
(212) 244-9494
fax (212) 244-9191
info@dramaleague.org
www.dramaleague.org
Roger T. Danforth, artistic director
Send pix & resumes directly to co.?: No
Usually casts: Casts through casting directors
    from Oct.–Nov. of each year.
Equity Letter of Agreement
Equity Showcase or Tiered Showcase

DJM PRODUCTIONS, INC.
The Helen Hayes Theater
240 W. 44 Street. Suite No. 5
New York, NY 10036
(646) 621-5171
info@DJMProductions.net
www.DJMProductions.net
Dave McCracken, producer
Send pix & resumes directly to co.?:
    Yes, but absolutely no visits.
Equity Showcase or Tiered Showcase
Non-Equity

DO GOODER PRODUCTIONS
359 W. 54 Street, 4FS
New York, NY, 10019-7507
(212) 581-8852
fax (212) 541-7928
dogooder@panix.com
www.panix.com/~dogooder
Mark Robert Gordon, founding artistic
    director
Joel Feltman, managing producer
Send pix & resumes directly to co.?: No
Usually casts: Only when posting a
    casting notice.
Equity Off-Broadway contract

*DOWNTOWN ART CO.
(212) 505-0835
fax (212) 505-0836
Ryan Gilliam, artistic director
Non-Equity; youth theatre only

DRAMA DEPT.
451 Greenwich Street, 7th fl.
New York, NY 10013
(212) 633-9108
fax (212) 633-9578
info@dramadept.org
www.dramadept.org
Douglas Carter Beane, artistic director
Michael S. Rosenberg, managing
    director
John Krasno, chief operating officer
Brian Fehd, general manager
Terry Jackson, production manager
Send pix & resumes directly to co.?: No
Equity Letter of Agreement

THE DREAM THEATRE
484 W. 43 Street, #14Q
New York, NY 10036
(212) 564-2628
Andrea Leigh, artistic director
Send pix & resumes directly to co.? Yes
Usually casts: At all times.
Equity Letter of Agreement
Equity Showcase or Tiered Showcase

THE DRILLING COMPANY
107 W. 82 Street, #1A
New York, NY 10024
(212) 229-8310
fax (212) 877-0099
DrillingCompany@aol.com
Hamilton Clancy (a.k.a. Joe Clancy), artistic
    director
Send pix & resumes directly to co.?: No
*Company actively attends showcases to seek
new talent.*

DUMBO THEATER EXCHANGE (DTX)
FDR Station Box 603
New York, NY 10150
DTX@prodigy.net
http://pages.prodigy.net/DTX
Luke Leonard, and S. Melinda Dunlap,
    artistic directors
Send pix & resumes directly to co.?: Yes
Equity Showcase or Tiered Showcase
Non-Equity

*DUO THEATRE
PO Box 1200
Cooper Station
New York, NY 10276
(212) 598-4320
duotheatre@aol.com
Michael Alasa, associate artistic director
Anthony Ruiz, assistant artistic director
Send pix & resumes directly to co.?: Yes
Usually casts/accepts pix & resumes:
    Ongoing.
Equity Showcase or Tiered Showcase

EMERGING ARTISTS THEATRE
518 Ninth Avenue, Suite 2
New York, NY 10018
(212) 627-5792
Eattheatre@aol.com
www.eattheatre.org
Paul Adams, artistic director
Send pix & resumes directly to co.?: Yes
Usually casts/accepts pix & resumes: Always.
Equity Showcase or Tiered Showcase

ENCOMPASS NEW OPERA THEATRE
138 S. Oxford Street, Suite 1A
Brooklyn, NY 11217
(718) 398-4675
fax (718) 398-4684
encompassopera@yahoo.com
Nancy Rhodes, artistic director
Joseph McConnell, managing director

Send pix & resumes directly to co.?: Yes to
Attn: Nancy Rhodes, artistic director
Usually casts/accepts pix & resumes: Casting
project-by-project
Seeks only strong legit singers.

ENDANGERED IMPROV
70 University Place, #5
New York, NY 10033
(212) 505-8068
Michael Horn, managing director
Ann Bowen, artistic director
Send pix & resumes directly to co.?: Yes
Usually casts/accepts pix & resumes: Casts
quarterly; accepts pix & resumes always.
Non-Equity
*This is a membership company; dues are
$50 per month to cover production costs.*

THE ENSEMBLE STUDIO THEATRE
549 W. 52 Street
New York, NY 10019
(212) 247-4982
fax (212) 664-0041
postmaster@ensemblestudiotheatre.org
www.ensemblestudiotheatre.org
Curt Dempster, founder/artistic director
Susann Brinkley, executive director
Send pix & resumes directly to co.?:
Yes, send to Attn: Casting Director.
Usually casts/accepts pix & resumes:
Throughout the year.
Equity Showcase or Tiered Showcase

FAUX-REAL THEATRE COMPANY
158 Grand Street, Apt. 4R
Brooklyn, NY 11211
(718) 384-5635
Mark Greenfield, artistic director
Send pix & resumes directly to co.?: No
Usually accepts pix & resumes: Show by show.
Equity Showcase or Tiered Showcase
Non-Equity
Works with an ensemble-based company.

FOLKSBIENE YIDDISH THEATRE, INC.
45 E. 33 Street
New York, NY 10016
(212) 213-2120
fax (212) 213-2186
staff@folksbiene.org
www.folksbiene.org
Zalmen Mlotek, executive director
Send pix & resumes directly to co.?: Yes
Usually casts/accepts pix & resumes:
Year-round.
Seeks Yiddish- or German-speaking performers.
Equity Off-Broadway contract
Operates under Actors' Equity Association.

407 PRODUCTIONS/407 VOICES
245 Eighth Avenue, #120
New York, NY 10011
The407Voices@aol.com
Oscar Phelps, artistic director

Chris Lucas, producer
Send pix & resumes directly to co.?:
Yes, send to Attn: Oscar Phelps
Usually casts: Year-round
Equity Off-Broadway contract
Equity Letter of Agreement
Equity Showcase or Tiered Showcase
Non-Equity

FREESTYLE REPERTORY THEATRE
120 W. 86 Street, Suite 1A
New York, NY 10024
(212) 362-4978
www.freestylerep.org
Laura Livingston, artistic director
Michael Durkin, executive director
Send pix & resumes directly to co.?: Yes
Usually casts/accepts pix & resumes: When
advertised in *Back Stage.*
Non-Equity

THE GALLERY PLAYERS OF PARK SLOPE
199 14 Street
Brooklyn, NY 11215
(718) 832-2594
info@galleryplayers.com
www.galleryplayers.com
Heather Siobhan Curran, president
Matt Shicker, publicist
Send pix & resumes directly to co.?: No
Equity Showcase or Tiered Showcase

GENESIUS THEATRE GUILD
520 Eighth Avenue, Suite 329
New York, NY 10018
(212) 244-5404
fax (212) 591-6503
info@genesiusguild.org
www.genesiusguild.org
Thomas Morrissey, artistic director
Stephen Bishop Seely, director of new play
development
David Leidholdt, director of new musicals
development
Kristina Latour, casting director
Send pix & resumes directly to co.?: Yes
Usually casts/accept pix & resumes: Year-round.
Equity Contract
Equity Letter of Agreement
Equity Showcase or Tiered Showcase
Non-Equity

GENESIS REPERTORY/GENESIS FILMS
Corporate & mailing address:
28-25 33rd Street, Suite #D4
Astoria, NY 11102
(718) 932-3577/press contact (646) 226-0370
genarts@aol.com
press contact: MWWrightgroupPR@aol.com
www.genesisrep.org
Jay Michaels, Mary Elizabeth MiCari, Robert F.
Saunders, and Michael Fortunato, general
managers
Send pix & resumes directly to co.?: Yes

Usually casts/accepts pix & resumes: Fall.
Equity Contract
Equity Showcase or Tiered Code

GILGAMESH THEATRE GROUP
425 W. 46 Street, 3A
New York, NY 10036
(212) 581-8956
Suzanne von Eck, artistic director
Send pix & resumes directly to co.?: No
Usually casts: Year-round.
Equity Showcase or Tiered Showcase

THE GLINES, INC.
240 W. 44 Street
New York, NY 10036
(212) 354-8899
John Glines, artistic director
Send pix & resumes directly to co.?: Yes,
    but only when company requests them.
Equity Contract
Equity Letter of Agreement
Equity Showcase or Tiered Showcase
Non-Equity

*GO-FORTH PRODUCTIONS
8 Remsen Street
Staten Island, NY 10304
(718) 987-4939 (also fax)
Email Bbig931719@aol.com
Bruce Biggins, producer-director
Elisa Di Simone, co-producer-choreographer
Send pix & resumes directly to co.?: Yes
Usually casts/accepts pix & resumes: Ongoing
    for season.
Equity Off-Broadway contract
Equity Showcase

GOLDEN SQUIRREL THEATRE
230 Riverside Drive, Apt. 14D
New York, NY 10025
(212) 749-3002
Gstheatre@aol.com
Steven Somkin, artistic director
Equity Showcase or Tiered Showcase
Non-Equity

H.A.D.L.E.Y. PLAYERS
207 W. 133 Street
New York, NY 10030
(212) 368-9314 (same fax #)
Gertrude Jeannette, artistic director
Equity Showcase or Tiered Showcase
Non-Equity

HARBOR THEATRE COMPANY
160 W. 71 Street, PHA
New York, NY 10023
(212) 787-1945
fax (212) 712-2378
www.harbortheatre.org
Stuart Warmflash, artistic director
Send pix & resumes directly to co.?: No
Usually casts/accepts pix & resumes: August.
Equity Showcase or Tiered Showcase

THE HEIGHTS PLAYERS
26 Willow Place
Brooklyn, NY 11201
(718) 237-2752
www.heightsplayers.org
Ed Healy, president
John Bourne, membership/reservation chairman
Non-Equity

*HERE ARTS CENTER
145 Sixth Avenue, ground fl.
New York, NY 10013-1548
(212) 647-0202
info@here.org
www.here.org
Kristin Marting, executive director
Send pix & resumes directly to co.?: Yes
Usually casts/accepting pix & resumes: Year-round.
Equity Showcase or Tiered Showcase

HIU PRODUCTIONS
(JAPANESE ACTORS GROUP)
229 E. 14 Street, #2W
New York, NY 10003
(212) 252-3476
fax (212) 475-5624
haiyushudan@hotmail.com
www.hiu-ny.com
Takuro Arai & Motoki Kobayashi, executive
    directors
Send pix & resumes directly to co.?: No
Usually casts/accepts pix & resumes: Three
    months before productions open (a month
    before rehearsals begin).
Non-Equity

HORIZON THEATRE REP
41 E. 67 Street
New York, NY 10021
(212) 737-3357
fax (212) 737-5103
info@htronline.org
www.HTRonline.org
Rafael DeMussa, artistic director
Equity Showcase

HORSE TRADE THEATER GROUP
85 E. 4 Street
New York, NY 10003
(212) 777-6088
fax (212) 777-6806
office@horsetrade.info
www.horsetrade.info
Kimo DeSean, artistic director
Erez Ziv, managing director
Send pix & resumes directly to co.? No
Usually casts/accepts pix & resumes: Varies;
    advertises when accepting pix & resumes.
Equity Off-Broadway contract
Equity Letter of Agreement
Equity Showcase or Tiered Showcase
Non-Equity
*Manages the Kraine Theater, Red Room, and
Under St. Mark's.*

THE HYPOTHETICAL THEATRE COMPANY, INC.
The New 14th Street Y
344 E. 14 Street
New York, NY 10003
Reservations: (212) 780-0800 x254
Media Contact: Ron Lasko/Spin Cycle
    (212) 505-1700
htc@nyc.rr.com
www.hypotheticaltheatre.org
Amy Feinberg, artistic director
Send pix & resumes directly to co.?: No
Usually casts: Auditions through agent submis-
    sions via Breakdown Services in early fall,
    winter, and spring.
Equity Tier II Showcase

THE ILLYRIA THEATRE CO.
3299 Cambridge Avenue
Riverdale, NY 10463
(917) 538-7341
Illyriamc@aol.com
Maggie Moore, artistic director
Mark Cortale, executive founding director
Send pix & resumes directly to co.?: No
Equity Off-Broadway contract

IMPACT THEATRE COMPANY
190 Underhill Avenue
Brooklyn, NY 11238
(718) 390-7163
ImpactTheatre@yahoo.com
Tim Lewis, artistic director
Send pix & resumes directly to co.?: Yes;
    send pix & resumes to Attn: Tim Lewis.
Usually casts/accepts pix & resumes: Anytime
Non-Equity

IMUA! THEATRE COMPANY
PO Box 286934
New York, NY 10128-0009
(212) 828-2444
fax (775) 542-6850
imuatheatr@aol.com
www.imuatheatre.org
Kaipo Schwab, artistic director
Hope Innelli, managing director
Send pix & resumes directly to co.?: Yes
Usually casts/accepts pix & resumes:
    Year-round.
Equity Letter of Agreement
Equity Showcase or Tiered Showcase
Non-Equity

INNERACT PRODUCTIONS:
138 South Oxford Street, Suite 2C
Brooklyn, NY 11217
(718) 230-1323
mail@inneractpd.com
www.inneractpd.com
John Shevin Foster, artistic director
Send pix & resumes directly to co.?: Yes.
Usually casts/accepts pix & resumes:
    Year-round.
Non-Equity

INTAR HISPANIC AMERICAN ARTS CENTER
PO Box 756
New York, NY 10108-0756
(212) 695-6134
fax (212) 268-0102
intarnewyork@aol.com
Max Ferra, artistic director
Lorenzo Mans, literary manager
Send pix & resumes directly to co.?: Yes
Usually casts/accepts pix & resumes:
    Year-round.
Equity Off-Broadway contract
Equity Letter of Agreement

INTERBOROUGH REPERTORY THEATER (IRT)
154 Christopher Street, 3B
New York, NY 10014
(212) 206-6875
IRTonline@yahoo.com
www.irt.dreamhost.com
Jim Sable, managing director
Vivian Lyn Hasbrouk, TYA artistic director
Jonathan Fluck, executive director
Luane Davis Haggerty, artistic director
Send pix & resumes directly to co.?: No
Usually casts/accepts pix & resumes: Advertise
    fall/winter in trade papers.
Equity Showcase or Tiered Showcase
Non-Equity

IRISH ARTS CENTER
553 W. 51 Street
New York, NY 10019
(212) 757-3318
fax (212) 247-0930
info@irishartscenter.org
www.irishartscenter.org
Pauline Turley, executive director
Send pix & resumes directly to co.?: Yes
Usually casts/accepts pix & resumes: End of
    summer/fall.
Equity Letter of Agreement

IRISH REPERTORY THEATRE
132 W. 22 Street
New York, NY 10011
Admin. ofc.: (212) 255-0270
Box ofc.: (212) 727-2737
info@irishrep.org
www.irishrep.org
Charlotte Moore, artistic director
Ciaran O'Reilly, producing director
Send pix & resumes directly to co.?: No
Equity Off-Broadway contract
Equity Letter of Agreement

*IRONDALE ENSEMBLE PROJECT
PO Box 150604
Brooklyn, NY 11215-0604
irondalerT@aol.com
www.irondale.org
Jim Nielsen, artistic director
Terry Greiss, executive director
Equity Letter of Agreement

*JEAN COCTEAU REPERTORY
Bouwerie Lane Theatre
330 Bowery
New York, NY 10012
(212) 677-0060
cocteau@jeancocteaurep.org
www.jeancocteaurep.org
David Fuller, producing artistic director
Send pix & resumes directly to co.?: No
Usually casts: Spring (April, May).
Equity Letter of Agreement
Non-Equity

JEWISH REPERTORY THEATRE
c/o 92nd Street Y
1395 Lexington Avenue
New York, NY 10128
(212) 415-5550/5575
jewishrep@yahoo.com
www.jrt.org
Ran Avni, artistic director
Send pix & resumes to directly co.?: No
Usually casts/accepts pix & resumes: Prior to
   each show.
Equity Off-Broadway contract

THE JEWISH THEATER OF NEW YORK
Mailing Address:
P.O. Box 845
Times Square Station
New York, NY 10108-0845
(212) 494-0050
thejtny@aol.com
www.jewishtheater.org
Tuvia Tenenbom, artistic director
Send pix & resumes directly to co.?: Yes, send
   to mailing address.
Usually casts/accepts pix & resumes: Show by show.
Equity Off-Broadway contract
Equity Letter of Agreement
Equity Showcase or Tiered Showcase

JUDITH SHAKESPEARE COMPANY
PO Box 60
Times Square Station
New York, NY 10036
(212) 592-1885
www.judithshakespeare.org
Philip Hernandez, executive producer
Joanne Zipay, artistic director
Send pix & resumes directly to co.?: Yes
Usually casts/accepts pix & resumes: All year.
Equity Tiered Showcase

KAIROS ITALY THEATER
77 Bleecker Street, #1412
New York, NY 10012
(212) 254-4025
fax (433) 346-2615
info@kitheater.com
www.kitheater.com
Laura Caparrotti, artistic director
Non-Equity
Actors must speak fluent Italian.

KEEN COMPANY
520 Eighth Avenue, Suite 328
New York, NY 10018
(212) 216-0963
fax (212) 216-9629
www.keencompany.org
Carl Forsman, artistic director
Eileen O'Reilly, producer
*Send pix & resumes directly to co.?:*Yes
*Usually accepts pix & resumes:*Use a casting
   director; general auditions in Jan. and April.
Equity Tier III Showcase

THE KILLING KOMPANY
21 Turn Lane
Levittown, NY 11756
(212) 772-2590
fax (212) 202-6495
killingkompany@killingkompany.com
www.killingkompany.com
Jon Avner, artistic director
Send pix & resumes directly to co.?: Yes
Usually casts/accepts pix & resumes: Twice a
   year—see *Back Stage* for casting notices.
   Will also accept submissions.
Equity Contract
Equity Showcase or Tiered Code
Non-Equity

KINGS COUNTY SHAKESPEARE COMPANY
138 S. Oxford Street, #1C
Brooklyn, NY 11217
(718) 398-0546
KCSCShakes@nytw.zzn.com
www.kingscountyshakespeare.org
Deborah Wright Houston, artistic director
Send pix & resumes directly to co.?: Yes;
   c/o Vicki Hirsch, casting director, at
   above address.
Casts/accepts pix & resumes: Year-round.
Equity Showcase or Tiered Showcase

LA MAMA E.T.C.
74-A E. Fourth Street
New York, NY 10003
(212) 254-6468
web@lamama.org
www.lamama.org
Ellen Stewart, artistic director and founder
Send pix & resumes directly to co.?: No
Usually casts/accepts pix & resumes: Show by show.
Equity Contract
Equity Letter of Agreement
Equity Tiered Showcase
Non-Equity
*Has three separate theatres under different
contracts.*

LABYRINTH THEATER COMPANY
c/o HBO Films
1114 Sixth Avenue, 26-23
New York, NY 10036
(212) 512-1232
fax (212) 512-1480

lab@labtheater.org
www.labtheater.org
Philip Seymour Hoffman and John Ortiz,
    co-artistic directors
Oliver Dow, executive director
Marieke Gaboury, general manager
Send pix & resumes directly to co.?:
    No; casts through agents.
Usually casts: Show by show.
Equity Letter of Agreement

THE LARK THEATRE COMPANY PLAY
DEVELOPMENT CENTER
939 Eighth Avenue, Suite 301
New York, NY 10019
(212) 246-2676
fax (212) 246-2609
info@larktheatre.org
www.larktheatre.org
John Clinton Eisner, producing director
Steven H. David, managing director
Send pix & resumes directly to co.?: Yes
Usually cast/accepts pix & resumes:
    Anytime.
Equity Contract
Equity Letter of Agreement
Equity Showcase or Tiered Showcase

LATIN AMERICAN THEATRE ENSEMBLE
PO Box 18
Radio City Station
New York, NY 10101
(212) 397-3262 (same fax #)
elportonlateNYC@aol.com
Margarita Toirac, executive producer
Send pix & resumes directly to co.?: Yes
Usually casts/accepts pix & resumes: Always.
Non-Equity

LIGHTNING STRIKES THEATRE
COMPANY
PO Box 7329
New York, NY 10116
(212) 713-5334
lstc@lightningstrikes.org
www.lightningstrikes.org
John McDermott, artistic director
JulieHera DeStefano, managing director
Send pix & resumes directly to co.?: Yes
Usually casts/accepts pix & resumes:
    All year-round.
Equity Off-Broadway contract
Equity Letter of Agreement
Equity Showcase or Tiered Showcase

LINCOLN CENTER THEATER
Mitzi E. Newhouse Theater
150 W. 65 Street
New York, NY 10023
(212) 362-7600
www.lct.org
Andre Bishop, artistic director
Bernard Gersten, executive producer
Equity Contract

*LIVE THEATRE GANG
270 Convent Avenue, Suite 8D
New York, NY 10031
www.livetheatregang.com
Reed McCants, artistic director
Ah-Keisha McCants, co-artistic director
Send pix & resumes directly to co.? Yes
Usually casts/accepts pix & resumes: Year-round.
Non-Equity

THE LOOKING GLASS THEATRE
422 W. 57 Street
New York, NY 10019
(212) 307-9467
lgtheatre@aol.com
www.thelookingglasstheatre.homestead.com
Justine Lambert, artistic director
Ken Nowell, managing director
Send pix & resumes directly to co.?: Yes
Usually casts/accepts pix & resumes: Show
    by show.
Equity Showcase or Tiered Showcase

LOVE CREEK PRODUCTIONS, INC.
Mailing address:
c/o Granville
162 Nesbit Street
Weehawken, NJ 07086-6817
(212) 769-7973
creekread@aol.com
Le Wilhelm, managing director
Philip Galbraith, Kirsten Walsh, Tony White,
    Sybil Simone, Jon Oak, artistic directors
Beverly Bullock, artistic director Shakespeare
Geoff Dawe, associate artistic director
    Shakespeare
Cynthia Granville-Callahan, literary
    manager/development
Kelly Barrett, Moira Boag, managerial coordination
Usually casts/accepts pix & resumes: Year-round—
    audition approximately 4 times a year.
Casting: (At times other than announced audi-
    tions; Only submit, if you know a company
    member/are familiar with our work). State if
    you are interested in company membership
    or casting only.
    Love Creek Productions
    21-44 45 Avenue , #4
    Long Island City, NY 11101
Equity Showcase or Tiered Showcase
Non-Equity

MABOU MINES
The TOny, ROn, NAncy, and DAvid (TORONADA)
The 122 Community Center
150 First Avenue
New York, NY 10009
(212) 473-0559
fax (212) 473-2410
office@maboumines.org
www.maboumines.org
Collective artistic leadership
Send pix & resumes directly to co.?: No
Equity Contract

MAGIC CIRCLE OPERA REPERTORY
ENSEMBLE, INC.
200 W. 70 Street, Suite 6-C
New York, NY 10023
(212) 724-2398
mcore@nyc.rr.com
Ray Evans Harrell, artistic director
Stephanie Weems, executive director
Stan Tucker, conductor
Liliana Morales, choreographer
Kenneth Newbern, musical coach
Send pix & resumes directly to co.?:
    Yes. Send to: Magic Circle Mgmt.,
    Attn: Harrell/Weems, at above address.
Usually casts/accepts pix & resumes: Before
    auditions.
This is a chamber opera company.

MANHATTAN ENSEMBLE THEATER
55 Mercer Street
New York, NY 10013
(212) 925-1900
fax (212) 925-1947
info@met.com
www.met.com
David Fishelson, artistic director
James E. Sparnon, producing director
Send pix & resumes directly to co.?: Yes
Usually casts/accepts pix & resumes:
    Year-round.
Equity Off-Broadway

*MANHATTAN THEATRE CLUB
311 W. 43 Street, 8th fl.
New York, NY 10036
(212) 399-3000
fax (212) 399-4FAX (4329)
www.manhattantheatreclub.com
Barry Grove, executive producer
Lynne Meadow, artistic director
Nancy Piccione/David Caparelliotis, casting
    directors
Send pix & resumes directly to co.?: Yes
Usually casts/accept pix & resumes: Fall.
Equity contract (Equity LORT B & D)
Equity Letter of Agreement

THE MARLOWE PROJECT
PO Box 090039
Brooklyn, NY 11209-0001
(212) 465-7428
Marloweproject@aol.com
Jeff Dailey, artistic director
Send pix & resumes directly to co.?: No
Usually casts/accepts pix & resumes:
    Just before auditions.
Non-Equity

MA-YI THEATRE CO.
520 Eighth Avenue. Suite 309
New York, NY 10018
(212) 971-4862
fax (212) 971-4876
info@ma-yitheatre.org

www.ma-yitheatre.org
Jorge Z. Ortoll, executive director
Ralph B. Peña, artistic director
Send pix & resumes directly to co.?: Yes
Usually casts/accepts pix & resumes: Year-round.
Equity Letter of Agreement

MCC THEATER
Mailing address:
145 W. 28 Street, 8th fl.
New York, NY 10001
(212) 727-7722
fax (212) 727-7780
mcc@mcctheater.org
www.mcctheater.org
Robert LuPone, Bernard Telsey, artistic directors
Send pix & resumes directly to co.?: No
Usually casts/accepts pix & resumes: All the time.
Casting:
    Bernard Telsey Casting
    145 W. 28 Street
    New York, NY 10001
Equity Letter of Agreement

MEDICINE SHOW THEATRE ENSEMBLE
Mailing address:
549 W. 52 Street, 3rd fl.
New York, NY 10019
(212) 262-4216
medicineshowtheater@juno.com
www.medicineshowtheatre.org
Barbara Vann, artistic director
Send pix & resumes directly to co.?: Yes
Usually casts/accepts pix & resumes: Show
    by show.
Equity Showcase
Non-Equity

MELTING POT THEATRE COMPANY
Mailing Address:
2444 Broadway, Suite 231
New York, NY 10024
(212) 330-7211
fax (212) 874-6054
larry@meltingpottheatre.com
www.meltingpottheatre.com
Larry Hirschhorn, artistic director
Sean Patrick Flahaven, managing director
Send pix & resumes directly to co.?: No
Usually casts/accepts pix & resumes: Early fall
    or spring.
Equity Letter of Agreement

METROPOLITAN PLAYHOUSE
220 E. Fourth Street, Second fl.
New York, NY 10009
(212) 995-8410
connect@metropolitanplayhouse.com
www.metropolitanplayhouse.org
Alex Roe, artistic director
Send pix & resumes directly to co.?: Yes
Usually casts/accepts pix & resumes:
    Year-round.
Equity Showcase or Tiered Showcase

MINT THEATER COMPANY
311 W. 43 Street, Fifth fl.
New York, NY 10036
(212) 315-9434
mint@minttheater.org
www.minttheater.org
Jonathan Bank, artistic director
Ted Altschuler, associate director
Send pix & resumes directly to co.?: No.
Usually casts/accepts pix & resumes:
    Show by show.
Equity Off-Broadway contract
Equity Letter of Agreement

*MODA ENTERTAINMENT, INC.
(212) 873-3324
info@modaentertainment.com
www.modaentertainment.com
Shannon Mulholland, producer
Equity Off-Broadway contract
Equity Letter of Agreement
Equity Showcase or Tiered Showcase
Non-Equity

THE JOHN MONTGOMERY THEATRE
COMPANY, INC.
(Bi-coastal, producing theatre in NYC and L.A.)
153 E. 57 Street, Suite 14F
New York, NY 10022
(212) 758-3820
JMTCinc@aol.com
www.jmtcinc.com
Suzanne Bachner & Trish Minskoff, artistic
    directors
Send pix & resumes directly to co.?: Yes
Usually casts/accepts pix & resumes: Year-round.
Equity Off-Broadway contract
Equity Showcase or Tiered Showcase
Non-Equity

MORNING GLORY PRODUCTIONS
50 Westminister Rd., #4E
Brooklyn, NY 11218
(212) 726-0400
Jahidah@hotmail.com
www.Jahidah-Kerry.com
Jahidah Diaab, director-producer
Angela Valentine, assistant director-producer
Send pix & resumes directly to co.?: Yes
Usually casts/accepts pix & resumes:
    Winter–spring.
Send pix & resumes to: Angela Valentine &
    Niki Boone, Casting Directors, at the
    above address.
Non-Equity

MUSICAL THEATRE WORKS
440 Lafayette Street
New York, NY 10003
(212) 677-0040
fax (212) 598-0105
reception@mtwnyc.org
Thomas Cott, artistic director
Randy Ellen Lutterman, executive director

Send pix & resumes directly to co.?: No
Usually casts/accepts pix & resumes: No.
Equity Letter of Agreement

NAKED ANGELS
9 Desbrosses Street, Second fl.
New York, NY 10013
(646) 214-7939
fax (212) 609-9099
info@nakedangels.com
www.nakedangels.com
Tim Ransom, artistic director
Kourtney Keaton, managing director
Send pix & resumes directly to co.?: No
Usually casts/accepts pix & resumes: On
    announced productions via their casting
    director
Equity Mini Contract
Equity Letter of Agreement
Equity Showcase or Tiered Showcase

NATIONAL ASIAN AMERICAN THEATRE
COMPANY
674 President Street
Brooklyn, NY 11215
(718) 623-1672
Mia Katigbak, artistic producing director
Send pix & resumes directly to co.?: Yes
Usually cast/accepts pix & resumes: Show to show.
Equity Showcase or Tiered Showcase

NATIONAL BLACK THEATRE, INC.
2031-33 National Black Theatre Way
a.k.a. Fifth Avenue
New York, NY 10035
(212) 722-3800
Dr. Barbara Ann Teer, founder and CEO
Send pix & resumes directly to co.?: Yes
Usually casts/accepts pix & resumes: Oct.–June.
Equity Showcase or Tiered Showcase
Non-Equity

NEC THEATRE & TV (NEGRO ENSEMBLE
COMPANY)
303 W. 42 Street, Suite 501
New York, NY 10036
(212) 582-5860
fax (212) 582-9639
1967nec@aol.com
www.negroensemblecompany.org
O.L. Duke, producing director
Frieda Nerandis, executive producer
Send pix & resumes directly to co.?: Yes
Usually casts/accepts pix & resumes: Year-round.
Equity Off-Broadway contract

NEUROTIC THEATRICAL COMPANY
465 W. 23 Street, #2C
New York, NY 10011
(212) 242-3657
Steve Diefenderfer, administrative director
Guy Bernotas, artistic director
Send pix & resumes directly to co.?: Yes
Usually casts/accepts pix & resumes: Open-ended.
Equity Showcase or Tiered Showcase

THE NEW ENSEMBLE THEATRE CO., INC.
444 W. 49 Street, #3B
New York, NY 10019
(212) 613-5796
newensemble@aol.com
www.newensemble.com
Steven McElroy, artistic director
Send pix & resumes directly to co.? Yes.
Usually casts/accepts pix & resumes: Ongoing.
Equity Showcase or Tiered Showcase.

NEW FEDERAL THEATRE
292 Henry Street
New York, NY 10002
(212) 353-1176
www.newfederaltheatre.org
Woodie King, Jr., producing director
Pat White, company manager
Send pix & resumes directly to co.?: Yes
Usually casts/accepts pix & resumes:
   Year-round.
Equity Off-Broadway contract
Equity Letter of Agreement

NEW GEORGES
Mailing address:
109 W. 27 Street, Suite 9A
New York, NY 10001
(646) 336-8077
info@newgeorges.org
www.newgeorges.org
Susan Bernfield, artistic director
Send pix & resumes directly to co.?: Yes
Usually casts/accepts pix & resumes: Ongoing.
Equity Showcase or Tiered Showcase

THE NEW GROUP
410 W. 42 Street
New York, NY 10036
(212) 244-3380
fax (212) 244-3438
info@thenewgroup.org
www.thenewgroup.org
Scott Elliott, artistic director
Geoffrey Rich, executive director
Send pix & resumes directly to co.?: No.
Casting director:
   Judy Henderson
   330 W. 89 Street
   New York, NY 10024
Equity Letter of Agreement

NEW PERSPECTIVES THEATRE
COMPANY
Mailing address:
750 Eighth Avenue, No. 601
New York, NY 10036
(212) 730-2030
www.newperspectivestheatre.org
Melody Brooks, artistic director
Send pix & resumes directly to co.?: Yes
Usually casts/accepts pix & resumes: Ongoing.
Equity Showcase or Tiered Showcase
Non-Equity

NEW YORK GILBERT & SULLIVAN
PLAYERS
251 W. 91 Street, 4C
New York, NY 10024
(212) 769-1000
fax (212) 769-1002
info@nygasp.org
www.nygasp.org
Albert Bergeret, artistic director
Send pix & resumes directly to co.?: Yes
Usually casts/accepts pix & resumes: Sept.
   for early Oct. auditions. May schedule
   more auditions in March.
Equity Letter of Agreement

NEW YORK THEATRE WORKSHOP
79 E. Fourth Street
New York, NY 10003
(212) 780-9037
fax (212) 460-8996
info@nytw.org
www.nytw.org
James C. Nicola, artistic director
Lynn Moffat, managing director
Send pix & resumes directly to co.?: Yes
Usually casts/accepts pix & resumes:
   Year-round.
Casting director: Jack Doulin
Equity Off-Broadway contract

NORTH AMERICAN CULTURAL
LABORATORY (NACL THEATRE)
Mailing address:
PO Box 2201
Times Square Station
New York, NY 10108
Summer office address:
NaCl Catskills
110 Highland Lake Rd.
Highland Lake,. NY 12743
Summer: (845) 557-0694; Winter:
   (718) 398-4589
nacl@nacl.org
www.nacl.org
Brad Krumholz, Tannis Kowalchuk, &
   ensemble
Send pix & resumes directly to co.?:
   Letters of interest only.
Usually casts/accepts pix & resumes: Year-round.
*Only those interested in the philosophy of perma-
nent ensemble, actor training, and collaboration
should inquire.*
Non-Equity

NUYORICAN POETS CAFE
236 E. Third Street
New York, NY 10009
(212) 465-3167
hotline (212) 505-8183
www. nuyorican.org
Rome Neal, artistic theatre director
Miguel Algarin, producer
Equity Showcase or Tiered Showcase
Non-Equity

NY ARTISTS UNLIMITED
212 W. 14 Street, #2A
New York, NY 10011
(212) 242-6036
fax (212) 989-8864
nyartunltd@aol.com
Melba LaRose, artistic director
Send pix & resumes directly to co.?: Yes
Usually casts/accepts pix & resumes:
    Throughout the year.
Equity Contract
Equity Letter of Agreement
Equity Showcase or Tiered Showcase
Non-Equity

THE OASIS THEATRE COMPANY INC.
PO Box 1153
Madison Square Station
New York, NY 10159
(212) 307-7014
www.oasistheatre.org
Brenda Lynn Bynum, artistic director
James Jenner, managing director
Send pix & resumes directly to co.?: Yes
Usually casts/accepts pix & resumes:
    At all times.
Equity Contract (currently a "Special
    Appearance" contract)

THE OBERON THEATRE ENSEMBLE
545 Eighth Avenue, Suite 402
New York, NY 10018
donovanjohnson@oberontheatre.org
www.oberontheatre.org
Donovan Johnson, artistic director
Brad Fryman, managing director
Send pix & resumes directly to co.?: Yes
Usually casts/accepts pix & resumes:
    Year-round.
Equity Showcase or Tiered Showcase

ODYSSEY THEATRE ENSEMBLE
416 Broadway, Suite 3
Brooklyn, NY 11211
(212) 591-0447
casting@odysseyensemble.com
www.odysseyensemble.com
Rachel Macklin, producing artistic director
Shana Solomon, associate artistic director
Send pix & resumes directly to co.?: Yes
Usually casts/accepts pix & resumes:
    Show-by-show basis.
Equity Showcase or Tiered Showcase
Non-Equity

ONTOLOGICAL-HYSTERIC THEATER
Office: 260 W. Broadway
New York, NY 10013
(212) 941-8911
Theatre: Ontological at St. Mark's Theater
St. Mark's-Church-in-the-Bowery
Second Avenue and 10th Street
(212) 420-1916
Box office: (212) 533-4650

www.ontological.com
Richard Foreman, artistic director
Equity Contract
Equity Letter of Agreement

OUTREACH THEATRE, INC.
"THEATRE OF DREAMS"
1219 77 Street
Brooklyn, NY 11228
(718) 680-3319
Bob Paton, artistic director
Send pix & resumes directly to co.?: Yes
Usually casts/accepts pix & resumes:
    Show by show.
Equity Contract
Equity Letter of Agreement
Equity Showcase or Tiered Showcase
Non-Equity

OVERLAP PRODUCTIONS
Cooper Station, PO Box 595
New York, NY 10276-0595
(917) 554-4870
Tania@overlapnyc.org
www.overlapnyc.org
Susanna L. Harris & Tania Inessa Kirkman,
    co-artistic directors
Sendn pix & resumes directly to co.?: Yes
Usually casts/accepts pix & resumes: Rolling.
Equity Showcase or Tiered Showcase

PAN ASIAN REPERTORY THEATRE
520 Eighth Avenue, Suite 314, 3rd fl.
New York, NY 10018
(212) 868-4030
fax (212) 868-4033
panasian@aol.com
www.panasianrep.org
Tisa Chang, artistic/producing director
Send pix & resumes directly to co.?: Yes
Usually casts/accepts pix & resumes: Show
    by show.
Equity Off-Broadway contract
Equity Letter of Agreement

THE PAPER BAG PLAYERS
Mailing address:
225 W. 99 Street
New York, NY 10025
Studio address:
185 E. Broadway
New York, NY 10002
(212) 362-0431
Judith Martin, artistic director
Send pix & resumes directly to co.?: Yes
Usually casts/accepts pix & resumes: Year-round.
Equity Guest Artist Contract

THE PEARL THEATRE COMPANY
80 St. Mark's Place
New York, NY 10003
Box office: (212) 598-9802
www.pearltheatre.org
Shepard Sobel, artistic director
Equity LORT "D" contract

THE PECCADILLO THEATER COMPANY
Bank Street Theatre
155 Bank Street
New York, NY 10014
(212) 633-6533 (same fax #)
Dan Wackerman, artistic director
Kevin Kennedy, general manager
Send pix & resumes directly to co.?: No
Casting: Casting director on per show basis.
Equity Showcase or Tiered Showcase

*PECULIAR WORKS PROJECT
595 Broadway, Second fl.
New York, NY 10012-3222
(212) 529-3626
fax (212) 529-3626
info@peculiarworks.org
www.peculiarworks.org
Ralph Lewis, Catherine Porter, and Barry Rowell,
    co-directors
Send pix & resumes directly to co.?: No
Does not accept pix & resumes.
Equity Showcase

PERKASIE THEATRE COMPANY
338 W. 19 Street, #3B
New York, NY 10011
(212) 924-8699
fax (212) 564-1497
sckeim@hotmail.com
Steven Keim, artistic director
Send pix & resumes directly to co.?: Yes
Usually casts/accepts pix & resumes: Anytime.
Equity Showcase or Tiered Showcase

PING CHONG & COMPANY
47 Great Jones Street
New York, NY 10012
(212) 529-1557
fax (212) 529-1703
pingchong@earthlink.net
www.pingchong.org
Ping Chong, artistic director
Bruce Allardice, managing director
Send pix & resumes directly to co.?: Yes
Usually casts/accepts pix & resumes: Year-round,
    depending on project.
Non-Equity

PINK, INC.
152 E. 23 Street
New York, NY 10010
(212) 253-6666
fax (212) 253-6646
us@pinkinc.org
www.pinkinc.org
Debra Roth, artistic director
Send pix & resumes directly to co.?: No
Usually casts/accepts pix & resumes: Never.
Non-Equity

PIPER THEATRE PRODUCTIONS
Mailing Address:
Box 1274
Yonkers, NY 10702

www.alltheworldsastage.org
Rachel McEneny, executive producer
John P. McEneny, artistic director
Beth Elliott, company manager
Send pix & resumes directly to co.?: Yes
Usually casts/accepts pix & resumes: Winter, spring.
Equity Showcase or Tiered Code
Non-Equity

PLAYWRIGHTS/ACTORS CONTEMPORARY
THEATER
c/o Juel Wiese
105 W. 13 Street, 5G
New York, NY 10011
(212) 242-5888
Jane Petrov, artistic director
Juel Wiese, managing director
Send pix & resumes directly to co.?: Yes
Accepts pix & resumes: Anytime.
Equity Showcase or Tiered Showcase

PLAYWRIGHTS HORIZONS
416 W. 42 Street
New York, NY 10036
(212) 564-1235
Tim Sanford, artistic director
Send pix & resumes directly to co.?: Yes
Usually casts/accepts pix & resumes: All times.
Casting:
    James Calleri, casting director
    Alaine Alldaffer, casting associate
    Mo Marshall, casting associate
    Kristen Jackson, casting assistant
Equity Contract

PREGONES THEATER
571 Walton Avenue
Bronx, NY 10451
(718) 585-1202
fax (718) 585-1608
info@pregones.org
www.pregones.org
Magalie Gonzalez, general manager
Send pix & resumes directly to co.?: Yes
Usually casts/accepts pix & resumes: Every
    three months.
Equity Letter of Agreement

THE PRESENT COMPANY
520 Eighth Avenue, Suite 311
New York, NY 10018
(212) 279-4455
fax (212) 279-4466
info@presentcompany.org
www.presentcompany.org
Elena K. Holy, producing artistic director
Send pix & resumes directly to co.?: Yes
Usually casts/accepts pix & resumes: Year-round.
Equity Showcase or Tiered Showcase
Non-Equity

PRIMARY STAGES COMPANY
Office address:
131 W. 45 Street
New York, NY 10036

Theatre address:
354 W. 45 Street
New York, NY 10036
(212) 840-9705
fax (212) 840-9725
Box office: (212) 333-4052
www.primarystages.com
Casey Childs, executive director
Andrew Leynse, artistic director
Tyler Marchant, associate artistic director
Nicole Cavaliere, general manager
Send pix & resumes directly to co.?: Yes
Usually casts/accepts pix &resumes: Rolling.
Equity Off-Broadway contract
Equity Letter of Agreement

PROSPECT THEATER COMPANY
520 Eighth Avenue, Suite 307, Third fl.
New York, NY 10018
(212) 594-4476
fax (212) 594-4478
artistic@prospecttheater.org
www.prospecttheater.org
Cara L. Reichel, producing artistic director
Melissa Huber, managing director
Genevieve Miller, casting director
Send pix & resumes directly to co.?: Yes, but not
    via email.
Usually casts/accepts pix & resumes: Ongoing.
Equity Showcase or Tiered Showcase

THE PROTEAN THEATRE COMPANY
484 W. 43 Street, #31-O
New York, NY 10036
www.ProteanTheatre.com
James McClure, producing director
Owen Thompson, artistic director
Send pix & resumes directly to co.?: Yes
Equity Showcase or Tiered Showcase

THE PUBLIC THEATER
425 Lafayette Street
New York, NY 10003
(212) 539-8500
www.publictheater.org
Or www.joespub.com
George C. Wolfe, producer
Mara Manus, executive director
Michael Hurst, managing director
Jordan Thaler/Heidi Griffiths, casting directors
Send pix & resumes directly to co.?: Yes.
Usually casts/accepts pix & resumes: All year.
Equity contract.
Equity Letter of Agreement
Equity LORT contract at the Delacorte Theater,
    Central Park.

PUERTO RICAN TRAVELING THEATRE
Mailing Address:
141 W. 94 Street
New York, NY 10025
Theatre:
304 W. 47 Street
New York, NY 10036

(212) 354-1293
Miriam Colon Valle, artistic director
Send pix & resumes directly to co.?: Yes
Usually casts/accepts pix & resumes: Show
    by show.
Equity Off-Broadway contract
Equity Letter of Agreement
Equity Showcase or Tiered Showcase
Non-Equity

PULSE ENSEMBLE THEATRE
PO Box 1533
Radio City Station
New York, NY 10101
(212) 695-1596
pet@pulseensembletheatre.org
www.pulseensembletheatre.org
Alexa Kelly, artistic director
Send pix & resumes directly to co.?: Yes
Usually casts pix & resumes: Fall.
Equity Showcase or Tiered Showcase

THE PYRAMID THEATRE ARTS FOUNDATION
159 W. 53 Street, Suite 21F
New York, NY 10019
(212) 541-8293
Nico Hartos, artistic director
Send pix & resumes directly to co.?: Yes
Usually casts/accepts pix & resumes:
    Show-by-show basis.
Equity Contract
Equity Letter of Agreement
Equity Showcase or Tiered Showcase
Non-Equity

*QUEENS THEATRE IN THE PARK
Mailing Address:
PO Box 520069
Flushing, NY 11352
Theatre:
Flushing Meadows Corona Park
Flushing, NY
(718) 760-0686
fax (718) 760-1972
QTIPARTS@aol.com
www.queenstheatre.org
Jeffrey Rosenstock, producing director
Send pix & resumes directly to co.?: No
Usually casts/accepts pix & resumes: By
    request only.
Equity Letter of Agreement (Mainstage)
Equity Mini Contract (Studio)

*QUEST THEATER ENSEMBLE
21-27 37th Street
Astoria, NY
(212) 560-0961
questtheater@earthlink.net
www.questtheater.org
Tim Browning, artistic director
Send pix & resumes directly to co.?: Yes
Usually casts/accepts pix & resumes: Pix &
    resumes always welcome—generals in spring.
Equity Showcase or Tiered Showcase

RATTLESTICK PRODUCTIONS
224 Waverly Place
New York, NY 10014
(212) 627-2556
fax (630) 839-8352
info@rattlestick.org
www.rattlestick.org
David Van Asselt, artistic director
Sandra Coudert, managing director
Louise Geddes, literary manager
Mildred Normandy, marketing director
David Elliott, director of new play development
Kevin Downes, business manager
Send pix & resumes directly to co.?: Yes
Usually casts/accepts pix & resumes: EPA's twice
    a year.
Equity Letter of Agreement

RED BULL THEATER
PO Box 250863
New York, NY 10025
(212) 414-5168
info@redbulltheater.com
www.redbulltheater.com
Jesse Berger, artistic director
Send pix & resumes directly to co.?: Yes
Usually casts/accepts pix & resumes: Year-round.
Equity Off-Broadway contract
Equity Letter of Agreement
Equity Showcase or Tiered Showcase
Non-Equity
All of the above TBD per project.

REPERTORIO ESPANOL
Gramercy Arts Theatre
138 E. 27 Street
New York, NY 10016
(212) 889-2850
fax (212) 686-3732
info@repertorio.org
www.repertorio.org
Gilberto Zaldivar, executive producer
Rene Buch, artistic director
Robert Weber Federico, artistic associate
    producer
Send pix & resumes directly to co.?: Yes
Usually casts/accepts pix & resumes: Ongoing.
Non-Equity

REV THEATRE COMPANY
302 W. 51 Street, 4D
New York, NY 10019
(212) 581-5377
rhandrc@earthlink.net
Rosemary Hay, artistic director
Rudy Caporaso, co-artistic director
Send pix & resumes directly to co.?: Yes
Usually casts/accepts pix & resumes: Year-round.
Equity Showcase or Tiered Showcase
Non-Equity
*REV's focus is on classical material, particularly
Shakespeare and the Jacobean writers. Pix &
resumes accepted only from performers with
classical training and experience.*

REVELATION THEATER
Mailing address:
PO Box 2632
New York, NY 10108
Theatre address:
334 W. 39 Street
New York, NY 10018
(212) 947-7000
fax (212) 947-7008
www.revelationtheater.org
Leslie L. Smith, artistic director
Send pix & resumes directly to co.?: No
Usually casts/accepts pix & resumes:
    By production.
Equity Off-Broadway contract

REVERIE PRODUCTIONS
520 Eighth Avenue, Suite 317
New York, NY 10018
(212) 244-7803
fax (212) 244-7815
info@reverieproductions.org
www.reverieproductions.org
Colin D. Young, artistic director
Send pix & resumes directly to co.?: Yes.
Usually casts/accepts pix & resumes:
    Show-by-show basis.
Equity Tiered Showcase

RIANT THEATRE
PO Box 1902
New York, NY 10013
(646) 623-3488
TheRiantTheatre@aol.com
www.theriantheatre.com
Van Dirk Fisher, artistic director
Send pix & resumes directly to co.?: Yes
Equity Contract
Equity Letter of Agreement
Equity Showcase or Tiered Showcase
Non-Equity

ROOTS&BRANCHES THEATER
132 W. 31 Street
New York, NY 10001
(212) 273-5297; (212) 273-5298
fax (212) 695-9070
roots&branches@jasa.org
Arthur Strimling, artistic director
Lauren Scott, general manager
Send pix & resumes directly to co.?: No
Usually casts/accepts pix & resumes:
    Never.
Non-Equity

**THE ROUNDABOUT THEATRE
COMPANY**
Administrative Offices
231 W. 39 Street, Suite 1200
New York, NY 10018
(212) 719-9393
fax (212) 869-8817
www.roundabouttheatre.org
Todd Haimes, artistic director

Ellen Richard, managing director
David Steffen, marketing director
Julia C. Levy executive director, external
    affairs
Equity Contract

*RUDE MECHANICALS
Murray Hill Station
PO Box 1913
New York, NY 10156
(212) 414-5136
rude@rudemechanicals.org
www.rudemechanicals.org
Eric Siegel, artistic director
Matthew Lawler, executive director
Send pix & resumes directly to co.?: Yes
Usually casts/accepts pix & resumes:
    Year-round.
Equity Showcase or Tiered Showcase

RYAN REPERTORY COMPANY
Harry Warren Theatre
2445 Bath Avenue
Brooklyn, NY 11214
(718) 996-4800
ryanrep@juno.com
John Sannuto, artistic director
Barbara Parisi, executive director
Michael Pasternack, technical director
Send pix & resumes directly to co.?: Yes
Equity Showcase or Tiered Showcase
    (adult-mainstage)
Non-Equity (children's theatre)

SAGE THEATER COMPANY
205 W. 15 Street, #2M
New York, NY 10011
(212) 929-3423
fax (212) 645-7684
antoniolay@aol.com
Richard Lay, artistic director
Steven Thornburg, director of Sage Acting
    School
Send pix & resumes directly to co.?: Yes
Usually casts/accepts pix & resumes:
    Show by show.
Equity Showcase or Tiered Showcase
Non-Equity

SALAAM THEATRE (SOUTH ASIAN
LEAGUE OF ARTISTS IN AMERICA)
16 W. 32 Street, Suite 10C
New York, NY 10001
(212) 330-8097
fax (212) 579-5537
info@SALAAMtheatre.org
www.salaamtheatre.org
Geeta Citygirl, artistic director
Send pix & resumes directly to co.?: Yes
Usually casts/accepts pix & resumes:
    Always.
Send pix & resumes to: Attn: Geeta Citygirl,
    c/o SALAAM Theatre at the above
    address.

Equity Letter of Agreement
Equity Showcase or Tiered Showcase
Non-Equity

SALAMANDER REPERTORY THEATRE
484 W. 43 Street, Apt. 14D
New York, NY 10036
(212) 695-2358
Joel Leffert, artistic director
Send pix & resumes directly to co.?: No
Usually casts/accepts pix & resumes: When
    project is available.
Equity Showcase or Tiered Showcase

SALT & PEPPER MIME THEATRE
138 S. Oxford Street, Suite 1D
Brooklyn, NY 11217
(718) 398-4979
fax (775) 252-1272
spmime@netzero.net
Ms. Scottie Davis, artistic director
Send pix & resumes directly to co.?: Yes
Usually casts/accepts pix & resumes: Year-round.
Equity Letter of Agreement
Equity Showcase or Tiered Showcase
Non-Equity

*SECOND STAGE THEATRE
307 W. 43 Street
New York, NY 10036
(212) 787-8302
fax (212) 397-7066
info@secondstagetheatre.com
www.secondstagetheatre.com
Carole Rothman, artistic director
Carol Fishman, managing director
Send pix & resumes directly to co.?: Yes—
    all casting inquires should be sent to the
    above address.
Usually casts/accepts pix & resumes: Varies.
Equity Off Broadway "C" contract

SHADOW BOX THEATRE
325 West End Avenue, 12B
New York, NY 10023
(212) 724-0677
fax (212) 724-0767
sbt@shadowboxtheatre.org
www.shadowboxtheatre.org
Sandra Robbins, artistic director
Marlyn Baum, managing director
Elaine Brand, administrator
Send pix & resumes directly to co.?: Yes
Usually casts/accepts pix & resumes:
    Sept. & Dec. for casting/accept resumes
    all year.
Childrens' musical puppet productions;
    school creative arts residencies.
Non-Equity

*THE SHAKESPEARE PROJECT
109 W. 27 Street, #9A
New York, NY 10001
(646) 336-8050
fax (646) 336-8051

scargle@shakespeareproject.org
www.shakespeareproject.org
Scott Cargle, artistic director
Send pix & resumes directly to co.?: Yes
Usually casts/accepts pix & resumes: Spring.
Equity Letter of Agreement

SHEA THEATRE
503 W. 42 Street, Suite #306
New York, NY 10036
(212) 581-1933
Carolyn Williams, artistic director
Send pix & resumes directly to co.?: Yes.
Usually casts/accepts pix & resumes:
    Weekdays only.
Send to Attn: Artistic Director Also works
    to cast the company's productions.
Non-Equity.

*SHOOTING STAR THEATRE
40 Peck Slip
In the South Street Seaport
New York, NY 10038
(212) 791-STAR
MTPres1@aol.com
Anita Brown, artistic director
c/o Montauk Theatre Productions
Send pix & resumes directly to co.?: Yes
Equity Contract
Non-Equity
*For some productions, AEA Guest Artist
or Special Appearance Contracts*

SHOTGUN PRODUCTIONS, INC.
165 E. 35 Street, Suite 7J
New York, NY 10016
(212) 689-2322
fax (718) 291-9354
PRK4257@aol.com
www.shotgun-productions.org
Linda S. Nelson, producing director
Patricia R. Klausner, managing director
Send pix & resumes directly to co.?: No
Usually casts/accepts pix & resumes:
    Cast per project, fall and spring.
Equity Showcase or Tiered Showcase

SIGNATURE THEATRE COMPANY
630 Ninth Avenue, Suite 1106
New York, NY 10036
(212) 967-1913
Theatre:
555 W. 42 Street
New York, NY 10036
(212) 967-1913
www.signaturetheatre.org
Box office: (212) 244-PLAY
James Houghton, artistic director
Kathryn M. Lipuma, executive director
Send pix & resumes directly to co.?: No
Usually casts/accepts pix & resumes:
    Varies.
Casting director: Bernard Tesley Casting
Equity Letter of Agreement

FRANK SILVERA WRITERS' WORKSHOP
PO Box 1791
Manhattanville Station
New York, NY 10027
(212) 281-8832
fax (212) 281-8839
playrite@earthlink.net
www.fsww.org
Garland Lee Thompson, founder/executive
    director
Send pix & resumes directly to co.?: Yes
Usually casts/accepts pix & resumes:
    Ongoing.
Equity Showcase or Tiered Showcase

THE SIMON STUDIO
PO Box 231469, Ansonia Station
New York, NY 10023
(212) 841-0204
rhsstudio@hotmail.com
www.simonstudio.com
Roger Hendricks Simon, artistic director
Send pix & resumes directly to co.?: Yes
Usually casts/accepts pix & resumes:
    All year.
Equity Contract
Equity Letter of Agreement
Equity Showcase or Tiered Showcase
Non-Equity

SIX FIGURES THEATRE COMPANY
PO Box 88
Planetarium Station
New York, NY 10024-0088
(212) 696-8931
info@sixfigures.com
www.sixfigures.com
Kimberly I. Kefgen, artistic director
Cris Buchner, associate artistic director
Loren Ingrid Noveck, literary manager
Kim S. Donovan, development director
Richard Hodge, production manager
Send pix & resumes directly to co.?: No.
Usually casts/accepts pix & resumes:
    Once a year, in the spring.
Equity Tiered Showcase

SOHO REP
Office/mailing address:
86 Franklin Street
New York, NY 10013
Theatre address:
46 Walker Street
New York, NY 10013
sohorep@sohorep.rog
(212) 941-8632
fax (212) 941-7148
www.sohorep.org
Alexandra Conley, executive director
Daniel Aukin, artistic director
Send pix & resumes directly to co.?: No
Usually casts/accepts pix & resumes:
    Depends.
Equity Showcase or Tiered Showcase

*SOHO THINK TANK AT OHIO
THEATRE
66 Wooster Street
New York, NY 10012
(212) 966-4844
fax (212) 625-3461
www.sohothinktank.org
Robert Lyons, artistic director
Eric Jungwirth, producing director
Send pix & resumes directly to co.?: Yes
Usually casts/accepts pix & resumes:
    Year-round.
Equity Showcase or Tiered Showcase

*SOURCEWORKS THEATRE
332 Bleecker Street, Suite F19
New York, NY 10014
(212) 946-4471
fax (212) 923-4552
info@sourceworks.org
www.sourceworks.org
Mark Cannistraro, producing artistic
    director
Equity Contract
Equity Letter of Agreement
Equity Showcase or Tiered Showcase
Non-Equity

ST. BART'S PLAYERS
109 E. 50 Street
New York, NY 10022
Information (212) 378-0217
Box office (212) 378-0248 or
    (212) 378-0222
http://members.aol.com/bartsweb
Bob Berger, Merrill Vaughn, and Veronica
    Shea, co-chairs
Send pix & resumes directly to co.?: Yes
Usually casts/accepts pix & resumes: Sept.,
    Dec., & Feb.
$40.00 annual membership fee
76th anniversary season
Non-Equity

STREETLIGHT PRODUCTIONS, INC.
110-64 Queens Blvd., PMB #175
Forest Hills, NY 11375-6347
(212) 769-7755
fax (212) 202-4107
streetlight@nyc.rr.com
www.streetlightproductions.org
Deborah Mathieu-Byers, artistic director
Stephen P. Byers, managing director
Send pix & resumes directly to co.?: Yes
Usually casts/accepts pix & resumes:
  . Year-round.
Produces in Manhattan.
Equity Showcase or Tiered Showcase
Non-Equity

*STUDIO 42
332 Bleecker Street, #E48
New York, NY 10014
(212) 330-7122

www.studio-42.org
Alison Albeck, producing director
Bradford Louryk, artistic director
Jen Wineman, artistic director
Send pix & resumes directly to co.?: Yes
Usually casts/accepts pix & resumes:
    Year-round.
Non-Equity

SUNDOG THEATRE, INC.
Mailing address:
PO Box 10183
Staten Island, NY 10301-0183
(718) 816-5453
www.SundogTheatre.org
Susan Fenley, artistic director
Scott Benedict, managing director
Send pix & resumes directly to co.?: Yes
Usually casts/accepts pix & resumes:
    Mostly accept pix per show, however,
    actors/playwrights can send anytime.
Equity Showcase or Tiered Showcase

TADA!
15 W. 28 Street, Third fl.
New York, NY 10001
(212) 252-1619
tada@tadatheater.com
www.tadatheater.com
Janine Nina Trevens, artistic director
Bonnie J. Butkas, managing director
Peter Avery, education director
Send pix & resumes directly to co.?: No
(Tada! is a youth theatre co.)
Non-Equity

TARGET MARGIN THEATER
138 S. Oxford Street, Rm. 5A
Brooklyn, NY 11217
(718) 398-3095
fax (718) 398-3613
info@targetmargin.org
www.targetmargin.org
David Herskovits, artistic director
Darren Critz, managing director
Greig Sargeant, casting director
Yuri Skujins, literary manager
Lenore Doxsee, production manager
Send pix & resumes to directly co.?: Yes
Usually casts/accepts pix & resumes:
    Year-round.
Equity Letter of Agreement
Equity Showcase or Tiered Showcase

TAWKING DAWG REPERTAWRY
THEATRICAL PLAYERS, LTD.
22-60 37 Street
Astoria, NY 11105-1906
TawkingDawg@aol.com
Francis J. Balducci, artistic director
Peggy Swisher, press secretary
Send pix & resumes directly to co.?: Yes
Usually casts/accepts pix & resumes: April.
Equity Showcase or Tiered Showcase

*TEATRO CIRCULO, LTD.
250 W. 26 Street, Fourth fl.
New York, NY 10001
(212) 242-4460
teatrocirculo@aol.com
Jose Cheo Oliveras, artistic director
Send pix & resumes directly to co.?: Yes
Usually casts/accepts pix & resumes: All year.
Non-Equity

THALIA SPANISH THEATRE
41-17 Greenpoint Avenue
Sunnyside, NY 11104
(718) 729-3880
fax (718) 729-3388
info@thaliatheatre.org
www.thaliatheatre.org
Angel Gil Orrios, executive/artistic/casting
    director
Kathryn Giaimo, administrative director
Soledad López, managing director
Send pix & resumes directly to co.?:
    Yes, to Attn: Angel Gil Orrios.
Usually casts/accepts pix & resumes:
    Year-round.
Non-Equity

THEATRE FOR A NEW AUDIENCE
154 Christopher Street, #3D
New York, NY 10014
(212) 229-2819
fax (212) 229-2911
info@tfana.org
www.tfana.org
Jeffrey Horowitz, artistic director
Dorothy Ryan, managing director
Send pix & resumes directly to co.?: No
Usually casts/accepts pix & resumes: Never.
Equity LORT "D" contract

THEATER FOR THE NEW CITY
155 First Avenue
New York, NY 10003
(212) 254-1109
fax (212) 974-6570
tnctheater@aol.com
www.theaterforthenewcity.net
Crystal Field, executive director
Send pix & resumes directly to co.?: Yes
Usually casts/accepts pix & resumes:
    Show-by-show basis.
Equity Showcase or Tiered Showcase

THEATER TEN TEN
1010 Park Avenue
New York, NY 10028
(212) 288-3246, ext. 3
theatr1010@aol.com
http://members.aol.com/theatr1010
Judith Jarosz, producing artistic director
Send pix & resumes directly to co.?: Yes
Usually casts/accepts pix & resumes:
    All year round.
Equity Tiered Showcase

THE THEATRE AT HOLY CROSS
329 W. 42 Street
New York, NY 10036
(212) 246-4732
fax (212) 307-5033
Jim Patterson, president
Pat Shankeman, secretary/treasurer
Send pix & resumes directly to co.?: Yes
Usually casts/accepts pix & resumes:
    Show-by-show basis.
Equity Showcase or Tiered Showcase

THE THEATRE-STUDIO INC.
750 Eighth Avenue, Suite 200
New York, NY 10036
(212) 719-0500
A.M. Raychel, artistic director
Equity Contract
Equity Letter of Agreement
Equity Showcase or Tiered Showcase
Non-Equity

THEATREWORKS/USA
151 W. 26 Street, 7th fl.
New York, NY 10001
(212) 647-1100
info@theatreworksusa.org
www.theatreworksusa.org
Barbara Pasternack, artistic director
Ken Arthur, managing director
Robin D. Carus, casting director
Send pix & resumes directly to co.?: Yes
Usually casts/accepts pix & resumes:
    Year-round.
Equity Contract
Equity Letter of Agreement

*THE THEMANTICS GROUP
(917) 975-1428
casting@themantics.org
www.themantics.org
Jay Aubrey, producing director
Blake Lawrence, artistic manager
Send pix & resumes directly to co.?: No
Usually casts/accepts pix & resumes:
    As requested for individual show
    auditions.
Equity Showcase or Tiered Showcase

13TH STREET REPERTORY
COMPANY
50 W. 13 Street
New York, NY 10011
(212) 675-6677
ThirteenSt@aol.com
www.13thstreetrep.org
Edith O'Hara, artistic director
Robert Kreis, associate art. director
Send pix & resumes directly to co.?: Yes
Usually casts/accepts pix & resumes:
    Ongoing.
Non-Equity
*Casts only with the company; accepts
pix & resumes for new members.*

*TODO CON NADA TIMES SQUARE
AT TODO 45
Mailing address:
PO Box 2352
New York, NY 10108-2352
Office address:
445 W. 45 Street, 4th fl.
New York, NY 10036
(917) 679-8228
todoconnada@aol.com
www.alternativebroadway.com
Aaron Beall, executive director
Send pix & resumes directly to co.?: Yes
Usually casts/accepts pix & resumes:
    Ongoing with cover letter.
Casting:
    Aaron Beall
    c/o Todo Con Nada Times Square at Todo 45
    PO Box 2352
    New York, NY 10108-2352
Equity Showcase or Tiered Showcase
Non-Equity
Also under the Hebrew Actors Union

29TH STREET REP
212 W. 29 Street
New York, NY 10001
(212) 465-0575
www.29thstreetrep.com
Tim Corcoran, David Mogentale, co-artistic
    directors
Send pix & resumes directly to co.?: No
Usually casts/accepts pix & resumes: Never.
Equity Contract
Equity Letter of Agreement
Equity Showcase or Tiered Showcase

UJAMAA BLACK THEATRE
New Yorker Hotel
W. 34 Street and Ninth Avenue, 9th fl., Suite 952
New York, NY 10001
(212) 642-8261
twgoodgod@aol.com
Titus Walker, artistic director
Send pix & resumes directly to co.?: Yes,
    send pix & resumes to:
    PO Box 4383,
    Grand Central Station
    New York, NY 10163.
Usually casts/accepts pix & resumes: Year-end.
Non-Equity

UNTITLED THEATER CO. #61
235 W. 102 Street, Suite 16S
New York, NY 10025
(212) 387-2043
edwardeinhorn@untitledtheater.com
www.untitledtheater.com
Edward Einhorn, artistic director
David Einhorn, producing director
Send pix & resumes directly to co.: Yes
Usually casts/accepts pix & resumes: Ongoing.
Equity Off-Broadway contract
Equity Showcase or Tiered Showcase

*URBAN STAGES
Office address:
17 E. 47 Street
New York, NY 10017
(212) 421-1380
fax (212) 421-1387
Theatre address:
259 W. 30 Street
New York, NY 10001-2809
urbanstage@aol.com
www.urbanstages.org
Frances Hill, artistic director
T.L. Reilly, producing director
Send pix & resumes directly to co.?: Yes
Usually casts/accepts pix & resumes: Open.
Casting: Stephanie Klapper
Equity Mini-Contract

VICTORY THEATRICAL
127 W. 95 Street, #2
New York, NY 10025
(212) 866-5170
fax (212) 866-1119
victoryth@aol.com
www.literallyalive.com
Brenda Bell, artistic director
Send pix & resumes directly to co.?: Yes
Usually casts/accepts pix & resumes: Early fall
    (Sept.); early winter (Jan.).
Non-Equity

THE VILLAR-HAUSER THEATRE
DEVELOPMENT FUND, INC.
c/o 188 E. 93 Street, #2B
New York, NY 10128
(917) 304-6823
lvillarhauser@aol.com
Ludovica Villar-Hauser, artistic director
Send pix & resumes directly to co.?: No
Usually casts/accepts pix & resumes: As
    advertised in *Back Stage*, show by show.
Equity Off-Broadway Contract
Equity Showcase or Tiered Showcase
Non-Equity

VINEYARD THEATRE
108 E. 15 Street
New York, NY 10003
(212) 353-3366
fax (212) 353-3803
www.vineyardtheatre.org
Douglas Aibel, artistic director
Bardo Ramirez, managing director
Send pix & resumes directly to co.?: No.
Usually casts/accepts pix & resumes:
    Submissions only.
Equity Letter of Agreement

VITAL THEATRE COMPANY
432 W. 42 Street, Third fl.
New York, NY 10036
(212) 268-2040
office@vitaltheatre.org
www.VitalTheatre.org

Stephen Sunderlin, artistic director
Julie Hamberg, associate artistic director
Lisa Brenner, literary manager
Carrie Libling, director of children's theatre
Send pix & resumes directly to co.?: Yes,
    address to Casting; for children's theatre,
    send to Director of Children's Theatre.
Usually casts/accepts pix & resumes: Year-round.
Equity Showcase or Tiered Showcase (mainstage)
Non-Equity (children's theatre)
*Playwrights can visit our website for submission
guidelines.*

VOICE & VISION
520 Eighth Avenue, #308
New York, NY 10018
(212) 268-3717
fax (212) 268-5462
vandv@vandv.org
www.vandv.org
Jean Wagner, artistic director
LeeAnne Hutchison, associate artistic director
Send pix & resumes directly to co.?: No
Usually casts/accepts pix & resumes: As needed.
Equity Tier II Showcase

VORTEX THEATER COMPANY, INC.
Sanford Meisner Theater
164 Eleventh Avenue
New York, NY 10011
(212) 206-1764/(212) 206-1765
Robert Coles, co-artistic director
Anthony John Lizzul, co-artistic director,
    managing director,
Send pix & resumes directly to co.?: No
Usually casts: Hold individual auditions for
    each play; general audition at least twice
    a year.
Casting: In-house.
Equity Tiered Showcase

*WATERLOO BRIDGE THEATRE CO.
401 Prospect Avenue
Brooklyn, NY 11215
waterloobridgetc@cs.com
www.waterloo.itgo.com
J. Brandon Hill, artistic director
Chris Bakolias, managing director
Non-Equity

WAXING MOON THEATRE COMPANY
c/o Cathrine Goldstein
1438 Third Avenue, Suite 18E
New York, NY 10028
Waxingmoon01@aol.com
(212) 769-8471
Cathrine Goldstein, founder/artistic director
Send pix & resumes directly to co.?: Yes; send
    to Cathrine Goldstein at above address—
    send pix & resumes only.
Usually casts/accepts pix & resumes:
    As needed; year-round.
Equity Showcase
Non-Equity

WESTBETH THEATRE CENTER
111 W. 17 Street
New York, NY 10011
(212) 691-2272
fax (212) 924-7185
general@westbethent.com
Arnold Engelman, president
Send pix & resumes directly to co.?: No
Usually casts/accepts pix & resumes:
    Show by show.
Equity Off-Broadway contract
Equity Letter of Agreement
Equity Showcase or Tiered Showcase

*WINGS THEATRE COMPANY, INC.
154 Christopher Street
New York, NY 10014
(212) 627-2960
Box office (212) 627-2961
fax (212) 462-0024
jcorrick@wingstheatre.com
www.wingstheatre.com
Jeff Corrick, artistic director
Robert Mooney, managing director
Send pix & resumes directly to co.: Yes
Usually casts/accepts pix & resumes:
    Year-round.
Equity Tier IV Showcase

WOMEN'S PROJECT & PRODUCTIONS
Administrative Offices:
55 West End Avenue
New York, NY 10023
Theatre:
Women's Project Theatre
    (formerly Theatre Four)
424 W. 55th Street
New York, NY 10019
(212) 765-1706
fax (212) 765-2024 (Administrative)
info@womensproject.org
www.womensproject.org
Julia Miles, founder & artistic director emeritus
Marya Cohn, acting artistic director
Georgia Buchanan, managing director
Send pix & resumes directly to co.?: Yes—
    for consideration for company's reading
    series only. Put to Attn: Literary Manager.
    Actors with agents preferred.
Usually casts/accepts pix & resumes:
    2–3 months prior to production; agent
    submissions only.
Equity Letter of Agreement

WORDSPACE THEATRE WORKSHOP
347 W. 55th Street, 4H
New York, NY 10019
(212) 586-8368
Paul Pierog, artistic director
Send pix & resumes directly to co.?: Yes
Usually cast/accepts pix & resumes: Ongoing.
Currently involved in video production.
Also sometimes does stage productions.
Non-Equity

THE WORKING THEATER
128 East Broadway
PO Box 892
New York, NY 10002-0892
(212) 539-5675
fax (212) 614-9821
Mplesent@aol.com
www.theworkingtheater.org
Mark Plesent, producing director
Robert Arcaro, artistic director
Send pix & resumes directly to co.?: No
Usually casts/accepts pix & resumes: During
production—resumes sent April of each year.
Equity Letter of Agreement

THE WORKSHOP THEATER COMPANY
312 W. 36 Street, 4th fl.
New York, NY 10018
(212) 695-4173; (212) 695-3384
Tony Sportiello, artistic director
Membership Company
Send pix & resumes directly to co.?: Yes
Usually casts/accepts pix & resumes: Anytime.
Equity Showcase or Tiered Showcase

THE XOREGOS PERFORMING COMPANY
496 Ninth Avenue, 4A
New York, NY 10018
(212) 239-8405
Shela Xoregos, producing director
Send pix & resumes directly to co.?: Yes
Usually casts/accepts pix & resumes: Year-round.
Equity Showcase or Tiered Showcase
Non-Equity

YANGTZE REPERTORY THEATRE OF
AMERICA
Mailing address:
c/o Maryknoll Sisters Center
10 Pinesbridge Rd.
Maryknoll, NY 10545
Office address:
#2 Mott Street, Suite 706
New York, NY 10013
*Moving to new office address on Lafayette Street,
at the end of Oct. 2003:*
(914) 941-7575
fax (914) 923-0733

joannawychan@juno.com
www.yangtze-rep-theatre.com
Dr. Joanna Chan, artistic director
Cathy Hung, company manager
Christopher Thomas, technical consultant
Send pix & resumes directly to co.?: Yes
Usually casts/accepts pix & resumes: During
auditions which are announced in ads in
Back Stage.
Non-Equity

YORK SHAKESPEARE COMPANY
PO Box 30771
S. Farmingdale, NY 11735
(646) 623-7117
yorkshake@aol.com
www.yorkshakespeare.org
Seth Duerr, artistic director
Send pix & resumes directly to co.?: Yes
Usually casts/accepts pix & resumes:
At all times.
Non-Equity

THE YORK THEATRE COMPANY
The Theatre at Saint Peter's Church,
Citicorp Center
619 Lexington Avenue
New York, NY 10022-4610
(212) 935-5824
fax (212) 832-0037
Box office: (212) 935-5820
mail@yorktheatre.org
James Morgan, artistic director
Louis Chiodo, consulting managing director
Send pix & resumes directly to co.?: Yes
Usually casts/accepts pix & resumes: Anytime.
Equity Contract
Equity Letter of Agreement

YOUNG PLAYWRIGHTS INC.
Young Playwrights Festival
306 W. 38 Street, #300
New York, NY 10018
(212) 594-5440
writeaplay@aol.com
www.youngplaywrights.org
Sheri M. Goldhirsch, artistic director
Equity Mini Contract

Casting Directors and Talent Agencies

FROM *ROSS REPORTS*

New York Casting Directors

AAAVOICECASTING
123 West 18th Street, 7th Floor
New York, NY 10011
(212) 675-3240

ABC PRIMETIME CASTING
157 Columbus Avenue, 2nd Floor
New York, NY 10023

AMERIFILM CASTING, INC.
195 Chrystie Street,
Suite 502G
New York, NY 10002

THE ASTORIA PERFORMING
ARTS CENTER
31-60 33rd Street, #B-9
Long Island City, NY 11106

BACKGROUND, INC.
20 West 20th Street,
Suite 228
New York, NY 10011
(212) 609-1103

BRADLEY BARON
P.O. Box 1023
Fort Lee, NJ 07024
(201) 313-1107

HARRIET BASS CASTING
648 Broadway, #912
New York, NY 10012
(212) 598-9032

JERRY BEAVER CASTING
484 West 43rd Street, #19-N
New York, NY 10036
(212) 244-3600

BREANNA BENJAMIN CASTING
PO Box 21077-PACC
New York, NY 10129
(212) 388-2347

JAY BINDER CASTING
321 West 44th Street, Suite 606
New York, NY 10036

BLOCK CASTING
Box 170, 1710 First Avenue
New York, NY 10128
(212) 332-9777

BLUE MAN PRODUCTIONS
599 Broadway, 5th Floor
New York, NY 10012
(212) 226-6366

NORA BRENNAN CASTING
752 West End Avenue
New York, NY 10025
(212) 531-1825

KRISTINE BULAKOWSKI
CASTING
Prince Street Station,
P.O. Box 616
New York, NY 10012
(212) 769-8550

CBS ENTERTAINMENT
51 West 52nd Street, 5th floor
New York, NY 10019

CTP CASTING
207 West 25th Street, 6th Floor
New York, NY 10001
(212) 414-1931

JAMES CALLERI CASTING
416 West 42nd Street
New York, NY 10036
(212) 564-1235

DONALD CASE CASTING INC.
386 Park Avenue South,
Suite 809
New York, NY 10016
(212) 889-6555

CASTING CONNECTION
Producers only call:
(609) 926-2209
(See also listing under California Casting Directors)

CASTING HOUSE
443 Greenwich Street, Fifth Floor
New York, NY 10013
(212) 965-9994

CASTING SOLUTIONS
231 West 29th Street,
Suite 601
New York, NY 10001
(212) 875-7573

CHANTILES VIGNEAULT
CASTING, INC.
39 West 19th Street, 12th Floor
New York, NY 10011

ROZ CLANCY CASTING
76 Wilfred Avenue
Washington Crossing, NJ 08560

DAVE CLEMMONS CASTING
265 West 30th Street
New York, NY 10001
(212) 594-7434

RICH COLE
648 Broadway, Suite 912
New York, NY 10012
(212) 614-7130

JODI COLLINS CASTING
9 Desbrosses Street,
Second Floor
New York, NY 10013
Complete Casting
(212) 265-7460

BYRON CRYSTAL
41 Union Square West,
Suite 316
New York, NY 10003

SUE CRYSTAL CASTING
251 West 87th Street, #26
New York, NY 10024
(212) 877-0737

MERRY L. DELMONTE
Casting & Productions, Inc.
575 Madison Avenue
New York, NY 10022

DONNA DESETA CASTING
525 Broadway, Third Floor
New York, NY 10012

JOAN D'INCECCO CASTING
fax: (201) 265-6016

DOWNSTAIRS CASTING
428 Broadway, Fifth Floor
New York, NY 10013
(212) 625-5638

PENNIE DU PONT
36 Perry Street
New York, NY 10014
(212) 255-2708

EXTRAS CASTING BY
BOOKED
9 Desbrosses Street, Suite 513
New York, NY 10013
(212) 925-6010

SYLVIA FAY
71 Park Avenue
New York, NY 10016

ALAN FILDERMAN CASTING
333 West 39th Street, #601A
New York, NY 10018
(212) 695-6200

LEONARD FINGER
34 Morton Street
New York, NY 10014

JUDIE FIXLER CASTING
P.O. Box 127
Green Farms, CT 06838
(203) 254-4416

JANET FOSTER
3212 Cambridge Avenue
Riverdale, NY 10463

FOX BROADCASTING COMPANY
1211 Avenue of the Americas
New York, NY 10036
(212) 556-2400
*(See also listing under L.A.
Casting Directors)*

GILBURNE & URBAN CASTING
80 Varick Street, Suite 6A
New York, NY 10013
(212) 965-0745

GODLOVE & COMPANY
CASTING
151 West 25th Street, 11th Floor
New York, NY 10001
(212) 627-7300

AMY GOSSELS CASTING
1382 Third Avenue
New York, NY 10021
(212) 472-6981

JOEY GUASTELLA CASTING
85-10 151st Avenue, #5B
Queens, NY 11414

JIMMY HANK PROMOTIONS
209 West 104th Street, Suite 2H
New York, NY 10025
(212) 864-2132

CAROL HANZEL CASTING
48 West 21st Street, 7th Floor
New York, NY 10010
(212) 242-6113

AMANDA HARDING
(See Koblin/Harding Casting)

HEERY CASTING
230 North Second Street, Suite 1A
Philadelphia, PA 19106
(212) 238-9240

JUDY HENDERSON &
ASSOCIATES CASTING
330 West 89th Street
New York, NY 10024
(212) 877-0225

HERMAN & LIPSON
CASTING, INC.
630 Ninth Avenue, Suite 1410
New York, NY 10036

HOUSE FILMS
53 West 36th Street, #305
New York, NY 10018
(212) 645-8462

HOUSE PRODUCTIONS
450 West 15th Street,
Suite 202
New York, NY 10011
(212) 929-0200

STUART HOWARD
ASSOCIATES, LTD.
207 West 25th Street,
Suite #601
New York, NY 10001
(212) 414-1544

HUGHES MOSS CASTING LTD.
484 West 43rd Street, Suite 28R
New York, NY 10036
(212) 307-6690

IMPOSSIBLE CASTING
122 West 26th Street, 6th Floor
New York, NY 10001
(212) 255-3029

INPRODUCTION CASTING
589 8th Avenue, 20th Floor
NewYork, NY 10018
(212) 868-4047

AVY KAUFMAN CASTING
180 Varick Street, 16th Floor
New York, NY 10014

KEE CASTING
424 Park Avenue South, #128
New York, NY 10016
(212) 725-3775

JUDY KELLER CASTING
140 West 22nd Street, 4th Floor
New York, NY 10011

KIPPERMAN CASTING, INC.
12 West 37th Street, 3rd Floor
New York, NY 10018
(212) 736-3663

STEPHANIE KLAPPER CASTING
122 West 26th Street, Suite 1104
New York, NY 10001
(646) 486-1337

KOBLIN/HARDING CASTING,
C/O C.S.A.
(212) 995-5336
*(See also listing under Los
Angeles Casting Directors and
C.S.A. Los Angeles)*

ANDREA KURZMAN
CASTING INC.
122 East 37th Street, 2nd Floor
New York, NY 10016
(212) 684-0710

MIKE LEMON CASTING, C.S.A.
413 North 7th Street, Suite 602
Philadelphia, PA 19123
(215) 627-8927

KELLI LERNER CASTING,
Artistic Endeavors LLC
330 West 56th Street, Suite 25E
New York, NY 10019
(212) 459-9293

LIZ LEWIS CASTING PARTNERS
129 West 20th Street
New York, NY 10011
(212) 645-1500

VINCE LIEBHART CASTING
1710 First Avenue, #122
New York, NY 10128

JOAN LYNN CASTING
39 West 19th Street, 12th Floor
New York, NY 10011
(212) 675-5595

MTV/MTV2 TALENT
1515 Broadway, 23th Floor
New York, NY 10036
(See also MTV/TRL)

MTV/TRL
1515 Broadway, 23rd Floor
New York, NY 10036
*(See also MTV Network under
L.A. Casting Directors)*

MACKEY SANDRICH CASTING
180 Grand Street, Third Floor
New York, NY 10013
(212) 343-3660

MADLAND CASTING,
The Astoria Performing Arts
Center
31-60 33rd Street, #B-9
Long Island City, NY 11106

JOEL MANALOTO CASTING
1480 York Avenue, Fourth Floor
New York, NY 10021
(212) 517-3737

MARGOLIS-SEAY CASTING
333 West 52nd Street,
Suite 1008
New York, NY 10019

MBC CASTING
325 West 38th Street
New York, NY 10018
(212) 564-7214

MCCORKLE CASTING LTD.
575 8th Avenue, 18th Floor
New York, NY 10018
(212) 244-3899

ABIGAIL MCGRATH, INC.
484 West 43rd Street, Suite 37-S
New York, NY 10036

MCHALE BARONE
30 Irving Place, Sixth Floor
New York, NY 10011

BETH MELSKY CASTING
928 Broadway, Suite 300
New York, NY 10010
(212) 505-5000

NORMAN MERANUS CASTING
201 West 85th Street, 16-D
New York, NY 10024

MATTHEW MESSINGER
CASTING
244 West 72nd Street
New York, NY 10023

MITCHELL/RUDOLPH CASTING
440 Park Avenue South,
   11th Floor
New York, NY 10016
(212) 679-3550

MUNGIOLI THEATRICALS, INC.
207 West 25th Street, 6th Floor
New York, NY 10001
(212) 337-8832

ELISSA MYERS CASTING
333 West 52nd Street,
   Suite 1008
New York, NY 10019

NICKELODEON
1515 Broadway, 38th Floor
New York, NY 10036

STEVEN O'NEILL
VP of Casting–NBC
30 Rockefeller Plaza, Room 1628E
New York, NY 10112

ORPHEUS GROUP CASTING
165 West 46th Street, Suite 405
New York, NY 10036
(212) 957-8760

MICHELE ORTLIP CASTING
(508) 696-0944

PALADINO CASTING
35 East 21st Street, 2nd Floor
New York, NY 10010
(212) 228-5500

JOANNE PASCIUTO INC.
17-08 150th Street
Whitestone, NY 11357

THE PHILADELPHIA
CASTING CO., INC.
114 Chestnut Street, 3rd Floor
Philadelphia, PA 19106
Number for actors only:
(215) 592-7577

POMANN SOUND
2 West 46th Street, #PH
New York, NY 10036
(212) 869-4161
Michele Pulice Casting
www.michelepulicecasting.com

TUFFY QUESTELL/ T.E.C.
CASTING
P.O. Box 859
Bronx, NY 10462
(718) 792-8447

LAURA RICHIN CASTING
33 Douglass Street, Suite #1
Brooklyn, NY 11231
(718) 802-9628

TONI ROBERTS CASTING, LTD.
1133 Broadway, Suite 630
New York, NY 10010

CHARLES ROSEN CASTING, INC.
140 West 22nd Street, 4th Floor
New York, NY 10011

JUDY ROSENSTEEL CASTING
43 West 68th Street
New York, NY 10023

CINDI RUSH CASTING, LTD.
27 West 20th Street, Suite 404
New York, NY 10011

PAUL RUSSELL CASTING
159 West 25th Street, Suite 1009
New York, NY 10001

HOWARD SCHWARTZ
RECORDING/HSR NY
420 Lexington Avenue, Suite 1934
New York, NY 10170
(212) 687-4180

BRIEN SCOTT
71-10 Loubet Street
Forest Hills, NY 11375
(818) 343-3669
*(See also listing under Los
Angeles Casting Directors)*

SELECTIVE CASTING BY
CAROL NADELL
P.O. Box 1538
Radio City Station, NY 10101-1538

SHANE/GOLDSTEIN CASTING
311 West 43rd Street, Suite 602
New York, NY 10036
(212) 445-0100

MARK SIMON CASTING
10 Rockefeller Plaza, Suite 1014
New York, NY 10020

CAROLINE SINCLAIR CASTING
c/o The Zipper Theatre
336 West 37th Street
New York, NY 10018
(212) 279-1002

WINSOME SINCLAIR &
ASSOCIATES
2575A Eighth Avenue
New York, NY 10030
(212) 281-4044

SIRIUS CASTING
(347) 661-7591
siriuscasting@aol.com

SKYRME, LEWIS, & FOX
CASTING
459 Columbus Avenue, #164
New York, NY 10024
(212) 724-1121

SIDRA SMITH CASTING
60 West 129th Street, Suite 7E
New York, NY 10027
(212) 831-6810
*(See also listing under Los
Angeles Casting Directors)*

SPIKE TV
1515 Broadway, 40th Floor
New York, NY 10036
*(See listing for Spike TV under
Los Angeles Casting Directors)*

SPOTTY DOG PRODUCTIONS
236 West 27th Street,
   Sixth Floor
New York, NY 10001
(212) 463-8550

STARK NAKED PRODUCTIONS,
INC./ELSIE STARK CASTING
39 West 19th Street, 12th Floor
New York, NY 10011
(212) 366-1903

ADRIENNE STERN
80 Eighth Avenue, Suite 303
New York, NY 10011

STRICKMAN-RIPPS, INC.
65 North Moore Street,
   Suite 3A
New York, NY 10013
(212) 966-3211

DANI SUPER & JOHN MABRY
(212) 414-0823

HELYN TAYLOR CASTING
140 West 58th Street
New York, NY 10019
*(See also listing under Los
Angeles Casting Directors)*

BERNARD TELSEY CASTING
145 West 28th Street,
   12th Floor
New York, NY 10001
(212) 868-1260

TODD THALER CASTING
130 West 57th Street, #10A
New York, NY 10019

THEATREWORKS/USA
151 West 26th Street,
   Seventh Floor
New York, NY 10001

VH1
1633 Broadway, Sixth Floor
New York, NY 10019

VIDEOACTIVE TALENT
1780 Broadway, Studio 804
New York, NY 10019
(212) 541-8106

VOICEHUNTER.COM
P.O. Box 286
Weston, CT 06881-0286
(800) 867-9532

WALKEN/JAFFE CASTING
Georgianne Walken and Shiela
Jaffe cast for film and T.V. including
principals for The Sopranos.
(For The Sopranos background
casting, see Grant Wilfley Casting.)

WARNER BROS. TELEVISION
CASTING
1325 Avenue of the Americas,
   32nd Floor
New York, NY 10019
(212) 636-5145
(See also Los Angeles Casting
Directors)

JOY WEBER CASTING
440 West End Avenue
New York, NY 10024
(845) 647-3849

KATHY WICKLINE CASTING
1080 North Delaware Avenue,
   Suite100
Philadelphia, PA 19125
(215) 739-9952

GRANT WILFLEY CASTING
60 Madison Avenue, Room 1027
New York, NY 10010
(212) 685-3537

LIZ WOODMAN CASTING
11 Riverside Drive, #2JE
New York, NY 10023
(212) 787-3782

WORLD CASTING
(a.k.a. World Promotions Inc.)
216 Crown Street, Suite 501
New Haven, CT 06510
(203) 781-3427

New York Talent Agencies

ABOUT ARTISTS AGENCY, INC.
(SAG-AFTRA-EQUITY)
1650 Broadway, #1406
New York, NY 10019
(212) 581-1857

ABRAMS ARTISTS AGENCY
(SAG-AFTRA-EQUITY)
275 Seventh Avenue, 26th Floor
New York, NY 10001
(646) 486-4600
(See also listing under Los
Angeles Talent Agencies)

ACCESS TALENT, INC.
(SAG-AFTRA)
37 East 28th Street, Suite 500
New York, NY 10016
(212) 684-7795

ACME TALENT & LITERARY
(SAG-AFTRA-EQUITY-WGA)
875 Sixth Avenue, Suite 2108
New York, NY 10001
(212) 328-0388

BRET ADAMS, LTD.
(SAG-AFTRA-EQUITY)
448 West 44th Street
New York, NY 10036
(212) 765-5630

AGENTS FOR THE ARTS, INC.
(SAG-AFTRA-EQUITY)
203 West 23rd Street, 3rd Floor
New York, NY 10011
(212) 229-2562

MICHAEL AMATO AGENCY
(SAG-AFTRA-EQUITY-WGA)
1650 Broadway, Room 307
New York, NY 10019
(212) 247-4456-7

AMERICAN INTERNATIONAL
TALENT AGENCY
(SAG-AFTRA-EQUITY)
303 West 42nd Street,
   Suite 608
New York, NY 10036
(212) 245-8888
fax: (212) 245-8926

BEVERLY ANDERSON
(SAG-AFTRA-EQUITY)
1501 Broadway, Suite 2008
New York, NY 10036
(212) 944-7773

ANDREADIS TALENT
AGENCY, INC.
(SAG-AFTRA-EQUITY)
119 West 57th Street,
   Suite 711
New York, NY 10019
(212) 315-0303

ARCIERI & ASSOCIATES, INC.
(SAG-AFTRA)
305 Madison Avenue,
   Suite 2315
New York, NY 10165
(212) 286-1700

THE ARTISTS GROUP EAST
(SAG-AFTRA-EQUITY)
1650 Broadway, Suite 610
New York, NY 10019
(212) 586-1452
(See also listing under Los
Angeles Talent Agencies)

ASSOCIATED BOOKING
CORPORATION
(SAG-AFTRA-EQUITY)
1995 Broadway, Suite 501
New York, NY 10023
(212) 874-2400

THE RICHARD ASTOR AGENCY
(SAG-AFTRA-EQUITY)
250 West 57th Street, #2014
New York, NY 10107
(212) 581-1970

ATLAS TALENT AGENCY, INC.
(SAG-AFTRA-EQUITY)
36 West 44th Street, Suite 1000
New York, NY 10036
(212) 730-4500

BARRY-HAFT-BROWN
ARTISTS AGENCY
(B-H-B) (SAG-AFTRA-EQUITY)
165 West 46th Street, Suite 908
New York, NY 10036
(212) 869-9310

BAUMAN, REDANTY & SHAUL
(SAG-AFTRA-EQUITY)
250 West 57th Street,
   Suite 2223
New York, NY 10107
(212) 757-0098
(See also listing under Los
Angeles Talent Agencies)

PETER BEILIN AGENCY, INC.
(SAG-AFTRA)
230 Park Avenue, Suite 200
New York, NY 10169
(212) 949-9119

THE BETHEL AGENCY
(SAG-AFTRA-EQUITY)
311 West 43rd Street, Suite 602
New York, NY 10036
(212) 664-0455

BLOC NYC (SAG-EQUITY)
41 East 11th Street, 11th Floor
New York, NY 10003
(212) 905-6236
(See also listing under Los
Angeles Talent Agencies)

JUDY BOALS, INC.
(SAG-AFTRA-EQUITY-WGA)
208 West 30th Street # 401
New York, NY 10001
(212) 868-0924

DON BUCHWALD & ASSOCIATES
(SAG-AFTRA-EQUITY-WGA)
10 East 44th Street
New York, NY 10017
(212) 867-1200, 1070
(See also listing under Los Angeles Talent Agencies)

CARRY COMPANY
(SAG-AFTRA-EQUITY-WGA)
Empire State Building
350 Fifth Avenue, Suite 1702
New York, NY 10118
(212) 768-2793
(See also listing under Los Angeles Talent Agencies)

CARSON-ADLER AGENCY, INC.
(SAG-AFTRA-EQUITY)
250 West 57th Street, Suite 2030
New York, NY 10107
(212) 307-1882

THE CARSON
ORGANIZATION, LTD.
(SAG-AFTRA-EQUITY)
The Sardi's Building
234 West 44th Street, Suite 902
New York, NY 10036
(212) 221-1517

MARY ANNE CLARO TALENT
AGENCY, INC.
(SAG-AFTRA-EQUITY)
1513 West Passyunk Avenue
Philadelphia, PA 19145
(215) 465-7788

COLEMAN-ROSENBERG
(EQUITY)
155 East 55th Street, Suite 5D
New York, NY 10022
(212) 838-0734

COLUMBIA ARTISTS
MANAGEMENT, INC.
(AFTRA)
165 West 57th Street
New York, NY 10019
(212) 841-9500

CORNERSTONE TALENT
AGENCY
(SAG-AFTRA-EQUITY)
37 West 20th Street, Suite 1108
New York, NY 10011
(212) 807-8344

CUNNINGHAM, ESCOTT,
DIPENE & ASSOCIATES
(SAG-AFTRA-EQUITY)
257 Park Avenue South, Suite 900
New York, NY 10010
(212) 477-1666
(See also listing under Los Angeles Talent Agencies)

GINGER DICCE TALENT
AGENCY
(SAG-AFTRA-EQUITY)
56 West 45th Street, Suite 1100
New York, NY 10036
(212) 869-9650

DOUGLAS, GORMAN,
ROTHACKER
& Wilhelm, Inc. (DGRW)
(SAG-AFTRA-EQUITY)
1501 Broadway, Suite 703
New York, NY 10036
(212) 382-2000

EWCR & ASSOCIATES
(SAG-AFTRA-EQUITY)
311 West 43rd Street, Suite 304
New York, NY 10036
(212) 586-9110
(See also listing under Los Angeles Talent Agencies)

EASTERN TALENT
ALLIANCE INC.
(SAG-AFTRA-EQUITY)
1501 Broadway, Suite 404
New York, NY 10036
(212) 220-9888

DULCINA EISEN ASSOCIATES
(SAG-AFTRA-EQUITY)
154 East 61st Street
New York, NY 10021
(212) 355-6617

ELECTRIC TALENT, INC.
(AFTRA)
172-13 Hillside Avenue,
   Suite 202
Jamaica Estates, NY 11432
(718) 883-1940

FLAUNT MODEL & TALENT INC.
(SAG-AFTRA)
114 East 32nd Street, #501
New York, NY 10016
(212) 679-9011

THE JIM FLYNN AGENCY
(SAG-AFTRA-EQUITY-WGA)
208 West 30th Street, Suite 401
New York, NY 10001
(212) 868-1068

FRESH FACES AGENCY, INC.
(SAG-AFTRA-EQUITY)
2911 Carnation Avenue
Baldwin, NY 11510-4402
(516) 223-0034

FRONTIER BOOKING
INTERNATIONAL, INC.
(FBI) (SAG-AFTRA-EQUITY)
1560 Broadway, Suite 1110
New York, NY 10036
(212) 221-0220

GWA (G. WILLIAMS AGENCY)
(SAG-AFTRA-EQUITY)
525 South Fourth Street, #365
Philadelphia, PA 19147
(215) 627-9533

THE GAGE GROUP
(SAG-AFTRA-EQUITY)
315 West 57th Street,
   Suite 408
New York, NY 10019
(212) 541-5250
(See also listing under Los Angeles Talent Agencies)

GARBER TALENT AGENCY
(SAG-AFTRA-EQUITY)
2 Pennsylvania Plaza,
   Suite 1910
New York, NY 10121
(212) 292-4910

GENERATION TV (SAG-AFTRA)
20 West 20th Street, #1008
New York, NY 10011
(646) 230-9491

GERSH LITERARY & TALENT
AGENCY
(SAG-AFTRA-EQUITY)
41 Madison Avenue, 33rd Floor
New York, NY 10010
(212) 997-1818
(See also listing under Los Angeles Talent Agencies)

VERONICA GOODMAN AGENCY
(SAG-AFTRA-EQUITY)
34 North Black Horse Pike
Runnemede, NJ 08078
(856) 795-3133

GREER LANGE TALENT AGENCY,
INC.
(SAG-AFTRA-EQUITY)
3 Bala Plaza West, Suite 201
Bala Cynwyd, PA 19004
(610) 747-0300

PEGGY HADLEY
ENTERPRISES LTD.
(SAG-AFTRA-EQUITY)
250 West 57th Street,
   Suite 2317
New York, NY 10107
(212) 246-2166

HARDEN-CURTIS ASSOCIATES
(AFTRA-EQUITY)
850 Seventh Avenue, Suite 903
New York, NY 10019

HARTIG-HILEPO AGENCY, LTD.
(SAG-AFTRA-EQUITY)
156 Fifth Avenue, Suite 1018
New York, NY 10010
(212) 929-1772

HENDERSON-HOGAN
AGENCY, INC.
(SAG-AFTRA-EQUITY)
850 Seventh Avenue,
    Suite 1003
New York, NY 10019
(212) 765-5190

INDEPENDENT ARTISTS
AGENCY
(formerly Carlson Menashe Artists)
(SAG-AFTRA-EQUITY)
159 West 25th Street,
    Suite 1101
New York, NY 10001
(646) 486-3332

INGBER & ASSOCIATES
(SAG-AFTRA-EQUITY)
274 Madison Avenue,
    Suite 1104
New York, NY 10016
(212) 889-9450

INNOVATIVE ARTISTS
TALENT & LITERARY AGENCY
(SAG-AFTRA-EQUITY)
235 Park Avenue South,
    Seventh Floor
New York, NY 10003
(212) 253-6900
*(See also listing under Los
Angeles Talent Agencies)*

INTERNATIONAL CREATIVE
MANAGEMENT
(SAG-AFTRA-EQUITY-WGA-AGMA)
40 West 57th Street
New York, NY 10019
(212) 556-5600
*(See also listing under Los
Angeles Talent Agencies)*

JORDAN, GILL &
DORNBAUM, INC.
(SAG-AFTRA-EQUITY)
1133 Broadway, Suite 623
New York, NY 10010
(212) 463-8455

STANLEY KAPLAN TALENT
(SAG-AFTRA-EQUITY)
139 Fulton Street,
    Room 503
New York, NY 10038
(212) 385-4400

KAZARIAN/SPENCER &
ASSOCIATES, INC.
(SAG-EQUITY-AFTRA)
162 West 56th Street,
    Suite 307
New York, NY 10019
(212) 582-7572
*(See also listing under Los
Angeles Talent Agencies)*

KERIN-GOLDBERG &
ASSOCIATES
(SAG-AFTRA-EQUITY)
155 East 55th Street, Suite 5D
New York, NY 10022
(212) 838-7373

ARCHER KING LTD.
(SAG-AFTRA-EQUITY-WGA)
317 West 46th Street, Suite 3A
New York, NY 10036
(212) 765-3103

KOLSTEIN TALENT AGENCY
(SAG-AFTRA-EQUITY)
65 Washington Avenue, Box 297
Suffern, NY 10901
Casting Line: (845) 357-7692

THE KRASNY OFFICE, INC.
(SAG-AFTRA-EQUITY)
1501 Broadway, Suite 1303
New York, NY 10036
(212) 730-8160

LALLY TALENT
AGENCY, L.L.C. (LTA)
(SAG-AFTRA-EQUITY)
630 Ninth Avenue, #800
New York, NY 10036
(212) 974-8718

THE LANTZ OFFICE
(SAG-AFTRA-EQUITY)
200 West 57th Street, Suite 503
New York, NY 10019
(212) 586-0200

LIONEL LARNER, LTD.
(SAG-AFTRA-EQUITY)
119 West 57th Street, Suite 1412
New York, NY 10019
(212) 246-3105

LEADING ARTISTS, INC.
(SAG-AFTRA-EQUITY)
145 West 45th Street, Suite 1204
New York, NY 10036
(212) 391-4545

BRUCE LEVY AGENCY
(SAG-AFTRA-EQUITY)
311 West 43rd Street, Suite 602
New York, NY 10036
(212) 262-6845

BERNARD LIEBHABER AGENCY
(SAG-AFTRA-EQUITY)
352 Seventh Avenue
New York, NY 10001
(212) 631-7561

THE LUEDTKE AGENCY, LLC
(SAG-AFTRA-EQUITY-WGA)
1674 Broadway, Suite 7A
New York, NY 10019
(212) 765-9564

MODELS ON THE MOVE
MODEL & TALENT AGENCY
(SAG-AFTRA)
1200 Route 70, Barclay Towers,
    Suite 6
P.O. Box 4037
Cherry Hill, NJ 08034
(856) 667-1060

WILLIAM MORRIS AGENCY, INC.,
TALENT AND LITERARY AGENCY
(SAG-AFTRA-EQUITY-WGA-DGA)
1325 Avenue of the Americas
New York, NY 10019
(212) 586-5100
*(See also listing under Los
Angeles Talent Agencies)*

NICOLOSI & CO., INC.
(SAG-AFTRA-EQUITY)
150 West 25th Street, Suite 1200
New York, NY 10001
(212) 633-1010

NOUVELLE TALENT
MANAGEMENT, INC.
(SAG-AFTRA)
20 Bethune Street, #4A
New York, NY 10014
(212) 352-2712

OMNIPOP INC. TALENT AGENCY
(SAG-AFTRA-EQUITY)
55 West Old Country Road
Hicksville, NY 11801
(516) 937-6011
*(See also listing under Los
Angeles Talent Agencies)*

FIFI OSCARD AGENCY INC.
(AFTRA-EQUITY-WGA-DGA)
110 West 40th Street, Suite 1601
New York, NY 10018
(212) 764-1100

DOROTHY PALMER TALENT
AGENCY, INC.
(SAG-WGA)
235 West 56th Street, Suite 24K
New York, NY 10019
(212) 765-4280

MEG PANTERA,
THE AGENCY INC.
(SAG-AFTRA-EQUITY)
1501 Broadway, Suite 1508
New York, NY 10036
(212) 278-8366

PARADIGM
(SAG-AFTRA-EQUITY)
500 5th Avenue, 37th Floor
New York, NY 10110
(212) 703-7540
*(See also listing under Los
Angeles Talent Agencies)*

PLAZA-7 (SAG-AFTRA)
160 North Gulph Road
King of Prussia, PA 19406
(610) 337-2693

PROFESSIONAL ARTISTS
(SAG-AFTRA-EQUITY-WGA)
321 West 44th Street,
    Suite 605
New York, NY 10036
(212) 247-8770

RADIOACTIVE TALENT INC.
(R.T.I.)
(SAG-AFTRA-ASCAP)
(Mailing Address Only)
350 Third Avenue, Box 400
New York, NY 10010
(917) 733-4700
Reinhard Talent Agency, Inc.
(SAG-AFTRA-EQUITY)
2021 Arch Street, Suite 400
Philadelphia, PA 19103
(215) 567-2000

GILLA ROOS, LTD.
(SAG-AFTRA)
16 West 22nd Street,
    3rd Floor
New York, NY 10010
(212) 727-7820

S.E.M. TALENT, INC.
(SAG-AFTRA-EQUITY)
(212) 330-9146

SCHIOWITZ/CLAY/ROSE, INC.
(SAG-AFTRA-EQUITY)
165 West 46th Street,
    Suite 1210
New York, NY 10036
(212) 840-6787
*(See also listing under Los
Angeles Talent Agencies)*

SCHULLER TALENT/
NEW YORK KIDS
(SAG-AFTRA-EQUITY)
276 Fifth Avenue, # 204
New York, NY 10001
(212) 532-6005

ANN STEELE AGENCY
(SAG-AFTRA-EQUITY)
330 West 42nd Street,
    18th Floor
New York, NY 10036
(212) 629-9112

STONE-MANNERS AGENCY
(SAG-AFTRA-EQUITY)
900 Broadway, Suite 803
New York, NY 10003
(212) 505-1400
*(See also listing under Los
Angeles Talent Agencies)*

PETER STRAIN &
ASSOCIATES INC.
(SAG-AFTRA-EQUITY)
1501 Broadway, Suite 2900
New York, NY 10036
(212) 391-0380
*(See also listing under Los
Angeles Talent Agencies)*

TALENT HOUSE AGENCY
(EQUITY)
311 West 43rd Street,
    Suite 602
New York, NY 10036
(212) 957-5220

TALENT NETWORK GROUP
(AFTRA)
111 East 22nd Street,
    Third Floor
New York, NY 10010
(212) 995-7325

TALENT REPRESENTATIVES
(SAG-AFTRA-EQUITY-WGA)
20 East 53rd Street, #2A
New York, NY 10022
(212) 752-1835

TALENTWORKS
(SAG-AFTRA-EQUITY)
220 East 23rd Street, #400
New York, NY 10010
(212) 889-0800
*(See also listing under Los
Angeles Talent Agencies)*

TOP CAT TALENT AGENCY, INC.
(SAG)
1140 Broadway, Suite 701
New York, NY 10001
Casting Directors Only:
(212) 447-4504

TAMAR WOLBROM, INC.
(SAG-AFTRA)
130 West 42nd Street,
    Suite 707
New York, NY 10036
(212) 398-4595

HANNS WOLTERS
INTERNATIONAL INC.
(SAG-EQUITY)
10 West 37th Street,
    Third Floor
New York, NY 10018
(212) 714-0100

ANN WRIGHT
REPRESENTATIVES
(SAG-AFTRA-EQUITY-WGA)
165 West 46th Street,
    Suite 1105
New York, NY 10036
(212) 764-6770

WRITERS & ARTISTS
AGENCY
(SAG-AFTRA-EQUITY-WGA)
19 West 44th Street,
    Suite 1410
New York, NY 10036
(212) 391-1112
*(See also listing under Los
Angeles Talent Agencies)*

BABS ZIMMERMAN
PRODUCTIONS, INC. (AGENCY)
(EQUITY)
305 East 86th Street
New York, NY 10028
(212) 348-7203

Los Angeles
Casting Directors

AKA CASTING
c/o Cole Avenue Studios
1006 North Cole Avenue
Hollywood, CA 90038
(323) 463-1600
*Casting Director Alan Kaminsky
casts commercials, industrials,
infomercials, print advertising
and voiceovers.*

ASG CASTING, INC.,
C.C.D.A.
10200 Riverside Drive,
    Suite 205
Toluca Lake, CA 91602
(818) 762-0200
*Arlene Schuster-Goss, Casting
Director, and Justin Radley,
Associate Casting Director,
cast for commercials and
T.V. reality shows through
agents. Union. Please don't
phone or visit.*

MELISSA ABESERA
CASTING
400 North Orange Drive
Los Angeles, CA 90036
(323) 931-5622
fax: (323) 931-1799
abeseracasting@aol.com
www.abeseracasting.com
*"I take comedy seriously and
real people too." Specializing
in real people.*

CECILY ADAMS CASTING
CBS Studio Center
4024 Radford Avenue,
    Building 2, Room 102
Studio City, CA 91604
*Cecily Adams, Casting Associate
G. Charles Wright, and Casting*

Assistant Carolyn Wilson cast film and T.V. No phone calls please.

JOE ADAMS CASTING
8383 Wilshire Blvd.,
    Suite 750
Beverly Hills, CA 90211
(323) 677-0066
Casting Director Joe Adams and Assistant Kara Edwards cast feature films. Don't phone, fax, or visit. Interviews by appointment only. Accepts photos-resumes by mail only. Attends showcases/ accepts showcase invitations. Currently casting State Evidence (Indie Feature), Happy Hour *(Sony/ Screen Gems),* Brown & Stein *(Indie Feature), "IF" and* Beauty Shop *(the sequel to* Barbershop*). Also currently producing films.*

SANDE ALESSI CASTING
13731 Ventura Blvd.
Sherman Oaks, CA 91423
Sande Alessi, C.S.A. casts principal work on music videos, commercials, lower budget features, industrials, print, etc. Union/Nonunion. Do not phone, fax or visit. Interview by appointment only. (See also listing for The Casting Couch Inc.)

STACY ALEXANDER
(323) 752-8345
(See VH1)

JOHNNY ALMARAZ
(323) 654-0273

JILL ANTHONY
(See Mossberg/Anthony Casting)

APEX CASTING
4335 Van Nuys Blvd.,
    Suite 354
Sherman Oaks, CA 91403
(818) 784-1100
www.apexcasting.com
Casting Directors: Johnny Franzen and Kirk Hoffman. Cast commercials, infomercials, films, music videos, print advertising, T.V., and voiceovers. Los Angeles and New York castings available. Union. Nonunion. Interviews by appointment only. Accepts photos, resumes, and tapes by mail only. Submitted materials will not be returned. Accepts showcase invitations. Please do not visit.

DEBORAH AQUILA
Casts films. Union. Don't visit. Accepts tapes by request only. (See C.S.A.)

NICOLE ARBUSTO
(See Dickson-Arbusto Casting)

KAREN ARMSTRONG
(See DeLaurentiis Productions)

JULIE ASHTON CASTING
5225 Wilshire Blvd.,
    Suite 414
Los Angeles, CA 90036
(323) 933-2278
fax: (323) 933-2578
Julie Ashton (Casting Director); Toni Magon (Casting Associate) cast for film and T.V. and "The Ortegas" for FOX.

CARRIE AUDINO
1600 Rosecrans Blvd.
Building 4B, 1st Floor
Manhattan Beach, CA 90266
(310) 727-2955
Carrie Audino, Casting Director. Casting Associate: Amanda D. Mahoney. Casting Assistant: Sari Knight. Casts for films and T.V. through agents only. Please don't phone, fax, or visit. Interviews by appointment only. Accepts photos and resumes by mail only. Please do not send unsolicited tapes. Attends showcases and accept showcase invitations. Union.

DAVID AULICINO
(See Viacom Productions)

PAMELA AZMI-ANDREW
Sonic Magic Studios
8522 National Blvd.,
    Suite 106
Culver City, CA 90232
(310) 558-3682
(888) 714-4337
(additional address)
P.O. Box 15564
North Hollywood, CA 91615
Casting Director Pamela Azmi-Andrew and assistant Michael Morillo cast T.V. Pilots, Episodic, Feature Films, Specials. Don't phone, fax or visit. Interviews by appointment only. Accepts photos-resumes by mail only. Indicate SAG membership on photos. Tapes will not be returned.

PATRICK BACA
(See Nassif & Baca Casting)

RISE BARISH CASTING, C.C.D.A.
5th Street Studios
1216 5th Street
Santa Monica, CA 90401
(310) 456-9018
(310) 458-1100
Casts commercials and features. Union. Accepts photos by mail only.

ANTHONY BARNAO
c/o The Lex Theater
6760 Lexington Avenue
Los Angeles, CA 90027
(323) 663-7973

MATTHEW BARRY, C.S.A.
4924 Balboa Blvd., #371
Encino, CA 91316
(818) 759-4425

FRAN BASCOM, C.S.A.
Columbia Pictures Television
3400 Riverside Drive, #765
Burbank, CA 91505
(818) 972-8339
(See also listing for Days of Our Lives *under Los Angeles-based Daytime Serials)*

PAMELA BASKER CASTING
(818) 506-7348

LISA BEACH
(323) 468-6633
Casts Features.

BELSHE CASTING
c/o Redondo Mail
996 Redondo Blvd.
Long Beach, CA 90804
Long Beach Office:
(562) 430-2299
BelsheCasting@aol.com
Casting Director Judy Belshe casts infomercials, commercials, industrials, and the occasional film. Actors' submissions will be accepted through various online services. Belshe is also author of several books available through e-mail to Judy. Classes also available.

BRETT BENNER
(See Romano/Benner Casting)

TERRY BERLAND
CASTING, CCDA
2050 South Bundy Drive
Los Angeles, CA 90025
(310) 571-4141
www.terryberlandcasting.com
Terry Berland C.C.D.A. Karmen Leech, Casting Assistant. (See also Westside Casting)

AMY JO BERMAN, C.S.A.
(310) 201-9537
Director of Casting, HBO.
(See HBO).

JUEL BESTROP
(See Jeanne McCarthy & Juel Bestrop Casting)

SHARON BIALY, C.S.A.
P.O. Box 570308
Tarzana, CA 91356
(818) 342-8630
fax: (818) 342-8744
Sharon Bialy and Sherry Thomas cast film, theatre, and T.V. Accepts photos by mail only.

TAMMARA BILLIK CASTING, C.S.A.
13547 Ventura Blvd., #688
Sherman Oaks, CA 91423
(818) 623-1631
Tammy Billik casts films and T.V. through agents only. Union.

JOE BLAKE
(See Westside Casting)

BARBIE BLOCK
(See Sally Stiner Casting)

GENE BLYTHE
(See Touchstone Television/ABC Entertainment Television Group)

CHARLIE BOGDAN CASTING
8899 Beverly Blvd.
Los Angeles, CA 90048
(310) 248-5296
fax: (310) 248-5297
Casts commercials and film.

EVE BRANDSTEIN CASTING
16001 Ventura Blvd.
Encino, CA 91436
(818) 386-2611

JACKIE BRISKEY, C.S.A.
4024 Radford Avenue,
    Admin. Bldg. Suite 280
Studio City, CA 91604
(818) 655-5601
Casts a soap & primetime T.V. Don't phone, fax, or visit. Interviews by appointment only. Accepts photos-resumes by mail only. Accepts tapes by request only. Please include height & age range on all submissions. Attends show-cases. (See also listing for Passions *under Los Angeles-based Daytime Serials)*

AMY MCINTYRE BRITT
(See listing under CFB Casting)

STEVE BROOKSBANK
(See Slater/Brooksbank Casting)

ANDREW BROWN
(See Paramount Pictures Features Casting)

BROWN-WEST CASTING
7319 Beverly Blvd., #10
Los Angeles, CA 90036
(323) 938-2575
brownwest@sbcglobal.net
Ross Brown & Mary West cast for films, theatre, T.V. Union. Don't phone, fax, or visit. Accepts photos by mail only.

MARY V. BUCK
(See Warner Bros. Television Casting)

BUENA VISTA MOTION PICTURE GROUP, (DISNEY FEATURE FILMS, TOUCHSTONE PICTURES)
500 South Buena Vista Street
Burbank, CA 91521
(818) 560-7510
Marcia Ross (Senior VP of Casting), Donna Morong (VP of Casting), Gail Goldberg (VP of Casting), and Kate Lacey (Feature Film Casting Coordinator) cast feature films through agents only. Don't phone, fax, or visit. Accept photos/resumes by mail only. NO UNSOLICITED VIDEOTAPES. Attends showcases.

PERRY BULLINGTON
(See MacDonald/Bullington Casting)

LEAH BUONO
(818) 736-3821
"Nickelodeon Talent Department"

JACKIE BURCH, C.S.A.
c/o Pearl Wexler (agent)
(310) 550-1060

BURROWS/BOLAND CASTING
(310) 503-4719
Bbcasting@aol.com
Casting Directors, Victoria Burrows and Scot Boland cast films and T.V. Don't phone, fax, or visit. Interviews by appointment only. Photos/resumes/tapes by mail only. Occasionally attends showcases.

CBS
7800 Beverly Blvd., #284
Los Angeles, CA 90036
(323) 575-2335
Peter Golden (Senior VP, Talent & Casting); Lucy Cavallo (VP, Casting),

Fern Orenstein (VP, Casting), and Karen Church (VP, Casting) cast for T.V. Accepts photos by mail only.

CFB CASTING
Office 1: (310) 820-9751
Office 2: (310) 993-5473
Permanent Service:
    (323) 822-3688
Amy McIntyre Britt and Anya Colloff cast films & T.V.

IRENE CAGEN, C.S.A.
(323) 525-1381
(See C.S.A.)

AKUA CAMPANELLA, C.S.A.
2630 Lacy Street
Los Angeles, CA 90031
(323) 222-1656
Casts film, T.V., commercials, theatre. No phone calls.

PAMELA CAMPUS, C.C.D.A.
(818) 897-1588

REUBEN CANNON & ASSOCIATES, C.S.A.
5225 Wilshire Blvd., Suite 526
Los Angeles, CA 90036
(323) 939-3190
Reuben Cannon and Kim Williams cast films & T.V. Union & nonunion. Accepts tapes by request only.

BLYTHE CAPPELLO
(See listing for Spike T.V.)

CATHI CARLTON
(See Westside Casting)

CARSEY WERNER MANDABACH COMPANY
CBS Studio Center
4024 Radford Avenue,
    Building 3
Studio City, CA 91604
(818) 655-6218
Rick Pagano (Head of Casting), Janet Farris (Associate).

FERNE CASSEL
Casts films. (See C.S.A.)

ALICE S. CASSIDY
fax: (323) 931-4381
Casts animated series, films & T.V. through agents only. Union. Don't visit. Attends showcases.

THE CASTING COMPANY
8242 West Third, Suite 250
Los Angeles, CA 90048
(323) 653-1200
Jane Jenkins & Janet Hirshenson cast films & T.V. through agents only. Don't phone or visit.

THE CASTING
CONNECTION
LA Producers, Directors,
Agents ONLY:
(818) 991-2716
Casting Directors: Annette
Benson, Diane Kirman, Sal
Dupree. No phone calls. No
submissions accepted at this
time. (See also listing under
New York Casting Directors)

CASTING SOCIETY OF
AMERICA®, (C.S.A.)
606 North Larchmont Blvd., 4B
Los Angeles, CA 90004
(323) 463-1925
www.castingsociety.com
The following registered casting
directors receive mail at the
above address & phone number:
A: Sande Alessi, Deborah
Aquila, Maureen Arata, B: Patrick
Baca; Deborah Barylski, Judith
Bouley, Kate Brinegar, Jackie
Burch, C: Irene Cagen, Craig
Campobasso, Ferne Cassel,
Lindsay Chag, D: Anita Dann,
Leslee Dennis, Sarah Dalton
Donlan, Dorian Dunas, Nan
Dutton, E: Kathryn Eisenstein,
F: Nancy Foy, Lisa Freiberger,
Jean Sarah Frost, G: Michael
Greer, H: Milt Hamerman,
Theodore Hann, Natalie Hart,
Nina Heninger, Tory Herald,
Dawn Hershey, Richard Hicks,
J: Elisabeth Jereski, Tara-Anne
Johnson, K: Tracy Kaplan, Kerry
Karsian, Thom Klohn, Amanda
Koblin, Joanne Koehler, Ronna
Kress, L: Jason La Padura, Ruth
Lambert, Shana Landsburg,
Geraldine Leder, Lisa London,
M: Liz Marx, Robert McGee,
Joseph Middleton, Lisa Mionie,
N: Robin Nassif, Marjorie Noble,
Patricia Noland, O: Gillian O'Neill,
Lori Openden, P. Mark Paladini,
R: Pamela Rack, Robyn Ray,
Barbara Remsen, Gretchen
Rennell-Court, Stacey Rosen,
Renée Rousselot, Jennifer Rudin,
Elisabeth Rudolph, S: Cathy
Sandrich, Julie Selzer, Bill Shepard,
Amanda Sherman, Margery
Simkin, Catherine Stroud, Andrea
Stone, T: Judy Taylor, Mark Tillman,
Joy Todd, W: Samuel Warren,
Rosemary Welden, Geri Windsor,
Barbara Wright, Y: Rhonda
Young, Ronnie Yeskel, Z: Lisa
Zarowin, Gary Zuckerbrod.

THE CASTING COUCH, INC.
13731 Ventura Blvd.
Sherman Oaks, CA 91323
(818) 623-7040
info@extrascastingguild.com
Sande Alessi, Jennifer Alessi, and
Kristan Berona cast background
actors for commercials, films,
industrials, music videos, print
and T.V. Union/Nonunion. Do
not phone, fax, or visit. Interviews
by appointment only. No 8x10's
please. Computer database
registration preferred—
(818) 623-7040. (See also listing
for Sande Alessi Casting)

LUCY CAVALLO
(See CBS)
Central Union/Central Non-Union
220 South Flower Street
Burbank, CA 91502
(818) 562-2700
Registration Info:
(818) 562-2755
Cast extras for films, T.V., commer-
cials, etc. SAG/AFTRA/nonunion.
Must register with company for
extra work. Call for registration
info. Registration in office.

CERVANTES CASTING
The Casting Studios
200 South La Brea, 2nd Floor
Los Angeles, CA 90036
(323) 954-0007
Casting Director: Toni Cervantes.

LINDSAY CHAG
(See C.S.A.)

DENISE CHAMIAN
Casts films & T.V. through agents
only. (See C.S.A.)

FERN CHAMPION CASTING
8255 Sunset Boulevard
Los Angeles, CA 90046
(323) 650-1280
Fern Champion, Casting Director.
Scott Rosen, Casting Associate.

CHELSEA STUDIOS
11530 Ventura Blvd.
Studio City, CA 91604
(818) 286-9400
The following Casting Directors
recieve mail and phone calls at
Chelsea Studios: Susan Havins,
Dea Vise, Megan Foley, Vicki
Goggin, Craig Colvin, Paul Ventura,
Susan Tyler (818) 506-0400,
Lynne Quirion, Billy Damota.

KAREN CHURCH
(See CBS)

LORI COBE-ROSS
2005 Palo Verde Avenue, #306
Long Beach, CA 90815
(562) 938-9088

ANDREA COHEN
CASTING
Casting Director Andrea Cohen
and Casting Associate Laurie
Shapiro cast flims and T.V.
through agents only. Interviews
by appointment only. Union.
(please contact through C.S.A.)

CHADWICK COHN
(See listing for Thunderstruck
Casting)

JOANNA COLBERT
CASTING
9720 Wilshire Blvd.,
4th Floor
Beverly Hills, CA 90212
Joanna Colbert (Casting
Director) and Richard Mento
(Associate) cast films. Don't
phone, fax or visit. Accepts
photos-resumes by mail only.
Attends showcases. Accepts
showcase invitations.

AISHA COLEY, C.S.A.
7336 Santa Monica Blvd., #611
West Hollywood, CA 90046
(323) 882-4144
(See also listing under 20th
Century Fox Feature Film
Casting)

ANNELISE COLLINS CASTING,
C.S.A.,C.C.D.A.
3435 Ocean Park Avenue,
Suite 112
Santa Monica, CA 90405
(310) 586-1936
www.annelisecast.com
No promo material sent in will
be returned. (See also The
Casting Studios)

ANYA COLLOFF
(See listing under CFB Casting)

CRAIG COLVIN
Craig Colvin & Company
Casting
11530 Ventura Blvd.
Studio City, CA 91604
Agents: (818) 286-9345
Classes: (818) 286-9347

COMPASSIONATE CASTING
On Your Mark
451 North La Cienega Blvd., #12
Los Angeles, CA 90048
(310) 360-9936

RUTH CONFORTE
CASTING, C.S.A.
3620 Barham Blvd.,
    Building Y, #201
Los Angeles, CA 90068
(818) 771-7287
*Casts T.V., feature films,
commercials, industrials,
videos.*

DAN COWAN
(323) 937-0411
(See Lien/Cowan Casting)

ALLISON COWITT, C.S.A.
(818) 501-0177
(See Fenton-Cowitt Casting)

ELAINE CRAIG VOICE
CASTING, INC., C.C.D.A.
6464 Sunset Blvd., Suite 1150
Los Angeles, CA 90028
(323) 469-8773
www.elainecraig.com
*Casts animated features,
commercials & voiceovers.
Don't visit. Accepts tapes
(audio/video).*

CRASH CASTING-
COMMERCIALS
(See On Your Mark)

CREATIVE EXTRAS
CASTING (CEC)
2461 Santa Monica Blvd., #501
Santa Monica,, CA 90404
(310) 391-9041
Registration: (310) 203-7860
Hotline: (310) 203-1459
*(CEC) Vanessa Portillo casts
background primarily for T.V.
and films. Call (310) 203-7860
for registration info. Don't
phone, fax, or visit the office
unless specifically asked to do
so. Accepts photos by mail only;
always include phone numbers
and union status on pictures.
No children. All those who
wish to register must be able
to legally work in the US. We
never charge a fee to register.*

PATRICK CUNNINGHAM, C.S.A.
2630 Lacy Street
Los Angeles, CA 90031
(323) 222-1656
fax: (323) 225-7815
pscrox@aol.com
*No drop-ins or follow-up calls.
Follow up by mail or will view
VHS tapes only if he requests
them. Tapes will not be returned.
No phone calls please.*

DIC ENTERTAINMENT
4100 West Alameda Avenue
Burbank, CA 91505
(818) 955-5400
*Marsha Goodman casts
animated features, T.V. &
voiceovers through agents
only. Don't phone or visit.*

JOE D'AGOSTA
(310) 652-8123

BILLY DAMOTA, C.S.A.
c/o Chelsea Studios
11530 Ventura Boulevard
Studio City, CA 91604
(818) 286-9400

BILL DANCE CASTING
4605 Lankershim Blvd.,
    Suite 401
North Hollywood, CA 91602
For Production Personnel Only:
    (818) 754-6634
Extras & Actors Only:
    (818) 725-4209
www.BillDanceCasting.com
*Bill Dance, Terence Harris, Bill
Marinella, Gary Davies, and
Darren Shepherd cast background
actors and day players for films,
T.V., commercials, industrials,
infomercials and music videos.
Registration is Monday–Friday
starting promptly at 12 noon.*

ERIC DAWSON
(See Ulrich/Dawson/Kritzer Casting)

SHAWN DAWSON
(See Ulrich/Dawson/Kritzer Casting)

DEHORTER CASTING, LLC.
MGM
10250 Constellation Blvd.,
    Second Floor, Suite 2060
Century City, CA 90067
(323) 586-8964
fax: (323) 264-1210
classes: classes@dehortercasting.
    com
*Casting Director Zora DeHorter
casts films, theatre and T.V. Union.
Through agents/managers only.
Interviews by appointment only.
Accepts photos/resumes/tapes
(video) by referral only. Attends
showcases.*

RICHARD DE LANCY &
ASSOCIATES
4741 Laurel Canyon Blvd.,
    Suite 100
Valley Village, CA 91607
(818) 760-3110
www.delancy.com

*Casts films, industrials, print
ads, T.V. and educationals. See
website for casting information.*

DELAURENTIIS PRODUCTIONS
10061 Riverside Drive,
    Suite 101
Toluca Lake, CA 91602
(909) 599-5838
*Karen Armstrong, Head of Talent.
NO phone calls—mail only!*

ELINA DESANTOS
P.O. Box 1718
Santa Monica, CA 90406
(310) 829-5958
Casts films & theatre.

DICKSON-ARBUSTO CASTING
3875 Wilshire Blvd., Suite 701
Los Angeles, CA 90010
(213) 739-0556
*Joy Dickson and Nicole Arbusto
cast film, T.V., and theatre. Accepts
headshots and resumes by mail.*

CONCETTA DI MATTEO
(See Long/Di Matteo Casting)

DISNEY CHANNEL
3800 West Alameda Avenue,
    Suite 529
Burbank, CA 91505
(818) 569-7500
*Adam Bonnett (VP Original
Series) and Matt Jackson
(Director, Talent Development)
cast for T.V. (episodic & feature),
on-air promos, voiceovers. Union
& nonunion. Don't phone or visit.*

DISNEY ENTERTAINMENT
PRODUCTIONS/TALENT
RESOURCES
T.D.A. 329R
P.O. Box 3232
Anaheim, CA 92803-3232
Audition Hotline:
    (714) 781-0111
*Megan Bywater, Dana Hinton
(Casting Directors) cast for Disney
Entertainment Productions. Talent
may access the www.disney.com
Keyword: Auditions, or call the
hotline. Please DO NOT send
tapes (audio or video) or CDs
unless requested.*

DIVISEK CASTING,, C.C.D.A.
6420 Wilshire Blvd.,
    Suite LL100
Los Angeles, CA 90048
(323) 655-7766
*Barbara Divisek & Karen Divisek
cast commercials, films, industrials, print ads, T.V., voiceovers.*

PAM DIXON
10351 Santa Monica Blvd.,
    Suite 200
Los Angeles, CA 90025
(310) 432-4852

MICHAEL DONOVAN
CASTING, C.S.A., C.C.D.A.
8170 Beverly Blvd.,
    Suite #105
Los Angeles, CA 90048
(323) 655-9020
fax: (323) 655-9021
Michael Donovan casts film, T.V.,
commercials, and theatre. Union
& nonunion. Accept pictures and
resumes by mail.

CHRISTY DOOLEY
CBS Television
7800 Beverly Blvd., #3371
Los Angeles, CA 90036
(323) 575-4501
Casts soaps & T.V. Union. Don't
phone or visit. (See also listing for
The Bold and the Beautiful)

BRIAN DORFMAN
(See Touchstone Television/ABC
Entertainment Television Group)

DOWD/REUDY CASTING
The Casting Studios
200 South La Brea
Los Angeles, CA 90036
(323) 665-1776
Mick Dowd & Tom Reudy cast
commercials, industrials, print
ads, voiceovers.

MARY DOWNEY PRODUCTIONS
705 North Kenwood
Burbank, CA 91505
(818) 563-1200
fax: (818) 563-1585
Casts new talent competition
including vocalists, comedians &
hosts, T.V. Also books celebrities
on Prime Time series & specials.
Union & non-union. Don't phone
or visit. Currently casting Best
Damn Sports Show Period/Fox
Sports Net.

DREAMWORKS CASTING
100 Universal Plaza
Universal City, CA 91608
(818) 733-9300
Leslee Feldman, head of casting;
Christi Soper, Wendy Schwam;
Steve Zegans and Celeste Leger
(Assistants) cast films & T.V.
through independent casting
directors. Animated projects are
cast through the office.

JENNIFRE DUMONT
jdumontcasting@aol.com
Casts for films, industrials and T.V.
Please submit comedians only.

CAROLYN DYER
14118 Archwood Street
Van Nuys, CA 91405
(818) 786-5586

E! ENTERTAINMENT TELEVISION
5750 Wilshire Blvd.
Los Angeles, CA 90036
(323) 954-2400
Dan Gibson (Director of On-Air
Talent/Casting) & Gina Merrill
(Casting Executive) cast extras,
T.V. & voiceovers. AFTRA. Don't
phone or visit.

ABRA EDELMAN
(See Goodman/Edelman Casting)

SUSAN EDELMAN CASTING
12413 Ventura Court, #300
Studio City, CA 91604
(818) 506-7328
Susan Edelman, C.S.A. cast for
T.V. series, miniseries, and movies
of the week.

DONNA EKHOLDT, C.S.A.
(Big Ticket Television Casting)
Sunset-Gower Studios
1438 North Gower, Bldg. 35, Box 45
Los Angeles, CA 90028
(323) 860-7425
Donna Ekholdt (Senior V.P. Talent
Development & Casting) and
Meredith Layne (Manager of
Casting) cast for T.V. Don't phone,
fax, or visit. Accepts photos by
mail only. Attends showcases.

BRITT ENGGREN
(See Rodeo Casting)

STEVEN ERDEK
(See Westside Casting)

DANIELLE ESKINAZI CASTING,
C.C.D.A.
The Casting Underground
1641 North Ivar Street
Los Angeles, CA 90028
(323) 465-9999
www.daniellecasting.com

FELICIA FASANO
(See Betty Mae Casting)

FENTON-COWITT CASTING,
C.S.A.
(818) 345-3434
Mike Fenton & Allison Cowitt cast
films, T.V., voiceovers through
agents only. Don't phone or visit.

LISA FIELDS CASTING
Silverlayne Studios
1161 North Las Palmas
Los Angeles, CA 90048
(323) 468-6888

FINN/HILLER CASTING
588 North Larchmont Blvd.
Los Angeles, CA 90004
(323) 460-4530
Sarah Halley Finn, C.S.A., Randi
Hiller, Casting Directors. Casts films.

SARAH HALLEY FINN
(See Finn Hiller Casting)

MALI FINN CASTING, C.S.A.
8284 Santa Monica Blvd.
West Hollywood, CA 90046
(323) 848-3737
Casting Director Mali Finn and
Casting Associate David Rapaport
cast films and T.V. Accepts photos
from union and nonunion talent
by mail only. Office Manager:
Jonathan Leeder.

JULIA FLORES/FLORES CASTING
9121 Atlanta Avenue, #430
Huntington Beach, CA 92646
(714) 965-4669
florescasting@mindspring.com
Casts for theatre, regional theatre,
national tours.

MEGAN FOLEY COMMERCIAL
CASTING, C.C.D.A.
Chelsea Studios
11530 Ventura Blvd.
Studio City, CA 91604
(818) 286-9350
Casts commercials, films,
industrials, theatre, T.V.

FOX BROADCASTING COMPANY
10201 West Pico Blvd.
Los Angeles, CA 90035
(310) 369-1000
Marcia Shulman (Executive Vice
President Casting), Bob Huber
(Senior Vice President of Casting),
Pauline O'Con (Vice President of
Casting). (See also listing under
New York Casting Directors)

EDDIE FOY III CASTING
11380 Foxglove Lane
Corona, CA 92880
(909) 272-2931
(818) 414-2519
c/o dick clark productions
3003 West Olive Avenue
Burbank, CA 91505
Casts films & T.V. (specials and
M.O.W.s). Accepts photos by
mail only.

DELIA FRANKEL
(See Sony Pictures Television)

CARRIE FRAZIER, C.S.A.
(310) 201-9537
Casts features through agents only. Don't phone, fax, or visit. (See HBO)

DEAN FRONK
(818) 325-1289
(See Pemrick/Fronk Casting)

FUNKY FERRETS CASTING
200 South La Brea Avenue,
Second Floor
Los Angeles, CA 90036
(323) 954-0007
Jacob Ferret and Robert Ferret cast commercials & films. Union only. Please don't phone, fax, or visit.

GALLEGOS/CARRAFIELLO CASTING
(GC CASTING)
639 North Larchmont Blvd., #207
Los Angeles, CA 90004
(323) 469-3577
Dennis Gallegos and Meghan Carrafiello cast commercials, films, industrials, infomercials, print ads, T.V., voiceovers.

NICOLE GARCIA
c/o MADtv
Hollywood Center Studios
1040 North Las Palmas, Bldg. 3
Hollywood,, CA 90038
(323) 860-8975
Do not phone or visit. Accepts pictures and resumes by mail only. Attends showcases. (See also listing for MADtv under Los Angeles Talk/Variety shows)

SCOTT GENKINGER
(See Junie Lowry-Johnson Casting)

JEFF GERRARD CASTING
(818) 782-9900
Casting Director Jeff Gerrard casts features, commercials, voiceovers, industrials, infomercials, music videos, print ads, soaps, theatre, T.V. Union & non-union. Associate is Tom Carnes. Accepts photos.

MICHELLE GERTZ CASTING, C.S.A.
(Please contact through C.S.A.)
606 North Larchmont Blvd., 4B
Los Angeles, CA 90004
Casting Director also credited as Michelle Morris Gertz, C.S.A. No unsolicited submissions.

DAN GIBSON
(323) 954-2446
(See E! Entertainment Television)

JANET GILMORE, C.S.A.
Raleigh Manhattan Beach Studios
1600 Rosencrans Avenue,
Bldg. 4-B, 1st Floor
Manhattan Beach, CA 90266
(310) 727-2290
Casts films and T.V. with Megan McConnell.

JAN GLASER
(See Gerald I. Wolff & Associates)

LAURA GLEASON CASTING, C.S.A.
19528 Ventura Blvd., #370
Tarzana, CA 91356
(818) 881-6643
Laura Gleason, C.S.A., casts films, T.V., soaps & theatre. Please don't phone, fax, or visit. Interviews by appointment only. Videotapes are accepted but will not be returned. Accepts photos and resumes by mail only. Attends showcases. Union.

CHARISSE GLENN CASTING, C.C.D.A.
Office Phone: (818) 735-7372
fax: (818) 735-7964
cgcast@flash.net
www.cgcasting.com
Casts commercials, industrials, infomercials and voiceovers through agents only.

GLICKSMAN/WALD CASTING
(310) 305-2222
Susan Glicksman C.S.A. and Alex Wald C.S.A. cast for T.V. and film.

VICKI GOGGIN
Vicki Goggin & Associates
Casting
Chelsea Studios
11530 Ventura Blvd.
Studio City, CA 91604
(818) 286-9331
Casts commercials.

GAIL GOLDBERG, C.S.A.
(818) 560-7509
(See Buena Vista Motion Picture Group)

PETER GOLDEN
(See CBS)

DANNY GOLDMAN & ASSOCIATES, C.C.D.A.
1006 North Cole Avenue
Los Angeles, CA 90038
(323) 463-1600
Casts commercials, industrials, infomercials, print ads, voiceovers. Union & nonunion. Accepts photos by mail only.

LIBBY GOLDSTEIN
(See Junie Lowry-Johnson Casting)

LOUIS GOLDSTEIN & ASSOCIATES
CASTING/PARADOX CASTING
P.O. Box 691037
West Hollywood, CA 90069
(310) 552-8257
(See also On Your Mark Studios)

GOLDWASSER/MELTZER CASTING
13029-A Victory Blvd., #366
North Hollywood, CA 91606
(213) 683-3742
Carol Goldwasser, C.S.A. and Howard Meltzer, C.S.A. cast T.V. series, animated series, film, T.V., theatre. Union. Accepts photos and tapes by mail only. Indicate union membership on photos. Tapes will not be returned. Interviews by appointment only. Attends showcases.

JEFF GOLOMB
(new contact info pending)

GOODMAN-EDELMAN CASTING, C.S.A.
(310) 473-1280
Elisa Goodman & Abra Edelman cast films, T.V., cable movies of the week, cable features, independent features, animated series/features. Union. Accepts photos-resumes by mail only. Indicate SAG membership on photos. Accepts tapes upon request only. Tapes will be returned if a SASE is provided. In order to save time and money send ONE photo-resume only. Do not send separate pictures and resumes to Elisa and Abra. We can only keep one in the office; duplicates are thrown away. Script Queries can be sent to Abra Edelman directly at 16170 Kennedy Road, Los Gatos, CA 95032.

MARSHA GOODMAN
(See DIC Entertainment)

MARILYN GRANAS, C.C.D.A.
220 South Palm Drive
Beverly Hills, CA 90212
(310) 278-3773
Casts animated features, commercials, films, industrials,

*T.V., voiceovers. Don't phone,
fax or visit. Interviews by
appointment only. Accepts
photos by mail only.*

NANCY GREEN-KEYES, C.S.A.
4924 Balboa Blvd., #371
Encino, CA 91316
(818) 759-4425

JEFF GREENBERG
CASTING
Paramount Studios
5555 Melrose Avenue,
    Marx Bros. Bldg., #102
Los Angeles, CA 90038
(323) 956-4886
*Jeff Greenberg, C.S.A. casts
films, theatre & T.V. Collin Daniel
(associate), Justine Hempe
(associate), Geralyn Flood
(assistant). Union. Accepts
photos/resumes and tapes
(audio/video) by mail only.
Attends showcases.
Do not visit.*

HARRIET GREENSPAN
c/o Nickelodeon
2600 Colorado Avenue
Santa Monica, CA 90404
(818) 386-2186

AARON GRIFFITH
8440 Santa Monica Blvd., #200
Los Angeles, CA 90069
(323) 654-0033
aaron@castingdirector.nu
*Casts films and television.
Union. Don't phone.*

AL GUARINO
2118 Wilshire Blvd., #995
Santa Monica, CA 90403
(310) 829-6009
*Casts films, television and
theatre.*

SHEILA GUTHRIE, C.S.A.
Paramount Studios
5555 Melrose Avenue,
Bluhorn Bldg., Room 128
Hollywood, CA 90038
(323) 956-5578
*(See also Paramount Television
Casting)*

HBO
2049 Century Park East,
    36th Floor
Los Angeles, CA 90067
(310) 201-9200
*Carrie Frazier (VP of Feature
Casting), Amy Jo Berman
(Director of Casting–Feature
Films).*

KIM HARDIN
(213) 694-0316

JEFF HARDWICK
CASTING, C.C.D.A.
12439 Magnolia Blvd., #296
Studio City, CA 91607
(818) 752-9898
jhcasting@sbcglobal.com
*Jeff Hardwick, C.C.D.A., casts
T.V., commercials, and film.
Submissions accepted—no
drop-offs. Union, nonunion.*

SUSAN HAVINS, C.C.D.A.
Chelsea Studios
11530 Ventura Blvd.
Studio City, CA 91604
(818) 286-9311
*Susan Havins, Hal Havins cast
commercials.*

RENÉ HAYNES, C.S.A.
1314 Scott Road
Burbank, CA 91504
(818) 842-0187
*Casts or consults on feature films
and television films. Specializes
in talent searches for projects
with specific casting needs,
such as the large Vietnamese
language cast in the independent
feature* Green Dragon. *Has an
extensive knowledge of Native
American talent throughout
North America (USA & Canada).
Accepts photos by mail only.*

HELGOTH AND
ASSOCIATES CASTING
1607 North El Centro,
    Suite 19
Hollywood, CA 90028
(323) 462-5021
Helgocast@msn.com
*Casting director Steve Helgoth
and assistant Janet Campbell
cast films, theatre, T.V. Accepts
photos-resumes by mail only.
Don't phone, fax, or e-mail.*

HENDERSON/ZUCKERMAN
CASTING, C.S.A.
16161 Ventura Blvd., #106
Encino, CA 91436
(818) 788-8909
fax: (818) 788-8991
*Cathy Henderson, C.S.A. &
Dori Zuckerman, C.S.A. and
Dana Olson (Casting Assistant)
cast films & T.V. Don't
phone or fax. Interviews by
appointment only. Accepts
photos-resumes by mail only.
Attends showcases.*

RICHARD HICKS
CASTING, C.S.A.
(213) 368-6400
Casts film, theatre, T.V.

RANDI HILLER
(See Finn/Hiller Casting)

MARC HIRSCHFELD
(See NBC)

JANET HIRSHENSON
(See The Casting Company)

HISPANIC TALENT CASTING
OF HOLLYWOOD
P.O. Box 46123
Los Angeles, CA 90046
(323) 934-6465
*Bill Hooey casts commercials,
films, T.V. Union & nonunion.
Accepts photos by mail only.*

BETH HOLMES CASTING,
C.C.D.A.
Loudmouth Studios
13261 Moorpark Street, #201
Sherman Oaks, CA 91423
(818) 501-5625
www.bethholmescasting.com
*Casts commercials and director's
reels mostly through agents.
Union and Nonunion. Don't
phone, visit or personally drop
headshots. Prefer headshots sent
through the mail only. Monica
Eisenbeis–Vice President;
Kirkland Moody–Associate.*

BILL HOOEY
*(See Hispanic Talent Casting
of Hollywood)*

BOB HUBER
*(See FOX Broadcasting
Company)*

VICTORIA HUFF, C.S.A.
5700 Wilshire Blvd.,
    Suite 500 North
Los Angeles, CA 90036
(323) 634-1260
Casts films, theatre, T.V. Union.

JULIE HUTCHINSON, C.S.A.
(818) 777-8327
*VP of Feature Film Casting,
Universal Studios. Casts films.
Union. Don't phone or visit. Agent
submissions only. (See Universal
Studios Feature Film Casting)*

HYMSON-AYER CASTING
(310) 577-3433
fax: (310) 577-3480
*Casting Directors: Simon Ayer
and Beth Hymson Ayer cast T.V.*

IDOLMAKERS CASTING
(See On Your Mark)

DONNA ISAACSON, C.S.A.
(310) 369-1824
Casts animated features & films through agents only. Union. (See 20th Century-Fox, Bldg 12, Room 201)

RICK JACOBS
Lifetime Television
Vice President, Talent
2049 Century Park East, Suite 840
Los Angeles, CA 90067
(310) 556-7564

JANE JENKINS, C.S.A.
(323) 938-0700
(See The Casting Company)

LORNA JOHNSON
8615 Tamarack
Sun Valley, CA 91352
(818) 252-6155

KALMENSON & KALMENSON
Voice Casting
(Mailing Address)
5730 Wish Avenue
Encino, CA 91316
(Studio: Auditions/Classes)
105 South Sparks Street
Burbank, CA 91506
(Auditions/Classes):
     (818) 342-6499
fax: (818) 343-1403
Kalmenson@earthlink.net
www.Kalmenson.com
Cathy and Harvey Kalmenson (Partners/Casting Directors) along with their casting team of eight, cast voiceovers only for radio/T.V. commercials, industrials, infomercials, CD-ROMs & interactive, voices of toys, books on tape, animated series/features, among others. Auditions by appointment only. Please do not visit. Union and nonunion casting. Accept audio demos by mail only, submitted by agents only. Attend showcases and accept showcase invitations. Also offer highly regarded voiceover workshops for all levels.

ELLIE KANNER, C.S.A.
10880 Wilshire Blvd., Suite 1101
Los Angeles, CA 90024
(310) 234-5082

CHRISTIAN KAPLAN, C.S.A.
(310) 369-1883
Casts animated features & films. Don't phone, fax, or visit. (See 20th Century-Fox, Bldg 12, Room 201)

TRACY KAPLAN, C.S.A.
(310) 559-3306
(See C.S.A.)

LISA MILLER KATZ, C.S.A.
4000 Warner Blvd., Building 131
Burbank, CA 91522
(818) 954-7586
Casts films & T.V. Accepts photos by mail only.

SARAH ELIZABETH KATZMAN
(323) 468-6633

LORA KENNEDY
(See Warner Bros. Features Casting)

PEGGY KENNEDY
(See listing under Debi Manwiller)

N LEE SONJA KISSIK
Magic Casting
1660 Cougar Ridge Road
Buellton, CA 93427
(805) 688-3702

AMY KLEIN, C.S.A.
12021 Wilshire Blvd., #263
Los Angeles, CA 90025
(310) 478-6068
Casts films & T.V. Union. Don't phone, fax, or visit. Accepts photos-resumes by mail only. Attends showcases.

BETH KLEIN
(See Viacom Productions)

HEIDI KLEIN, KLEIN CASTING
(818) 759-6761

ROBIN KLEIN, KLEIN CASTING
(818) 759-6761

THOM KLOHN
Casts films, T.V. Don't phone, fax, or visit. Interviews by appointment only. Accepts photos-resumes by mail only. Attends showcases and accepts showcase invitations. Attends plays and screenings. Union. (See C.S.A.)

EILEEN MACK KNIGHT
12031 Ventura Blvd., Suite 4
Studio City, CA 91604
(818) 753-9585
Currently casting The Bernie Mac Show *and* The Proud Family *(Disney animated series).*

KATHY KNOWLES
Fifth Street Studios
1216 Fifth Street
Santa Monica, CA 90401
(310) 458-1100

KOBLIN/HARDING CASTING
(c/o C.S.A.)
(310) 785-9779
Casting Directors Amanda Harding, C.S.A. and Amanda Koblin, C.S.A. cast for T.V., theatre and film. Please don't phone or fax. (See also listing under New York Casting Directors)

AMANDA KOBLIN
(See Koblin/Harding Casting)

DOROTHY KOSTER CASTING
Crystal Sky Productions
1901 Avenue of the Stars,
     Suite 605
Los Angeles, CA 90067
(310) 843-0223
Casts films & T.V. Don't visit.

ANNAMARIE KOSTURA
(See NBC)

CAROL KRITZER
(See Ulrich/Dawson/Kritzer Casting)

DEBORAH KURTZ, C.C.D.A.
c/o Stella Studios
11751 Mississippi Avenue,
     Suite 140
Los Angeles, CA 90025
(310) 477-6555
Casts commercials, T.V. & features.

L.A. CASTING GROUP, INC.
Los Angeles Center Studios
1201 West 5th Street, Suite F-240
Los Angeles, CA 90017
(213) 534-3888
Extras Registration Line:
     (213) 5343892
www.lacgroup.com
Michael Schiavone (Casting Director), Joe Marino (Casting Director), Leah Olympia (Casting Assistant), Emmanuel Agus (Casting Assistant) cast films, T.V., commercials, extras, music videos, soaps and print advertising. Union. Nonunion. Interviews by appointment only. Do not visit. Do not fax.

ROSS LACY CASTING
The Casting Studios
200 South La Brea
Los Angeles, CA 90036
(310) 358-7558

LINDA LAMONTAGNE
P.O. Box 1371
Culver City, CA 90232
(310) 559-3314

LANDAU CASTING, C.C.D.A.
Fifth Street Studios
1216 Fifth Street
Santa Monica, CA 90401
(310) 458-1100
*Judy Landau & Katherine Landau
cast commercials.*

LANDSBURG/FIDDLEMAN
CASTING
13455 Ventura Blvd.,
   Suite 214
Sherman Oaks, CA 91423
*Casting Directors Shana
Landsburg and Teri Fiddleman
cast CD-Roms & interactive,
films, T.V. Accepts photos-
resumes by mail only.*

LA PADURA/HART CASTING
100 Universal City Plaza,
   MT 6149
Universal City, CA 91608
*Casting Directors: Jason
LaPadura C.S.A., Natalie Hart
C.S.A., Laura Adler (Associate),
Keri Owens (Associate), Russell
Scott (Assistant).*

MEREDITH LAYNE
Big Ticket Television
Sunset-Gower Studios
1438 North Gower, Building 35,
   Box 45
Los Angeles, CA 90028
(323) 860-7425
*Meredith Layne, C.S.A. (Manager
of Casting) casts for T.V. Union
only. Don't phone, fax, or visit.
Accepts photos by mail only.
Attends showcases. Interviews
by appointment only. (See also
separate listing for Donna
Ekholdt)*

SALLY LEAR, C.S.A.
838 North Fairfax Avenue
Los Angeles, CA 90046
Don't phone or visit.

KELI LEE
*(See Touchtone Television/ABC
Entertainment Television Group)*

CAROL LEFKO
P.O. Box 84509
Los Angeles, CA 90073
(310) 888-0007
*Casts film, T.V., theatre and
commercials.*

ALEXA LESKYS
(See Viacom Productions)

KATHLEEN LETTERIE
(See The WB)

GAIL LEVIN
*(See Paramount Pictures
Features Casting)*

HEIDI LEVITT CASTING, C.S.A.
7201 Melrose Avenue, Suite 203
Los Angeles, CA 90046
(323) 525-0800
*Casting Director: Heidi Levitt.
Casting Associate: Mia Levinson.
Casts films & T.V.*

LIBERMAN/PATTON CASTING
4311 Wilshire Blvd., #606
Los Angeles, CA 90010
(323) 462-9175
*Meg Liberman, C.S.A., Cami
Patton, C.S.A., Tim Payne
(Casting Associate), Nelia Morago
(Casting Director), Sandi Logan
(Casting Director), Christal Karge
(Casting Assistant) & Margaret
Pearson (Assistant) cast films, T.V.,
animated series/features, theatre,
voiceovers through agents
only. Don't phone, fax, or visit.
Interviews by appointment only.
Accepts photos-resumes from
agents/managers only only. Does
not accept unsolicited tapes.*

AMY LIEBERMAN CASTING
601 West Temple Street
Los Angeles, CA 90012
(213) 972-7374
*Amy Lieberman, C.S.A. is
Casting Director for the Mark
Taper Forum and the Ahmanson
Theatre.*

SHARON CHAZIN LIEBLEIN
(See Nickelodeon)

LIEN/COWAN CASTING,
C.C.D.A.
7461 Beverly Blvd., Suite 203
Los Angeles, CA 90036
(323) 937-0411
*Michael Lien & Dan Cowan cast
commercials.*

TRACY LILIENFIELD, C.S.A.
CBS Studio Center
4024 Radford Avenue, Sound
   Building, Second Floor
Studio City, CA 91604
(818) 655-5652
Casts for T.V.

ROBIN LIPPIN, C.S.A.
(please contact c/o C.S.A.)
606 North Larchmont Blvd., 4B
Los Angeles, CA 90004
*Casts T.V., MOWs, pilots &
features through agents only.
Union. Don't phone, fax, or visit.*

*Interviews by appointment only.
Accepts photos-resumes by
mail only. Attends showcases.
Currently casting the new NBC
series* Happy Family.

MARCI LIROFF
P.O. Box 57948
Sherman Oaks, CA 91413
(818) 784-5434
*Casts films. Interviews by
appointment only.*

LONDON-STROUD CASTING,
C.S.A.
c/o C.S.A.
(323) 668-0875
*Lisa London, C.S.A. & Catherine
Stroud, C.S.A. cast films & T.V.
Union. Accepts photos by mail
only. (See also C.S.A.)*

BEVERLY LONG, C.C.D.A.
Moorpark Studios
11425 Moorpark Street
Studio City, CA 91602
(818) 754-6222
*Casts commercials &
Independent films.*

CAROLYN LONG
(See Long/Di Matteo Casting)

LONG/DI MATTEO CASTING
The Bakery
10709 Burbank Blvd.
North Hollywood, CA 91601
(310) 225-5267
*Carolyn Long and Concetta Di
Matteo cast for features. Photos
and resumes are accepted.
Phone calls are accepted but
actors are asked to keep phone
calls at moderation. Conduct T.V./
workshops for actors; phone the
office for information.*

MOLLY LOPATA, C.S.A.
13731 Ventura Blvd., Suite A
Sherman Oaks, CA 91423
(818) 788-0673
*Casts for T.V. through agents
only. Don't phone, fax, or visit.*

JUNIE LOWRY-JOHNSON
CASTING, C.S.A.
c/o 20th Century-Fox
10201 West Pico Blvd.
Bochco Bldg, Room 232
Los Angeles, CA 90035
(323) 956-4856
c/o Paramount
5555 Melrose Avenue
Von Sternberg Building,
   Room 104
Los Angeles, CA 90028

Junie Lowry-Johnson, Scott Genkinger, Ron Surma, and Libby Goldstein cast for film and T.V. Junie & Scott are currently casting NYPD Blue; Junie & Ron are casting Star Trek; Junie & Libby are casting Six Feet Under and Deadwood.

LINDA LOWY CASTING, C.S.A.
5225 Wilshire Blvd.,
    Suite 718
Los Angeles, CA 90036
(818) 733-0669

PENNY LUDFORD CASTING
1069 Dolores Road
Altadena, CA 91001
Penny Ludford, C.S.A. casts for T.V. (including MOW, pilots), independent films, music videos, commercials and industrials. Don't phone, fax, or visit. Interviews by appointment only.

MTV NETWORK
2600 Colorado Avenue
Santa Monica, CA 90404
Rod Aissa (Vice President of Talent Development and Casting). Actors/actresses, on-air hosts, comedians may send pictures-resumes and video demos by mail only. Attends showcases. Don't phone or visit.

MACDONALD/BULLINGTON CASTING
c/o C.S.A.
(310) 383-1474
Perry Bullington, C.S.A., Bob MacDonald, C.S.A., & Victor Martinez.

BETTY MAE CASTING
1023 1/2 Abbot Kinney Blvd.
Venice, CA 90291
(310) 396-6100
Felicia Fasano, Mary Vernieu cast features and T.V.

SUZIE MAGREY
(See On Your Mark Studios)

FRANCINE MAISLER, C.S.A.
Sony Studios
10202 West Washington Blvd.
Jimmy Stewart Building,
    Room 207
Culver City, CA 90232
(310) 244-6945
Casts films. Don't phone or visit.

MAMBO CASTING
1139 Hacienda Place
West Hollywood, CA 90069
(323) 650-9190
fax: (323) 650-9194
orlette@mambocasting.com
www.mambocasting.com
Casting Director Orlette Ruiz casts film, T.V. and voiceovers. Don't phone, fax, or visit. Interviews by appointment only; through agents only. Accepts tapes (audio/video) by mail only. Union. Nonunion.

SHEILA MANNING CASTING, INC.
508 South San Vicente Blvd.
Los Angeles, CA 90048
(323) 852-1046
Sheila Manning: Casting Director. Cast animated features, commercials, industrials, infomercials, music videos, print ads, soaps, T.V., theatre & voiceovers. Union & nonunion. English and Spanish-language commercials.

DEBI MANWILLER,
Pagano/Manwiller Casting
c/o "24"
6250 Canoga Avenue
Rick Pagano, Debi Manwiller & Peggy Kennedy cast film & T.V. through agents only. Accept photos and resumes by mail only. No phone calls.

MINDY MARIN,
Bluewater Ranch Entertainment
    Inc./Casting Artists, Inc.
1433 Sixth Street
Santa Monica, CA 90401
(310) 395-1882
Mindy Marin, C.S.A., casts films.

MARTIN CASTING, INC.
Digital Casting Studios
1040 North Las Palmas, #30
Los Angeles, CA 90038
Melissa Martin, C.C.D.A. casts commercials, & print ads through agents only. No phone calls or e-mails, please.

TONY MARTINELLI
(See 20th Century Fox Television)

RICKI G. MASLAR
4130 Cahuenga Blvd., Suite 108
Universal City, CA 91602
(818) 769-6800
Additional phone: (818) 761-8986
(additional address)
5036 Coldwater Canyon
Sherman Oaks, CA 91423

LARAY MAYFIELD/MCCOY FILMS
c/o Silverlayne Studios
1161 North Las Palmas
Los Angeles, CA 90048
(323) 468-6888
Casts films through agents only. Also casts commercials. Union. Don't phone, fax or visit.

BRIGID MCBRIDE
(See Westside Casting)

VALERIE MCCAFFREY, C.S.A.
4924 Balboa Blvd., #172
Encino, CA 91316
(818) 785-1886
Casts Feature Films. Union. Interviews by appointment only. Through agents only. Accepts photo-resume and videotapes by mail only. Please don't visit.

MCCANN-KNOTEK ASSOCIATES
8350 Santa Monica Blvd.,
    Suite 201
Los Angeles, CA 90069
(310) 854-0656
fax: (310) 854-6370
Hank McCann and Robert Knotek (partners) cast films, theatre, T.V. through agents only. Union. Don't phone, fax, or visit. Interviews by appointment only. Audio/video tapes will not be returned.

BARBARA MCCARTHY
(See Paramount Pictures Features Casting)

JEANNE MCCARTHY & JUEL BESTROP CASTING
5225 Wilshire Blvd., Suite 418
(323) 934-8363
Casting Directors Jeanne McCarthy, Juel Bestrop, and Natasha Cuba cast for films and some high-end pilots. (See also C.S.A.)

MEGAN MCCONNELL, C.S.A.
Raleigh Manhattan Beach
    Studios
1600 Rosencrans Avenue
Bldg. 4-B, 1st Floor
Manhattan Beach, CA 90266
(310) 727-2290
Casts films and T.V. with Janet Gilmore. Don't phone or visit.

CYDNEY MCCURDY
2460 North Lake Avenue,
    Suite 111
Altadena, CA 91001
(818) 569-3055

KELLY MCDONALD
(See Spelling Television)

VIVIAN MCRAE, C.S.A.
P.O. Box 1351
Burbank, CA 91507
(818) 848-9590

ELIZABETH MELCHER
(See Powell/Melcher Casting)

GINA MERRILL
(See E! Entertainment Television)

JEFF MESHEL
(See NBC)

JOSEPH MIDDLETON, C.S.A.
10201 West Pico Blvd.
Building 89, Suite 448
Los Angeles, CA 90035
Monika Mikkelsen
(310) 396-6100

ANNA MILLER CASTING
P.O. Box 2567
Winnetka, CA 91396
(818) 517-9743
Casts mainly principals for commercials, some extras, films, industrials, infomercials, music videos & T.V., mostly through agents but will accept general submissions as well. Union & nonunion. Accepts photos by mail only.

KEVIN MILLER CASTING
c/o Chelsea Studios
11530 Ventura Blvd.
Studio City, CA 91604
(310) 358-7021
Casts films, commercials, infomercials, music videos, print advertising, T.V. Union, nonunion. Don't phone, fax, or visit. Accepts photos-resumes by mail only. Attends showcases.

RICK MILLIKAN, C.S.A.
Sony Pictures Entertainment
10202 West Washington Blvd.
Clark Gable Building,
   Room 204
Culver City, CA 90232
(310) 244-3188
Rick Millikan and associate Diana Jaher cast for The Guardian.

MIONIE/STRINGER CASTING
*Lisa Mionie, C.S.A. and Eileen Stringer, Casting Directors.
(See C.S.A.)*

RICK MONTGOMERY CASTING
(310) 841-5969

BOB MORONES CASTING
4130 Cahuenga Blvd., Suite 309
Universal City, CA 91602
(818) 761-5353
Bob Morones, C.S.A. (Casting Director), Veronica Collins (Casting Associate), Bonita Deneen (Casting Trainee) cast independent feature films, T.V. pilots, series & specials as well as commercials. Accept photos by mail only. Accept tapes (audio/video). Attend showcases.

DONNA MORONG, C.S.A.
(818) 560-7875
(See Buena Vista Motion Picture Group)

MOSSBERG/ANTHONY CASTING
4024 Radford Avenue, Trailer 800
Studio City, CA 91604
(818) 655-4154
Julie Mossberg & Jill Anthony cast animated features/series, T.V. Don't phone, fax, or visit. Interviews by appointment only. Accept photos-resumes by mail only. Attend showcases. Currently working on ABC's Less than Perfect *and* Related By Family *for FOX.*

JOHN MULKEEN
CASTING, C.S.A.
1728 Alvira Street
Los Angeles, CA 90035
(323) 938-6556
Casts commercials, industrials & T.V. (See also On Your Mark Studios)

ROGER MUSSENDEN C.S.A. &
ELIZABETH TORRES, C.S.A.
10536 Culver Blvd., Suite C
Culver City, CA 90232
(310) 559-9522
Cast films & T.V. Accept photos by mail only.

BRIAN MYERS
4924 Radford Avenue,
   Bungalow 5
Studio City, CA 91604

NBC
3000 West Alameda Avenue
Burbank, CA 91523
(818) 840-3774
Marc Hirschfeld (Executive VP of Casting); Jeff Meshel (VP of Casting); Annamarie Kostura (VP of Daytime Casting) (818) 840-4410; Sonia Nikore (VP of Casting); Grace Wu (VP of Casting).

ROBIN NASSIF
(See Nassif & Baca Casting)

NASSIF & BACA CASTING
(818) 528-2080, x2
Patrick Baca, C.S.A. and Robin Nassif, C.S.A. cast films, pilots, MOWs and theatre. Union. Unsolicited submissions via agent or manager only at this time. Please don't phone, fax, or visit. Interviews by appointment only.

NANCY NAYOR
CASTING, C.S.A.
6320 Commodore Sloat Drive
Los Angeles, CA 90048
(323) 857-0151
Casts films & T.V. Don't phone, fax or visit. Accepts photos by mail only.

DEBRA NEATHERY
4820 North Cleon Avenue
North Hollywood, CA 91601
(818) 506-5524
Casts films, commercials, industrials & voiceovers.

BRUCE H. NEWBERG, C.S.A.
(323) 468-6633
(See C.S.A.)

NICKELODEON
2600 Colorado Avenue,
   Second Floor
Santa Monica, CA 90404
(310) 752-8402
Sharon Chazin Lieblein (Head of Casting–Nickelodeon/Nick at Nite/TV Land/Nicktoons). Susana Martinez (assistant). Casts T.V., voiceovers, extras, and animated series/features. Union/Nonunion. Don't phone, fax, or visit. Interviews by appointment only. Accepts photos-resumes by mail only. Only send tapes upon request. Tapes will not be returned. Attends showcases.

NICOLAU CASTING,
C.S.A., C.C.D.A.
8910 Holly Place
Los Angeles, CA 90046
(323) 650-9899
Kris Nicolau casts commercials, film, theatre. Union. Accepts photos by mail only.

SONIA NIKORE, C.S.A.
(818) 840-3835
(See NBC)

WENDY O'BRIEN, C.S.A.
automatic sweat
221 North Robertson Blvd., #F
Beverly Hills, CA 90211
(310) 271-2650
Casts for films, T.V.

PAULINE O'CON
*(See Fox Broadcasting
Company)*

JENNY O'HAVER & COMPANY,
C.C.D.A.
(323) 650-9010
*(See also On Your Mark
Studios)*

ON LOCATION CASTING
1223 Wilshire Blvd., PMB #409
Santa Monica, CA 90403
(310) 772-8181
Registration: (310) 229-5332
Talent Hotline: (310) 284-3549
OLCCasting@hotmail.com
*Tina Kerr (Casting Director)
casts union and nonunion
background actors for films
and T.V. Don't phone, fax, or
visit. Interviews by appointment
only. Accepts photos and
resumes by mail but recommends having a digital photo
taken at registration. Attends
showcases and accepts show
showcase invitations.*

ON YOUR MARK
451 North La Cienega Blvd., #12
Los Angeles, CA 90048
(310) 360-9936
*Houses the following casting
offices: John Mulkeen, Susie
MaGrey, Crash Casting, Louis
Goldstein, Jenny O'Haver, Lisa
Pantone, Phyllis Ricci, Idolmakers
Casting, Compassionate Casting.
Casting directors cast for commer-
cials, films, music videos, print
advertising, T.V. Interviews by
appointment only.*

LORI OPENDEN
500 South Buena Vista
Animation Building,
    Suite 1E 28
Burbank, CA 91521
*(Please see also listing under
UPN)*

FERN ORENSTEIN
(See CBS)

GREGORY ORSON, C.S.A.
8000 Sunset Blvd.
Los Angeles, CA 90046
(323) 848-3615

RAQUEL OSBORNE CASTING
rockio@sbcglobal.net
*Casts extras, film & T.V. Union &
nonunion. Submissions accepted
only on request or by email.*

JESSICA OVERWISE, C.S.A.
17250 Sunset Blvd., #304
Pacific Palisades, CA 90272
(310) 459-2686
*Casts films, T.V., theatre and
commercials through agents.
Union. Don't phone or visit.
Accepts photos and resumes
by mail.*

RICK PAGANO,
PAGANO-MANWILLER CASTING
4024 Radford Avenue,
    Building 3, #111
Studio City, CA 91604
*Rick Pagano & Debi Manwiller
cast film & T.V.*

MARVIN PAIGE, C.S.A.
P.O. Box 69434
West Hollywood, CA 90069
(818) 760- 3040
*Casts features, T.V., and celebrity
events. Production and Talent
Consultant for television
Biography series and other documentaries. Accepts photos,
resumes, and tapes (audio/visual)
by mail only. Union. Attends
showcases.*

LISA PANTONE, C.C.D.A.
c/o On Your Mark Studios
1134 Berkeley Drive
Glendale, CA 91205
lisa@lisapantone.com
www.lisapantone.com
*Lisa Pantone casts award
winning, independent films,
commercials, reality shows,
music videos, and theatre. (See
also On Your Mark Studios)*

JOHN PAPSIDERA, C.S.A.
automatic sweat
221 North Robertson Blvd.,
    Suite F
Beverly Hills, CA 90211

PARAMOUNT PICTURES
FEATURES CASTING
Paramount Studios
5555 Melrose Avenue
Bob Hope Building, Room 206
Hollywood, CA 90038
(323) 956-5444
fax: (323) 862-1371
*Gail Levin (Senior VP, Features
Casting), Andrew S. Brown*

*(Director, Features Casting),
Barbara McCarthy (Manager,
Features Casting), cast
films only.*

PARAMOUNT TELEVISION
CASTING
5555 Melrose Avenue
Bluhdorn Building,
    Room 128
Hollywood, CA 90038
(323) 956-5578
*Sheila Guthrie (Senior VP,
Talent & Casting), Danielle Diller
(Casting Associate), Damona
Resnick (Casting Administrator).
Elizabeth Boykewich-Torres (Pilot
Season Casting Consultant).
Interviews by appointment only.
Attends showcases.*

CAMI PATTON
(See Liberman/Patton Casting)

JOEY PAUL CASTING
Hollywood Center Studios
1040 North Las Palmas,
    Building 33
Hollywood, CA 90038
(323) 860-8989
Ms. Joey Paul Jensen, C.S.A

PEMRICK/FRONK CASTING
14724 Ventura Blvd., Penthouse
Sherman Oaks, CA 91403
(818) 325-1289
*Donald Paul Pemrick, C.S.A.,
Dean E. Fronk and Elizabeth
Hollywood (Casting Assistant)
cast films and T.V. Union.*

MERCEDES PENNEY
CASTING
224 East Olive Avenue, #205
Burbank, CA 91502-1234
(818) 842-2270
Epaainc@aol.com

NANCY PERKINS
*(See Universal Network
Television)*

PENNY PERRY
500 South Sepulveda Blvd.,
    Suite 310
Los Angeles, CA 90049
*Casts films, theatre, T.V. through
agents only. Also packages films.*

KARI PEYTON CASTING
1145 North McCadden Place
Los Angeles, CA 90038
(323) 462-1500
fax: (323) 462-1661
*Not accepting photos and
resumes at this time.*

BONNIE PIETILA
20th Century Fox
10201 West Pico Blvd.,
    Trailer 730
Los Angeles, CA 90035
(310) 369-3632
Casts films & T.V. Producer:
The Simpsons.

GAYLE PILLSBURY
(See Zane-Pillsbury Casting)

PLASTER CASTING
1161 North Las Palmas Blvd.
Los Angeles, CA 90038
Not accepting photos and
resumes at this time.

CHRISTY POKARNEY
Omega Entertainment
8760 Shoreham Drive
Los Angeles, CA 90069
(310) 855-0516
Casts films & T.V. Accepts
photos by mail only.

HOLLY POWELL
(See Powell/Melcher Casting)
Powell/Melcher Casting
5555 Melrose Avenue,
    Bungalow 25
Los Angeles, CA 90038
(323) 956-4260
Casting Directors Holly Powell,
C.S.A., Elizabeth Melcher;
Casting Associate Helen
Diament and Casting Assistant
Tara Treacy cast T.V., including
UPN's One on One *and* Eve.

LYNNE QUIRION
Chelsea Studios
11530 Ventura Blvd.
Studio City, CA 91604
(818) 286-9400

CLAUDIA RAMSUMAIR
(See The WB)

MARK RANDALL
CASTING
1811 North Whitley, #401
Los Angeles, CA 90028
(323) 465-7553

JOHANNA RAY &
ASSOCIATES, C.S.A.
1022 Palm Avenue, #2
West Hollywood, CA 90069
(310) 652-2511
Johanna Ray primarily casts
films. Only accepts headshots
when related to a current
project. Accepts unsolicited
film work only if it contains
professional T.V./film work.

ROBI REED & ASSOCIATES
6605 Hollywood Blvd., Suite 100
Los Angeles, CA 90028
Robi Reed-Humes casts films,
T.V. & voiceovers. Don't phone,
fax, or visit.

JOE REICH
Manager, Casting Administration
Walt Disney Television
500 South Buena Vista,
INP Building, Room 107 F
Burbank, CA 91521-2343
(818) 560-6877
Does not accept photos and
resumes. Does not actively cast.

JOAN RENFROW
Onyx Productions
5550 Wilshire Blvd., Suite 301
Los Angeles, CA 90036
(323) 692-9830
Casts commercials.

TOM REUDY
(323) 954-0007
(See Dowd/Reudy Casting)

PHYLLIS RICCI
(See On Your Mark Studios)

RODEO CASTING
7013 Willoughby Avenue
Rodeo Studios
Los Angeles, CA 90038
(323) 969-9125
Britt Enggren casts commercials &
print ads. Don't phone, fax, or visit.

ROMANO/BENNER CASTING
c/o C.S.A.
606 North Larchmont Blvd., 4B
Los Angeles, CA 90004
Debby Romano, C.S.A., Brett
Benner and Robyn Owen, casting
directors.

VICKI ROSENBERG &
ASSOCIATES
10201 West Pico Blvd., #80/10
Los Angeles, CA 90035
(310) 369-3448
Vicki Rosenberg, C.S.A.; Alexis
Frank Koczara, Associate; Beth
Sekul, Assistant. Casts for CBS'
Judging Amy.

DONNA ROSENSTEIN
c/o Disney
500 South Buena Vista Street
Old Animation Bldg. 3A11
Burbank, CA 91521-1809
(818) 560-7837
Casting Director Donna Rosenstein,
C.S.A. casts films and T.V. Dylann
Brander: Casting Associate.

Please don't phone, fax or visit.
Casting through agents only. Do not
send unsolicited videotapes. Union.

MARCIA ROSS, C.S.A.
(818) 560-7510
(See Buena Vista Motion Picture
Group)

PATRICK J. RUSH CASTING,
C.S.A.
3400 Riverside Drive, Suite 700
Burbank, CA 91505
(818) 977-7560
Casting Directors, Patrick J. Rush,
C.S.A. casts films & T.V. Don't
phone, fax, or visit. Interviews by
appointment only. Accepts
photos-resumes by mail only.

MARNIE SAITTA
CBS The Young and the Restless
7800 Beverly Blvd., Suite 3305
Los Angeles, CA 90036
(323) 575-2803

GABRIELLE SCHARY, C.C.D.A.
Sessions West Studios
2601 Ocean Park Blvd., Suite 120
Santa Monica, CA 90405
(310) 450-0835
(310) 450-9228
www.sessionsweststudios.com

LAURA SCHIFF
(818) 954-5781

ARLENE SCHUSTER-GOSS
(See ASG Casting)

EMILY SCHWEBER
(310) 364-0474
Casting Director Emily Schweber
casts films. Accepts photos-
resumes by mail only.

BRIEN SCOTT, C.S.A.
18034 Ventura Blvd., Suite 275
Encino, CA 91316
(818) 343-3669
Casts films, T.V. Don't phone, fax,
or visit. Interviews by appointment
only. Accepts photos/resumes/
postcards by mail only. Attends
showcases/accepts showcase
invitations. (See also listing under
New York Casting Directors)

TINA SEILER
P.O. Box 2001
Toluca Lake, CA 91610
(818) 382-7929
tinacasting789@yahoo.com
Casts films, industrials, infomercials,
theatre, T.V. & voiceovers and reality
shows. Principals and extras. Union
& nonunion. Don't phone or visit.

LILA SELIK CASTING,
C.C.D.A.
1551 South Robertson Blvd.,
   #202
Los Angeles, CA 90035
(310) 556-2444
www.castingbylilaselik.com
*Lila Selik (Casting Director,
dialogue coach and acting
teacher) casts CD-ROMs &
Interactive, commercials, films,
industrials, infomercials, music
videos, print ads, theatre, T.V. &
voiceovers through agents only.
Info (agent name and phone,
actor's name) must be on front of
pictures and on back of resumes!
Also casts for DGA "Directors
Workshops." Union & nonunion.
Please don't phone, fax, or visit.
No personal deliveries by
actors/models.*

FRANCENE SELKIRK-
ACKERMAN
*(See Shooting From The Hip
Casting)*

SELZER CASTING, C.S.A.
(323) 468-3215

JULIE SELZER, CASTING
DIRECTOR
(See C.S.A.)

TONY SEPULVEDA, C.S.A.
(818) 954-7639
(See Warner Bros. Television)

SESSIONS WEST STUDIOS
2601 Ocean Park Blvd.,
   Suite 201
Santa Monica, CA 90405
(310) 450-0835

PAMELA SHAE
(See Spelling Television Inc.)

SHANER/TESTA CASTING
3875 Wilshire Blvd., Suite 700
Los Angeles, CA 90010
(213) 382-3375
*Dan Shaner and Michael Testa
cast films & T.V. Accept photos
by mail only.*

AVA SHEVITT
Village Studio
519 Broadway
Santa Monica, CA 90401
(310) 656-4600
*Casts commercials, film, T.V.,
and teleconference. Offers
digital clips posted to web
page & session delivered
on CD.*

SHOOTING FROM THE
HIP CASTING
Zydeco Studios
11317 Ventura Blvd.
Studio City, CA 91604
(818) 506-0613
*Francene Selkirk-Ackerman
and assistant Tracy Mueller
cast commercials, film shorts,
industrials, infomercials, music
videos, print advertising, T.V. &
voiceovers. Union & nonunion.
Don't phone, fax or visit. Accepts
photos by mail only. Accepts
tapes (audio/video) by mail only.
Tapes will not be returned.
Attends showcases and improv
shows occasionally.*

SHOWTIME NETWORK
(See Viacom)

MARCIA SHULMAN
*(See Fox Broadcasting
Company)*

MARK SIKES, C.S.A.
Pioneer Valley Productions
8909 24th Street
Los Angeles, CA 90034
(310) 652-9599
*Casts films, T.V. & commercials.
Union & nonunion. Accepts
photos-resumes by mail only.
Interviews by appointment only.*

JOAN SIMMONS
P.M.B. #108
38-180 Del Webb Blvd.
Palm Desert, CA 92211-1256
(760) 360-4423
JRS-Presents@Prodigy.Net
*Casts theatre. Union &
nonunion. Interviews by
appointment only. Accepts
photos-resumes by mail only.
Accepts tapes by mail only.
Attends showcases.*

CLAIR SINNETT
CASTING
531 Main Street, #1135
El Segundo, CA 90245
(310) 606-0813
sinnett@earthlink.net
www.actorsworking.com
*Clair Sinnett, Aaron Revoir
and (NY & LA Associates) cast
films, industrials, commercials,
theatre & movies for television.
Union. Don't phone, fax, or visit.
Attends theatre & industry
showcases in Los Angeles and
New York City.*

MELISSA SKOFF
CASTING, C.S.A.
11684 Ventura Blvd., Suite 5141
Studio City, CA 91604
(818) 760-2058
Additional Phone: (818) 760-2058
fax: (323) 468-4555
(Additional address):
   11684 Ventura Blvd.,
   #5141Studio City, CA 91604
*Casts, films, T.V., theatre &
commercials through agents only.
Accepts photos by mail only.*

SLATER/BROOKSBANK
CASTING
4151 Prospect Avenue
The Cottage, #102
Los Angeles, CA 90027
*Casting Directors: Mary Jo Slater,
C.S.A., Steve Brooksbank,
C.S.A., and Beth Blanks. Casting
Associate: John Villacorta.*

SIDRA SMITH CASTING
(310) 428-5578
tellsid@aol.com
*Casts for animated series/features,
commercials, films, industrials,
infomercials, music videos,
print advertising, theatre, & T.V.
Union/Nonunion. Interviews by
appointment only. Attends showcases. (See also listing under
New York Casting Directors)*

J.S. SNYDER & ASSOCIATES
1801 North Kingsley Drive, #202
Los Angeles, CA 90027
(323) 465-4241
*Stephen Snyder casts commer-
cials, films, industrials, print ads,
theatre & T.V.*

STEPHEN SNYDER
(323) 465-4241
(See J.S. Snyder & Associates)

SOBO CASTING
Castaway Studios
8899 Beverly Blvd., Lobby
Los Angeles, CA 90048
(310) 248-5296
*Amy Sobo and Jane Sobo,
casting directors. Accept photos
and resumes but please do not
seal envelope.*

SONY PICTURES
ENTERTAINMENT
9336 West Washington Blvd.
Culver City, CA 90232
(310) 244-4000
Production offices for episodic T.V.

SONY PICTURES TELEVISION
9336 West Washington Blvd.
Culver City, CA 90232
(310) 202-3444
Dawn Steinberg (Senior VP Talent & Casting) and Adrianna Porcaro, Assistant; Delia Frankel (Director of Casting). Please don't phone or visit. Interviews by appointment only. Accepts photos and resumes by mail only. Does not accept unsolicited tapes under any circumstance. Attends showcases and accepts showcase invitations.

CHRISTI SOPER
(See DreamWorks Casting)

SPELLING TELEVISION
5700 Wilshire Blvd.,
    Suite 575
Los Angeles, CA 90036
(323) 965-5784
Pamela Shae (Senior VP of Talent) and Kelly McDonald (Executive Director of Talent) cast T.V. Don't visit. Interviews by appointment only. Accept photos-resumes by mail only. Attend showcases.

SPIKE TV
2600 Colorado Avenue
Santa Monica, CA 90404
(310) 752-8240
Blythe Cappello; Director of Casting and Talent Development. (See also listing under New York Casting Directors)

PAMELA STARKS CASTING
(323) 571-1800
starkscasting@earthlink.net
Casts commercials primarily. (Will consider casting other projects.)

SALLY STINER
CASTING, C.S.A.
9336 West Washington Blvd.
Stage 11 Offices, Room 1
Culver City, CA 90232
(310) 392-3197
Casting Directors Sally Stiner and Barbie Block.

STANZI STOKES CASTING
(818) 762-8448

STUART STONE, C.C.D.A.
8899 Beverly Blvd., First Floor
Los Angeles, CA 90048
(310) 248-5296
(323) 866-1811
Casts voiceovers and infomercials only!

CATHERINE STROUD
(See London/Stroud Casting)

CHADWICK STRUCK
(See listing for Thunderstruck Casting)

LORI SUGAR CASTING
5933 West Slauson Avenue
Culver City, CA 90230
Judith Holstra and Lori Sugar cast films & T.V. Accept photos by mail only. Accept audio/ videotapes but they will not be returned. SAG members only please.

RON SURMA
(See Junie Lowry-Johnson Casting)

MONICA SWANN
CASTING, C.S.A.
Sunset Gower Studios
1438 North Gower Street
Los Angeles, CA 90028
Office: (323) 468-3776
fax: (323) 468-3774
Casts films & T.V.

MARYCLAIRE
SWEETERS
(See Westside Castin)

TLC/BOOTH, INC.
6521 Homewood Avenue
Los Angeles, CA 90028
(323) 464-2788
Loree Booth and Leland Williams are independent casting directors.

YUMI TAKADA
CASTING, C.C.D.A.
2105 Huntington Lane,
    Suite A
Redondo Beach, CA 90278
(310) 372-7287
yumicasting@earthlink.net
Casts commercials, films, industrials, infomercials, music videos, print ads & voiceovers. Union & nonunion. Specializes in casting of Asians for all areas. Don't phone, fax or visit. Audio/video tapes will not be returned.

MARK TAPER FORUM
601 West Temple Street
Los Angeles, CA 90012
(213) 972-7374
Amy Lieberman, C.S.A. is Casting Director for the Mark Taper Forum and the Ahmanson Theatre.

JAMES F. TARZIA CASTING
7130 Hollywood Blvd., Suite 24
Hollywood, CA 90046
(323) 874-9217
JTWEHO@yahoo.com
www.jamestarzia.com
James F. Tarzia casts films & T.V. through agents only. Union. Don't phone or fax.

HELYN TAYLOR CASTING
1412 North Crescent Heights
    Blvd., #104
West Hollywood, CA 90046
Casts features, commercials, & theatre. Union. Don't phone, fax, or visit. (See also listing under New York Casting Directors)

MARK TESCHNER
CASTING, C.S.A.
ABC Television Center
4151 Prospect Avenue
General Hospital Building
Los Angeles, CA 90027
(323) 671-5542
Casts films, soaps & T.V. Specializes in casting of actors for daytime dramas. Don't phone, fax or visit. (See also listings for General Hospital under Los Angeles-based Daytime Serials)

MICHAEL TESTA
(See Shaner/Testa Casting)

JAMIE THOMASON
Disney TV Animation
500 South Buena Vista Street
FGW Building, Suite 1110
Burbank, CA 91521

THUNDERSTRUCK CASTING
11718 Barrington Court, Suite 265
Los Angeles, CA 90049
(310) 572-2898
Casting Directors Chadwick Cohn & Chadwick Struck cast commercials, films, T.V., music videos, and print advertising. Chad and Chad are both currently working at Paramount Studios. Please don't visit. Accepts photos by mail only. Indicate SAG/AFTRA affiliation. Attends showcases.

JOEL THURM, C.S.A.
Hollywood Center Studios
1040 North Las Palmas,
    Building 24
Los Angeles, CA 90038
Casts films, T.V. Don't phone, fax or visit. Interviews by appointment only. Accepts photos-resumes by mail only.

TILLMAN/JOHNSON-PLATE
CASTING
(c/o C.S.A.)
606 North Larchmont Blvd., 4B
Los Angeles, CA 90004
*Casting Directors Mindy
Johnson-Plate and Mark Tillman,
C.S.A. cast films and T.V. Don't
phone, fax, or visit. Interviews
by appointment only. Accepts
photos and resumes by mail only.
Attend showcases and accept
showcase invitations. Union.*

JOY TODD CASTING CORP.
www.Joytodd.com
*Casts feature films. Union. Don't
phone, fax, or visit. Accepts
video tapes w/SASE. (See C.S.A.)*

TONDINO-WARREN CASTING
2550 North Hollywood Way,
    Suite 204
Burbank, CA 91505
(818) 843-1902
*Gennette Tondino & Ted Warren
cast films.*

TOUCHSTONE TELEVISION/
ABC ENTERTAINMENT
TELEVISION GROUP
500 South Buena Vista Street
Burbank, CA 91521-4651
(818) 460-7313
fax: (818) 460-6903
*Gene Blythe (Executive VP,
T.V. Casting); Keli Lee (Senior
VP, Casting), Brian Dorfman
(VP, Casting-Comedy); Ayo
Davis (Director, Drama
Casting).*

20TH CENTURY FOX
FEATURE CASTING
10201 West Pico Blvd.
Los Angeles, CA 90035
(310) 369-1824
*Donna Isaacson (Executive
VP of Casting); Christian
Kaplan (Vice President of
Feature Casting); Aisha coley
(Vice President of Casting);
Michael Hothorn (Director
of Feature Casting); Seth
Yanklewitz (Manager of
Feature Casting).*

20TH CENTURY FOX
TELEVISION
10201 West Pico Blvd.
Building 88, Room 212
Los Angeles, CA 90035
(310) 369-4265
*Tony Martinelli (Director,
Casting); Ryan May (Assistant).*

TYLER CASTING, C.C.D.A.
c/o Chelsea Studios
11530 Ventura Blvd.
Studio City, CA 91604
(818) 506-0400
*Casting Director Susan Tyler
casts commercials, films, T.V.,
voiceover and promotional.
Union & nonunion. Accepts
photos by mail only.*

UPN (UNITED PARAMOUNT
NETWORK)
11800 Wilshire Blvd.
Los Angeles, CA 90025
(310) 575-7000
*Judith Weiner (SR VP of Casting),
Dana Theodoratos (Manager of
Casting), Lori Openden
(Consultant).*

ULRICH/DAWSON/KRITZER
CASTING
4705 Laurel Canyon Blvd., #301
Valley Village, CA 91607
(818) 623-1818
*Robert Ulrich, C.S.A., Eric
Dawson, C.S.A., Carol Kritzer,
C.S.A. and Shawn Dawson
C.S.A. cast T.V. and film through
agents only. Union. Don't
phone, fax.*

UNIVERSAL NETWORK
TELEVISION
100 Universal Plaza
Building 1320, Suite 4-M
Universal City, CA 91608
(818) 777-0437
*Nancy Perkins (Senior VP of
Talent & Casting).*

UNIVERSAL STUDIOS FEATURE
FILM CASTING
100 Universal City Plaza
Building 2160, Suite 8A
Universal City, CA 91608
(818) 777-8327
fax: (818) 866-1403
*Julie Hutchinson (VP of Casting);
Liz Salem (Coordinator, Feature
Casting); and Aaron Harper
(Casting Assistant). Agent
submissions only.*

VH1
2600 Colorado Avenue
Santa Monica, CA 90404
(310) 752-8345
Stacy.Alexander@Vh1staff.com
*Stacy Alexander, Director of
Casting. Accepts photos-resumes
and tapes (audio/video) by mail
only. Please do not phone, fax or
visit. Interviews by appointment*

*only. Attends showcases and
accepts showcase invitations.
Casting through agents only.
Union or nonunion. (See also
VH1's listing under New York
Casting Directors)*

BLANCA VALDEZ CASTING,
C.C.D.A.
1001 North Poinsettia Place
West Hollywood, CA 90046
(323) 876-5700
*Casting Director: Blanca Valdez.
Casts commercials, Voiceovers,
Print, T.V., Film. Bilingual:
Spanish/English*

VALKO/MILLER CASTING
12003 Guerin Street
Studio City, CA 91604
(818) 754-5414
*Nikki Valko, C.S.A. and Ken Miller,
C.S.A. cast for T.V. and Film.*

MINA VASQUEZ
8306 Wilshire Blvd., #1918
Beverly Hills, CA 90211
(323) 669-1723

PAUL VENTURA
Chelsea Studios
11530 Ventura Blvd.
Studio City, CA 91604
(818) 286-9400
Casts commercials.

VIACOM PRODUCTIONS
10880 Wilshire Blvd., Suite 1101
Los Angeles, CA 90024
(310) 234-5035
*Beth Klein (Sr. VP of Casting,
Viacom Productions and
Showtime), David Aulicino
(Manager of Casting, Viacom
Productions) and Alexa Leskys
(Casting Associate) cast for T.V.
Please do not visit.*

THE VOICECASTER
1832 West Burbank Blvd.
Burbank, CA 91506
(818) 841-5300
casting@voicecaster.com
www.voicecaster.com
*Huck Liggett, Martha Mayakis and
additional staff cast for animated
series/features, CD-ROMs & interactive, commercials, industrials,
infomercials, T.V. and voiceovers.
Don't visit. Interviews by appointment only. Accepts audio demos
by mail only. Union/Nonunion
and celebrity casting. Also offers
audition, animation and voiceover
workshops for all levels.*

THE WB
411 North Hollywood Way
Building 34-R, Room 161
Burbank, CA 91505
(818) 977-6016
*Kathleen Letterie (Executive
Vice President of Casting);
Claudia Ramsumair (Director of
Casting); Tess Sanchez (Director
of Casting); Michelle Furtney
Goodman (Assistant to Kathleen
Letterie); Susan Grennan
(Assistant to Claudia Ramsumair
and Tess Sanchez).*

DEBE WAISMAN CASTING
11684 Ventura Blvd., PMB #415
Studio City, CA 91604
(818) 752-7052
Extra Registration Hotline:
(310) 535-1325
fax: (818)752-7054

DAVA WAITE CASTING, C.S.A.
CBS Studio Center
4024 Radford Avenue,
Bldg. #7, 2nd Floor
Studio City, CA 91604
(818) 655-5050
fax: (818) 655-8233

KATY WALLIN CASTING
1918 West Magnolia Blvd.
#206
Burbank, CA 91506
(818) 563-4121
www.katywallin.com
*Katy Wallin, C.S.A. (Producer,
Casting Director), Sheila Conlin
and Tara Johnson cast film,
T.V., and has a division of the
company that casts commercials.
Associate: Anita Johnson Lusk.
Assistant: Sondra Jovel. Accepts
photos by mail only. Also offers
casting suites available for rental
on a daily and weekly basis.*

WALT DISNEY FEATURE
ANIMATION
2100 Riverside Drive
Burbank, CA 91506
(818) 460-9192
*Jen Rudin, Casting Director,
and Matthew Jon Beck, Casting
Associate, cast animated features
& films.*

WARNER BROS. FEATURE
FILM CASTING
4000 Warner Blvd.
Burbank, CA 91522
(818) 954-6000
*Lora Kennedy (Senior VP of
Features Casting).*

WARNER BROS. TELEVISION
CASTING
300 Television Plaza,
Bldg. 140, 1st Floor
Burbank, CA 91505
(818) 954-6000
*Mary V. Buck (Senior VP);
Tony Sepulveda (VP), Wendi
Matthews (VP), Tony Birkley
(Manager), Lisa Loia (Manager)
cast for T.V. (See also NY Casting
Directors: Meg Simon, VP)*

SAMUEL WARREN, C.S.A.
(323) 462-1510
*See C.S.A.) Casts commercials,
films & T.V. Don't phone or visit.
(See also C.S.A. and San Diego
listings)*

TED WARREN
(818) 843-1902
(See Tondino/Warren Casting)

MIMI WEBB-MILLER
CASTING
171 Pier Avenue
Santa Monica, CA 90405
(310) 452-0863
fax: (310) 581-5277
mwmcasting@aol.com
*SAG, Real People and Location
Commercial Casting.*

WEBER & ASSOCIATES
CASTING
10250 Constellation Street,
Suite #2060
Los Angeles, CA 90067
(310) 449-3685
*Paul Weber, C.S.A. and
Associate Ivy Isenberg cast
T.V. and features. Don't phone,
fax. Interviews by appointment
only. Accepts photos, resumes,
and tapes (audio/video) by mail
only. Union. Feel free to send
postcards for openings or
updates.*

APRIL WEBSTER
CASTING
800 Main Street, #310
Burbank, CA 91506
(818) 526-4242
*April Webster, C.S.A. and
Casting Associate Mandy
Sherman cast for features,
television, and theatre.
Currently casting ABC's Alias
and 111 Gramercy Park.*

JUDITH WEINER
(310) 575-7008
(See UPN)

ALYSSA WEISBERG
CASTING
(310) 889-9557
*Office casts Film/Television/
Theatre. Submissions accepted
by agents and managers only.
Don't phone, fax. Interviews by
appointment only.*

MARY WEST
(See Brown/West Casting)

WESTSIDE CASTING
STUDIOS
2050 South Bundy Drive
West Los Angeles, CA 90025
(310) 820-9200
fax: (310) 820-5408
*Full-service casting facility
with eight studios. Top of the
line equipment including DSL
and digital cameras. Casting
Directors: Cathi Carlton, Joe
Blake, Mary Claire Sweeters,
Brigid McBride, Steve Erdek,
Terry Berland, Mimi Webb
Miller. Cast commercials, films,
voiceovers, music videos,
print advertising. Please do
not phone or fax. Union.*

GERALD I. WOLFF &
ASSOCIATES, INC.
1135 South Beverly Drive,
Second Floor
Los Angeles, CA 90035
(310) 277-6200
*Casting Directors Gerald I. Wolff,
Jan Glaser, C.S.A. and Christine
Joyce cast films. Assistant:
Robert Moreno. Union. Don't
phone, fax, or visit. Interviews by
appointment only. Audio/video-
tapes will not be returned. No
drop-ins. All submissions by mail
only. Attends showcases.*

GERRIE WORMSER
CASTING
2160 Century Park East,
207 North
Los Angeles, CA 90067
(310) 277-3281
*Casts T.V., film, commercials,
industrials, infomercials, music
videos, print advertising, soaps,
theatre, and voiceovers. Also
a Talent Coordinator. Don't
visit. Interviews by appointment
only. Accepts photos, resumes
and tapes (Audio/Video) by
mail only. Union/Nonunion.
Attends showcases. Talent
Consultations.*

DOUGLAS WRIGHT CASTING
10061 Riverside Drive, #196
Toluca Lake, CA 91602
(323) 912-1195
Casting Director Douglas Wright casts feature films and theatre. Accepts photos-resumes by mail only. Attends showcases and accepts showcase invitations via mail only. Please do not send unsolicited videotapes or visit.

GRACE WU
(818) 840-2045
(See NBC)

NAOMI YOELIN
854 19th Street
Santa Monica, CA 90403
(310) 829-9764

BONNIE ZANE
(See Zane-Pillsbury Casting)

DEBRA ZANE, C.S.A.
5225 Wilshire Blvd., Suite 601
Los Angeles, CA 90036
(323) 965-0800
Debra Zane (Casting Director) and Tannis Vallely (Casting Associate) cast films. Do not visit.

ZANE-PILLSBURY CASTING
585 North Larchmont Blvd.
Los Angeles, CA 90004
(323) 769-9191
Bonnie Zane, C.S.A.; Gayle Pillsbury, C.S.A. Cast for T.V. Union. Don't phone or visit.

GARY ZUCKERBROD, C.S.A.
(818) 526-4332

DORI ZUCKERMAN
(See Henderson/Zuckerman Casting)

Los Angeles Talent Agencies

AKA TALENT AGENCY
(ATA, AFTRA,SAG)
6310 San Vicente Blvd., Suite 200
Los Angeles, CA 90048
(323) 965-5600

A.S.A. TALENT (SAG-AFTRA)
4430 Fountain Avenue, #A
Hollywood, CA 90029
(323) 662-9787

ABOVE THE LINE AGENCY
(SAG-WGA-DGA)
9200 Sunset Blvd., Suite 804
West Hollywood, CA 90069
(310) 859-6115

ABRAMS ARTISTS
AGENCY, INC.
(ATA-AFTRA-EQUITY)
9200 Sunset Blvd., 11th Floor
Los Angeles, CA 90069
(310) 859-0625
(See also listing under New York Talent Agencies)

ACME TALENT & LITERARY
(ATA-AFTRA-EQUITY-WGA-DGA)
4727 Wilshire Blvd., #333
Los Angeles, CA 90010
(323) 954-2263
(See also listing under NY Talent Agencies)

ACTORS L.A./L.A. ACTORS
GROUP AGENCY
(SAG)
12435 Oxnard Street
North Hollywood, CA 91606
(818) 755-0026

AGENCY FOR THE
PERFORMING ARTS, INC.
(ATA-AFTRA-EQUITY-WGA)
9200 Sunset Blvd., 9th Floor
Los Angeles, CA 90069
(310) 888-4200

AGENCY WEST
ENTERTAINMENT
(a.k.a. J.E.O.W. Entertainment)
(SAG-AFTRA-EQUITY-WGA)
5750 Wilshire Blvd.,
  Suite 640 North
Los Angeles, CA 90036
(323) 857-9050

AIMÉE ENTERTAINMENT
ASSOCIATES
(SAG-AFTRA)
15840 Ventura Blvd., Suite 215
Encino, CA 91436
(818) 783-9115

ALLURE MODEL & TALENT
AGENCY
(ATA-AFTRA)
5556 Centinela Avenue
Los Angeles, CA 90066
(310) 306-1150

ALVARADO REY AGENCY
(ATA-AFTRA)
8455 Beverly Blvd., Suite 410
Los Angeles, CA 90048
(323) 655-7978

AMATRUDA BENSON &
ASSOCIATES (ABA)
(SAG)
9107 Wilshire Blvd., #500
Beverly Hills, CA 90210
(310) 276-1851

AMSEL, EISENSTADT &
FRAZIER, INC.
(ATA-AFTRA-EQUITY)
5757 Wilshire Blvd., #510
Los Angeles, CA 90036
(323) 939-1188

ANGEL CITY TALENT
(ATA-AFTRA-EQUITY)
4741 Laurel Canyon Blvd.,
  Suite 101
Valley Village, CA 91607
(818) 760-9980

ARTIST MANAGEMENT
AGENCY
(SAG-AFTRA)
1800 East Garry Street, #101
Santa Ana, CA 92705
(949) 261-7557
(See also listing under San Diego Talent Agencies)

THE ARTISTS AGENCY
(ATA-AFTRA-EQUITY-WGA)
1180 South Beverly Drive,
  Suite 400
Los Angeles, CA 90035
(310) 277-7779

THE ARTISTS GROUP, LTD.
(SAG-AFTRA-EQUITY-WGA)
10100 Santa Monica Blvd.,
  #2490
Los Angeles, CA 90067
(310) 552-1100
(See also listing under New York Talent Agencies)

THE AUSTIN AGENCY
(SAG-AFTRA-EQUITY)
6715 Hollywood Blvd.,
  Suite 204
Hollywood, CA 90028
(323) 957-4444

BADGLEY CONNOR TALENT
AGENCY
(SAG-AFTRA-EQUITY)
9229 Sunset Blvd., #311
Los Angeles, CA 90069
(310) 278-9313

BAIER/KLEINMAN
INTERNATIONAL
(SAG-AFTRA)
3575 Cahuenga Blvd. West,
  #500
Los Angeles, CA 90068
(323) 874-9800

BALDWIN TALENT, INC.
(SAG-AFTRA)
8055 West Manchester, #550
Playa Del Rey, CA 90293
(310) 827-2422

BOBBY BALL AGENCY
(ATA-AFTRA-EQUITY)
4342 Lankershim Blvd.
Universal City, CA 91602
(818) 506-8188
*(For additional MP/TV
Department info, please see
listing under Defining Artists)*

BARON ENTERTAINMENT
(SAG-AFTRA)
5757 Wilshire Blvd.,
Suite 659
Los Angeles, CA 90036
(323) 936-7600

BAUMAN, REDANTY & SHAUL
(ATA-AFTRA-EQUITY)
5757 Wilshire Blvd., #473
Los Angeles, CA 90036
(323) 857-6666
*(See also listing under New York
Talent Agencies)*

MARIAN BERZON
TALENT AGENCY
(ATA-AFTRA-EQUITY-WGA)
336 East 17th Street
Costa Mesa, CA 92627
(949) 631-5936

BONNIE BLACK TALENT &
LITERARY AGENCY
(SAG-AFTRA-WGA)
12034 Riverside Drive,
Suite 103
Valley Village, CA 91607
(818) 753-5424

THE BLAKE AGENCY
(SAG-AFTRA-EQUITY)
1327 Ocean Avenue,
Suite J
Santa Monica, CA 90401
(310) 899-9898

BLOC TALENT AGENCY, INC.
(SAG-EQUITY)
5225 Wilshire Blvd,
Suite 311
Los Angeles, CA 90036
(323) 954-7730
*(See also listing under New York
Talent Agencies)*

BRADY, BRANNON & RICH
(ATA-AFTRA)
5670 Wilshire Blvd., Suite 820
Los Angeles, CA 90036
(323) 852-9559

BRAND MODEL & TALENT
(SAG-AFTRA)
1520 Brookhollow Drive, #39
Santa Ana, CA 92705
(714) 850-1158

BRESLER-KELLY &
ASSOCIATES
(ATA-AFTRA-EQUITY)
11500 West Olympic Blvd.,
Suite 352
Los Angeles, CA 90064
(310) 479-5611

DON BUCHWALD &
ASSOCIATES, PACIFIC
(AFTRA-EQUITY-WGA-DGA)
6500 Wilshire Blvd., #2200
Los Angeles, CA 90048
(323) 655-7400
*(See listing under New York
Talent Agencies)*

BUCHWALD TALENT GROUP
(AFTRA)
6500 Wilshire Blvd., Suite 2210
Los Angeles, CA 90048
(323) 852-9555

CAREER ARTISTS
INTERNATIONAL
(SAG-AFTRA-WGA)
11030 Ventura Blvd., #3
Studio City, CA 91604
(818) 980-1315

CONAN CARROLL &
ASSOCIATES
(EQUITY-WGA)
6117 Rhodes Avenue
North Hollywood, CA 91606
(818) 760-4730

CARRY COMPANY TALENT
REPRESENTATIVES
(SAG)
1631 21st Street
Santa Monica, CA 90404
(310) 913-0035
*(See also listing under New York
Talent Agencies)*

CASSELL-LEVY, INC. (CLINC.)
(ATA-AFTRA)
843 North Sycamore Avenue
Los Angeles, CA 90038
(323) 461-3971

CASTLE-HILL ENTERPRISES
(SAG-AFTRA-EQUITY)
1101 South Orlando Avenue
Los Angeles, CA 90035
(323) 653-3535

CAVALERI & ASSOCIATES
TALENT & LITERARY AGENCY
(SAG-AFTRA-WGA-DGA-
EQUITY)
178 South Victory Blvd.,
Suite 205
Burbank, CA 91502
(818) 955-9300

CHAMPAGNE TROTT TALENT
AGENCY (ATA)
9250 Wilshire Blvd., #303
Beverly Hills, CA 90212
Talent Division: (310) 205-3111
Model Division: (310) 275-0067

THE CHASIN AGENCY
(SAG-AFTRA-DGA-WGA)
8899 Beverly Blvd., #716
Los Angeles, CA 90048
(310) 278-7505

CHATEAU-BILLINGS TALENT
(SAG-AFTRA)
5657 Wilshire Blvd., #200
Los Angeles, CA 90036
(323) 965-5432

CINEMA TALENT AGENCY
(SAG-AFTRA)
2609 West Wyoming Avenue,
Suite A
Burbank, CA 91505
(818) 845-3816

CIRCLE TALENT ASSOCIATES
(ATA-AFTRA-EQUITY)
433 North Camden Drive,
Suite 400
Beverly Hills, CA 90210
(310) 285-1585

W. RANDOLPH CLARK
COMPANY
(SAG-AFTRA)
13415 Ventura Blvd., Suite 3
Sherman Oaks, CA 91423
(818) 385-0583

CLEAR TALENT GROUP
(SAG-AFTRA-EQUITY)
10950 Ventura Blvd.
Studio City, CA 91604
(818) 509-0121

COLLEEN CLER TALENT
AGENCY (SAG-AFTRA)
178 South Victory, #108
Burbank, CA 91502
(818) 841-7943

COAST TO COAST TALENT
GROUP, INC.
(ATA-AFTRA-EQUITY-WGA)
3350 Barham Blvd.
Los Angeles, CA 90068
(323) 845-9200

COMMERCIAL TALENT
(ATA-AFTRA)
9255 Sunset Blvd., Suite 505
Los Angeles, CA 90069
*Infomercials, industrials.
Interviews by appointment
only. Accepts photos-resumes
by mail only.*

CORALIE JR. THEATRICAL
AGENCY
(SAG-AFTRA-EQUITY-WGA-AFM)
4789 Vineland Avenue,
Suite 100
North Hollywood, CA 91602
(818) 766-9501

CREATIVE ARTISTS AGENCY, LLC
(ATA-AFTRA-EQUITY-DGA-
WGA-AFM)
9830 Wilshire Blvd.
Beverly Hills, CA 90212-1825
(310) 288-4545

THE CROFOOT GROUP, INC.
(AFTRA)
23632 Calabasas Road, #104
Calabasas, CA 91302
(818) 223-1500

THE CULBERTSON GROUP, LLC
(ATA-AFTRA)
8430 Santa Monica Blvd.,
Suite 210
West Hollywood, CA 90069
(323) 650-9454

CUNNINGHAM-ESCOTT-
DIPENE/LOS ANGELES
(ATA-AFTRA-EQUITY)
10635 Santa Monica Blvd., #130
Los Angeles, CA 90025
Commercials: (310) 475-2111
Children's Division:
(310) 475-3336
Print Division: (310) 475-7573
*(See also listing under New York
Talent Agencies)*

DDO ARTISTS AGENCY
(SAG)
8322 Beverly Blvd., #301
Los Angeles, CA 90048
(323) 782- 0070

THE DANGERFIELD AGENCY
(SAG-EQUITY)
4063 Radford, Suite 201C
Studio City, CA 91604
(818) 766-7717

DEFINING ARTISTS
(a subsidiary of Bobby Ball
Agency)
(AFTRA-ATA)
4342 Lankershim Blvd.
Universal City, CA 91602
(818) 985-8886

DIVERSE TALENT GROUP
(ATA-AFTRA-WPD)
1875 Century Park East,
Suite 2250
Los Angeles, CA 90067
(310) 201-6565

CRAIG DORFMAN &
ASSOCIATES
(SAG-AFTRA)
(323) 655-5850

DRAGON TALENT, INC.
(SAG)
8444 Wilshire Blvd.,
Penthouse Suite
Beverly Hills, CA 90211
(323) 653-0366

EWCR & ASSOCIATES
(ATA-AFTRA-EQUITY-WGA)
280 South Beverly Drive,
Suite 400
Beverly Hills, CA 90212
(310) 278-7222
*(See also listing under New York
Talent Agencies)*

ELLIS TALENT GROUP
(ETG) (SAG)
4705 Laurel Canyon, Suite 300
Valley Village, CA 91607
(818) 980-8072

FERRAR-MEDIA ASSOCIATES
(SAG-AFTRA)
8430 Santa Monica Blvd., #220
Los Angeles, CA 90069
(323) 654-2601

FILM ARTISTS ASSOCIATES
(SAG)
4717 Van Nuys Blvd.,
Suite 215
Sherman Oaks, CA 91403
(818) 386-9669

5 STAR TALENT AGENCY
(ATA-AFTRA)
2312 Janet Lee Drive
La Crescenta, CA 91212
(818) 249-4241

FLICK EAST-WEST
TALENTS, INC.
(SAG-AFTRA)
9057 Nemo Street, Suite A
West Hollywood, CA 90069
(310) 271-9111

FONTAINE MUSIC
(SAG-AFTRA)
205 South Beverly Drive,
Suite 212
Beverly Hills, CA 90212
(310) 471-8631

GFTA GWYN FOXX
TALENT AGENCY
(ATA-AFTRA)
4401 Wilshire Blvd.,
Second Floor
Los Angeles, CA 90010
(323) 937-7776

THE BARRY FREED CO.
(SAG-AFTRA-EQUITY-WGA)
468 North Camden Drive,
Suite 201
Beverly Hills, CA 90210
(310) 860-5627

ALICE FRIES AGENCY, LTD.
(SAG-AFTRA-DGA-WGA-
packaging)
1927 Vista Del Mar Avenue
Hollywood, CA 90068
(323) 464-1404

THE GAGE GROUP, INC.
(ATA-AFTRA-EQUITY-WGA)
14724 Ventura Blvd.,
Suite 505
Sherman Oaks, CA 91403
(818) 905-3800
*(See also listing under NY Talent
Agencies)*

DALE GARRICK
INTERNATIONAL AGENCY
(ATA-AFTRA-WGA)
1017 North La Cienega Blvd.,
Suite 109
West Hollywood, CA 90069
(310) 657-2661

GEDDES
(SAG-AFTRA-EQUITY)
8430 Santa Monica Blvd.,
Suite 200
West Hollywood, CA 90069
(323) 848-2700

THE LAYA GELFF AGENCY
(SAG-AFTRA-EQUITY-WGA-
DGA)
16133 Ventura Blvd., #700
Encino, CA 91436
(818) 996-3100

THE DON GERLER AGENCY
(SAG)
3349 Cahuenga Blvd. West, #1
Los Angeles, CA 90068
(323) 850-7386

THE GERSH AGENCY
(ATA-AFTRA-EQUITY-WGA)
232 North Canon Drive
Beverly Hills, CA 90210
(310) 274-6611
*(See also listing under New York
Talent Agencies)*

MICHELLE GORDON &
ASSOCIATES
(SAG-AFTRA-EQUITY-WGA)
260 South Beverly Drive,
Suite 308
Beverly Hills, CA 90212
(310) 246-9930

GRANT, SAVIC, KOPALOFF &
ASSOCIATES
(SAG-AFTRA-WGA-DGA)
6399 Wilshire Blvd., Suite 414
Los Angeles, CA 90048
(323) 782-1854

GREENE & ASSOCIATES
(SAG-AFTRA)
7080 Hollywood Blvd.,
   Suite 1017
Hollywood, CA 90004
(323) 960-1333

BUZZ HALLIDAY & ASSOCIATES
(ATA-AFTRA-EQUITY)
8899 Beverly Blvd., Suite 715
Los Angeles, CA 90048
(310) 275-6028

VAUGHN D. HART &
ASSOCIATES
(SAG-AFTRA-EQUITY)
8899 Beverly Blvd., #815
Los Angeles, CA 90048
(310) 273-7887

BEVERLY HECHT AGENCY
(ATA-AFTRA-WGA)
12001 Ventura Place,
   Suite 320
Studio City, CA 91604
(818) 505-1192

HERVEY-GRIMES TALENT
AGENCY
(SAG-AFTRA)
10561 Missouri Avenue, #2
Los Angeles, CA 90025
(310) 475-2010

THE DANIEL HOFF AGENCY
(SAG-AFTRA-EQUITY)
1800 North Highland Avenue,
   #300
Los Angeles, CA 90028
(323) 962-6643

HOLLANDER TALENT GROUP,
INC.
(SAG-AFTRA)
14011 Ventura Blvd., Suite 202
Sherman Oaks, CA 91423
(818) 382-9800

THE HOUSE OF
REPRESENTATIVES
(ATA-AFTRA-EQUITY)
400 South Beverly Drive, #101
Beverly Hills, CA 90212
(310) 772-0772

HOWARD TALENT WEST
(ATA-AFTRA-EQUITY-DGA)
10657 Riverside Drive
Toluca Lake, CA 91602
(818) 766-5300

ICON TALENT AGENCY (SAG)
3800 Barham Blvd., Suite 303
Los Angeles, CA 90068
(323) 845-1480

IDENTITY TALENT AGENCY
(ATA)
7080 Hollywood Blvd.,
   Suite 1009
Hollywood, CA 90028
(323) 469-1100
submissions@idtalent.com

INNOVATIVE ARTISTS, TALENT &
LITERARY AGENCY, INC.
(ATA-AFTRA-EQUITY-WGA-DGA)
1505 10th Street
Santa Monica, CA 90401
(310) 656-0400
*(See also listing under New York
Talent Agencies)*

INTERNATIONAL CREATIVE
MANAGEMENT INC. (ICM)
(ATA-AFTRA-EQUITY-WGA-
   DGA-AFM)
8942 Wilshire Blvd.
Beverly Hills, CA 90211
(310) 550-4000
*(See also listing under New York
Talent Agencies)*

JS REPRESENTS
(SAG)
6815 Willoughby Avenue,
   Suite # 102
Los Angeles, CA 90038
(323) 462-3246

KM & ASSOCIATES
(SAG-AFTRA-EQUITY-DGA)
4922 Vineland Avenue
North Hollywood, CA 91601
(818) 766-3566

KAZARIAN-SPENCER &
ASSOCIATES, INC.
(ATA-AFTRA-EQUITY)
11365 Ventura Blvd.,
   Suite 100, Box 7403
Studio City, CA 91604
(818) 769-9111
*(See also listing under New York
Talent Agencies)*

SHARON KEMP (SAG)
447 South Robertson Blvd., #204
Beverly Hills, CA 90211
(310) 858-7200

WILLIAM KERWIN AGENCY
(SAG-AFTRA-EQUITY)
1605 North Cahuenga Blvd.,
   Suite 202
Hollywood, CA 90028
(323) 469-5155

ERIC KLASS AGENCY
(SAG-AFTRA-EQUITY)
139 South Beverly Drive, #331
Beverly Hills, CA 90212
(310) 274-9169

PAUL KOHNER INC.
(ATA-AFTRA-EQUITY-WGA)
9300 Wilshire Blvd., #555
Beverly Hills, CA 90212
(310) 550-1060

L.A. TALENT
(ATA-AFTRA-EQUITY)
7700 West Sunset Blvd.
Los Angeles, CA 90046
(323) 436-7777

L.J. & ASSOCIATES
(AFTRA)
17328 Ventura Blvd.,
   PMB 185
Encino, CA 91316
(818) 345-6960

L.W. 1, INC. (SAG)
7257 Beverly Blvd., Second Floor
Los Angeles, CA 90036
(323) 653-5700

THE LEVIN AGENCY
(SAG-AFTRA)
8484 Wilshire Blvd., #750
Beverly Hills, CA 90211
(323) 653-7073

THE ROBERT LIGHT AGENCY
(AFTRA)
6404 Wilshire Blvd., #900
Los Angeles, CA 90048
(323) 651-1777

KEN LINDNER &
ASSOCIATES, INC.
(SAG-AFTRA)
2049 Century Park East, #3050
Los Angeles, CA 90067
(310) 277-9223

LOVELL & ASSOCIATES
(ATA-AFTRA-EQUITY)
6730 Wedgewood Place
Los Angeles, CA 90068
(323) 876-1560

JANA LUKER AGENCY
(SAG-AFTRA-EQUITY-WGA)
1923 1/2 Westwood Blvd., #3
Los Angeles, CA 90025
(310) 441-2822

MGA/MARY GRADY AGENCY
(SAG-EQUITY)
221 East Walnut Street,
   Suite #130
Pasadena, CA 91101
(818) 567-1400

MADEMOISELLE TALENT &
MODELING AGENCY
(SAG)
10835 Santa Monica Blvd.,
   #204A
Westwood, CA 90025
(310) 441-9994

MALAKY INTERNATIONAL
(SAG-AFTRA)
10642 Santa Monica Blvd., #103
Los Angeles, CA 90025
(310) 234-9114

ALESE MARSHALL
AGENCY (MODELS,
COMMERCIALS & FILM)
(SAG-AFTRA)
23639 Hawthorne Blvd., #200
Torrance, CA 90505
(310) 378-1223

MAXINE'S TALENT AGENCY
(SAG-AFTRA-WGA)
4830 Encino Avenue
Encino, CA 91316
(818) 986-2946

MCCABE/JUSTICE, LLC
(ATA-AFTRA-EQUITY)
8285 Sunset Blvd.,
   Suite 1
Los Angeles, CA 90046
(323) 650-3738

MEDIA ARTISTS GROUP
(SAG-AFTRA-WGA)
6300 Wilshire Blvd.,
   Suite 1470
Los Angeles, CA 90048
(323) 658-5050

MERIDIAN ARTISTS AGENCY
(SAG-AFTRA-EQUITY)
9229 Sunset Blvd, #310
Los Angeles, CA 90069
(310) 246-2600

METROPOLITAN TALENT
AGENCY
(ATA-AFTRA-EQUITY-WGA)
4526 Wilshire Blvd.
Los Angeles, CA 90010
(323) 857-4500

MIRAMAR TALENT
(SAG)
7400 Beverly Blvd.,
   Suite 220
Los Angeles, CA 90036

THE MORGAN AGENCY
(SAG-AFTRA-EQUITY)
7080 Hollywood Blvd.,
   Suite 1009
Los Angeles, CA 90028
(323) 469-7100

WILLIAM MORRIS AGENCY
(ATA-AFTRA-EQUITY-WGA-DGA)
151 El Camino Drive
Beverly Hills, CA 90212
(310) 859-4000
*(See also listing under New York
Talent Agencies)*

H. DAVID MOSS & ASSOCIATES
(SAG-AFTRA-EQUITY)
733 North Seward Street,
   Penthouse
Los Angeles, CA 90038
(323) 465-1234

SUSAN NATHE & ASSOC./CPC
(ATA-AFTRA)
8281 Melrose Avenue, Suite 200
Los Angeles, CA 90046
(323) 653-7573

OMNIPOP, INC.
(SAG-AFTRA-EQUITY)
10700 Ventura Blvd., 2nd Floor
Studio City, CA 91604
(818) 980-9267
*(See also listing under New York
Talent Agencies)*

THE ORANGE GROVE
GROUP, INC.
(ATA-AFTRA-EQUITY-WGA-
   DGA-AGMA-AGVA)
12178 Ventura Blvd., Suite 205
Studio City, CA 91604
(818) 762-7498

ORIGIN TALENT (SAG-AFTRA)
4705 Laurel Canyon Blvd.,
   Suite 306
Studio City, CA 91607
(818) 487-1800

OSBRINK TALENT AGENCY
(SAG-AFTRA)
4343 Lankershim Blvd., Suite 100
Universal City, CA 91602
(818) 760-2488

PTI TALENT AGENCY (ATA)
14724 Ventura Blvd.,
   Penthouse Suite
Sherman Oaks, CA 91403
(818) 386-1310

PACIFIC WEST ARTISTS
(SAG)
12500 Riverside Drive,
   Suite #202
North Hollywood, CA 91607
(818) 755-8544

PAKULA/KING AND ASSOCIATES
(SAG-AFTRA-EQUITY)
9229 Sunset Blvd., Suite 315
Los Angeles, CA 90069
(310) 281-4868

PARADIGM
(ATA-AFTRA-EQUITY-WGA)
10100 Santa Monica Blvd.,
   25th Floor
Los Angeles, CA 90067
(310) 277-4400
*(See also listing under New York
Talent Agencies)*

THE PARADISE GROUP
TALENT AGENCY
(AFTRA)
8721 Sunset Blvd., Suite 209
Los Angeles, CA 90069
(310) 854-6622

PINNACLE COMMERCIAL TALENT
(ATA-AFTRA-EQUITY)
5757 Wilshire Blvd., #510
Los Angeles, CA 90036
(323) 939-5440

PLAYERS TALENT AGENCY
(SAG-AFTRA)
13033 Ventura Blvd., Suite N
Studio City, CA 91604
(818) 528-7444

PRIVILEGE MODEL & TALENT
AGENCY
(SAG-AFTRA)
14542 Ventura Blvd., #209
Sherman Oaks, CA 91423
(818) 386-2377

PRODUCTIONS PLUS
NATIONWIDE TALENT
AGENCY/WEST COAST OFFICE
(AFTRA)
19300 South Hamilton Avenue,
   Suite 240
Gardena, CA 90248
(310) 324-5544

PROGRESSIVE ARTISTS
AGENCY CORP.
(SAG-AFTRA-EQUITY-WGA-DGA-
   PGA)
400 South Beverly Drive, #216
Beverly Hills, CA 90212
(310) 553-8561

QUALITA DELL'ARTE: ARTISTS &
WRITERS DI QUALITA
(SAG-AFTRA-EQUITY-WGA-DGA)
5353 Topanga Canyon Road,
   Suite 220
Woodland Hills, CA 91364
(818) 598-8073

REBEL ENTERTAINMENT
PARTNERS, INC.
(ATA-AFTRA-DGA-WGA)
8075 West Third Street, #303
Los Angeles, CA 90048
(323) 935-1700

CINDY ROMANO MODELING &
TALENT AGENCY
(SAG-WGA)
P.O. Box 1951
Palm Springs, CA 92263
(760) 323-3333

SDB PARTNERS, INC.
(SAG-AFTRA-EQUITY)
1801 Avenue of the Stars, #902
Los Angeles, CA 90067

SMS TALENT, INC.
(ATA-AFTRA-EQUITY)
8730 Sunset Blvd., #440
Los Angeles, CA 90069
(310) 289-0909

THE SAMANTHA GROUP
TALENT AGENCY (SAG)
300 South Raymond Avenue, #11
Pasadena, CA 91105
(626) 683-2444

THE SARNOFF COMPANY INC.
(SAG-AFTRA-WGA-DGA)
10 Universal City Plaza,
     Suite 2000
Universal City, CA 91608
(818) 753-2377

THE SAVAGE AGENCY
(AFTRA-EQUITY-ATA)
6212 Banner Avenue
Los Angeles, CA 90038
(323) 461-8316

JACK SCAGNETTI TALENT
AGENCY
(SAG-AFTRA-EQUITY-WGA)
5118 Vineland Avenue, #102
North Hollywood, CA 91601
(818) 762-3871

IRV SCHECHTER COMPANY
(SAG-AFTRA-WGA-DGA)
9460 Wilshire Blvd., #300
Beverly Hills, CA 90212
(310) 278-8070

SCHIOWITZ/CLAY/ANKRUM
AND ROSS, INC.
(SAG-AFTRA-EQUITY)
1680 North Vine Street,
     Suite 1016
Los Angeles, CA 90028
Theatrical/Literary:
     (323) 463-8355
*(See also Schiowitz/Clay/Rose
listing under New York Talent
Agencies)*

SANDIE SCHNARR TALENT
(SAG-AFTRA)
8500 Melrose Avenue, #212
West Hollywood, CA 90069
(310) 360-7680

JUDY SCHOEN & ASSOCIATES
(ATA-AFTRA-EQUITY)
606 North Larchmont Blvd., #309
Los Angeles, CA 90004
(323) 962-1950

KATHLEEN SCHULTZ
ASSOCIATES
(SAG-AFTRA-EQUITY-WGA)
6442 Coldwater Canyon,
     Suite 206
Valley Glen, CA 91606
(818) 760-3100

DON SCHWARTZ
ASSOCIATES, INC.
(SAG)
1604 Cahuenga Blvd. #101
Hollywood, CA 90028
(323) 464-4366

SCREEN ARTISTS AGENCY
(AFTRA)
4526 Sherman Oaks Ave
Sherman Oaks, CA 91606
(818) 789-4896

DAVID SHAPIRA & ASSOCIATES
(SAG-AFTRA-EQUITY-WGA)
15821 Ventura Blvd., #235
Encino, CA 91436
(818) 906-0322

SHAPIRO-LICHTMAN, INC.
(SAG-AFTRA-EQUITY-WGA-
     DGA)
8827 Beverly Blvd.
Los Angeles, CA 90048
(310) 859-8877

SIERRA TALENT AGENCY
(SAG)
14542 Ventura Blvd., #207
Sherman Oaks, CA 91403
(818) 907-9645

SIGNATURE ARTISTS
AND MODELS
(SAG)
6700 West Fifth Street
Los Angeles, CA 90048

MICHAEL SLESSINGER &
ASSOCIATES
(SAG-AFTRA)
8730 Sunset Blvd., #270
Los Angeles, CA 90069
(310) 657-7113

SONJIA WARREN BRANDON'S
COMMERCIALS UNLTD., INC.
(ATA-AFTRA)
190 North Canon Drive, Suite 302
Beverly Hills, CA 90210
(323) 655-0069
*Another division: SWB Theatrical
& Children's Commercial*

CAMILLE SORICE TALENT
AGENCY
(SAG-AFTRA-WGA)
Mailing Address:
13412 Moorpark Street, Suite C
Sherman Oaks, CA 91423
(818) 995-1775

SPECIAL ARTISTS AGENCY
(ATA-AFTRA)
345 North Maple Drive, #302
Beverly Hills, CA 90210
(310) 859-9688

SCOTT STANDER &
ASSOCIATES, INC.
(SAG-AFTRA-EQUITY)
13701 Riverside Drive, Suite 201
Sherman Oaks, CA 91423
(818) 905-7000

STARCRAFT TALENT AGENCY
(SAG-AFTRA)
1516 North Formosa
Los Angeles, CA 90046
(323) 845-4784

STARWILL PRODUCTIONS
TALENT AGENCY
(SAG-WGA)
433 North Camden Drive,
     Fourth Floor
Beverly Hills, CA 90210
(323) 874-1239

THE STEVENS GROUP
(SAG-AFTRA)
14011 Ventura Blvd., Suite 201
Sherman Oaks, CA 91423
(818) 528-3674

STONE-MANNERS AGENCY
(ATA-AFTRA-EQUITY-WGA)
6500 Wilshire Blvd., Suite 550
Los Angeles, CA 90048
(323) 655-1313
*(See also listing under New York
Talent Agencies)*

PETER STRAIN &
ASSOCIATES, INC.
(ATA-AFTRA-EQUITY)
5455 Wilshire Blvd.,
     Suite 1812
Los Angeles, CA 90036
(323) 525-3391
*(See also listing under New York
Talent Agencies)*

MITCHELL K. STUBBS &
ASSOCIATES
(ATA-AFTRA-EQUITY-WGA-DGA)
8675 West Washington Blvd.,
     Suite 203
Culver City, CA 90232
(310) 838-1200

SUTTON, BARTH &
VENNARI, INC.
(ATA-AFTRA)
145 South Fairfax Avenue,
   #310
Los Angeles, CA 90036
(323) 938-6000

TALENTWORKS
(ATA-AFTRA-EQUITY)
3500 West Olive Avenue,
   Suite 1400
Burbank, CA 91505
(818) 972-4300
(formerly Gold/Liedtke &
Associates and H.W.A.
Talent Representatives)
*(See listing under New York
Talent Agencies)*

HERB TANNEN & ASSOCIATES
(ATA-AFTRA)
10801 National Blvd.,
   Suite 101
Los Angeles, CA 90064
(310) 446-5802

THE THOMAS TALENT
AGENCY
(SAG-AFTRA-EQUITY)
6709 La Tijera Blvd., #915
Los Angeles, CA 90045
(310) 665-0000

ARLENE THORNTON &
ASSOCIATES
(SAG-AFTRA)
12711 Ventura Blvd., #490
Studio City, CA 91604
(818) 760-6688

TILMAR TALENT AGENCY
(SAG)
4929 Wilshire Blvd.,
   Suite 1020
Los Angeles, CA 90010
(323) 938-9815

TISHERMAN AGENCY, INC.
(SAG-AFTRA)
6767 Forest Lawn Drive, #101
Los Angeles, CA 90068
(323) 850-6767

UNITED ARTISTS AGENCY
(SAG-AFTRA-DGA-WGA)
14011 Ventura Blvd., Suite 213
Sherman Oaks, CA 91423
(818) 788-7305

UNITED TALENT AGENCY
(ATA-AFTRA-DGA-WGA)
9560 Wilshire Blvd., #500
Beverly Hills, CA 90212
(310) 273-6700

US TALENT AGENCY (SAG)
485 South Robertson Blvd.,
   Suite #7
Beverly Hills, CA 90211

VISION ART MANAGEMENT
(SAG-WGA-DGA)
9200 Sunset Blvd., Penthouse 1
Los Angeles, CA 90069
(310) 888-3288

THE VISSION AGENCY
(AFTRA)
1801 Century Park East,
   24th Floor
Los Angeles, CA 90067
(310) 553-8833

VOX, INC.
(formerly Talent Group, Inc. (TGI))
(SAG-AFTRA)
5670 Wilshire Blvd., Suite 820
Los Angeles, CA 90036
(323) 655-8699

THE WALLIS AGENCY
(SAG-AFTRA)
4444 Riverside Drive, #105
Burbank, CA 91505
(818) 953-4848

BOB WATERS AGENCY, INC.
(SAG-AFTRA-EQUITY)
4311 Wilshire Blvd.,
   Suite 622
Los Angeles, CA 90010
(323) 965-5555

ANN WAUGH TALENT AGENCY
(SAG-AFTRA-EQUITY)
4741 Laurel Canyon Blvd., #200
North Hollywood, CA 91607
(818) 980-0141

SHIRLEY WILSON &
ASSOCIATES, INC.
(SAG-AFTRA-WGA)
5410 Wilshire Blvd., #510
Los Angeles, CA 90036
(323) 857-6977

WORLD CLASS SPORTS
(ATA)
880 Apollo Street, #337
El Segundo, CA 90245
(310) 535-9120

WRITERS & ARTISTS AGENCY
(ATA-AFTRA-EQUITY-DGA-WGA)
8383 Wilshire Blvd., Suite 550
Beverly Hills, CA 90211
(323) 866-0900
*(See also listing under New York
Talent Agencies)*

STELLA ZADEH &
ASSOCIATES
(AFTRA-DGA-WGA)
17328 Ventura Blvd.
Encino, CA 91316
(818) 424-2226

ZANUCK, PASSON,
AND PACE INC.
(SAG-AFTRA-EQUITY)
4717 Van Nuys Blvd., #102
Sherman Oaks, CA 91403
(818) 783-4890

Contributors

Marc Bernstein has written the popular column "Actors and Income Taxes" in *Back Stage* for over twenty-four years. He prepares income tax returns nationwide for people in the entertainment industry. In addition to his tax practice, Marc is an educator and a professional musician.

Catherine Castellani is a playwright, audio dramatist, and a feature contributor to *Back Stage*. Her work has been heard on National Public Radio and seen on stages in New York, Los Angeles, and San Francisco, including La Tea, the Eclectic Theatre Company, and Climate Theater. She has had residencies at the Ucross Foundation and the MacDowell Colony. She lives in New York.

Luke Thomas Crowe has worked as a bartender, picture-framer, equipment-truck driver, data processor, and writer, among other pursuits. He taught classes in film, animation, and sound recording/design as an NHSI faculty member at Northwestern University in Chicago. Luke received a Fine Arts degree in Motion Pictures, Television, and Recording Arts from Florida State University. Currently, he's an editorial associate at *Back Stage*.

Amelia David brings to her feature articles and *Back Stage* comedy column "Laughing Matters" her passion for performance—both from her own experiences on stage, screen, in commercials, cabaret, and recordings, and from her background as a cabaret/comedy booking manager and publicist for New York's Duplex cabaret. There she developed and promoted the careers of literally thousands of performers. She continues to see comics' dreams come true on a regular basis.

Native New Yorker **Margaret Emory** has worked as a talent agent for the past fourteen years. She is currently with Dulcina Eisen Associates. A member of Phi Beta Kappa and an honors graduate of Princeton University—as well as a graduate of the Neighborhood Playhouse School of Theatre—Margaret has been a performer and director, and headed a national Shakespearean company. She founded the Emory Seminars, a program on the business of acting, which she has taken to schools and universities. She writes the "Ask an Agent" column for *Back Stage*.

David Fairhurst is an actor and freelance writer. He has appeared in more than thirty New York and regional theatre productions, a dozen independent films, and television programs such as *Law and Order, Ed,* and *Sex and the City*. In the early 1980s he was a member of the folk-punk band The Splitting Headaches. He holds B.A. degrees in English and psychology from the University of Pennsylvania, an M.F.A. in acting from New School University, and is a lifetime member of The Actors Studio.

David Finkle has written frequently about the arts in numerous publications.

Bonnie Gillespie is an author, journalist, casting director, and former *Back Stage* columnist. Her books include *Casting Qs: A Collection of Casting Director Interviews* and *Self-management for Actors*. She provided casting consultant services on several independent short films and stage plays, working as casting coordinator for the Fox series *Mr. Personality, Paradise Hotel,* and *Project X*. She also provides career-consulting services to actors and is a frequent guest speaker at acting studios and bookstores in Los Angeles.

Born in Cleveland, **Phyllis Goldman** earned a B.S. degree in education at Ohio State University, with a major in dance. As a performer she worked in concerts and shows, in summer stock and Off-Broadway. Her writing has appeared in publications including *Back Stage, The Forward, Interview, Pointe, Elle,* and *Dancer*. She recently completed her first novel, *East Side Story,* and a screenplay, *Unbuttoned*. She is married, with three daughters. (Two are professional dancers and one is a fashion stylist.) She has four grandchildren.

Erik Haagensen is *Back Stage*'s copy chief and "Making Musicals" columnist, and has also written for *Show Music Magazine* and other publications. A Richard Rodgers Award-winning playwright-lyricist, his work has been seen Off-Broadway, in numerous regional theatres, and in the U.K. Erik holds a Bachelor's degree in Theatre from Northwestern University and a Masters degree in musical-theatre writing from New York University. He lives on Manhattan's Upper West Side with his partner, casting director Joseph McConnell.

Simi Horwitz is an award-winning on-staff feature writer for *Back Stage*. She covers newsworthy theatre artists (in her weekly "Face to Face" column) and trends in theatre.

Leonard Jacobs, *Back Stage* associate news editor, was founding editor of Theatermania.com and has written reviews and features for such publications as *The Village Voice, Theater Week,* and *American Theatre* since 1990. A playwright, director, producer, and dramaturg, he is an expert on late nineteenth-century American theatre and has lectured at Princeton and Yale. He is writing the first-ever biography of playwright Clyde Fitch and recently contributed a chapter on Fitch to an anthology of post-Civil War plays.

Los Angeles-based freelance writer **Anne Kelly-Saxenmeyer** covers the theatre and the actor's trade for *Back Stage West.* She has also contributed to the *L.A. Weekly,* the *Los Angeles Downtown News,* and the *Santa Monica Mirror.* She has a background in dance and holds a B.A. in English from UCLA.

Michèle LaRue is a professional actress (AEA, SAG, AFTRA) and editor. A member of The East Lynne Company and New Jersey Repertory Company, she performs with theatre troupes in New York City and the regions, and tours four one-woman plays nationally. Her writing has appeared in *American Theatre, Theatre Crafts* magazine, and *Equity News,* among others, and she is a member of Drama Desk. Her relationship with *Back Stage* spans twenty years, most recently as a senior editor.

Michael Lazan writes theatre reviews, book reviews, features, and the "Arts and the Law" column for *Back Stage.* He is also a playwright who has had works produced at such companies as the Rattlestick Theatre Company and Ensemble Studio Theatre, among many others. He is, as well, an attorney in private practice in New York City.

Dany Margolies has been an arts journalist for nearly a decade, writing for Los Angeles-based publications that include *Back Stage West, The Malibu Times,* and *Nitelife After Dark.* She currently serves as managing editor at *Back Stage West,* and is a member of the Los Angeles Drama Critics Circle and a substitute host for "Arts in Review" at KPFK FM Los Angeles.

Rick Pender has been an award-winning theatre writer for *CityBeat,* Cincinnati's alternative newsweekly, since its founding in 1994. In 1998 he became its Arts and Entertainment editor. He was named Ohio's best critic in 2002 by the Society of Professional Journalists. Rick is vice-chairman of the American Theatre Critics Association (ATCA); he has mentored young critics at several ATCA seminars. He is also a regional correspondent for *Back Stage* and assistant editor of *The Sondheim Review.*

Jenelle Riley is the film and television reporter for *Back Stage West* and the author of numerous plays, including *Heart Murmurs and Brain Matter, Comfortably Numb,* and *Unholy Matrimony.* She also penned the short films *Auditions* and *Safety.*

Lisa Jo Sagolla is a choreographer, a dance critic for *Back Stage,* and the author of *The Girl Who Fell Down: A Biography of Joan McCracken.* She teaches dance at Columbia University, Marymount Manhattan College, and the School of the Dance Theatre of Harlem.

Elias Stimac has worked as an entertainment writer and critic in New York and Los Angeles, with over twenty years of experience in the field. He regularly contributes to national publications and websites, including *Back Stage,* and also writes scripts for the stage and screen. In addition, Elias makes time for his other artistic pursuits, including acting, directing, painting, and photography. He can be reached through his production company at www.loanstarstage.com.

Esther Tolkoff is a writer and reviewer for *Back Stage.* She has written for *AudioFile Magazine, The New York Times,* and for universities and other organizations. She was editor of City College's *Alumnus Magazine* and associate editor of the newspaper *New York Teacher,* where she won several awards. She has performed her own comedy monologue and has also appeared in independent films and in small theatres in New York.

Laura Weinert has been a staff writer and theatre critic for *Back Stage West* for the last four years. She teaches creative writing at the Central Juvenile Hall in Los Angeles as a part of InsideOut Writers. She has also written freelance for the *Los Angeles Times.*

Mark Dundas Wood writes features, reviews, and columns ("Backlot Buzz," "Off the Bookshelf") for *Back Stage,* and has also contributed to *American Theatre, Theater Week,* and *The Oregonian.* He holds an M.F.A. degree in dramaturgy from Columbia University and serves as a dramaturg for New Professional Theatre and Broad Horizons Theatre Company in New York City. Mark is an associate editor of this handbook. He lives in Hell's Kitchen, Manhattan.